UNDERDOG!

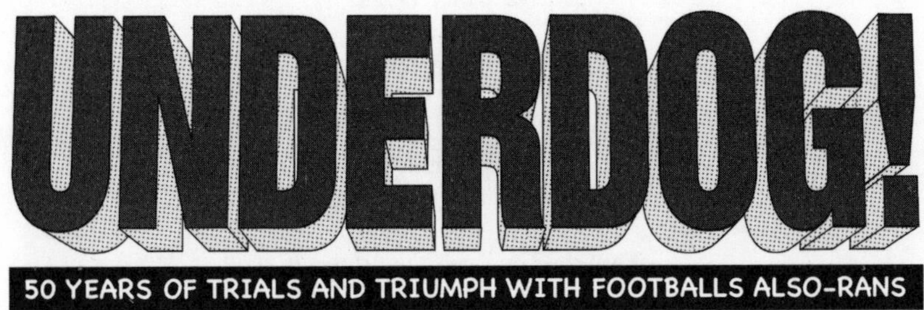

By Tim Quelch

Pitch Publishing Ltd
A2 Yeoman Gate
Yeoman Way
Durrington
BN13 3QZ

Email: info@pitchpublishing.co.uk
Web: www.pitchpublishing.co.uk

Published by Pitch Publishing 2011

A CIP catalogue record for this book is available from the British Library.

13-digit ISBN: 9781908051134
Typesetting and origination by Pitch Publishing.
Printed and bound in Great Britain by MPG Books Limited.

THANKS

I would like to thank the large number of people who helped me so much in writing this book. If I have overlooked anyone please accept my apology. I am deeply grateful to the former professional footballers who have given me generous amounts of their time: Martin Dobson, Geoff Nulty, Steve Kindon, Ken and Alan Ballard, Keith Tucker and Bob Seith. I am very appreciative for the terrific support I have received from other authors, notably Ivan Ponting, who encouraged me to write this book as well as granting me full use of his eloquently-written work. Niall Couper generously allowed me wide usage of his fascinating interviews with former Wimbledon F.C. players and managers. David Bull provided me with excellent Southampton F.C. material and a wide range of contacts. Roger Sinden allowed me full access to his lovingly assembled histories of Hastings United. David Steele generously gave me access to his illuminating Carlisle United material and very helpfully checked my draft chapters on the club. Justin Horton and Huw Richards also generously granted me access to their publications and helped with my draft Oxford United and Swansea City chapters. Paul Camillin gave me full access to his absorbing interviews with ex-Brighton & H.A. players. David Saffer granted me access to helpful material within his Bobby Collins biography. Dave Thomas and Phil Whalley kindly gave me their permission to reproduce large extracts of their superb interviews with former Burnley F.C. players. Graham Brookland at Aldershot Town was extremely helpful, too, in providing background information, obtaining club photos and in proof-reading my draft chapter on the club's history.

I am very appreciative of all the publishing companies who have given me permission to reproduce extracts from copyright work: Eaglemoss, Random House Group Ltd., Bloomsbury Publishing plc, Lennard Associates Ltd, John Blake Publishing Ltd., Seaview Media, The History Press, Little, Brown Books, Football World, Desert Island Books, Penguin

Books, Mainstream Books and Harper Collins. Some of the material I have used in the production of this book has lost its reference source or the acquired rights ownership could not be identified. I have endeavoured to seek permission from all rights owners. If I have inadvertently infringed copyright please accept my sincere apologies. I am writing this book to raise funds for the Alzheimer's Society. All of my royalties will be donated to this source. I hope, therefore, that any inadvertent breach will be considered kindly.

I am also greatly indebted to supporter websites: notably Ian Grant & Matt Rowson at Watford's 'Blind, Stupid and Desperate', Paul at Bristol City's 'Three Lions and a Robin', Tony Scholes at Burnley's Clarets Mad, Phil Whalley of Clarets' Archive, Workington's Workipedia site, QPR's Independent Review site, Fulham's Hammy End Chronicle, Swansea's scfc.co.uk and Dave at Leeds' 'Mighty Whites' site. Rival supporters came to my aid, too, including Rod Robbins and Nigel Woodcock. National and local newspapers and football magazines have provided rich sources of material. Thanks go to the *Aldershot News & Mail, Backpass* magazine, *BBC Radio Bristol, Bletchley Gazette, Burnley Express, Cumberland News,* Brighton *Evening Argus, Daily Mail, Daily Mirror, Guardian, Hastings & St. Leonards Observer, The Independent, Lancashire Evening Post; Mail on Sunday; News of the World, Oxford Mail; Sunday Pictorial; Daily Sketch;* Carlisle *Times & Star*; *The Times; Northampton Chronicle & Echo, the Observer & Observer magazines, South Wales Evening Post, Sunday Express, The Sunday Times, Watford Observer, Charles Buchan's Football Monthly, Four Four Two* and *When Saturday Comes* magazines. All of the above sources have helped me to present a more rounded portrait, not only of the football, but also of life in Britain over the last fifty years. A would like to extend a big thank you to photographer Ian Morsman for use of his excellent Aldershot Town shots, Howard Talbot for his terrific Burnley FC photography, the Press Association, Getty Images and Action Pictures for permission to use their excellent material, Burnley FC Chief Executive, Paul Fletcher M.B.E. for use of shots of his wonderful goal at Leeds in 1974, Pete Oliver at Burnley FC for use of 1972-73 Second Division Championship-winning team photo and the F.A. various clubs for use of programme covers.

Finally, I would like to express my gratitude to my wife, Liz, and to my daughter, Lydia, for indulging my labour of love, to my friends, notably Phil Whalley and Roger King for proof-reading earlier drafts and suggesting helpful amendments and to my publishers for their supportive and experienced guidance throughout the production of this book.

Tim Quelch: July 2011

CONTENTS

INTRODUCTION: Exiled From Main Street 11

KIND OF BLUE 1958 – 1962 13

THE 1958/59 SEASON 15
Chelsea v Wolverhampton Wanderers 15
Norwich City v Tottenham Hotspur (F.A. Cup fifth round) 19
Yet more World Cup disappointment 25
'Never had it so good'? 27

THE 1959/60 SEASON 29
Brighton & Hove Albion v Aston Villa 29
The age of innocence or the age of naivety? 35
West Ham United v Huddersfield Town (F.A. Cup third round) 40
England v Sweden 42
The motorway age arrives 44

THE 1960/61 SEASON 47
Hastings United v Wisbech Town 47
Brighton & Hove Albion v Burnley (F.A. Cup fourth round) 53
Freeing the soccer slaves 57

THE 1961/62 SEASON 60
Brighton & Hove Albion v Leyton Orient 60
A short history of tractor boys in Suffolk 76
Burnley burn out 81
Beyond the Fringe 82
Farewell to the season of the underdog 82

'PLEASE PLEASE ME' 1962 – 1970 85

THE 1962/63 SEASON 87
Tonbridge v Hastings United 87
Disoriented O's chimed out 100
Suffering Suffolk 102
Brighton rocked 105
The case for the defence 108
1963: a year of living pruriently 111

THE 1964/65 SEASON 113
Brighton & Hove Albion v Darlington 113
The Cobblers' glass slipper 130
'A Hunting We Will Go': Carlisle's Twin Promotions 139
Worked over by Workington 142
'Fade to Grey' 144

THE 1965/66 SEASON 146
Northampton Town v Fulham 146
Ramsey's World Cup-winning formula 162

THE 1966/67 SEASON 166
Wisbech Town v Hastings United 166
A tale of two 'Jocks' 175
And a tale of A. Stock 180
'… It's all part of my Autumn Almanac' 186

THE 1967/68 SEASON 189
Tottenham Hotspur v Manchester City 189
'Paint it Black' 196
'It's the economy, stupid' 197

THE 1968/69 SEASON 199
Preston North End v Chelsea (F.A. Cup fourth round) 199
'Street Fighting Man': The end of the Sixties 209

THE 1969/70 SEASON 211
Burnley v West Bromwich Albion 211
World Cup willies 217

'I DON'T BELIEVE IN MIRACLES' 1971 – 1979 219

THE 1970/71 SEASON 221
Colchester United v Leeds United (F.A. Cup fifth round) 221
Sound of the Seventies 226

THE 1971/72 SEASON 230
Burnley v Hull City 230
Hereford's gain: Barrow's loss 237

THE 1972/73 SEASON 243
Preston North End v Burnley 243

THE 1973/74 SEASON 248
Leeds United v Burnley 248

THE 1974/75 SEASON 261
Burnley v Wimbledon (F.A. Cup third round) 261
Carlisle United v Burnley 270

THE 1975/76 SEASON 283
Blackpool v Burnley (F.A. Cup third round) 283

THE 1976/77 SEASON 289
Carlisle United v Matlock Town (F.A. Cup third round) 289

THE 1978/79 SEASON 304
Brighton & Hove Albion v Burnley 304
Watford's 'Miracle Maker' 312
'Video Killed the Radio Star': the end of the Seventies 324

'BLUE MONDAY' 1980 – 1987 327

THE 1980/81 SEASON 329
Oxford United v Burnley 329
'Maxwell's Silver Hammer': Bust to boom and back again 331

THE 1981/82 SEASON 342
Swansea City v Leeds United 342
Bristol City: the price of loyalty 357
Put out more flags: the Falklands factor 367

THE 1986/87 SEASON 371
'They came to bury Burnley… ': a near death experience 371

'RISE' 1987 – 2010 375

THE 1987/88 SEASON 377
Wimbledon v Liverpool (F.A. Cup final) 377
'Two Tribes': Fear and loathing in Thatcher's Britain 402

THE 2007/08 SEASON 406
Exeter City v Aldershot Town 406
'Things Can Only Get Better': the Nineties and Noughties 431
Final Word 433

REFERENCES 435

INTRODUCTION

Exiled From Main Street

I have never been attracted by easy, vicarious glory. Even as a kid I rooted resolutely for the Indians (sorry, Native Americans). Southern Dixie stole my affection for no better reason than they were the underdogs in the US Civil War. So, it was destined that my choices of favourite football teams should follow a similar pattern. I do not drool over failure, though. I simply believe that success should be hard-earned. What sets my pulse racing is a team of doughty competitors punching well above their weight, determined to beat their retreat when the going gets really tough.

Although I have remained largely faithful to one team, Burnley, for over forty years, I am no monogamist. I have always had an unstoppable urge to lend a struggling club my Jonah-like support. Ironically, my life as a football supporter began in the First Division, at Stamford Bridge, in the late fifties, but in those days Chelsea were a cash-strapped, faltering First Division side en route to Division Two. As soon as Tommy Docherty had transformed them into swish King's Road slickers my interest began to wane. By that time I had developed affections for two local sides – Brighton & Hove Albion and Hastings United – as they immediately dropped like stones.

I came haltingly to football. My dad first tried to kindle an interest when I was five. He presented me with a birthday gift of a leather ball. We tried it out on a soggy surface in a deserted recreation field on a glowering autumn afternoon. The ball became impossibly heavy with excess moisture, barely trickling away from my flailing kicks. This did not seem like fun.

A year or so later I had to move to a new school in a distant town. Here, I discovered that Chix bubble gum football cards were hard currency. Staring at their crudely coloured images I couldn't imagine what the fuss was about. Most of the footballers were captured in stiff, perfunctory poses, their faces devoid of expression. They didn't seem to be having fun, either.

However, the faraway places they represented – Huddersfield, Sheffield and Burnley – seemed as exotic as the Black Hills of Dakota. Gradually my curiosity increased but it wasn't until I came across a 1957 football annual – *The Big Book of Football Champions* – in a local Woolworths store, that my interest took hold. Seeing that I was absorbed by the book, my father seized his Jesuit moment and bought it for me.

The pictures were quite different from those on the cards. Here was drama aplenty. There were shots of the ball yanking the goal net amid broken-toothed celebrations. There were lunging, muscular tackles by beefy defenders with furrowed expressions, while slight forwards writhed at their feet in pain. There were ballistic Brylcreemed goalkeepers, clad in thick jerseys, their flat caps dislodged by their frozen acrobatics. Thick, cloying mud was everywhere as if football was trench warfare. Unlike the cards, these snapshots conveyed excitement, action and suspense. I was so entranced by the seized moments of high drama that I tried emulating them in our shared orchard. Perhaps dad was alarmed by my grimacing, clawing, twisting tableaux for he decided then to take me to my first game.

This book is about growing up and becoming old with professional football. It is one 'Baby Boomer's' account of how football has evolved over the last fifty years, stretching from an unfair wage cap to unsustainable freedom and from one World Cup disappointment in Sweden to yet another in South Africa. Meanwhile in the world outside, we have lurched from one Middle East crisis – Suez – to several others, each with potentially more devastating consequences. So, in the words of the Average White Band, 'Let's Go Round Again'.

KIND OF BLUE 1958–1962

'Expect nothing. Live frugally on surprise'
Alice Walker, 1973

THE 1958/59 SEASON

Chelsea v Wolverhampton Wanderers

'When'
30 August 1958

Dad warned me that Chelsea would be cannon fodder. They had won the Football League in 1955 adopting a rugged style of play but then fell away quickly. In a cartoon of the time, one character remarks, 'I see Chelsea have won', to which his companion replies: 'They can't have, they won last week.' Inconsistency ran through them like the lettering on seaside rock. Massive victories sat alongside humiliating defeats. When asked what he thought of this Chelsea defence, their prospective coach, Tommy Docherty, replied that 'A jellyfish has more shape.' It is difficult to reconcile the opulent Chelsea Football Club of today with the infuriatingly inconsistent 'Drake's Ducklings'. Alan Hansen had yet to say 'You'll never win anything with kids.'

August 30th 1958 was a day of swooning heat. The huge glass roof at Paddington station incubated the warmth from the sun and that from its many copper-domed steam locomotives. Wispy, shimmering vapours conveyed the scent of sulphur, tar and scorched oil. Ruddy-faced men in open-necked shirts and loose flannels heaved strapped, swollen, brown leather suitcases into the crammed chocolate and cream carriages. Meanwhile, intricately curled or pony-tailed women stood aside, coolly issuing instructions. Some wore flared floral skirts with broad black belts while others sported straight shift dresses. Many of these couples or young families were off to the Cornish Riviera: to St Ives, Newquay or Looe. The summer of '58 was the high-water mark of holiday rail traffic. Thereafter, many more families turned to the road.

London was bulging with tourists. Many chose the parched parks where they could stretch out under the cooler canopies of the flaking plane trees. Despite the baking temperatures we made for Lyons Corner House cafeteria, where we joined the throng jostling with trays in search of elusive seats. It seemed that the protective metal covers provided for our fatty, soggy meals were as superfluous as any hope of taste or nourishment. Eating out in the fifties was generally a functional, joyless duty. The tube that rocked and rolled from Earl's Court to Fulham Broadway was packed, too, compressing the overpowering odour of tobacco. Every breath was worth twenty un-tipped. From then I knew what life must be like for a laboratory beagle.

Outside the ground there were programme sellers, emphasising the second syllable in their hoarse cries for custom – proGRARMS! There were badge sellers, too, selling small, blue star-shaped plastic brooches containing a selection of photographs of favourite players: Jimmy Greaves, Peter Brabrook and Ron Tindall. I chose one of Jimmy Greaves sporting a crew cut. He was smiling mischievously. It was a prophetic pick. Climbing the steep stairwell on to the open western terraces, it was obvious that this was a huge crowd. It was recorded as being over 61,000. I had never seen so many people squeezed into such a restricted space. Feeling the full force of the sun's glare, many found that they were overdressed. Thick Harris tweed sports jackets were removed, ties were unfastened and chests exposed but still the beady sweat trickled down so many flushed faces. Someone tried to make a paper hat out of a newspaper. It was a poor effort attracting much good-natured ridicule. On the public address system they were playing a song from the popular musical, *My Fair Lady.* Stanley Holloway declaimed in a gruff, atonal cockney voice, 'With a little bit of luck, with a little bit of luck, someone else'll do the blinkin' work.' Chelsea needed no luck or help on this scintillating afternoon as they murdered Wolves. Jimmy Greaves recalled in his book, *Greavsie*:

> *We didn't get off to the best of starts. Bobby Mason put Wolves ahead after only two minutes, but we were far from being fazed by that. There were certain games when I took to the pitch and just knew I was going to have one of those games when everything would go my way. From my first touch of the ball, I felt comfortable. I was relishing the big match occasion, confident of my own ability, sure that I would feature among the goals. In our first real attack of note, I corkscrewed past Ron Flowers and Gerry Harris before playing a one-two with Peter Brabrook. Though shackled by Bill Slater, when receiving the ball back from Peter I felt confident enough to hit it first time. I'd seen a gap just to the left of Malcolm*

Finlayson and aimed for that. Whenever I was presented with such an opportunity, I never hit the ball with all the power I could muster because I didn't have to. When I saw an opening, I would simply pass the ball through the space knowing no one would reach it. Malcolm Finlayson couldn't and we were level.

Jimmy Greaves scored five times that day and each goal seemed a carbon copy of the one before. Time and again he latched on to a sharp pass, anticipating its weight and angle expertly. Without hesitation he instantly made perfect contact with the ball, caressing it into his path. He drew Wolves' central defenders towards him only to flash past them with a shimmy and a dab on the accelerator. Each time Wolves' keeper, Finlayson, advanced, but Jimmy was too quick, too sharp for him. With meticulous timing and accuracy Greaves pushed the ball past Finlayson and into the net. No explosive finish was necessary. This was the hallmark of a master craftsman.

After half an hour Chelsea were 4-1 up. The Wolves defenders were not just red-faced on account of the heat. Billy Wright took unmerciful stick. He looked laboured and cruelly exposed, hardly a credible contender for England's most capped player. The young men around us were cooing 'Ooh Beverley' at him. He looked sheepish, as if he could actually hear their banal jibes above the raucous commotion. Wright had recently married Joy Beverley, who was a member of a popular trio of female singers, the Beverley Sisters. There was little fuss. He took a day off from training. She took a few hours off from her rehearsal. Just a few gathered at the Poole registry office. Joy's sister, 'Babs', described it as 'a quiet affair'. No Berkshire castle and host of angelic harpists for Billy and Joy. No tanker of pink champagne, either, and no celebrity magazine to pick up the tab.

Although Bill Slater reduced the deficit with a penalty before half-time, Chelsea seemed well out of sight. At the interval, Wolves' manager, Stan Cullis, yanked the nails out of Billy Wright's palms and instructed Slater to mark Greaves instead. It made little difference. Greaves continued to exploit Wolves' square defence with his lightning reactions. Only a spoilsport linesman denied him a double hat-trick. Cullis might have been the 'Iron Manager' but he was a consummate sportsman, too. He told the *London Evening News* reporter: 'What a player [Greaves is]. Someone's just said he doesn't run around enough. He wouldn't have to do that for me.'

Stan Cullis was a shrewd tactician. He adopted a command and control management style as befitted an old-school army man. Wing Commander Reep's statistical analyses revealed to him that 50 per cent of goals came from no more than one pass and 80 per cent from not more than three passes.

Consequently, he wanted his team to make no more than three passes in reaching their opponents' penalty area. So convinced was he by the greater efficacy of the long ball that it was this aspect of the Hungarians' play which impressed him most, while watching their mauling of England at Wembley in 1953. Cullis favoured a pressing game, principally in his opponents' half. He expected his muscular wing-halves, Clamp and Flowers, to move up close behind his five forwards in a Panzer-like assault which was designed to overwhelm and demoralise the opposition.

Cullis was prepared to accommodate a flair player like Peter Broadbent providing he operated within his tight tactical plan. Cullis demanded that his fast, raiding wingers were supplied with long balls to catch defences at their thinnest. He frowned at a short forward pass. He was cross at a short lateral pass and apoplectic at a back pass, unless made in an emergency. Elaborate passing movements had no part in his plan. His full-backs were told to tackle hard and then find a forward quickly and accurately. His wingers were told to 'hit the corners' but to make for goal if the opportunity arose. He insisted that his players always supported the man in possession. His players were physically and mentally tough and extremely fit. Cullis maintained that his tactics were always fair and constructive but not all pressmen agreed. Ken Jones of the *Daily Mirror* described one Wolves performance, one year later, as 'crash-bang soccer with hardly one breath of imagination or intelligence to break the monotony of crash tackles and aimless passes'.

By contrast, Jimmy Greaves recalled that his 'lovely old manager', Ted Drake, rarely gave his team any instruction about how they should play. Chelsea did not have a coach to fill this gap. The arrival of Tommy Docherty three years later would address this deficit, but would also create territorial tension between him, as coach, and Ted Drake, as manager. As happened at Arsenal, when a Young Turk, Ron Greenwood as coach, clashed with an older Turk, George Swindin as manager, the result was a turkey on the pitch.

Jimmy described Ted Drake as an 'all the best' manager because, according to him, that was the sum of Ted's pre-match advice. It was small wonder that Chelsea were exasperatingly inconsistent as they played much more by instinct than design. According to Jimmy Greaves' jocular accounts, Chelsea seemed like a pub team that happened to be in the First Division.

However, Jimmy recognised in his book, *The Heart of the Game,* that: 'The majority of managers in the late fifties were figureheads. Perhaps it was because managers ran a club in every sense of the word that they didn't have time to supervise training or turn their minds to tactical ploys. Many managers doubled up as the club secretary, a throwback to the pre-war years ...Their duties could also involve match-day catering.' Many managers at

…hen largely desk-bound. Few had the public profile or …ers command today. Although Ted Drake distinguished …uit manager when he joined Chelsea in 1952, this was …e unusual step of leading the players' training sessions. …ch and tactician, he was less well equipped than those that …mmy Docherty and Dave Sexton.

… by what I saw. The drama of the freeze frame had been … exhilaration of the moving picture. I came to understand … game with sudden changes of pace, rapid speed of thought … acceleration. If I was less startled by the natural talent and …ue on show this was because Jimmy Greaves made it look so

…script to this stunning victory, four days later Chelsea played at …st 4-0. Any designs I might have had about becoming a glory hunter were knocked back into lugubrious shape. Anything else would have been an offence to karma.

Norwich City v Tottenham Hotspur (FA Cup fifth round)

'I Got Stung / One Night'
18 February 1959

The fifties proved to be a golden age for the underdog, particularly in the FA Cup. For example, Third Division (North) side Port Vale reached the semi-finals in 1954 having beaten both of their First Division opponents, Cardiff City and FA Cup holders, Blackpool. Frequently, the poor state of pitches during the winter months helped the underdog, enabling them to compete on more even terms. The 1959 FA Cup winners, Nottingham Forest, came perilously close to defeat in the third round on an iced, rutted surface at Tooting & Mitcham while Liverpool, then a Second Division side, lost their balance on Worcester City's ice rink. And, of course, the maximum wage cap and the feudal 'retain and transfer' system enabled smaller clubs to retain their most talented players for longer periods. After Third Division side Southampton had thrashed top-flight team Manchester City 5-1 at Maine Road in 1960, they kept their two wingers, who created so much mayhem – the tricky Terry Paine and tearaway John Sydenham. Both eventually played for their parent club in the top tier.

Norwich City's cup run in '58/59 started inauspiciously. They were languishing in 16th place in the newly-formed Third Division. Their manager, Archie Macaulay, a distinguished former Arsenal and Scottish international right-half, had come under intense pressure from the fans. Early in the season he became barricaded in his office as disillusioned supporters protested loudly in the street outside. In keeping with the dismal mood, City struggled to beat amateurs Ilford, a lowly-placed Isthmian League side, at home in the first round. The Canaries were actually a goal behind at half-time and only secured victory late in the game.

In the second round, Norwich first drew at Swindon and were then under the cosh in the replay. However, after home keeper Ken Nethercott had to retire hurt, the previously disgruntled Norwich crowd got behind their depleted side. Suddenly, the ground began to pulse and pound with vociferous passion. As Swindon melted in the heat they generated, the dapper, crew-cut Canadian Errol Crossan netted the goal which put City through to face Manchester United at home in the third round.

The occasion was a triumph for the terse, poker-faced Archie Macaulay. Despite taking merciless flak from the fans, he kept his nerve. Macaulay knew his team could play. He just needed to convince his players. His shrewd positional changes helped. Ron Ashman, with over 400 senior games behind him, was converted into a solid, thoughtful left-back, where he found a steady partner in Brian Thurlow. To accommodate Ashman's move, Roy McCrohan was switched to right-half, where he operated in a defensive capacity. Macaulay also restored the twinkling Bobby Brennan to the left wing, when most supporters thought he was finished. Meanwhile on the opposite flank, Errol Crossan, nicknamed 'Cowboy' because of his Canadian roots, was encouraged to run with paralysing directness at opposing defences. The little Irishman, Jimmy Hill, was given greater licence to exercise his craft in midfield. In turn, Terry Allcock was instructed to push up more to partner the predatory Terry Bly. The tactical changes worked like a dream. Confidence began to surge through the once choking Canaries.

Matt Busby took no chances. He fielded his strongest side including his expensive new recruit Albert 'Golden Boy' Quixall. Bobby Charlton, Dennis Viollet, Bill Foulkes, Warren Bradley and Irish international keeper, Harry Gregg, all played. Although Munich must have still been fresh in their minds, United's league form had recovered remarkably. They would finish the season as First Division runners-up to Wolves.

Norwich's skipper, Ron Ashman, won the toss and compelled United to face the low, dazzling winter sun. The afternoon was so numbingly cold that 35 fans needed the assistance of the St John's Ambulance brigade. As for the players, they had their work cut out in just keeping their feet. A thin, crusty carpet of snow covered a rock-like Carrow Road surface. But the treacherous conditions did not wholly account for the ruthless way in which Norwich swept their famous opponents aside.

Macaulay instructed his team to hustle United from the start and to sit tightly on their inside trio of forwards: Charlton, Viollet and Quixall. Nevertheless, United made the better start. Fortunately, Charlton slipped when through on goal and Thurlow managed to clear another effort off the line. But, thereafter, Norwich seized total control. United's wing-halves, Freddie Goodwin and Wilf McGuinness, became bewildered by the skill and thrust of Hill and Allcock while the full-backs, Carolan and Foulkes, were undone by Brennan's sparkling footwork and Crossan's speed. The quality of Norwich's football was unbelievable. Only an outstanding display of goalkeeping from United's Harry Gregg kept the final score down to 0-3.

The star of the occasion was local-born centre-forward Terry Bly, who on this shivering afternoon simply roasted United's centre-half, Ronnie Cope. Macaulay commented, 'Using his speed and balance, Bly had all the room he needed in the middle and could have had half a dozen goals.' Bly settled for two. The first came after 31 minutes. Terry Allcock's penetrative pass gave Bobby Brennan the opportunity to run to the byline whereupon he sent a skidding centre into United's box. Bly's sprint proved far too quick for the slipping and sliding Manchester defenders. Without hesitating, Bly blasted the ball past Gregg. Although a retaliatory attack resulted in Viollet heading wide, Norwich were deservedly in front at the break. Norwich goalie Ken Nethercott had only one save to make before half-time, when he dealt competently with Scanlon's curling shot.

Norwich were uncontainable at the start of the second half. Bly's header hit the crossbar, releasing a shower of snow. Bobby Brennan's shot hit the post and Terry Allcock's effort was blocked on the line. Gregg had to hurl himself this way and that to keep the rampant Canaries at bay. It couldn't last. And it didn't. On the hour, Bly beat Foulkes and raced down the left wing. Making an unaccustomed error, Gregg could only parry Bly's high cross, allowing Crossan to head into the empty net. Norwich continued to pour forward. Gregg saved brilliantly from Bly. Allcock's shot fizzed past the post and Crossan's effort was disallowed. But with only two minutes remaining, Norwich added to United's humiliation. Having beaten the hapless Cope once again, Bly was left with a clear run on goal. He cut in from the left and sent a searing right-foot drive past Gregg at his near post.

Bly remembered: 'I only had a few touches of the ball during the game but after each touch it seemed to end up in the net.' The headlines of the local *Pink'n* read 'Bly, Bly Babes. It was glory, glory all the way.' Bly had nearly given up the game during the previous season because of a serious cartilage injury. During the fifties, treatment of sports injuries was primitive. Players rarely recovered from medial or cruciate knee injuries and even cartilage problems could ruin their careers.

Ron Ashman confessed, 'It's difficult to work out just what happened to us. One minute we were a struggling Third Division team lucky to be in the third round. Then, overnight, we had this conviction we could beat anyone. You see, it wasn't just that we had taken United to the cleaners. There were good players in our team, a lot of good players. We weren't a kick and rush side and it just needed something to set it off. Beating United did that for us. Home advantage is a tremendous thing in the FA Cup, but as time went on we honestly believed we could win anywhere against anyone.'

Macaulay commented: 'They all laughed when I said we could beat Manchester United but I knew our men to be capable of winning. I planned two lines of defence. Right-half, Roy McCrohan stayed back with the centre-half, Butler, and the full-backs, while left-half Matt Crowe operated in front. As soon as a Norwich move broke down, Terry Allcock doubled back with Crowe. That way we were able to break up most of their moves before they started. I reckoned full-back Billy Foulkes could be beaten so I told our inside-left, Jimmy Hill, to stay on the wing with Bobby Brennan and that was where our goals came from. It worked to perfection.'

Norwich's next opponents were Cardiff City, who were preparing for a top-flight return. Once again, Bly was the two-goal hero, chipping the Cardiff keeper for his second-half winner. In a battle of the birds, yellow prevailed over blue (3-2), setting up a trip to that old boiler of a cockerel, Spurs.

Spurs' boss, Bill Nicholson, was a hard taskmaster. He expected the highest standards from his players on and off the pitch. He was a shrewd tactician, too, one of the sharpest around. Nicholson's head wasn't turned by a 10-4 victory in his first game in charge. He recalled that 'too many silly goals were given away'. Spurs leaked 95 league goals during the '58/59 season – relegation form. Creative genius Danny Blanchflower was partly to blame. Too often, he neglected his defensive duties. But Blanchflower's cavalier performances were not Nicholson's only problem. His whole team was misfiring. Cliff Jones, signed for a record fee from Swansea, looked more like an apprentice than the world-class winger he was to become. As talented as he was, Johnny Brooks performed fitfully at inside-forward; 'always better in a winning side', was Nicholson's terse view. Nicholson needed a dynamic ball-winner. Hearts' Dave Mackay fitted that bill, but he did not arrive until March.

A consistent goalscorer was needed to play alongside Smith, but the Spurs boss had to make do with Dave Dunmore, temporarily. Chelsea's

Les Allen was a better option. He would not arrive until later in the year as a result of a shrewd swap involving Brooks. Ultimately, Jimmy Greaves would deliver a better solution. In 1961, Nicholson paid AC Milan £99,999 for him. The goalkeeping position was vulnerable, too. Nicholson did not rate either John Hollowbread or Ron Reynolds. Only Dundee's keeper, Bill Brown, would satisfy his need.

Archie Macaulay knew Spurs' defensive organisation was shaky and their morale, fragile. He believed his team had a chance, particularly with 20,000 Norwich fans accompanying them to a grey, murky White Hart Lane, doubling the number that had grumpily attended City's home games a few months before. Norwich was in the grip of cup fever. Tickets were at a premium. Work schedules went haywire. Almost everyone knew the mournful, yet oddly inspiring, Carrow Road anthem, 'On the Ball City'. The club were on the local paper's front pages for weeks.

Macaulay knew he had to stop Spurs from playing. Norwich's pressing game wasn't pretty. Their tackling was tough, ultra tough. Everyone defended, from the front to the back. But chances still came. Thankfully, Ken Nethercott was in excellent form, making three smart saves before the interval. Ron Ashman recalled, 'We had to keep things tight because Spurs had some outstanding individual players. They had to be pinned down and in a cup-tie atmosphere you are bound to get rugged stuff. We needed a goal to settle us down.'

The Norwich players were buoyant at half-time. They had done half their job well. Their hosts had not hurt them and seemed dispirited. Shortly after the break, Norwich showed they could sting as well as tame. After 65 minutes, Terry Allcock drove them deservedly into the lead. Just as Macaulay hoped, Spurs began to fragment. Drooping postures and resigned looks abounded. Jones' murderous pace deserted him. Like his colleagues, he ran into blind alleys, wandering ineffectively along the left wing where he was barracked by the impatient home supporters. With Spurs unravelling, Hill, Allcock and Bly had good chances to make the tie safe but they spurned them. Time was almost up when Dunmore chased a loose ball on the left flank. He centred immediately. Hearing Cliff Jones' call to 'leave it', Bobby Smith dummied the cross, allowing the out-of-sorts Welsh winger to volley home the equaliser. Ashman was aghast, saying: 'It was the one defensive error we made. We never expected Dunmore to retrieve the ball after Jim Iley sliced a shot towards the touchline. But he did. I managed to get a hand to the shot but couldn't stop it.'

For the replay, Danny Blanchflower was restored at inside-right in place of Harmer. Welsh international right-winger, Terry Medwin, came in for Brooks and Eddie Clayton took over from Dunmore. Norwich were unchanged. Carrow Road was like a cauldron with 38,000 people crammed in. Blanchflower remarked, 'I have played all round the world in some of the world's greatest stadiums, but I have never experienced an atmosphere like that. The crowd is worth a goal start for Norwich. The anthems, the cheers are always in your ears. There is no way you can shut them out.' There was no way of shutting out the Norwich players, either.

Spurs almost went ahead through Bobby Smith but Nethercott saved his shot superbly. 'At my age one good save a match is enough,' cracked the veteran custodian. He wasn't troubled again. Roared on by a febrile crowd, Norwich swarmed all over Spurs. The crucial breakthrough came in the 63rd minute. Ashman chipped into the box; he later conceded it was a miskick. The Spurs defenders were slow to react to a deflection. Bly unhesitatingly drove the loose ball past Hollowbread. The misty night sky was rent with a thunderous roar.

At the final whistle the delirious crowd poured on to the pitch. Still Ashman found enough space to dance an excited jig with a policeman, whose sense of duty took second place to his all-consuming excitement. Lugubrious but sporting, Bill Nicholson said, 'Norwich are a good side and they kept coming at us all the time. Good luck to them in the next round.' Norwich were drawn away at Sheffield United, who were managed by Joe Mercer, Macaulay's former Arsenal colleague.

The wily Mercer had successfully introduced *catenaccio* to Bramall Lane – a back four with a 'sweeper' operating behind to seal any gaps and take care of other opponents breaking from deep positions. The blunting Blades, with the immaculate Joe Shaw operating as their sweeper, conceded just seven goals in 17 league games. But eagle-eyed Archie Macaulay noticed that their right-back, Cec Coldwell, did not cover the centre-half as well as England full-back Graham Shaw did on the left. He decided that Norwich should probe United's left flank in order to draw Joe Shaw over to that side and attempt to exploit the space left by Coldwell, on the Blades' right, by pinging a long pass into the inside-left channel for Bly or Hill to latch on to. The move had to be played at pace and the pass executed with great accuracy. It needed to be delivered far enough out to keep Sheffield goalie, Hodgkinson, at home, but not so far out that United's wing-halves could snuff out the danger.

However, on a bright Sheffield afternoon, City's hopes seemed eclipsed when Ken Nethercott dislocated his right shoulder after diving at the feet of United's left-winger. At that point Norwich were already a goal down as Russell's deflected shot looped over the unlucky Nethercott. Macaulay insisted that Nethercott should come off and Brennan, a winger, should go in goal. But the captain, Ashman, overruled his manager, telling his keeper:

'If you go off we have no chance of equalising. You go back in goal, Ken, and we'll keep Sheffield out of your reach.' Ashman was as good as his word, and late in the game Brennan's mazy dribble set up the unmarked Crossan for an easy equaliser. Nethercott bravely stood at his post for over an hour, enduring excruciating pain. He would never play for Norwich again. Sandy Kennon replaced him in the replay. Having jumped jail, Norwich surged into a 2-0 lead in the replay. Brennan turned his marker, Coldwell, before thumping a drive into the top right-hand corner. Then Bly seized upon a defence-splitting pass and dinked a delicate shot over the advancing Hodgkinson. Although the Blades' arch-poacher, 'Doc' Pace, punished Kennon when he fumbled Hamilton's low shot, Bly restored City's two-goal lead after the break, blasting home from close range. Sheffield's Gerry Summers headed in from a late corner to produce a tense finish but Norwich held out.

In the semi-final at White Hart Lane Norwich were paired with Luton, then a declining First Division side. Despite dominating the early play the Canaries missed several gilt-edged chances. Allan Brown made them pay by heading the Hatters into a first-half lead from Billy Bingham's precise cross. Although Brennan equalised after the break, capitalising upon a miscued header to score with a scorching drive, Norwich could not make their superiority count. In fact, Norwich were indebted to their shaky keeper, Kennon, as it was his acrobatic save which denied Luton a late winner.

In the replay at St Andrew's, Norwich again had the better of the early play but found ex-England goalie Ron Baynham in international form. On the one occasion when the City forwards managed to beat him, Brendan McNally cleared off the line. Norwich were then left to rue their fortune as Northern Ireland's World Cup hero, Billy Bingham, stabbed home a second-half winner. At Wembley, Luton played poorly in losing to ten-man Nottingham Forest. The Norwich players felt they would have made a better fist of the occasion but settled for their new celebrity status.

Yet more World Cup disappointment

In the immediate post-war years, English football seemed to suffer from a 'Little Englander' mentality. We were slow to join the World Cup competition. We seemed complacent, feeling we had nothing to prove after beating world champions, Italy, 4-0 in Turin in 1948. What then followed in Brazil, two years later, was a very nasty surprise. Our World Cup defeat by the fledgling USA side emphasised our sagging status. Having insulated ourselves from modern tactical thinking, we were ruthlessly torn apart by the Hungarians in 1953, and again in 1954, just prior to the World Cup finals in Switzerland. Despite prestigious victories in friendly internationals against recently-crowned world champions West Germany in the autumn of 1954, and against Brazil, the world champions-in-waiting in 1956, when it came to the 'real thing', a World Cup tournament, we faltered serially.

We were slow to join the European Cup competition, too. The 1955 Football League champions, Chelsea, were discouraged from joining by our football authorities. Thanks to Matt Busby's determination, Manchester United joined the competition during the 1956/57 season, but they were eliminated by the mighty Real Madrid. Of course, we will never know what Manchester United might have achieved had their side not been tragically decimated at Munich. However, succeeding champions, Wolves, stumbled immediately. Stan Cullis, their manager, boasted of his team's international prowess having defeated the cream of European club sides – Honved, Spartak Moscow and Real Madrid – in friendlies. But once tested in an official competition, they came up well short of the required standard.

So did England in the 1958 World Cup finals in Sweden although they were depleted by the Munich tragedy and an injury to Tom Finney, arguably their best outfield player. They were eliminated at the group stage after a play-off defeat by the USSR. After winning the Jules Rimet Trophy, Brazilian skipper, Hideraldo Luiz Bellini, paid England the equivocal compliment: 'England gave us the hardest match. They were better than [finalists] Sweden, very good in defence, and played practical football.'

If this was praise with a faint insult it was probably fair. Helped by Bill Nicholson's shrewd defensive tactics, England managed to blunt Brazilian brilliance in Gothenburg, achieving a creditable 0-0 draw. It was Brazil's only game in Sweden that they failed to win. Like England, Scotland fell at the first hurdle. It was left to our underdogs, Northern Ireland and Wales, to surpass expectations.

Prompted by the midfield brilliance of Danny Blanchflower and Jimmy McIlroy and the penetrative wing play of Peter McParland and Billy Bingham, Northern Ireland beat Czechoslovakia in a group play-off. But their brave fight ended in the last eight. The Irish were already missing key players through injury. Their absurdly punishing itinerary did the rest. Having held France in the first half, spurning an excellent scoring opportunity, they eventually ran out of puff and were overrun.

Wales qualified for the quarter-finals after heroically defeating Hungary 2-1. There, they faced Brazil. Unfortunately, injury robbed them of the talismanic John Charles but thanks to Jack Kelsey's agility in goal, their plucky defence was breached just once, by Pele, with less than twenty minutes remaining.

'Never had it so good'?

This was neither a vintage time for British football nor one for the country at large. Despite Harold Macmillan's confidence, our consumer boom of the late fifties was not founded upon a strong, sustainable economy. Our textile industry was already in decline because of the strength of foreign competition. Shipbuilding would suffer a similar fate as would other heavy industries. The jobless total rose by almost 500,000 in 1958; it was the highest annual rise in ten years.

In 1938, Neville Chamberlain feared that if Britain entered a European war it could not afford it would cease to be a world power. He was right. Britain fared worse, economically, from victory than West Germany, Italy and Japan ultimately did from defeat. Despite taking our place as a world player in the 1950 Korean conflict, the scale of our decline was emphasised just six years later at Suez. Here, the Americans made us back off, threatening to withdraw essential international monetary aid. The ill-conceived campaign ended less like the snarl of a bulldog and more like the yap of a poodle. Before Suez, we produced a series of self-reverential war films which celebrated British courage with either stiff-upper-lipped or jaunty conviction. After Suez, we were more circumspect. The 1959 British film *Yesterday's Enemy* even suggested that we were not always honourable in combat. We clung doggedly to our world policing role, though, as if we were still an imperial power.

Although we embarked upon decolonisation and retagged Empire Day as Commonwealth Day, immigration from Commonwealth countries created tensions in our poorer areas where the competition for housing and jobs was more acute. This, plus sexual jealousy, was the background to the 1958 riots in Nottingham and Notting Hill. The unnamed photographer in Colin McInnes' novel, *Absolute Beginners* (1959) remarked: 'I don't understand my country anymore … the English race has spread itself all over the damn world … no one invited us … yet when a few hundred thousand come and settle among our fifty millions we just can't take it.'

In the late fifties, our selective interpretation of past glory clouded our vision of the future. The European Economic Community was inaugurated in 1958 without us. We appeared unconcerned, remaining suspicious of European economic and political ties. At the base of this suspicion was a fear of being taken over. It was this fear which prompted former Labour Prime Minister, Clem Attlee, to sneer: 'Very recently this country spent a great deal of blood and treasure, rescuing four of 'em from attacks by the other two.' More far-sighted politicians like Ted Heath and George Brown were in a minority when it came to recognising the benefits of stronger ties with Europe. This remains a vexed political issue, notably among Conservatives.

However, we were generally much more upbeat about the American cultural invasion although we sent Jerry Lee Lewis packing in 1958 on account of his marriage to his 13-year-old cousin. We fawned over US popular music, films and TV shows like *I Love Lucy, Wagon Train* and *Bilko*. American film star Tony Curtis epitomised the popular 'Italian Look'. The hula hoop craze of 1958 was an American innovation, too. With imitation being the sincerest form of flattery, we had our Elvis facsimile in Cliff Richard while Adam Faith plagiarised 'hiccupping' Buddy Holly. Television adverts, heavily influenced by stateside 'Mad Men', provided jingles which dislodged our youngsters' love of traditional nursery rhymes. Even the highly patriotic *Eagle* comic drew upon glossy American production values. In short, American culture seemed 'cool', whereas British traditions seemed staid, fusty or 'square'.

THE 1959/60 SEASON

Brighton & Hove Albion v Aston Villa

'Living Doll'
22 August 1959

Thinking I needed a fuller portfolio of struggling causes, Dad interrupted my stay with relatives in Crawley to take me to nearby Brighton. It was yet another day of sparkling sunshine in one of the hottest summers on record. We caught a Southern Electric train which was already full by the time we had wriggled in. A smouldering heat infused the button-clothed, horsehair seats, releasing stale scents of perfume and tobacco. Not that there were any spare places to sit. Squeezed into a stuffy, overcrowded corridor, I wondered what might happen at Chelsea that afternoon. We had not returned to Stamford Bridge since that epic first game despite my hankering for more. Having administered the drug, Dad left me with 'cold turkey' for almost 12 months. But he had to work most weekends.

Leaving its penultimate stop in its wake, the humming train accelerated past the shrivelled, straw-strewn fields, already plundered by the locust-like combine harvesters. If this signalled the last days of summer, the tropical temperature did not. As the hazy outline of the South Downs came into view, my sense of anticipation sharpened. Behind them, my dad told me, was the Goldstone Ground, the home of Brighton & Hove Albion. As we swayed towards our destination, a kindly home supporter told us about what had been happening at his beloved club. Brighton were then a middling Second Division side.

Brighton had been promoted from Division Three (South) in April 1958, after a switchback run-in. Their success hinged upon the outcome of their crucial final home fixture with Watford. Brighton did not choke, thrashing the Hornets 6-0 in front of a capacity crowd of 31,038. The hero was 20-year-old local lad, Adrian Thorne, who scored five times. Adrian later recalled to Paul Camillin in the book *Match of My Life*:

> *I could sense the determination in the team. Glen Wilson was a superb skipper: a hard, efficient, tireless worker in midfield. He with Don Bates [a Sussex County cricketer] and Kenny Whitfield formed a superb midfield trio throughout that season and stopped any sort of attacks from Watford that night. Up front we tore them apart, annihilating them with three quick goals. Bang, bang, bang. Effectively the game was over. I happened to get on the end of everything that came my way. In other matches you get the same number of chances, but not put them away.*

Adrian thought Brighton's genial manager, Billy Lane, protected him at the start of his professional career. He explained to a Brighton *Evening Argus* reporter: 'I had come from a sheltered environment and when I first went into the senior dressing room and heard all the swearing I thought, "What have I got into?" Billy was aware of this and would ask the players not to use bad language when I was there. That was rather embarrassing for me but Billy could be a bit touchy about language. I thought he did a good job for the club and was the first manager to get them promotion.'

Lane strengthened his squad by bringing in a six foot striker, John Shepherd, from Millwall, young inside-right Ronnie Clayton and left-winger Freddie Jones from Arsenal, and Workington's wing-half Jack Bertolini. Realising he needed more skill and experience, Lane signed Manchester City full-back Roy Little in October 1958 for £4,850. Little had been an FA Cup winner with City in 1956. Arsenal's winger, Mike Tiddy, joined too, as did Reading's leading goalscorer, Tommy Dixon. With the season drawing to a close, Lane paid £7,000 for Leicester City's creative Scottish inside-forward, Ian McNeill.

After their first four games in Division Two, Brighton were in bottom place. Nine goals were put past them at Middlesbrough in the opening fixture with Brian Clough scoring five. At the end of the game, Brighton's skipper, Glen Wilson, asked the referee for a touch of the ball as he hadn't managed one during the game. Gradually the tide turned. Dixon and Shepherd shared 27 league goals, while young Thorne chipped in with ten as Brighton completed their season in 12th place – a remarkable turnaround.

Although Albion's average attendance in Division Two grew by 36 per cent to around 22,400 their costs were rising. There was the West Stand reconstruction to pay for. But Lane still managed to persuade his board to find another £15,000 to bring in Newcastle's 24-year-old reserve centre-forward Bill Curry for the start of the '59/60 season. It seemed incredible that Newcastle were prepared to shed a striker who had netted 21 First Division goals in just 33 appearances. There again, Curry had the fast, predatory Len White ahead of him. Although it took Curry a few games to find his feet he demonstrated that he was the 'real deal'. By April 1960, he had scored 26 league goals including three hat-tricks. That £15,000 fee seemed like a snip. A Brighton *Evening Argus* reporter recalled:

> *Bill Curry had that rare gift of hovering in the air. He seemed to do so while making up his mind whether to direct the ball either into the back of the net or to the feet of a better placed colleague. This ability he shared with the great headers of the game although the nearest Curry came to international level was one appearance for England under-23s while a Newcastle player. Ask any Albion fan today who saw Curry what they remember best about him, and they will confirm that not only was his aerial power extraordinary but his pace and bravery for a player of no more than 5ft 10in was something worth going a long way to see. Those spring-heeled leaps were all about matchless timing. Bill scorned any notion of lurking in the box and poaching chances created by others. He mixed it with the toughest of the tough and could kick with the best. Off the park he was a perfect gentleman and when Billy Lane saw him score a hat-trick at Fratton Park the previous season his eyes lit up on learning afterwards that the man he wanted had an exemplary track record on and off the pitch.*

There was quite a buzz about Curry on our cramped train but no one was in any doubt that newly-relegated Aston Villa would be a tough proposition. Only two years before they had won the FA Cup, controversially defeating Manchester United, thereby denying the 'Busby Babes' the first 'double' of the twentieth century.

Joe Mercer, the former Everton, Arsenal and England wing-half, took charge of the leaking Villa just before Christmas 1958. Joe was one of the 'new-style' coaching managers. His managerial career had begun inauspiciously, though. Sheffield United were relegated in 1956 at the end of his first season in charge, as were Villa in 1959. Nevertheless, when he left Sheffield in 1958 the Blades were no longer a club 'well in the red'. They were poised for a return to the First Division. Mercer restored Villa's fortunes quickly, too, taking them back to the top flight after one full season in charge. Despite suffering a stroke in 1964, he and Malcolm Allison then set about transforming the fortunes of languishing Manchester City.

Mercer had turned down Arsenal before taking on what some saw as a poisoned chalice at Aston Villa. Mercer explained: 'My reasoning was that I still had to prove myself as a good manager and in Villa there was scope ... [although] the impression was that the place was morbid and lifeless. The club seemed choked by tradition. Tradition can be a wonderful friend but a dangerous enemy.' He demanded a free hand to develop his way of playing. Despite losing his first three games in charge he was encouraged by what he saw. He said, 'The boys responded to me. There was no defeatism among them and the spectators in those days were still loyal. Things began to improve. By Easter we were in the semi-final of the FA Cup and five points clear of the relegation places. But I think the effort the lads made for me in the cup cost them too much; I am sure it advanced the retirement of captain, Peter Aldis.'

Mercer knew that success in football is always founded upon a sound defence. He had demonstrated this at Bramall Lane. Although he helped tighten up the Villa defence the problem then shifted to the attack as his forwards suffered a goal drought; only six goals were scored in their vital last eight league games. Nevertheless, a 0-0 draw at relegation rivals Manchester City in the penultimate game seemed sufficient to keep them up. It was not to be. City beat Leicester in their final game, while West Bromwich's 88th-minute equaliser, against Villa, sent Mercer's side down by a point and .001 of a goal.

Joe Mercer remembered 'The foundations for our return to the First Division were laid in the dressing room after the West Bromwich game ... It was only the second time in their 85-year-old history that Villa had slipped into the Second Division but there was no recrimination from the directors. I bought a few players: Jimmy MacEwan, a right-winger from Raith, Bobby Thompson from Wolves at inside-right and Jimmy Adam from Luton Town, who played in four different positions.' Although given £25,000 by the Villa board for team strengthening, Mercer invested the money in a new training ground. He said: 'It was the right decision I am sure. Villa's young players could not have made the progress they have without the ground.'

While allocating long hours to 'administrative work' – Mercer was always at the office at 9.00am and sometimes did not return home until past midnight – he refused to be office-bound. He said, 'I liked to be with the players between ten and twelve every morning, sometimes coaching them.'

He picked out his sessions with his talented centre-forward Gerry Hitchens as one of his most significant achievements. Mercer recalled:

> *Gerry's reaction to my coaching gave me my greatest satisfaction. Gerry obviously had all the skills but could not co-ordinate them to best effect. He could kill a ball perfectly but then he would freeze on it, giving the defender time to get in his tackle. He also came back square to the ball instead of half-turning to see the opposition coming in. By putting Gerry into this situation in training, hour after hour, doing the right thing eventually became automatic. His fantastic speed and stamina helped him pass players to the byline but then he had a habit of bringing the ball back to his right foot, giving the defence time to recover. By improving his left foot he was able to cross first time. We were also able to improve his shooting. All golfers will appreciate his trouble; he was trying to knock the cover off the ball. We managed to slow his strike down and this did the trick.*

Hitchens was absent for the Brighton game but he would become Villa's leading scorer during this season. He was en route to fame and fortune as an England international and Serie A striker. Hitchens remained in Italy for nine years – a record stay for a British footballer – playing for Inter, Torino, Atalanta and Cagliari.

Upon arrival at Hove station, it was readily apparent that there was going to be an almighty crush. Easing ourselves out of the train, we were forced to shuffle up the steps and over the packed, extended footbridge that spanned both sets of platforms and the adjacent sidings. The queue for the entrances started almost upon leaving the footbridge. While caught up in this churn, my dad managed to reach out to a badge seller, buying me another plastic star-shaped brooch. Rather guiltily I found it was one of Peter McParland, Villa's forceful, free-scoring left-winger. It was his reckless charge which deprived Manchester United of their goalkeeper, Ray Wood, for most of the 1957 FA Cup Final. Wood sustained a broken cheekbone and concussion but, as was the way back then, he heroically returned to play as a wobbly right-winger, frequently dabbing his nose with smelling salts. To add insult to inflicted injury, McParland then smashed in two second-half goals – a bullet header and an unstoppable drive – past deputy United keeper,

Jackie Blanchflower, to win the cup for Villa. In the World Cup, though, McParland's heroics were without controversy

Drenched with sweat on account of the searing sun and the compressed crowd, my legs buckled and my head swam. The stand roofs seemed to oscillate in the humid heat. Propped up by my dad, we eventually pushed through the ratcheting turnstiles and made for a less crushed spot at the highest part of the East Terrace. Some 31,484 people eventually crammed into the ground. More condensed than Stamford Bridge, the terraces seemed to shake with the pounding of so many feet when the blue and white striped team ran out.

For this game, Mercer was forced into making a number of changes. He had to replace Hitchens with the veteran former England international Jackie Sewell, who had played at Wembley against the Magical Magyars in 1953. The former Burnley left-back, Doug Winton, was drafted in, while young Terry Morrall deputised for the experienced Jimmy Dugdale at centre-half. Mercer moved Jimmy MacEwan to inside-right, allowing Jimmy Adam to take the right wing slot. But if this was a makeshift team, they did not play like one. Brighton were under the cosh from the very start and went a goal down before half-time. Villa's scorer was MacEwan. I think, but I am not sure, that Brighton equalised after the break. John Shepherd is credited with the goal. Then, after what I dimly remember as a period of Brighton pressure, Villa won the game through Jackie Sewell. It was his last goal for the club. Brighton's scorer, John Shepherd, was also about to depart, too, for his final league club, Gillingham. It was remarkable that the predatory but injury-prone Shepherd should have become a professional footballer after polio had left him paralysed during his early years.

On that scorching afternoon, an image of McParland's pace and power remains. He was so dominant, so strong in the air, thumping the ball venomously with his forehead, and so muscular on the ground with an explosive shot from either foot. Each loose ball was contested hungrily, no tackle shirked. While happy to run at his full-back, he was not content to hug the touchline. He created mayhem in the box with his aerial power. There he would jostle aggressively for space, levering himself above the mix to produce whiplash headers. I was later surprised to find that McParland was then marginally less than six feet tall, weighing just over 12 stones. He seemed larger than that. But this was the size of the man's performance.

After the game, Dad and I walked down to the sea. When I later read the introductory passages of Graham Greene's novel *Brighton Rock*, I was reminded of that day. 'They came in by train from Victoria every five minutes, rocked down Queen's Road...stepped off in bewildered multitudes into fresh and glittering air: the new silver paint sparkled on the piers, the cream houses ran away into the west like a pale Victorian water-colour...' A vivid image of that occasion remains. The sea, mildly rippled by an onshore breeze, scintillated in the lowering evening sunlight. Trolley buses hummed along the packed promenade, their extended arms click-clacking at the joints in the overhead cables. We bought candyfloss at the Palace Pier where even the vicious rat-a-tat-tat of the tail-gunner video game – a relic from a World War Two training exercise – could not drown the screaming from the perilous helter-skelter. Here, terrified punters were shot out above the sea in their lurching descent. Ah, 'those hazy, lazy, crazy days' of an unforgettable summer.

The age of innocence or the age of naivety?

There were 36 hat-tricks scored in the First Division alone in this season. Compare that figure to the record for the Premiership 2008/9 season – just six! On this first day of the season, Jimmy Greaves scored one in a remarkable 4-4 home draw with Preston North End. In the return game, on a grisly December day of high wind and rain, Jimmy went two better, scoring all five of Chelsea's goals in a stupendous 5-4 victory. Cliff Jones was another hat-trick hero on day one, as Spurs shot down the woeful Magpies 5-1 at St James' Park. Bill Curry might have had a wry smile.

Over the season, there was a succession of bewildering results. Having lost 3-1 at Fulham, Wolves bared their yellowed teeth in the return fixture, winning 9-0. Wolves also scored ten against Manchester City in two league games, hammering City 6-4 at Maine Road. Shaking off a dreadful start to the season, Newcastle slaughtered Everton 8-2 and Manchester United 7-3, prompting Matt Busby to buy West Bromwich's defensive wing-half, Maurice Setters.

Even circumspect Aston Villa, who netted a comparatively modest 29 league goals in their first 17 Second Division fixtures, scored 21 in their next three, thrashing Charlton 11-1 and tonking both Bristol City and Scunthorpe 5-0, with Hitchens scoring ten times. As can be seen in photographs of the time, defenders seemed as rare as ospreys while voracious, virtually unopposed forward lines bore down on goal. Greaves recalled this as the 'final year in football's age of innocence, the last in which just about every game was played in a very open and attacking manner'.

But for 'innocence' read also 'unprofessional', for preparations at many top clubs were little better than shambolic, not helped by the poor training facilities and lack of qualified coaching. For example, First Division Blackpool had no dedicated training ground and no indoor gym. It was small wonder that Stan Matthews was allowed to train alone on the Blackpool sands. It was not unusual for top clubs to use their ground's cinder car park as a practice area. Unsurprisingly, more emphasis was placed upon fitness training than ball work.

Noel Cantwell was appalled by the lax training standards he found at Old Trafford after joining United from West Ham in 1960. Cantwell told Leo McKinstry, author of *Jack and Bobby*, that:

> *There was no proper coaching whatsoever. Nobody, but nobody at Old Trafford knew anything about coaching. Training was so boring it would drive you mad. We would just have a few laps, a five-a-side, and sometimes a game at the back of the stands, where people kicked the f*** out of each other. With people like Bill Foulkes and Harry Gregg around anything could happen. I remember Harry once bit Shay Brennan, sank his teeth right into him because Shay didn't pass the ball. Out on the field, there did not seem to be any system or pattern. We were just a team of individuals ... At West Ham we'd had modern training gear. But at Old Trafford, it was all great big old sweaters and socks full of holes. We were given boots in training that were like cut-off wellingtons. It would remind you of being in prison.*

The situation at Manchester City seemed no better. Denis Law was shocked at what he found there after transferring from Huddersfield in March 1960 for a British record fee of £55,000. In his autobiography, *The King*, Law wrote:

> *Apart from Bert Trautmann, only Ken Barnes and George Hannah could really play – it seemed to me the rest were runners or players past their best ... At City the kit was in rags. The training under Jimmy Meadows was poor. It was just running and more running. There was nothing to inspire the younger players and no work on developing skills or tactics. When I went to Italy, it was a different world: the training was excellent, completely different from anything I had experienced in*

England, and everything was done with a ball at your feet, even the running. We hardly ever saw a ball at Manchester City – and it wasn't just City: many other English clubs, Manchester United among them, prepared their players in this way. The weak theory at the time was if the ball was kept away from players during the week, on a Saturday they'd be that much more eager for it. Speaking personally, I needed the ball to work with in order to improve. My career wasn't in athletics; when I trained for football, I wanted to do it with a ball.

Trainee Norman Hunter was horrified by the indiscipline he found at Leeds. So was a young Billy Bremner, who said: 'Training was just doing laps, a kick-about with a ball but no ball on Friday, just sprints. We went to play a very important game towards the end of the season at Blackburn Rovers. I remember thinking: "I wonder where we're going to eat." In the end, we stopped off at a cafe and had beans on toast. It was all a bit of a rush, nothing had been arranged. And this was the most important game of the season. We lost 3-2. Even as a young fellow, I thought, "We haven't really prepared well for this game".' Freddie Goodwin's opinion was that 'Many of the side just seemed to play for themselves. And Jack [Charlton] was part of that. He was an undisciplined player when I joined.' Don Revie was enraged by Jack's behaviour in practice matches, which Jack seemed to treat as a joke. Even Jack later admitted that his habit of racing about all over the park was 'totally unprofessional'.

Despite the studious perfectionism of Fulham captain Johnny Haynes, he had difficulty imposing his high standards upon his colleagues, especially arch-joker Tosh Chamberlain. On 5 December 1959, his team travelled to Leeds with high expectations of an away victory. With five minutes left before kick-off, Fulham were still short of three first-team players, though. England international Jim Langley had decided that he, George Cohen and Alan Mullery would walk from their city centre hotel to the ground, taking in some of Langley's old haunts. Langley had previously played for Leeds. Unfortunately, 'Memory Lane' proved far too forgettable and the trio ended up at the rugby league ground in Headingley at the other side of the city. Only a big bribe persuaded a passing motorist to save their bacon. By the time they arrived at Elland Road, Fulham manager, Bedford Jezzard, had already stripped off. Not that it mattered. Fulham still won 4-1.

By contrast, Burnley, Spurs, Newcastle and West Ham used modern, innovative training methods while at Wolves, under Stan Cullis, and Sheffield Wednesday, under Harry Catterick, strict, well-drilled game plans were devised. Burnley would rehearse rigorously a variety of bewildering free-kick routines. So would Spurs, under Bill Nicholson. It was Nicholson's novel idea to use his big centre-half, Maurice Norman, in an attacking role at corners and free kicks.

West Ham's choice of kit reflected their modern beliefs. Following the Hungarian example, they adopted the lightweight boots, the trimmed-down shin pads, the lighter, cooler, V- and polo-necked short-sleeved shirts, and the shorter shorts. Their away shirts had a swish Continental design: twin hoops across the chest, one in claret and one in sky blue. West Ham were renowned for their 'Cassettari café society'. This was the afternoon meeting place of West Ham luminaries such as Malcolm Allison, Noel Cantwell, John Bond, Dave Sexton, Frank O'Farrell and Jimmy Andrews. Here, new theories about tactics and formations were formulated and debated with passionate intensity. In the '60-61 season, West Ham became one of the first English clubs to use a 4-2-4 formation, although Manchester City's 'Revie Plan' of the mid-fifties utilised an earlier version, derived from the 'Magical Magyars'.

Elsewhere, there was less of an appetite for the shock of the new. For example, at Blackpool some senior players resisted Ron Suart's modern innovations. Ron was a fully-qualified FA coach. He had replaced Blackpool's wily and much-loved old-school boss, Joe Smith. The Tangerines' flying winger Bill Perry recalled with author Mike Prestage:

> *[Before Ron Suart arrived] we had no coach, rarely had team talks or discussions. Joe Smith never did much talking because he trusted us to go out and do our best. He was a fatherly figure. He once screwed up a newspaper article on the talents of Jimmy Greaves, telling us: 'Just go out and play your own game.' [On the other hand] … Ron Suart was full of the new ideas of the day. Instead of players being left to do their own thing on the field they were taught set plays and tactics. I was 28 years old and being asked to do things I'd never tried before and wasn't capable of doing. I told him, 'Look Ron, it is alright talking to a young kid of 18 to 20 about something like this because they are at an age where they can adapt but I'm too long in the tooth to change my style.'*

Even some of the more far-sighted coaches lacked basic professionalism. For example, Walter Winterbottom prepared poorly for England's 1959 summer tour to South America. He failed to acclimatise his players for the blazing temperatures and high altitudes of Mexico and Peru. Consequently, his team crumbled to humiliating defeats in both games, just as they did in the intense heat of Belgrade 12 months before.

In his *Empire News* column in 1959, the journalist and former England international David Jack concluded: 'Make no mistake, this is crisis time for England. The game we gave to the world is no longer played with the required skill in these islands.' Jack blamed poor team selection. Nottingham Forest's FA Cup-winning manager, Billy Walker, blamed the lack of craft in the inside-forward and wing-half positions. Even Johnny Haynes, an inside-forward of Wayne Rooney's stature, was not excused. Walker complained that English coaches were suppressing individual flair. Charles Buchan, editor of *Football Monthly*, blamed tactical intransigence. He said: 'We will not accept the facts that long wing-to-wing passes and long kicks upfield by full-backs are useless. And that players trying to run, or dribble, round opponents are doomed to failure.'

Burnley and Northern Ireland playmaker Jimmy McIlroy shared Buchan's frustration. In 1960, Jimmy wrote, 'I wish I could interest every club in the country in FOOTBALL. I mean football, which doesn't include "getting stuck in", "fighting" or "belting the ball". I believe skill and fight are opposites – the complete footballer possesses a blend of both – but the emphasis should be very much on skill. If we are to equal the best in Continental football the tough stuff must be erased from our game, to make way for more subtlety, delicacy and softness of touch.'

Perhaps distracted by Wolves' 'cosmetic' triumphs against Honved and Real Madrid, and by England's friendly victories over West Germany and Brazil, we had been slow to learn our Hungarian lessons in spite of the modern tactical thinking demonstrated by Bill Nicholson, Joe Mercer, Malcolm Allison, Ron Greenwood, Tommy Docherty, Don Revie, Alan Brown and Burnley captain Jimmy Adamson. Writing in his book *One Hundred Caps and All That* in 1961, ex-Wolves and England captain Billy Wright concluded: 'Our whole approach to the game has marked time while the rest of the world, unfettered by a grand history and ponderous league system, has galloped by at the double.'

Wright had played in the England sides which were thrashed twice by Hungary. After watching his former club side, Wolves, torn apart in both home and away legs by Barcelona's fluid counter-attacks in the European Cup competition of 1959/60, he commented: 'I used to think it was right for a team to go out and play the game naturally; to work things out as the game developed. That was until I met the crack Continental sides. They showed football played to a highly organized plan … It is the big difference between English football and the best of the game abroad.'

At home, football and cricket remained largely insulated from a world that was leaving Britain behind. Up until 1962, professional cricket still staged an annual representative contest between the 'Gentlemen' and the 'Players'. The administration of the game epitomised the 'old school tie' ethos. We would not recover the Ashes until the early seventies, and only after the appointment of a curmudgeonly, professional and shrewdly tactical leader in Ray Illingworth. At national and club levels, professional football was little different from cricket. It was still gripped by what Anthony Sampson described in *Anatomy of Britain* as, 'club-amateur' influences. At a number of leading clubs, directors attempted to select the team, as at Newcastle, recruit new players without involving the manager, as at Luton, or provide half-time instruction, as at Bolton. Even at the national level, Walter Winterbottom was not even entitled to pick his own team without the input of an FA committee made up of the 'great and the good', but with no experience of managing professional football. Ultimately, we would look to another ultra-professional tactician, Sir Alf Ramsey, to change that practice and restore our international prowess.

West Ham United v Huddersfield Town (FA Cup third round)

'Why'
13 January 1960

Alongside Southampton's amazing smash-and-grab raid, one of the most astonishing results among the '59/60 FA Cup third-round ties, came at a frost bitten, snow-covered Upton Park where the pitch was pronounced fit for play only two hours before the Wednesday afternoon kick-off. Even more surprisingly, the victims were one of our most modern-thinking clubs.

Leaving aside the 300 Terriers fans travelling in hope, a regulation home victory was predicted. Little did we know that a new star was about to be unveiled. Improbably, he was on the side of the Second Division underdogs, and even more improbably he took the form of a decidedly frail 19-year-old. I heard the lad had earned his chance by scoring in the first game at Leeds Road. Now he proceeded to take his place in the limelight – if the hazy shade of winter grey could be so described.

As he limbered up, he looked as if he had duped his team-mates – a ballboy in the Huddersfield stripes. But if his slender physique suggested he might be out of his depth, his technique instantly refuted this. From the first kick he was in the thick of the action. No nerves, no hesitancy, he was immediately on the money. Time and again he took on the slipping and sliding Hammers, retaining a mesmerising sureness of touch. With a feint here and a shimmy there, he persistently bewildered his markers, deftly evading their lunging tackles and employing his darting pace to accelerate away from trouble. Never selfish, he continually probed for openings which his team-mates could exploit, employing an expansive range of raking passes to ravage West Ham's jittery defence. His stamina was astonishing: pushing forward at lightning speed when the ball was won and tenaciously chasing opponents down when it was lost. He never let the home defenders settle, constantly harrying and hurrying them, haring from one to another like a frisky sheepdog. His appetite for the ball seemed uncontainable as he continually returned to the edge of his own box to give his keeper, Ray Wood, an attacking outlet. Supremely confident, but never arrogant, he seemed oblivious to the aggravation his precocious talent might be arousing. As it was, he had it his way. The chapped, foot-stamping, ear-tingling crowd was steadily won over. Setting aside their partisan passions, the home fans began to acknowledge his genius. If this was a 'ballet on ice' then its choreographer and leading performer was Denis Law.

As early as the 12th minute, the young Scotsman had the ball in the net only to be frustrated by an offside flag. The reprieve was short. Scampering around West Ham's midfielders, he released Ledger with a penetrative through ball. The right-winger crossed crisply and quickly for the inside-left, Massie, to thump home an unstoppable header. In the 23rd minute Ledger was again the provider, albeit fortuitously. When West Ham's keeper, Dwyer, fumbled his centre, Huddersfield left-half and captain, McGarry, tucked away the gift. Although West Ham reduced the deficit on 38 minutes through left-winger Musgrove, Huddersfield's two-goal lead was restored just before the break when Les Massie prodded in Jack Connor's pass.

Any hopes West Ham might have had of a second-half recovery were extinguished soon after the resumption. Seeing that Ken Brown was having difficulty in controlling the ball on the tricky surface, Law struck instantly, dispossessing the West Ham centre-half and sending Connor clear. The visitors' centre-forward made no mistake, finding goal with a zipping shot that evaded Dwyer's dive. With 20 minutes left, Connor doubled his account with an acute-angled shot that left Dwyer helpless. Grasping the mantra, 'if you can't beat them …', the West Ham supporters began chanting 'we want six' while the ecstatic Huddersfield throng gave a full-throated rendition of their battle song 'Smile Awhile'. Law thought he had granted the ironic home fans' wishes but the referee played the party-pooper. Nevertheless, realising we had witnessed a performance of immaculate skill, we gave Denis Law and his impressive team thunderous applause as they left the field.

For West Ham, this was a further calamity as their season fell apart. As for Huddersfield, their glory was short-lived. Less than three weeks later, languishing Luton would extinguish their heightened FA Cup ambitions with a solitary goal. Huddersfield had already lost their talismanic manager, Bill Shankly, to Liverpool. Soon they would lose their brilliant inside-right to Manchester City.

England v Sweden

'Sea of Love'
28 October 1959

But the bite of the underdog was not solely felt by our top league clubs for, in the autumn of 1959, our national side was humbled, too. The Football Association had reluctantly granted Walter Winterbottom his wish to select a younger side for the internationals against Wales and World Cup finalists, Sweden. His team included the England Under-23 caps: Stoke full-back Tony Allen; Burnley's John Connelly; the Middlesbrough pairing of centre-forward Brian Clough and winger Eddie Holliday; plus Birmingham centre-half Trevor Smith, who replaced the retired Billy Wright. This was possibly the youngest senior team to represent England. But if a poor Welsh side, already weakened by the absence of the Charles brothers, posed questions about England's technique, tactics and basic cohesion, the Swedes rammed home the unpalatable truths.

Sweden's team comprised a collection of part-timers: a store keeper, a fireman, a salesman, an electrician, a telephone worker, an engineer, a draughtsman, a businessman, two office clerks and a farmer. They achieved their comprehensive victory without five of their stars: Hamrin, Gren, Liedholm, Skoglund and Gustavvson, who were needed by their Italian league clubs. But just as the émigré English coach, Jimmy Hogan of Burnley, had inspired the emphatic Hungarian victories over his home country in 1953 and 1954, another Englishman, George Raynor of Barnsley, masterminded a further humiliation. Raynor had helped Sweden achieve Olympic glory and World Cup success. He was revered in his country of employment, but ignored in his country of birth. Here, his glittering CV was snubbed. Here, he had to find work as a Butlin's store man and as a part-time manager at Skegness Town. Here, the irony of his exclusion seemed lost on the crusty Football Association.

Goran Berger, the Swedish national football museum curator, remarked: 'It really seems amazing that England didn't want George Raynor when he came home. For us, he's simply the most successful national coach of all time. Incredibly popular, he changed the game here with his tactics and organisation. He taught himself how to coach, never took an exam in his life and yet he taught us how to win.'

Although a brilliant five-man move enabled John Connelly to give Winterbottom's new-look side the lead, England spent much of the game chasing flitting shadows. The Swedes simply mesmerised England with their precise passing, darting movement and changes of pace. Smith, still struggling with a calf injury, could not hold the lithe and forceful centre-forward, Agne Simonsson. So impressive was Simonsson's performance that Real Madrid offered him a contract immediately after the game. The Swedes scored three times with Simonsson grabbing a brace. They also created a host of other chances with the woodwork twice coming to England's rescue. England were out-thought, out-fought and thoroughly outplayed by a team with a superior tactical vision shaped by a self-taught English coach.

Bobby Charlton's late consolation goal restored a degree of respectability but failed to disguise the chasm in class dividing the two teams. Discounting the Republic of Ireland's victory of 1949, this defeat was only England's second on home soil to a foreign country. If our shortcomings were acknowledged, the remedies had not yet been found. The Swedes, like the Hungarians before them, had benefited from playing with a settled side, well schooled in a particular style of play. Raynor had persuaded the leading Swedish club sides to adopt the same way of playing. England's arcane, archaic, 'chop and change' selection process had prevented us from achieving that degree of stability, compounded by the limited time Winterbottom was allowed to spend with his squad.

Much criticised for his below-par performance, Brian Clough was never selected again. One incident epitomised his dispiriting experience. In failing to capitalise upon a goalscoring opportunity, he inadvertently stumbled with the ball nestling beneath him. He quipped bitterly: 'It was as if I was trying to hatch the bloody thing.'

'I feel like a football fifth columnist,' Raynor told the pressmen the night after Sweden's Wembley victory. 'I got some sort of satisfaction out of the result but not enough. I would much rather have been doing the same sort of thing for the country of my birth ... I want to work in England – *for*

England. They want me in Ghana, in Israel, in Mexico and in Sweden. I am a knight in Sweden and have a huge gold medal of thanks from King Gustaf. I have a letter of thanks and commendation from the Prime Minister of Iraq. My record as a coach is the best in the world. I don't smoke. I don't drink. I live for football.'

It was Raynor's idea to man-mark Hidegkuti in Budapest. This helped Sweden stall the Hungarian supply line and achieve an impressive 2-2 draw. Raynor was astute enough to realise this would be an exhausting task, detailing two Swedish players to undertake this task in turn, ensuring that they remained fresh. Despite being a spectator at the game, Walter Winterbottom failed to follow Raynor's lead when Hungary played at Wembley shortly afterwards and paid with a heavy defeat.

It would take a determined, Raynor-like tactician to sweep away the 'club amateur' fustiness: to assert winning tactical disciplines, prepare better, develop squad stability and cohesion, and turn a group of talented English players into a world-beating team, with its whole becoming greater than its collective parts. However, before this Ramsey-led revolution, the national side, like so many of the First Division teams of the day, comprised a clutch of glittering but disparate elements.

The motorway age arrives

1959 was the year in which 'the music died' with Buddy Holly perishing in a plane crash. It was also the year in which Fidel Castro seized control in Cuba. The Cold War became a frantic tussle for technological supremacy, ultimately ruinous in the Soviets' case. For around 25 years the space race provided a global scorecard of reputations. In October 1959, Lunik III sent back the first pictures of the 'dark side of the moon' to the underwhelmed Soviet scientists. But where the Soviet boffins found monotony, Pink Floyd found musical inspiration.

British feet remained firmly on the ground, though. In 1959, we had still to build *Evening Star*, our last steam locomotive. Meanwhile, the Japanese had begun work in developing their 135mph bullet train. While Dr Richard Beeching began his radical railway pruning exercise, our first motorway, the M1, opened. With the new Mini saloon expanding the range of affordable cars for lower income families, road was about to triumph emphatically over rail.

There was no change of government, though. The Tories, under Harold Macmillan's leadership, were returned to power in 1959 with a thumping majority. Although lampooned by the satirists of the early sixties, Macmillan was no sentimentalist. He knew our days as an imperial power were over. By the time he left office, four years later, the global map had been largely drained of its red hue. While the north-western clubs continued to dominate the Football League, the industrial map of Britain was changing fast, too, with economic power shifting inexorably from north to south. By 1960, 'King Cotton' was preparing to abdicate as a vast number of Lancashire mills 'weaved out', having failed to compete with cheaper manufacturers in the Far East. Over the next 20 years, what was once the cradle of the British industrial revolution became its casket.

Fantasies of British dominance persisted, however, as reflected by the huge popularity of Ian Fleming's 'snobbery with violence'. Here, we found superior British wit and courage confounding all, underpinned, even more improbably, by superior British technology. Fantasy was also at the heart of Keith Waterhouse's ironic novel *Billy Liar*, published in 1959, although a more sombre message lingers within Billy Fisher's serial escapism. It was if fantasy was a reclusive refuge for bright, aspiring, young working-class men, frustrated by the restrictions placed upon their ambitions. These were the 'in-betweeners' who, unlike their forbears, did not have their identity defined by war, but were still too young to enjoy the better career opportunities and greater social mobility of the sixties. Perhaps *Billy Liar* served as a metaphor for those who clung to the myths of Britain's past rather than facing up to the challenges of its present. Pathetically, the Crown chose to interpret one of those challenges as a fight for decency by prosecuting Penguin books for daring to print *Lady Chatterley's Lover*. The fustiness of Establishment thinking was epitomised by the prosecuting counsel's summing-up. He asked the members of the jury: 'Is it a book you would wish your wife or servants to read?'

At the end of the season we also bade a fond farewell to Tom Finney, the unassuming 'Preston Plumber', an extravagantly talented footballer who remained at Deepdale throughout his career. Jimmy Greaves said, '[Tom] was so adept with either foot that I could never make up my mind which one was the most effective when it came to shooting, passing, crossing and dribbling … His body swerves and feints mesmerised countless defenders. He could beat any opponent, find the space to make a telling pass when under pressure and he possessed a thunderous shot.' As proof of his indispensability, North End were relegated from the top flight 12 months after his retirement. They have not returned since.

If Tom's magnificent talent represented the crowning glory of the steam age, then the compelling artistry of Real Madrid reflected the swish potency of the jet age. At Hampden Park, in May 1960, Real produced a dazzling display to lift the European Cup for the fifth year in succession. Their sumptuous performance was played on the same bumpy surface which was blamed for the turgid 1-1 draw in the Home International between Scotland and England several days before. To emphasise the scale of Real's superiority over British opposition, they defeated Barcelona, the contemptuous conquerors of Wolves, by 6-3 in one semi-final, while Eintracht Frankfurt, their thrashed opponents at Hampden, annihilated Rangers 12-4 in the other. Only two British teams threatened to challenge Real's supremacy: Burnley, the recently-crowned Football League champions, and Bill Nicholson's Spurs. Jimmy Greaves recalled: 'This Burnley team was brimming with outstanding individual players, and they were encouraged to play with emphasis more on skill than sweat and stamina. In an era when quite a few teams believed in the big boot, they were a league of gentlemen.' However, Spurs were waiting in the wings ready to seize their crown. In the '60/61 season Spurs embarked upon a stunning double-winning triumph and then three years later they would become the first British club to raise a European trophy. As improbable as it might have seemed then, 'The times they were a-changing.'

THE 1960/61 SEASON

Hastings United v Wisbech Town

'Apache'
20 August 1960

It might have been the beginning of Britain's motorway age, but this game harked back to the years of gloomy austerity. I made my acquaintance with Southern League football a few months after we resettled in the fading seaside resort of Hastings – 'popular with visitors since 1066' was the Royal Mail's strapline. Looking at the age profile of the teams before me it seemed apposite. Four players stood out in this respect: Len Duquemin and Norman Uprichard for Hastings, and Jesse Pye and Billy Elliott for the fenland town of Wisbech.

Len Duquemin, the 1959 Southern League Player of the Year, was introduced as this season's captain. In Len's obituary, written for the *Independent* in April 2003, Ivan Ponting described him thus:

> *The Guernsey-born marksman, a ceaselessly competitive study in perpetual motion on the pitch, was a quiet, gentle, engagingly unassuming fellow away from the action, and it was not difficult to imagine him moving tranquilly among the monks as he tended their garden during the German occupation of the Channel Islands in the Second World War … Duquemin scored 134 goals in 308 senior games for Spurs his solitary Football League club and, despite his lack of extravagant natural ability, he was considered a key man by both manager and team-mates as he helped to lift the Second Division title in 1949/50, then the First Division crown in the following campaign. Arthur Rowe's team won renown for their flowing push-and-run style, which involved*

> *slick interchanges of short, accurate passes as they swept from one end of the pitch to the other. It was a fresh, swashbuckling approach which lit up the post-war soccer scene and won lavish plaudits for the ball-playing likes of the inside-forwards Eddie Baily and Les Bennett, the wing-half and skipper Ronnie Burgess, the wingers Les Medley and Sonny Walters, and a full-back named Alf Ramsey, who one day would lead England to World Cup glory. But there was a need, too, for players who would run ceaselessly when they were not in possession, providing extra passing options for their artistic colleagues; they didn't always get the ball and rarely took the eye, but without them the system would have foundered. One such was the wing-half Billy Nicholson, destined to become the most successful manager in Spurs history, and another was Duquemin, whose honest sweat was an important lubricant to the smooth running of Rowe's captivating machine.*

Duquemin was tenacious. At Spurs, he saw off the challenges posed by signings Dave Dunmore from York and Alfie Stokes, before succumbing to Bobby Smith's greater youth and potency in 1958. Typically, it was his goal at Sheffield Wednesday which secured the First Division title for Spurs in 1951. As an industrious battler for the cause, Bill Nicholson recognised in Len a kindred spirit. They remained close friends long beyond their playing days.

However, when Len arrived at Hastings he was 36 years old. He seemed middle-aged. People of his generation lived harder lives impeded by basic nutritional standards and less advanced health care. But whether muscular or wiry, so many men of Len's age seemed tough, battle-hardened, no-nonsense individuals. Footballers of the forties and fifties appeared suited to military wear – maybe with an army beret sliding towards their right ear and a lapelled khaki tunic gathered above their waist. But age did wither them. Today, a man looking like Len did in 1960 would be considered to be 30 years older. And it wasn't all about appearances, either. Following Arthur Rowe's mantra, Len still tried to 'make it simple' but he could no longer 'make it quick'. In this game, his first for Hastings, it wasn't long before the griping brigade got on his case. 'Duquemin's too slow,' they muttered. 'He holds up the whole forward line.' If a striker of today bagged 25 goals in a season, as Len did in 1960/61, they would expect resounding applause. Churlish Hastings supporters worked to a meaner standard.

Opposing Len was another star centre-forward of the forties and early fifties: 40-year-old former Treeton collier, Jesse Pye. Pye began his football career in 1938 when he signed for Sheffield United. With the outbreak of hostilities he joined the army, serving in North Africa and Italy. After being demobbed, he signed first for Notts County and then for Wolves, whom he represented with distinction, scoring twice in their 1949 FA Cup Final victory over Leicester City. He played for England in a 'Victory International' and was then capped against the Republic of Ireland in 1949. It became England's first home defeat against a 'foreign' side. Pye was never selected again. However, he scored 95 times in 209 games for Wolves before moving on to Luton in 1952, where he helped a young Gordon Turner hone his predatory goalscoring abilities. He completed his Football League career at Derby. Pye moved to Wisbech in 1957, becoming the landlord of the Mermaid Inn in the Market Place before opening a sweet shop. In 1960, he took over at Fenland Park.

Also facing Len was the feisty and combative former Bradford, Burnley, Sunderland and England left-winger Billy Elliott, then in his 35th year. Elliott is probably the only Football League player to be dismissed – a very unusual event in the fifties – for 'a look of intent' as if looks could kill. His aggressive competitiveness on the field was legendary. In writing Billy's obituary for the *Independent* in 2008, Ivan Ponting had this to say: 'In action [Billy] was a study in high-velocity pugnacity laced with deceptively subtle skills. His attacking speciality was racing beyond his marker to reach the byline, then driving a low cross into the penalty area, often through a tangled forest of legs, for conversion by lurking marksmen.'

Former Burnley and Northern Ireland inside-forward, Jimmy McIlroy, said it wasn't always thus. Referring to a time when Burnley had a particularly small forward line, he told Burnley author Dave Thomas:

> *Having softened up his marker, Elliott proceeded to send over a series of head-height crosses at rocket-like speed. The ball was like concrete in those days, and, when wet, weighed a ton. The laces left a nice imprint on your forehead. Who the hell wanted to head the ball when it came across at the speed that Elliott belted it? There was understandable reluctance to head any of his crosses. Elliott became thoroughly fed up of this during one game. At last he lost patience. Glowering menacingly at us*

*midget forwards, he demanded: 'Which one of you f***ers keeps f***ing ducking? I'm wasting my f***ing time here.'*

The two goalkeepers on show had pedigree, also. Hastings had Norman Uprichard, a member of Northern Ireland's 1958 World Cup squad. According to one long-standing Pompey supporter, he remains the best goalkeeper to represent Portsmouth, better, even, than the likes of Alan Knight or David James, 'at least when he was sober'. The Wisbech keeper was the courageous former Norwich custodian Ken Nethercott, a hero of Archie Macaulay's FA Cup giant-killers of '59.

We queued in the town centre for the football bus beneath the cawing, wheeling gulls. At least the shops' canopies gave us some relief from the scorching sun while we waited to board. Among the parade of shops, Mutton's announced that 'everything is reduced' with 'many bargains for the fuller figure'. Perhaps you came out dressed as lamb. Cobley's advertised Daks which were described as 'ideal for the weekend', 'tough and handsome', 'mostly at £5 / 15'. A sketch was shown of a twenty-something man in a challenging pose, legs splayed and hands on hips, demanding we saw some serious Cavalry Twill action. There were posters, too, advertising 'All Star Wrestling on Hastings Pier' with both 'Dr. Death' and 'Shirley Crabtree, the 19½ stone giant from Halifax' [later known as 'Big Daddy'] topping the bill. Meanwhile, at the White Rock Pavilion, there were the 'Fol-de-Rols: the famous song and laugh show' with Jack Tripp. 'Bexhill Donkey Races' were also billed with a small sketch of a donkey so we were clear what was on show. With Mastins' department store still employing cash canisters that whizzed back and forth on wires, there was a sense that little had changed since pre-war days. Only Coombes Motors' advertisement for the 'new Vauxhall Victor at £723 12/6d, including Purchase Tax' gave notice of the modern consumer boom. For female household drudgery of the early fifties had been relieved, nationwide, by a vast expansion in labour-saving devices: washing machines, fridges and vacuum cleaners. Home comfort had increased, too, with many more houses having inside bathrooms and toilets. The massive increase in television ownership also presented a serious challenge to the post-war popularity of professional football and the cinema.

Once seated inside a green and cream Maidstone & District bus, the temperature became overwhelming. Even with every top window slid well back, we had to mop our streaming faces continually, almost gagging in the heat's intensity. Slowly, the bus climbed the steep hill out of town, its engine growling and its interior fittings vibrating alarmingly. The gearbox rebelled on the sharp slopes, crunching and grinding, before a lower gear was conceded. Frequently, the bus paused as if waiting for a second wind before juddering forward with arthritic zeal. The stench of mucky oil and petrol swept through the upper deck, mingling with the sour smell of tobacco and producing a dizzying sensation. Eventually, we found enough height to gaze back across the town's roof tops towards the gleaming Pevensey Bay and the indistinct silhouette of Beachy Head. It was hardly the weather for football.

Having arrived, it was readily apparent that a sizeable crowd had gathered. It was later confirmed as 3,749, respectable by modern League Two standards. Most supporters were basking on the grass bank which ran the length of the eastern flank, as if this was a popular picnicking spot. Many of these fans were shielding their eyes from the burning sun as they surveyed the verdant pitch and the distant sea beyond. But here there was some relief from the dazzling heat. The flag bearing the town's ancient crest fluttered in a welcome breeze which wafted tinny music from the tannoy system around the ground in wavering volume. It was my introduction to 'Ladies of Calcutta'. This bright brassy tune was one of only three records played at all home games until the Mersey beat finally infiltrated the PA box in 1963, forcing the stubborn incumbent to admit that, contrary to local prejudice, the sixties had arrived. The other two stalwarts in the club's record collection were '76 Trombones' and the parochial rallying cry of 'Sussex by the Sea' which was always cranked up as the team took the field. It wasn't exactly *Expresso Bongo*.

Although Billy Elliott had lost his former pace, he was far too quick for Hastings' lumbering, disorganised defenders. Without knowing, then, who he was, his daunting presence remains. In a flickering, over-exposed snatch of film stored inside my head, there he is, grim-faced and fiercely focused, accelerating along the left flank in the blinding glare of the sun, fizzing one low centre after another across the hapless Hastings box. Elliott might have learnt his Turf Moor lesson the hard way but he'd learnt it well. On this afternoon he seemed unstoppable.

After just 90 seconds, Wisbech were ahead as Jessie Pye rifled home a free kick. His shot was so venomous that the ball cannoned off the board behind the goal and back into play before anyone quite realised what had happened. Almost from the restart, Elliott crossed for Pye to nimbly side-step several inept challenges and flick in his second. With only 15 minutes gone, Elliott was the provider once more as Pye completed his hat-trick with a vicious volley. Goalkeeper Norman Uprichard could only admire Pye's finishing power. Capitalising on Elliott's low raking crosses, there was no need of Pye in the sky. The Treeton collier may have been 40 years old, but he retained the predatory instincts of his youth.

Hastings then retaliated. Their right-winger, Micky Bull, pulled a goal back seven minutes later, and then Len Duquemin lashed home a second. But even before the half-hour mark was reached, Wisbech restored their two-goal advantage. This was like a primary school game. After Ronnie Clayton, the ex-Brighton forward, had fluffed a second-half penalty, Wisbech added a fifth, crushing Hastings' newly-assembled side with disdain. Heaven knows whether Uprichard was sober or not. It hardly mattered. Even from my inexperienced perspective, I could see how little protection he was given. Just two weeks later, he was out of the side along with four of his colleagues. He would not regain his place until the season was almost over.

That sunny day in a generally disappointing summer was soon eclipsed by a sopping autumn as wave after wave of Atlantic fronts drenched the British Isles. *Apache*'s twanging Hawaiian chords became the soundtrack for those damp, dull days. Before each game I would wait for the football bus in a town centre café, morosely looking out at the spattering rain through condensation-beaded windows. The moist air inside was as heavy with the pungent odour of sweaty plastic macs as with stewed tea and chips. It was as if Giles' cartoon images of the British seaside – a wet, grey, choppy Channel resort inhabited by a demonic granny, anarchic kids and buffeted parents – was inspired by a day trip to Hastings.

As testament to the huge volume of rain that fell during those autumn months, steam trains were restored on the electrified routes through Lewes where the Ouse flood waters reached platform level. And as if Hastings United's cavalry was not slow enough already, the Agincourt conditions of that autumn and winter slowed it to a dead halt. In game after game, they slumped off to the derision of a dwindling crowd. It didn't matter that Len Duquemin scored goals with apparent ease because more were conceded. I learnt quickly to feed off the leanest of pickings.

With Hastings being as bad as they were, I placed extra amounts of hard-earned pocket money into our church collection in the hope of bribing a divine reprieve. It was the most egotistical, mercenary, small-minded version of religion ever conceived. It was appropriate, then, that my parents should arrange my confirmation as an Anglican. While a rare victory represented a full glass of blessings, the frequent defeats were indictments of moral failure. I came easily to a persecution complex. Two years later, the world faced mutually-assured destruction. The Cuban missile crisis was intensifying alarmingly. With his creation in peril God might have had bigger things on his mind, and yet I was sure he had ordered Ramsgate Athletic to punish me for missing church.

Brighton & Hove Albion v Burnley (FA Cup fourth round)

'Poetry in Motion'
28 January 1961

Burnley were the current Football League champions. They had just beaten a very strong Hamburg side, featuring German international Uwe Seeler, 3-1 in the first leg of the European Cup quarter-final. Alan Ridgill of the *Sunday Pictorial* described Burnley thus: 'Here was the almost perfect soccer machine – as smooth running as a Rolls-Royce and yet packing the punch of a centurion tank.' And yet Burnley was a small-town club supported by a population of just 80,000. This was a third of the size of Brighton and Hove with its population of 246,000. Burnley also spent less in assembling its title-winning side (£13,000) than Brighton had in creating a middle-of-the-table Second Division team (over £30,000). But this cup tie was billed as a contest between the 'giants' of Burnley and the 'minnows' of Brighton.

In his programme notes, Brighton's normally genial manager, Billy Lane, sounded stressed. He wrote, 'I am not "flannelling" when I state that here at the Goldstone we have the most loyal and understanding supporters of any club. I, as well as many other managers, know that when things are not going too well they are recipients of many letters of abuse, etc. Not so with our supporters, in fact I have received many letters of encouragement. It certainly makes a manager's job far easier in times when everything appears to be adverse. Well, supporters, here's a big "thank you" from the players and myself for your loyalty to the club.'

After a long period of stability under the chairmanship of the kindly Major Carlo Campbell, the club had become mired by boardroom squabbles. The new chairman, Alec Whitcher, was under pressure. He had blocked a takeover bid by the Alliance Building Society, displeasing many supporters who thought a vital investment opportunity had been missed. Whereas Campbell had treated Lane like a son, protecting him from censure during the tough times, the often grumpy Whitcher was more demanding. He was particularly critical of Lane's dealings in the transfer market, which had cost the club in excess of £30,000 without conspicuously improving the squad. Whitcher even reprimanded Lane for smiling with a visiting manager after a home defeat. With internal politics causing so much unhappiness, Lane decided this season would be his last at the club. He became the manager of non-league Gravesend & Northfleet, leading them to a stirring FA Cup run in 1962/63.

According to John Vinicombe of the Brighton *Evening Argus*: 'The Goldstone dressing room in the late fifties comprised two camps: those who got on with the manager and those who did not. Whatever the rights and wrongs of his ten-year reign, there can be no argument about Albion's success in that period.'

Not helped by disruptions behind the scenes, Brighton started the 1960/61 season poorly. At the end of October they were in bottom place, a point behind a Luton Town side that was slaloming towards Division Four. Lane had agreed surprisingly to Bill Curry's transfer request at the start of the new season. Lane seemed disinclined to hang on to players who were unhappy at the club, irrespective of their importance. Adrian Thorne would be another case in point. Curry scored 26 league goals in 49 appearances for Brighton. Given his value it seemed inconceivable that he should be allowed to move to similarly-placed Derby County for just £12,000 – around £3,000 less than his purchase price in 1959. It did not look like good business.

Billy Lane replaced Curry with Chelsea inside-forward Tony Nicholas, who had fallen out with his Chelsea manager, Ted Drake. Despite making his debut for Chelsea as an 18-year-old, his career was stalling at Stamford Bridge. Goaded by Drake's criticisms after a narrow defeat in the Burnley snow, the outspoken Nicholas kicked a hole in Drake's office door. He explained: 'Eventually I accepted the chance to join Brighton just to get away from Ted, but two weeks later he got the sack and after I went Tommy Docherty was appointed and I think that would have suited me as he liked a runner.' However, the former England youth international had no qualms about joining Brighton. He liked manager Billy Lane, whom he described as a 'gentleman', and enjoyed life in the town. This deal cost Brighton £15,000.

Lane had already signed Middlesbrough's reserve centre-forward, Dennis Windross, during the close season. His acquisition proved to be a mistake, though. Despite scoring 43 goals for Middlesbrough's reserves in the season before, Windross struggled to make the grade at Brighton. Lane also splashed out £15,000 on Everton's inside- or outside-left, Bobby Laverick. The fast and powerful Laverick proved to be exasperatingly inconsistent, though, despite chipping in with ten league goals. Only the enthusiastic Tony Nicholas, a quick, mobile forward with a strong shot, proved an immediate success, although he was not a forceful leader of the line in the Curry mould. He ended the season as top scorer with 13 goals in 27 games, netting four goals in the vital end-of-season victories against Huddersfield (2-1) and Stoke (2-0) which ultimately secured Brighton's safety.

Republic of Ireland international full-back Joe Carolan was also added to the squad, at a cost of £10,000, to replace the veteran Roy Little. A composed defender, Carolan was signed from Manchester United in December 1960 after playing 66 senior games at Old Trafford as an integral member of the post-Munich side. He had became surplus to Busby's requirements after Irish colleague Noel Cantwell joined United. Before the season was out, former Villa, Manchester United and Chelsea midfield enforcer Stan Crowther joined Brighton too. He no longer had any appetite for the game, though; his contract was cancelled after he refused to play for Brighton's third team. Crowther had been an England under-23 international, an FA Cup winner with Villa in 1957, and an FA Cup finalist with the Munich-depleted Manchester United side in 1958 – a season in which he received special dispensation to play for both Villa and United in the same competition. At Brighton, he made less than a handful of appearances. He later reflected, bitterly, 'Football for me was wasted years. If I had my time over again it would be the last business I would choose as an occupation.' How sad.

Before Burnley arrived, Brighton's unbeaten six-match run had lifted them into mid-table. The Albion had recorded 3-1 home victories over a strong Liverpool side in the league and over Bill Curry's new club, Derby County, in the third round of the cup.

January 28th was a wild, wet day. The train had to almost pick its way between the sodden, sagging, sullen marshes and the grey, grubby, foam-flecked sea. Shrouds of rain were driven across our path by the gusting wind. Already saturated in our walk to the station, our clothing steamed gently inside the carriage. A further soaking awaited us on the open Goldstone Ground terraces. Fortunately, the rain became patchier once we arrived. It was just as well because the glistening pitch was already pitted with small pools of water, particularly in the grassless goalmouths. Here, the groundsmen set about their forking and sanding duties industriously. As they moved in our direction, each prod of their forks emitted a hiss of earthy complaint. Despite the awful weather, a large crowd of 28,672 congregated. Many fans, like us, occupied the exposed East Terrace, but our discomfort was soon forgotten as the game got underway. The match was a corker, in the very best traditions of FA Cup ties.

It was expected that the boggy conditions would sap Burnley's pace, and yet the ploughed field did not appear to incapacitate them. The Clarets started strongly with their fast raiding wingers, Connelly and Pilkington, making early inroads and their quick, mobile centre-forward, Ray Pointer, pulling Brighton's centre-half, Roy Jennings, all over the place. But it was their powerful left-half, Brian Miller, who struck the first blow after 25 minutes. He beat Brighton's young keeper, Charlie Baker, with a typically emphatic effort.

As the game progressed the pitch churned up, enabling Brighton to compete more equally. They began to stall Burnley's free-flowing moves and attack with greater menace. With just two minutes remaining of the first half, wing-half Jack Bertolini broke through the Burnley defence to equalise. The roar was incandescent.

Lifted by their success, Brighton began the second half boldly, but their momentum was upset when Joe Carolan headed into his own net after 52 minutes. Undaunted, Brighton's right-back, Bob McNicol, seized his moment, atoning also for his partner's error. Having run 50 yards with the ball at his feet, he decided to let fly from 35 yards. McNicol had never scored for Brighton before but no one would have known. Having made perfect contact, the ball flashed into the Burnley net, leaving their keeper, Adam Blacklaw, a helpless spectator. It was one of the most sublime goals seen at the Goldstone Ground. In trite harmony, the leaden sky parted, briefly allowing a shaft of wan sunlight to filter through.

So, with an hour gone Brighton were back on terms. Now hope turned to belief. Driven on by the excited crowd, the Albion pushed forward resolutely. Seven minutes later, the much-maligned Dennis Windross put Brighton ahead. Having been written off by some as the centre-forward who 'couldn't hit a cow's arse with a banjo', this was a particularly sweet moment for Windross. Even Billy Lane had conceded that 'Dennis has taken a little time to settle down'. In their frenzied delight, the Brighton fans had wholly forgiven Windross. However, Burnley were not yet beaten. For all their silky skills, Burnley were a resilient bunch. They responded immediately, pouring forward in numbers. With the Brighton defenders losing their footing in the oozing mud, Burnley's arch-poacher, Jimmy Robson, slipped in to snatch an equaliser. For the remaining 17 minutes both teams slugged it out toe to toe. But despite close calls at either end, the deadlock could not be broken.

Ultimately, this splendid 3-3 draw would have little significance for either side. Burnley progressed to the semi-final, where they lost to 'double'-winning Spurs. They also failed to defend a two-goal lead in Hamburg. And to complete a hat-trick of woes, Aston Villa eliminated them from the newly-introduced Football League Cup competition after a semi-final replay. But that wasn't all. The Football League also fined Burnley £1,000 for fielding a reserve side against Chelsea prior to their return game with Hamburg. As for Brighton, they held on to their Second Division status, thanks to a late surge, but following Billy Lane's much-lamented resignation, troubled times lay just ahead.

Freeing the soccer slaves

During the 1960/61 season, the maximum wage ceiling was abolished in the Football League. Led adroitly by Fulham's 32-year-old inside-forward, Jimmy Hill, the 2,700-strong Professional Footballers' Association (PFA) successfully challenged the feudal power of the clubs. The crisis came to a head in November 1960. The Football League tried to see off the mounting dispute by proposing that the clubs raise their maximum wage from £20 to £30 per week, and offer players longer contracts. At this time, each player was on a one-year deal. This afforded them and their families very little security. Tom Finney remembered: 'The retained players were called in one-by-one and it would be something along the lines of "well, you've had a good season and we're offering you the same terms as last season, sign here", and he would sign a blank form and they would fill the terms in later.' The clubs held the whip hand.

In 1959, the average national wage was just over £11 per week, but a top variety entertainer earned much more. For example, Fulham's chairman, Tommy Trinder, earned £100 per week for compering the TV show *Sunday Night at the London Palladium*. So, while the leading professional footballers were able to earn substantially more than their predominantly working-class supporters, they were generally paid much less than other entertainers. Billy Wright, England's captain with over 100 international caps, did better than most. He estimated that he earned around £2,000 per year from club and country alone. That amounts to around £79,500 per year in modern currency, which, of course, is less than some present Premiership players earn in a week. On top of that, he and other top players benefited from the commercial opportunities emerging in the late fifties. For example, Johnny Haynes advertised Brylcreem, Tom Finney advertised Shredded Wheat and Jimmy Greaves endorsed Bovril. Wright, too, had considerable earnings outside the game. Although the maximum wage created an artificially level playing field, this did not ensure parity of earnings, even in the First Division. Those differences sharpened down the divisions. For example, an average Third Division player in 1959 would earn about half of what Wright drew in basic club wages alone. Some clubs partially circumvented the wage restriction with the use of bonuses and 'under the table' payments, which caused a scandal when uncovered at Sunderland.

To the astonishment of the Football League chiefs and the anger of the players, the clubs rejected the Football League's proposals. Hill immediately summoned rallies in London, Birmingham and Manchester. The players' attitudes hardened. They demanded a percentage of their transfer fees and an end to the enslaving 'retain and transfer' system. The 'retain and transfer' system meant that while a club held a player's registration, it could hold on to him or transfer him as it saw fit, irrespective of the player's wishes. Inside-forward George Eastham was already on strike, refusing to play again for his registered club, Newcastle, and demanding a transfer to a club of *his* choosing.

There had been threats of strike action before 1960, but now the players had a new weapon – the Football Pools. In the previous season, the Football League had sold their fixture rights to the Pools companies for over £250,000 a year. This contract was now in jeopardy. The public sympathised with the players. So did the politicians – on both sides of the House. This was a fight that the clubs were destined to lose.

The clubs tried to win the propaganda war by publicising details of their players' earnings, including bonuses, in their matchday programmes. This was done in reaction to Danny Blanchflower's and Jimmy Hill's allegations of 'soccer slavery'. With the strike imminent, the clubs made a vain attempt to sway public and professional opinion, emphasising the dire financial consequences facing them if the wage restriction was ended. Billy Lane wrote in the Brighton programme on 14 January 1961: 'I have always advocated that players should have better terms, provided the cash to cover increased wages comes through the turnstile. There are, in my opinion, 60 per cent of League clubs running at a loss. Now that the maximum wage scale may be abolished the Albion can no longer pay the maximum wage [approximately £25 per week] to players playing in the League side [although] this has been the practice of the club during the past ten years.' In Brighton's case, this was not shroud-waving.

Despite their protests, the clubs realised that the game was up. They had to give way. A consortium of clubs, led by West Bromwich Albion, including a group from Lancashire, tried to revive the original Football League proposal and insert a new maximum wage of £30 per week. But it was too late. Fulham had already broken ranks. Their chairman, Tommy Trinder, announced he was going to pay his international captain, Johnny Haynes, £100 per week to keep him at Craven Cottage. We were already losing our top players to Italy. Lured by the lustre of the Italian lira during the early sixties, Denis Law, Jimmy Greaves, Joe Baker and Gerry Hitchens decided to follow John Charles' example, and sample the Mediterranean sun.

Experience abroad suggested that better pay led to better football. But the abolition of the wage cap came when our gates were falling and clubs were finding it harder to make ends meet. The clubs in the Third and Fourth

Divisions were already leaning heavily upon supporters' contributions to keep their heads above water. During the 1960/61 season, supporter contributions to Third and Fourth Division clubs totalled £370,000 (about £14 million today) whereas the clubs' total revenue from transfer sales amounted to only £37,000, ten times less.

At the end of the 1960/61 season, almost a third (800) of the 2,800 registered players were released. The cost of increasing wages was met through greater redundancies. Ironically, one of those to be released was the PFA chairman, Jimmy Hill, after he struggled to recover from a knee injury.

The abolition of the maximum wage began to shift power from the autocratic clubs to their previously disenfranchised players. This trend was accentuated by a 1963 High Court judgement which ruled that the 'retain and transfer' system was an unlawful restraint of trade. However, it would take the Bosman judgement of 1995 to complete the reversal of the pre-1961 balance of power between club and player. With the abolition of the wage ceiling, top players began to develop a taste for the things that the extra money could buy. Although far from being the rich kids of today, many top players in the sixties began to separate themselves from their working-class roots.

THE 1961/62 SEASON

Brighton & Hove Albion v Leyton Orient

'Wonderful Land'
7 April 1962

The 1961/62 season proved to be the ultimate Jonah experience. Chelsea and Brighton were relegated and Hastings were only spared a further demotion because they had nowhere left to fall. Dad decided that I was in need of salvation and took me to see the surprise package of Second Division football: Leyton Orient. This was a team that appeared to be punching way above their weight.

Under Alec Stock, that shaman of lower division success, Leyton Orient won the Third Division championship in 1956 for the first time in their history. Because they were frequently shorn of their best players, such as Vic Groves, Stan Charlton, Len Julians, Tom Johnston and Phil Woosnam, the O's spent most of the following five seasons looking anxiously down the table. With nearby Spurs embarking upon their record run of success, Orient's gates continued to slide, falling to an average of 11,000 during the 1960/61 season, over 5,000 lower than during their championship year of '55/56. By this time, Alec Stock had moved on to Queens Park Rangers in search of a new challenge. His assistant, Les Gore, again deputised, having filled Stock's boots when Alec spent several months reviving Roma's fortunes in Serie A. Stock's magic wasn't confined to modest surroundings.

Orient's performances during the 1960/61 season had given no hint of what was to follow. From mid-September 1960 until New Year's Day 1961, they went without a home victory. A return to the Third Division seemed likely. Thankfully, craggy, battling Tom Johnston was enticed back into the fold. His 16 goals enabled the O's to finish in 19th place, three points clear of the relegation zone. The Brisbane Road pitch had hardly helped. In a season of almost relentless rain, six matches were postponed, putting strains on the club's meagre coffers.

The abolition of the maximum wage in 1961 meant further financial difficulty for Orient chairman Harry Zussman and his board. Ignoring the credible claims of the ever-faithful Gore, Harry astonished the football world by recruiting Johnny Carey as his new manager in the summer of 1961. Author Ivan Ponting described Carey thus: 'Johnny Carey was a thoroughbred footballer who exuded class and calmness as Manchester United's first post-war captain and one of the most accomplished full-backs the British game has produced. A soft-brogued Dubliner who earned the epithet "Gentleman John" for his scrupulous fairness and unruffled demeanour no matter how dire the circumstances, Carey won every domestic prize available to him. His collection of honours included the Footballer of the Year award in 1949, an accolade underlined by the identity of the only previous holder, Stanley Matthews.' Despite taking Blackburn up to the First Division in 1958 and helping restore Everton's ailing fortunes – his first game in charge was a 10-4 defeat at Spurs – he was sacked by Goodison director and Littlewoods Pools magnate, John Moores, in the back of a taxi in the spring of 1961. Everton were then placed fourth in Division One, their highest post-war position. The jibe to a beleagured football manager, 'taxi for Mr X', remains to this day. Carey's riposte was to name his new Woodford home as 'Moores's Folly'.

As surprising as Carey's sacking had been, his brilliant, pint-sized midfielder, Bobby Collins, thought he understood why. Collins told his biographer, David Saffer, that 'Johnny insisted that we enjoyed our football. The only flaw he had was that he wasn't hard enough with the players and some did take liberties. Discipline was not tight enough and this stopped him from becoming a great manager. Top managers need a ruthless streak, as players do, if they want to make it at the highest level.' Ex-Evertonian Harry Catterick was appointed in Carey's place. He was a very different kettle of fish. Under his authoritarian management, Everton seized the First Division title in 1963 playing a winning combination of deft and daunting football.

During the 1959/60 season, Carey was given over £100,000 to spend – a huge transfer budget then. It was only just enough to keep Everton in the top flight. By sharp contrast, at Orient, Carey was forced to rely largely upon an inherited squad. But what seemed a ragbag of fledgling, dormant or discarded talent was, in fact, a close-knit group of able and mentally strong players with a driving desire for success.

Carey's *modus operandi* was a slow but sure build-up of play, using flowing passing movements. It was the way he had played under Matt Busby. He abhorred belting a long ball up the middle which he saw as a gift to the opposition. He instructed his goalkeepers to pass or throw the ball out to his defenders 'along the floor' instead of trading in the lottery of an aerial punt. Although Carey had a clear notion of how the game should be played, he was not hot on detail. Apart from exhorting his players to 'fizz it about', 'knock it around' and 'give and go', Carey never involved himself in the tactical or technical details. He left that to his coach, Eddie Baily, a former Spurs and England international, who completed his playing career at Orient. Carey's strengths lay in his unruffled demeanour and his capacity to exude calm confidence at times of stress – a steadying influence.

Eddie Baily was quite different, although he, too, had learnt to play his football in the 'right way', having been an integral part of Arthur Rowe's fluid 'push and run' title-winning side of 1950/51. Carey's choice of Baily as his coach was an inspired one. Whereas Carey was laid-back, measured and urbane, Baily was excitable, confrontational and profane. But Baily was also astute, skilful and vastly experienced. Carey was wise enough to buy a terrier and let it bark for itself. Baily was given the scope to hone the players' technique and sharpen their tactical awareness, geeing them up with choice vernacular. He was equally prepared to put his arm around their shoulders. Baily was a man after their own hearts.

As a coach, Baily placed a high premium on ball work. He organised afternoon skills sessions for selected players, helping them lift their game. As a tactician he expected his wingers to track back and help the full-backs. But he was not interested in a spoiling game. He wanted his team to play fluently – to pass and move, to play neat one-twos in tight spots and entertain the crowd.

Johnny Carey had history with the Orient fans. It was he, as manager of Blackburn, who lured their record goalscorer, Tom Johnston, to Ewood Park in 1958 for £15,000 to complete Rovers' successful promotion push. Johnston outstayed Carey at Ewood by one year, scoring 14 times as Rovers comfortably retained their First Division status. But by the summer of '61, the Scottish warrior with the withered arm – a legacy of an earlier mining accident – had reached his 34th birthday. Although his Orient team-mates felt otherwise, Carey considered Johnston too old for his side and offered him a coaching job at a reduced salary. Johnston was unimpressed and left to join Gillingham in Division Three. Errol 'Cowboy' Crossan, another hero of Norwich's 1959 FA Cup run, also left, returning to his native Canada. This left Carey with a first-team squad of 18 players. More worryingly, he was without a regular goalscorer following Johnston's departure.

Dave Dunmore was signed from West Ham during the closing months of the 1960/61 season in exchange for young Alan Sealey, who would become the star of the 1965 European Cup Winners' Cup Final. Despite

Dunmore's obvious skills – he had a good shot, a great touch and held up the ball well – he had failed to establish himself at Upton Park and White Hart Lane. He had an imposing physique but seemed disinclined to make the most of it. On first sight, he seemed an unlikely replacement for Johnston.

Fellow forward Malcolm Graham had hardly ripped up trees, either. Troubled by a knee injury which had threatened to end his career, the largely left-footed striker scored just seven times during the previous season, his first at Brisbane Road. Orient chairman, Harry Zussman, was set to offload him to Swindon but the Robins were not prepared to meet the £500 signing-on fee that Graham wanted. Graham had been a regular goalscorer at Barnsley in the late fifties but a cartilage problem had blighted his stay at Bristol City after his move there in 1959. Orient's little left-winger, Terry McDonald, was signed from West Ham's youth team where he had played alongside Bobby Moore. Although McDonald had a reasonable strike rate for a winger – one in five – he seemed unlikely to take on Johnston's share. Long-serving right-winger Phil White was an occasional goalscorer only, as was the creative inside-forward, Ronnie Foster. Surely, opposing defences would have little to fear from this Orient forward line?

The strength of the Orient squad lay in its defence. The half-back line comprised the defensive Cyril Lea and the more attacking Malcolm Lucas, both signed from amateur clubs. They were bolstered by the rock-like, super-fit centre-half, Sid Bishop. During the 1961/62 season, Lea and Lucas became recognised as the best wing-halves in the division. Both were ultimately rewarded with full Welsh caps. But Bishop's contribution was pivotal, too. At right-back was the classy, fiercely competitive former amateur international, Stan Charlton, who, in 1958, had returned from a three-year spell at Arsenal. A master of the sliding tackle, Charlton proved to be an inspirational leader. Partnering him was ex-'Busby Babe' and converted centre-forward Eddie Lewis. What Lewis lacked in pace he made up for in excellent positioning. His sharp anticipation enabled him to nick the ball off faster opponents. The brave Frank George and the dependable Scot, Bill Robertson – a league title winner with Chelsea in 1955 – shared the goalkeeping duties. To give a yardstick of what Orient achieved in 1961/62, the current Doncaster side probably have a better chance of reaching the top flight than that Orient team did. But Carey's plucky, well-coached side found unrecognised strengths. United by tremendous camaraderie, fired by accelerating self-belief and fed with smart tactical awareness, they proceeded to move mountains.

Their season began promisingly with a creditable 0-0 draw at recently-relegated Newcastle. While Lucas sat on the crafty Ivor Allchurch, McDonald came close to snatching victory. However, two days later, Southampton inflicted a 'Paineful' 3-1 home defeat after a frenetic duel. Any fears that this was to be business as usual were dispelled as five victories were reeled off in succession. A 2-0 home win was recorded over Clough-less Middlesbrough with Lucas scoring with a 30-yarder. Further long-range efforts from Foster and McDonald turned the tables at the Dell. Then Walsall were thumped 5-1 at Fellows Park with Graham scoring a devastating 12-minute hat-trick. But as September drew to a close, Orient's form began to stutter. Only two wins and three draws came in the next nine league games. Nevertheless, a fighting 3-3 draw was secured at table-topping Liverpool on 28 October. The O's took the lead three times. And each goal was a corker. There was Foster's swift half-volley but then Dunmore trumped his towering header with a ferocious 30-yarder. Roger Hunt (twice) and Leishman kept the Reds on terms although McDonald might have nicked the points at the death. Unfortunately, his close-range effort hit the post. The Anfield fans applauded the gallant O's off the pitch. These were more sporting times.

But two days later, a return trip to Lancashire proved disastrous. The O's suffered a 5-1 defeat at First Division Blackpool in a League Cup replay. They recovered swiftly, though. On the following Saturday, they beat bottom-placed Charlton 2-1 at a sunny Brisbane Road. Another brace from Dunmore proved just enough to subdue their battling opponents. A wasteful 0-0 draw then followed at struggling Leeds but this halting show was merely a prelude for a run of nine consecutive league victories.

First up were leaking Brighton on a bright, cold 18 November. Undone by a series of dreadful defensive errors, the Albion were thumped 4-1. A sterner test awaited the O's at Scunthorpe's Old Show Ground. But with Orient's defence restraining the Lincolnshire poacher, Barrie Thomas, the O's outshone their hosts under the Old Show's lights (2-0). A pair of 2-0 home victories followed, over Norwich and Newcastle. Dunmore scored yet another brace against the Canaries, watched by an appreciative Cliff Richard. Ronnie Foster was then the star of the pre-Christmas show at a frosty Ayresome Park as Orient won 3-2, thereby recording a 'double' over the Teessiders. With the festive season coming crisp and clear, the O's were invigorated sufficiently to record a second 'double', this time over lowly Swansea with Dunmore netting all four of their goals. Further 'doubles' followed, in early January, as two middling Midlands sides were vanquished – Walsall at home (3-0) and Derby away (2-1). Dunmore's brace of penalties proved very helpful.

The FA Cup tested their mettle more. Having seen off the buzzing 'Bees' of Brentford (2-1) after a third-round replay, second-placed O's were in a confident mood to take on the First Division leaders, Burnley, at Turf Moor. Burnley were in frightening form, particularly at home. They had contemptuously dismissed Alec Stock's Queens Park Rangers 6-1 in the previous round and had thrashed Manchester City 6-3 two weeks before. But defending well in numbers, Orient hit Burnley on the break. Ronnie Foster put them ahead after converting Graham's cushioned header back across goal. Burnley scraped a fortuitous draw through an 83rd-minute goal from Gordon Harris. Harris' typically fierce drive had found goal via the post, but there was a suspicion that he had used his hand first to control the ball. The replay at Brisbane Road on Tuesday 6 February was a belter. Less hampered by counter-attractions, 31,000 fans came to lend their excited support.

Veteran comedian Arthur 'hello playmates' Askey provided the pre-match entertainment, larking around in a blue and white beret and tracksuit. Arthur Askey was one of many showbiz celebrities and impresarios who took advantage of Harry Zussman's ultra-hospitable boardroom. Others included Cliff Richard, Lew and Les Grade and Bernard Delfont.

As for the game, Orient began in whirlwind style. Twice the ball thudded against the Burnley woodwork. But after an hour's play, largely dominated by Orient, Burnley's left-half, Brian Miller, stole in at a right-wing corner to score with a header that entered the net via the underside of the bar. 'Gallant Orient Go Out Fighting', declared the *Mirror*, 'this was the great Cup robbery! Orient had out-played, out-run and out-shone glamorous Burnley. But they lacked the goal touch that mattered.' Twenty-five years later these two teams would meet again in a 'do or die' Fourth Division scrap. It would determine Burnley's future existence as a football club. Nothing is for ever.

Before the Burnley tie, Orient were only one point behind leaders Liverpool, and five points ahead of nearest rivals, Southampton, powered by George O'Brien's and Tommy Mulgrew's goals and Terry Paine's trickery. However, the Burnley games seemed to drain the team's stamina and disturb their momentum. Straddling Orient's FA Cup defeat, relegation-doomed Bristol Rovers (2-3) and mid-table Preston (0-2) came to Brisbane Road and won. Plymouth then consigned the O's to a hat-trick of league losses and their fourth defeat on the bounce. Plymouth were now only two points behind Orient.

The Plymouth game marked the debut of the veteran Wolves and England right-winger Norman Deeley. Carey had shelled out £12,500 for the tiny, but dynamic and muscular, wingman because of a serious knee injury sustained by the skilful Phil White. With Wolves' old guard losing their bite, Deeley was offloaded. Carey's only other acquisition was Gordon Bolland, a 19-year-old Chelsea inside-forward who had been a member of the Blues' 1960 FA Youth Cup-winning team. He was sold for £5,000 in March 1962 as Chelsea faced the drop into Division Two.

On 24 February, Orient stemmed their poor run by winning 1-0 at Stoke. The Potters were reinforced by the returning 46-year-old Stanley Matthews, veteran ex-Preston and Villa striker Tommy Thompson, and the lithe, free-scoring former Manchester United and England star, Dennis Viollet. However, these vaunted forwards made no impression upon the stubborn O's defence, leaving Dunmore's 25-yard drive to steal the points. A week later, at a chilly Brisbane Road, the O's managed to hold a strong Sunderland side to a 1-1 draw having conceded a third-minute opener. Both Deeley and Bolland impressed in their home debuts. Deeley's 55th-minute equaliser was rather fortunate, though, being a speculative cross-cum-shot that floated over the head of Sunderland keeper Jim Montgomery. Carey looked on with envy at Sunderland's expensively assembled squad. Over £100,000 had been spent on Brian Clough (£45,000), George Herd (£40,000) and centre-half Charlie Hurley (£20,000), although 'Old Big 'Ead' was ruled out through injury. This was a blessing as Clough's brace in mid-October had sealed a narrow 2-1 win. The point which Orient won here would prove crucial on the final day.

Orient were now finding wins harder to come by. Just two came in their six March fixtures. However, thanks to a brilliant 25-yarder from Terry McDonald, they seized both points at Bury, where another stout defensive display was required. A ferocious long-distance drive from Graham also enabled Orient to subdue gritty Charlton at the Valley (2-1). Although an uncharacteristic error by Stan Charlton gifted Liverpool a last-minute equaliser on 17 March, this had been another epic contest. The champions-elect were bulging with present and future international stars including Roger Hunt, Ian St John, Gerry Byrne and Ian Callaghan. But they were indebted to a past England international, Alan A'Court, for their point. Left-winger A'Court slammed in both of Liverpool's goals, ensuring that Graham's and Lucas' spectacular strikes were not in a winning cause.

On the Saturday preceding the Brighton game a more resilient Leeds side, then in 21st place, came to Brisbane Road and shut up shop (0-0). Having lost Dunmore to a thigh injury at Charlton, the O's had to contend with not only a make-shift centre-forward, but also a hobbling one. An early injury to full-back, Lewis, resulted in him being pushed up front. Fortunately, Revie's men were only interested in saving a point for they rarely troubled the Orient goal. Leeds' outstanding performer was Bobby

Collins, Carey's former midfield maestro. He had been surprisingly released by Everton. Their negligent loss would become Leeds' restorative gain as the 'Little General' became the lynchpin of Don Revie's upwardly-mobile Leeds.

Frustrated at having dropped a point against Leeds, Carey sought to make up lost ground at the Goldstone on 7 April. Brighton and Orient were heading in opposite directions, not that their balance sheets gave any guide. Although hardly rich, Brighton had splashed out almost £50,000 on their squad whereas Orient had spent only a third of that figure.

George Curtis had been appointed as Brighton's manager after Billy Lane left in the previous summer. Curtis had been a nimble inside-forward with Arsenal before the war and with Southampton afterwards. He had been dubbed 'twinkle toes' at the Dell not only by his appreciative fans but also by his frustrated team-mates. After spending the 1952/53 season with the French side Valenciennes, he completed his playing days as player-manager with Chelmsford City. George also preached the new coaching gospel. He had gained his FA coaching qualifications at Lilleshall before accepting a coaching post at Sunderland in 1957. Here, he worked under a fellow coaching enthusiast, the censorious but shrewd Alan Brown. George Curtis seemed an ideal replacement for Lane.

The senior Brighton players thought otherwise, however. Nicholas later told an *Evening Argus* reporter:

> *I like to think that I had helped keep Brighton up [in 1960/61]. When George came he only bought one player – Joe Caven from Airdrie. I reckon Brighton got done paying £15,000 for him. He came with a reputation of being a free-scoring centre-forward and didn't get one for us. The trouble was that we needed new players but there wasn't sufficient money. We needed two or three good 'uns. If we had had another two or three players we could have done quite well instead of finishing bottom. George's idea was to make world-beaters of people with little or no ability ... There is a complete difference between managers and coaches and George was definitely a coach. When George took over he told all the players, 'any problems, don't see me, see Joe Wilson'. George just didn't want to know. Once, when I went to see him for the refund of a taxi fare of 9/6d., he handed me a*

> *ten shilling note. I started to walk out of the office and he called me back and asked for the change. He wasn't joking. Don't get me wrong, George was a charming chap, a gentleman and a good coach, but a dead loss as a manager and I think he knew it.*

Inside-forward, Ian McNeill added, 'George Curtis ruined the club. Yet he was the best coach I worked under. He kept saying he wanted youngsters in the team but they weren't good enough. He'd coach one style during the week but, on a match day, he would be calling for distance balls over the heads and all the preparations went out of the window. Bob McNicol was a firm crowd favourite who had played in practically every game until Curtis brought in David Smith from Burnley. At training we'd form up in opposing sides and, after being left out, Bob really clattered into George. Next time, George made sure he had Bob in his team.'

George seemed a strange cove. His programme notes for the Blackburn FA Cup tie included a quote from the medieval Persian poetry of Omar Khayyam, prefaced by his own impenetrable thoughts. George wrote: 'We all appreciate some of the players' problems. Some appreciate them all. Our players, the young ones in particular, are paying the price of experience and circumstance by criticism. In the end it will reward them richly. Meantime this quote might well encourage them: "The Ball no question makes of ayes and noes, But right or left as strikes the player goes; And He that tossed thee down into the Field, He knows about it all, He knows."'

Lurching from the obscure to the obvious, during his introduction to Norwegian football he pointed at a leather football and solemnly told his new Rosenborg side, 'this is a ball', prompting his best striker to retort: 'George, don't go too fast, now.'

Creditably, or perhaps naively, George explained his choice of tactics in his programme notes for the Orient game. He wrote: 'At Huddersfield it was agreed that [right-winger] Mike Tiddy would play a flanking mid-field game in order not only to draw Ray Wilson [a World Cup winner in '66] further from his goal line to present a vacant wing area behind him, into which either Nicholas or Caven might move, but to 'ferret' for the ball should the wing-half prepare to move into attack. Tony Nicholas' role as a support man for Caven proved not without successes, for two scoring chances were created, from which, unfortunately, Tony's shots were off target. This afternoon, for example, we might well anticipate the wanderings of Deeley and McDonald.' Prescient George Curtis appeared to be on the same wavelength as his former Southampton team-mate, Alf Ramsey. George had difficulty in translating his tactical awareness into winning game plans, though. After occupying a mid-table position at New Year, the Albion had nosedived into bottom place by 7 April. The 'Orient' programme advertised the Hollywood blockbuster *El Cid* at the Astoria. The club was certainly in need of a white knight.

During the autumn period, Brighton took some heavy beatings on the road. Southampton hammered them 6-1 at the Dell and both Plymouth and Newcastle subjected them to 5-0 drubbings. Defensively, the Albion were a mess. Tony Sitford was at fault for at least two of the goals conceded in their 4-1 defeat at Orient. The warning signs had been evident as early as August when injury-depleted visitors Swansea were allowed to pull back a two-goal deficit to grab a 2-2 draw. After beating Middlesbrough on 28 October, Brighton did not record another league victory until the festive period – eight games later – when they managed to beat Bristol Rovers both at home and away. These twin victories pushed them up to 16th place. But with their confidence still shaky, the rot finally set in after an FA Cup drubbing at home by First Division Blackburn. Only a home 3-2 win against newly-promoted Walsall on 24 March arrested their free fall. It was their first league victory in three months. Recalled Bobby Laverick scored a brace. The tide did not turn, though, with Brighton remaining rooted to the bottom. A victory on 7 April was as vital for them as for their visitors. While Brighton were at full strength, Carey had to replace his injured centre-forward, Dunmore, with Gordon Bolland. Ron Foster slotted into Bolland's place at inside-right.

It was a dull, passionless day. Even the chilly north-easterly wind could not disperse a grey mist that smudged the sea, sky and surrounding downs. The draping clouds appeared to coalesce with the rippling sea water in an enveloping gloom. It was hard to believe that little more than a year had passed since we had stepped out of Hove station, oblivious to the gusting wind and rain, eagerly anticipating victory over the Football League champions. Here, the home fans shuffled towards the terraces, only too aware of the dank cold. The average home gate of 13,000 represented a 2,500 fall on the previous season although only 1,000 short of what high-flying Orient were drawing. Orient fans had congregated on the eastern terraces. They were chirpily expectant. I had yet to follow a successful side so I was perplexed by their carping criticisms of Bolland, Graham and McDonald. I had no idea that a deluge of blessings could generate such impatience. Their maligned heroes began by attacking the North Stand at the Old Shoreham Road End.

The game jolted into a snarling dogfight on a rutted glue pot of a surface. It was hardly the place for flowing football. There was no composure, just frantic tussles, hopeful punts and hasty clearances with possession ping-ponging between the straining sides. While Brighton hunted as a compressed pack, the Orient players were better at spreading the play, allowing both McDonald and Deeley greater freedom to run at the home full-backs. Following one such break on the left, McDonald cut in and, with his favoured right foot, hammered the bobbling ball goalwards. Brighton's keeper, Charlie Baker, could only parry his skimming shot, allowing Ronnie Foster a simple finish. In the remaining 15 minutes before half-time, Brighton upped the tempo but their attacks lacked cohesion and were easily snuffed out by the redoubtable Orient defence.

As the half-time scores were shown on the coded metal plates, the Shadows hit 'Wonderful Land' came over the public address system. It sounded regretful rather than joyful – perhaps appropriately, given the glum mood of the Brighton fans.

The second half was more open. Brighton's inside-forward Ian McNeill managed to get the ball down and provide more thoughtful and incisive service for his tearaway forwards, Nicholas and Laverick. The Orient defence came under greater pressure. But with Brighton pushing forward in search of an equaliser the O's forwards enjoyed more space at the other end. Little Terry McDonald had a lot of the ball. From my lofty position he looked very young, frail and vulnerable, almost as if he was an altar boy dragooned into playing. But up close he looked tougher, more streetwise. There was no doubting his ability. Once in possession he was calm and assured, continually drawing Joe Carolan towards him, only to confound the Eire international with his quick feet, darting by on the inside or outside and pumping one cross after another into the crowded Brighton box. Whereas McDonald was nimble and nifty, Deeley was forceful and direct, frequently making a beeline for goal with a scurrying motion, using his surprising upper body strength to shrug off the challenges. With Orient failing to capitalise upon their excellent wing service, Brighton remained in the hunt until the very end. But it was to no avail. The Albion were no better at converting their chances than the O's.

Orient deserved their narrow victory although Brighton boss, George Curtis, felt differently, remarking: 'There was sufficient collective effort for our lads to have bagged both points and it was disappointing, to say the least, in recording the manner in which Leyton scored the only goal of the match. Results at our end of the table most certainly didn't help us. Anyway we can only help ourselves. We MUST help ourselves during the remaining six matches.' Despite George Curtis' desperation, Brighton were unable to rescue themselves. A disappointing 2-2 home draw with

Charlton was followed by a 3-1 defeat at Preston. Contrary to expectation, the Albion recorded two home victories on the bounce – only their sixth and seventh of the season – beating Norwich 2-1 on Good Friday and, much to Orient's delight, defeating Plymouth 3-2 a day later. But it was not enough to save them. Their final two fixtures at Norwich and Derby ended in lame defeats. One year after Billy Lane had left them, Brighton were back in Division Three. Their final tally of 42 league goals was just one more than Barrie Thomas managed to score alone that season for Scunthorpe (31) and Newcastle (10).

Tony Nicholas told a Brighton *Evening Argus* reporter:

> *When I went to Brighton it was on a two-year contract. After the first year the maximum wage had been abolished and when that changed so did the contracts. The first-team players were on £20 a week. I thought I should get more, but the board turned me down in no uncertain fashion. 'More money, Nicholas?' they chorused. 'What a nerve. The players have taken the club down and you come in here asking for an increase. No. There isn't any.' In the end I got £28 a week to play for Chelmsford City in the Southern League … There had to be something radically wrong for that situation to come about. After all, Brighton had been a Second Division club. Nobody at Brighton could say I didn't give 100 per cent and the crowd liked me. I thought, 'Why should I be stuck at the same pay level as some that weren't so good?' [Brighton inside-forward] Ian McNeill was of the same opinion and I don't think we were the only ones.*

It seemed incredible that one of the country's brightest prospects, just two years before, chose to abandon a still promising Football League career at the age of 24 years. While the abolition of the maximum wage favoured the best players at the biggest clubs it did less for those with small, cash-strapped sides. Added to its financial woes, Brighton was a club divided and duly paid the price as they slid haplessly towards the Fourth Division.

As for Orient, their win at Brighton put them three points clear of Plymouth but it failed to revive their home form. A week later, another promotion-chasing side, Scunthorpe United, came to Brisbane Road and snatched the points with a solitary goal. It was scored within 30 seconds of the start by the Iron's inside-left, John McGuigan, who intercepted a misplaced pass by Mal Lucas. Although Dunmore was recalled he seemed troubled still by his thigh injury. Despite dominating the game, Orient could not score. While fifth-placed Scunthorpe moved within three points of Orient, Plymouth's progress was stalled by a 2-1 defeat at Bury. Orient's main rivals, though, were Sunderland, who had put together a string of victories. Their 2-1 away win at Luton was their fourth on the spin, putting them just two points behind the O's.

Orient's poor home form threatened to scupper their promotion chances. After beating Walsall in mid-January, eight home games had passed by without a win. The goals had dried up. After Foster's goal at Brighton the O's went five and a half hours without scoring again. A nervous 0-0 draw, at home against Luton on Good Friday evening, was the third consecutive game in which they had failed to score. McDonald was desperately unlucky, though, that his 52nd-minute effort was ruled out. Yet another 0-0 draw came on the following day at Norwich. Their ragged showing deserved no better. Meanwhile, Sunderland were hammering Newcastle 3-0. They were only two points behind with a game in hand. The O's seemed to be bottling it.

Injuries and poor form forced Carey to reshuffle his pack. Former Chelsea inside-forward Derek Gibbs was recalled for the return game at a sunny Kenilworth Road. It was his first game for six months. Foster was also restored to the team although not fully fit, while Bolland and young Billy Taylor were excluded. Bizarrely, Luton fielded two goalkeepers with ex-England international Ron Baynham filling in at centre-forward. The O's fans despaired as Luton took an eighth-minute lead through wing-half Bob Morton. Then, to compound their misery, Dave Dunmore fluffed a penalty 11 minutes later. The news from Roker Park was not good. Sunderland were thrashing Rotherham. Orient's promotion prospects appeared to be draining away.

However, Derek Gibbs seized his brief moments of glory. Just before the break he equalised with a volley and ten minutes into the second half he put the O's in front by converting McDonald's cross. But just a minute later Orient were downcast once again as Luton's Brendan McNally squared the game with a swiftly-taken free kick. Or so they thought, for much to their relief, the referee ordered the kick to be retaken. Luton's chance had gone. Despite laying siege to the O's goal for the next 20 minutes, Luton could not prevent Mal Lucas from giving his side an unassailable lead with a venomous volley from 25 yards. However, having beaten Rotherham 4-0, Sunderland remained hot on Orient's heels. Scunthorpe were not out of the race, either. Their brace of 2-1 victories – at home to Preston and away at Huddersfield – meant they were only three points behind with a game in hand. Plymouth and Southampton were now out of contention, though.

The tension was gripping everyone at the club. Director Les Grade proposed offering the Rotherham players an £800 reward to beat Sunderland in the return game on Easter Tuesday. At his behest, Stan Charlton and Dave Dunmore drove to Rotherham and reluctantly put the offer to the Millers' captain, Roy Lambert. Their mission was a fiasco. Although desperate to keep their quest a secret, both Dunmore and Charlton were easily recognised in the crowd. A queue of autograph hunters gathered around them. As for the game, Clough's hat-trick gave Sunderland an easy victory. Sunderland overtook Orient on goal average. But Scunthorpe were out of it, having lost their return home game with Huddersfield.

Everything depended upon the final games. If Sunderland won theirs at Swansea they would be promoted, unless the O's beat Bury by a better score. To add more spice to the mix, Swansea needed a point in order to secure Second Division safety.

Roy Horobin, the *Sunday Express* football correspondent, described Orient's home game with Bury thus:

> *Five minutes from the end of this memorable game … Malcolm Graham scored the greatest goal of his life – and burst into tears. He chased a long pass from Norman Deeley and raced past former Newcastle centre-half, Bob Stokoe. Then, drawing Chris Harker from his goal, he dribbled round the goalkeeper and slammed the ball into the net. But it was all too much for him and as the delirious crowd … raced on to the field to acclaim him, so he hung his head as the tears streamed down his face … It will always be remembered as Graham's day. Coming into the side only because of an injury to Ronnie Foster, he had already put Orient on the road to victory after 14 minutes when he jumped like a stag to nod the ball into the roof of the net with Harker desperately clutching the empty air … Every man in this Orient side played himself into the ground and chased every ball until he was ready to drop. Bury, who played throughout as great sportsmen, never gave up – but they could muster just one shot at goal.*

It was not quite as straightforward as Roy reported, however. Sunderland had led 1-0 for most of their game at Swansea. Regular bulletins from the Vetch Field were broadcasted by the BBC Light Programme. Among the 21,678 crowd at Brisbane Road there were a few fans with transistor radios pressed to their ears, passing on the news from South Wales. It was a nail-nibbling, lip-chewing, anxious afternoon. Orient's bursting joy at Graham's 14th-minute opener was tempered quickly by the disappointing news that Brian Clough had put Sunderland ahead. Over 200 miles away at the Vetch Field, the *South Wales Evening Post* reporter was recording:

> *Far more composed and often showing superior skill, Swansea Town ensured Second Division football next season by holding Sunderland to a 1-1 draw in what was undoubtedly the most exciting match of the campaign ... Although it took them 66 minutes to equalise through Brayley Reynolds they played with more confidence and verve ... Sunderland's policy seemed to be 'to hold what we have'. Clough, always a potential danger, was remarkably well held by Mel Nurse while Herbie Williams and Reg Davies limited the scope of Willie McPheat and George Herd. Only on very isolated occasions did wingers Harry Hooper and Jackie Overfield get the better of Swansea's full-backs, Harry Griffiths and Alan Sanders. As for John King – not nearly as busy as Jim Montgomery – he did a man-sized job despite a troublesome thigh injury, for which he received a pain-killing injection during the interval ... Reynolds crowned another good showing by getting the all-important goal – his 20th this season. He had some hectic duels with the talented Hurley [but] it was from wingers Morgans and Barry Jones that the greatest threat came ... Webster, though closely marked, was always probing and Peter Donnelly contributed much ... The crowd of 18,100 which included about 2,000 from Sunderland had plenty to interest them and there was some well-deserved applause at the end for the Swans' gallant and successful fight in the last few weeks to retain Second Division status, which they have held longer than any other club ... Sunderland*

chief, Alan Brown, had this to say: 'We expected a struggle but our players were tensed up and though they tried hard, Swansea played harder.'

The clock had just eased past 4.15pm when an excited commotion spread around Brisbane Road, which quickly developed into a full-throated roar as it became known that Reynolds, the abrasive Welsh striker with the Elvis quiff, had equalised for Swansea. He had saved the O's season. Harry Zussman had promised Swansea's boss, Trevor Morris, a new hat if the Swans denied Sunderland and helped send the O's up, but knowing full well what that result was worth, Morris held out for a new bespoke suit, which he duly received.

After the game at Brisbane Road, the champagne flowed. Harry Zussman, the ever-jovial Orient chairman, was almost incoherent with joy. He and Jack Young, the club president, recalled a time 13 years before when Leyton Orient were facing the uncertainty of a Football League re-election process. Then, as young businessmen, they felt unable to watch any more of Orient's crucial final home game with Southend, which the O's were losing 1-0. Instead, they sought the refuge of the club's tiny office. While they were discussing how they might secure the necessary votes, a roar went up from the crowd. Wally Pullen had equalised and Orient's immediate Football League future was assured. Now, with Orient promoted to the top flight, their fortunes had been transformed. Zussman bubbled, 'I just can't believe it. It's marvellous but here [pointing at Johnny Carey] is the man who has done it all.' Carey, as modest as ever, simply said: 'I'm happy for this great-hearted club, but credit must go to a bunch of lads who played their hearts out.'

Carey was correct. A key ingredient of Orient's success was their work rate, not only in creating the openings but in bolting the defence. When Norman Deeley joined the club, he was surprised to find he was expected to track back as well as bomb forward. He had been employed as an out-and-out attacker at Wolves. It was this determination to defend from the front, to cover so tightly for one another, that made Orient such a hard team to beat. Orient conceded 40 goals during the 1961/62 season, less than a goal per game. Only Liverpool conceded fewer with 38. Even meanly defensive Sunderland conceded ten more goals than Orient. As managers Alf Ramsey, Bill Nicholson, Cliff Britton, Alan Brown and Joe Mercer understood, to create a successful side you must always start at the back.

Another feature of Orient's remarkable triumph was their ability to score many of their goals from distance. This is particularly surprising given the greater weight of the leather ball at that time, although diminutive Burnley winger Brian Pilkington contended that it was all a matter of timing. He certainly scored some corkers in his time at Burnley – two came in the European Cup run of 1960/61. The high ratio of successful long distance shots suggested that attackers were not closed down as quickly then as they are today. The positioning of the goalkeepers was probably less good, also. I recall being surprised that Gordon Banks produced relatively few spectacular saves – his brilliant diving stop from Pele's header, excepted. He explained that he worked so hard on his positioning – continuously practising stopping shots and headers from different angles and heights – that there was less need for him to be a gymnast.

A short history of tractor boys in Suffolk

In 1962, a version of the 'American Dream' still prevailed in the Football League. Unlike in Spain, Italy and South America, where a junta of powerful clubs cornered the honours, it was still possible here for a humble club to achieve top-flight glory. Burnley had demonstrated this in 1960 although, for all their limitations in cash and support, they were then an established First Division side. By contrast, the rise and rise of Ipswich Town was positively *Rocky*-like. They had only joined the Football League in 1938. They were still a Third Division club in 1957. And yet, come May 1962, they were First Division champions. They were only the second Football League club to win the First Division title at their initial attempt – Preston were the first, in 1888/9.

It was quite by chance that Ipswich Town became a Football League club at all, let alone a successful one. The seed was sown during the mid-thirties after the Arsenal chairman, Sir Samuel Hill Wood, suggested to his friend, John Murray Cobbold, that he might care to watch a game at Highbury rather than have a day at the races as was his wont. It was a Damascus-like experience for Cobbold. He enjoyed the occasion so much that he came away with the firm intention of turning his local amateur side, Ipswich Town, into the 'Arsenal of East Anglia'. Cobbold took charge of the club and put them immediately on a professional footing, securing a place for them in the Southern League, then the strongest English non-league competition. Ipswich won the Southern League championship in their first season. Cobbold then set about campaigning for his club's election to the Football League. He was clearly a persuasive man because Ipswich began life in the Third Division (South) at the start of the 1938/39 season. Cobbold enlisted the highly experienced Scott Duncan as his manager. It was a wise decision. At the end of his first season in charge, Duncan had taken Ipswich to seventh place. After war stopped play, Ipswich were forced to rebuild from scratch. During the austere post-war period, progress proved to be much slower. Although Ipswich finally won a Second Division place in 1954, their stay lasted for one year only. Then came the Ramsey revolution.

Ramsey reinvented himself. He came from a working-class background. He had a taste for jellied eels and the simple life. And yet he knew he had to smarten up his act if he was to make his name as a successful football club manager. It was not enough that he'd had a glittering playing career. Like John Major, he encased himself in an elocution straitjacket. He needed to be credible within the social circles he was expected to inhabit. At Ipswich this included the club 'aristocracy', the Cobbolds. The trouble was, when Ramsey tried to 'toff it up', he sounded like Harold Steptoe. In the year that Ramsey took over at Ipswich the national press were having a field day with Professor Alan Ross's study of 'U and non-U' linguistic conventions. It was a source of amusement to many and not only the 'plebs'. The aristocratic novelist, Nancy Mitford, had her tongue in her chic when she pronounced that it was non-U (that is, not 'upper class') to use the term 'toilet' instead of 'lavatory'. Although absurd, the debate emphasised the strength of class snobbery existing in post-war Britain.

Ramsey's diction was so formal, so clipped, so contrived, that when he used the f-word it was as if the Queen had farted. He was not the only club manager to try to toff it up, at least while on duty. Take the stilted, florid prose adopted by Harry Potts at Burnley or George Curtis at Brighton in their programme notes. These were the strained attempts of working-class men at proving themselves in an elitist climate. With educational snobbery being rife in those times, they felt obliged to present themselves in refined tones. When alone with their teams they were much more relaxed and informal. In public, they were constantly on guard. Ramsey once quipped that a crisis in the Cobbolds' boardroom was 'a shortage of sherry'. He knew where he belonged.

For all that, Ramsey was his own man. Although vastly experienced in domestic and international football and shrewd in knowing what made a team tick, he wasn't sold on the new coaching ideas. He was disinterested in obtaining coaching qualifications. Perhaps he was reluctant to subject himself to formal examination? He seemed self-conscious about his rudimentary education. He was a traditionalist when it came to training methods, too. Alf was not a tracksuit manager, despite sporting one when in charge of England's World Cup squad. At Ipswich he was quite prepared for his trainer, Jimmy Forsyth, to organise the fitness training: the weights, the sprints and long-distance running, supplemented with a bit of shooting practice and impromptu 5-a-side games.

What singled Ramsey out as a brilliant manager was his use of tactics. He had an elephant-like memory of games he had seen, even those played months before. He could recall the various runs his players made, the positions they took up, how they laid the ball off, which way they turned when challenged, how quickly and accurately they passed. He shared this knowledge with them, showing them how they might improve. He introduced voluntary skills sessions during the afternoons. These helped to sharpen up the accuracy of his players' short passing. While he expected his team to play in a certain way, his game plans were conceived in the knowledge of what was achievable. His pragmatism allowed room for professional development, though. Ordinary footballers became better under Ramsey. Some became extraordinary, like Jimmy Leadbetter.

Although largely a private man, Ramsey fostered a close-knit team which championed his aims and methods and reflected his focus and self-belief. Thanks to Ramsey's tactical acumen, his Cinderella-like Ipswich side had a ball at the start of the sixties although, soon after their crowning glory, the midnight chimes struck.

In 1960/61, Ipswich won the Second Division title with an average gate of 15,095. This was scarcely better than Orient's during their promotion season. The Cobbolds were comparatively well-off but their club was not rich. As was the case at Orient, Alf Ramsey had to make do with a collection of misfits and cast-offs. Typical of his captures was the ploddingly orthodox inside-left, Jimmy Leadbetter. Leadbetter was nicknamed 'Sticks' or 'Steptoe' on account of his wasted, geriatric appearance. In truth, he looked more aged than TV cop, George Dixon. And Dock Green police had no concept of a retirement policy. Ramsey breathed new life into Leadbetter's spindly legs and deceptively frail frame, turning him into a deadly playmaker.

Leadbetter was converted into an unorthodox left-winger who held back in the manner of Zagallo. Like the faster Brazilian, Leadbetter looked to pick up the ball deep inside his own half. This move enticed opposing full-backs to move uncertainly towards him – few full-backs were then comfortable about crossing the halfway line – allowing Leadbetter to ping deadly long balls into the spaces they left behind. The predatory twin central strikers, Crawford and Phillips, exploited these opportunities to the hilt. But this tactical innovation would not have worked without Leadbetter's skill in executing his passes so adroitly, consistently finding the right areas at the right pace and height. Among Jimmy's previous clubs, neither Chelsea nor Brighton had any idea he harboured such a lethal talent. Ramsey recognised the potential that others had missed.

Ramsey unearthed other jewels in the bargain bins. He signed left-back John Compton from Chelsea for £1,000, centre-half Andy Nelson from West Ham for £8,500, and outside-right Roy Stephenson from Leicester for £3,000. None of these players had become established first-teamers at their previous clubs. But Ramsey knew better. It was a testament to his skill that no fewer than five Ipswich players collected Third, Second and First Division championship medals under his management – an unprecedented feat. The 'famous five' were goalkeeper Roy Bailey, signed from Crystal Palace; left-half John Elsworthy; inside-left Ted Phillips; right-back Len Carberry (spotted while on national service) and Jimmy Leadbetter. His other buys were Ray Crawford, Portsmouth's disaffected reserve centre-forward – an absolute steal at £5,000 – Billy Baxter, a tough young Scottish defender snatched from junior football for a pittance, and inside-forward Doug Moran, bought from Falkirk for £12,300 after Ipswich won the Second Division title.

Alf Ramsey's preferred system of play was a fluid version of a 4-2-4 formation which morphed into 4-4-2 when possession was lost. As Ray Crawford pointed out, it took the players time to practise the tactic smoothly. He recalled that Jimmy Leadbetter covered the left post at corners but was initially so slow in moving upfield that he would play the opposition onside. But once the teething problems were sorted out, the system worked like a well-oiled machine.

Tactically, Ipswich's success was founded upon a physically strong, quick-covering defence, reinforced by its backtracking wingers, Leadbetter and Stephenson. Like Mercer, Ramsey knew that success depended upon having a strong defence. He also adopted the mantra of his former boss, Arthur Rowe: 'make it simple, make it quick'. Like Stan Cullis, he wanted his team to move the ball quickly, attempting to reach the opponents' penalty area in no more than three passes. But he was no advocate of 'kick and rush'. These passes needed to be made quickly but with precision. With Leadbetter, particularly, but also with Stephenson, he had the right men to provide this quality of service.

However, he still required the powerful running and the ferociously accurate shooting of Ted Phillips and Ray Crawford up front to turn the tactical advantage into goals. Crawford was a real handful for defences. He had strength, an alert eye for a half-chance and commanding aerial ability. But Phillips was more intimidating. Tall and wiry with a weathered complexion, Ted exuded hardness. You wouldn't have expected to find Ted in a tanning studio unless it was of the hide-leathering sort. His blistering shot was once timed at an incredible 94mph. And that's with a much heavier ball than that used today. Even more impressively, Phillips could apply swerve to his shooting. So, if the opposing keeper was not knocked senseless by his explosive shots, he was likely to be dumbfounded by their curve. Burnley goalie Adam Blacklaw recalled a game at Turf Moor, in August 1961, when he was first introduced to the power of Ted's shooting. Although Adam was a big, beefy lad, he remembered how Ted worked him over with a series of 30-yard thunderbolts which made the crowd gasp. Ted scored with one such effort. Adam didn't see the ball until it was past him. He saw Phillips line up the shot. Then, wham, the ball was in the back of the net. Adam hadn't moved an inch. It was a breathtaking effort.

In 1960/61, Ipswich were promoted to the top flight having scored 100 league goals – Phillips scored 30 and Crawford 40. In winning the First Division championship, the pair scored a further 61 goals between them – Phillips 28 and Crawford 33 – in a team total of 93. Crawford was considered good enough to play for England. However, his club side's strength was greater than a sum of its individual talents.

Crucially, Ipswich inflicted two league defeats upon 'double' champions, Spurs, in their race for the title. Having lost 3-2 at Portman Road in the previous autumn, Spurs were expected to exact revenge in the return game on the evening of 14 March. On a threadbare pitch, slick Spurs began by taking the game to their opponents. Wing-halves Blanchflower and Marchi pushed up in support of their voracious forwards. But this approach suited Ipswich's counter-attacking game plan. Without Dave Mackay to close him down, Ted Phillips ran riot in the spaces left in the Spurs defence, scoring twice with clinical shots. Ted had more to offer than just brute force. While Spurs' attacks foundered on Ipswich's defence, superbly marshalled by Elsworthy, the visitors created havoc on the break. Both Stephenson and Moran had shots which smacked against the bar. Here was a side assembled for only £30,000 completely outplaying a team that cost over a quarter of a million. Spurs were reckoned to be one of the best clubs in Europe. Their narrow defeat by Benfica in the semi-final of the European Cup would prove that.

Ipswich's opponents were slow to combat Ramsey's tactical plan. This was partly because TV and video coverage was so limited then. Besides, there wasn't the depth or breadth of tactical scrutiny that there is today. Spurs' boss, Bill Nicholson, cottoned on quicker than most, though. In the Charity Shield game at Portman Road in August 1962, he told his wing-halves to mark Leadbetter and Stephenson tightly, leaving the full-backs to tuck in alongside the centre-half, Norman, to repel Crawford, Phillips and the other inside-forward, Moran. The innovation worked like a dream. Ipswich were thrashed 5-1. Their party was over.

Burnley burn out

On 3 March 1962, Burnley led the First Division with 42 points, four ahead of Spurs in second place and five in front of Ipswich. They also had games in hand. The Clarets had just hammered West Ham 6-0, taking their total league goals tally to an incredible 90. They were equally successful in the FA Cup, threatening to emulate Spurs' double-winning feat of the year before. And yet they failed to grasp either prize, finishing up as runners-up in both competitions. Burnley's manager, Harry Potts, seemed reluctant to make changes when his side began to stumble. It was rumoured that playmaker Jimmy McIlroy had been 'tapped up' by an Italian club just before the final. This might have explained his below-par performance at Wembley although Jimmy's view was that he and his team simply ran out of steam. There was little doubt that he often played when not fully fit, such was his importance to his side. So, burnout seemed to be the most likely explanation. Burnley would never be as good again.

Before the mandatory wage cap and the feudal 'retain and transfer' system were removed, a talented, tactically astute 'David', like Burnley or Ipswich, could defeat the richer, more fancied 'Goliaths' over the long, rugged haul of an English First Division football season. But even then money shouted. As with Ipswich's championship in 1961/62, Burnley's league title victory in 1959/60 was a triumph against the odds.

Thereafter, those odds grew ever longer for a team like Burnley. Situated in a small, economically-declining community, Burnley's team, like its town, required more resources than it could muster in order to thrive. The imminent abolition of the footballers' maximum wage not only disturbed the balance sheet, it also meant that the team could no longer rely upon attracting the best young talent. That talent would go increasingly to the highest bidder. As a small-town club with limited means greater efficiencies needed to be found while facing increasing competition from richer clubs. There were also other leisure attractions to contend with. Burnley FC was forced to consider how it should market itself within the confines of a declining local economy. The 'sell to survive' policy was born in this climate. Regrettably, that policy could only work while the club remained as a force in the top flight and was seen to give its talented youngsters an earlier opportunity to shine on the big stage. By so doing, Burnley could still hope to compete with and confound the more lucrative enticements offered by larger clubs. However, it needed its youth policy to deliver at a high rate of productivity to plug the gaps left by its departing stars. Once the harvest began to fail, the team fell away, and, with the law of diminishing returns biting deeper into its prospects, the club slid downwards to that traumatic day in May 1987.

Beyond the Fringe

Harold Macmillan's government brought about modernisation in the mines, the railways, schools and universities and achieved large-scale decolonisation, and yet he and his ministers seemed crusty and out of touch. At least that seemed to be the view of a 'Baby Boomer' generation that had come of age in this time of greater opportunity. Partly because of their growing frustrations, satire became chic.

A new satirical nightclub opened in London called 'The Establishment'. This attracted the controversial American comedian Lenny Bruce, who traded in edgy examinations of sensitive issues including racial prejudice. *Private Eye* produced its first scrappy editions and, much as it might appear tame now, the *Beyond the Fringe* revue scoffed at 'establishment' sacred cows. Take the Second World War, for example. Up until the mid-fifties, the British film industry churned out a series of plucky wartime dramas like *The Battle of the River Plate*, *Reach for the Sky* and *The Desert Rats*. To mock these tales of selfless courage was considered almost sacrilegious, at least by those who insisted that Britain should be forever great and grateful. But while Peter Cook, Dudley Moore, Jonathan Miller and Alan Bennett were criticised, notably in the provinces, for trivialising a war that they had been spared, this accusation could not be levelled at Joseph Heller, whose novel, *Catch-22*, first appeared here in 1961. Heller had served as a bombardier with the US Air Force, flying missions over Nazi-occupied Italy in support of the Allied invasion. His grotesquely funny satire savaged, with nihilistic abandon, the euphemisms, moral pretensions and organisational chaos of war. In a year when Britain seemed to be declining and Cold War tensions mounting, gallows humour had more resonance.

Farewell to the season of the underdog

Ipswich and Orient, the massive underdogs of '61/62, had their days; spectacularly brilliant ones, at that. To complete a hat-trick of improbable triumphs, little Dundee interrupted Rangers' domination of the Scottish League, before proceeding, even more improbably, to a European Cup semi-final a year later. Not to be outdone, Fourth Division Rochdale reached the final of the League Cup, only to lose 4-0 on aggregate to Norwich City of Division Two. Although a number of First Division sides shunned the new cup competition, this was still an impressive feat. It was perhaps appropriate, then, that during this season of surprises Johnny Byrne of Crystal Palace became the first Third Division player to be picked for England. Not that he remained a small guy for much longer. In March 1962 he was transferred to West Ham for £65,000, a record deal between English teams. Having spent two seasons insensate with serial surrender, Orient's, Ipswich's and Dundee's fantastic achievements not only restored my hope of something better; they also nudged that hope closer to expectation. These teams proved that a lack of resources need not be an insurmountable barrier. Apparently unpromising talent could be harnessed to devastating effect. Where a team was prepared to make the very most of its individual and collective talents, there were potential wonders to behold. It was high time for 'Please Please Me'.

'PLEASE PLEASE ME' 1962–1970

'Like all dreamers, I mistook disenchantment for truth'
Jean-Paul Sartre, 1964

THE 1962/63 SEASON

Tonbridge v Hastings United

'Let's Dance'
17 November 1962

It had been a poor summer. Despite an unexpectedly vibrant victory over Argentina, England performed disappointingly in the Chile World Cup finals. Arthur Hopcraft's lugubrious verdict in his book *The Football Man* was, 'Far from knowing all there was to know about the game, we found that we had been left years behind it. We even looked old. Our shorts were longer, thicker, flappier than anyone else's, so that our players looked like Scoutmasters struggling to keep pace with the troop.' The brilliance of Brazil's Garrincha ended our joyless jamboree in the quarter-finals.

The Pakistani cricket team also took a brief look at the grey, chilly English weather before shrivelling into submission. Meanwhile, things were not going well for Prime Minister Harold Macmillan. With sterling in trouble, his Cabinet divided and his popularity rating slumping to 36 per cent, Macmillan sacked seven ministers and conducted other ministerial changes affecting 40 per cent of Government posts. Jeremy Thorpe, a Liberal, sniped: 'Greater love hath no man than he lay down his friends for his life.'

Southern League Hastings United conducted their 'Night of the Long Knives' purge, too. New manager Ted Ballard announced, 'I promise you that next season we will be at least more like a football club … and every endeavour will be made to give you the football you and the town deserve.'

Tim Kelly's rash bid for glory in 1960/61 had saddled the little seaside club with an annual wage bill of almost £13,000, around £500,000 in modern currency. Relegation resulted in the release of all 15 professionals, including Len Duquemin. This left just a handful of local hopefuls signed on amateur terms. Although this small, cheerless band was augmented by a clutch of cheap 'cast offs', only centre-half John Ashen and ex-Chelsea keeper Ian Agate justified their pay. These two were kept very busy indeed.

In that bleak winter, a team largely comprising the halted and the lamentable waited in vain for a divine miracle. Local pub players gave the Pilot Field a wide berth lest they were dragged in. Nevertheless, the '61/62 austerity drive worked. Despite the dismal results on the pitch – an anorexic 14 points accrued from five wins and four draws with 115 goals conceded – the club secured a profit of £1,480, approximating to £53,000 today. Helped by the 53 per cent reduction in wages, the 1960/61 deficit of £1,763 was reversed spectacularly, even on the back of an average gate of 780, which was 50 per cent down on the previous year.

In these more brutal times, a beleaguered football manager like Tim Kelly might well be sent packing with a flea in his ear, but the *Hastings & St Leonards Observer* correspondent was more gracious, describing Kelly as 'a victim of the economy axe', and believing that he left Hastings with his 'reputation untarnished'. Kelly achieved a win percentage of 16 per cent in his previous two seasons in charge. For new manager Ted Ballard, the only way forward was up.

Ballard, a former lower-division defender with Brentford, Southampton and Orient, was a shrewd cookie. He had made a good fist of managing neighbouring Ashford Town, a small Southern League club set in a railway community of 28,000 residents. His budget seemed to comprise twigs and twine and yet he consistently assembled competitive sides. Hastings must have seemed a more attractive proposition, though, with its much larger population of 68,000 – well over twice the size of Ashford and almost on a par with that of First Division heavyweights, Burnley. Besides, Ted had completed his playing career at Hastings United.

Like the best of non-league managers, Ted had a sharp eye for the neglected and unrecognised talent that lurked beneath the Football League radar. According to his sons, Ken and Alan, Ted was constantly on the lookout for better players. He spent hours watching midweek games all over the southern counties – league and non-league. As his Hastings captain, Keith Tucker, pointed out:

> *Ted kept a careful note of all the players that caught his eye. He put their names in his little black book. He knew exactly what players he needed and who might best fit in. And once he fancied a player he wouldn't let go. He tried to get me at Charlton but the manager wouldn't release me. Ironically, I was put on the transfer list shortly afterwards.*
>
> *Wigan came in for me, offering big money for those*

> *times. They had a rich director with a big coach business. So I went north. But Ted didn't give up. After he found that I had gone to Wigan, he phoned me at the end of my first season there, telling me what he was planning at Hastings and how much he wanted me to be his captain. Eventually he persuaded me to come back south although I was offered league football – at Stockport – on better money, too. Ted was very persistent and very persuasive. Mind you, when I phoned Ted back to say I had decided to join him I thought he'd be pleased, but he just moaned: 'Bloody hell, why are you phoning me now? I'm trying to get a piano out of the road.' That was Ted all over.*

Keith, formerly with Charlton, was one of Ted's first recruits at Hastings. Keith said:

> *Ted had a fantastic knowledge. He might have had his narky temper, but he was very methodical. He knew exactly what he wanted from his players. That 1962 team came from all over the place, but he was determined to get most of us living in the town so we could train together and become a tight unit, which we were. Only two lived outside. Ted sorted out digs for us, and a local builder gave us jobs. We settled in quickly. From the start Ted got us into good routines. It was really important to him that the full-backs developed a close understanding with their wingers. So he had us working on that until it became instinctive. He believed the wingers needed to back us up in defence. He wanted us to attack, but also keep things tight at the back. He had us practising the free kick routines, too. He was such a perfectionist. When big Joe White played up front we'd try to find his head; he was such a brilliant header of the ball, but Ted didn't like 'hoofball'. He was happy for Joe to work the opposing defenders, using his strong physique, but this was done to give the ball players, like Terry Marshall, more room to play in. Ted stressed that he wanted us to pass along the ground. 'That's what the best teams do,' he'd say.*

It was good fun playing under Ted, but he was strict, mind. He always spoke his mind, and he trained us hard, very hard. He didn't go in for the long distance runs so much as the sprints. We had this routine where a group of us would jog around the perimeter of the Pilot Field. Then, the bloke at the back had to try to sprint to the front, while the others did their best to outpace him. It was utterly knackering. Yet we did this over and over again. This was the sort of fitness that matches demand. Even during that dreadful winter in which we didn't play for two months, Ted had us training on the sands and at White Rock baths. We always kept up our standard of fitness.

As Ken Ballard confirmed, Ted was a good coach. He said: 'Dad taught me how to defend, how to position myself. Like the best coaches he knew that a successful side must have a strong, well-organised defence. He used the swivel system to reduce the chances of his defenders being caught square.' Ken explained that, in those days, 'it was unusual to find a manager, like Dad, who was prepared to give detailed instructions. I played under Dad's friend and former team-mate, George Curtis, at Stevenage. He was an FA coach. George was Brighton's manager when Dad came to Hastings. George was such a nice man but never told us how he wanted us to play. Sid Bishop, the former Orient centre-half, was the same when he took over from Dad at Hastings.'

Alan Ballard illustrated how hard his Dad could be. He recalled a time at Ashford when a head injury to centre-half John Harris forced Ted to withdraw his player from the fray. Alan said: 'John was dazed but Dad brought him round and had almost persuaded him to go back on when this woman supporter came from behind the barrier to have a closer look at John. Shocked at how battered he was, she exclaimed, "Oh … My … God!" whereupon John took fright and refused to shift from the bench. Dad was absolutely livid.' With the privations and horrors of war still fresh in their memories, many men of Ted's generation worked to tougher standards.

Keith Tucker remembered Ted's desperation to win. He recalled:

We were playing Ashford. It was shortly after Ted had started at Hastings, and he was determined to put one over his former club. Anyway, we struggled to get the better of them despite bossing the play. At half-time we came in at 1–1. Ted went ballistic and started throwing hot cups of tea at us. One whistled just past Eddie Stone's ear causing him to complain, 'Boss, there was no sugar in that.' Things didn't get any better after half-time. So by the end, Ted was really stoked up. So much so that he threw all of our wage packets into the bath. There we were scrambling around in the dirty water trying to find our money. Someone picked out one sopping packet, weighed it in his hand and shouted: 'This one seems a bit heavier. It must be yours, Terry.' Terry Marshall was our most highly-paid player. Even when Ted got mad, we'd still end up having a laugh.

*Ted was such a ducker and diver, always on the lookout to spring an advantage. We were playing at Barry in that season. Knowing I had a Welsh background and could put on a convincing 'Valleys' accent, Ted told me to impress the ref with my Taffy lingo when we tossed up. Ted didn't want the ref penalising us because we weren't Welsh. Anyway, we were struggling for a while so I started to get mad, effing and blinding at the others, completely forgetting I was supposed to be Welsh. The referee races up to me and tells me that he's booking me not only for bad language but also for taking the p***. It was the only time I was ever booked in my career. Thanks Ted!*

Ted knew I was a tough tackler and good at reading the game. I wasn't that fast, but I had good positional sense. When Jeanne and I got married, Ted told my wife: 'If he (pointing at me) gives you any trouble just slap a number seven on your back. He's got no pace, you know. He'll never catch you.'

Mind you, Ted could be tight. We'd handed over a bill to him from a café we'd stopped at on the way to a game. Ted studied the receipt before demanding to know 'who's had two cups of tea?' We couldn't believe it. He even took the 2d when it was reluctantly handed over!

Ken Ballard added, 'Dad didn't take any prisoners. If he didn't think you were up to it, he'd tell you straight.' Ken tells of an occasion when Ballard's trainer was instructed to release two young trialists who were not up to the required standard. 'Our trainer was softer than Dad, though, and didn't like to tell the lads straight out. This incensed Dad. "OK I'll do it myself then!" he snapped and marched into the changing room where the young lads were sharing a bath with the senior players. "You two," he says. "I won't be needing you any more. A waste of soap and water!" Grimacing with embarrassment, the rest of us had to avert our eyes. Harsh, eh?'

Alan Ballard recalled that 'Dad got good people to work with him, too – assistants like Jock McGuire, the Scottish physio. I once had a foot injury and Jock spotted it straight away without me having to tell him. He was that good at his job.'

Keith agreed, saying: 'Ted had Jimmy Hernon as his reserve team coach, too. Jimmy had such amazing skills. He had been a real star in the 1940s and '50s. He played under Bill Shankly.' Keith was right. Hernon had real pedigree. So much so that Bolton forked out £16,000 for him just after the war. Here, Jimmy played alongside the likes of Nat Lofthouse. Hernon certainly left a lasting impression with former BBC football commentator, Kenneth Wolstenholme. Ken once said of Hernon: 'With one deft drop of the shoulder and a quick shimmy, Jimmy could leave defenders in a heap on the floor. He charmed me.' Reflecting upon the paucity of talent around Hernon in one game, Wolstenholme added, 'He stood out like an expensive jewel at a jumble sale.' Jimmy was certainly appreciated at Hastings, where he helped Ted turn a club of 'no-hopers' into one of the stronger non-league sides in the land. That was before Ted's relationship with Hastings United's board soured in the summer of 1964. Jimmy Hernon fitted in well with this happy, ribbing team. With his wonderful self-deprecating humour, Jimmy once said 'I started at the top and, with a lot of effort, gradually worked my way down.' There were no 'Fancy Dans' in Ted's team.

Southampton Football Club's summer tour of Brazil in 1948 had opened Ted's eyes to the possibilities of 'total football'. It was a trip he shared with future England boss Alf Ramsey and Brighton manager George Curtis. It was meant to be an English masterclass but the roles of teacher and pupil were reversed very quickly. Shortly before his death in 2008, Ted told Aiden Hamilton, author of *An Entirely Different Game*, 'They [the Brazilians] were all footballers in the team – 11 footballers which British football never used to be then. You played to the position you were in. We had full-backs who were good kickers of the ball but couldn't beat a man to save their life. And that was playing for England, as well … It was an entirely different game. They paralysed us.' Ted and his colleagues found that even a reserve Brazilian goalkeeper could perform outstandingly acrobatic ball skills. Having presumed Brazilian football to be 'a load of rubbish', Ted munched a lot of humble pie. As a consequence, Ted looked to recruit the most skilful footballers he could find for all positions.

Ted's team of '62 was founded upon two strong, experienced full-backs: Bill Cockburn, formerly of Burnley and Gillingham, and Keith Tucker. He had two tough-tackling but creative wing-halves: Alan 'Spider' Brown, whom Ted successfully converted from an ineffective centre-forward, and Eddie Stone, once of Crystal Palace and Charlton. Stone had a ferocious shot to add to his armoury. Ted had a bit of a headache about his centre-half. Having splashed out £1,500 (around £54,000 in modern currency) on Southampton stopper John Page, he found that the overweight defender was not mobile enough for the job and replaced him quickly with the muscular ex-Tunbridge Wells and former Hastings pivot, Gerry Boon.

Up front, Ted collected an embarrassment of riches. Inside-forward Terry Marshall was his stellar close-season signing. Marshall had signed for Newcastle in December 1958 together with Wisbech Town colleague, goalkeeper, Bryan Harvey. Charlie Mitten, the Newcastle boss and ex-Manchester United star, had shelled out £7,000 for Marshall but, unlike Harvey, Terry did not made the grade, managing just five First Division appearances in three seasons. Those extravagantly talented inside-forwards, George Eastham and Ivor Allchurch, blocked his path. But as Ted Ballard found, Terry could disappear in a scrap. He wasn't very physical. And if his head went down he couldn't do a thing right. Marshall returned to Wisbech in 1961 but found it hard readjusting to non-league football, despite helping the Fenmen to the Southern League First Division title in May 1962. But Ballard was alert to Marshall's potential and built a fluent attack around his pace, neat touch and eye for goal.

For good measure, Ted recruited Marshall's Wisbech team-mate, the tricky, skilful outside-right Bela Olah, who was a former Hungarian youth international. Olah had played in Northampton Town's Fourth Division promotion-winning side in 1961 after escaping alone to Britain, aged only 18, following the Hungarian Revolution of 1956. Ted's other 'ace' was Gordon Burden, a little left-winger with scorching pace and a gigantic heart. Burden had played much of his football under Ballard at Ashford Town, having had a brief professional career at Doncaster Rovers. In reserve Ted had Alan Back, a former Charlton amateur, who would eventually blossom into one of the most dangerous right-wingers in Southern League football. Like Burden, Back had everything in his locker – speed, skill and devastating finishing power.

The centre-forward slot proved troublesome, though. Ted decided quickly that the lanky Alan Brown, a former reserve forward at Brighton, was better employed as a half-back. He turned to ex-Orient, Ramsgate and Tunbridge Wells forward Dai Davies instead. The mobile Davies proved to be a good finisher, once putting three goals past Peter Taylor, Brian Clough's future sidekick, in a 7-1 victory at Burton, but Ted was not entirely satisfied. Eventually, fisherman Joe White was chosen for the part. Like Boon, the burly White had previously played for Hastings. He made an early impact on his return, scoring four times in an astonishing 8-1 drubbing of promotion rivals Dover at their Crabble ground.

The inside-left position was passed around also. Ted went to the Hastings Central Cricket Ground to persuade South African and Sussex county cricketer, Dennis Foreman, to take on the role. Foreman had played 211 games for Brighton, scoring 63 goals, but his knees were troubling him so his tenure was brief. Trainee accountant and former Orient and Romford inside-forward, Clive Lloyd, eventually assumed the mantle.

Finally, Ted began the season by selecting Ian Agate as his first-choice goalkeeper. Agate was one of just two players inherited from Ted's predecessor. Agate had been an FA Youth Cup winner with Chelsea in 1958/59, playing alongside Jimmy Greaves. It had been thought that the agile but error-prone Agate would play second fiddle to new signing Bob Charles, a former Southampton regular and England youth international. However, Ted decided that 16-stone Bob was carrying too much weight, and selected Agate ahead of him. This turn of events prompted Bob to up sticks and head for Weymouth. But Ted wasn't entirely happy with Ian Agate, either. Ian mixed spectacular stops with sloppy mistakes. He was at fault for at least one of the goals in the promotion battle at Tonbridge in November. Keith Tucker said, 'Ted asked Ian after the game "Are your eyes all right?" Ian seemed to lose the ball in the floodlights. So, Ted brought in Alf Bentley to replace him. Alf was a good keeper – so brave. He'd played at Coventry and Gillingham. Not much got past him. And he made sure his defence was well-organised, too.'

Although Hastings made a slow start to the season, drawing three and losing one of their opening four league games, it was readily apparent that this was a much stronger side. After their FA Cup elimination by a snappy Maidstone United team including future Manchester United and England star David Sadler, they thrashed injury-depleted Tunbridge Wells Rangers 8-0. A 3-2 victory over Jackie Milburn's Yiewsley, their third on the bounce, followed on a sunny Saturday at the end of September. This win enabled Hastings to shoot up to third spot. Having endured two seasons of abject humiliation I was never without my oxygen mask, so unaccustomed was I to this lofty success.

The Yiewsley game gave me my first and last sighting of Jackie Milburn as a player. By then, the former Newcastle and England centre-forward was 38 years old. He was about to be recruited as Alf Ramsey's successor at Ipswich after Ramsey accepted the England job. On an afternoon of shimmering warmth, Milburn provided a final glimpse of the sublime skill and power he commanded in his pomp. It came late in the first half after Hastings had taken a two-goal lead. Up until that point Milburn had seemed content to fan measured passes out to either wing as if conducting a leisurely coaching session. Carrying greater weight than in his prime, he jogged into the vacant spaces awaiting an 'out ball' from his defenders. Undeterred by the quality of the pass, he was able to control the ball instantly, turning away from any challenge with a nonchalant shrug before feeding his more industrious colleagues.

With the half-time break beckoning, he decided upon a different approach. Receiving the ball in the centre circle and with his back to goal, he shaped to play a lateral pass to his right-winger, only to fool his marker by spinning on a sixpence. Immediately, the afterburners were flicked on and we saw a snatch of that explosive acceleration which had terrified defenders during the early fifties. Caught on their heels by Milburn's burst of speed, the Hastings markers were swiftly bypassed. The full-backs were forced to converge but before they could intercept Milburn's run, he let fly from around 20 yards. Making a perfect connection, the ball fizzed goalwards. The keeper, Agate, hurled himself to his right but to no avail. The ball evaded his groping palms, flashing just past the apex of the post and crossbar before thwacking against the corrugated wall at the back of the covered terrace. Those who had stood in the path of Milburn's shot took rapid evasive action. Recovering from his sprawling dive, Agate blew out his cheeks in relief, while his defenders looked at one another, less in accusation, more in respect of Milburn's power. Standing next to me, a grizzled older man peeled back a smile. With a knowing flick of his balding head, he remarked in a strangely lilting accent: 'WOR' Jackie, eh!'

By mid-November, Hastings were behind leaders, Margate, only on goal average. Their next opponents were third-placed Tonbridge who were then managed by 'happy' Harry Haslam. Haslam had been a full-back in the immediate post-war years with Rochdale, Oldham, Brighton, Orient and Hastings, before becoming a football manager, initially with amateurs Eastbourne United, but finally with Second Division Sheffield United. At Tonbridge, Haslam recruited a number of players with Football

League pedigree. The side he selected for the Hastings game included three players with recent top-tier experience: Joe Carolan, a Republic of Ireland international full-back previously with Brighton; Alan Shackleton, the former Burnley, Leeds and Everton centre-forward; and Gerry Francis, a black South African winger who had played for Leeds and York City. Like Ted Ballard, Haslam had a knack of picking up misplaced gems. During the late sixties he discovered a highly promising teenage full-back called Malcolm Macdonald, although it was Bobby Robson, as Fulham's temporary manager, who converted the youngster into a powerful centre-forward.

Haslam was prepared to look far and wide for untapped talent. It was as a result of the networks he established in South America that the gifted Argentinean midfielder, Alex Sabella, was brought to Bramall Lane in 1978 for £160,000. It was a shrewd purchase. While Sabella was unable to prevent the Blades' relegation in 1979, the young playmaker oozed class. I can vouch for that having endured his almost single-handed demolition of Burnley in September 1978. Haslam then made a sizeable profit on the deal, selling him on to First Division Leeds in 1980 for £400,000. It was through Haslam's Argentinean connections that Keith Burkinshaw was able to bring Ossie Ardiles and Ricky Villa to Spurs after the 1978 World Cup.

It was rumoured that Haslam had been offered 17-year-old Diego Maradona, but could not afford the £200,000 asking price so he went for Sabella instead. This was probably the nearest that Sheffield has come to receiving the hand of God. Although his spell at Sheffield United ended unhappily, Harry Haslam had shown at Luton how well he could manage on a shoestring budget. He took over from Alec Stock in 1972, having been the club's promotions manager. Within two years, he'd guided the cash-strapped Hatters back into Division One. It was the completion of Luton's restorative return journey. They had lost their top-flight place in 1960 and by 1965 found themselves in the basement. Having reached the top flight in 1974, Harry didn't have too much to play with but against the odds almost managed to keep his side there.

November 17 1962 was a grey, greasy, grimy day. I had spent the morning in the gloom of the back room completing my geography homework, drawing a map of the East Midlands, carefully listing the main industries of each of its principal towns and cities: hosiery for Leicester, bicycles and lace for Nottingham, steel for Corby and Wellingborough, boots and shoes for Northampton. In the sixties our towns and cities were still characterised by what they manufactured. How quaint that now seems. As I was studiously compiling the map I listened peripherally to *Brian Matthew's Saturday Club*. Amid the rockabilly standards emerged a song that immediately grasped my attention. Its opening jabbed me sharply in the chest: the stomping drum 'intro', like the beat from a Sioux war dance, the nasal, nerdy vocal that followed, punctuated by an insistent, staccato organ riff. It was a raw, ragged 'frat' rocker as if put together in some kids' garage, but oh so compelling. So, this was Chris Montez's 'Let's Dance'. The lads at school had gone on about it for weeks. Now it had insinuated itself within me. It urged my rapid strides to the station. 'Hey baby won't you take a chance …' It fired the throbbing diesel, too, as it lurched around the wet, wooded curves to Tonbridge. 'Say that you'll let me have this dance …' It suppressed the anodyne music from the Angel Ground's PA. 'Well let's dance, let's dance …' It became embedded in the pulsating, tingling rhythms of the game. 'We'll do the Twist, the Stomp, the Mashed Potato, too, any old dance that you wanna do. But let's dance, well let's dance …' I need no photographic record. 'Let's Dance' illuminates this dimly-lit, drizzle-shrouded day forever.

The game was a cracker, played in front of a condensed, excitable crowd of 2,000-plus. After 16 minutes Hastings were ahead. Centre-forward Dai Davies set up Terry Marshall, who shook off two Tonbridge defenders and slid the ball so coolly past Fred Crump, the advancing keeper. It was as if Terry had become Jimmy Greaves. Ken Ballard recalled: 'Terry had so much talent. But his head dropped when things weren't going well. Then, Dad used to yell at us "for God's sake don't give him the ball!"' But this was Marshall's tenth goal of the season. He was then playing with complete assurance, showcasing the ability that had once attracted Charlie Mitten at Newcastle. Clustered on the stacked railway sleepers, the Tonbridge supporters were not disheartened. They poured continuous encouragement into the ear of their quick, compact left-winger, Johnny Dennis. 'C'mon Johnny, you can roast this guy. He's useless', they'd said, gesticulating at Bill Cockburn, our craggy right-back. Actually, Bill was Johnny's master, adroitly anticipating the winger's crude push-and-run stratagem whereas on the opposite flank Keith Tucker was having a tougher challenge contending with the sinuous swerves and nimble footwork of Gerry Francis. But according to Ted Ballard, 'Keith played Francis beautifully' that afternoon.

Just before half-time, Tonbridge equalised, helped by Francis, although the goal was a gift. Ian Agate misjudged Francis' swirling cross, spilling the ball at the feet of Alan Shackleton. The tall, wiry 'Shack' didn't spurn opportunities as simple as these and proceeded to clip the ball into the back of the empty net.

After the break my Tonbridge 'pals' and I were treated to a masterclass of left-wing play. If Johnny Dennis was the great pretender, Gordon Burden was the real deal. Gordon may have been small, but he was tough, skilful and exceedingly fast. Time after time he whizzed past Joe Carolan, his distinguished marker, as if he did not exist. Gordon was simply uncontainable. In the ensuing months, I would honour the memory by drawing stubby left-wingers belting around the margins of my school exercise books.

Ken Ballard recalled how 'Dad knew what havoc Gordon could cause. His attacking tactics were quite simple. "Get the ball and give it to Gordon."' With 20 minutes left, Dai Davies did just that. Burden streaked along the left flank leaving a succession of dumbfounded defenders in his spattering wake. Anticipating Marshall's speed he fired a fast, low, fizzing centre across the Tonbridge goalmouth. Marshall latched on to the chance in a flash, haring into position and rifling a ferocious first-time drive past the statuesque Crump. His skidding shot was so fierce that the ball ricocheted off the board behind the goal and back into play, fooling many into believing that the post had been struck. Only the referee's signal confirmed that Hastings were ahead again. This was finishing power of the highest order. Amazingly, I was watching this quality display from my formerly derided home team.

Harry Haslam seemed to be an easy-going, jocular character, but his teams were always strongly competitive. His class of '62 was no different. Increasing pressure was applied to the Hastings goal. Fortunately, Tonbridge's finishing was less competent than their approach work. With just a few minutes remaining, it appeared that Hastings would cling on to a precious victory. But they were finally undone by Ronnie White's moment of glory. Keith Tucker recalled: 'I knew Ronnie at Charlton. He had bags of skill. One minute he was playing on the Hackney Marshes, the next he was playing for Charlton in Division One. It was incredible. He could do fantastic things with a ball.' Ronnie certainly backed Keith's judgement here. He was positioned around 20 yards from goal and hemmed in by determined defenders, but somehow he created a sliver of space. It was just enough for him to chip a perfectly placed shot over the head of keeper Agate and find the back of the net. I can still replay that goal in my head, its execution becoming steadily slower as if my recorder is spluttering with age. The ball arcs lazily over the heads of our defenders. Agate's upward leap is silhouetted against the pallid glow of the floodlights. The ball eludes him, dropping gently below the bar and plopping into the net. There is a momentary stillness, both on the makeshift terracing and in the upper tier of the ancient pavilion. Then, in a snap second everyone else seems to be leaping around, waving their arms in the air. Some jabbing jibes came my way. As disappointed as I was, I had to concede that this was a worthy end to a terrific game.

Almost half a century has passed since that day. Upon emerging from

Tonbridge station, the London–Hastings train passes the site of the old Angel Ground. But the only connection with the past remains with the name of the shopping complex – the Angel Centre – which stands where the ramshackle ground once was. The adjacent sidings have become a car park. The steam locomotive shed now houses track maintenance stock. The throaty roar of the diesel has been superseded by the smooth, quiet acceleration of the electric train. Perhaps there are less than a hundred people who can recall this compelling contest. Soon all memories will be gone. The only evidence of that game will remain in a dog-eared programme or two and in a rarely-examined press archive in the local library. This is the fate of parochial passions.

With neither side having further FA Cup commitments, Ted Ballard invited his friend and former Saints team-mate, George Curtis, to bring his senior Brighton team to Hastings for a friendly on the following Saturday. Although Brighton had fallen upon hard times, I expected their first team to be too strong for my resurgent side. Not so. Apart from a combative display from their left-half, Bill Cassidy, sluggish Brighton were beaten comprehensively. Gordon Burden murdered the Brighton right-back, Sid Jest, setting up a host of chances for his colleagues. Reserve right-winger Alan Back scored a brace in the opening half an hour, the first coming in under a minute. The scale of Hastings' superiority was much greater than the final 2-0 scoreline suggested.

However, just two days later, reality bared its teeth. Hastings were paired with Premier Division Chelmsford City in a second-round Southern League Cup game. Expensively-assembled City used this home tie to celebrate the turning on of their new floodlights. And they made sure that nothing would spoil their party. Hastings were thrashed 5-1. All of the Chelmsford first team were full-timers. Up front they had Tony Nicholas, formerly of Brighton and Chelsea, on £28 per week (roughly equivalent to £1,000 per week today) and Bobby Mason, the former Wolves star, on £35 per week (approximating to £1,200 per week now). Both were paid more than anyone in George Curtis' Brighton team and were almost three times better off than anyone in Ted Ballard's side.

Ambitious Chelmsford proved to be far too strong. They had the greater skill with Mason pulling the strings at inside-forward, threading a succession of exquisite balls through Hastings' back line for Nicholas and others to exploit. Collectively, City had greater pace, too, although Burden caused the home defence some discomfort. More significantly, City had greater stamina, a product of their full-time status. Chelmsford's fourth and fifth goals came late in the game when Hastings were running out of puff, having spent 80 minutes doggedly chasing their opponents. If Hastings had any pretensions of reaching the Football League this was the daunting standard that they would have to meet. Saturday's victory over Brighton now seemed pyrrhic. However, Ted Ballard soon had his lads geed up again. Five league victories followed on the bounce with 22 goals scored. It seemed that Hastings were well placed to seize the Southern League First Division title. Life was swimmingly sweet. Then, on the evening of Boxing Day 1962, a savage blizzard swept across southern Britain. The town shuddered under the weight of successive snowfalls. Ash, cinders and brown salt pocked the treacherous ice sheets but the wan winter sun could not loosen their grip. From December until March, Hastings United, 'like a cold lasagne', were 'suspended in deep freeze'.

Disoriented O's chimed out

Having clawed their way into the First Division in April 1962 with a small, unfancied squad, John Carey's Orient side became the bookies' favourites for the drop. With chairman Harry Zussman prioritising ground improvements, Carey made no additions to his team during the close season. After taking just one point from their opening four fixtures, it seemed as if Orient had overreached themselves. Although unlucky to lose their home game with West Bromwich at the end of August, they recovered by beating hapless West Ham 2-0 three days later on a blisteringly hot afternoon. One week after, Orient trumped this by beating a visiting Manchester United team, including Denis Law, by 1-0. Terry McDonald, the 22-year-old left-winger, scored the winning goal in the last minute, recalling: 'I latched on to a loose ball and sprinted to the centre edge of the penalty area. I could see big Maurice Setters and Tony Dunne coming to challenge me, so I drove the ball right-footed past David Gaskell into the top right-hand corner.' Orient's win was no fluke. Reg Drury of *Reynolds News* reported: 'That United survived until the 89th minute was mainly due to the acrobatics of keeper Gaskell. Bolland might have had a hat-trick.'

Buoyed by these terrific victories, Orient went one step further by hammering visitors Everton, the 'cheque-book' champions-elect, in the following midweek game. Orient's three goals were scored by Deeley, Bolland and Dunmore in a whirlwind four-minute spell just after the break. This hat-trick of victories lifted Orient up to 12th position. Despite beating struggling Fulham 2-0 at Craven Cottage at the end of September, Orient's form unravelled thereafter. They did not register a further league win until 15 April, when Bolton were beaten at Burnden Park by Dunmore's second-half goal. By then, relegation was almost a certainty. Carey belatedly attempted to strengthen his side by recruiting 29-year-old left-winger Malcolm Musgrove from West Ham for £11,000 and 27-year-old former Wolves inside-forward Bobby Mason from Chelmsford City for £15,000. Mike Pinner, an amateur international and trainee solicitor, kept goal in 19 games, too. It was to no avail. Before signing out, however, Orient managed to defeat eighth-placed Liverpool 2-1 at home, helped by a rare goal from centre-half Sid Bishop.

Orient scraped together 21 points over this long, hard, icy season. Almost half of these points were accumulated before the end of September. Alongside Pompey's pitiful return in 1958/59, this was the lowest points total accrued by a relegated First Division side since Leeds went down in 1947. Just as Orient's returns dwindled, so did their gates. Their opening home fixture with Arsenal drew in 26,300, yet their final league victory, over Liverpool, attracted just 8,273. Harry Zussman hadn't needed those 5,000 extra spaces, after all.

Mal Lucas told Tony McDonald, author of the splendid *Leyton Orient: the untold story of the O's best-ever team*, 'Teams don't always function as well when they are under the type of constant pressure we found ourselves under … one main difference I found in the First Division was there were opposition players who wouldn't follow me. So if our move broke down, I'd find that there was a spare player behind me in space and we couldn't seem to counteract that kind of situation.' Terry McDonald added:

> *There was too much onus on David Dunmore to score, although Malcolm Graham weighed in with nine goals, but there wasn't much support from the rest and the ratio of goals from midfield was poor. We had to do so much more defending as a team, even most of the forwards, which meant leaving Dave Dunmore isolated … We were more defensively minded so I wasn't skipping past full-backs and getting crosses in like I had been doing in the Second Division. I never saw three or four of our players in the box waiting for the ball. When we did go forward we had no six-yard-box goalscorer … the inside-forwards had to come back deep and pick up balls inside our own half, starting moves from there, and then try and get in the box as well. On very heavy pitches, it must have been hard work for them. You*

> *would have been hard pressed to find another pitch in the Football League as heavy and so lacking in turf than the notorious Brisbane Road mud heap. There was a lack of possession, too, because you had to work that bit harder to get the ball, especially away from home ... In our promotion season we could play our football instinctively and with ease at times, in the top flight we got muscled out of it.*

Orient failed because the club could not afford to strengthen its side sufficiently. Terry McDonald reckoned that around half of the positions needed replacements but Johnny Carey's response was, 'We haven't got the money, my hands are tied.'

As Burnley and Blackpool demonstrated at the start of their recent Premiership seasons, bubbling team spirit can deliver remarkable results. But sooner rather than later the better teams get up to speed. Their coaching boffins find ways of neutralising the newcomers' game plans. In short, the underdogs are 'found out'. What might work well over a cup run works less well over a lengthy league campaign. Quality tells. Once greater pressure is applied to the defences of these 'upstarts', mistakes – both forced and enforced – become commonplace. Like a punch-drunk boxer caught on the ropes, the small guys begin to take increasingly heavy hits. Despite their collective commitment to defence, Orient shipped 81 goals in their 42 league games in 1962/63. The 'one for all, all for one' team ethic, which often sustains these gallant battlers, started to fragment. The odd slip turns quickly into a slide. And once the luck starts to run out, a trickle rapidly becomes a torrent.

Suffering Suffolk

The 1962 Football League champions, Ipswich, came perilously close to joining Orient on their return journey. In 1962 Ramsey had an ageing side. Eight of his squad were aged 30 years or older; their best days were behind them. But only one addition was made during the summer – 28-year-old Bobby Blackwood, a winger or inside-forward, was signed from Hearts for £10,000. Although Ipswich's average gate during their championship season was only 22,559, almost half that of Spurs, this should have given the club enough resources to strengthen the team. Certainly, Brighton spent more with less support. Perhaps Ramsey did not want to change a winning combination? All 28 of his players were retained in 1962.

As England's boss, Alf Ramsey was prepared to chop and change. But at Ipswich, loyalty seemed to tie his hands. He appeared contorted by guilt at leaving Leadbetter out of a European Cup tie, having acknowledged his importance to Ipswich's title success. He seemed blind to the fact that his tactical plan had been rumbled. After Spurs had thrashed his side 5-1 in the 1962 Charity Shield, Alf seemed not to have a Plan B. Ray Crawford told Mike Donovan of the excellent *Backpass* magazine: 'Alf got wingers Jimmy and Roy Stephenson to play 20 yards deep in their own half. Those days, full-backs wouldn't go beyond the halfway line so it gave our two plenty of space. Nobody thought of pushing them on to Jimmy and Roy, not even Bill Nicholson at Spurs ... But Bill had worked it out by the time we played Spurs in the Charity Shield the following season. He pushed Dave Mackay and Danny Blanchflower on to our wingers ... Others caught on, too.' But Alf Ramsey stubbornly believed the 5-1 defeat was due to individual failings rather than sussed-out tactics.

Only one point was taken from Ipswich's first three games – a 3-3 home draw with Blackburn Rovers on the hot, opening day of the season. Although Blackpool were thumped 5-2 at home on Tuesday 28 August, league form stuttered. In fact, Ipswich's form was so shaky, that after losing 3-1 to Arsenal on a grey afternoon at Highbury in late November, they fell into the relegation zone – only two points better off than bottom-placed Orient. During that autumn they suffered heavy home defeats by Birmingham (1-5) and Manchester United (3-5). Ipswich's previously robust defence disintegrated. Keeper Roy Bailey got the yips, making a series of costly errors. Meanwhile, at the other end the goals were drying up – Ipswich's final tally of 59 league goals was almost 40 per cent down on the championship season. Their prestigious 2-1 victory over AC Milan, the eventual European Cup winners, was entirely cosmetic. The first leg, played in an almost empty San Siro Stadium, was lost 0-3. Ipswich's 14-1 thrashing of Floriana (of Malta) had counted for nothing.

It was not just age, form and injury which were withering the Football League champions. There was unrest over pay, too. Both Crawford and Billy Baxter held out for better terms. Ray Crawford realised that his England team-mates were earning substantially more. While Ipswich were prepared to pay him only £30 per week, his England colleague Johnny Haynes was receiving over three times as much.

On the 25 October 1962 Alf Ramsey decided to accept the offer of the England job. But he found it hard to let go of his creation. So much so, that he remained at Portman Road until the threat of relegation was lifted – six months later! Meanwhile, his successor, Jackie Milburn, remained sidelined, unable to proceed with the necessary strengthening. Ramsey told Milburn, perhaps disingenuously, that while the team lacked strength in depth, the club had no money for reinforcements. This hiatus caused ructions in the boardroom. Long-serving director Ernest Steel was so incensed by his colleagues' prevarication that he resigned, accusing the other board members of being Ramsey 'yes men'. Milburn had been handed a poisoned chalice. Although the team were the reigning Football League champions, the club seemed organised like a small, parochially-minded non-league outfit. After Bill Slater, the former Wolves and England half-back, turned down the Ipswich job, there were only two applicants for the post: Stockport's boss, Reg Flewin, who later went on to manage Hastings United, and Milburn. This said a lot about the club's standing in the football fraternity.

As the icy winter turned eventually to a chilly, soggy spring, Ipswich were still in big trouble. They had been beaten heavily at home by the lucrative champions-elect, Everton (0-3), and by Spurs (2-4), and thrashed at West Bromwich (1-6). Their prospects of staying up seemed as bleak as Orient's. Ipswich's remaining fixtures included a number of 'four-pointers'. They recovered a semblance of their championship form, winning six and drawing four of their final 12 games. It was just as well. Ipswich were only four points clear of the relegation places on the final day of the season. Moreover, two of those points had been acquired in controversial circumstances. The *People* had alleged that their 2-0 home victory over Sheffield Wednesday on Saturday 1 December had been 'fixed'. Three Wednesday players – centre-forward David 'Bronco' Layne, England centre-half Peter Swan and wing-half Tony Kay – each admitted to placing £50 fixed-odds bets which would pay rich dividends if their team lost at Ipswich, and if York beat Oldham and Lincoln beat Brentford. As it turned out, both Oldham and Brentford won. Peter Swan maintained in his book *Peter Swan: Setting The Record Straight* that 'there was nothing out of the ordinary about either of [Crawford's] goals' which won the game. As it happened, Ipswich survived in the First Division for one more year only.

No provision had been made by Ramsey to replace the older members of his team. There was no youth policy at the club and no effective scouting network. Milburn had to rebuild from scratch. He was forced to sell Crawford – his only regular goalscorer – in order to finance essential replacements. He looked for cheaper acquisitions north of the border. This was not a success. Billy Baxter told Rob Hadgraft, author of *Ipswich Town: Champions of England 1961-62*: 'Perhaps Milburn's biggest mistake was getting too many Scots together, for they started drinking and misbehaving and he couldn't do anything with them.'

Ray Crawford told *Backpass* writer, Mike Donovan: 'Jackie was a wonderful man, but as a manager he didn't have a clue. He'd turn up for training at 10am and you'd see him standing there with a cigarette in one hand and a cup of coffee in the other with his foot on the ball, saying: "Good morning lads. We'll have a good day today …" [Whereas] Alf knew what he wanted. He got the players to play in a certain style. If you didn't do what he wanted you'd be out of the side.' The strategy was shot and the discipline had disappeared.

After scoring 100 league goals in their Second Division championship season of 1960/61 and 93 in winning the First Division title a year later, Ipswich were relegated at the end of the 1963/64 season, having scored 56 league goals and conceded 121. Ramsey's triumph was a one-off. It would take Ipswich a further four years to regain their place in the top flight.

Brighton rocked

Following Albion's demotion, George Curtis rung the changes. Nine of his first-team squad departed. Full-backs Joe Carolan and Bob McNicol went to Tonbridge and Gravesend respectively. As for the forwards, Tony Nicholas joined Chelmsford, Ian McNeill signed for Southend, Bobby Laverick was sent to Coventry, Mike Tiddy returned to his native Cornwall to play for Penzance and Joe Caven returned to Scotland, joining Raith Rovers. Finally, Alan Brown joined Hastings while Tony Sitford followed McNicol to Gravesend. Put together, these players had cost the club over £50,000 in transfer fees, yet their departures had yielded almost nothing. Worryingly, Brighton were growing few of their players. Only wing-half Robin Upton and goalkeeper Brian Powney had emerged as promising home-grown talent, although a young centre-half, Norman Gall, brought in from Gateshead, seemed a good prospect. Once again cash-strapped Brighton were forced to spend.

George Curtis recruited Bert McGonigal, a goalkeeper from Glentoran; Jimmy Collins, a Scottish inside-forward from Spurs at a cost of £8,000; Bill Cassidy, a Scottish wing-half from Rotherham for £6,000; Peter Donnelly, an inside-forward from Swansea for £6,000; plus Jim Cooper, an outside-left, and William Bailey, a centre-forward, from Airdrie. The new recruits lined up alongside a number of surviving regulars: Bobby Baxter at left-back; Jack Bertolini, Roy Jennings and Steve Burtenshaw, the well-established half-back line; and Johnny Goodchild up front. Despite shelling out £20,000 on new signings (worth around £700,000 in today's values or £6 million in present transfer currency), Curtis was unable to improve Brighton's performances.

In late September, his team lost their home League Cup game by 1-5 to a Portsmouth side largely comprising reserves. Ironically, Pompey received a £50 fine from the Football League for fielding an under-strength team. A shocking 2-4 home loss to Reading followed on 6 October. Reading arrived at the Goldstone as one of the worst travellers in the division. But they were far too good for the Albion. This defeat dumped Brighton into bottom position. The fans began to lose patience with Curtis. Only 6,556 turned up for the Albion's 1-0 win over Carlisle three days later. Even an unexpected 5-1 win at Bradford Park Avenue in early December failed to allay concerns about George Curtis' management.

George received his cards on 1 February. A dismal 0-0 home draw with Southend in the Goldstone snow was the final straw. George Curtis had won less than a quarter of the 74 league games he was in charge for. He would have greater success in Norway, guiding Rosenborg to the Premiership title during the late sixties, although their fans complained about his defensive tactics. He was much less effective, however, when he took charge of Norway's national side. George was at his best in a coaching capacity. Former Arsenal and Scotland keeper, Bob Wilson, had a very high opinion of him. Wilson said, 'George had a wonderful manner and fantastic knowledge. He was a truly outstanding coach and a real gentleman.' George continued to coach youngsters until dementia blighted his later years.

George, Ted Ballard and Alf Ramsey took different lessons from their shared Brazilian tour in 1948. Alf sought ways of neutralising more gifted teams. He used canny game plans, such as the withdrawn wingers, at Ipswich, and his 'wingless wonders' of '66, to put his side ahead of more skilful opponents. On the other hand, George aimed to raise the skill levels of those he coached, whether they were professionals or aspiring youngsters. He borrowed what were then novel ideas from the Brazilians such as head-tennis and their throw-in routines. However, as a manager, George proved less capable than his two contemporaries of converting his knowledge into winning football. Although Ted did not share Alf's distrust of flair players, endeavouring always to produce entertaining football, his talents were confined to non-league football.

Despite his obvious shortcomings as Brighton's manager, George made two important contributions to the future success of the club with his twin signings of Jimmy Collins and Bill Cassidy. Both Collins and Cassidy played crucial roles in Brighton's revival under succeeding manager, Archie Macaulay.

Jimmy Collins recalled how 'George was a bit of a flash character and that's why I liked him. When we met to discuss the move, he rolled up a copy of the *Daily Mirror* and showed me how one of the Hungarian stars of the time, Hidegkuti, did a trick. That convinced me to come.' But once he had signed, Jimmy quickly realised what a mess the club were in. Discipline was poor and relationships seemed strained. On his own admission, Jimmy did not help on either score. He told Brighton *Evening Argus* reporter, John Vinicombe, in 2001: 'Some of the players were dreadful and I made myself unpopular by letting them know I thought they were no good. They had some good ones, of course, like Roy Jennings and Jack Bertolini, but I found the style in which the team played such a contrast to the good passing and movement they played at Spurs. Albion just hoofed it and chased after the ball a bit in the Wimbledon style. It upset me.'

Jimmy confessed he even had a punch-up with some team-mates. There was an early set-to with Scottish winger, Jimmy Cooper. Jimmy explained: 'The fights all occurred during five-a-sides. I had a bit of a temper. I was a bit of a miserable little so and so. I was always moaning and snapping at my team-mates on the field and was probably made captain because I had the biggest mouth. I was anti-establishment, a rebel. I regret being like that. It's not nice to make yourself unpopular and it meant I didn't enjoy my football like I should have done. I've now become more tolerant.' Jimmy enjoyed a drink, too, which didn't help. He explained that he was 'keen on off-the-field action. I sought out the nearest pub. I had, as I've said, a bad attitude.'

George's replacement, Archie Macaulay, had steered Norwich to an FA Cup semi-final in 1959 and to promotion to the Second Division a year later. In October 1961, he was appointed as West Bromwich Albion's manager, commanding an annual salary of £3,000 – worth around £111,000 a year today, a tidy pay cheque for a manager in the early sixties. Macaulay struggled, though. In his first season in charge, only a late five-match run of victories rescued the Baggies from trouble. His second season proved to be the club's worst campaign in eight years. With the Hawthorns' average gate dropping by 4,500 – a massive fall of 20 per cent – Macaulay left the club in April 1963 to be replaced by ex-Sheffield United star and Peterborough manager, Jimmy Hagan.

Archie was a tougher character than George. He had no qualms about laying down the law. Several Brighton players reported having run-ins with him. Even with better discipline in place he had little time to turn around Brighton's season, arriving, as he did, just before Easter. Despite winning his first game in charge at highly-placed Notts County, a further relegation followed. During this season of ice, snow and postponements, the unpalatable truth was that the Brighton board had paid out more than

£30,000 in transfer fees to end up with almost a 25 per cent reduction in revenue and another demotion. In fact, the club had paid out around £100,000 in transfer fees since its promotion to Division Two, recouped very little of that in sales and was now two divisions worse off, having lost half of its average gate.

The case for the defence

A major topic of discussion in the 1962/63 British football season was 'blanket defences'. Respected football journalist Ivan Sharpe commented in the *News of the World Football Annual 1963-64*:

> *Perhaps it was because defensive tactics played a prominent part of the 1962 World Cup games in Chile. This may have been the reason why English football developed this bugbear and menace last season. Whatever the cause, the trend was regrettable, especially as this dulling effect on the game as a spectacle arrived at an inopportune time. The sponsors of Manchester City's five half-backs formation denied that this was primarily a defensive system but improved attack was not discernible in the team's actual performance. Such a system might prove attractive if the right type of player were available – mobile, nippy, versatile; able to advance or retire as the flow of the game demanded … players who have had experience at both forward and half-back. But this essential was not there when I watched the City.*

During the mid-fifties, Les McDowall's Manchester City were regarded as a stylish, innovative side, renowned for their 'Revie Plan', based on the Hungarians' use of a deep-lying centre-forward. But Revie then fell out with McDowall following a spat over his holiday arrangements, and moved on to Sunderland. In any event, by that time City were an ageing side. Former City goalkeeper Bert Trautmann, told Alan Rowlands, author of *Trautmann, the Biography*: 'The problem was we no longer had the talent at the club, we just did not have players that were good enough.' With resources stretched and no youth policy to speak of, City were pushed into replacing many of their departing stars with frugal lower-division signings. Whereas the City side of the mid-fifties was one of the stronger teams in Division One, contesting successive FA Cup finals, by the close of the decade they were fighting a rearguard action against relegation.

Desperate for a quick fix, Les McDowall papered over the cracks by paying a record fee for Denis Law in 1960. It didn't take Law long to realise how bad things had become at Maine Road. He became so concerned by the paucity of City's resources – their depleted squad, primitive training facilities and ragged kit – that he took off to Italy as soon as he could. McDowall's adoption of an ultra-defensive formation in 1962/63 was his last throw of the dice. He hoped that curmudgeonly tactics would compensate for his side's lack of potency. He deployed two backs to cover the centre of the defence while five half-backs sat in front of them. Bobby Kennedy and Roy Chatham wore inside-forward shirts but assumed defensive duties only. City made do with three forwards – the veteran George Hannah, as an orthodox, creative inside-forward, plus two strikers; Peter Dobing and Alex Harley. Only Harley, with 23 league goals, reached double figures that season, while his side scored a miserly 58 goals. Not that the defence fared any better for McDowall's defensiveness – 102 goals were conceded! There was a succession of fearful drubbings. For example, West Ham twice gave City six of the worst while Wolves thrashed them 8-1 at Molineux.

Leicester were more successful with their defensive tactics although this won them few friends. The press were certainly unimpressed. After the Foxes shut up shop in the FA Cup semi-final with Liverpool, having taken the lead, one paper headlined 'Leicester City's cul-de-sac'. Another remarked derisively: 'A 10-1 system as sound as a castle dungeon.' Defeated Liverpool manager, Bill Shankly, carped: 'This can never be football. It is bad for the game and the best way of emptying the terraces.' Many agreed. At first, Leicester manager Matt Gillies dismissed the criticisms glibly, claiming that his team consisted of 'players, not forwards or defenders'. But he then promised: 'You have my assurance that Leicester will go to the final with the idea of showing just what they can do.' He needn't have bothered. Manchester United's attacking fluency made his pledge irrelevant.

The Potteries pair, Stoke City and Port Vale, were also criticised for their defensiveness. Nottingham Forest had their detractors as well, including some of their own supporters. They took particular exception to manager Andy Beattie's selection of an extra centre-half, Peter Hindley, in place of a centre-forward.

My first direct experience of the new defensiveness arrived when Hinckley Athletic visited Hastings United in March 1963. Hinckley was then a hosiery manufacturing town with a population of no more than 40,000. Its modest football club was largely overlooked on account of its proximity to Leicester, Coventry and the two Birmingham teams. It rarely attracted gates of more than a few hundred.

During the 1962/63 season, Hinckley Athletic were managed by Dudley Kernick, a former Birmingham City and Torquay player and a qualified FA coach. Like Ted Ballard, Kernick knew how to create a competitive team with limited resources. Assembling a number of cast-offs from local league sides, Kernick turned his little club into unlikely promotion contenders. He began by making them hard to beat, reducing the number of goals they conceded by a half. He was helped by having a vastly experienced captain in Peter Aldis. Aldis had played 262 times for Aston Villa, starring in their controversial FA Cup victory over Manchester United in 1957. He had been well regarded by Villa's boss, Joe Mercer. Aldis had the distinction, too, of scoring with a 35-yard header, which remained as a world record until 2009. It was Aldis' only goal in competitive football. More importantly, Aldis knew how to make Hinckley's defence one of the tightest in the division.

Saturday 9 March 1963 dawned stormy and sopping. Having been frustrated for almost two months by the Arctic occupation, an accumulation of Atlantic fronts made up for lost time. Congregating impatiently at the Western Approaches, one by one they roared in, flooding the thawing land and leaving oozing sludge where the crumpling snow had previously been. Hastings United's Pilot Field pitch was turned into a hissing quagmire even before the game began.

From my untutored perspective, Hinckley's strategy seemed timid. Whenever Hastings gained possession, eight or more of their players clustered behind the ball. Hastings mounted attack after attack only to find their route to goal barred by a double rank of defenders. With Hinckley's defensive tactics drawing Hastings forward, the visitors found gaps to exploit on the break. Despite having so much of the ball, Hastings were two goals down at the interval. Failing to recognise what I had seen, I put this down to bad luck. Despite the mud-plastering conditions, the sheeting rain and buffeting wind, I thought the game could be saved. I was wrong. Hinckley were so cool and skilful in defence, never resorting to aimless clearances. As soon as they won possession, their alert forwards scampered off ready to plunder the growing gaps in Hastings' back line. Hinckley let the ball do the work, employing the most direct approach possible. Several of their players occupied positions at odds with their shirt numbers. I was bewildered. I had yet to see Cassius Clay's demolition of the colossus Sonny Liston. I thought that all-out defence was only employed by those facing impending defeat. I was at the base of a new learning curve.

1963: a year of living pruriently

'Sexual intercourse began in 1963 (which was rather late for me) – Between the end of the *Chatterley* ban and the Beatles' first LP.' So wrote poet Philip Larkin in *Annus Mirabilis*. Here, Larkin reflected sardonically on the nation's prurient interest in the Profumo Affair, the details of which came to light in March 1963.

John Profumo was the Secretary of State for War in the Macmillan government. His affair with Christine Keeler, reputedly the mistress of an alleged Russian spy, was a major scandal not only because of the national security implications, but also because he tried to conceal the affair when questioned in the House of Commons. Once his deceit was discovered, the repentant Profumo was forced to resign. The Profumo Affair also damaged the reputation of Prime Minister Harold Macmillan, who tried to insist: 'I was determined that no British government should be brought down by the action of two tarts.' However, Macmillan also resigned, a few months later, due to ill health. The satirical magazine *Private Eye* had a field day mocking the Tory slogan 'Life's better under a Conservative', and spoofing Macmillan's 1957 boast with 'We Have Never Had It So Often'. The morally discredited Tories became a laughing stock. Despite Alec Douglas-Home's best efforts, electoral defeat beckoned. Contrasted with Harold Wilson's promise of a 'white heat' technological revolution, grouse moor tweeds seemed hopelessly out of step, at least to the new 'Baby Boomer' electorate. Their impatience with the apparently anachronistic, nepotistic and 'amateurish' way in which the country was run was a catalyst for change.

Apart from providing superior coverage of Southern League results and tables, the *News of the World* and the *People* devoted copious space to the sordid details of the Profumo affair. For pubescent boys like me, brought up in a hot-house, single-sex school, this was an absolute joy. Fed by a never-ending stream of salacious gossip, my friends and I obsessed about what Christine Keeler and Mandy Rice-Davies got up to. We ogled at their slinky, alluring poses in clinging sweaters and tight skirts or less – much less. We fantasised about their daily 'romps'. Seduced so hopelessly by lurid sexual stereotypes, it was impossible to think of them doing mundane things like mooching around Tesco or unblocking a plughole. Their lives seemed consumed by palpitating sexuality. Then bloody Millicent Martin mucked things up. She was the smug chanteuse on the Saturday evening satirical TV show, *That Was The Week That Was*. Parodying the *Funny Girl* Broadway number, she sneered, 'People who read the *People* are the muckiest people in the world.' Dad was so affronted he immediately cancelled both the *People* and the *News of the World*. Thank you, *TW3*.

In terms of national security, the Profumo Affair was far less important than Kim Philby's defection. Its greater significance lay in the alarmed reactions it prompted among the conservatively-minded, an attitude which was still rife across all classes. They were fearful that greater economic freedom was licensing growing promiscuity among younger people. The wider availability of birth control and pornography were cited as contributory factors. Not that adolescent sexual behaviour in fifties Britain seemed any more restrained according to a fifties research study. Around half of the young adults interviewed admitted they had sex before marriage and approximately 30 per cent said their weddings were 'shotgun' affairs. But the outrage at the Profumo Affair was also stirred by wounded patriotism as if our national decline had been brought about by lapses in decency that the Profumo Affair seemed to epitomise. Not that the sixties featured the permissive *sex and drugs and rock 'n' roll* extravaganza that some made out. While the nouveau riches of deified pop stars, swish photographers, chic fashion designers and iconic models enjoyed less restricted lives, licensed in part by their massive incomes and glossy fame, the rest of us were constrained by more conservative standards. Remember, the decade opened with an obscenity trial – the *Chatterley* ban. It ended with one, too – the prosecution of the underground magazine, *OZ*, in 1971. Here, the Crown failed to restrain a sexually rampant *Rupert Bear*. In between, the Musicians' Union refused to allow the Stones to play 'Let's Spend the Night Together' on the *Eamonn Andrews Show*. Leaving aside our taste for saucy seaside smut, as perpetrated by the likes of Benny Hill, this so-called 'permissive' age didn't seem that laid-back to me.

THE 1964/65 SEASON

Brighton & Hove Albion v Darlington

'Ticket to Ride'
26 April 1965

The '64/65 season was a bleak, anguished affair for Hastings United. It was also Ted Ballard's last at the club. Having guided Hastings to promotion in 1963 and placed the club among the 20 strongest non-league outfits in the country, he was deeply frustrated that he could not take his team further. Money was in very short supply. Although helped by a local benefactor, the club still had to find around £4,000 (about £130,000 in today's values) for a set of floodlights which were installed in late 1963. On top of this, the average gate had fallen from a 2,000-plus figure during Hastings' promotion year of 1963. Two years later, with troubles off the pitch dampening what was happening on it, the average gate barely exceeded 1,000. Ted was offered the managerial post at local rivals Dover, but the Hastings board refused to release him.

In early 1965, the club announced that it was £3,000 in debt, a sum which was on a par with its annual wage bill. In the face of mounting debt – reputedly, £75 was being lost each week – the Hastings United Supporters' Club made a one-off donation of £50. As well-intentioned as it was, this gift was no more than a token gesture. The lottery scheme was stalling, too, placing yet more strain on the shrivelling revenue stream. A wage cut had already been imposed and several players had been released – three after Ted's angry reaction to a dismal 0-3 defeat at Guildford in early November. The rebuked players had apparently blamed Ted for not arranging a proper pre-match meal. They wanted steak. Ted provided toast. Modern nutritionists might have sided with Ted. But then it was different. Steak was the goal standard.

Hastings' entry into the midweek Kent Floodlight League had hardly helped matters. The club had hoped that this higher calibre competition would prove more attractive to supporters than the reserve games. Not so. The midweek home gates averaged only 500. Moreover, these 20 or so fixtures placed further strain on the squad's shrinking resources. Several first-team players totted up around 70 games that year. No wonder the team collapsed in an exhausted heap before they were dumped back in Division One.

In February 1965, Ted Ballard called a meeting of 16 south-eastern non-league clubs to consider the possibility of forming a regionally-based league. Non-league attendances had been falling sharply during the early sixties. Reductions of 50 per cent were not uncommon. Most of the Southern League Premier Division clubs were situated in far-flung locations – Telford, Worcester, Cheltenham, Weymouth, Bath, Yeovil, Rugby, Nuneaton, Cambridge (both City and United), Wisbech and King's Lynn. Unsurprisingly, there was growing interest in a more locally-based competition. It was reported that Wimbledon had no immediate financial concerns, having two rich benefactors on board, but they were an exception among the southern-based clubs; not that their state of grace would last for much longer. Southern League outfit Deal Town, however, had not been able to pay their players for several weeks.

This situation was not peculiar to non-league clubs. By the mid-sixties, Football League gates had dropped by almost 40 per cent from the post-war high in 1949/50. Alarmed at the sharp fall in gate revenue, the Football League met in early 1965 to consider reimposing a wage ceiling. But, of course, the cork was now out of the bottle. Nobody had the bottle to jam it back in. Nevertheless, Tom Finney was just one of several former stars who regretted the abolition of a wage ceiling. He wrote an article called 'Pampered and Overpaid', stating: 'I was one who fought against the maximum wage, arguing that footballers should be paid what they are worth. But today, when the sky's the limit, I'm afraid the trouble is that many are paid too much for too little … I could not name 50 players, or indeed a dozen, who are worth £100 a week. And too often, I fear, this fantastic sort of money goes to their heads rather than to their feet.' Remember, this was written in 1964, not 2011! Not that many Southern League salaries were anything like £100 per week. In 1964, Hastings centre-forward George Francis was reputedly on around £14 per week. He was one of Hastings' more highly-paid professionals, having previously scored 144 goals in 313 Football League appearances with Brentford, QPR and Gillingham.

Ted resigned from his post at Hastings United at the end of the 1964/65 season. Disillusioned, he left football for good, becoming a local publican. It seemed such a waste.

While Hastings were struggling in an adverse financial climate, Brighton were prospering on the back of renewed investment supplied by chairman Eric Courtney-King and fellow director Harold Paris. During the 1963/64 season, Brighton's boss, Archie Macaulay, began to assemble the side that would storm out of Division Four in style one season later. In December 1963 Archie signed Dave Turner, a young, dynamic wing-half who had been playing in Newcastle's reserves. Turner quickly found his place in Archie's side. Bill Cassidy, an industrious utility player, was shifted to inside-left to accommodate him. York's goalscoring winger, Wally Gould, was also brought in, as was Swindon's skilful inside-forward, Jack Smith.

Without doubt, the most eye-catching of Macaulay's signings was that of 32-year-old former Spurs and England centre-forward Bobby Smith in May 1964. Brighton *Evening Argus* reporter, John Vinicombe, wrote in 2001: 'Just imagine Michael Owen joining Albion. That was the impact Bobby Smith made when he quit Tottenham Hotspur for the Seagulls in May, 1964. Smith remains arguably the biggest name ever to sign for the club. The fans adored him as he hit the goals which earned Albion promotion in his first and only full season with the club. In his day, Smith had similar superstar status to Owen. He was a top-flight icon, a Cup-winning hero and a renowned England goalscorer. More Didier Drogba than Owen in style, he was a barnstorming centre-forward with a touch of flair and a prolific marksman.'

The programme for the opening league game with Barrow told us: 'Fifteen England caps spanning four years, 220 goals for Spurs, two FA Cup-winners' medals and a European Cup-Winners' Cup medal – those are just some of the highlights in Bobby's career that began with Langdale Boys' Club in Yorkshire. After nearly 14 years in first-class football, Bobby has joined Albion and shaken the entire soccer world. Few dreamed that he would come to Brighton, but here he is, large as life!'

Smith began his Football League career at Chelsea, where he scored 30 goals in 86 games before moving to White Hart Lane in December 1955 for £16,000. As the Brighton programme stated, 'There have been few more courageous wearers of an England shirt than Smith, who on November 20th last year was a national hero after Northern Ireland were crushed 8-3 at Wembley. Yet that was to be Bobby's last appearance. He couldn't have ended on a finer note. It will not take long for Bobby's fame to stir the Goldstone and lead Albion back into the higher class of football that Brighton and Hove deserve.'

Brighton's chairman, Eric Courtney-King, was bursting with pride at the club's capture of Smith. Seizing the slot that is normally reserved for the manager's notes, Eric wrote in the programme for the Barrow game: 'This signing shows just how eager we are to climb to our rightful place in the Football League, and we all wish Bobby a happy and successful stay with us ... I am seldom courageous enough to make predictions of any kind on the subject of professional football but this is one of those occasions when I am encouraged to do so. I believe there will be a larger number of fans at this, our first match of the season, than we have seen at the Goldstone Ground for quite a long time.'

Eric was right. Over 20,000 supporters turned up on a scalding August day to see Bobby Smith score two – including a stunning diving header – and Jimmy Collins, one, in a 3-1 victory. This attendance more than doubled the average turnout for the previous season (9,300) and was the largest Goldstone crowd since their promotion to Division Two. Archie Macaulay set out his stall. He wanted Brighton to succeed by playing stylish, attacking football. Barrow might not have been great shakes – they had just been re-elected having finished the previous season in 92nd spot. Nevertheless, Archie's selection of five attacking players showed the strength of his conviction. Supporting Bobby Smith at centre-forward were two free-scoring wingers – Wally Gould and John Goodchild – plus two creative inside-forwards with an eye for goal in Jack Smith and Jimmy Collins. As for the rest, Mike Hennigan, a new signing from Southampton, was chosen at centre-half, assisted by Alan Sanders at right-back and Norman Gall at left-back. Jack Bertolini and Dave Turner filled the wing-half berths. In goal, Brian Powney was preferred to Bert McGonigal.

Stirred by Brighton's immediate success, an even bigger crowd (22,697) was attracted by the midweek visit of Oxford United on 25 August. Oxford were a much tougher proposition than Barrow. It had taken the Oxford boss, Arthur Turner, seven seasons to transform a mediocre, suburban non-league side – previously known as Headington United – into a forceful, scrapping Fourth Division outfit which was capable of turning over strong First Division opposition. Oxford had dumped Blackburn out of the FA Cup a few months before. It was some makeover. Turner – previously a First Division manager at Birmingham City – even refused a top-flight managerial position with Leeds in 1959 after his board of directors matched Leeds' salary offer. Like Ted Ballard at Hastings, Turner encouraged his players to live locally, helping them find work in the vicinity. In those days the local Morris car and Pressed Steel plants offered plentiful jobs. On the back of the economic boom of the late fifties, Oxford's working 'town' began to emerge from beneath its academic 'gown'. Cowley became almost as well known as Corpus Christi with its gleaming cars rivalling the dreaming spires. The rebranded Oxford United FC epitomised the city's ascendant working image. The club drew upon the support of the local production workers, offering tough, uncompromising ambition. There was nothing abstract or theoretical about Turner's teams. Southern League titles and Football League entry followed after Turner persuaded his board to put the club on a full-time professional basis.

Andrew Ward and John Williams wrote in their book, *Football Nation*, 'Oxford United owned their ground, had capital reserves of £52,000 and owned seven properties. There were eighteen full-time professional players, ten part-timers and five groundstaff boys. The wage bill was £400 per week, and gates varied from 4,500 to 17,000 according to the attraction. It was a convincing case. Oxford were elected to the Football League in 1962.'

If Turner was responsible for setting his club up, his forthright, dynamic skipper, Ron Atkinson, drove it forward. Ward and Williams wrote:

> *Ronnie Atkinson had various nicknames. One was 'The Tank'. Another was 'The Oil King'. When he changed for a match he rolled over the top of his shorts so that they were high on his legs, exposing as much of his thick, muscular thighs as was decent. He looked more like a weightlifter than a footballer. Then he got out a bottle of olive oil and coated his legs until they glistened in the floodlights … he worked as a representative for a hardware store and cleaned windows with his team-mate Bud Houghton … He would tackle the wall to get himself aggressively wound up. He led his team out of the dressing room like an explosion rather than a chore. He announced his presence to the crowd by whacking the ball up in the air … Arthur Turner particularly enjoyed watching Ronnie Atkinson lead out his team. It gave Turner the same kind of feeling as when his team went one-nil up.*

Brighton had achieved an impressive 'double' over Oxford during the previous season. But, handicapped by an arm injury to new centre-half Hennigan, Archie's archers couldn't pierce Arthur's armour (0-0). Come April, Arthur Turner's side would accompany Brighton into Division Three with the second-meanest defence in the Football League. They, too, were men on a mission.

Despite beating a strong Rochdale side on a sunny 5 September (3-0) with goals from Collins, Jack Smith and Goodchild, Brighton's early form was erratic. Archie Macaulay was not happy. He wrote in the Rochdale programme: 'At Hartlepools our lads were well below form and disappointingly gave away a very silly equalising goal in the closing seconds of the game [1-1].'

Archie seemed no happier in his notes for the midweek return fixture with Newport County on 15 September. A League Cup defeat at Millwall left him bitterly disappointed as he was denied a reunion with Norwich, the club he took to an FA Cup semi-final, in the next round. A subsequent 0-2 league defeat at Millwall did not improve his mood. In fairness, Brighton had been asked to play four games in a week. To add to his worries, Albion were nursing a growing injury list.

Robin 'Nobby' Upton, who had replaced Turner in the Newport game, suffered more than anyone. *Evening Argus* reporter John Vinicombe wrote: 'Just when a bright Albion career lay in prospect, he broke his right leg twice inside four months and was never the same player again … So frequent were his visits to hospital, specialists and treatment rooms that Upton managed only 44 first-team appearances from 1962 to 1967 yet remained cheerful and wonderfully optimistic. This was far from easy when watching training and matches propped-up by crutches.'

On a brighter note, we had a wonderful Indian summer in 1964. September delivered day after day of basking sunshine. The still-warm English Channel glittered invitingly as if it was July. The weather was so enticing that Southdown Motor Services used the Brighton programme to advertise its extended range of late coach holidays. Alongside other adverts placed by local hotels was one for the Carrington Marriage Bureau, where 'a wonderful match may begin' and 'many a happy home team has started'. You got down to business quickly at the Carrington.

On 19 September Bobby Smith was on target again, scoring twice against 91st-placed Bradford City. But even with fleet-footed Peter Knight adding a third this was not enough to beat the determined Bantams (3-3). Archie's anguish hardened after successive defeats at Chester (1-3) and York (1-2). Brighton had fallen to 13th position. This was not what the board of directors had in mind.

Brighton's form in October was much better, helped in part by the signing of 29-year-old former Spurs and Wales international full-back Mel Hopkins for £8,000. Four victories came on the bounce. Torquay (3-1), York (3-1) and Notts County (6-0) were beaten at home, while Lincoln were defeated at Sincil Bank (1-0). Archie's five-star attack was beginning to sparkle.

If Bobby Smith was the celebrity performer, Jimmy Collins was the team's driving force. A Brighton programme described him thus: '... Jimmy, 26, has proved one of Albion's best inside-forwards since the war. He proved easily one of the outstanding players in the Fourth Division last term and would have stood out in better company. Northampton Town fancied him and there were other clubs who noted the trickery and cunning of Albion's skipper. Since the end of last season Jimmy has married a local girl and is keener than ever to settle down in Brighton and Hove.' Collins would eventually play 221 games for Albion in a six-year stay, scoring 48 goals – a tremendous return for a midfielder.

Jimmy Collins told reporter John Vinicombe in 2001: 'If I hadn't have met Wendy I'd have ended up a fat alcoholic blob. She straightened me out. Meeting and marrying Wendy was the best thing I ever did ... Brighton had big crowds for a club in the lower divisions. Archie did a good job and it was an exciting season. Six of us got into double figures that season. I don't think that will ever happen again. It was unbelievable. I remember I got the first goal against Barrow and the hundredth, thanks to the lay-off by Bobby Smith, against Darlington ... I remember Archie turfed me out of a snooker hall once. He didn't like his players in snooker halls.'

On 24 October, Doncaster Rovers came to town. Although Bobby Smith had been injured in the 4-0 rout of visiting Lincoln during midweek, Brighton were confident of extending their winning home run to five games. But Archie exercised a measure of caution, singling out Rovers' danger man, Alick Jeffrey, in his programme notes. Archie wrote: '[Jeffrey is] one player who is contributing much towards Rovers' revival. You will recall he received a serious broken leg injury. It was thought that his career was ended but through sheer guts and determination this young player has brought himself back to fitness, and our lads will have to be on the alert to contain this fine forward.'

Peter Whittell accounts for Alick's star-crossed career in his biography: *The Life Story of Doncaster Rovers Legend Alick Jeffrey*. Jeffrey had made his senior debut for Doncaster Rovers in Division Two in 1954. He was merely 15 years old. His precocious talent was so great that he was selected for the England under 23 side at the age of 17. Manchester United assistant manager, Jimmy Murphy, took notice. He told his boss, Matt Busby, that the boy appeared to be as gifted as Duncan Edwards. Even the normally reserved Stanley Matthews gave Jeffrey unreserved praise, describing him as a 'football genius'. Alick impressed everyone who saw him play. He had wonderful balance and scored spectacular goals. By the age of 18 he was an established player, having scored 34 goals in 71 league appearances.

Matt Busby was so keen to land the youngster that he was prepared to smash the British transfer record for a teenager. Busby even went as far as to make a 'good faith' payment of £200 to Jeffrey, just to assure the boy that he would be on his way to Old Trafford as soon as negotiations were completed. £200 was a lot of money back then – roughly equivalent to Jeffrey's half-year wages. He wasn't greedy. He spent a chunk of the money on a fridge for his mum. But during an under 23 international with France Jeffrey broke a leg. There were complications. Rehabilitative care in the mid-fifties was often primitive at best. Jeffrey struggled to regain fitness. In 1957, after a year of fruitless efforts, he reluctantly gave up the fight. He received £4,000 compensation. Doncaster got £15,000. With his career in ruins, Jeffrey subsequently decided to move to Australia. Here, he began to play football again. After four years in Australia, Jeffrey wanted to return to England.

George Raynor was then the manager of non-league Skegness Town. With his outstanding coaching skills ignored by both our league clubs and the FA, George was forced to find work at Butlin's, Skegness. Here, at least, his talents were appreciated. He was invited to manage the local side – Skegness Town – during his spare time. George agreed. Just as he had done in Sweden, George made an immediate impact. He transformed the fortunes of the flagging, dilapidated club. Then, the returning Jeffrey caught his eye. George extended a helping hand. Jeffrey responded. Playing for Skegness Town was not beneath this young man's dignity. George, the international master coach from Barnsley, devised a new rehabilitation programme for Jeffrey. It worked better than anything tried before. While not providing a miracle cure, Jeffrey regained much of his former fitness. Most importantly, George taught Alick how to cope with his limitations. Jeffrey knew he would never be the star he had once seemed destined to become. He didn't let his head drop, though. After a year spent rebuilding his strength, stamina and speed, he found that he was good enough to return to full-time professional football. He was offered a further contract with Doncaster Rovers. Time, however, had not been kind to the Rovers. In the intervening years, they had fallen from the Second Division into the Fourth. Jeffrey made a tentative return – 20 senior games, four goals. But it did not take him long to remind us of what we had missed. During the 1964/65 season he played in each of Doncaster's 46 league games, scoring an incredible 36 goals – 43 per cent of Doncaster's final tally. He would net 95 goals for Donny in his second spell with the club before his departure for Lincoln in 1969.

Alick Jeffrey never cursed his ill luck. He counselled: 'Don't weep for me, think of those lads in Munich. If I hadn't broken my leg, I would probably have been on that plane.' The *Independent* journalist, James Lawton, wrote after Jeffrey's premature death in 2000: 'He always said that he had nothing to complain about. He had a lot of pleasure in life. He had a family he loved, one that was proud of him. There was a purpose in everything. He broke his leg but he didn't die in a Munich snowdrift. Once he was a wonder boy but, for him, life rolled on, and for this alone he was grateful.'

On that bright, warm Saturday on 24 October, Alick was a real menace. Brighton were hard-pressed to contain him. He led the charge as Doncaster pushed forward while veteran Bill Leivers and his fellow defenders restricted Brighton's free-scoring attack to just one goal – netted by Bill Cassidy. With Bobby Smith incapacitated by a groin injury and his namesake suffering from a badly gashed ankle, Brighton could not summon enough firepower to subdue Donny (1-1). But the draw was good enough to raise Albion to third position, their highest placing so far.

Hampered by injuries to key players, Brighton performed inconsistently during the following month, dropping out of the promotion places. The top-of-the-table clash with Bradford Park Avenue on 7 November proved to be a big attraction. Almost 21,000 spectators came along on a bright, raw afternoon to watch an exciting 2-2 draw. Bradford's attack was led by a prolific goalscorer, Kevin Hector. He would score 113 goals in 176 appearances for Park Avenue before moving to Derby County in 1966. It was there that Hector established his reputation as one of our leading strikers of the late sixties and early seventies. He scored 147 more goals for the Rams, helping them lift the First Division championship in 1972 – under Clough and Taylor – and again in 1975, under Dave Mackay. He also represented England twice, once in the disappointing World Cup qualifier against Poland in 1973. In this promotion battle, he and fellow striker, Jim Fryatt, kept the Brighton defence at full stretch. Although both Jack and Bobby Smith scored for Brighton, it wasn't enough to seal victory. Nevertheless, Brighton went up one place to fourth.

Archie's FA Cup ambitions disappeared at the first hurdle at Ashton Gate on a day of gusting wind and slanting rain. Wrexham bore the brunt of Albion's anger at the Goldstone a week later. The gate was lower than hoped. On a grey afternoon, 14,477 came to see successful efforts from Goodchild, Bobby Smith, Cassidy (2) and Gould secure an easy 5-1 victory. Promotion-seeking Tranmere had more of a bite, though, on the following Friday night. Goals from Bobby Smith and Cassidy were in vain as Brighton lost 2-4. But, rejuvenated by a free weekend – a legacy of their early FA Cup exit – Brighton visited Barrow on a glowering, teeming Saturday afternoon on 12 December and turned on a scintillating display in the Holker Street mud, winning 4-1 with goals from Bobby Smith (2), Gould and Goodchild. It was their biggest away victory of the season.

Back into their stride, Brighton hammered Hartlepools 5-0 at a freezing, foggy Goldstone on the Saturday before Christmas. Bobby Smith and Gould scored a brace apiece and Collins added a fifth. Perhaps Christmas shopping duties were to blame for the smaller crowd of 12,667, the lowest home gate of the season. But the shuddering cold probably played a part, too. Snow then fell over the Christmas period. However, both games with Halifax went ahead. Albion won the Boxing Day game at the Goldstone 2-1 with goals from Gould and Cassidy, loudly cheered by the 19,000-plus delighted home supporters. Bill Cassidy's match-winning goal was the icing on the cake. Cassidy was a Goldstone favourite. He always gave his all in Albion's cause. He made people laugh, too. *Evening Argus* reporter John Vinicombe wrote:

> *Bill played every game as though it was the Cup Final. The highly-charged 90 minutes that he put in either at wing-half, inside-forward or occasionally centre-forward, were particularly effective in the lower divisions where the need to fight for the right to play was paramount. Moreover, Bill knew full well that he had to make up for lack of pace by extra physical effort. A tackle from Cassidy did not contain an option of coming back for more although there was not a bad bone in his body and a joke was never very far away from a stream of Scottish oaths. Being a good pro, Bill took his football very seriously but was blessed with an intuitive knack of relieving tension by a timely quip or gesture. When Bill donned the cap and bells it did more for morale than a torrent of invective from manager Archie Macaulay. Flagging spirits soared when Bill was up to his pranks. Archie, a fellow Scot, valued his joker in the pack. He knew full well that a happy dressing room can often be the launch pad of a successful side. This proved to be the case in the 1964/65 Fourth Division championship campaign when Bill's ten goals in 24 games proved a most acceptable ratio amid so much competition for places. It used to be said in the old days of pre-overseas*

imports that a manager needed to guard against getting too many players from north of the border at one time in case they formed a too powerful group. That was not a problem for Archie. After all he was one of them although he tended to treat some of the players like a laird might boss his tenants. Perhaps Cassidy tended to be overshadowed by the star quality of the championship side. But [his] ten vital goals had an important bearing on the destination of the pennant. Injury prevented him from figuring in all but two of the last 14 matches. Old knocks were catching up. He came back after a hernia the previous season and then broke a small bone in his back while there was a spate of knee problems. By the summer it was time for Cassidy to leave the Albion. Archie gave him a free transfer.

Bill moved to Southern League Chelmsford City, where he won a Southern League championship medal. Here again, he was applauded as a cult hero. Then he moved to Cambridge United, helping them win the Southern League title and gain Football League entry. It was here that his Albion nickname, 'Thunder boots', was revived, as he scored 56 goals in 120 appearances at the Abbey Stadium. Cambridge United manager Ron Atkinson – the former Oxford captain – appreciated Cassidy's 'crash-bang-wallop' style. Thereafter, Bill's life was not a happy one. When he was 42 years old he suffered a thrombosis. He became registered as a disabled person. Worse was to follow. In the eighties, Bill spent a period in prison, having been found guilty of burglary and handling charges. He died at the young age of 54 years. Jimmy Collins, his closest friend at Albion, told John Vinicombe: 'A man couldn't have had a better friend. He had his down spells, but he made you laugh. I loved that man.'

Brighton's 3-1 home win over Crewe in January saw the debut of the ill-fated Barry Rees at right-half. Tragically, Barry was killed in a road accident just before Albion won the Fourth Division championship in April. Promotion rivals Millwall were beaten 2-0 at the Goldstone on 16 January and struggling Southport were beaten at Haig Avenue, a week later, in front of a miserly 2,286 crowd. A storm-tossed 4-4 draw with Chester on 6 February broke a seven-game winning sequence. However, with Robin Stubbs, the leading Fourth Division marksman, well marshalled by Norman Gall, Torquay were then beaten 1-0 at Plainmoor on 13 February, a day of dappled sunlight. According to John Vinicombe, Archie Macaulay was so pleased with the result that he converted the return trip into an almighty bender.

Nevertheless, Brighton were back in shape in time for the following trip to Meadow Lane where Notts County were beaten 2-1 on a day of grey, damp, penetrating cold. Once again, Jack Smith was on target, as was Cassidy. A hat-trick of victories ensued including a 5-0 romp against Chesterfield at the Goldstone. Goodchild grabbed two goals and Gould one but in answering the case for the defence, Mel Hopkins joined in the fun with a debut goal. A crowd of almost 21,000 clapped and cheered. Brighton seemed well ensconced in third place.

Brighton's 11-match unbeaten run came to an end in the mud and snow at a bright, blustery Belle Vue on 6 March. Here, Alick Jeffrey inspired Doncaster to a 2-1 victory in front of a 10,000-plus crowd, despite Bobby Smith scoring on his return to action. Bradford Park Avenue proved no more hospitable two weeks later (0-2). Although this was a promotion battle, only 6,300 locals considered it worthy of their interest. Five years later, Park Avenue ceased to be a Football League club after Cambridge United were elected to take their place.

On the following Monday there was another promotion four-pointer at Spotland, Rochdale. Norman Gall recounted his experience of this fiery game to author Paul Camillin in his *Match of My Life* book. Norman said:

> *This was a cracking game … [It was] quite a tetchy affair – which wasn't helped by some poor refereeing … Kevin Howley awarded Rochdale a penalty, claiming an Albion defender had punched the ball out … when in fact it had been Brian [Powney]. We were livid, and all the more so when the penalty was converted. We fought back to equalise through Johnny Goodchild – only for Rochdale to take the lead again. Jimmy Collins equalised for us a second time, before the incident occurred which makes the game stand out in my mind as certainly the most eventful of my career.*
>
> *Myself and Rochdale forward, Bert Lister – a big stocky six-foot-plus centre-forward – were chasing a loose ball towards the byline in front of the main stand. I knew he wasn't going to go for the ball – so neither did I. I stood my ground and we both barged into each other. He went into the wall and I went over the top and into the home*

> *supporters. As I went into the crowd I felt a blow to the back of my head. As I got to my feet, still in the crowd, I found everyone was trying to hit me. I put my hands up to protect myself, instinctively pushing out at the baying mob. I managed to get away from the crowd and back on to the side of the pitch, but then Lister started wrestling with me. We were both on the ground for a few seconds before the other players ran in to separate us. Howley came over and straight away sent us both off. Lister went off being cheered by the Rochdale fans, and I was told by Jimmy Collins, the captain, to go down injured so they could buy some time and reorganise the defence. That upset the crowd even more. Howley then ordered me to get off. Archie Macaulay came out to put his arm around me and console me, but as we were walking off the pitch towards the tunnel we were pelted with rubbish, fruit, pies and all sorts by their fans. At that point Archie bailed out and left me to walk back to the dressing room on my own. I took the brunt of the supporters' pelting as I left the field of play and I remember looking down at my shirt. It was covered in rubbish but at the same time I was thinking how important the point could be.*

Norman duly served a seven-day suspension, meaning he missed the 3-1 home win over Southport on the 26 March, in which Collins (twice) and Gould were on target. He also missed the tense 2-2 draw at promotion-chasing Oxford, too, in front of a 13,429 crowd. Here, Jack and Bobby Smith were Brighton's marksmen.

Brighton entered the final straight in good shape. A midweek 2-1 victory at Wrexham on 3 April, with goals by Jack Smith and Gould, moved Brighton into second spot. Despite losing 4-1 at lowly Bradford City on Friday 6 April, the damage was repaired immediately with a crucial 2-1 midweek home win over promotion rivals, Tranmere. Norman Gall recalled: 'We went top of the league by beating Tranmere ... [They] had gone 1-0 up after I made a mistake with a short back pass which let in their striker to score but Bobby Smith drew us level [with only 15 minutes remaining] and I then headed in a corner in the final minute at the South Stand End. Wally Gould picked me out from the left and I got above the Rovers defence and headed home. That win took us above our opponents and put us head of the division with four games to play.' Over 24,000 supporters attended this game, making it Brighton's biggest gate of the season, thus far.

All that remained were the three Easter games plus a rearranged fixture with Darlington at home at the end of April. First up was the Good Friday game at Edgeley Park, Stockport, played in warm spring sunshine on a bone dry, rutted surface. Urged on by a large contingent of Albion fans in the 10,000-plus crowd, Brighton cruised to a 4-1 victory with goals from Goodchild, Bobby Smith, Gould and Collins. However, winter then made a sudden, unwelcome return with temperatures plummeting overnight. Easter Saturday dawned icy and wet with the rain then turning to snow. Brighton lost their footing at Feethams where Darlington won comfortably by 2-0. Despite this setback, Brighton managed to cling on to pole position. The conditions for the return game with Stockport on Easter Monday were scarcely better, but Brighton had little difficulty despatching their opponents 3-1 with goals from Collins, Jack Smith and Goodchild. Now only five points separated the seven teams contesting the four promotion places. But, for Brighton, the equation was simple. If they won their final home game against Darlington, on Monday 26 April, they would be promoted as champions.

It was only in the late afternoon that Tony and I decided to go. Having pooled our depleted resources, we had just enough for our rail fares and admission. We hurriedly set off barely two hours from kick-off. Our electric train seemed to saunter sadistically along the coastal line meaning that the whale-backed downs approached with infuriating slowness. Outside, there was a celebration of succulent spring growth. The golden evening sunlight dazzled in the criss-cross dykes. Fresh foliage fluttered on a serene breeze. A scent of cut grass wafted in at each of our interminable stops. The evening's beauty clamoured for attention but kick-off preyed on our minds. We changed trains at Brighton, scampering between the platforms, trying to catch the fastest connection.

By the time we had arrived at Hove station, the game had begun. As we left the train, the sound of the crowd made an immediate shuddering impact. We sprinted over the footbridge and then down the eerily empty street to the first set of turnstiles. Once inside, we were confronted with a bulging crowd – later reported to be in excess of 31,000. With the Eastern Terrace full to bursting we headed towards the South Stand, making our way along the well between its upper and lower sections. There seemed to be no space at all. But a sudden spilling motion granted us a narrow ledge, which we seized. With the crowd recoiling we had to defend our slender foothold staunchly, grabbing at a stanchion to prevent us from toppling backwards. Thereafter, we were forced to stand mainly on tiptoe. But still our vision was obstructed. We couldn't see the goal immediately in front of us. It was the one that the Brighton lads were attacking in their blue facings and white sleeves.

We could see Jimmy Collins, though, deep in midfield: busy, buzzing, bustling, angrily brushing off his obstructive opponents, twisting one way, then the other, looking for an opening with prickly resolve. But we had to rely upon the crowd to know whether one of his raking passes had found its mark. A sudden crescendo, like the ignition of a jet engine, signified that it had. And then, with the added thrust of an afterburner, there seemed to be a chance of a goal. But a cascading sound, like surf surging over the pebbles, suggested that the opportunity had been lost. It was pointless asking what was happening. We had no way of hearing one another above the din. And besides, those around us had no better idea of what was happening than we did. We had to content ourselves with snatched glimpses and audio clues. We could see the Brighton wingers at the starts of their runs. There was Gould, upright, composed and direct, shrouded in the shadow of the West Stand. On the opposite flank there was Goodchild, hunched and scurrying, catching the full glare of the setting sun. But sight of them would be lost as soon they approached the box or veered towards a corner. Stretching upwards as far as we could go, we could just see the Darlington keeper at the height of his leap, grasping the ball, under pressure from the heads of the Brighton forwards. But that was as good as it got.

We continued to be storm-tossed, as if caught in an Atlantic squall. Urged on by the increasingly vociferous crowd, Brighton cranked up the momentum. Darlington were pushed further and further back. At least, that was the implication. Certainly, sightings of the Darlington players in advanced positions became rarer. The visitors had not come to pay homage, though. They were determined to compete – by fair means or foul. Judging by the crowd's mounting anger it seemed as if they were opting for the latter. The Brighton trainer made several sprints towards the Darlo end. His appearances were accompanied by shrill whistles, so piercing that we had to cover our ears. It was as if he was the culprit. With boos also bellowed out at regular intervals, we presumed that the Darlo hitmen were hard at work.

Then it happened. It simply had to. The crowd's strength appeared overpowering. It seemed as if the ball was being sucked into the Darlington net by its collective gasps. We discovered later that Bobby Smith had put Jimmy Collins in on goal and Jimmy had finished clinically. The resulting roar was volcanic. The South Stand shook with so many bodies pogoing in no space at all. A chaotic, tumbling surge followed, giving us a brief glimpse of Collins being hugged by his team-mates. It was his 17th league goal of the season and Brighton's 100th. Soon afterwards, we gathered that Jack Smith had added another. The mayhem of the first goal was repeated with even greater fervour. With the Darlington defence unravelling, Brighton were home and dry. When the third went in – Gould's 21st league goal – the promotion party began. Brighton's three years of hurt had been gloriously expunged. Perversely, the third goal seemed to spark a Darlington revival. A balding wing-half called Ray Yeoman began to stride forward purposefully. But to no avail. Although their tall centre-forward scored with a rasping shot in front of the North Stand, Brighton's title was safe.

As the final whistle blew, thousands of fans clambered over the perimeter wall and on to the pitch. But Tony and I decided to leave quietly. I was pleased at Brighton's triumph, of course. I had followed them for six years, reading their match reports avidly, always looking out for their results and periodically going to their games. I wanted them to do well. But this didn't feel like my night of joy. Instead, I felt like a party-crasher. I had thought that Brighton's promotion might have compensated for Hastings' sad decline. It didn't. I was beginning to learn what monogamy means.

The 1964/65 triumph was another feather in Archie's cap. He had brought together a team that had, for the most part, performed superbly. It was also a vindication of the investments made by the board of directors under Eric Courtney-King. The signing of Bobby Smith was a huge success. But there was still some uncertainty why such a big name in English football should have joined Fourth Division Brighton. John Vinicombe pursued this in an interview with Bobby, conducted in 2008. John wrote:

> *So how come Bobby went from the First to the Fourth Division for a cut-down £5,000 fee just six months after winning his last cap for England? There were suggestions a gambling problem hastened his Spurs departure, that he was available for an almost giveaway price so Spurs could be rid of any potential embarrassment as swiftly as possible. But Smith denied he had got into difficulties through his love of a bet and insisted his move was made for footballing reasons.*
>
> *Smith said: 'I liked a flutter. You won some, you lost some. I was happy doing it as long as I didn't get*

> *into any trouble. But I never did. I left Spurs because (manager) Bill Nicholson told me he was going to replace me. I thought, I can't stay somewhere I'm not wanted. Bill Nick let me go for a small fee to help me get a move more easily as a reward for what I had done for the club.'*
>
> *Smith did, though, join Albion via a bookmaker. Smith said: 'I knew Georgie Gunn, who was a bookie who supported Brighton. He rang me up and said come down. He was a nice fellow and Brighton were interested so I said yes. I never regretted it. I enjoyed every minute … I can't praise Brighton and their fans high enough. I knew I was treated as a bit of a hero when I came because I'd had a bit of success and the goals came naturally but everyone played their part in that side. We had a good set of lads who got on and developed a strong team spirit.'*

Smith refuted the story that Macaulay suspended him for a fortnight because he reported back for pre-season training in July 1965 at an overweight 15 stone, but he was adamant a money row with Macaulay saw him sacked three months later. Smith said: 'I was writing an article for the *People* and getting £500 for it. Macaulay said he wanted £400 and that if he didn't get it he would terminate my contract. He was due to leave and I had been asked to take over as manager but the board told me they had to go with his decision to sack me. I was annoyed. I thought then, "that's me finished with pro football". It was not a nice way to go out.'

Bobby Smith left Brighton in the summer of 1965. It was a premature departure. Team-mate Robin Upton observed: 'I thought Bobby Smith was a terrific player ... at home. You didn't see much of him away.' But Smith might have served Albion well for a year or so more. Instead, he chose to join newly-relegated Hastings United in October 1965. The former Orient centre-half, Sid Bishop, had recently replaced Ted Ballard as Hastings' boss, playing as well as managing. Smith and Bishop had apparently been friendly when they were both playing in London. It was reputed that Smith was offered £65 a week to play for Hastings – a huge sum (worth around £100,000 per year today) for a club said to be in financial difficulty. Regrettably, the move was not a success. But more of that comes later.

The Cobblers' glass slipper

In April 1965, Northampton were promoted to the First Division behind Newcastle. They rose from the Fourth Division to the First in just five years. Sadly, they would return just as quickly, becoming the first 'Grand Old Duke of York' club in Football League history. Their rise and fall fitted snugly within the sixties, having been promoted from the Fourth Division in 1961 and relegated back there in 1969. Dave Bowen, a former Northampton, Arsenal and Wales half-back, was the club's manager between 1959 and 1967 – eight years of wildly switchback fortunes. He also found time to manage the Welsh national side for half this time, having been appointed to the post in 1964, and remaining in charge for ten years. Although courted by Olympiakos, Dave Bowen's heart remained with Northampton, his adopted home town, and where he began his professional career as a wing-half in 1947.

Bowen deserves enormous credit for what he achieved at the County Ground, a playing arena that the club shared with Northamptonshire County Cricket Club. In the late fifties and early sixties, Northampton could not be described as a big town. Its population was just over 100,000. Its rugby union side commanded at least as much local press coverage as its premier football team.

Northampton Town was not a rich club. The board of directors comprised a coach company owner, two farmers, a chemist shop owner, a builder, a timber merchant, a restaurateur and a leather trader – all hard-working, well-intentioned and financially secure but certainly not loaded. Players did not join the Cobblers for financial gain. As Mark Beesley explained in his captivating book *Northampton Town: A Season in the Sun*: 'The money wasn't great, as more than one of the "grass root" Northampton '60s players intimated ... "We were on £25 per week if we weren't in the first team but we could make that up to £35 by getting there," one player told me .... "We were on the same sort of money as the men in the [boot and shoe] factory, who we would play skittles with in the pub on a Thursday night." These wage levels were substantially less than the £50 per week received by Swindon players for winning promotion to Division Two, in 1963, behind Northampton. They were no better than what Southern League outfit Chelmsford City were prepared to pay their best player, either. Northampton did not draw vast crowds. In 1959/60, Bowen's first season in charge as player-manager, Northampton attracted an average gate of 8,310.

Nevertheless, Bowen knew how to make the most of limited resources. Helped by his extensive football networks, which included his strong

Highbury connections, Bowen persuaded many talented, if overlooked, players to come to the County Ground. He was a sharp negotiator, too. Most of his incoming transfers were made at knock-down prices.

Bowen knew how to create effective, tactically smart teams – ones that remained vigorously competitive, hard-working, mentally strong, close-knit and mutually supportive. Bowen had no qualms about signing 'leaders' – Theo Foley and Cliff Holton were good examples. He never saw strong characters as representing any threat to his authority. He always looked to improve his side, no matter how well it was performing. Bowen was renowned for replacing one successful forward with a better one. He switched players' positions not just to cover a gap but to maximise a player's contribution. In his first years in charge he converted his centre-half, Laurie Brown, into a makeshift but highly successful inside-left. He also decided that his right-winger, Mike Everitt, would be more effective as a tough-tackling left-back.

Talented local youngsters were not neglected, either, under Bowen's management. Young centre-half Terry Branston and fledgling forwards Barry Lines, Don Martin and Jim Hall developed so well that they played for him in Division One. Bowen and his faithful assistants – 'Roly' Mills, Jack Jennings and 'Joe' Payne – formed a formidable coaching team. Like Bowen, Payne was a Welshman. Jennings originated from the north of England. Only Mills was born and bred in the town, and yet all four were passionately committed to Northampton, as if they knew no other place. Their canniness matched their loyalty. Even experienced professionals learned to raise their game under Bowen and his assistants.

Although Bowen was a regular trader in the transfer market, he constructed his sides carefully, inducting newcomers into well-established teams. As a testament to his team-building skills, five members of the side that won promotion in April 1961 – goalkeeper Norman Coe, full-back Mike Everitt, wing-half or inside-forward Derek Leck, centre-half Terry Branston and winger Barry Lines – played for him in Division One four years later. In fact, that group swells to seven if Republic of Ireland full-back Theo Foley and Geordie winger Tommy Robson are taken into account. They joined the 'Northampton Express' one year after it left its first stop.

Bowen knew exactly what players he needed for a small-town club like Northampton to thrive. Listed among his early priorities were two fast wingers who could provide consistently accurate crosses for bludgeoning, bustling, brawny central strikers. The plan might have been unremarkable but Bowen's choice of exponents was inspirational. Local left-winger, Barry Lines, met Bowen's needs so well that he played regularly in all four divisions, including 40 games in Division One. Such was Lines' skill and reliability that his faster, more direct rival, Tommy Robson, was sold to Chelsea in 1965 to boost Bowen's modest top-flight survival fund.

The right wing had a longer cast list, though. Bela Olah, a tricky former Hungary youth international and future Hastings United star, helped set Northampton on their way out of the bottom division in 1960. However, it was the ex-Arsenal right-winger, Mike Everitt, prior to his defensive conversion, who took over the baton as the Cobblers closed in on promotion. In the higher division, former Romford wide-man, Roy Sanders, took on the mantle temporarily before Billy Hails was captured from Peterborough, in time to propel Northampton to the Third Division championship in 1963. Ultimately, the former Kettering and Luton right-winger, Harry Walden, seized the part as Northampton sped to Division One. But once there, Walden had to concede his place, temporarily, to Joe Broadfoot, a highly talented but ultimately disappointing £27,000 purchase from Ipswich.

Having experimented successfully with Laurie Brown playing alongside forceful centre-forward Mike Deakin, Bowen set his eye on a more powerful model in Cliff Holton. Brown had moved on to Highbury, where Holton had made the first of his 200 league appearances in 1950. Holton had already blasted in 42 league goals in taking Watford out of the bottom division in 1960. Acknowledging Holton's imposing presence, Bowen immediately made him club captain, unceremoniously deposing his newly-appointed skipper, Theo Foley. Any tension this created was dissipated quickly, though. A supremely confident Holton announced to his new team-mates: 'You provide the crosses and I'll provide the goals.' He was as good as his word. Having been signed just hours before his first game at Selhurst Park, he duly demolished Palace with a thunderous hat-trick.

Bowen had an uncanny knack of sensing when his players had peaked. He allowed Mike Deakin to move on to Aldershot in 1961 after he had scored 31 goals in only 44 appearances – a strike rate that most managers would give their right arms for. However, Bowen knew what he was doing. Deakin's career fizzled out soon after his move. In order to restore his favoured vanguard, Bowen recruited a 'chip off the old block' in Alec Ashworth, whose 'playboy image' had allegedly ruffled feathers at Luton. Bowen was unfazed that Ashworth and Holton seemed to be birds of a feather in that respect – quite rightly, as the pair proceeded to terrorise Third Division defences. Holton and Ashworth shared 21 goals in the opening ten fixtures of the 1962/63 season.

Although Holton scored 52 goals in only 60 games under Bowen, the Northampton boss seemed quite relaxed about forging a deal which took his talismanic but ageing striker to the Valley in that dreadful winter of

'63. There were other fish in the sea. And as far as strikers go, they didn't come much bigger or bolder than Frank Large. Once linked up, Large and Ashworth duly steamrollered the opposition, taking Northampton to the 1962/63 Third Division championship. Ashworth was the club's leading goalscorer with 25 goals in 30 appearances while Large, a former QPR centre-forward, smashed in 18 goals in 20 games, including two hat-tricks. As proof of their combined power, Ashworth scored three goals and Large bagged two as Reading were ravaged 5-0 at the County Ground on 30 March 1963. Northampton galloped to the Third Division title, which was duly won on 11 May, with a 4-0 drubbing of local rivals Peterborough at London Road. To exact extra sweetness from the occasion, two former 'Posh' players – Billy Hails and Ray Smith – put themselves on the scoresheet.

Northampton Town's heavy artillery helped the club net a century of goals in winning the Third Division title. But Bowen knew that all successful teams had to be tight at the back, too. In the lower divisions, a rough, tough discipline was required. Therefore, he set about assembling a set of physically obdurate defenders, who had no qualms about doling out the rough stuff, diving in where it hurts. After watching Theo Foley, Exeter's left-back, knock lumps out of Mike Everitt in 1961, Bowen thought, 'this chap could do a good job for me', and promptly signed him for the start of his Third Division campaign. All of Bowen's defenders were uncompromising. They were prepared to put their bodies on the line in the call of duty. John Kurila, Terry Branston and, ironically, Mike Everitt, were exactly what Bowen had in mind. It was the rugged treatment that these guys meted out week in, week out that enabled Bowen's more constructive players – Barry Lines, Derek Leck and Joe Kiernan – the scope to operate creatively in front of them.

As author Mark Beesley indicated, Northampton Town's success was a triumph of planning and realism. As the going got tougher, Bowen rammed home his pragmatic message with his players. He insisted: 'We've got one point to start with. Let's see if we can hang on to it and see if we can pinch two.' With Bowen's teams, defence was a shared responsibility. Wingers were expected to track back and if they didn't Foley and Bowen would scream at them to comply. When Joe Broadfoot showed little appetite for Town's battling style, Bowen's record signing was dropped promptly. Bowen's players operated at a punishing work rate. If they didn't, they did not play. Bowen and his coaches always insisted upon the highest standards of fitness.

As Northampton rose through the divisions, Bowen knew that he required a greater injection of quality. But quality normally costs a lot. Despite the rising gates – an average crowd of 13,422 watched the Cobblers'

Third Division triumph – Bowen realised that if he was to buy a better player he had to cash in some prized assets. The club didn't have the cash to do otherwise. So, before the start of their first season in Division Two, out went Alec Ashworth to Preston North End for £22,000, making Northampton a handy £12,000 profit. It was also a good move for Ashworth, who helped his new club to the following season's FA Cup Final. With his departure, Frank Large was left to lead the line without a big-hitting strike partner. Peter Kane was re-signed from Arsenal and youngsters Don Martin, Jim Hall and Billy Best stepped up. But, despite some promising performances, notably from Don Martin, these four mustered only 17 goals between them. Large, too, found goalscoring more difficult in the higher division. Perhaps this was why he was allowed to leave for Swindon for £10,000 in March 1964.

Having lost their primary marksmen and encountered better opposition, Northampton's goal standard fell by a half during 1963/64. Just 58 goals were scored. Large's tally of 12 goals was the only one to reach double figures. Nevertheless, Northampton's combative style enabled them to reach a comfortable mid-table position by the season's end. Bowen's boys proved adept at defending a single-goal advantage – nine out of their 16 league victories were achieved by the narrowest of margins. Less frugally, promotion-bound Sunderland were trounced 5-1 in the ice and snow of the County Ground. Here, Bowen out-thought his wily counterpart, Alan Brown, by equipping his players with baseball-style boots to achieve greater traction in the slippery conditions. The occasion was also a personal triumph for young Corby-born striker Don Martin, who scored a couple as Northampton completed a prestigious 'double' over their well-heeled opponents.

By trading in Ashworth and Large, Bowen found he had enough in the coffers to land Colchester's goalscoring inside-forward, Bobby Hunt, for £20,000. Hunt had scored 99 times in 164 games for the Layer Road club, although not in the bulldozing, bull-headed style of Ashworth or Large. Author Mark Beesley described Hunt as 'a jaunty individual, with a flair for twists and turns which enabled him to shrug off defenders and deliver incisive crosses and shots.' Here was a creator as well as a taker of goals. However, apart from scoring a memorable hat-trick against Jackie Milburn's beleaguered Ipswich in September '64, Hunt's goal touch seemed to desert him at the County Ground. Bowen knew, though, that he needed Hunt's all-round striking ability if Northampton were to progress.

But with Bowen missing a brawny, bustling leader of the line, he turned to a former Barnet, England and Great Britain amateur international,

Bobby Brown, who was surplus to requirements at Vicarage Road. Although Brown was not considered good enough for Third Division Watford, Bowen recognised the six-foot striker's potential. After all, he had played nine times in Division One for Fulham. Bowen knew Brown was not the finished article. He needed the opportunity to develop his game under the guidance of Bowen's coaching team. While Brown played only a handful of games during the 1963/64 season, he progressed so well that he became Northampton's leading goalscorer in both of the seasons which followed.

Although goalkeeper 'Chic' Brodie had performed well in the Third Division title-winning side, Bowen thought that, with Northampton's star rising, he needed a top-flight keeper. Blackpool's reserve custodian, Bryan Harvey, met his specifications, having played regularly in Division One for Newcastle under Charlie Mitten. Harvey had joined Newcastle in 1958 alongside Wisbech team-mate Terry Marshall, who later became Hastings United's top gun.

Finally, Bowen decided that he needed more craft in midfield if his team was to make further progress. In stepped 'strolling' Joe Kiernan, a 21-year-old former Sunderland apprentice, for a ridiculously low price of £2,000. Bowen needed Foley's persuasive charm to land him, though. Once Foley had curled his arm around Joe's shoulder there was no escape. Kiernan played 18 games in the 1963/64 season, demonstrating quickly the class that took him to the brink of the senior Scottish side.

Bowen was not afraid to take risks in improving his side. The greater risk, though, was the state of Bowen's health. He was still troubled by rheumatic fever. He had been forced to take a two-week rest in 1962. Now, with the illness returning, Bowen had to down tools once more. For a short time, it looked as if Bowen would resign. Fortunately, his health improved sufficiently for him to return to action.

Bowen added two more players to his squad in advance of their triumphant 1964/65 season. Right-winger Harry Walden was signed from Luton in exchange for Town's Billy Hails, and centre-forward Charlie Livesey was signed from Watford for £17,000. The quick, tricky Walden was expected to offer greater firepower than Hails but he turned out to be a much better maker than taker of goals.

The same could be said of Charlie Livesey. Livesey was a class act, an entertainer both on and off the pitch. Bowen had seen what the strapping Livesey could do. He had noted the lad's budding talent at Southampton in 1958. He saw him blossom as Jimmy Greaves' partner at Chelsea a year later. Livesey had strength and speed. He was adept at shielding the ball from rugged defenders. He had a lovely touch and possessed a fierce shot.

Moreover, he scored spectacular, solo goals with the breezy swagger of Frank Worthington. He had netted 17 times in 39 First Division games for Chelsea in a two-year stay. The problem was that he tended to lose concentration. His application wasn't always what it should have been. He was a joker in the pack, a card. That was why his stay at Chelsea was cut short. That was why he languished at Gillingham for two years. However, Livesey had rediscovered his zest for the game after moving to Watford in 1962. At Vicarage Road, his 26 goals in 64 games almost took the Hornets to the Second Division in April 1964. This was good enough for Bowen. Livesey was only in his mid-twenties. He still had room for growth. He seemed worth the risk. Bowen could see him leading the line in the top flight. Quality of his kind was rarely available at the price that the Cobblers could afford.

Northampton began their promotion campaign on Bank Holiday Monday, 24 August 1964. They had been denied a Saturday home start on account of a clash of fixtures with the County Cricket Club. At a smoggy Ayresome Park, Bowen sent the following team out to do battle with Middlesbrough: Harvey, Foley and Everitt, Leck, Branston and Kiernan, Walden, Hunt, Livesey, Martin and Lines. Frustratingly, Northampton lost to a last-minute goal from Boro's Arthur Horsfield. And despite an unexpected 2-0 victory at Maine Road, Manchester, where Hunt scored with a scorching 20-yarder, Northampton's early form gave no hint of what was to come. Indeed, after a 0-2 loss to Southampton at a sweltering Dell on 5 September, the Cobblers had dropped to 17th position.

A narrow 1-0 home victory over Newcastle on 8 September signalled a remarkable upturn in form. An unbeaten 16-match run followed, lifting Northampton into top spot. Ironically, it was champions-elect, Newcastle, who brought their run to an end in the return game on 12 December. Cobblers' Morpeth-born left-winger, Tommy Robson, was stretchered off after only 15 minutes. As hard as the ten men battled, they could not halt the Geordie tide. Newcastle crushed them 5-0, replacing them as the divisional leaders.

Northampton's autumn run of success did not depend upon the goalscoring abilities of one or two strikers. This was very much a team effort. Twelve of them opened their accounts during that run. Although Bobby Brown, Don Martin and Tommy Robson would eventually top the charts with 13 league goals each, 11 others chipped in with important strikes. This was a team that never knew when it was beaten. On several occasions, Northampton won or saved games with goals scored in the final five minutes. For example, Branston's 88th-minute header saved a point at

Fratton Park on 7 October after his team had trailed 0-2 after 22 minutes, and 2-3 with only two minutes left. It was only at Newcastle in December and at Plymouth in April (2-5) that Northampton were forced to settle for damage limitation. And on both occasions they had been reduced to ten men.

Bowen ensured that his teams remained resilient, quick to bounce back from defeat. Northampton lost only six games in gaining promotion to Division One in 1965 and none at home. There was never a time when one defeat followed another. Bowen looked to maintain a settled side but never missed an opportunity to strengthen the team if it was flagging. For example, Bowen forked out £10,000 to bring Ken Leek back to the County Ground immediately after the drubbing at Newcastle. He was fortunate that his directors backed him as much as they could. Bowen wasn't averse to improvising, either. For example, he once played his converted full-back, Mike Everitt, in another unaccustomed position, at inside-right. Talk about the Midas touch! Everitt's sizzling 25-yard drive made sure that Manchester City returned home with nothing except bruised pride (2-0).

Bowen was lucky that his defenders remained largely free of injury. Unfortunately, Terry Branston was an exception, after being carried off with cartilage damage in a 1-1 draw at Norwich on 20 March. Here, Bryan Harvey made yet another magnificent penalty save – he made six that season. But Branston's misfortune became Graham Carr's opportunity. The 20-year-old Geordie, a former apprentice and father of comedian Alan Carr, acquitted himself impressively. Twenty-two years later, Graham Carr would lead another successful Northampton side out of the Football League basement.

On 17 April 1965, Northampton achieved 'the impossible' – promotion to the top flight just four years after leaving the bottom division. Only 6,800 were there to witness the fabulous feat as the game was played at Gigg Lane, Bury. Here, the Shakers were well and truly stirred. Northampton won 4-1 with Joe Kiernan snatching an early goal and Don Martin scoring a couple. Bobby Brown also celebrated his extended run at centre-forward by scoring, too. It was his 12th league goal of the season. Although expected to be an understudy to Livesey, Brown seized his chance in early January and never let go during the promotion run-in, proving to be a more reliable finisher than his feted rival.

Charlie Livesey would have one more chance to prove his worth in the top flight. Alas, the opportunity slipped from his grasp. After Livesey failed to make an impact on the bigger stage, a regretful Bowen decided that Charlie no longer had the 'right stuff'. In November 1965, he was transferred to Brighton for £6,000. As was the case at Watford, Livesey quickly rediscovered his form in the lower division. His powerful displays and keen anticipation helped set up numerous opportunities for his new Albion colleagues. Although Brighton were then only a mid-table Third Division side, Alf Ramsey became interested in Livesey's performances as the England boss prepared for the World Cup finals. For Bowen, this merely underlined what Livesey might have achieved had he shown greater application. Livesey completed his Football League career with Brighton, scoring 37 goals in 146 appearances before transferring to Crawley Town, of the Southern League, in 1969. He later became a painter and decorator. Tragically, he died of asbestosis in 2005, aged only 67 years.

On a balmy Saturday evening on 24 April, Northampton completed their league programme with a 1-1 home draw with relegation-threatened Portsmouth. A crowd of 20,660 crammed into the three-sided County Ground to acclaim their heroes, many squeezed on to the duckboards that covered the cricket outfield. It was a joyous occasion for their opponents, too, as the point salvaged by Wilson's 84th-minute equaliser was just enough to save their bacon and send Swindon down instead. It was a fitting way for Pompey's Jimmy Dickinson to end his long career, on his 40th birthday.

When interviewed on national radio, Bowen was circumspect about how Northampton might fare in Division One. Bowen said: 'When we came out of the Fourth Division, people said we would probably struggle in the Third and when we came out of the Third Division people said we would probably struggle in the Second ... Nothing is impossible in football with the right kind of people around you if they are prepared to dedicate themselves. It is all down to the boys.'

But Bowen was not fooled. He knew he faced a Herculean task in keeping Northampton in the top flight with a war chest of just £25,000. He knew the club would do well to draw in crowds of more than 20,000. With Northampton's major footwear industry in decline, another casualty of stronger competition abroad, the town's prospects were not auspicious, either. Bowen looked covetously at Bury's brilliant inside-forward, Colin Bell, Swindon's powerful right-winger, Mike Summerbee, Millwall's terrific young keeper, Alex Stepney and Dundee's wing wizard, Charlie Cooke. But this was mere window shopping. They were all out of his price range. Bowen had to content himself by clinging on to his prized playmaker, Joe Kiernan, as Arsenal and Everton sniffed around. Rumours circulated that offers of around £40,000 had been made. It came to nought. Northampton would begin life in the top flight with the squad that had achieved promotion. Joe Mercer, Bowen's friend and former Arsenal team-mate, regarded

Northampton's promotion as 'a miracle' and rightly so. Just as Joe said, this was a greater triumph against the odds than England's World Cup victory.

'A Hunting We Will Go': Carlisle's twin promotions

While Northampton were defying the odds with their ballistic rise up the Football League, Carlisle were attempting to follow suit, securing consecutive promotions in 1963/64 and '64/65, which lifted them into the stratosphere of the Second Division. The architect of their amazing revival was new manager and former player, Alan Ashman. Ashman took over in the most inauspicious of circumstances. His call came during the worst winter of the last 60 years. With the country ice-bound, Third Division Carlisle were relegation-bound. Worse still, they were booted out of the FA Cup by visiting Gravesend & Northfleet, a struggling Southern League side. The manager, Ivor Powell, paid for this ignominious defeat with his job.

At the time of his summons, Ashman was chicken farming, although he managed to find some time to revive the fortunes of Northern League side Penrith. Ashman had previously been a deadly marksman with Carlisle, especially good with his head. So, it was no surprise when he purchased a 'headmaster' in Hugh McIlmoyle.

Since his startling introduction into the big time, McIlmoyle's career had stalled. He had made an unexpected appearance for Leicester in the FA Cup Final of 1961. Here, he took the place of the disciplined top scorer, Ken Leek. Despite performing creditably at Wembley in an injury-depleted side, he was given few opportunities at Filbert Street thereafter. A year after Leicester's FA Cup Final defeat, McIlmoyle was transferred to Second Division Rotherham for £8,000. But the young Scot struggled to make an impact at Millmoor, scoring four times in 12 appearances. It was said that Ashman had not seen the 23-year-old play before signing him for £5,000 in early 1963. Ashman later admitted, 'I knew he was good but I didn't know he was that good.' For McIlmoyle wasted little time in repaying Ashman's faith. He proceeded to score goals – stacks of them. McIlmoyle arrived too late to avert Carlisle's relegation to Division Four in May 1963, although he scored twice on his debut as the Cumbrians beat Notts County 4-2. It was in the following season that McIlmoyle revealed what damage he could inflict upon opposing defences. By the turn of the year, he had plundered 30 league goals, gloriously exploiting the wing service provided by Sammy Taylor and Frank Kirkup and the intelligent midfield prompting of ex-Newcastle and Swansea inside-forward, Reg Davies.

Not that he had to share the strike burden alone. For much of the season, he was ably accompanied by Joe Livingstone, a brawny central striker who had been Brian Clough's understudy at Middlesbrough. Unlike Clough, Livingstone was not just a 'fox in the box'. He was prepared to scrap and graft outside the area, too, working the defenders, creating gaps, giving McIlmoyle more scope to exercise his deadly talent. As opposing sides gradually wised up to McIlmoyle's threat, his rich pickings dwindled. After New Year, he managed just nine more goals. However, both Livingstone (20) and Johnny Evans (16) made sure that the goal rush did not cease. Their lethal firepower shot Carlisle to promotion behind champions Gillingham, who clinched the title on goal average, despite scoring barely half of Carlisle's 113 goals. Following his February '64 transfer from Stockport, the small but nippy Evans scored at a rate of over a goal per game. This included a hat-trick in a 6-0 drubbing of Doncaster plus four two-goal returns.

Like Dave Bowen at Northampton, Alan Ashman had to work on a very tight budget. Incoming moves needed to be financed by outgoing ones. Eyes, therefore, turned to McIlmoyle as the next 'cash cow'. His 44-goal haul for the 1963/64 season had prompted excited chatter up and down the Football League. Withering Wolves were the first to make a move, though. In the late fifties, Wolves had little difficulty in racking up 100 goals per season. Now they were struggling to reach half that total. McIlmoyle was targeted as their potential saviour. Although Stan Cullis surprisingly lost his job in September, managerless Wolves still went ahead with the deal. When, in October 1964, the Carlisle board were offered £30,000 for McIlmoyle, they felt they couldn't refuse. While McIlmoyle was unable to prevent Wolves' slide into the Second Division, the proceeds from his sale enabled Ashman to assemble a championship-winning side that would meet Wolves there.

To replace McIlmoyle, Ashman signed the nomadic 'kingmaker', Frank Large. Fearsome Frank was the perfect foil for the sprightly Johnny Evans. In came wily playmaker Willie Carlin, too, all 5ft 5in of him, from Halifax at a bargain fee of £10,000, albeit a record one for both Carlisle and the Shaymen. He would take over the midfield duties from Reg Davies. Carlisle United historian, David Steele, described Carlin as 'a pugnacious little player who could both make and score goals.' He later became a key member of Clough and Taylor's rejuvenated Derby side. His stock was rising. Left-winger Ron Simpson, the only Carlisle-born player in the side, was also signed from Sheffield United and the versatile Jimmy Blain was brought in from Rotherham. These two would patrol the flanks.

It wasn't just the attack that needed to be recalibrated, though. Ashman realised there needed to be a tightening at the back as well. So, in came

Stan Harland, a robust defensive wing-half from Bradford City. He would progress to Football League Cup glory with Swindon five years later. The alliance he created with Tommy Passmoor and captain Peter McConnell provided the fulcrum of Carlisle's defensive strength. Not that Carlisle's full-backs, Terry Caldwell and Hugh Neill, were deficient. Nor were Allan Ross and Joe Dean 'between the sticks'. As with Dave Bowen's Northampton, Carlisle's success owed much to the all-round competitive strength of its team. Ashman had turned a once failing side into one that was hard to beat.

If there was any misgiving about McIlmoyle's October departure, Johnny Evans made light of this by netting six times in nine games. His rush of goals helped Carlisle to five victories, including a vital one at Ashton Gate. With Carlisle up to fourth spot, behind Brentford, Bristol Rovers and Grimsby, it was clear that this team was not out of its depth. However, the FA Cup defeat at non-league Crook Town in November was a major embarrassment. To make matters worse, the 1-0 defeat actually flattered Carlisle. Thereafter, their form wobbled. Barnsley and Colchester were despatched with interest but then Brentford thrashed them 6-1 at a freezing, foggy Griffin Park, on the Saturday before Christmas. Carlisle fell to seventh place.

Public interest appeared to be waning. Almost 12,000 supporters had turned up for the August Bank Holiday 1-1 draw with Port Vale. Yet less than half that number watched the 4-1 victory over Colchester on 12 December. Fortunately, the Football League paired Carlisle with Workington over the festive period. These home and away clashes certainly whetted local appetites. The Brunton Park game, won 1-0 by Carlisle, attracted over 14,000 fans while the return at Borough Park, also won by Carlisle 1-0, brought in almost 12,000. Although a 1-2 home defeat by the divisional leaders, Bristol Rovers, followed on 2 January, this setback was righted quickly with a 3-1 win over fifth-placed Grimsby a week later. Four victories followed on the bounce, taking Carlisle into second place, one point behind Cliff Britton's big-spending Hull City, who had overtaken the previous leaders, Bristol Rovers. Carlisle and Hull then faced one another on 20 February. With so much at stake, 17,174 supporters piled into Brunton Park. Perhaps predictably, the game ended as a tough 0-0 stalemate, although a late Hull 'goal' was ruled out controversially. But Carlisle were now well into their stride. Of their 12 remaining fixtures, eight resulted in victories. Six of these were achieved by a single-goal margin. This was a side that kept its nerve under pressure.

Carlisle's final three fixtures were crammed into the Easter weekend. Each of Carlisle's five challengers had a chance of overhauling them. Over 16,000 local fans turned up on a bright 16 April for the Good Friday clash with fifth-placed Bristol City. A rare strike from Stan Harland helped salvage a crucial point. Although the Easter Monday game against third-placed Mansfield, at Field Mill, was lost 0-2 in front of a crowd of almost 14,000, Ashman knew that victory in the return fixture on Easter Tuesday would secure both promotion and the Third Division championship. Realising that Carlisle were on the brink of an historic moment, a crowd of 18,764 squeezed and squirmed into Brunton Park for the final game. The tension inside the ground must have been overwhelming and yet Ashman's lads showed no sign of nerves. They had a job to do and they proceeded to do it in style, storming into a 3-0 interval lead. Capitalising upon the excellent service provided by Simpson and Blain, Frank Large put the Cumbrians two up early in the game. Then, just as the half-time break approached, Johnny Evans added a third after yet another superb cross found him in space. The Stags had been shot. With all anxieties dissipated, the second half was a breeze; a mass party began in celebration of Carlisle's highest placing in their 44-year-old league history. Surprisingly, Carlisle's running partner in their promotion was Bristol City, not Hull. Fred Ford's Bristol had snatched the remaining promotion place away from Cliff Britton after winning their final three games.

Worked over by Workington

But the 'Underdog of the Season' award should have surely been presented to Third Division Workington, for reaching the quarter-finals of the League Cup for the second year in succession. Their run began with a 9-1 annihilation of beleaguered Cumbrian rivals, Barrow, at home. It continued with a 1-0 victory at Third Division Scunthorpe and then featured an incredible 5-1 thrashing of First Division side Blackburn Rovers at Ewood Park, following a 0-0 draw in Workington.

Former Workington full-back John Ogilvie told freelance reporter John Walsh: 'Up here, we were lucky to get a draw. Rovers had ten internationals in their side. They were a good team. We went to Blackburn for the replay on Bonfire Night. It was pouring down. Our trainer, George Aitken, said to us before the game, "Remember they said the *Bismarck* couldn't be sunk." Well, we just paralysed them. We would have beaten anyone that night. Kit Napier scored twice. He was a very quiet lad, very shy and didn't like being roughed up but he had a hell of a shot. If you gave him any space, he'd get goals.'

Workington followed up this incredible result by thumping Second Division Norwich 3-0 in round four. Although their run eventually ended in a quarter-final replay, their opponents, Tommy Docherty's King's Road swingers, were given an almighty shock. Former Chelsea star, Peter Osgood, was sat in the dugout for the first game at Borough Park. He recalled in his book *Ossie: King of Stamford Bridge*: 'Out on the field little Workington were working the Chelsea stars over. We fought to leave with a 2-2 draw but not until a nail-biting finale when Workington had a goal disallowed.' Kit Napier's equaliser had earned the Reds a second chance.

Although Chelsea won the replay at Stamford Bridge, Workington's performance surpassed all expectations. Osgood remembered the game vividly as well he might, as it was his first senior appearance at the age of 17 years. He recalled:

> *Workington were good and for long periods outplayed us, to the frustration and annoyance of the crowd who had assumed that their performance up there was due to home advantage and the 'little club rising to the big occasion' syndrome and that we would demolish them here at Stamford Bridge. On their side was a guy called Keith Burkinshaw, who became better known for his stint as manager at Tottenham Hotspur during the 1970s and 1980s. We were not looking good and my debut was turning into a damp squib. With nine minutes remaining George Graham glided through the midfield and found me with an intelligent pass on the edge of the area. I slipped through and swerved right past the Workington keeper, and clipped the ball across him and into the back of the net. I had no time to savour the moment because before we knew it Tommy Knox had thumped another shot against the post and I was there to tap it firmly home.*

Nevertheless, this doughty Cumbrian team had represented its small industrial town, comprising just 30,000 residents, with great distinction.

And yet this was nothing new for Ken Furphy's boys. In the previous season, when Workington were still a Fourth Division side, their League Cup run had also featured four victories, albeit against more modest opposition. They beat Third Division Oldham, away, 5-3; Fourth Division Southport, at home, 3-0; Second Division Huddersfield, at home, 1-0; and Third Division Colchester, at home, 2-1, before being hammered 6-0 at

Upton Park. 'Budgie' Byrne scored a hat-trick with five of the goals coming in a bewildering 32-minute spell.

The catalyst for Workington's triumphant resurgence was the appointment of Ken Furphy as the club's player-manager. Although Furphy began his career as a footballer with Everton in 1950, he spent most of his playing days in non-league and lower division circles with Runcorn, Darlington and Workington. This gave him a keen understanding of how to achieve success at this level. According to former Reds' full-back John Ogilvie, 'Furphy was one of the best tacticians the club ever had. He'd give you the lowdown on our opponents. He'd tell you which player went this way or that and who'd go down. He must have had them closely watched.' Furphy brought higher professional standards to Workington. He introduced improved training regimes. He reorganised the side, helping some players find more effective positions. Furphy also developed the club's youth team, entering it, for the first time, in the FA Youth Cup competition.

One of Furphy's last signings for Workington was among his best. 'Kit' Napier was a 20-year-old Scot, who had failed to settle at either Blackpool or Preston. He quickly became a crowd-pleaser at Borough Park, scoring 25 times in 58 appearances, before moving on to Newcastle for £18,000. In 1966, he transferred to Brighton for £8,500, where he became their leading goalscorer in all but one of the six seasons he spent on the south coast, netting 84 times in 256 league appearances. After falling out with his Brighton boss, Pat Saward, he rejoined Ken Furphy at Blackburn, the club he had once humiliated as a Red.

After Furphy left for Watford (he later managed Sheffield United), Workington had one further tilt at fame, in 1965/66, when their push for promotion to the Second Division ended six places short. Thereafter, a steady decline set in, concluding with their ejection from the Football League in 1977 in favour of Wimbledon. By then, their gates had plummeted from a healthy 5,000 or so to fewer than 1,000. But their heroics of almost 50 years ago are an undimmed memory for those who were there.

'Fade to Grey'

On 30 January 1965, Labour Housing Minister Richard Crossman made the following entry in his diary: 'What a faded, declining establishment surrounded me. Aged marshals, grey, dreary ladies, decadent Marlboroughs and Churchills. It was a dying congregation gathered here and I'm afraid the Labour Cabinet didn't look too distinguished either. It felt like the end of an epoch, possibly even the end of a nation.' This was one of many morose reflections on the death of Winston Churchill. But as Crossman knew very well, it was no good wallowing in our 'heroic' past; there was work to be done. The country – particularly the industrial North and Midlands – was still sullied by slum, derelict and prefabricated housing which needed to be demolished and replaced with modern, purpose-built homes. Too many people were without basic amenities – adequate shelter being the most urgent need. The 1967 BBC Wednesday Play *Cathy Come Home* rammed that point home better than any government inquiry. Beneath the vapid gloss of 'swinging' England there was a grim, grimy, gritty reality, closer to the abject poverty illustrated in the 1967 film, *The Whisperers*, than to the atavistic preening depicted in *Darling*, nearer the harshness of *Z Cars* than the cosiness of *Dixon of Dock Green*.

This was the year that we also bade farewell to Stanley Matthews, who finally retired from professional football at the age of 50. *News of the World* sports editor, Frank Butler, wrote in testimony: 'There will never be another Stanley Matthews in our time. That is why it is fitting that the first knighthood to a professional footballer should go to a man who in thirty-three years as a professional has shattered so many records ... He broke Billy Meredith's long-standing record by becoming the oldest active player in first-class football ... Matthews is not only unique as the most fantastic dribbler and soccer entertainer the world has known but also because of his modesty and good conduct both on and off the field. Never in thirty-three years did he have his name taken and he never knew how to foul!'

Lest we forget, Stan Mortensen was the forgotten hat-trick 'hero' of the 1953 FA Cup Final. Matthews had an insipid game apart from his late, crucial intervention. And yet according to the myth, this was the 'Matthews Final'. When Mortensen died in 1991, one jaundiced hack speculated whether his burial might be dubbed the 'Matthews funeral'. But in our eagerness to demythologise past glories, we might do well to remember the newspaper editor's quip in John Ford's western, *The Man Who Shot Liberty Valance*: 'When the legend becomes fact, print the legend.'

THE 1965/66 SEASON

Northampton Town v Fulham

'Somebody Help Me'
23 April 1966

Bedford Jezzard took over as Fulham's first-team manager in 1958. He had previously been the youth-team manager for two years. It was a big step up but he had Frank Osborne, Fulham's long-standing general manager, to assist him. During the 1920s Frank became the first Fulham player to win an England cap. Frank had an excellent relationship with the board of directors, which helped Jezzard settle into his new role. Also helping to maintain club stability was physiotherapist and trainer, Frank Penn. Frank Penn had joined Fulham in 1915 – six years before Osborne. Although Osborne had spent much of his playing career at Spurs, Penn was strictly a one-club man. While he never had official responsibility for team affairs, there is little doubt that Penn played his part in developing the homely Fulham culture and their attractive style of play.

After taking Fulham to the First Division in 1959, Jezzard managed to keep them there for the next five seasons. There were various close calls, though, most notably during the 1961/62 season. Ironically, this was the year in which Fulham came within a whisker of reaching Wembley. Unfortunately for them, they were undone by a combination of bad luck and Jimmy McIlroy's magic as Burnley progressed to the final instead.

The 1959/60 season proved to be Jezzard's best. Thereafter, Fulham became rooted in the bottom half of the table. Apart from Maurice Cook's 15-goal return in 1962/63, they were largely dependent upon Graham Leggat's goals to keep them out of trouble. By 1964, there was an urgent need for team strengthening. It seemed strange, then, that in March of that year, the Fulham board decided to cash in their major asset: wing-half, Alan Mullery. Spurs boss, Bill Nicholson, was looking to replace his long-serving and ageing captain, Danny Blanchflower. The White Hart Lane board were prepared to splash out £72,500 for the dynamic midfielder – a record outgoing fee for Fulham. Jezzard was deeply unhappy about the deal, compounded by the fact that his chairman, Tommy Trinder, had negotiated the transfer behind his back. It was left to Mullery to announce the news of his imminent transfer to his shocked manager and team-mates during the half-time break in a home league game with Liverpool on 14 March 1964. Remarkably, his team recovered their composure to defeat Liverpool with a second-half goal from Reg Stratton.

Being a comparatively small club in an expensive area and facing fierce local competition, Fulham needed to make greater economies. The club's gates had fallen by a quarter since 1960 to around 21,000. Mullery's sale might have been necessary but its manner and timing left much to be desired. A bond of trust was broken between the board and the manager. When Jezzard's mentor, Frank Osborne, decided to retire in October 1964, Jezzard called it a day, too. He declined the board's revised job offer, one in which he was given full managerial control. Although still short of his 40th birthday, he turned his back on football for good, preferring to take charge of a family-run pub in nearby Hammersmith. Trainer Frank Penn followed him out of Craven Cottage, having decided to retire at the age of 69 years. Sadly, Frank's retirement proved to be very short. He died a year later in St Pancras Hospital. So ended a productive and happy management partnership; it was one that had done so much to sustain Fulham's top-flight status. What happened after tore the club apart.

According to Dennis Turner, author of *Fulham: the Complete Record*, 'Chairman Trinder wanted to make Fulham a more "professional" club … The choice of Vic Buckingham was very unfortunate. In a relatively short space of time, his radical changes left the club facing relegation from the First to the Third Divisions in successive seasons.' Yet he arrived at the Cottage in January 1965 with very impressive credentials.

Vic Buckingham had been a successful manager of West Bromwich Albion during the fifties. During his six years in charge at the Hawthorns he guided them to an FA Cup triumph in 1954, narrowly missing out on the 'double' because of a late loss of league form. In his playing days during the thirties and forties, Buckingham had been a classy wing-half with Spurs. After retiring as a player, he began coaching Oxford University and Pegasus, quickly developing a reputation as a deep and original thinker. Success came rapidly as he steered Pegasus to victory in the FA Amateur Cup at Wembley. From there he moved into the Football League, cutting his managerial teeth at Bradford in 1951.

Buckingham had expansive vision. At the Albion, he introduced a version of Arthur Rowe's short-passing 'push and run' style of play, which was so successful in taking Spurs to the league championship in 1951. However, he made an important modification. He used the long ball as a swift and shrewdly-timed spring, employing his centre-forward, Ronnie Allen, in a deep-lying role to prompt dangerous counter-attacks. Buckingham insisted that all of his players should both attack and defend, depending upon the state of the game. He encouraged constructive play. He preferred that the goalkeeper threw the ball to one of his defenders instead of launching it. He wanted his defenders to use short accurate passes instead of long, hopeful punts.

Buckingham broke new ground by taking his Albion side on tours of the USSR, Canada and the USA, in order to fly the flag and flex their muscles. He left them in 1959 having achieved a succession of top-six placings and a series of impressive FA Cup displays. In his time at the Hawthorns, he recruited a number of outstanding players – Bobby Robson, Derek Kevan, Graham Williams and Maurice Setters – all of whom gained representative honours. After leaving the Hawthorns in 1959, he steered Ajax to the Dutch title at the end of his first season in charge. He returned to England a year later to take over from Harry Catterick at Sheffield Wednesday – Catterick having moved on to Everton. Despite having to contend with the match-fixing scandal involving Peter Swan, David Layne and Tony Kay, Buckingham consolidated his reputation as a top manager by achieving upper-half positions in all three seasons he was in charge at Hillsborough.

As Dennis Turner records, Buckingham's attempts at changing 'too much, too soon, ended in tears ... players like Cook, Langley, Keetch, Leggat, O'Connell, Key and Marsh were all moved on. A clear-out might have been justified but not to have replaced them with veterans like Terry Dyson [the former Spurs winger] and Mark Pearson [the former Manchester United and Sheffield Wednesday forward], both well past their "buy-by" dates. Relegation was only avoided in his first full season by the appointment of the outstanding Dave Sexton, as coach, at the turn of 1966.'

In 1964/65, Fulham finished in 20th position, avoiding relegation by four points. It was their worst season since 1961/62 – hardly surprising, perhaps, given the disruption behind the scenes. This time, they could not rely upon Graham Leggat to save them. Injury restricted him to just 17 appearances. Fortunately, young Rodney Marsh stepped up, impressing with his swaggering skill. He scored 17 league goals while no one else managed to reach double figures. It was just as well that Fulham were continuing to produce young talent. With home support continuing to drop, there was little in the coffers for new purchases. Although over 36,000 watched Fulham recover from a first-half deficit to beat Manchester United 2-1 on

5 September, the average league gate in 1964/65 fell by a further 4,000 to 17,562. Only Blackburn and Burnley had less support.

The 1965/66 season threatened to be much worse. After a brave 3-4 defeat at fifth-placed Spurs on 19 February, Fulham were rooted at the foot of the table, having won only five times. Their last victory had been on New Year's Day against Arsenal (1-0), six games before. Until Sexton assumed first-team coaching duties in January 1966, replacing Ronnie Burgess, Fulham had suffered a succession of heavy poundings. They had lost at home to Aston Villa (3-6), away at Manchester United (1-4), away at West Bromwich (2-6), at home to Burnley (2-5) and away at Leicester (0-5). In his quiet, methodical way, Sexton helped Fulham to tighten up their defence. After the festive five-goal thumping at Filbert Street, just four goals were conceded in their next five games. And three of these fixtures were against top-five sides – Burnley, Chelsea and Manchester United. Although the narrow defeat at Spurs smarted, Fulham had hurt their hosts that afternoon. It had been the first time that Fulham had scored more than two goals since they beat Everton 3-2 on 16 October. The introduction of youngsters Steve Earle and Les Barrett had given their attack greater potency. Both scored at White Hart Lane. Despite these green shoots of recovery, Fulham were in great peril. They were bottom; a point worse off than 21st-placed Blackburn and five points below Northampton, who were just outside the relegation zone. Time was drawing short; there were 13 games left in which to save themselves. However, a remarkable transformation was nigh. The visit of champions-elect Liverpool, on 26 February, provided the catalyst.

Liverpool were in fine form. Only a surprising 1-2 FA Cup third-round defeat to Chelsea, on an Anfield ice rink, disturbed their eight-match unbeaten sequence, comprising seven league victories and a draw. Liverpool had scored four goals in each of their preceding three games. Fulham looked set for a dismal afternoon. The side that had lost so narrowly at Spurs was retained. In goal was the Northern Irish international keeper, Jack McClelland. He had been signed from Arsenal in 1964 as cover for the injured first-choice keeper, Tony Macedo. Macedo had been a former England under 23 international, who had served Fulham well in almost 350 senior appearances. Now, McClelland replaced him on grounds of form not fitness. The full-backs were the forthcoming World Cup hero, George Cohen, and Brian Nichols, who had replaced former England left-back, Jim Langley. Langley had left to join the Queens Park Rangers revolution masterminded by manager Alec Stock and chairman Jim Gregory. Bobby Robson played at right-half, the position in which he enjoyed so much success with England in the '60/61 season. Centre-half John Dempsey had replaced the departed Bobby Keetch. Dempsey would later win FA Cup and European Cup Winners' Cup medals with Chelsea after his £70,000 move in 1969. He would also represent the Republic of Ireland, winning 21 caps. Stan Brown played at left-half, having been successfully converted from centre-forward.

Steve Earle took over the right-wing berth from Johnny Key, who had left to join Coventry, then en route to Division One under Jimmy Hill. Although not physically robust, Earle was quick and skilful with an eye for goal. He proceeded to score 11 vital goals in just 15 league games during the latter part of the season. At inside-right was Graham Leggat. He was approaching the end of his illustrious career with Fulham. Like Earle, Leggat troubled opponents as much with his goalscoring as with his sparkling wing play. Before his controversial £20,000 transfer to Birmingham in December 1966, Leggat scored 127 league goals in 251+3 appearances. Like Tom Finney, Leggat could more than fill in at centre-forward. Indeed, it was largely in this role that he scored 16 league goals in helping Fulham stay up at the end of this troubled season.

Although Johnny Haynes played with the number 9 on his back, his was a midfield role. The maverick Rodney Marsh, who had started the season in the number 9 shirt, was a more orthodox centre-forward, but he lost his place after the 0-5 debacle at Leicester. Following a dispute with Buckingham, Marsh joined former team-mate Jim Langley at Loftus Road. The £15,000 that QPR paid for him became one of the biggest bargains of the sixties, as his goals helped the Loftus Road club rise through the divisions to reach the top flight in 1968, seizing the Football League Cup en route in 1967. In 1972 Malcolm Allison paid QPR £200,000 to take Marsh – then an England international – to Manchester City in a doomed attempt to seal the First Division championship. Allan 'Sniffer' Clarke, the 19-year-old Walsall striker, became Marsh's replacement at Fulham for a fee of £35,000. Clarke made a slow start after his protracted transfer but progressed rapidly, thereafter, to become one of our greatest goalscorers.

Haynes' former shirt number (10), the one he wore 56 times for England, was taken by Mark Pearson, a former Manchester United inside-forward, who rose to prominence after the Munich tragedy. Finally, another Fulham youngster, Les Barrett, played wide on the left, replacing the former Spurs winger, Terry Dyson. Barrett was exceptionally quick and had the confidence to take on and beat opposing full-backs. But he was no showboater. There was a menacing end product to his dazzling wing play. He could be relied upon, not only to provide a stream of dangerous crosses, but also to finish off what others created. He scored 75 league goals in 420+3 appearances for the Cottagers. Whether it was at the behest of Buckingham or Sexton, the belated, but essential, inclusion of Earle and Barrett proved to be a masterstroke in securing Fulham's First Division survival.

It was Steve Earle's two goals – one in each half – which enabled Fulham to defy the odds and beat the mighty Liverpool. With a new surge of confidence, Fulham visited Aston Villa two weeks later and thrashed them 5-2 with Earle and Leggat scoring a brace apiece and Barrett also making his mark. Sunderland were next on their hit list and were duly despatched 3-0 with Leggat scoring a further two. Playing away no longer held any terrors as West Ham were overcome 3-1 at Upton Park. Earle, Barrett and Leggat shared the spoils. West Bromwich had also given Fulham a hiding earlier in the season. Once again, the tables were turned as Johnny Haynes chipped in with a rare pair of goals to secure a 2-1 home victory. The five-match winning sequence was broken when title-chasing Leeds came to the Cottage on Good Friday. The game attracted the highest home crowd of the season – almost 39,000 – but Fulham could not repeat their Liverpool triumph (1-3). However, four days later, the Cottagers took their revenge on Revie's side, winning with Mark Pearson's goal. On the following Saturday, second-half goals from Earle, Leggat and Bobby Robson overturned Sheffield Wednesday's interval lead (4-2). However, Leicester delivered a nasty shock on the following Monday evening. The Foxes came, saw and conquered easily, winning 4-0. Nevertheless, Fulham's surge of seven victories had lifted them off the bottom – they were in 21st place with 29 points. Their incredible run of form had enabled them to build up an 11-point lead over doomed Blackburn. Nevertheless, Northampton remained two points in front. Crucially, though, the Cobblers had played one game more. This meant that the Northampton versus Fulham game on 23 April assumed a huge significance. A victory for either side would almost certainly consign the losers to relegation.

Northampton's reward for reaching the top rung was a daunting early fixture list – Everton, away, followed by Arsenal and Manchester United at home. For the opening game at a sunny, sultry Goodison Park, Bowen put out his strongest team. He knew Terry Branston, his tough-tackling centre-half, was still nursing a bruised ankle. But he needed him to deal with Everton's powerhouse centre-forward, Fred Pickering. Bowen took the risk. With 20 minutes remaining it looked as if his gamble had paid off. The Cobblers were holding Everton at 1-1. Then, Branston's ankle buckled and with it went Northampton's chances. A lucky deflection enabled Pickering to restore Everton's lead and the hosts proceeded to run away with the game (2-5).

Perhaps Bowen should have had more faith in Graham Carr, Branston's deputy, because he substituted ably in the ensuing 1-1 home draws with Arsenal and Manchester United. In both games Northampton battled back from being a goal behind. Hunt's late equaliser against United was a 20-yard scorcher. But the Cobblers were equally indebted to their skipper, Theo Foley, at right-back, who kept George Best on a tight rein. It would be a very different affair when the sides next met at the County Ground, in an FA Cup tie in 1970. Then, George Best revelled in the mud, nonchalantly putting six past the Northampton keeper, Kim Book.

But the next four games revealed just how tough life would be. A goalkeeping howler from Harvey and another fortunate deflection gifted Newcastle the points at St James' Park (0-2). Burnley then gave the Cobblers the Willies at Turf Moor. While Scottish right-winger Willie Morgan gave Vic Cockcroft a torrid afternoon, his team-mate, Willie Irvine, capitalised by scoring a hat-trick (1-4). West Bromwich's Jeff Astle followed suit in the next game at the County Ground (3-4). This was Northampton's first league home defeat since 18 April 1964. Table-topping Burnley then repeated the Turf Moor indignity a few days later, with 'Willie-the-wisp' Irvine again on target (1-2). Tommy Robson's searing 30-yard opener had counted for nowt. Northampton were bottom.

More exasperation followed. Forest's right-winger, Kear, denied Northampton their first Division One win by equalising in the closing seconds of their game at the City Ground (1-1) on 18 September. Although Blackburn were beaten 1-0 at Ewood Park in the League Cup, mud, driving rain and Ron Springett held Northampton up at home against Sheffield Wednesday (0-0). Bowen's former club, Arsenal, were also fortunate to scrape a draw when they met his current employers at Highbury on Tuesday 28 September. The local derby at Filbert Street on 2 October took a similar course as Gordon Banks performed a series of magnificent saves to keep Northampton at bay. He was unable to stop Foley's penalty, however (1-1).

On 9 October, the sequence of draws was broken after Sheffield United's left-back, Ken Mallender, hammered home an early 25-yard drive to nick the points for the visiting Blades (0-1). The Cobblers' collywobbles returned. Fulham crushed them 5-0 in the midweek League Cup game in London. Leeds, with Giles and Bremner in irrepressible form, went one goal better on the following Saturday (1-6). Northampton finally broke their duck against the current European Cup Winners' Cup champions, West Ham, on a radiant late October afternoon at the County Ground. Ken Leek's impudent back-flick found goal with ten minutes left, delighting the 15,000 home fans (2-1). But the away daze continued at a blustery Roker Park on 30 October (0-3). Bowen was unimpressed with his team's showing, accusing his players of showing a lack of effort. Harry Walden was so put out by the criticism that he submitted a transfer request, only to withdraw it later after calming down.

Bowen knew he needed more quality. But naturally, he had to sell first in order to buy. So, Ken Leek was sold to Fourth Division strugglers Bradford City for £10,000. Livesey and Leck were also transferred to Brighton for £7,000 and £6,000 respectively. Robson was the next to go, to Chelsea for £30,000. This allowed Bowen the funds to bring in the lightning fast, goalscoring right-winger Joe Broadfoot from Ipswich for £27,000 and Manchester United's Welsh international inside-forward Graham Moore for £15,000. But it was his home-grown policy which came to his aid when Aston Villa called at the County Ground on a bright but chilly 6 November. Here, Jim Hall returned from his hamstring injury with a bang – well, actually two bangs – as within ten minutes of kick-off he had a brace of goals to his name. Although Hall had to retire hurt with a recurrence of his hamstring problem, Northampton clung on to win (2-1). Northampton rose out of the relegation zone. Next up were Liverpool at Anfield. Once again class told. With Peter Thompson turning Theo Foley inside out, the deputy keeper, Coe, had to perform heroics to keep Shankly's men down to five (0-5). Town were back in bottom place. Consequently, Bowen made several changes for the visit of Spurs on 20 November. New signing Joe Broadfoot made his debut, partnered by Don Martin. Bobby Brown came in for Bobby Hunt. Even without Greaves, who was laid low with hepatitis, Spurs proved too strong for Northampton. Dave Mackay ran the show, thumping in a 35-yard drive before setting up Frank Saul for Spurs' second.

For the trip to relegation rivals Fulham on 27 November, Bowen restored Robson on the left wing for his valedictory appearance. Bowen was looking to nail the Chelsea deal. Helped considerably by an injury to Fulham's keeper, Macedo, the Cobblers won 4-2, with ex-Cottager Bobby Brown scoring a hat-trick. Fortune continued to smile on Bowen's boys when lowly Blackpool came to town a week later. Having taken a two-goal lead early in the second half, the visitors were denied a deserved last-minute equaliser because the match officials failed to see that the ball had crossed the goal line. Blackpool's furious protests were made in vain. Northampton's fortunate victory lifted them out of the relegation places.

Two weeks before Christmas, Northampton travelled to their other relegation rivals, Blackburn. It had been a wretched season for Rovers. A summer polio epidemic had resulted in the postponement of their opening games. They also lacked their former firepower. Twin strikers Andy McEvoy and John Byrom had notched over 50 league goals between them in the previous season. But depleted by injury and poor form, the pair mustered less than a quarter of that figure this time around. Their manager, 'Jolly' Jack Marshall, had little cause for mirth. With McEvoy and Byrom ruled out of the Northampton game, he was woefully short of attacking options. He was compelled to employ his powerful Welsh international centre-half, Mike England, as a makeshift centre-forward, accompanied by former Bury striker, George Jones. Marshall was also without his tricky former England midfielder, Bryan Douglas, but he had emerging England star Keith Newton at right-back and burly ex-England captain Ronnie Clayton in a defensive midfield role. Northampton had already beaten a much stronger Rovers team at Ewood Park in the League Cup in September. They were confident of another away victory. But Blackburn's recent home form had belied their lowly position. Despite suffering three consecutive away defeats they had thumped Newcastle (4-2) and Nottingham Forest (5-0) in their previous two home games. On a damp, drab December afternoon Blackburn gave Northampton one hell of a hiding. Helped by Jones' hat-trick, Blackburn won 6-1, allowing them to leapfrog over their visitors and rise two places.

New £15,000 signing Graham Moore was brought in for the fiery, festive home fixture with Tommy Docherty's Chelsea. Although Moore scored on his debut, his 79th-minute leveller proved to be in vain as George Graham stole the points five minutes later (2-3). In the return match at Stamford Bridge, a day later, ex-Cobbler Tommy Robson was chosen to replace Bobby Tambling, whose father had died suddenly. While Robson did not make much impact against his former team-mates, Barry Bridges did. His 83rd-minute back-header, from Venables' cross, sealed the game (0-1). Northampton did better in their New Year game at Bramall Lane. Despite going behind to a hotly-disputed Mick Jones goal, the Cobblers battled to earn a deserved point through goals by Martin and Lines (2-2). The Blackburn drubbing was avenged a week later, although it was a close-run thing (2-1). West Ham were then held at a snowy Upton Park (1-1) but Bowen saw this as a point lost after his side's first-half dominance.

Once again a slip quickly became a slide. After Nottingham Forest ended Northampton's interest in the FA Cup (1-2), Bowen was forced to endure three painful defeats on the spin. Helped by Branston's early error, Everton enjoyed a comfortable 2-0 victory at the County Ground. Then, back on the road, both Manchester United and Stoke inflicted 6-2 defeats upon reeling Town. Bowen and his coaching assistant, Joe Payne, had prepared for the Old Trafford fixture by watching the Reds beat Benfica 1-0 in the European Cup quarter-final home leg. A fat lot of good it did them for

Busby's team proceeded to murder the Cobblers. United were two up within ten minutes and 4-1 up after only half an hour. Although Northampton battled to restore a semblance of pride, they could not prevent Charlton rifling in three goals. Around 35,000 United fans enjoyed the carnage. Northampton's only consolation was that Benfica suffered greater indignity in the return leg as *El Beatle*, George Best, ran amok in Lisbon, scoring twice in an unforgettable 5-1 triumph.

But whereas Manchester United had simply outclassed Northampton, Bowen's boys capitulated weakly against unremarkable Stoke. Their cause wasn't helped when John Ritchie battered Coe, the goalie, in scoring a controversial first-minute opener. Coe and Northampton struggled to recover while Ritchie, a former Kettering centre-forward, went on to record a hat-trick.

Despite the many heavy hits Northampton took, they were a resilient, competitive bunch. For the visit of Newcastle on a bright, blustery 19 February, Bryan Harvey was recalled, as were Branston and Foley in place of Carr and Cockcroft. Just 14,500 fans attended, around 800 fewer than the average gate in their promotion season. However, Martin gave the Cobblers the perfect start, heading in Broadfoot's free kick after 15 minutes. Moore doubled the lead in the 32nd minute when he pounced upon Brown's deflected shot. Nine minutes after the break, Martin sealed victory when he volleyed in Brown's cross. Jim Iley's 90th-minute goal for the visitors was of no consolation. With Blackburn losing 3-1 at Villa and Fulham losing at Spurs, this had been Northampton's day. They had a four-point lead over Blackburn and a five-point advantage over Fulham. There was still much to fight for.

On the following Saturday at a swampy Hawthorns, Martin was once again on target. Despite being under the cosh for most the game, Northampton had a gilt-edged opportunity to steal both points. Frustratingly, Brown's miscued shot slithered wide of an open goal (1-1). He paid for that error with his place. In the next week, Bowen spent the remaining £26,000 of his survival fund on George Hudson, the high-scoring former Coventry, Peterborough and Accrington centre-forward.

'Teddy boy' George Hudson had scored 136 goals in 222 league games. He wasn't over the moon about the transfer, though. He was settled in his club house at Coventry and was worried about where he would live if he moved on. He tried to remonstrate with the Sky Blues' manager, Jimmy Hill, but to no avail. It was a done deal. The Coventry fans were equally upset about his move. Bowen was cock-a-hoop though, believing that Hudson's goals would keep Northampton up. Bowen's confidence rubbed off on the home fans; 21,548 poured into the County Ground on a sunny Saturday 5 March to watch Hudson make his debut against Leeds. He didn't disappoint. After only 11 minutes he crossed sharply for Lines to power a header past Sprake and two minutes later he scored a scintillating individual goal, lifting the ball delicately over Jack Charlton before running around him and blasting in a ferocious volley from just inside the box. Although Mike O'Grady promptly reduced the deficit, Northampton defended stubbornly to record a notable victory. That resilience was on show a week later, too, as John Kurila scored an 89th-minute goal to hold visiting Nottingham Forest to a 3-3 draw.

However, Bowen was furious with his team after a lame 1-3 defeat at Hillsborough on 19 March. According to author Mark Beesley, Broadfoot's commitment was called into question. This was a team that relied upon unstinting, sweated labour. Maximum effort was demanded of everyone. Mark Beesley wrote that Joe reacted to Bowen's reproach by replying, 'I can't help it … a leopard can't change its spots.' As a result of that ill-advised remark, Broadfoot was promptly sidelined. However, Bowen did relent and selected Broadfoot for the dogfight with Fulham. But Broadfoot failed to arrive on time. He tried to explain that his car had broken down but Bowen wasn't listening. Broadfoot was never selected again and left for Millwall in the summer.

After Bowen's irate outburst at Sheffield, Northampton embarked on an unbeaten five-game run. They were unlucky not to beat neighbouring Leicester in the County Ground snow after hitting the woodwork three times (2-2), but recovered from a half-time deficit to beat Villa (2-1) in a Birmingham blizzard. Champions-elect, Liverpool, were held to a 0-0 home draw on 9 April, and thanks to Don Martin's 49th-minute goal, Stoke were beaten 1-0 three days later. George Hudson's immaculate chip gave Northampton a 35th-minute lead at White Hart Lane but Jimmy Greaves' late penalty denied them both points. That pleasing run seemed to have set them up well for their relegation decider with Fulham on 23 April 1966.

With relatives living in Northampton, I was kept regularly in touch with the Cobblers' fortunes. I still have many of the local press cuttings they sent me, although I have mislaid almost all of the programmes. The only surviving one dates from November 1960, when Hastings United played at the County Ground in the first round proper of the FA Cup. Northampton won 2-1, with Hastings' goal scored by Keith Smith, brother of Bobby. Examining the programme's adverts, there is little to suggest that the swinging sixties had arrived. They seemed more reflective of 'the Archers' than 'Mad Men'. Tomkins of St Andrew's Road promised us that their seeds came 'fresh from our own farms'. Suitably reassured, I turned to Ennals & Castell Ltd of Weston Street, who boasted they were the leading local Massey-Ferguson distributors. Whatton's of Hartwell reckoned it was *the* place for wood – 'always a home winner', they added excruciatingly. And there was the Cromwell old-world garden restaurant where one could 'dine, wine and relax' – hardly distinctive selling points for a restaurant. Almost in desperation, the proprietor added 'It's new! It's old! It's unique! It's beautiful!' In the early sixties, it seemed as if a typical Northampton fan was probably a son or daughter of the soil, good with their hands, familiar with farm machinery, but reticent about going out; so much for 'Twist and Shout', then.

I have often found the football passions of others infectious. It was no different with my Northampton-based relatives. Slowly but surely I ingested the Northampton bug, so much so that the team's perilous situation held my attention as the crucial Fulham match drew closer. Eventually, I decided I would make a rare trip north and take in the game. Supplementing my memory with scrapbook remnants and an old diary entry, this is what I recall.

Around 2pm on that thinly-clouded, mild spring afternoon, my relatives and I joined the throng of 24,500 supporters filing their way towards the County Ground. At least the slow walk helped deal with the mounting 'butterflies'. For once squeezed inside the small ground, where there was no room to move, the tension coiled constrictively. The home supporters became increasingly pensive; their conversations seeming more fractured. Attempts at laughter seemed contrived and exaggerated. The smokers drew heavily on their fags. Others chewed meditatively. Some flicked inattentively through their programmes. Everyone was impatient for the game to start. Eventually the teams emerged to a full-throated roar. Each of the players sprinted towards their respective ends, relieved, no doubt, to dissipate their strained nerves after the stifling incubation of the dressing room.

After their thumping home defeat by Leicester, Fulham manager Vic Buckingham dropped Les Barrett, moved Leggat back to the left-wing and recalled midfield maestro Johnny Haynes, who had recovered from a calf injury. Despite his lack of goals, Allan Clarke, Fulham's recent signing from Walsall, continued to lead the line. Northampton were unchanged with Mackin continuing to deputise for Foley at right-back. The captains tossed for choice of ends. Northampton began by attacking the Hotel End.

Before kick-off on Saturday 23 April the bottom of the First Division table was:

	Played	Won	Drawn	Lost	For	Against	Points
17 Sunderland	39	13	7	19	47	69	33
18 Aston Villa	38	13	6	19	63	72	32
19 Sheffield Wed.	36	12	7	17	50	58	31
20 Northampton	39	9	13	17	51	84	31
21 Fulham	38	12	5	21	59	80	29
22 Blackburn	36	7	4	25	51	77	18

Northampton grasped the initiative immediately. They swarmed forward with furious energy. With only a few minutes gone, Moore thumped a header against the bar. Walden's follow-up shot was blocked on the line. The swaying crowd oohed and aahed. Fulham were all at sea, swamped by a surging claret tide. The foraging Cobblers seized upon each of the visitors' desperate clearances as if they were an excited pack of retrievers in eager pursuit of a thrown stick. Their midfielders poured forward in support of their strikers. Fulham reeled backwards. With the midfield conceded, Joe Kiernan picked up the ball and ran and ran right into the heart of the Fulham defence. The Cottagers backed off – too much, it seemed. They allowed the clever playmaker the time and space to line up a shot. Kiernan grabbed the opportunity. The ball sped goalwards. McClelland could only parry his stinging effort. The ball ran loose. In a flash, Hudson pounced on the spill and prodded Northampton into the lead. A cataclysmic roar erupted, fuelled as much by pent-up anxiety as ecstatic delight. Hudson soaked up the adulation, although Kiernan deserved the credit. 'Bowen was right,' growled an already hoarse guy next to me. 'Hudson will save our season.' But there was a long way to go. Only 13 minutes had passed.

To our great dismay, the lead lasted just six minutes. Oddly, Hudson's goal seemed to calm Fulham's nerves as much as Northampton's. The visitors began to play their football neatly. The siege subsided. Having more room and composure to press forward, Fulham's left-back, Brian Nichols, pushed up. Midfielders Mark Pearson and Bobby Robson suddenly found room for a swift exchange of passes close to goal. Robson was left with a clear sight of the target. He did not hesitate, placing his shot carefully inside Coe's left-hand post. The Northampton keeper hadn't a chance. Only the stumbling cheers of the Fulham supporters disturbed the glum silence that descended upon the Hotel End. Robson's joy was short-lived, though. Twelve minutes later, he misplaced his clearing header from Walden's cross. It found the unmarked Kiernan lurking outside the visitors' penalty area. Kiernan's quickly-despatched shot fizzed past

McClelland and Northampton were back in front. The County Ground once again rocked and roared with incandescent glee.

Northampton went for the kill. Fulham were placed under renewed pressure. Just before the break, reserve right-back John Mackin floated a free kick into the Fulham box. There seemed to be some confusion as the ball cleared McClelland and dropped into the net. But the excited roar was stifled almost instantly. International referee Jack Taylor had awarded a free kick. There had been a prior infringement, apparently. This was the cue for much disgruntled muttering. Nevertheless, the surrounding home fans seemed content that their side had their noses in front. Their job was half done.

Fifteen minutes after the break came the moment which probably sealed Northampton's fate. Following a sharp breakaway, Hudson was put in on goal. He shot immediately but straight at the Fulham keeper. With Hudson's shot too hot to handle, McClelland pushed the ball up into the air. Spinning wildly, the ball looped back over the goalie's head and towards the open goal. Only with a frantic clawing motion did McClelland push the ball away – but too late, surely? It looked as if it had already crossed the line. Hudson appealed. So did Kiernan, but to no avail. Referee Taylor, having been caught out by the speed of Northampton's break, was well out of position. He could not confirm that a goal had been scored. Neither could his linesman, who had slipped at the critical moment. Play continued. It seemed that Northampton had been denied cruelly. 'I'll tell you what, Taylor,' shouted someone in front of me, 'why don't you stick to your bleeding chops because all yer doin' here is breaking our bleeding hearts.' Taylor was a butcher by trade.

Three minutes later, Fulham jumped jail. George Cohen raced down the right flank and centred crisply for Earle to turn his low cross past Coe. The home fans were incensed. Bellicose boos and screeching whistles poured forth. 'F***ing robbed!' hissed my neighbour. 'Yer bleeding cheats!' But Northampton had only themselves to blame. After the break they had sat back, attempting to hold on to what they had. It was a catastrophic tactical error. After conceding so much space in midfield they allowed the momentum to pass to the visitors. In truth, Fulham could and should have levelled before Earle's 65th-minute equaliser. Leggat was particularly culpable, having wasted several presentable chances.

Revived by Earle's equaliser, Fulham attacked with increasing conviction. Northampton had to defend obstinately. A draw was not a disastrous result as they still held a two-point lead over Fulham, despite their London rivals having a game in hand. But with three minutes remaining, Leggat streaked down the left flank and floated over a centre for Earle to place his header wide of Coe from ten yards. In the Hotel End, heads sunk and shoulders slumped but out on the pitch Northampton reacted in the only way possible. They pushed everyone forward, bar their keeper. This left them hopelessly unguarded at the back. In the final minute Haynes, positioned deep inside his own half, brought the ball calmly under control. He seemed oblivious to the battle raging around him. Did anything faze this guy? Spotting Earle in acres of space, he clipped an immaculate pass into the winger's path. Earle was 60 yards from goal, unmarked, with no one in front of him except Coe. Taking Haynes' pass smoothly in his stride, off he galloped. There was no chance of anyone catching him. The horribly exposed Coe advanced rapidly but Earle was too composed, too confident to be disconcerted by this. In one sinuous movement he waltzed around the stricken custodian and planted the ball into the empty net for the winning goal and his hat-trick.

The now silent Hotel End could only look on in despair. Earle wheeled away to receive the congratulations of his exultant team-mates. The deflated home fans began to shuffle towards the exits. They had no answer to the jeers of the jubilant Fulham contingent. 'Goin' down, goin' down, goin' down …', the away fans chanted, swarming all over the pitch at the final whistle. Underdog had devoured underdog. Fulham were out of the relegation zone, having leapfrogged Northampton. Now only a miracle could save Bowen's team. Fulham's smash-and-grab raid had almost certainly saved their bacon and cooked Northampton's goose.

Although Bowen's boys beat Sunderland two days later, bravely recovering from a first half deficit (2-1), they needed to win their final game at sunny Blackpool and hope that other results went their way. They were disappointed on both counts. Alan Ball ran them ragged at Bloomfield Road. The Cobblers limped to a three-goal defeat (0-3). Villa's 3-0 home victory over Arsenal confirmed their fate. Northampton's pumpkin parade had begun.

Many years after, winger Barry Lines told his local paper, the *Bletchley Gazette*:

> *I was really sad that we went down so quickly but it would only have been a matter of time because we couldn't have maintained it, not without some benefactor coming in with a huge amount of money that would've signed players that kept us up. The really disappointing aspect of it was that we went back down so quickly and finished up back in the Fourth Division. The only thing, from my point of view, is that by the time we'd been*

> *up and back again, there were very few grounds in the country that I hadn't actually played on. And, of course, I had the distinction of being the first player to score for the same club in all four divisions!*

Seventeen months later, I went to the Goldstone Ground, Hove to watch Brighton take on Northampton in a Third Division game. The match was played on a bright, gusty, late September afternoon. Brighton were becalmed in the third tier while Northampton had been recently relegated from Division Two. The Cobblers had endured a dismal season in which they scored only 47 goals and mustered just 30 points. Although Hudson, Brown, Hunt and Broadfoot had left the club soon after Northampton's drop from the top flight, many of the club's First Division regulars remained for a further demotion. Even the return of the talismanic Frank Large could not prevent a further fall. Northampton's previously irrepressible momentum and mighty morale had eroded. Their method had become pocked with self-doubt, leaving the club on meagre rations. The Cobblers took as many heavy hits in the Second Division as they had done in the First, except that it became the turn of Palace (1-5), Preston (1-5), Ipswich (1-6), Hull (1-6), Portsmouth (2-4), Cardiff (2-4) and Wolves (0-4) to administer their chastisement.

On 30 September 1967 Northampton won at Brighton, by 2-0, with goals from Large and Hall, but it was a wretched game. Neither side could deal with the erratic course of the ball in the windy conditions, particularly given the Goldstone Ground's rock-like surface. The players had as much ball control as a dog with a balloon. With young Don Martin leaving for Blackburn several months later – for what was then a club record fee of £36,000 – and Jim Hall and Billy Best moving on also, it seemed as if the club had been forced to pawn their future. Bowen included former Wolves and England wing-half Ron Flowers in his side to face Brighton. Player-coach Flowers would eventually succeed Bowen as manager, but only after ex-Spurs' midfielder Tony Marchi had experienced a brief and unsuccessful period in charge. Although the Cobblers hung on to their Third Division status at the end of the '67/68 season, a year later they found themselves back in the basement. By then, their average attendance had slumped to under 7,000. To compound their woes, just six years after competing in the top flight, Northampton were forced to apply for re-election to the Football League. Not that Fulham's immediate future was much more cheery. Although Allan Clarke's 24 league goals helped Fulham retain their First Division status at the end of the 1966/67 season, the trapdoor opened one year after, and, like the Cobblers, they kept falling, ending up in Division Three by 1969.

Sadly, an unlikely triumph like Northampton's often becomes a rod with which to beat ensuing failure rather than a cause for commemorative pride. As former Wolves boss, Stan Cullis, muttered after his sacking at Molineux: 'I'd only created a yardstick that people could criticise me against.' We raise modest expectations at our peril. Given the limited resources available to Bowen, the scale and speed of his side's climb was one of the most remarkable achievements in the history of British football.

Ramsey's World Cup-winning formula

Alf Ramsey's World Cup preparations were in tatters after a disastrous 'Little World Cup' tournament held in Brazil in the summer of 1964. Brazil hammered England 5-1 in the opening game with Pele running riot. England's Johnny Byrne recalled: 'Pele had unbelievable skill but it was only when you were chasing him that you realised that he could motor like an Olympic sprinter – it was all I could do to keep pace with him – and he had the ball at his feet.' A shell-shocked Ramsey dropped five players for the turgid 1-1 draw with Portugal five days later. Meanwhile, Argentina beat Brazil 3-0. Merciless in their use of spoiling tactics, Argentina successfully subdued the brilliant Pele and his fluent team-mates. And orchestrating their game plan was an imposing 6ft 4in defender by the name of Antonio Rattin. In due course, his infamy would grace a Wembley World Cup quarter-final. Argentina became the tournament winners after beating England 1-0 in the final game. Here, in Brazil, England had been out-thought and outplayed. Ramsey realised that if his team were to beat gifted, sophisticated sides such as Brazil and Argentina, he had to adopt better tactics. If flair was dispensable, vision, organisation, discipline and commitment weren't. With the World Cup two years away he had much to ponder.

Up until the end of 1965, Ramsey had persisted with a 4-2-4 formation. It had proved largely successful against Home Tournament and European opposition, but unconvincing against the might of Brazil and Argentina. In an unattributed press cutting, Ramsey explained (probably after England's World Cup victory): 'A vital requisite for successful 4-2-4 is a pair of attacking wingers with the ability and speed to take on defenders, to get past them, take the ball to the goal line and pull it back. This always presents the biggest problem for goalkeepers. It became apparent to me that we hadn't got the wingers who could give us the service we wanted because of the way that defences had tightened up. If the winger did get past a full-back he was always confronted by another covering player. We had to think of something else.' That something else was a 4-3-3 formation, although Ramsey's World Cup-winning version was more of a 4-1-3-2 model with

Nobby Stiles operating as a holding midfielder. He denied that Argentina's performance in 1964 had prompted his thinking, stating: 'The Argentines usually played with at least five, and sometimes more, players crowding the middle of the field. Their object seemed mainly to avoid defeat. Mine has always been to win.'

His victorious game plan did not emerge as a 'Year Zero', 'Damascus-like' brainwave. The Brazilians had flirted with his tactical ploy in winning the 1958 World Cup in Sweden. But Ramsey first realised its winning potential after successfully experimenting with the system in a practice match between the England seniors and his under 23 side in June 1965. Unbeknown to the under 23s, Ramsey instructed the seniors to adopt the 4-3-3 formation, while their juniors were told to play their natural game. The upshot was that the senior midfield trio of Bryan Douglas (Blackburn), Johnny Byrne (West Ham) and George Eastham (Arsenal) overran the youngsters. The under 23s were bewildered as to how they might counter their opponents' total control. Nevertheless, Ramsey proceeded cautiously. During the 1965 summer tour, he continued to select two orthodox wingers – Terry Paine (Southampton) and Derek Temple (Everton) against West Germany (won 1-0), and Paine and John Connelly (Manchester United) against Sweden (won 2-1). England's subsequent poor performances against Wales (0-0), Northern Ireland (won 2-1) and Austria (lost 1-2) forced a more radical change.

If the Battle of Waterloo was won on the playing fields of Eton then England's World Cup victory was rehearsed on a playing field of Madrid. On 8 December 1965, England met the current holders of the European Nations Cup, Spain, in a friendly at Real Madrid's Bernabeu Stadium. It was a bitterly cold evening. With the Bernabeu's frosty surface glistening in the glare of the floodlights, only 25,000 chilled souls could be enticed from their warm homes. They were totally unprepared for what they saw.

In Madrid, Ramsey decided to go for broke. He told an unnamed reporter, 'The numbers my men will wear are nothing more than a means of identifying them for the spectators.' Ramsey's back four of George Cohen (Fulham), Jack Charlton (Leeds), Bobby Moore (West Ham) and Ray Wilson (Everton) seemed reassuringly tight. Nobby Stiles (Manchester United) sat in front of them, sealing off Spanish routes to goal and providing a link between defence and attack. Meanwhile, his midfield, comprising George Eastham (Arsenal), Bobby Charlton (Manchester United) and Alan Ball (Blackpool) combined creativity with powerful probing. The forwards – Joe Baker (Arsenal) and Roger Hunt (Liverpool) – also defended from the front, continually hounding and harrying when possession was lost, forcing the Spanish defenders into a succession of distributional errors.

The Spanish full-backs were thrown by the absence of wingers to mark. Consequently, they were lured into uncertain areas, causing their defence to lose its shape. The emerging gaps on the flanks were then ruthlessly exploited by England's fast, overlapping full-backs. Meanwhile, Alan Ball ran here, there and everywhere, foraging in advanced positions, taking on the perplexed Spanish defenders, pulling them all over the place and creating space for others to plunder. Here, he was giving notice of his remarkable show of stamina and skill that would grace the latter stages of the World Cup Final. As early as the eighth minute, Ray Wilson crossed to the far post for Joe Baker to nip in and nod the ball past the Spanish keeper, Iribar, one of five survivors from the 1964 European Nations Cup Final team. Even when an injury to Baker forced a reshuffle, with Hunter replacing Bobby Charlton in midfield, there was no disturbance to England's devastating fluency. The Spaniards were left chasing phantoms. Just before the hour, Roger Hunt emphasised England's total superiority by scoring their second goal, having benefited from some sharp interplay between the liberated Moore and the fleet-footed Cohen.

The Spanish manager said afterwards: 'England were phenomenal, far superior in the experiment and their players.' And yet after this resounding endorsement, Ramsey still clung on to his wingers – Connelly, Paine and Ian Callaghan (Liverpool) played one game each in the three turgid World Cup group games. England's performance against Argentina in the quarter-finals was unimpressive also. Had it not been for Antonio Rattin's self-destructive behaviour, Argentina might have won. In the end Ramsey was indebted to Ron Greenwood's inventive 'near post' drills as Geoff Hurst's flicked header, from Martin Peters' pinpoint cross, gave England a narrow victory against their depleted South American opponents. It wasn't until the semi-final against Portugal that England really displayed the proficiency they had shown in Madrid. The rest, as we all know, is history. Certainly, England benefited substantially from being the host nation and in playing all of their games at Wembley, but this was still a victory against the odds. There were stronger nations participating in this tournament. Notwithstanding the world class credentials of Bobby Charlton, Gordon Banks and Bobby Moore, as at Ipswich, Ramsey had used an enterprising tactical plan to put his side ahead of opponents with greater natural talents.

Jimmy Greaves made these comments in his book, *The Sixties Revisited*:

> *England's success in the World Cup spawned an army of imitators and suddenly clubs were playing the 4-3-3*

> *way with the emphasis heavily upon defence. I speak from painful memory when I say that it made life harder for goalscorers. Penalty areas became as packed as Piccadilly in the rush hour and goals, the lifeblood of the game, were hard to come by … New phrases were starting to creep into the language of the game: work rate; the overlap; tackling back; running off the ball; centre-backs; sweepers; midfield anchormen … The coaches were in charge and their tactics started to squeeze the goals out of football just as I had seen in my brief spell in Italy.*

In non-league football, the new defensive tactics were seized upon as a means of redressing inequalities of strength. Defensive shields emerged everywhere, often proving sufficiently robust to subdue the less talented forwards competing at this level. Sterile stalemates became commonplace, leeching the excitement from the non-league game, and accelerating the decline in attendances which, at league level, had prospered in the immediate aftermath of England's World Cup success.

THE 1966/67 SEASON

Wisbech Town v Hastings United

'Release Me'
29 April 1967

Question: 'What do the following have in common – Hastings United, the 1996 BBC drama *Our Friends in the North*, alleged large-scale corruption in the Metropolitan Police force and the *Oz* underground magazine obscenity trial in 1971?

Answer: Mr James Humphreys.

Hastings United Through Time author, Roger Sinden, recalled: '[In 1965] the new chairman of United was James Humphreys, whose major passion was greyhound racing at a time when there were moves afoot to bring racing to Hastings. He had joined the board in June 1965 and was chairman by mid-season.'

It was understandable that Jim Humphreys should have been received so cordially by the club. Humphreys seemed a personable chap, charming, even, and more importantly he had a viable plan for reviving Hastings United's fortunes: dog racing. He planned to use the Pilot Field's perimeter space, once used by the town's former speedway team, as a dog track. The club were really hard-up. Humphreys seemed to be a successful businessman. He wasn't short of cash, it seemed, having an impressive spread at nearby Northiam. He was experienced in the gambling business. It looked as if a local dog track would benefit himself, the club and, maybe, the town, too. According to those closely connected with the club, nothing was known about the shadier aspects of Mr Humphreys' life.

As for the football team, former Orient centre-half, Sid Bishop, replaced Ted Ballard as Hastings boss also retaining a playing role. But according to Ken Ballard, Ted's son, Sid was not suited to management although he was still a good player. Ken, who played under Sid, thought that the former Orient stopper wasn't disciplined enough, leaving the players too much to their own devices. Certainly, Sid's early results were erratic. But

Humphreys' arrival heralded major changes. In came a string of pedigree performers, including former Chelsea, Spurs, Brighton and England centre-forward Bobby Smith and Welsh under 23 striker, Jim Ryan. With these reinforcements Hastings were fired into life, powering their way up the Southern League First Division after recording a string of devastating victories against Ramsgate (6-0), Deal (9-0), Gloucester (6-2) and Kettering (7-3). It seemed too good to be true. And, sadly, it was because James or Jimmy Humphreys had 'history'. Bit by little bit his 'history' was revealed.

In 1996, Colin Wills of the *Sunday Mirror* wrote an article at the launch of the TV serial *Our Friends in the North*. He wrote: 'BEHIND the sex and sleaze of TV's newest crime blockbuster lies a real-life story of police corruption. The drama served up in *Our Friends in the North* paints a glamorous picture of Soho in the Sixties. But millions of viewers will be unaware that it is based on true accounts of the blackest period in police history when hundreds of Britain's policemen were on the payrolls of gangsters. The parallels between the TV characters and real people are astoundingly close. Pornographer, Bennie Barratt, played by Malcolm McDowell, is drawn from Jimmy Humphreys, the Mr Big in Soho at the time. The "crusading cop", Roy Johnson, is the double of Frank Williamson, a senior police officer drafted in by then-Home Secretary, Jim Callaghan, to clean up Scotland Yard.' Wills said that Humphreys described the mood of the TV drama as 'very accurate'.

Coincidentally, in 1971, the editors of a 'hippie' magazine, *Oz*, were prosecuted under the obscene publication laws for producing a 'School Kids issue'. Among the magazine's features was a comic strip of an unusually libidinous Rupert Bear. A public outcry, led by John Lennon and a young John Birt, greeted the jail sentences meted out to *Oz*'s Richard Neville, Felix Dennis and Jim Anderson. The convictions were subsequently overturned on appeal, but this was only after Lord Chief Justice Widgery had apparently conducted some investigations of his own. Allegedly, he had sent his clerk to Soho to buy £20 worth of the hardest pornographic material he could find on open sale. Apparently, the contents of the offending *Oz* magazine paled by comparison. It was said that Widgery then realised that the *Oz* prosecutions were indefensibly discriminative.

According to Alan Travis, in his *Guardian* article of 13 November 1999, the collapse of the *Oz* trial prompted the new Home Secretary, Reginald Maudling, to examine why the Metropolitan Police Obscene Publications Squad had targeted *Oz* when there was much more lurid material on open sale. Maudling had become concerned at being seen to discriminate against the 'alternative society', particularly since the Obscene Publications Squad had targeted other underground magazines, also – *International Times* and *Frendz*. Maudling was not at all reassured by the answers he received from DCI George Fenwick, the head of the 'dirty' squad. To add to his concerns, Lord Longford's enquiry into pornography revealed that several porn merchants were allegedly bribing police officers. But Maudling's subsequent investigations came up against a wall of silence. According to Travis, in February 1972, 'Flying Squad' boss, Commander Kenneth Drury, was found to have spent a two-week holiday in Cyprus with James Humphreys. Humphreys was allegedly one of seven 'porn barons' named in Lord Longford's report. Drury attempted to excuse himself by claiming he had been looking for Ronnie Biggs, the escaped train robber. Not hot on geography, then.

Within weeks of this exposure, Maudling appointed Robert 'Mr Clean' Mark as the new commissioner of the Metropolitan Police Force. The hawk-featured Mark was also known as the 'Manchester Martinet' and the 'Lone Ranger from Leicester'. He was a fierce moral warrior. Despite Drury's exposure, Mark made little headway in uncovering the other culprits caught up in the supposed web of corruption.

Then, in April 1974, came a breakthrough. Jimmy Humphries was convicted of grievous bodily harm. His victim was a man who had allegedly been having an affair with his wife. In an article appearing in the *Independent* on 4 July 1994, Andrew Weir wrote:

> *On a promise of help with getting an early release, Humphreys started to amaze investigating detectives with his memory, supported by a diary of payments and meetings with detectives. A Sixties colleague mused over why Jimmy should turn grass, even if it was against policemen. 'The trouble with Jimmy was he had a pathological fear of going to jail. And in this business that's something of a liability.' In trials between November 1976 and July 1977 Humphreys and others gave evidence that led to 13 Yard detectives, two of them ex-commanders, being jailed for a total of more than 90 years. Some were sacked after internal tribunals. Many more were asked to retire or were invalided out.*

Humphreys' evidence was vital in the success of Robert Mark's clean-up campaign. Not renowned for his stand-up turns, Mark remarked, 'A good police force is one that catches more crooks than it employs.' He added: 'The real fear of pornographers was not of the courts but of harassment, either by strong-armed men seeking protection money or by the police doing, in effect, the same thing.'

Alwyn W. Turner, author of the modern history book *'Crisis? What Crisis?' Britain in the 1970s*, observed: '*The Sweeney* might show Flying Squad officers mixing with the criminal classes, but there was nothing in the TV series to indicate that, for example, James Humphreys, a leading Soho porn baron, "was considered a suitable guest to be invited to the annual dinner of the Flying Squad in the autumn of 1970".' Turner also alleged that a senior Met police officer of the time had offered 'to write for the spanking magazine *Janus*'. Talk about spare the rod and spoil the force.

For all his charms, 'Jim' Humphreys, as he was known at Hastings United, was strong-minded and ambitious. Quester, the *Hastings Observer*'s football correspondent, wrote after Humphreys' election as club chairman: 'That is the man at the helm of United. And we will know he's there, believe me.' Although Humphreys' overriding ambition was to establish dog racing locally he did not neglect the football club. It is possible that his injection of wealth helped bankroll the signing of Bobby Smith in October 1965.

Smith signed a two-year contract with a wage reputed to be £65 a week. Actually, it was considerably less than that – probably under £40 per week – but this was still a massive outlay for a small non-league club, equating to an annual wage now worth around £60,000. Although Smith later claimed that the club reneged on a promise to pay him a £1,000 signing-on fee, he seemed initially happy with the deal, stating that he was looking for a club near to his Brighton home. He also said he was pleased to be playing alongside Hastings' player-manager, Sid Bishop, who was described as an 'old friend from his London footballing days'. Smith explained: 'I'm not really match fit because I haven't been able to train for several weeks but it won't take me many days to get in condition again. I'm a big man and I have to watch what I eat and so on but too much has been made of this overweight business. That was not really what the business at Brighton was all about.'

Roger Sinden wrote: 'None of the Hastings team had met Smith before, let alone trained with him, and the speculation grew in the dressing room as to whether he would turn up. [Before his first game at Ashford, Kent] there were traffic jams in the town, contributing to Smith's delayed arrival, and the average gate of 650 was increased to 2,875. [Hastings midfielder] Bela Olah recalls that Smith sauntered into the dressing room eventually, with his football boots wrapped in newspaper under his arm. After a brief introduction Smith proposed tactics to Olah. Smith suggested that if there was a cross from the wing, it should not be at him but placed three or four feet in advance for him to run on to.' Apparently Bela Olah questioned whether Smith would be able to reach such a cross – perhaps indelicately, given concerns about Smith's weight and fitness – but Smith assured him that this would be fine as long as 'it wasn't hit too hard'. According to Roger Sinden, 'Bela found Bobby Smith a down-to-earth person, with no airs and graces … Smith was modestly disarming [about his previous international successes] saying all of that was in the past … Bela was quick to scotch the rumours about Bobby Smith's off-the-field drinking and said that he never saw any evidence of this. His interest in betting is well evidenced [though] … and [once] Sid Bishop had to drag Smith out of the [betting] shop to make sure that he started the game on time.'

Smith started well, scoring with a header in his debut game against Ashford and then netting two goals with nonchalant ease in his first home match against Dover. But the business strategy did not go to plan. Cecil Catt, then the Hastings United chairman, expected a crowd of between 4,000 and 5,000 to greet Smith's first appearance at the Pilot Field, whereas on a damp, grey afternoon only 3,223 turned up, no more than for a local derby with Tonbridge. Thereafter, Smith's appearances became increasingly fitful. He excused his absence on health grounds. Some claims seemed genuine, but according to the club, others were not. Crowds – home and away – lost patience with him. So did the Hastings management. There were three suspensions – one by the club and two by the FA. These were usually followed by frank, heart-to-heart discussions between the player and the club, leading to new but short-lived resolutions. In May 1966, the club thought they had gone far enough and decided to sack Smith only for the Southern League to uphold his subsequent appeal.

Hastings narrowly failed to achieve promotion at the end of the 1965/66 season. Although they scored over 100 league goals they conceded almost 60. Bishop resigned, joining Guildford City as a player only. He remarked much later, 'The wrong type of people were running the club [at Hastings] and I wasn't at all happy there.' He was replaced by former Watford, Fulham and Liverpool keeper Dave Underwood. Although Underwood had a reputation as being a 'jack the lad', his team played with greater discipline than under Bishop. Liam Brady's elder brother, Ray – a Rolls-Royce centre-back at this level – performed superbly in a tightly-organised defence, while Underwood's former Watford colleague, Tony Gregory, an FA Cup finalist with Luton in 1959, helped provide the necessary punch up front. Despite an embarrassing FA Cup defeat at Horsham, Hastings pushed themselves into the promotion places during the autumn and remained there all season, losing just five times.

Hastings seemed to be a happier side under Underwood. Much of that can be attributed to Underwood's breezy management. Ricky George played at Oxford, Hastings and Barnet before becoming an FA Cup hero at Hereford in 1972. He told Roger Sinden that 'Dave had a face like an old-time prize fighter; a broken nose, swollen lips. He also talked with a lisp. I was always notoriously late for games and I remember one Sunday we were playing the inmates of Ford Open Prison and Dave told me the kick-off was two o'clock. At five to two on the dot I rushed in breathlessly to find an empty dressing room. About a quarter of an hour later, big Dave strolled in with the rest of the players, grinning fit to burst: "Whoopth-a-daithy," he says, "I've thuthed you out Ricky, alwayth late. Kick-off'th at free." I loved the man, I truly did.' Underwood became club chairman at Barnet between 1977 and 1982. In his time at Underhill he signed Jimmy Greaves, who later thanked him for helping him in his struggle with alcoholism.

Despite enjoying success on the field during the 1966/67 season, Dave Underwood had to contend with growing cash shortages. After the comparatively lavish expenditure of the previous season, money was once again in short supply. Adult admission prices were raised to four shillings, forcing Humphreys to justify the decision in the local press. In November, it was announced that all of the players had been put on the transfer list. Two directors resigned and the club secretary was sacked. Thousands of begging letters were sent to local businesses. Then, leading goalscorer Jim Ryan was sold to Exeter City in January 1967 for a fee 'believed to be substantially less than the £1,000' originally quoted. In April 1967, another director, Ted Ive, resigned, insisting that the club's debts of £6,000 were unsustainable. He claimed the club was 'not ready for Premier Southern League football and that it needed to take drastic action to stop the financial drift'.

Underwood was not free of the Smith headache, either. In January 1967, San Francisco offered Smith $12,000 per year – over £80 per week – to play soccer with them, also dangling a $2,000 signing-on fee. Smith announced he was 'keen for a fresh start'. He was quoted in the national press as saying: 'I would be only too happy to put English football well and truly behind me. I have had enough.' He didn't discuss the offer with Underwood first, though, prompting his manager to declare angrily: 'Smith has been very quick to speak to the national press but though I have sent telegrams galore I have heard nothing from him and I am disgusted with the whole business.' As it happened, the US deal did not go through. Smith also expressed interest in managing Cheshunt FC after his former Spurs team-mate, Terry Medwin, left the job. But nothing came of that, either. Eventually, Smith was sacked by Hastings for failing once again to turn up for training. This time the Southern League did not uphold his appeal. So, in March 1967, Smith's chequered 17-month spell with Hastings came to a close. Smith made 34 starts in all competitions, scoring 16 goals. Despite his excessive weight, he was still a formidable footballer – too talented for second-tier Southern League football.

Like all good managers, Dave Underwood used his networks well. Although the club were struggling financially, he was allowed to bring in Dunstable centre-forward Bill Meadows, a former team-mate. Meadows had been a junior at Arsenal before spending several years at languishing Clacton. But at Dunstable he proved to be an excellent goal poacher. On first sight, he looked ungainly. He ran with a stiff-legged gait. And yet he was deadly in front of goal. During that run-in, he scored 14 league goals at almost a goal a game. Like Ricky George, Meadows was destined for greater things. Both played leading roles in Hereford's FA Cup run of 1971/72, which included a staggering defeat of First Division Newcastle United.

On 29 April 1967, Hastings travelled to Wisbech Town. Dad and I went with them. As it happened, we had resumed our football partnership just in time to bid a joint farewell to Southern League football. How fitting it was that Wisbech should be our opponents, for the Fenmen had been the visitors at my first game at the Pilot Field almost seven years before. Then, it was Dad who took me. In no time at all, I would begin taking him. In this interlude we went as a pair. This game would mark my release from Hastings – not only from the club but the town also, as first university and then work would take me to the opposite end of the country. I did not know this then, but this was almost a valedictory journey.

It was a glorious spring day of dozing warmth. There was just a whisper of a breeze to caress away all cares, inducing a state of somnolent calm. I'm not just talking about myself here. Looking around the Brentwood service station, our companions' heads appeared to be lolling, also. The driver must have got it bad because he drove like a snail on Mogadon. We were hopelessly late by the time we reached Cambridge. There, three players clambered out into a taxi and shot off across the Fens, forgetting that their kit was in the coach's boot. That torpid day certainly dulled our senses. Not that this brief flurry of activity injected any urgency into our lifeless driver. He continued as before, progressing at a funereal pace along the straight Fenland roads. It was the first time I had been as far east as this. The prairie-sized fields of black, silty soil stretched out for mile after mile, interrupted only by regimented lines of trees and sludgy, algaefied dykes. The sun dazzled in a huge cloudless sky while the horizon shimmered like a mirage, its haziness fed by the languidly drifting smoke from the smouldering field fires.

We reached Wisbech's ground at around 3.30. But the game had not started. It couldn't. The Hastings team had no kit. The local supporters greeted our entrance with a weary jeer. They seemed more bored than angry. One local fan proceeded to list all the clubs that had arrived late previously. It was a lengthy record. The drawn-out, dreamy drive had helped strip away any sense of atmosphere. The first half panned out accordingly – a scrappy, lethargic midfield stroll with a few half-hearted fouls and no end product.

After the interval Hastings showed greater appetite and verve and started probing the home defence. But it took a highly controversial refereeing decision to spur this dull contest into life. Wisbech's left-back had sustained what appeared to be a nasty ankle injury and proceeded to limp off the field midway inside his own half. At that very moment, Hastings defender Keith Rutter punted the ball towards Bill Meadows, who was positioned just inside the Wisbech half. The home defenders had spotted Rutter's intention and duly pushed up to catch Meadows offside. Once in possession, Meadows dawdled on the ball, expecting the referee's whistle to sound. But upon hearing our frantic calls to make for goal, he twigged. Even Bill was too quick for his markers when given a ten-yard start. Moreover, he was at his predatory best in one-to-one situations. Meadows easily rounded ex-Peterborough keeper Jack Walls and slammed the ball home.

Then, all hell broke loose. The former Birmingham forward, 'Bunny' Larkin, led the charge, almost going head-to-head with the referee, demanding that he rule out the goal. The referee remonstrated that he had not given the home left-back permission to leave the field. This meant he had played Meadows onside. Larkin was not appeased. His incensed tirade resulted in a booking. It might well have been worse. Larkin had acquired a reputation as a 'stormy petrel'. Once, at St Andrew's, he had been involved in a spectacular set-to with Tony Nicholas, then of Chelsea. It was clear that the intervening years had not dimmed his fire. The game degenerated into a squally spat, littered with crunching tackles and petulant abuse. The mood was hardly improved when Wisbech's left-winger, Spelman, was denied a blistering equaliser 16 minutes from time. It wasn't clear what the infringement was. In a fizzing, feisty finale only desperate goal line clearances from Ray Brady and Keith Rutter kept Hastings' lead intact. While the Hastings players hugged one another excitedly at the final whistle, believing that promotion was almost in their grasp, their opponents trudged off grumpily. This would be Jesse Pye's last season in charge. Over the previous decade, his team had won nine games on the spin against Hastings. Arguably, Wisbech would never be as good again. As for Hastings, promotion was confirmed a week later but it would prove to be a pyrrhic victory.

Ted Ive was right. Hastings were not strong enough for Southern Premier League football. Bill Meadows suffered a cartilage injury, leaving the club without a centre-forward. Two players with Football League First Division experience were signed; Tommy Harmer, once of Spurs, and Derek Leck, formerly with Brighton and Northampton, eventually came in. But by then, Hastings were in free fall. They were relegated at the end of the 1967/68 season having accumulated just 16 points.

New manager Reg Flewin, previously a First Division title winner with Portsmouth, appealed for public financial support. He pleaded: 'We have only 13 registered professionals on our books and one [Bill Meadows] is injured and unlikely to be available for selection for several weeks [it would be much longer than that]. Our wage bill for players and staff is about £350 per week [around £500,000 per year in modern currency] and overhead charges are approximately £100 per week. Our Tote Improvement Fund brings in about £90 per week and our gate money is between £200 and £250 per fortnight. Our income is therefore approximately £215 per week and our expenditure is £450 per week. We are launching a New Ticket Scheme in addition to the Tote and we must sell approximately 4,500 each week to break even.'

Reg Flewin was looking for 12 per cent of the local working population to contribute six per cent of their average weekly income to a lottery scheme in support of the town's football club. Many of his potential punters already did the weekly football pools in the hope of much greater riches. There were those who liked a flutter on the horses, too. So, there was little chance that Flewin would achieve his goal. Besides, this was a time of economic hardship, with devaluation just around the corner. Hastings was no longer a prosperous town. The holiday trade was flagging. Local jobs were harder to find.

Meanwhile, Jim Humphreys was losing interest. His dog track proposal wasn't winning favour. Football was not his main concern. In an attempt to draw a bigger crowd, he once experimented with pre-match jousting. It was a one-off affair, thankfully. A local knight was appointed complete with lance, shield, armour, the works. A suitably-robed steed was found, too, although it was a poor specimen, looking like mechanically recovered meat. The opposition wasn't any better. Demonstrating a commendable sense of decorum, the two nags refused to move, digging their hooves deep into the Pilot Field's cinder track. The 'knights' were left trying to poke one another from statuesque positions. Cue Stuart Hall. Never in the field of medieval conflict was so much embarrassment felt by so few.

Thereafter, Hastings United experienced the fate that befell many non-league clubs after the immediate post-war surge of interest. While passionately supported by a few, it became ignored by the majority. After the mid-sixties boom, four-figure crowds at the Pilot Field became very much the exception. Today, a club bearing the name of Hastings United continues to play there although the original club ceased to exist in the mid-eighties. Like its predecessor, the new club struggles to make ends meet in a cash-strapped place at a cash-strapped time. Whenever supporters of much bigger clubs claim that they are the most passionate, loyal fans in the country, I remain sceptical. It's hard to imagine that they are more dedicated than the painfully few supporters of these little non-league clubs. Not only do these fans bellow their minnows on, week in, week out, mostly in inhospitable places, with only a few hundred others – if that – for company, many of them also work tirelessly to help their clubs remain afloat. Instead of being derided as mad or sad, these committed fans should be applauded for showing what supporters can do for their clubs. As fans, we can, and, perhaps should, be more than consumers. Lest we forget, many club membership schemes offer as much of a stake as a Tesco loyalty card. Should that be the sum of our involvement?

A tale of two 'Jocks'

Jock Stein reckoned that 'the best place to defend is in the other team's penalty area'. Celtic's manager worked on basic principles. He believed that supporters wanted to see adventurous, attacking football, but he also knew that in order to deliver that successfully his team needed to be fit, supremely fit. He made sure that each and every one of his outfield players was capable of lasting an exhausting, scurrying 90 minutes. He insisted that the man on the ball was to be supported at all times. There had to be progressive options in all areas of the park. Intelligent running off the ball was mandatory. Everyone was expected to hunt hungrily for space. The full-backs were expected to overlap and the midfielders were urged to find threatening positions. Meanwhile, his wingers were required to track back and continually harass their opposite numbers. It was work, work, work. There was to be no letting up. The product was lovely to watch but punishing to play. Stein said: 'The difference between a really good side and a great side can often be the touch of the unpredictable. Call it a flash of genius, if you like. Or flair.' His team certainly had men with flair. There was 'jinking' Jimmy Johnstone, the flame-haired right-winger who could turn full-backs inside out. There was the muscular midfield visionary, Bertie Auld, who had an immaculate range of raking passes. There was Bobby Murdoch, who combined power with finesse in his playmaking role. He had delicacy of touch but ferocity of shot. And then there was buoyant Bhoy Tommy Gemmell, a roving turret at left-back. With players of this calibre, Celtic were capable of upsetting estimable opponents.

On 25 May 1967, Celtic became the first British club to contest the final of the European Cup. They had reached the final in style. Over two-legged ties they had hammered Zurich (5-0), made nonsense of Nantes (6-2), squeezed past Yugoslavian champions Volvodina (2-1) and disposed of Dukla Prague (3-1) in the semi-final. In keeping with Jock Stein's brand of 'total football', the goals were shared around. Centre-forward Steve Chalmers led with five, but full-back Tommy Gemmell chipped in with three, all scored in the two Zurich games.

On a brilliant, cloudless May evening in Lisbon, Celtic's opponents were Inter Milan. Italian club sides had dominated the European Cup competition since the Spanish and Portuguese giants were deposed in the early sixties. But their success had been founded upon a negative concept – the risk of defeat must be eliminated. The Italian gold standard was a clean sheet. Although Inter's boss, Helenio Herrera, vehemently rejected the notion, Inter had successfully practised this philosophy to the point of sterility. Herrera accepted that *catenaccio* (four defenders and a sweeper) was his invention, but maintained that his tactics were not purely defensive, pointing out that his left-back, Facchetti, operated also in an attacking role.

However, Celtic were determined to teach Inter a better way of winning. Stein remarked before the game: 'It is important for Celtic's players to think they can win every match [but] … if it should happen that we lose to Inter Milan, we want to be remembered for the football we have played.' For Jock Stein, style and substance went hand in hand. To demonstrate his point he showed his players a film of Real Madrid's masterclass at Hampden Park in May 1960. The fluidity of Real's shape and the fluency of their passing and movement were simply mesmerising. Stein insisted that the 'formation is not as important as the attitude' and that 'attack should be in the mind'. Only once, in this competition, had Celtic departed from this principle. That was when they shut up shop in Prague, having won the home leg 3-1. This only confirmed that they were better off sticking to their attacking principles.

Whereas Celtic approached the game in a relaxed frame of mind, the Inter players were stewing with nervous tension. For three days they had been incarcerated in a seafront hotel that Herrera had cleared of other guests. The hot-house atmosphere incubated the players' fears and paranoia, a situation hardly helped by Inter's disintegrating Serie A form. To make matters worse, they were without the injured Jair and Suarez, depleting them of their counter-attacking potency. Moreover, Mazzola, their other forward of note, was still suffering with the after-effects of flu.

Nevertheless, Inter stuck with their normal game plan. This involved attacking their opponents from the off to try to secure an early lead which they would then defend tenaciously. Mazzola almost gave Inter the perfect start in an opening raid when he headed against the veteran Ronnie Simpson's legs. But Mazzola did not have long to wait for a better opportunity. He started the move which resulted in Corso finding the centre-forward, Cappellini, with a defence-splitting pass. Craig was forced to bring him down and Mazzola wrong-footed Simpson from the spot. It had been an enterprising start by the Italians, but having gained this seventh-minute lead they reverted to type and pulled all but two forwards back. Rejoicing in the acres of space Inter conceded, Celtic proceeded to swarm all over them. Their twin strikers, Stevie Chalmers and Willie Wallace, attempted to lure Inter's central defenders out of position by alternately dropping deeper. Meanwhile, wingers Jimmy Johnstone and Bobby Lennox drifted inside, allowing the full-backs, Jim Craig and Tommy Gemmell, the space to bomb forward along the flanks.

Sarti, in the Inter goal, performed magnificently, producing one of the best goalkeeping displays in the history of the European Cup. He took hits from all directions but still managed to keep his goal intact with his astounding agility. However, he was indebted to the crossbar for denying blasts from Gemmell and Auld. With Celtic committing everyone to attack and Inter defending so deeply, the Italians weren't able to pick up everyone, particularly those breaking from deep positions. And that's how Celtic's equaliser came about on the hour. Murdoch's pass invited Craig to advance quickly down the right flank, and, with the Italians expecting a lofted centre towards the far post, the Celtic right-back swept a low pass into the path of his opposite number, Gemmell, who unhesitatingly hammered a shell-like shot into the top corner. Inter were played out. They could muster no response, other than a succession of high and hopeless clearances which were immediately gobbled up by the voracious Scots. Sure enough, with just six minutes remaining, Steve Chalmers deflected Murdoch's scuffed effort past Sarti and Inter were undone. The might of Italy had been toppled by a relatively unknown team from Scotland. That unfancied side, comprising only 'Glaswegians', had become the first British team to lift the European Cup. In crushing *catenaccio*, Stein had prospered where Cullis had foundered.

But while the *catenaccio* system was a bit peaky, it was not yet dead.

After the game, an enthralled Bill Shankly sought out his victorious compatriot. As Shankly entered the Celtic dressing room, he boomed out, 'John, [using Jock's Christian name] you've just become a bloody legend.' Not as far as Prime Minister Harold Wilson, was concerned, though. While he arranged knighthoods for Stanley Matthews, Alf Ramsey and Matt Busby, Jock Stein was ignored. Scottish heroics seemed to count for less. No wonder the Scots were so delighted with their 3-2 Wembley win over the new World Cup champions in April 1967.

1967 was also a proud time for another 'Jock' – Jock Wallace, the goalkeeper-manager of Berwick Rangers, who defied the might of Rangers in the Scottish FA Cup in January of that year. Wallace had a habit of overturning much stronger opponents. As player-manager of Bedford in 1964, he helped his Southern League side defeat Newcastle at St James' Park in the third round of the FA Cup. Bedford obviously learnt well from his lead as they then went on to defeat Brighton and Oxford respectively in the 1965/66 and 1966/67 FA Cup competitions. But his Berwick triumph took the biscuit. Rangers were en route to the European Cup Winners' Cup Final. They seemed far too strong for tiny, part-time Berwick Rangers.

Over 13,200 supporters crammed into Shielfield Park, Tweedmouth on that grey, misty January afternoon, a figure that almost matched the borough's population. Although over two-thirds of those attending were Rangers fans, at least 4,000 were local people, meaning that 25 per cent of townsfolk were there. They were in for the surprise of their lives.

For the first 37 minutes, Rangers attacked relentlessly. The game was as one-sided as it was predicted to be. Shot after shot rained in on the Berwick goal but Jock Wallace repelled everything fired at him. He played a blinder. Willie Henderson and Alex Smith were at fault for missing easy chances but nothing could detract from the quality of Wallace's performance. He was magnificent. Then, completely out of the blue, Berwick broke away for Sammy Reid to score. The Glasgow hordes looked on in stunned disbelief as the team in amber and black danced a jig of delight. For the remaining eight minutes of the first half normal service was resumed, with Rangers bearing down on Wallace's goal only for the 'Jungle Fighter' to confound each attack. After the interval, things got worse for Rangers. Willie Johnston broke his leg in a one-to-one challenge with Wallace. But Rangers continued to pour forward, spurning chance after chance – George McLean and Jim Forrest were particularly culpable. Then, with only five minutes remaining, Berwick broke away again. Only a brilliant save from visiting keeper Norrie Martin denied them.

When the final score was broadcast across the UK no one could quite believe it. It was assumed to be an error. Surely, the Rangers score was missing a one before the nought? With the post-match recriminations fermenting, Rangers' manager, Scott Symon, distanced himself from the humiliation. He stated: 'I am at a loss to understand how professional players can go into a game like that and apparently fail to understand the consequences of a defeat for the club. Our prestige has received a shattering blow. They, the players, were found wanting completely in ability and intelligence.' Rangers' chairman, John Lawrence, followed suit, stating: 'There is no doubt in my mind, that the only people who can be blamed for this defeat are the ones on the field, the players.' Symon reacted by transferring two of his scapegoats – Forrest and McLean – leaving him short of striking power for the European Cup Winners' Cup Final against Bayern Munich. Rangers lost 1-0 in extra time after a lacklustre display. Symon's impetuous reaction to the Berwick defeat weakened his stature at Ibrox. Little did the famous Glasgow club realise that their nemesis would soon become their saviour.

Jock Wallace never considered any cause lost until the final whistle sounded. His fierce competitiveness was frightening. Writing his obituary in July 1996, David McKinney of the *Independent* described Jock Wallace as

> *... a giant of Scottish football ... who ended Celtic's domination of the game in the 1970s and led Rangers to two domestic trebles within three years, the Glasgow club winning the league title, the League Cup and the Scottish Cup. Wallace had a frightening growl but a soft centre. The abiding image of him is that of the clenched fist, signifying the character he built into his teams – character which emanated from the man himself ... Leaning on his army background with the King's Own Scottish Borderers, Wallace reduced international football players to quivering wrecks after punishing training sessions on the Gullane sands. The exercise and the military precision with which he approached the job paid rich dividends.*

As a young, aspiring left-back at Ibrox, celebrity chef Gordon Ramsay had good reason to remember Wallace. He explained in the *Observer Sport Monthly* in 2002: 'Some people ask me today how I can be so firm – but when you worked under Jock Wallace there is no pussyfooting around when you want standards. I still remember him telling me they were letting me go. He was f***ing ruthless. We were only in there about five minutes and I wanted to cry but I couldn't cry because I wouldn't even dream of crying anywhere near Jock Wallace, and I wouldn't give him the pleasure of seeing me crying, and I wouldn't give the pleasure to my father of seeing me crying.'

Gary Lineker, the TV presenter and former England captain, recalls the terror he felt when Jock Wallace, then manager of Leicester City, 'pinned me against the dressing room wall at half-time and called me a lazy English this and that. We were 2-0 up and I'd scored both goals. I didn't score in the second half – I was still shaking!' It was small wonder that the Rangers forwards turned tail at the sight of Wallace before them: Braveheart indeed!

And a tale of A. Stock

The other remarkable act of 'giant-killing' in 1967 was Queens Park Rangers' Football League Cup triumph at Wembley. Those who dismissed Third Division Rangers' chances had obviously not paid attention to their performances as they cruised to the final, demolishing First Division Leicester 4-2 in the fourth round and thrashing Second Division Birmingham 7-2 on aggregate in the semi-finals. Rangers were also well on course for seizing the Third Division title. They finished 12 points in front of second-placed Middlesbrough, racking up over 100 goals with Rodney Marsh netting 30 of them. Marsh had been a steal from Fulham at £15,000. While his former boss, Vic Buckingham, saw Marsh as an unreliable maverick, his new boss, Alec Stock, saw him as a cavalier artist. Marsh was a swaggering presence in a bright attacking side which featured the 'Kosher Garrincha', Mark Lazarus, on the right wing and Roger Morgan on the left. Whereas Lazarus was fast, powerful and direct, Morgan was trickier. On Morgan's own admission he wasn't a tough competitor. But between them the two wingers contributed over a quarter of Rangers' league goals that season. Ex-Spurs 'double'-winning star, Les Allen, led the line. He hadn't lost his goal touch, either, as he weighed in with 16 league goals. Mike Keen also pushed up from midfield, notching six goals himself.

But for all their attacking flair, Rangers made sure they were tight at the back. Tony Hazel, Frank Sibley, Ron Hunt and former international Jim Langley maintained a redoubtable back line in front of the brilliant young keeper, Peter Springett, younger brother of England international, Ron. Rangers conceded a miserly 15 goals in 23 league games played at Loftus Road that season. They only let in eight more on their travels, too. This was a First Division side in waiting.

Rangers' Wembley opponents were West Bromwich Albion. Albion had played terrific, attacking football in winning the Football League Cup in 1966, crushing West Ham 4-1 in the second leg of the final. Their league form had been good, too, as they completed the '65/66 campaign in sixth spot having netted 91 goals with twin strikers, Jeff Astle and John Kaye, sharing 36 of these. The wingers, Clive Clark (a former Ranger) and Tony Brown, contributed a further 27 between them. However, Jimmy Hagan's side struggled in the following season, at least in the league. Although Albion breezed through the preceding rounds of the League Cup, handing out another hammering to West Ham (4-0), with Astle notching a hat-trick, their league form had stalled after winning 3-2 at Highbury on 22 October. Between then and their Wembley date on 4 March, Albion had mustered just three wins and ten points from 17 league games. The Twin Towers might have beckoned but so did the drop. There wasn't as much between these sides as the pundits thought.

Because of increasing defensive frailties, Hagan had been forced to bring in two centre-backs: John Talbut from Burnley for £30,000 and Eddie Colquhoun from Bury. The bird-watching goalkeeper, John Osborne, was also bought from Chesterfield to replace Ray Potter, who had been sold to Portsmouth. However, Dick Sheppard was brought back in goal for Wembley. He had kept goal in most of the earlier rounds.

Despite his defensive troubles, Hagan seemed unconcerned by the threat posed by Rodney Marsh. On the day before the game he made the dismissive remark, 'He is top scorer in the league because he is a striker in a successful team at the top of a lower division and playing confidently. Anyone can get goals in those circumstances.' Obviously, Hagan hadn't taken in Marsh's tremendous semi-final performances against Birmingham in which he scored three goals. His headed goal at St Andrew's – one of four scored by a rampant QPR – was something special. Marsh recalled that 'It was my best header. I actually got up so high that I nodded it down just under the crossbar.' Marsh added two more goals in the second leg, too.

For the first 45 minutes of the final, there was nothing to suggest that the pundits had called this wrongly. Queens Park Rangers appeared totally overawed. Hagan's side grasped the advantage with only seven minutes gone. West Bromwich right-back, Bobby Cram, pushed forward, transferring the ball sideways to Bobby Hope, who relayed it to fellow midfielder, Doug Fraser. Fraser immediately pinged the ball to Brown on the edge of the Rangers box. Although Brown was heavily tackled, the ball ran loose to 'Chippy' Clark, who had darted in from the left wing. Clark was a superb finisher. Finding himself inside the box with only keeper Springett to beat, he coolly wrong-footed the Rangers custodian before clipping the ball into the unguarded left-hand corner. In the 36th minute, Clark repeated his trick, once again assisted by his right wing 'oppo', 'Bomber' Brown, who had capitalised upon Astle's headed pass. Rangers were run ragged. Had it not been for Jim Langley's crucial interventions and Springett's agility, West Bromwich would have been well ahead by half-time. Stock's boys looked destined for a humiliating defeat.

This is where Alec Stock earned his corn. Nothing much fazed this wily operator. As player-manager of Yeovil, then a struggling Southern League side, he masterminded their victory over First Division Sunderland in the FA Cup competition of 1948/49. He was no one trick pony for he proceeded to resuscitate the fortunes of both Leyton Orient and AS Roma during the fifties, achieving further giant-killing exploits with the former. Ivan Ponting wrote in Stock's obituary in the *Independent* in April 2001:

> *Few football managers have achieved more with less than Alec Stock. Immensely ambitious despite eschewing a variety of opportunities to employ his gifts on a loftier plane, the dapper, disciplined, unfailingly courteous West Countryman emerged as a giant-killer supreme … Perhaps a tendency to worry persuaded him to avoid the merciless spotlight directed on the top echelons of the game, or maybe he preferred to build from his own foundations rather than inherit someone else's work, a situation which pertained more readily at a less exalted level. Whatever, it speaks eloquently for the talent and durability of Alec Stock that he entered League management as the country's youngest boss and left it as the oldest. Alec Stock was an old-fashioned, impeccably mannered football man, adept at fashioning silk purses from sows' ears and invariably popular with his players. It was appropriate that Fulham [whom he took to the 1975 FA Cup Final] should have clinched the First Division title on the day of his death, and how fitting it would be if his beloved Yeovil Town should attain League status in the coming weeks.*

Mark Lazarus later explained in an interview with a member of the Independent R's Review website:

> *I view [Alec Stock] with great admiration. I would say [it was] like a father and son relationship. He was the only man that could, or would, give me a clip around the ear and get away with it. He had been a captain in the Army, he knew how to handle and motivate people. If anyone had a problem, inside or outside of football, Alec would do his best to sort it out. I never played under any manager quite like Alec Stock. He was a very professional man and no one was in any doubt about who was in charge, a natural leader of men. I felt a great sadness when he passed away. I think of him as a great man … [At half-time at Wembley] he didn't shout, or rant and rave. He just said that we'd had a chance to soak up the atmosphere, we'd had our day out, and now it was time to go out and play like he knew we could. He never changed tactics or anything. He told us to go back out and enjoy ourselves. Don't get me wrong, Alec hated losing, but he must have realised that if he tore into us, we would have gone further into our shells. He said it was a beautiful day, so go out and enjoy it. Alec said exactly the right things.*

Rodney Marsh also recalled: 'We were beaten. Our heads were down. Alec told us to be a credit alright. But he also told us we were the better side and all we had to do was show it. He told us we could win. He told me: "Rodney, none of them can lace your boots. Go out and show them what good football, real football is all about. Go out and show the world you're the greatest."'

Stock's inspirational words transformed his team. Those players who had trudged into the dressing room so disconsolately left it so fired up that they were ready to scale mountains. Rangers tore into the Albion from the restart, hunting for the ball ravenously. Although much of Stock's morale-boosting talk had been directed at Marsh, others took inspiration, too, particularly Mark Lazarus, who proceeded to turn up the heat on West Bromwich's Welsh international left-back, Graham Williams. Neither Williams nor his colleagues could contain the powerful, reinvigorated Lazarus, who repeatedly made deep inroads into their territory.

Eighteen minutes after the break, Lazarus was brought down to the right of the Albion box. Les Allen lofted the resulting free kick towards the penalty spot, where Rodney Marsh's leap seemed to create confusion in the Albion defence, leaving left-winger, Roger Morgan, behind him, to head Rangers back into the game. In an interview conducted for the QPR website in 2008, Roger said: 'I still get a lot of stick from my children and other people about that goal! I didn't score that many with my head as it was not one of my greatest attributes, I can assure you. I thought I rose above the defender in the air and nodded home Les Allen's cross. But my kids say the ball hit me on the head and went in!' Having seen the video record, I'm with Roger's kids. Whether intentional or not, Morgan's goal turned the game.

Mark Lazarus told the Independent R's Review: '[After Roger scored] we were really up for it. Mike Keen had a great shot saved. Les took the corner and I hit a volley that was cleared off the line. We were slowly applying more pressure. Then Rodney got the ball in the middle of the park and off he went on a run towards their goal. Rodney says that he was looking for someone so that he could lay it off, but they just opened up so he kept going, shot and scored. From that moment, we knew we would win.'

Rodney's modest assessment was about right. Having wandered first one way and then the other, nonchalantly beating a couple of Albion defenders, he suddenly produced a right-foot shot which zipped across the Wembley turf and into the net off the left-hand post.

Albion were deflated. Confidence, composure and competitiveness hissed out of them like a nailed tyre. Rangers took control. Their skipper, Mike Keen, started to impose his authority in midfield, assisted by the industrious Frank Sibley, while Jim Langley discovered the elixir of youth as he skipped along the left flank in support of Rangers' mounting attacks. With only eight minutes remaining, Rangers' grinding pressure told, although their controversial winning goal was vehemently disputed by the incensed Albion defenders. Dick Sheppard had come out to grab a through ball. He appeared to be comfortably in possession when Rangers' centre-half, Ron Hunt, slithered into him at the end of a long forward run. Hunt's lunging right leg collided with Sheppard's head, whereupon the ball ran loose to Lazarus, who knocked it into the empty net. Referee Walter Crossley ruled that the goal should stand because he considered the collision to be an accident. He stated: 'Without foul intention the law says there can be no foul.'

Mark Lazarus commented after the game: 'I had a film over my left eye from early in the second half. Everything was blurred after a ball bounced badly and hit me in the eye. But when that chance came I knew it was going into the net.' As for Ron Hunt, whose robust challenge set up the goal, he claimed that Sheppard was not in possession when he went for the ball, saying: 'It was a 50–50 chance for Dick Sheppard and me. I kicked the ball.

It rebounded off the keeper. We collided quite hard as I went sliding on and we both went down.' The BBC film evidence is inconclusive.

Stock quipped a day or so later, 'We just turned over in bed on the Sunday morning and read about the final in the papers. I felt wonderful and I gave them all Sunday morning off training.' But after having a bit more time for reflection he made a more expansive assessment, stating: 'The important thing to us that season was winning promotion. The League Cup was just the icing on the cake. Our second-half performance against Albion was out of this world, and Rodney was in a class of his own. He rivals George Best as being the nearest thing there is to a genius in this game of ours.' Best and Marsh would ultimately play together at Craven Cottage.

Allen (£21,000) and Marsh (£15,000) were expensive signings by Rangers' standards, made possible by chairman Jim Gregory's investment in the club he had supported since he was a child. However, Stock's other signings were characteristically cut-price: veteran left-back Jim Langley was a free transfer from Fulham in 1965, Mark Lazarus cost only a small fee when signed from Brentford in 1966 and ex-Plymouth midfielder, Keith Sanderson, was not even a full-time professional when he signed in 1965. He doubled as a computer programmer. As for the other six members of his team, all were 'home-grown', expertly developed in Stock's 'academy'. Alec Stock was undoubtedly the architect of this astounding victory.

Mark Lazarus also acknowledged the important part played by Jim Gregory in Rangers' success. He said: 'Jim Gregory was one of us. He always came into the dressing room before a game, always had time for a word and a laugh and joke with everyone. He would often take the whole team out for a meal. I remember that Jim had a tremendous relationship with Les Allen. At the time it felt like everyone who was at QPR, from Jim Gregory down to the groundstaff boys, was part of the team. He was the instigator of everything good about the club. It was a wonderful time to be part of the club.' Jim Gregory put his money where his mouth was. Even top First Division players envied the £220 bonus that each member of his cup-winning team received. Gregory's only regret was that Rangers were denied automatic entry into the 1967/68 European Fairs Cup competition, because qualification rights were restricted to First Division sides.

Despite his obvious disappointment, even beaten Albion boss, Jimmy Hagan, complimented Rangers on their success. Showing greater generosity after the game than before, he said, 'I did not think at the time that two goals were enough. We should have gone for a third – especially against a side like Rangers. They finished the better side.'

Although West Bromwich pulled up their socks after Wembley,

securing First Division safety easily by winning eight and drawing two of their remaining 12 games, it was not enough to save Hagan's job. Better times would lie ahead for him, though, as he proceeded to revive Benfica's fortunes spectacularly during the early seventies. As for the Albion, they would return to Wembley, in the FA Cup, a year later under ex-Carlisle boss, Alan Ashman. This time they enjoyed better fortune, with Jeff Astle's extra-time belter beating much-fancied Everton.

Boosted by their cup victory, Queens Park Rangers achieved successive promotions. But First Division football proved to be a bridge too far, too soon, as they experienced immediate relegation. Alec Stock had to take a three-month leave of absence for health reasons during that campaign. A parting of the ways followed with Stock moving on to Luton Town. Nevertheless, after regrouping successfully, Rangers returned to the First Division in 1973 behind the champions, Burnley. This time they made a much better fist of life at the top. But by that time, Rodney Marsh had moved on to Manchester City.

Simon Hattenstone wrote in the Guardian in March 2010:

> *As a boy I adored and despised Rodney. He had ridiculous ability, amazing cheek, could do anything with a ball. He was the blond George Best. Whereas drink did for Best, laziness and gobbiness did for Marsh. He only played when he fancied it. But when he fancied it, boy did he play. When City bought him in 1972 we were top of the old first division, on track to secure the championship. We finished fourth. He played a mere nine times for England. There was a reason for that, too. When Alf Ramsey told him, "If you don't work harder I'll pull you off at half time," Marsh replied: "Crikey, Alf, at Manchester City all we get is an orange and a cup of tea." He was never picked again.'*

'... It's all part of my Autumn Almanac'

I didn't get the 'summer of love'. I was disqualified, not so much by age as by lack of opportunity. In fairness, I didn't try too hard. San Franciscan radiance didn't travel too well, at least not as far as sour, de-flowered

Hastings. Besides, I had winter in my blood. My compass pointed resolutely northwards. Lancaster was on my radar and independence was on my mind. In the meantime, I settled for the womb-like warmth of my local chess club, heavy with its aromas of polish, tea, toasted teacakes and cigars. Here, an ancient gas fire popped and flared all day, every day, whatever the weather. It was an ideal bolt-hole for the socially lame. Little was said, just a brief exchange of courtesies and then hours of silent, furrowed concentration to the accompaniment of so many ticking clocks. An elderly woman, clad in heavy woollens, shuffled mutely in and out of the oak-panelled room with trays of refreshment.

I loved this reclusive refuge, particularly on glowering winter afternoons. Periodically looking up from the chess board, I would watch the beaded raindrops on the window glass outside, their tiny inverted reflections of the rushing sky quivering in the wind. Gulls swooped, glided and circled above the grey, flaking Victorian tenements. Below them, the street lights flickered into life at the close of the day, staining the damp pavements with their dull light. Anonymous traffic swished past. And here in this haven from the storm, untouched and unnoticed by the passing years, the liturgy of chess was recited – the Queen's Indian, the Ruy Lopez, the Sicilian – in all its musty imperial, consular glory.

But if I was an equivocal subscriber to the present and a bashful advocate of the past, I was not alone, not by a long chalk. Take the Beatles, for instance. As much as they pushed the margins with their narcotic-influenced 'Tomorrow Never Knows' and 'Day in the Life' they seemed, as George Melly observed, 'at their happiest when celebrating the past'. George Harrison's dismissive take on the trippy, hippie San Francisco scene was 'a load of horrible, spotty drop-out kids on drugs'. Their *Sgt. Pepper's Lonely Hearts Club Band* album evoked, as historian Dominic Sandbrook put it, 'the fading memories of circuses, music halls and terraced streets'. The Kinks picked up the baton with their 1968 album, *The Kinks Are the Village Green Preservation Society*. In the Kinks' 1967 single, 'Autumn Almanac', Ray Davies sang: 'I like my football on the Saturday, roast beef on Sundays all right … This is my street and I'm never going to leave it …' (Pye/Reprise music). The Beatles and the Kinks championed an image of Englishness, then in retreat. Not everyone bought the West Coast eulogies of Scott McKenzie or the Flowerpot Men. It was almost as if we, like coy explorers, needed to remain in touch with our home roots. With the nation desperately in love with the long-running TV serial *The Forsyte Saga*, and Victorian fashions revived by Biba and Laura Ashley, that ambivalence about embracing the 'shock of the new' was probably more pervasive than caricatures of the age allow.

Where that ambivalence was tinged or gripped by fear, Mary Whitehouse and her cohorts struck a reassuring chord. She even claimed an unlikely rapport with Mick Jagger after meeting him on a TV panel show; talk about 'Sympathy for the Devil'. Despite her crankiness, Mrs Whitehouse made prominent and influential friends, including journalist Malcolm Muggeridge, MP Bill Deedes, anti-pornography campaigner Lord Longford and the housewives' choice, Cliff Richard. Even novelist Kingsley Amis, who thought Longford was 'a f***ing fool', shared Mrs Whitehouse's prejudices about cultural life in the late sixties. Seizing his scatter gun, Amis laid waste to the whole 'abortion-divorce-homosexuality-censorship-racialism-marijuana package' and 'the professional espouser of causes, the do-gooders, the archetypal social worker'. Meanwhile his poet friend, Philip Larkin, strafed trade unionists, students, immigrants and socialists of all kinds. Plenty of other contemporary writers shared Amis' and Larkin's concerns about the direction of modern life, if not Larkin's racism or Amis' splattering spleen. These included A.S. Byatt, Piers Paul Reid, Malcolm Bradbury and Anthony Powell. Their reactionary attitudes hardly supported Christopher Booker's thesis that the sixties was the age of *The Neophiliacs*. There seemed too many of us who abhorred the new. Perhaps Booker, the satirist, was just being satirical, though?

As historian Dominic Sandbrook stated in his book *White Heat*:

> *Whitehouse, Muggeridge, Amis and others spoke for millions of people who felt frightened or threatened by social and cultural change. These millions were unhappy that British power was so clearly in decline, felt let down by the Wilson government, and worried that the country they loved was changing beyond recognition. They were troubled that while church attendance was falling, the figures for divorce, abortion, delinquency and violent crime were all well on the rise. They saw the sixties not as years of liberation, but as an age of anxiety. And in the decade to come they would find their champion – a middle-aged, middle-class grocer's daughter from Grantham.*

THE 1967/68 SEASON

Tottenham Hotspur v Manchester City

'What a Wonderful World'
4 May 1968

Since Dad introduced me to football ten years before, Manchester City had remained in the shadow of their richer, slicker but ill-fated neighbours. During the early sixties the gap between the two sides grew, particularly after City's relegation in 1963, a fate that United only narrowly averted in that same year. But having jumped jail, United made a spectacular revival, winning the FA Cup at the end of that troubled '62/63 season. By 1965, United's First Division championship year, Maine Road was a sorry sight. Even in their relegation-haunted seasons of the late fifties and early sixties, City had managed to draw in average crowds of 32,000-plus. And yet only 8,015 deigned to turn up for their Second Division home game with Swindon on 16 January 1965. One of their players remarked: 'I've never felt as depressed in all the time I've been a professional footballer. It was ghastly playing a first-team match in front of all those vacant spaces.' Things were about to change, though.

Seven months after the Swindon 'no show', Joe Mercer was appointed as City's manager. He was not thought to be in the best of health, having suffered a stroke 12 months before. This setback had forced him to relinquish his previous post at Villa Park. Despite his wife's attempts at dissuasion, Mercer believed he was ready for the fray. He knew he could no longer be a tracksuit manager. He needed someone to do the running, someone who could knock his new team into shape. Mercer decided Malcolm Allison was his man. So he gave the ebullient coach a call. Allison's playing days had been cut short by tuberculosis but he had put aside his grief by committing himself wholeheartedly to coaching, acquiring a full range of FA badges. He established a reputation quickly as a physically demanding, innovative and shrewd tactician. Allison cut his teeth at West Ham where, according to a young Bobby Moore, Allison taught him everything he knew. Allison then managed Southern League side Bath City before moving to Plymouth Argyle. Mercer intervened as Allison was considering a coaching position with Raich Carter at Middlesbrough. Mercer persuaded him to come to Maine Road instead.

Allison believed that it was England's hammering by the Hungarians in 1953 that alerted him to the possibilities of coaching. Almost 50 years later, he told the *Observer* journalist, Jon Henderson:

> *What was amazing to me was how the Hungarians, by changing positions, made such a difference. Herbert Chapman's W-M formation (the full-backs and half-backs arranged in a W and the five forwards in an M) lasted for more than 25 years. Everyone copied this formation, so when the Hungarians changed their tactics and played with a deep centre-forward, they destroyed England. OK, they might have had some great players but they weren't that much better than us, not 6–3 and 7–1 better … Ramsey was at right-back and nearly all the goals came down that side. He couldn't handle the winger who was too quick for him. So when Ramsey became England manager, he adopted two deep wingers [as he did at Ipswich] to protect the full-backs so they couldn't get chased like he had been. He developed the 4–4–2 formation which was the 1966 World Cup-winning line-up. It got me thinking, too, that it was more about formations, about the way you played, than about great players.*

Mercer and Allison faced a huge challenge upon their arrival at City in July 1965. They found a squad of just 21 players made up of seasoned professionals and largely untried youngsters. City had completed the previous season in Division Two in 11th place. Allison believed that City needed to be tighter at the back. Mercer agreed. Allison's irrepressible enthusiasm and energy left an immediate and indelible mark upon his new squad. Former forward Neil Young told Ian Penney, author of *Manchester City: the Mercer – Allison Years*,

> *Under previous regimes the training sessions were basically run, run, run. There was no variation and*

> *we hardly saw the ball until the next game. Now we still ran but there was much more emphasis upon ball work ... We played a lot of five-a-side games and attack against defence ... The sessions were shorter and faster ... Joe would walk around taking in every detail. Later, Joe would say [to Malcolm], 'Why don't you try that?' 'What about this?' Joe was really a father figure to us. Nothing was too much trouble ... Joe and Malcolm encouraged me to shoot more often ... the theory being that goalkeepers were used to saving shots only from certain areas and anywhere else could cause them problems ... Another thing we'd do in training was head tennis ... we actually won [an FA tournament] against teams like Arsenal and Chelsea ... I think Malcolm was about twenty years ahead of his time. Malcolm was especially good as a psychologist. He used to make each one of us think we were the best in the world.*

City needed better players, though. Some of the existing squad were no longer good enough. Mercer brought in reinforcements: Mike Summerbee, a direct right-winger or centre-forward from Swindon for £35,000; Ralph Brand, a prolific goalscorer with Rangers, for £30,000; George Heslop, Everton's reserve centre-half, for £20,000; and, just before the March 1966 transfer deadline, midfielder Colin Bell, from Bury, for £45,000. Allison had set his heart on Bell. He was impressed with his stamina, speed and skill. As Neil Young observed, 'Bell could make 20, 30, 40-yard runs and defenders couldn't pick him up.' Allison played a canny game in landing Bell, bogusly emphasising his shortcomings to rival scouts. Meanwhile, several seasoned professionals departed. Out went powerful inside-forward Derek Kevan to Crystal Palace. Centre-forward Jimmy Murray and full-back Dave Bacuzzi joined Walsall and Reading, respectively, several months later. Mercer and Allison brought about an astonishing change in City's fortunes. At the end of their first season in charge, City were promoted as Second Division champions.

On 18 December 1965, I watched City overpower Crystal Palace at a squelching Selhurst Park. It was a startling display of indomitable, muscular professionalism. The star of the show was Mike Summerbee. Allison told Ian Penney: 'When I saw Summerbee playing in practice matches he was playing too deeply for an outside-right and I encouraged him to play further forward.' On this dark, wet December afternoon, Summerbee took this advice to heart, for he was the initiator of City's devastating counter-attacks. He was so quick, strong and versatile, audaciously confident about taking on the Palace defenders unaided. On this saturated surface he showed astounding sureness of touch. Time and again he collected the ball deep inside his own half and proceeded to run with blatant directness at the Palace goal. The home markers would attempt to close him down, but he had the quickness of feet and surge of acceleration to confound them. And while he created mayhem in Palace's defence, gaps opened up for his team-mates to exploit. Twice, midfielder Mike Doyle broke through to finish what Summerbee had set up. Palace had one of the meanest home defensive records in the division but City were in a different class.

City spent their first season back up in the top flight consolidating. They might have hoped for more because they got off to a sensational start. But having faltered, Allison looked for further reinforcements. To that end he persuaded Mercer to fork out £17,500 to bring Tony Book, his talismanic full-back, up from Plymouth. Book had played for Allison at Bath and Plymouth but he was then 31 years old. Too long in the tooth, feared Mercer, but Allison knew better. Having finally won his partner over, it didn't take Book long to assuage all doubts. Young concluded that 'Not many players got the better of Tony Book.' Allison experimented by using Book as a sweeper, an innovation that Mercer had used when at Sheffield United, but one that had been hardly employed in English football. Book was ideally suited to the role with his uncanny positional sense, his sharp reading of the game, his physical strength and accurate distribution.

Allison then caused his partner further consternation by bringing in left-winger Tony Coleman from Doncaster – 'a skinhead covered in tattoos' – for £12,350. Even Allison described him as a 'parole officer's nightmare'. Before the 1969 FA Cup Final, Coleman famously said to Princess Anne, 'Give my regards to your mum and dad.' He also once 'gate-crashed' a penalty kick which his team-mate Francis Lee was preparing to take, haring in and blasting the ball way over the bar. When the apoplectic Lee confronted him, Coleman 'explained' that he had 'just felt like it'. But Mercer conceded that despite Coleman's waywardness, the lad could play. Mark E. Smith, grouchy leader of waspish 'Mancabilly' band, The Fall, and lifetime City fan, reckoned that Coleman is the only City player he could write a song about.

During the 1967/68 season, goalkeeper Ken Mulhearn was brought in from Stockport. He was an excellent shot stopper. But City's signing of that triumphant season was undoubtedly Francis Lee – captured from Bolton for £60,000. Allison knew that Lee's dynamic speed over the first five yards and his bustling directness would hurt opposing defences. He wasn't wrong.

The 1967/68 season began slowly but City soon picked up the pace. When they beat Spurs comprehensively in December's 'ballet on ice' it was clear that they were strong title contenders. Their 5-1 demolition of Fulham on 16 March put them in pole position on goal average although not only United, but also Leeds and Liverpool, were breathing down their necks. Despite relinquishing their lead shortly afterwards, City managed to regain it as they prepared for their penultimate league fixture at White Hart Lane on a warm and overcast afternoon in early May.

After lifting the FA Cup in May 1967, Spurs failed to push on. Jimmy Greaves recorded in his biography, *Greavsie*:

> *The domestic season of 1967/68 was one of the unhappiest I ever experienced in football. The tremendous team spirit Spurs had shown in the previous season deserted us … We enjoyed a super [FA Cup] win over Manchester United after a replay … but we went down at Anfield in a replay … I finished with 23 goals, plus three in the FA Cup, but I was concerned about my overall form … I often felt tired and jaded but, most worrying of all, I realised my appetite for football wasn't the same. For a time during that season I actually contemplated retiring from the game … I think Bill Nicholson had noticed my lack of verve because he went out and bought Martin Chivers from Southampton for what was then a club record fee of £125,000 … When Martin arrived he took over from Gilly [Alan Gilzean] up front with Alan [Mullery] dropping back into a deeper role behind Chivers and myself. It wasn't an unsuccessful partnership, but there wasn't the fire of old. But that was true of the team as a whole. [At the end of the season] Bill sold Dave Mackay to Derby County and Cliff Jones to Fulham.*

There was a similar downbeat mood in the Spurs match programme 'Comment' section, where it was said: 'Last season we won the FA Cup and finished third in the Football League. This year we can make no such claim. In spite of our long unbeaten home run extending from November 1966 until Leicester defeated us here by a single goal last December – a sequence of 27 League and FA Cup matches – we missed our way in the autumn [when] we suffered our European Cup Winners' Cup knockout by Olympic Lyonnais that can only be described as a "Spurs disaster" … That experience deflated everyone at the club.' Joe Mercer or Malcolm Allison surely would have taken heart had they read these notes before the game.

Spurs lined up as follows: Pat Jennings in goal, Phil Beal and Cyril Knowles as the full-backs, Mike England and captain Dave Mackay as the centre-backs, Jimmy Robertson, Alan Mullery, Terry Venables and Alan Gilzean in midfield, with Greaves and Chivers up front. Jimmy Greaves and the departing Cliff Jones were the only Spurs players to reach a goal tally of double figures that season.

City were unchanged with Mulhearn in goal and Book and Pardoe at full-back. Seven years previously, I saw the strapping Pardoe score four goals in a schoolboy international at Wembley. In a 17-year career at City he played in every position bar centre-half and goalkeeper. At centre-back, the powerful Heslop was supported by tough-tackling Michael Doyle. In midfield there was the penetrative pass master, Alan Oakes, alongside Bell and Coleman, with Summerbee, Young and Lee in more advanced positions, although there was considerable fluidity and versatility about City's play. They had an impressive array of marksmen. Thus far, Coleman, Bell, Summerbee, Young and Lee had shared 64 league goals.

Clearly, Manchester City no longer needed my patronage. I had rooted for them all season on account of their previous struggles. But it was Spurs who were in greater need of spare sympathy. They were swamped immediately by the fury of City's attacks. Coleman and Lee continually stretched their full-backs while Summerbee put himself up against Mike England, pulling the Spurs centre-half one way and another with his wiry twists and turns, creating gaps for the foraging Bell to plunder. Not that Bell needed much space in which to operate. He proceeded to make one blind run after another, carving out even wider openings that Young and others could exploit. The bewildered Spurs defenders found it impossible to track the City players' dazzling movement, particularly Bell. Even when they seized upon a loose ball, Bell and others were immediately on top of them, harrying them into hurried, wayward clearances. Bell never stopped running. His energy level was incredible. With Spurs at sixes and sevens, City advanced their defensive line with Doyle released to supplement their incessant assaults on the home goal. This was siege warfare. Spurs were pressed back within their box like beleaguered defenders of a holed fortress. Greaves looked frantic with frustration while big Chivers was merely ornamental. It seemed inconceivable that City would not score. But Doyle,

Young, Coleman and Lee failed to put away the excellent opportunities that came their way.

Encouraged by their reprieve, Spurs gradually made a few cautious advances but these were so hesitant, so lacking in conviction, that they were easily snuffed out by the commanding Heslop and his fellow minders. And just as it seemed as if Spurs might reach half-time on level terms, City struck. In the 40th minute, a slick exchange between Book, Summerbee and Coleman enabled Bell to latch on to the ball at pace, glide past Mackay and find goal with a sweetly-struck drive that gave the diving Jennings no chance. Spurs were so overwhelmed that within 30 seconds of the restart, they almost gifted Young a second. Only Jennings' brilliance denied him. But the big Northern Irishman was powerless to prevent City's second goal less than a minute into the second half. Knowles had managed to keep out Young's snap shot, but the ball ricocheted to Bell, who rifled it low into the net at brutal velocity. With their position now apparently hopeless, Spurs started to find their feet. Not that City were much troubled, and 15 minutes from time Summerbee's skewed shot beat Jennings to secure two vital points. Although Greaves reduced the deficit in the 83rd minute from a spot kick, City might well have added two more as Lee blazed over and Young's shot clipped the top of the crossbar. Spurs' humiliation had been as great as that in December's 'ballet on ice'.

Allison told Ian Penney: 'The game at Tottenham was a brilliant tactical success. The plan was to isolate the ageing Dave Mackay in the centre of the Spurs defence. Francis Lee would pull Cyril Knowles wide on the right while Mike Summerbee would do the same with Mike England. This would leave a huge gap in the middle for the rampaging Colin Bell to run at Mackay. The plan worked beautifully … [Dave Mackay told Allison after his subsequent move to Derby] "I've never been so insulted in my life as I was on that day. You absolutely slaughtered us in that match. That was the reason I left Tottenham."'

After Leeds lost their midweek game at Arsenal, the City boys knew they needed only to win at Newcastle to take the title they had last secured in 1937. After a tense first half, City duly achieved their goal, winning in style by 4-3. Although United lifted the European Cup on a night of high emotion, City were rightfully our club team of the season. As refreshing and admirable as their title victory was, it seems inconceivable that I should have held a torch for a club that has such bloated resources now. Even back in 1968, it was evident that City were a big city club once again – hardly the mangy mutt that I had once petted.

Reflecting upon his City career, Malcolm Allison told Jon Henderson of the *Observer*: 'The first time I was at City, because we were doing badly when Joe and I arrived, everything I asked the players to do, they did. When I went the second time in 1979 there were a lot of successful players there, but they didn't want to work. They didn't want to train and they moaned and they dodged. They were non-professional.'

'Paint it Black'

In order to reach White Hart Lane I had to catch a train from Liverpool Street. It was crammed well before departure. But being one of the first to board, I was able to find a window seat next to a door. A black girl joined the train en route, hesitantly inserting herself into the all-white, male scrum. Because of the pressure of bodies she was compelled to arch her body above me, supporting herself awkwardly by stretching for the luggage rack rail above my head. This contorted position left her standing on tiptoe. I offered her my seat, unaware that my gesture would cause her more discomfort. Having risen unsteadily to my feet, it was only at my insistence that she reluctantly took my place. Coming from a town with an almost totally white population I was unaware of the potential sensitivity of her situation. I was simply obeying what I thought to be a common courtesy. I had assumed that her discomfort was merely due to shyness. It was only afterwards, when I recalled how uneasily she had cast her eyes around, that I considered that there might have been a more sinister explanation.

We had exchanged places just weeks after Enoch Powell's infamous 'rivers of blood' tirade. Powell's startling volte-face on the issue of immigration had stoked the fires of segregationalism and racism, particularly amid the white inhabitants of the declining heavy industrial communities of the West Midlands and the North. Although Powell's remarks had caused his political career to collapse as dramatically as the Ronan Point tower block, he received messages of support from hundreds of sympathisers across the country. After his dismissal from Ted Heath's shadow cabinet, some workers in Reading, Norwich and Southampton went so far as to strike in support of him. It seemed not to matter one jot that white British emigrants easily outnumbered the immigrants from the Asian sub-continent, Caribbean and elsewhere. As was the case in Smethwick, many local white inhabitants regarded their new black and Asian neighbours with suspicion, an aversion which had intensified in light of the declining job prospects. Not that the *Windrush* generation and other immigrants were made to feel welcome during the late forties and early fifties, when shortages of cheap labour threatened to disrupt our reviving economy. Then, we were still producing a wide range of goods that the rest of the world actually wanted. Racial animosity was the background to Patrick Gordon-Walker's controversial electoral defeat in 1964. I wondered how the nameless black girl got on with her white neighbours.

Although Johnny Speight and Warren Mitchell, script-writer and lead actor in the TV sitcom *Till Death Us Do Part,* lampooned the casual racism which was rife in sixties Britain, the satire was lost on many viewers. In fact, a large number readily identified with Alf Garnett's racial bigotry. It was doubtful whether the mixed race comedian, Charlie Williams, found his satirical target any better with a string of 'Enoch Powell' jokes. He scoffed that Powell's dying wish was to have several hundred 'Pakistanis dancing on his grave', adding, after a 'comedic' pause, that Powell wanted a sea burial. Williams was not alone. Like Williams, Jos White traded in 'Powell jokes', using the term 'Pakistani' like the white racists did, in a derogatory vein. Both Williams and White made their names on the tough working men's club circuit. They also appeared on the ITV show *The Comedians* alongside Bernard Manning. But where was their humour heading? Was it helping combat racism or simply playing to the racist gallery? Williams added further ambiguity by recognising Powell's view on immigration, saying: 'It sounds daft coming from me but in some ways you've got to go along with Enoch Powell. I reckon that immigration should be on a measured scale and under proper control.' But lest we forget, both as a Yorkshire miner and as a professional footballer, Williams had to battle for acceptance. When Williams played for Doncaster during the mid-fifties there were no more than a handful of black footballers in the British professional game. Through a combination of wit, determination and broad-shouldered affability, characters like Charlie Williams helped create a wider acceptance of black footballers in our game.

'It's the economy, stupid'

As in any age, there are always those who are predisposed to believe the worst. Not that there weren't genuine causes for concern in late sixties Britain. Britain's manufacturing industries continued to decline. Devaluation meant that our money went less far, while rising inflation and a stagnant economy ('stagflation') meant that wage rises became less affordable. Even where wage increases were granted, their value became lost quickly. It was unsurprising that the unions started to flex their muscles. But fears about mounting trade union militancy were largely overblown, at least until the early seventies. While industrial action increased sharply in 1968, prompting Barbara

Castle to present her doomed industrial relations strategy, *In Place of Strife*, the number of days lost to strikes was less than those lost to sickness. Between 1965 and 1974 industrial action was more prevalent in France and Italy than here. But perception is everything. The consumer boom of the late fifties and early sixties had sharpened the nation's appetite for the good life. The economy and the trade union militants were seen to be threatening that. Labour did not seem to be working. Communist infiltration of the trade union movement was suspected. And not only by the shroud-waving Conservative press. Wilson happened to agree. It was small wonder that as the economy slid backwards the nation slid to the right. Morose grumpiness became the mood of choice.

Mike Hodges got the picture. His 1971 film, *Get Carter*, which he based in Newcastle, was littered with images of late sixties decay. Here, we had battered back-to-back terraces, cheerless interiors, desolate industrial wastelands, run-down pubs, run-to-seed drinkers, gangland violence, vice, corruption, bleak couplings and shrivelled relationships. Bruce Robinson must have been impressed. His much later film, *Withnail and I*, splendidly covers a grubby thespian life on the dole, Camden-styled, circa 1969. Robinson introduced us to the feral, flat life of the period, lubricated with gargantuan quantities of drugs and booze. His images of late sixties squalor are as striking as those in *Get Carter*. Take the slum wrecking ball, swinging to the rhythm of Hendrix's 'All Along the Watchtower'; not so much 'swinging' as 'seedy' England.

But five typists from the Colt Heating and Ventilation Company in Surbiton did not subscribe to this gloom and doom. They decided they would help revitalise the flagging economy by working half an hour longer, each day, for no extra pay, thereby kicking off the 'I'm Backing Britain' campaign. The press picked up the cause; so did the Labour and the Conservative parties. Prince Philip sent his congratulations. Other firms followed suit. But then Bruce Forsyth climbed on board with an excruciating 'I'm Backing Britain' single. We had the 'I'm Backing Britain' mugs, too, with a union jack design. The Surbiton women's commendable gesture got lost in the tawdry commercial froth. Nothing rolls as fast through a vacuum as a bandwagon. It was almost a kindness when the trade union leaders dismissed the campaign as irrelevant to economic regeneration. One union forbade its members to take part. As if Enoch Powell wasn't unpopular enough within his party, he waded in with an alternative campaign titled 'Help Brainwash Britain'. 'I'm Backing Britain' collapsed within six weeks of its New Year start. It was back to morose grumpiness.

THE 1968/69 SEASON

Preston North End v Chelsea (FA Cup fourth round)

'Albatross'
25 January 1969

I finally left the South in 1968, the year of unrest. Martin Luther King had been gunned down in Memphis, triggering race riots across North America. With a strident Aretha Franklin demanding 'Respect' and a stomping James Brown insisting 'Say It Loud (I'm Black and I'm Proud)', US sprinters Tommie Smith and John Carlos gave the Black Panther salute from the Olympic podium. Soviet tanks ground Dubcek's liberal reforms into the Prague dust. Palestinian Sirhan Sirhan assassinated Bobby Kennedy. Paris seethed with revolt and South Africa's Prime Minister Vorster angrily cancelled the MCC tour upon hearing of Basil D'Oliveira's selection. We also had the two anti-Vietnam demonstrations outside the US Embassy in Grosvenor Square, the first of which turned ugly. However, our violent protests compared pallidly with what took place in Paris and, later, at Ohio State University.

I arrived at Lancaster in the damp, overcast autumn of 1968 to find the new university resembling a Klondike town. The place was a building site with mud everywhere. Discreetly isolated in rural splendour, our stay quickly became an exercise in experimental living. Joss sticks abounded, if only to subdue the rancid smell of our clothing. Vitamins were at a premium. They had a better diet on the *Bounty*. Christmas was duly celebrated with scurvy. Those young men who arrived with short back and sides, horn-rimmed glasses and sports jackets went home with flowing locks, John Lennon specs and beaded buckskin. Student relationships with the nearby city seemed less like 'town and gown' as 'town and clown'. *Withnail and I* had come to Lancaster.

I have Baz, a fellow student, to thank for bringing me back to Preston. To be truthful, I hadn't thought too much about them since I rooted for them in the 1964 FA Cup Final. The intervening years had not been kind to North End. Not that Baz agreed. If Baz's love of North End wasn't blind, it was certainly clouded with cataracts.

I first met Baz when he lurched drunkenly into the room my girlfriend shared with another female student. He didn't knock. He just barged right in clutching a small tin of Nescafe. I later realised that he looked upon the coffee tin as a swipe card. Seeing me sitting on one of the single beds, he narrowed his eyes, studying me blearily while he rocked unsteadily back and forth on his heels. I thought he might cut up rough, but no. He inquired in a gentle Lancashire growl whether I had ever seen Willie Irvine play. 'On the TV', I admitted. He contemplated that for a while before continuing in a deeper, louder, gruffer voice: 'Then you'll know how … (and here he paused, hitching himself up like a long jumper about to hit the runway*) how f***ing ex-cel-lent* he is, won't you.' I noticed how he bit down on his bottom lip just before he swore, spring-loading it, like a catapult, so he could propel his expletive at maximum velocity; it was almost as if he was vomiting the obscenity. He even stumbled forward with the force of his delivery. This was world class vulgarity.

Baz was an evangelist; a voice growling in the wilderness. He wanted to share his homage of Willie with everyone. Like a zealously bigoted Bible Belt preacher, he saw no reason to recognise others' privacy or priorities. Baz never picked his moments. He was a wild boor. And yet the women indulged him much like an unruly, all licks and paws, young retriever. They'd tolerate his intrusions, pat his mane of wavy, blond hair, and tug playfully at his straggling beard. He'd quieten then and, with a sleepy smile, proffer his tin of coffee. One day we found 'Willie Irvine is f**king excellent' sprayed on a pillar in the university's main square. It didn't tax the college's investigative powers too much. Baz was threatened with expulsion but was eventually excused. Perhaps he received a piss-artist-in-residence bursary?

On another occasion we were surprised to find him on a London-bound coach transporting anti-apartheid protesters to a demonstration. This was a new departure for Baz, or so we thought. Radical politics wasn't his strongest suit. Strong views he had aplenty, political issues, no. But then we twigged. He'd blagged his way on so he could get to an away game. Heaven help the protesters once Baz got going. And on the return journey that gruff voice would have been gruffer still, after 90 minutes of furious, obscene invective. Then he sounded like Lee Marvin. This is how Baz came to be known as 'Deepdale Throat'.

Being easily infected by others' passions, Baz's obsession with Willie Irvine prompted me to do two things: firstly, to find out more about the player, and secondly, catch a red and cream Ribble double-decker bus to

Preston to watch him play. I was probably Baz's one and only convert. He was suitably proud, clumsily curling an arm around my shoulders, pinching my cheeks, while the college women looked on in disbelief.

In his biography *Together Again*, Willie Irvine recounted to author, Dave Thomas: 'When Bobby Seith took over in 1967/68 he had a sinking ship to rescue in a very short space of time. It was a dispirited club which had just had a run of six successive defeats; new players couldn't be tempted to join and critics pointed anyway to the waste of money on previous purchases. Seith didn't do a bad salvage job and made an immediate difference ...' Bob Seith's persuasive charm snared Willie.

Willie Irvine had enjoyed two and a half successful years at Burnley, his parent club. Taking on the mantle of the immortal Ray Pointer, he made his first-team breakthrough in the late summer of 1964. In next to no time, he proved himself to be a top gun. In 144 starts in all senior competitions, Irvine scored 97 goals for Burnley. He was smart on the ground and strong in the air. He put himself about with a strut, insinuating himself into the tiniest of spaces to get a shot away, heaving himself above defenders with perfect timing to produce a flashing header. He would get up the noses of his opponents with his cocky, sometimes brash, 'gobby' manner. It was all part of the contest. The mind games matter almost as much as the quick feet. Like the very best strikers he was always ready to pounce on the half-chance, eyes keenly alert, primed, nerve ends sparking, leg muscles twitching in readiness, coiled to make that explosive spurt, just enough to put him ahead of his markers. It didn't need to be much. At this level, the slightest margins are decisive.

He played with George Best in Northern Ireland's colours. It was said that Ramsey regretted that – he wanted him for himself. Willie Irvine had the class of Jimmy Greaves. The lad who'd emerged from grinding poverty looked set for the richest prizes football could bestow. He was already big but seemed destined to be huge.

But then his world caved in. His leg was broken in a petulant FA Cup tie with Everton. One witness said it was a horror tackle. The crack could be heard at the back of the stand, apparently. It was January 1967. Irvine was aged just 23. Harry Catterick, the Everton manager, went into the dressing room to find him. Willie expected an apology. He didn't get one. '[Catterick] told me that it served me right, that I'd got what I'd been asking for.' There was a lot of bad blood.

Gradually the break healed, but something was wrong. Willie started to develop a limp, half an hour or so into a game. He began to fret. It spoilt things at home. The team wasn't doing so well, either. They started to let in many more goals. There was a spat between chairman Bob Lord and his team-mate Gordon Harris. Harris was moved on. It poisoned the air. Willie began to bridle at Burnley's exacting coach, Jimmy Adamson. As his confidence fell, the niggling got worse. 'Adamson just gnawed away at me in the back of my head ... I couldn't play for him ... His coaching was excellent, studious, thoughtful and creative. As a tactician he was outstanding ... but I just couldn't relate to him.' The goals started to dry up – down to one in three; a good rate for many strikers, not for Willie though. He was no longer an automatic selection. He looked for a way out. But in his desperation to go, Willie didn't look before he jumped. He said he had no idea how badly placed Preston were. But he still signed. That was in March 1968. Preston paid Burnley £45,000 for him. Willie got a £5,000 signing-on fee and a regular £75 per week wage plus appearance money. That was £15 more a week than he was getting at First Division Burnley. Preston could barely afford this, but they couldn't afford relegation, either. Willie was their get out of jail card.

Willie made his Preston debut at Portman Road, Ipswich on Saturday 16 March 1968. Preston were in 20th position, two points better off than Rotherham and bottom-placed Plymouth. Second-placed Ipswich had massive creativity in Danny Hegan and Colin Viljoen. They packed a powerful punch with veteran Ray Crawford, Frank Brogan and John O'Rourke. They thrashed Preston 4-0. Worse still, both Rotherham and Plymouth won, leaving Preston outside the drop zone on goal average only.

'Bloody hell,' thought Willie, 'what am I doing here, what have I done?' But on the following Monday, Preston narrowly beat Aston Villa 2-1 after conceding an early goal. Willie recalled: 'My goal was lucky. I was probably offside but strikers need luck and it came my way that day ... The crowd seemed to take to me straight away ... there was a run of eight unbeaten games and relegation, so close just weeks earlier, was avoided. In 11 games I scored six times. There was a hat-trick against Huddersfield [3-1].' 'Magnificent display by Irvine ... neither the wind, rain nor mud in atrocious conditions could stop the irrepressible Irvine', wrote *Lancashire Evening Post* reporter Norman Shakeshaft.

Willie's confidence returned. 'I felt ten feet tall. That's what strikers need – praise ... In truth the whole team played better as Seith's influence, man-management, coaching and tactics paid off, but fans see things more simply. Irvine had arrived, Irvine had scored goals and Irvine kept them up.' Willie must have had Baz in mind. Along with the other Preston 'Kopites' Baz was there, lustily growling out an adapted version of Manfred Mann's hit single 'Mighty Quinn'. 'Come on without, come on within, you'll not see nothing like Willie Irvine.' Willie's capacity for f***ing excellence was growing exponentially, helped further by his penalty goal which did for local rivals, Blackburn, at Ewood Park on Easter Saturday (1-0). Despite an apparently dodgy defeat at Bristol City, Preston finished on a high.

As the 1968/69 season hove into view, there was an air of expectation around the club. How often an unexpected reprieve revives momentum, leading to expansive and often unrealistic ambitions. Willie was happy with his lot. He had high hopes of Bob Seith, too, 'whose knowledge of the game was first class and who was very much respected and popular with the players.' Willie hit the ground running, scoring 13 goals in the opening 16 games. Willie's winning goal against Bristol City on 16 November (1-0), pushed Preston up to eighth spot. Having lost influential midfielder Alan Spavin and full-back John Ritchie to injury, Bob Seith described this as 'a wretched match' but Preston were then just three points outside the promotion places. No wonder Baz was so chuffed when we first met.

Regrettably, that was as good as it got as North End embarked upon a seven-match winless run, suffering a 4-0 defeat at Sheffield United, a 4-1 home defeat at the hands of Bolton and a 1-0 loss at Blackburn on Boxing Day. Preston slumped into 15th position. On the plus side, Bob Seith had helped tighten up the defence – there were 18 clean sheets that season. The main problem was Preston's lack of goals. If Willie didn't score then it was unlikely that anyone else would. Gerry Ingram was brought in from Blackpool as Willie's strike partner but he struggled to find his feet. His time would come two years later.

Bob Seith reacted to the slide by blooding two youngsters in midfield – 19-year-old Scot, Alex Spark, a composed, constructive box-to-box player, and 18-year-old Bolton boy, Ricky Heppolette, then the only Indian-born player in league football. Baz had high hopes that both youngsters would graduate into 'excellent' players, although neither were yet considered ready for the gold-star expletive.

The FA Cup helped Preston get back on track. Irvine scored twice and Temple once as Nottingham Forest were beaten emphatically (3-0) on 4 January 1969. All three goals were scored at the Town End; a penalty which Irvine smashed into the right-hand corner with Forest keeper Grummitt diving in the opposite direction, a crisp shot from ex-Evertonian Derek Temple after his forceful run bisected future Derby stars Terry Hennessey and Henry Newton, and a fine individual goal from Irvine, who waltzed around the stricken Grummitt before scoring. After a blank Saturday due to an arctic intrusion, reinvigorated Preston beat an almost bankrupt Aston Villa 1-0 at home. It was an ugly affair. Bob Seith pronounced that 'The most that can be said of this travesty of football is that we won ... Tommy Docherty [Villa's new boss] disagreed but Villa's idea, it seemed to me, was to frustrate and completely upset their opponents ... I would never allow my team to resort to those tactics.' Preston's scrambled winner came in the 95th minute as referee Pat Partridge added five minutes for Villa's persistent time-wasting.

The match programme for the fourth-round home tie with Chelsea contained a piece on the visitors' boss, Dave Sexton: 'Possibly the only case on record of a man being appointed "boss" by popular demand of the players!' During the early sixties, Sexton had been a successful coach at Stamford Bridge under the abrasive but dynamic Tommy Docherty. He had helped Tommy transform the club. Docherty had set aside years of drift under Ted Drake by bringing together a young, sparkling, energetic and highly competitive team that once again pushed for honours in the top flight. Peter Osgood and his team-mates rated Sexton's part in that revival highly. Had Tommy Docherty not undermined their combined efforts with some heavy-handed discipline, Chelsea might have gained more silverware than just the League Cup, which was won in 1965. But Docherty was such a larger-than-life character that after his fractious departure in 1967, he left a void at the club. Osgood remembered Sexton as an 'excellent coach, a deep thinker and a grafter'. Believing that he was the man to lead them out of the doldrums, a deputation of first-teamers approached the Chelsea board and respectfully offered their recommendation. Fortunately, the directors listened. The reserved and mild-mannered Sexton was a different kettle of fish to the maverick Docherty. After years of enduring Docherty's turbulence, Sexton's quieter persona appealed to them. Besides, Sexton had an impressive CV. He had just guided Arsenal to their highest placing in eight years, and had helped 'rescue' Fulham from relegation in the season before. He seemed to be the ideal candidate to turn things around. And he did just that.

Peter Osgood recounted to Martin King and Martin Knight in *Ossie: King of Stamford Bridge*: 'Immediately he explained to us what his strategy was going to be – he'd start with the defence and when that was shored up, concentrate on the midfield and then the forward line ... We stopped getting hammered week in, week out ... We started creating attacks again. By this time us boys up front were reaping the benefits and from being relegation candidates in November [1967] we finished in a highly respectable sixth place and reached the quarter-finals of the FA Cup.' Sexton strengthened his squad by bringing in Alan Birchenall, the Sheffield United striker with a sweet left foot, for £100,000, and Ian Hutchinson, a strapping, raw-boned striker from Southern League Cambridge United, for £5,000. Initially, the Chelsea lads couldn't understand what Sexton had seen in Hutchinson. They would find out shortly.

For the fourth-round FA Cup tie at Preston, Sexton selected Peter Bonetti in goal, Eddie McCreadie and 19-year-old Stewart Houston as the full-backs, David Webb and Ron Harris in the centre-back positions, John Hollins and John Boyle in central midfield with Peter Osgood and Charlie Cooke playing wide, and Alan Birchenall and Bobby Tambling as the central strikers. Chelsea came into this game in fifth position in Division One but they had suffered successive defeats: a 4-1 loss at Manchester City and a 2-1 reverse at home to Liverpool in front of a 51,872 crowd. Preston's much higher than average gate of 31,875 was small beer to their big city opponents.

Republic of Ireland international Alan Kelly picked himself in Preston's goal, while Seith went for a full-back pairing of George Ross and Jim McNab, young Alex Spark and Bill Cranston in central defence, a midfield of Derek Temple, Ken Knighton, Ricky Heppolette and Frank Lee, and Willie Irvine and Gerry Ingram up front.

Bob had hoped for better entertainment after a dire contest with Villa but he was to be disappointed. Saturday 25 January remained grey, hazy and nondescript. The same description could have been applied to the game. The BBC *Match of the Day* cameras were there. Creating a highlights package out of the dross on show was a real challenge. Apart from a wonderfully sinuous run by Peter Osgood, which ended with a low shot that whistled just wide of Kelly's left-hand post, this was a dour contest. Willie Irvine ran around a lot but his supply line was stamped out as Chelsea's strength and industry nullified North End's limited creativity. Ingram seemed out of his depth while his wingers, Lee and Temple, got little change out of their opposing full-backs. On the plus side, Preston defended tenaciously with a mature performance from their two youngsters. Chelsea didn't get too many sniffs of goal. Tambling might have done better with a shot that hit the post and Webb had a headed goal ruled out for an earlier infringement. But all in all, Preston deserved a second bite. I didn't know what I was going to say to Baz, though. I have had better times with my head in a bucket. I thought it prudent to keep this to myself.

Actually, Preston got a third bite. Floodlight failure brought the first replay to a premature close with Chelsea winning comfortably by 2-0. Seith had replaced the ineffective Ingram with the recovered Spavin, but Irvine's supply line hadn't improved. On the other hand, Sexton had selected young Hutchinson to play up front alongside Alan Birchenall to give his attack greater physical presence. This had made a difference. Both strikers were on the scoresheet before the lights went out.

Despite their fortunate reprieve, Preston suffered a huge loss in the second replay – a serious injury to Willie Irvine. It came after he had given Preston the lead. Despite Irvine's injury, Preston bravely kept Chelsea at bay until the final minute. Sadly, two late strikes from Webb and the dazzling Cooke turned the game on its head. Preston were out of the FA Cup. Worse still, they were left with a lame main striker. While he remained at Preston, Willie Irvine would not be the same player.

Willie explained in his biography: 'I had taken a whack that was to have serious effects ... David Webb was one of a complete posse of Chelsea hard men. He caught me with a scissors tackle which gripped my left leg. As I turned one way my left knee stayed where it was: game over for me. It was diagnosed as ligament trouble and I carried on playing, which is what we used to do in those days without the benefit of state-of-the-art medical technology. But I struggled, scored less and less with a yard of speed missing.'

Irvine scored just three more league goals that season while Preston finished just below halfway, in 14th position. With Irvine incapacitated, they scraped together only 15 goals in their final 16 league games. If Willie's 15 league goals were taken out of the equation, Preston would have been in a sorry mess. Thankfully, their defence remained proud and strong.

Not having the appropriate treatment, Willie Irvine's injury was aggravated. The pain in his knee became excruciating. A belated X-ray revealed that Willie had a chipped bone, and that calcification had made matters worse. An operation was needed. Further complications resulted after the surgeon cut through a nerve. Willie managed just 16 hobbling appearances during the 1969/70 season as Preston slid deeper and deeper into relegation trouble. Willie needed help up front, but now there was no money to bring anyone in: quite the contrary. The bank forced Preston into selling their better players before permitting any further spending. Ken Knighton was sold for a cut-price £45,000. Temple went off to non-league Wigan for just £4,000. I started to see less and less of Baz. He must have been inconsolable.

The only bright spots were Ricky Heppolette's progress and the blossoming of Archie 'Go Go' Gemmill. Gemmill would eventually play for Brian Clough at Derby County and Nottingham Forest. Clough was so keen to land Gemmill that he threatened to sleep outside Archie's house until he signed. Eight years later, Gemmill scored a magnificent World Cup goal for Scotland against Holland, albeit in a lost cause.

My lasting memory of Gemmill dates back to a very chilly Monday evening, on 16 March 1970. Relegation rivals Charlton were the visitors. In front of a 13,000 crowd, Gemmill produced a superlative performance which tore the Addicks apart. This was after Ray Treacy had headed the visitors into the lead. Gemmill bristled with spiky energy, wriggling in between the Charlton defenders, angrily shrugging off their clumsy restraints. Head down, hunched shoulders, ducking beneath the radar, he feigned to go one way before scurrying off in the other, showing for the ball all over the park, controlling it instantly, boring straight into the box, his quick feet taking him past one defender after another. Shooting on first sight of goal, he was unstoppable. Preston thrashed Charlton 4-1, lifting themselves just above the drop zone and leaving their visitors with the dregs.

It was a lonely swallow, though. Five of Preston's last seven games were lost and none won. Just four more goals were scored. The final indignity came on Monday 13 April, in front of an unsegregated crowd of over 34,000. First Division-bound Blackpool came to Deepdale and won with humiliating ease by 3-0. Ex-Blackburn, Everton and England centre-forward Fred Pickering scored a dismissive hat-trick and former Preston 'reject' Micky Burns played a blinder. Willie Irvine put in an appearance, but it was a pointless limping gesture. Preston failed to create a single chance. They were down and Bob Seith was out.

So was Willie, although his tetchy relationship with new manager, Alan Ball senior, stretched out until the New Year of '71. Then, a loan deal was struck with Pat Saward, Brighton's bubbly manager. After bidding farewell in a Boxing Day game at Tranmere, in front of a paltry crowd of 7,000, Willie headed off for a brief but glorious Indian summer by the sea.

Willie didn't hit it off with the new Preston manager (father of the World Cup hero, Alan Ball junior). But the gruff, confrontational Ball did a good job on a shoestring budget, taking North End back up as Division Three champions, at the first time of asking, alongside reviving Fulham. The so-called 'James Cagney of football' achieved this impressive feat with largely the same dispirited and disjointed squad that was relegated a year before, minus Temple, Gemmill and, for the most part, Irvine.

Ball sold Gemmill to Derby for £59,000 and made just two 'car boot sale' purchases: Bobby Ham, a diminutive striker from Bradford City, for £7,500, and Clive Clark, the veteran ex-QPR and West Bromwich winger. Ham would prove to be quite a bargain. He scored 11 vital goals in 30 league starts, partnering Gerry Ingram, who finally proved his worth by scoring 22 times. Preston gained promotion at rivals Fulham on Saturday 1 May, thanks to a header from young Ricky Heppolette (1-0). The *Match of the Day* cameras were there to record the august occasion. Three days later, Alan

Ball's magnificently revived team seized the Third Division championship with a 3-0 victory over Rotherham. Over 28,000 flocked to Deepdale to acclaim their triumph. I trusted that Baz was among them. I hoped he was. I hoped, too, that he had become reconciled to Willie's departure. I didn't find out for I never saw Baz again.

In January 1969, Chelsea's prospects seemed so much better than those of Preston. Chelsea finished the season in fifth place in Division One while Preston were languishing 31 places below them. Chelsea's average gate of 37,600 was almost three times the size of North End's at 13,471. And yet only 11 years before, Preston were better-placed than Chelsea. Preston completed the 1957/58 season as First Division runners-up, drawing an average crowd of almost 25,000, while Chelsea were nine places below them. Although Chelsea attracted a higher average gate of 37,000, their prospects seemed no better than their Lancastrian rivals. As proof of that, both sides were relegated at the start of the sixties. But then their fortunes diverged sharply, perhaps reflecting the state of the nation's economy. Preston were rooted in the declining industrial North while Chelsea were at the heart of 'swinging London'.

That gulf continued to grow. Within weeks of Preston's demotion in 1970, Chelsea snatched the FA Cup from Leeds' deserving grasp. Chelsea then went on to defeat Real Madrid, a year later, in the European Cup Winners' Cup Final. It seemed inconceivable, then, that the two sides would face one another in a league game before the new decade was out. But that's what happened. Saddled with crippling debts inflicted by the construction of a huge new stand, Chelsea stumbled and fell. They were relegated to Division Two in 1975. Meanwhile, Preston yo-yoed between the Second and Third Divisions. But their paths finally crossed at Stamford Bridge in December 1979. By then, Chelsea's average Second Division gate had fallen to 25,000, although this was still twice what Preston were able to draw.

Preston's decline after the fifties was a fate shared by many of their Lancastrian neighbours – particularly those in the county's smaller, declining industrial towns. Blackpool's First Division excursion in 1970/71 proved to be a one-season wonder, in spite of the talents of Micky Burns, Tommy Hutchison, Tony Green, Alan Suddick and veteran Jimmy Armfield, in his valedictory season. Once Blackpool dropped from the top flight they continued falling, albeit erratically, until they eventually reached the basement. The same fate would afflict Preston, Burnley and Bolton. Blackburn, too, dropped as far as Division Three during the seventies and eighties before reviving, helped by Jack Walker's millions. Although Liverpool and Everton have both remained in the top flight, at least since Liverpool's promotion in 1962, both Manchester clubs have tasted relegation in the intervening years – United in 1974 and City at various points during the eighties and nineties. In fact, City once sunk as low as the third tier before Joe Royle rescued them. Before the Premiership cartel emerged, no one was immune from failure.

'Street Fighting Man': The end of the sixties

On 20 July 1969, the 'Eagle' landed on the moon. A triumphant Neil Armstrong celebrated this miraculous feat with the immortal words: 'One small step for man, one giant leap for mankind.' Not that many parts of the developing world were listening. For independence had not guaranteed a new dawn or a giant step forward. Too many former colonies had succumbed to coups, dictatorships, civil unrest, wars and, in some places, widespread starvation, as in Biafra.

1969 seemed to mark a parting with youthful idealism. If Woodstock's three days of 'peace and music' represented its zenith, a brief interlude in which young hearts ran or slithered free, then Altamont signalled its nadir, particularly when coupled with the Manson nightmare and the nightly televised horror of Vietnam. Fittingly, *Easy Rider*, one of the films of the year, charted the death of a 'hippie' dream. Ironically, Fonda and Hopper's freedom ride was financed by a hard drugs deal underwritten by the habits of less free narcotic addicts. As Jack Kerouac found, uncomplicated freedom, on the road or elsewhere, is hard to come by.

In Britain, there was a different backlash against hippies. Enter the skinheads. They appeared to be living in the past. Their right-wing hatred resurrected the thirties as much as their braces did. In fact, hatred seemed to be their defining identity more than their bovver boots or their taste for reggae or Tamla Motown. By 1969, football had become stained by their hatred. Not that skinhead hatred was confined to football. Other targets included long-haired students, minority ethnic groups, notably those originating from the Indian sub-continent, and gay men. But the tribal nature of football proved particularly attractive to skinhead gangs looking for 'aggro'. Sewn on to their Crombie jackets or tattooed on to their bodies were their football club badges, their marks of distinction. Had England been scarred with sectarianism, other targets might have featured.

Football hooliganism wasn't a skinhead monopoly, though. Crowd trouble, both in and outside our grounds, had emerged four or five years before without any skinhead influence. Even in the late sixties and early seventies, terrace disorder was not purely down to skinheads. But with media coverage of football increasing following the 1966 World Cup, greater publicity was given to football-related violence and particularly that perpetrated by belligerent young men with insect-like shaven heads in narrowed, rolled-up jeans and intimidating footwear.

Combat can arouse intoxicating excitement. Former soldiers, such as Philip Caputo (*A Rumor of War*) have referred to its addictiveness, leaving many yearning for a return to action irrespective of their countervailing fears of death and disability. This is the central theme of the film, *The Hurt Locker*. The prospect of violence can also confer a sense of power on those prepared to use it. The bigger the occasion, the greater that sense of power and excitement is likely to be. Football has helped create the occasion with its vast pulling power. The media has then widened the platform. However, Hunter Davies, author of *The Glory Game,* qualified this, having spent an afternoon with a Spurs 'firm' at Coventry. He observed that the act of seizing a rival's territory, particularly when on 'enemy' soil, was more satisfying than inflicting harm.

In his book, *Among the Thugs*, American journalist Bill Buford graphically documented the pernicious nature of gang culture in shaping attitudes and behaviour. Having 'gone native', he described how the brutality of gang life infiltrated his urbane sensibilities, temporarily converting him from a well-mannered, considerate adult into one who ruthlessly pushed aside and barked thuggishly at a dithering older couple.

Explaining the class component of football-related gang behaviour is a lot trickier. Despite the media claims about 'designer hooligans' – 'thugs' who supposedly double as estate agents and bankers – the reality is that most football 'firms' or 'crews' comprise largely white, youngish, working-class men, who seem keen to exercise their warrior-like masculinity. That is not to say that economic status doesn't matter – it does. It is reflected in the gangs' bragging rights. During the eighties, the London-based 'firms' frequently derided their less well-off rivals in the North by flaunting their Pringle sweaters and Calvin Klein underwear. It hasn't always been about denim and Doc Martins.

Football hooliganism was not a new phenomenon in the mid-1960s. Football-related disorder not only preceded the sixties, it preceded the twentieth century. But there is little doubt that it took root and spread during the latter half of the sixties. It is doubtful, however, that John and Yoko had football 'aggro' in mind when they pleaded 'give peace a chance'.

THE 1969/70 SEASON

Burnley v West Bromwich Albion

'Bridge Over Troubled Water'
21 March 1970

In March 1970, the US President, Richard Nixon, stepped up B-52 bombing of the Ho Chi Minh Trail. It was a desperate and ultimately forlorn attempt to stop supplies being moved from North Vietnam, through Laos and Cambodia, to the Viet Cong, their fellow combatants in the South; so much for superior American firepower.

Over the previous six months, the Vietnam War had moved much closer to home. Al had made that difference. Al was an American student on a year's exchange. He came to Lancaster University in October 1969. It was a year-long reprieve, for his draft number was almost up. As the year progressed, so his wretched anguish mounted. He talked quickly and slept badly. On the night before the game, I kept him company while he indulged the former and coped with the latter. Our cheap cigarettes and cheaper coffee helped see us through.

Like Baz, Al was very fond of expletives. But while Baz would take the measured aim of an accomplished archer, Al would lay waste to his targets with Pom-Pom fury. Al would spit out his expletives, his face contorted with distaste. 'Tell me this,' he would exclaim, 'how the f***ing hell are we mixed up in a legitimate struggle for national unification. It's got f*** all to do with communist expansion. The gooks [he wasn't averse to using U.S. military slang] just want their country back. Jesus f***ing Christ don't you think its time! The f***ing French colonialists grabbed the country from them over a hundred years ago. Then, they wouldn't give it back – even after their hiding by the Germans.' After a brief pause for breath, his diatribe would continue: 'Jesus, they even got the defeated Japs to guard it for them after the Second World War! No wonder the Vietnamese are so p***ed off … All we're doing over there is wasting lives – theirs and ours. For what, may I ask? We're trying to prop up a corrupt, puppet government that no one wants except those leeches on the make. It's incapable of defending itself. And after the f***ing fiasco of Tet, we know we can't protect them, either, no matter how many million bombs we drop on the jungle trails.' It was if Al was desperately rehearsing his pitch to an imaginary draft board, hoping that a combination of honed logic and furious invective might save him from his appalling fate. We never found out what that was.

I had mixed feelings when Dave interrupted my abbreviated sleep, offering me my first trip to Turf Moor, Burnley. Dave was a West Brom fan. He noted my lapsed faith, pouring scorn upon my promiscuous wanderings, having 'tarted myself around', as he put it, at Leeds and, thanks to Baz, Preston. He discounted my dalliance with Morecambe. And I didn't tell him about my one-night fling, for 'old time's sake', with Brighton. Not that there was much fun to be had there. Despite the huge physical presence of Alex 'Boom Boom' Dawson, Brighton failed lamentably to blow down Walsall's walls. But the Brighton fans' chanting (to the tune of Hare Krishna) 'Walsall duck pond, Walsall duck pond, Walsall duck pond, Walsall duck pond; Quack-a- quack quack, Quack-a- quack quack, Quack-a- quack quack, Quack-a- quack quack', accompanied by pecking hand gestures, probably provided me with my most surreal experience on a British football ground.

Dave seemed to regard me as the sheepish shadow that haunts the dating agencies, the sorrowful soul who becomes the protective project of match-fixing friends. Anyway, he wanted some company. That's why he dangled, no, prodded his invitation. Besides, he had his newly-acquired Vauxhall Victor to show off. The V-bomber was a chic vehicle when the *Z-Cars* crews hit the road in 1962, but Dave's rusted wagon obliterated the memory. On the motorway we were well off the pace. Other traffic hissed by derisively. The heater was knackered and the smearing wipers weren't any better.

It was a foul day. Dirty, ragged clouds rolled in from the Irish Sea, dragging with them curtains of rain. Stepping out on to the greasy cobbled street, a blustery wind propelled stinging, spiteful rain into our screwed-up faces. All around us were the scars of industrial blight: the derelict mills, the oily canal and the weed-strewn, rusted marshalling yards. Yet beneath the drab and rain-darkened moors, stone-terraced Burnley appeared welcoming. The inviting light falling from the latticed windows, the flickering front room fires, did not mock our discomfort so much as draw us in, making it possible to feel at home here.

The football club, like its town, was a declining force. A newly-constructed, all-seated stand had been built at the western end but the southern flank was a cordoned-off demolition site. Post-war austerity characterised the remaining parts of the ground. Rusted girders dripped with the penetrating rain. In step with their surroundings, the kids exuded nonchalant toughness. It wasn't so much their bovver boots or their scuffed scarves, tied tightly to their wrists. None of them wore coats. They seemed oblivious to winter's late riposte. I was deeply impressed.

Harry Potts was no longer in charge. He had been pushed 'upstairs' as general manager, allowing former captain and favourite son, Jimmy Adamson, to take over team affairs. Harry's move had been made in order to keep Adamson at the club. After all, Adamson had an impressive reputation as a coach. Bobby Charlton rated him. He had been schooled for the England job to follow on from Walter Winterbottom after the Chile World Cup finals. Adamson spurned that opportunity, preferring to extend his playing career. So the post was offered to Alf Ramsey.

Burnley's bluff chairman, Bob Lord, thought that the Potts–Adamson partnership was his dream ticket, pairing Potts' impressive managerial track record with Adamson's glittering coaching skills. Besides, as manager and skipper, they had complemented one another so well during the club's glory days. In 1963, Adamson still thought so highly of Potts that he recommended him as a part-time adviser to the new England manager, Alf Ramsey. But after Adamson was appointed as first-team coach a year later, it wasn't long before their relationship became strained.

Adamson was steeped in modern tactical thinking. He had seen in Chile how defensively-minded the international sides were, recognising that new methods were needed to beat them. Potts was more of an old-school thinker, wedded to what had worked well for him in the past, not appreciating, perhaps, that he no longer had the surfeit of talent which could make up for any tactical deficiencies. Whereas the excitable, enthusiastic Harry Potts rarely gave detailed instruction about how he wanted his team to play, the ostensibly cooler Adamson was much more specific about what he wanted from his players, using training ground drills and blackboard diagrams to make his point. But it wasn't just a clash of ideas that was the problem. With the club's fortunes fading and its average attendances falling to 16,072, the lowest in the top flight, Burnley had to sell in order to survive. The growing pressure on the bottom line caused the cracks to widen in the Potts–Adamson relationship. Their differences in personality and style started to grate. From rubbing along famously they began to rub one another up the wrong way.

Former Burnley midfielder, Arthur Bellamy, had already broken into the first team when Jimmy Adamson was made coach in 1964. He told Burnley author, Dave Thomas:

> *Harry was never a great tactician but Jimmy introduced new routines, moves and free kicks. The way Burnley*

> *played could depend on who they were playing and team selections began to be made on the basis of who was the best man for a particular role. Jimmy was perhaps one of the first of the new tacticians, the first of the modern-day coaches and talkers. Harry was a great man and a great manager, but he was not a great coach in my opinion. He was a smoother of troubles and he gave players confidence. But Jimmy Adamson taught me to do things I didn't know I could do, like playing sweeper. Gradually Jimmy became more and more responsible for the training. Things became more planned and technical under Jimmy. The man from the next era was replacing the man of the old.*

Fellow midfielder, Martin Dobson, had good reason to feel grateful to Adamson, who had rescued his career after being rejected by Bolton. Martin added: 'Jimmy had us practising set plays for hours on end. Each time we erred, he hauled us back and we would start again. The delivery had to be spot on, the positioning had to be exact, the runs needed to be timed perfectly. Jimmy wouldn't accept anything less than perfection.'

One-club man Brian Miller was a Potts fan. In fact, he based his later managerial style upon that of his old team boss. But he was well aware of Harry's tactical limitations. Brian remembered an unusually heavy defeat at Ipswich in 1961, which Potts attributed to the humid conditions, failing to recognise how Ramsey's tactical plan had completely flummoxed them. Brian added: 'There was no inquest or fuss made [by Potts]. It was simply, "ah well, let's get on with the next game".'

Former left-back Les Latcham became a first-team regular in 1967 following the transfer of Alex Elder to Stoke. He told Dave Thomas how the atmosphere gradually soured between Potts and Adamson, commenting: 'It became increasingly clear that the partnership was not working and that Adamson wanted sole control. This was not an unnatural ambition. He had his own theories, tactics and aspirations. It meant however that there was growing confusion about exactly who was in charge, and if there is one thing that footballers want it is clarity.' Elder described how a once 'happy club' was becoming divided as the players were splitting into pro-Adamson and pro-Potts camps. He illustrated this by citing two examples concerning player selection: 'Ralph Coates came in for a game in his early days, played really well, and was told by Adamson he would start the next game. Potts overruled this. Willie Irvine tells the story that it was Adamson who decided he would not feature in one of the Fairs Cup games. It was Potts who informed him though and when Irvine asked why he was not playing, Potts replied it was Adamson's decision and it was nothing to do with him.' Clearly, this divisive situation wasn't helping anyone, least of all the team's prospects.

In February 1970, the change was made. Chairman Bob Lord appointed Adamson as team manager and Potts was 'pushed upstairs'. Surprisingly, it came about after Forest had been thrashed 5-0 at home, Burnley's fourth win in a five-match unbeaten run. It was clear, then, that this had been a planned decision, to which Harry Potts had not been privy. Although Potts graciously acknowledged Adamson's accession, saying 'I could not hand over to a better fellow', he was devastated to be excluded from the Gawthorpe training ground. Harry never lost his love of the place, rubbing his hands on icy mornings, excitedly exclaiming 'it's just like Switzerland'. As Martin Dobson observed, Harry found it hard to adjust to the role of general manager. He had been a father figure to many of his younger players. He had rescued Steve Kindon after he had been thrown out by his landlady and he had comforted Ralph Coates during a family bereavement. According to Dave Thomas, author of *Harry Potts: Margaret's Story*, Harry's wife, Margaret, harboured a grudge about the affair, feeling that her husband had been stabbed in the back. When she and Harry were denied a top-table place at the club's annual dinner she had no hesitation in speaking her mind. What had been a generally happy, close-knit club began to fragment.

It wasn't just the club management which was in a state of flux. The team was beginning to change markedly, too. Only full-back John Angus remained from the 1959/60 championship-winning side. But still young hearts ran free. Steve Kindon and Dave Thomas were the newish kids in town, complementing established home-grown stars like Ralph Coates and Brian O'Neil and astute signings like Frank Casper and Martin Dobson. Kindon and Thomas had graduated from the youth team that had won the FA Youth Cup in 1968. Before the Albion game, Adamson purred about the performances of his gifted youngsters who had done him proud in the 3-3 midweek draw at Old Trafford. Two-goal Thomas was singled out for special praise.

Not that Adamson's pre-match euphoria inhibited West Bromwich. A skidding strike from a midfielder, 'Bomber' Brown, fizzed over the glistening mud to give the visitors an early lead, prompting the Burnley Longside fans to chant inanely, 'Zigger, zagger, zigger, Astle is a n*****.' Jeff Astle was the Baggies' white, free-scoring centre-forward.

At this time, football had a dismal record in combating racism. This didn't just apply to what was happening on the terraces. Many football coaches had little compunction about writing off black British players peremptorily, often castigating their alleged lack of commitment, mental toughness and work rate. Few young black players managed to break through this stultifying discrimination. It is perhaps worth speculating whether, as a young hopeful, Pele would have been offered terms by a British club. Those who did break through had to contend with racist abuse, even from their colleagues and fans. When the black Bermudan striker, Clyde Best, made his mark in West Ham's front line during the early seventies, the home crowd greeted him with the chant 'We bought Clyde Best and covered him with chocolate. Ooh!' It was an adaptation of the reggae-style Cadbury's Fruit & Nut TV advert. Although meant affectionately, the chant seemed to suggest that Best's blackness was just a veneer, as if he was an honorary white. But perhaps that's reading too much into it.

Meanwhile, Burnley had worries about their top-flight status. A point at Old Trafford had not relieved their relegation woes. Stung by the early setback, they set about wresting control from the Baggies. Eventually, Tony Brown, Len Cantello, Graham Lovett and Bobby Hope were forced to concede the sodden midfield to the flitting Coates, the twinkling Thomas, the terrier-like O'Neil and the steadfast Bellamy. Increasing pressure became applied to West Bromwich's suspect defence.

Steve Kindon was in 'runaway wardrobe' mode. Making light of the heavy conditions, he continually powered in from the left, uninhibited by surface water, spattering mud and despairing tackles, to launch muscular assaults on the opposition's goal. Warming to his efforts, the 12,000-plus home crowd set aside their groaning, moaning and heckling and threw themselves into the fray, belligerently bellowing their side on. Suddenly, the promise was fulfilled. Kindon broke through on the left side of the Baggies' box, lashing home a fierce, rising drive past Albion keeper, Osborne. The visceral force of Kindon's shot unleashed a leaping, straining, tumult on the Longside. The sullen away support was treated to their jabbing gestures of derision. The Clarets fans' vociferous joy pierced the afternoon's dank greyness.

The rain grew in intensity as a premature dusk descended. The glare of the floodlights flashed and sparkled in the muddy pools appearing all over the pitch. As the second half progressed, the game became, quite simply, a trial of strength. It was one in which Burnley's youngsters were the more determined. By the time that Bellamy's slithering long-range effort had evaded a thicket of legs and found goal, neat football had been abandoned. The objective was now to propel the ball as far forward as possible and set off in dogged pursuit. Hacking it clear of the mud and puddles seemed to require Herculean power. We felt exhausted by association.

The crowd continued to urge Burnley forward, hurling encouragement and invective in equal measure, but the Clarets could not find another way through. It didn't matter. By then, West Brom had lost their way entirely. And soon would I. Little did I realise this, then, but a claret and blue potion had been injected into my veins. Life would never be the same again.

World Cup willies

With England expected to do well in the Mexico World Cup, Wilson hoped to trade on the feelgood factor. He planned a general election for immediately after the quarter-finals. Alas, it was to end in tears for both Ramsey and Wilson. Ramsey's class of '70 was touted as his strongest. But England's form had not been startling. Having lost to Yugoslavia in the 1968 European Football Championships, England weren't even the best international team in Europe, let alone the world. During 1968, their record had been unremarkable – inferior to both West Germany and Czechoslovakia. Although England progressed through the group stages in Mexico on the back of turgid 1-0 victories over Romania and Czechoslovakia, their 1-0 defeat by the brilliant Brazilians underlined the size of their task if they were to retain their crown. As it turned out, it wasn't the sublime Pele and his superb team-mates who brought about England's downfall; it was that durable old enemy, West Germany. Admittedly, bad luck, crucial goalkeeping errors and a mistaken substitution played a big part in their loss. With England's hopes evaporating in the searing heat of Leon, Harold Wilson's chances of electoral victory faded also.

Prior to England's World Cup elimination, Wilson held a lead in the electoral polls. Like England, Wilson was to suffer two late mortal blows. The press strike ended just in time for the nation to dwell on the bad news from Mexico; a trade deficit was also announced instead of the expected surplus. Actually, the deficit was not significant, the product of a one-off purchase of two jumbo jets. But it was enough to put Tory leader, Ted Heath, marginally ahead in the polls.

In going to the country, Wilson had little to crow about. His economic record was unprepossessing. His government had been battered by a succession of economic crises, climaxing with the devaluation fiasco of November 1967. The Department of Economic Affairs had achieved little other than to stir up jealous animosity with the Treasury. The five-year growth target of 30 per cent was hopelessly ambitious. In fact, Britain's production of manufactured goods continued to shrink during Wilson's time in office. Not that there was anything unusual about this. Between 1950 and 1970, Britain's share of world manufacturing exports fell from over a quarter to barely a tenth. To a large extent this decline was inevitable. Given our relatively small population and limited natural resources, it was impossible for us to sustain our Victorian Age supremacy as better-endowed nations came up to speed. This did nothing, of course, to dampen the preposterous expectations of those who believed that Britain's supremacy was a God-given right. What happened in the seventies gave us cause for sober reflection, particularly our status in the global football hierarchy.

‘I DON’T BELIEVE IN MIRACLES’ 1971–1979

‘As a dog returneth to his vomit, so a fool
returneth to his folly’
Proverbs chapter 26, v.11

THE 1970/71 SEASON

Colchester United v Leeds United (FA Cup fifth round)

'Resurrection Shuffle'
13 February 1971

Don Revie always made detailed game plans. He asked his coach, Syd Owen, to prepare elaborate dossiers on all opponents. Revie placed great value on these but Owen had reservations. Owen felt they bred an over-cautious approach. Leeds and England left-half, Norman Hunter, told Andrew Mourant, author of *Don Revie: Portrait of a Footballing Enigma*: 'I think we did pay the opposition too much respect. But whatever Don did at that time, you had to have respect for. Though looking back, I would never have a dossier to play against a team. I would make certain points. We analysed teams far too much.' Leeds and Scotland right-winger, Peter Lorimer, agreed. 'We used to play some teams at Elland Road that weren't entitled to be on the same pitch as us,' he claimed. 'He [Revie] was so thorough that at the end you were creating a bit of respect for a team you didn't have to fear.'

Former Workington boss Ken Furphy liked dossiers, too. Like Revie, he gathered detailed information about his opponents. Prior to Watford's FA Cup tie with Manchester United in 1969, Furphy provided a trenchant analysis of each of the United players. He told his team how softly centre-half Steve James headed the ball; how Nobby Stiles' sphere of influence was reduced because he had to mind James; how the keeper, Rimmer, was strong in the air but slow in getting down to low shots; how full-backs Francis Burns and Tony Dunne pushed up without ensuring sufficient cover; and how Best's volatility might offer something to exploit. Looking at the BBC TV coverage of his briefing session, a number of his players looked bemused, as if they were struggling to contend with the welter of detail. Football is a game of honed instinct. Too much instruction risks immobilisation. As forensic as Furphy's analyses were, their value seemed depleted by their volume. Perhaps Revie's preparations were tarnished in a similar way?

However, some of Revie's players found ways of filtering the information overload. Leeds and Scotland midfielder Billy Bremner told Andrew Mourant: 'I'd look at the dossier but I wasn't taking much in … The only time I would listen was when he [Revie] was talking about Continental players I didn't know.' Lorimer admitted: 'We knew how we were going to play anyway.'

While Revie created a superb team, his cautious, superstitious nature possibly held them back. Nevertheless, Leeds arrived at Colchester, on a bright Saturday afternoon in February 1971, as massive favourites. No one, other than Dick Graham and his boys, could have envisaged what would transpire. Listening in on our college kitchen radio, we couldn't believe our ears.

In 1971, Colchester were a mid-table Fourth Division side. They had never done or won anything of significance. Their ramshackle ground at Layer Road normally attracted crowds of around 5,000 or so to their league games. They weren't much better off than a top Southern League side. But on this day 16,000 supporters strained every rusting seam to get in.

Colchester's manager, Dick Graham, had previously been the boss of Crystal Palace and Orient. He was an unorthodox, controversial veteran who had greyed early in his service of the game. He was a scrapper, but kept his own counsel. He had no time for hype, idle banter or expansive predictions. His teams did his talking out on the pitch. Graham was only prepared to make three pre-match promises: one, his team would be as hard as nails; two, they would be as fit as butchers' dogs, and three, that everyone would be massively fired up for the fight. In order to get his players' heads in gear, Graham knew he had to coax some and bully others. Graham might have been a tough disciplinarian but there was nothing rigid about his management style. At Palace he impressed as a tactical innovator, being one of the first managers in the English game to introduce two centre-backs and adopt a squad system with players called in to perform specific tasks. Graham was always prepared to roll up his sleeves. He could be head cook and bottle-washer. In keeping almost bankrupt Orient afloat, he became a multi-tasking supremo, combining his management duties with that of groundsman, barman and fund-raiser. Graham didn't wilt in the face of massive obstacles. He tackled them head-on with bullish determination.

Colchester were an ageing side – six of their players were over 30. They became known as 'Grandad's Army'. Graham explained: 'I have to resurrect players. I look around to find men who have been discarded before their time and give them a new lease of life.' Ray Crawford was one of

Graham's 'Lazarus' signings, the 34-year-old having been snatched back from Southern League football at Kettering Town.

Crawford told Mike Donovan of *Backpass* magazine: 'I went to Kettering Town, who were a good, well-run club. They got me a rented house and a job. That was hard – having to work for a living! The chairman ran a dry cleaners and I had to knock on doors asking people if they had any dry cleaning. One bloke, with a fag in his mouth, came to the door and I asked the question. He looked at me, took the fag out of his mouth, and held it in his hand and said: "F*** off!" It hadn't been that long ago that I was playing in front of 40,000 at Highbury.' But then Hereford's player-manager, John Charles, convinced Crawford that he should still be playing league football. Prompted by his wife, Crawford contacted Dick Graham at Colchester and a deal was fixed. Graham paid both Kettering and Charlton £2,000 each (Charlton still held the player's registration) and Crawford was back in league football. Crawford recalled that 'Dick was good enough to have managed at a higher level. He was a great motivator and his training was hard but brilliant.'

Crawford was confident his side could beat Leeds. 'I always play well against Leeds,' he insisted. 'I always score goals against Jack Charlton.' Graham laid out his game plan. He told his team that they were to attack boldly from the start, they were to press Leeds in their own half, they were to harry them in packs, they were to get in their faces and never let them settle. He told his hard men, John Kurila (one of Dave Bowen's former enforcers) and John Gilchrist, to clamp down tightly on Allan Clarke and Johnny Giles and 'accompany them to the toilet, if necessary'.

Crawford later told Steve Morgan of *Four Four Two* magazine: 'We knew that the Leeds goalkeeper, Garry Sprake, was going through a bad time. So we decided to bombard him with crosses.' The burly Crawford gave Charlton a real going-over, too, jostling, barging and harassing him unmercifully, inducing a morass of wild errors. 'A dithering novice' was Geoffrey Green's withering assessment of Charlton's shaky performance. The normally self-assured league leaders became rattled quickly. They were being beaten at their own game.

After 18 minutes of incessant pressure, Colchester were awarded a free kick inside the Leeds' half, near the left touchline. Sprightly right-winger Brian Lewis, who was causing Leeds so much confusion by constantly swapping flanks, floated the ball high towards the far post. Under pressure from a posse of bustling Colchester players, Sprake flapped haplessly at the cross. Crawford moved in for the kill. Timing his run with precision, he brushed aside the bemused Charlton and leapt unmarked to produce a perfect glancing header. The ball flashed off the right side of his forehead and into the top right-hand corner of the net. Terry Cooper, the far-post sentry, barely twitched as the net bulged behind him. It was a classic Crawford goal. Once again it was *The Curse of the Jungle Boy*. Layer Road shuddered with the ecstatic roar of 16,000 voices. Ten minutes later they were whisked into dreamland.

Once again, it was Crawford who was the executioner. This time the goal was simply freakish. Although laying prone on the edge of the six-yard box following a tussle with Leeds' right-back Paul Reaney, Crawford somehow managed to swivel on his backside and poke the loose ball past the dumbfounded Sprake with his trailing left foot. Reaney, Charlton and Sprake all looked on in horror as the ball bobbled slowly towards goal, clipping the inside of the right-hand post before rolling in. There was a momentary pause as the wide-eyed crowd struggled to suspend their disbelief. But with Crawford's right arm raised in triumph, realisation overcame incredulity as yet another explosive cheer rocked the dilapidated ground.

Sprake's confidence was shattered. Although the Welsh international was a brilliantly agile goalie, he had become increasingly error-prone. And with his game unravelling, so his morale nosedived. This caused him to be even more impulsive and jittery. While playing at Anfield, Sprake had literally thrown one in, much to the delight of the onlooking Kop, who immediately broke into a rendition of 'Careless Hands'. But Revie stood faithfully behind Sprake – to a fault, perhaps. Certainly, the now shaky Sprake was blatantly culpable for Colchester's decisive third goal. Within ten minutes of the restart, Brian Lewis tested Sprake's nerve once more and yet again it deserted him. Lewis' exploratory lob into the box bounced awkwardly between the hesitant Sprake and the uncertain Reaney. Their momentary delay in dealing with a routine clearance proved fatal, for in powered Colchester's muscular Dave Simmons to jump between them and head the ball home. Brian Glanville reported in *The Sunday Times*: 'Charlton stood, hands dejectedly on hips, like a man contemplating the abyss.' Meanwhile, Crawford and Simmons were embracing one another excitedly in front of their adoring fans on the Layer Road terrace.

The Leeds players had been well briefed by Revie. It wasn't as if they hadn't been prepared for Dick Graham's highly-charged game plan. They had been explicitly told not to mix it with the Colchester lads and to concentrate on their own game. Yet they cast aside Revie's instructions, principally because Colchester managed to get up their noses so well. Instead of seeing off their exuberant opponents with their silky one-touch football, the Leeds players opted for fighting fire with fire. They reacted

Capital punishment: Jimmy Greaves scored five goals against Football League champions, Wolves at Stamford Bridge, August 1958 (Getty Images)

Jimmy Greaves (right) and Surrey county cricketer, Ron Tindall, Chelsea's hit men against Wolves in August 1958 (Author's collection)

Archie Macaulay, boss of giant-killing Norwich in 1959 and of Fourth Division champions Brighton in 1965 (Brighton & Hove Albion FC)

Danny Hylton (second right) has put Aldershot Town into an early lead at promotion rivals, Torquay United, in March 2008. Scott Davies (third right) scored a stunning 90th minute winner to help his side seize the Blue Square Conference Premiership title just over a month later. Joining in the celebrations here are Joel Grant (far left), Rob Elvins (second left) and Anthony Charles (far right) (Ian Morsman)

to the crash-tackling Colchester storm by following suit. Revie's tactical plan went careering out of the window in a litany of reckless tackles and headless, thumping exchanges. The formidable Leeds defence had seldom crumbled so wanly; their smoothly destructive midfield had rarely been so inept. In the absence of Bremner, Giles was expected to control the middle of the park but Colchester's tough little wing-half, John Gilchrist, was quick to get on his case. Instead of focusing upon his immaculate passing game, Giles was provoked into a series of petulant scuffles by his gleeful but gritty marker.

After the game, Gilchrist explained how he inadvertently knocked Giles out of his stride. 'Right at the start,' he said, 'Terry Cooper miscued this clearance up into the stand. "Blimey", I thought, "what sort of effort was that from an England full-back?" Trouble was, I must have said it aloud. And Giles overheard. "Never mind Cooper, how many caps have *you* got?" he shouted back. I couldn't let it go at that, so I told him, "None, but then I wasn't born in Ireland, where they give away caps with packets of cornflakes." Looking back, I think I'd have been better off keeping my trap shut. He's small, is Giles, but he can be bloody hard. I'll be carrying the marks from this match long after it has been forgotten.'

The irony was that Colchester's third goal reminded Leeds how good they could be. Suddenly, they began to play with paralysing power. Dick Graham said 'It was the most controlled demonstration of pure football I've ever seen in such circumstances.' Going for broke, Revie told Clarke to drop deeper while Giles was pushed further forward. With Leeds' penetrative passes finding their mark, Colchester were pushed back to the edge of their box. Dick Graham's players continued to run and run, trying to harry their opponents into errors, as before, but now they found Leeds players too quick and assured for them. The Leeds boys had previously allowed their hosts to lead them into blind alleys, whereas now they were despatching scampering runners to all parts of the park, stretching the home defenders and creating cracks in their huddled fortress. The iron grip, which Kurila and Gilchrist had so effectively applied, became loosened. Increasingly, the Colchester enforcers were bypassed by a succession of stunning one-twos. With consternation growing among the home fans, Hunter stole into the crowded area to head home Lorimer's corner. Leeds had 29 minutes to salvage both their cup dreams and their reputation. Colchester responded to the mounting pressure by producing a frenzy of torrid tackles and frantic lunges, but, with still 12 minutes left, Giles found sufficient space to nip in and nab Leeds' second. Gnawing anxiety gripped the home supporters as they saw their prospects of a historic triumph slipping away.

With both their confidence and energy draining, Colchester went for the 'Alamo' solution. Everyone was pulled back to man the rickety pump. Consequently, Colchester breakaways became briefer and rarer, although Crawford was given a sniff of a chance to seal the game. He confessed that he was 'just too bloody tired to kick the ball that should have given me my hat-trick.' Leeds were now bombarding the Colchester goalmouth incessantly. Just three minutes from time, Leeds' centre-forward, Mick Jones, connected perfectly with Peter Lorimer's cross. His header was goalbound before home centre-half, Brian Garvey, got in its way, diverting the ball into the arms of his alert keeper, Graham Smith. Colchester had won. It was the most amazing giant-killing act since Walsall beat the mighty Arsenal in 1933.

After the game, Ray Crawford commented: 'Leeds never got their passing game going until about the last 20 minutes when we couldn't get the ball off them.' He summarily dismissed Jack Charlton's complaint that there was 'virtually no grass on the ground and the pitch was very bumpy: what we call a great leveller.' 'Nonsense,' retorted Crawford. 'They just never got used to the pitch – it was a fantastic playing surface.' Looking again at the archive footage, Ray's assessment seemed fair. Even the goalmouths were still green and there seemed to be no problem about the ball running smoothly once Leeds were on top. After the game, Jack Charlton left Ray a note saying: 'Lucky bastard, best wishes, Jack'.

Dick Graham kept his pre-match promise that he would scale the crumbling walls of Colchester Castle if his side won. But the season would end in disappointment for both sides. In the next round Colchester were thumped by Everton. They also failed to win promotion. After West Bromwich's controversial victory at Elland Road in April, Leeds failed to win any honours, either. Dick Graham did have another taste of glory, though, when he guided his side to a Watney Cup triumph, beating First Division West Bromwich in the final. But shortly afterwards he lost his job after a boardroom reshuffle. He left with the sour reflection: 'If I had fielded a team of 11 carpenters they would have still expected it to have beaten Leeds United.'

Sound of the seventies

The introduction to John Peel's Radio One show was provided by Jimmy Page's scorching riff in 'Heartbreaker'. By Peel's innovatory standards, the music he showcased then didn't sound that groundbreaking, apparently stuck in the 'prog' grooves of the late sixties. Thank God, he found later liberation in the vibrancy of reggae and punk. But while much of the early inventiveness of progressive rock had degenerated into plodding pretension, newer, sharper sounds were to be heard from the emerging gay and women's liberation movements. Here we began to hear the rebel yells of the chronically oppressed and suppressed.

With the consumer boom releasing more women from household drudgery and improvements in education and contraception seeming to spur further freedoms, the role of women, particularly within marriage, became re-examined. In her sociological study *The Captive Wife*, Hannah Gavron discovered a mixed picture as far as female emancipation was concerned. She noted still 'the constant pressure on young women to play down and discipline an ambition that society at the same time constantly stimulates'. Although she recognised that modern marriages were more egalitarian than those of previous generations, for middle-class wives 'equality meant *independence*', whereas 'for the working-class it meant *closeness*'. She observed, too, that while many middle- and working-class wives had less difficulty in reconciling their roles as wives and workers, they had a greater problem in juggling their roles as *mothers* and workers. She also believed that educational improvements had done little to liberate working-class women. Most of them were without academic qualifications and left with dull, repetitive jobs. Working-class mothers were more likely to feel isolated than their middle-class counterparts.

Whereas Hannah Gavron used a scalpel in presenting her carefully-dissected observations, Germaine Greer went for the sledgehammer in her best-selling feminist polemic, *The Female Eunuch*, published in 1970. She lashed out angrily with the claim 'Women have very little idea how much men hate them.' With popular films around like *Straw Dogs* and *Carnal Knowledge* you could see her point. Greer believed that women are taught to hate themselves and repress their capacity for vitality, action, autonomy and self-expression. Even entertainment as apparently innocuous as *Monty Python* had its only female performer, Carole Cleveland, consigned to ironically titillating roles. My mother-in-law was not too impressed with women's lib, though. Having suffered the privations of the pre-war Tyneside depression, she dismissed 'this burning your bra nonsense' as 'wanton vandalism'.

In October 1970, the British Gay Liberation Front (GLF) was started by Bob Mellor and Aubrey Walter. Gay rights campaigner, Peter Tatchell, remembered: 'GLF was a glorious, enthusiastic and often chaotic mix of anarchists, hippies, left-wingers, feminists, liberals and counter-culturalists. It questioned marriage, the nuclear family, monogamy and patriarchy – as well as the wars in Vietnam and Ireland ... We saw society as fundamentally unjust and sought to change it ... GLF aligned itself with the movements for women's, black, Irish, working-class and colonial freedom. We marched for troops out of Ireland and against the anti-union Industrial Relations Act ... Our message was "innovate, don't assimilate".' It was hard to accuse the GLF of narrowing its targets.

Encouraged by the emergence of the GLF, Ged, a fellow student, decided he would announce his 'coming out' in a university lecture theatre, just before the arrival of a history professor. Oddly, he chose me as his confidant, although there was nothing confidential about this announcement. It was like the zealous testimony of a religious convert, made so loudly that a score of students turned to stare at us. There was no escape. While Ged told me of his 'Damascus' experience, his eyes fixed on mine with a feverish intensity, forcing my stilted smile. Although rendered mute by his revelation, Ged was blissfully unaware of my discomfort. He was too consumed with his exuberant rediscovery. From being an edgy, haunted, restless individual, he had suddenly found a sense of fulfilment and, with it, unexpected self-confidence. 'Good for him', I decided, once I had regained my composure.

The gay and women's liberation movements did much to question and erode what were previously considered to be the 'natural' differences between men and women. And here glam rock gave a hand, being both an expression of this liberation and a contributor to it. Gary Kemp, formerly of the new romantic band Spandau Ballet, recalled that 'Gender-bending was suddenly far more rebellious than drugs and violence.' The camp, androgynous, glamorous look was in, thanks not only to Marc Bolan and David Bowie, but also Lou Reed, Roxy Music and the proto-punk New York Dolls. In glum, grey, strike-ridden, power-stricken Britain we appreciated a dash of colour.

The consumer boom of the late fifties and early sixties saw the emergence of a wealthier, more individualistic, skilled working-class group. Many of their members proceeded to populate the burgeoning new towns, which sprung up around the fringes of our run-down city centres. Sociologists called them C2s. They were the potential readership that Rupert Murdoch courted when he reinvented the *Sun* newspaper in 1969. When the Tory manifesto, *A Better Future*, emerged from Ted Heath's Selsdon Park policy think tank in January 1970, it had resonance with this group. After all, they had their rising prosperity to protect. Unsurprisingly, many of them were attracted by greater tax cuts, stronger law and order, curbs on 'excessive' strike action, greater immigration controls and reductions in public spending.

Disingenuously, Wilson accused 'Heath's Selsdon Man [as] designing a system of society for the ruthless and the pushing, the uncaring. His message for the rest is: you're out on your own.' Actually, Ted Heath was not the callous creator of a suburban Frankenstein that Wilson made out. Although inclined to be prickly, huffy and standoffish, Heath was, at heart, a consensus politician. He gravitated towards the middle ground. Not a lot separated Heath's Tories from Wilson's so-called socialists. Over the next decade the divisions between the parties would grow significantly. As a result of the oil crisis, bitter industrial unrest and a substantial fall in the value of sterling, the British political 'post-war consensus' began to unravel.

THE 1971/72 SEASON

Burnley v Hull City

'Telegram Sam'
12 February 1972

It was a bleak mid-winter. As if the insurgent, damp cold wasn't bad enough, we had to contend with daily power cuts as Prime Minister Heath slugged out a losing battle with the miners. Heath never got to grips with the trade unions. His Industrial Relations Act was a disaster.

Eleven million days were lost to strikes in 1970, the highest total since the General Strike of 1926. The National Union of Miners (NUM) had not been a militant organisation in post-war Britain; quite the contrary. But its members were becoming increasingly frustrated. Their wages had slipped significantly behind those of many other manual labourers, and their annual holiday entitlement was still only two weeks when most workers were getting three. Moreover, miners were expected to put up with primitive conditions such as the appalling heat at the coalfaces, which forced many of them to work naked. Despite post-war modernisation, the British coalmining industry was still largely unmechanised. Helped by a reduced majority threshold for deciding industrial action, the NUM were ready to do battle.

In January 1972, the miners began their industrial action with a new and decisive tactic – the 'flying picket'. Saltley was its crowning glory; it was a vindication of Arthur Scargill's shrewd planning. Helped by sympathetic local car workers, the Birmingham-based coke depot was closed as 10,000 pickets overwhelmed the few hundred policemen deployed to keep the coke supplies flowing.

Thousands of factories were forced to work a three-day week. Millions of workers were laid off. In Burnley, Vokes Ltd told a hundred of its staff that there was no work for them. The town's Coronation Mill ran at 50 per cent production, operating on Wednesdays, Thursdays and Saturdays. Electrical heating was banned in shops, restaurants and other places of entertainment. The *Burnley Express* carried a picture of a barmaid at the Talbot Hotel cheerfully serving pints by candlelight. 'We can take it!' was the gritted message. In the worst tradition of 'Ballroom Blitz', Padiham Town Hall hosted a chilly 'Tots to Teens' dance, inhabited by scores of manic little girls scurrying around in hot pants. Despite the eclectic age range, no local teenagers would be seen embalmed there. The public were urged to restrict electrical usage to one room at home. Only the hospitals were spared the power cuts, although Burnley's Marsden Hospital had to borrow an army power generator to keep it going.

After seven weeks of misery, Heath endured a humiliating defeat, conceding almost all of the NUM's demands. The Barnsley strike leader, Scargill, crowed: 'Here was living proof that the working class had only to flex its muscles and it could bring governments, employers, society to a complete standstill.' It usually avails underdogs little to be so brazen in their moment of triumph, particularly when their victory is so complete and demeaning. Margaret Thatcher noted with distaste that 'There was no disguising that this was a victory for violence.' Her determination to restrain what she considered to be excessive trade union power led to bloody conflict in the years ahead. If Saltley was Heath's 'Bull Run' then Orgreave would be her 'Gettysburg'.

But the bloodiest conflict of that winter took place in Londonderry on Sunday 30 January when 13 unarmed civilians on a civil rights demonstration were shot dead by soldiers of the Parachute Regiment. The 'Troubles' claimed the lives of 72 innocent civilians, 43 soldiers, 11 policemen and five members of the Ulster Defence Regiment in 1972. It would be the worst annual death toll of the Ulster conflict.

After a promising start to life in Division Two, Burnley's subsequent performances did little the lift the glum mood. Welsh winger Leighton James had emerged as a major talent, though, scoring seven times in his first 11 games. He was twice on target as visiting Middlesbrough were thumped 5-2 on 13 November although, arguably, Burnley's star performer that afternoon was 'super sub' Steve Kindon, who created so much havoc in Boro's defence with his bullish power and thoroughbred pace. Jimmy Adamson told James Lawton of the *Daily Express*: 'There is no more powerful runner in English football than Steve Kindon. When he is feeling good in himself he frightens opposing defences right out of their skins.' And yet a few weeks later, following a succession of fitful performances, an exasperated Adamson told his young striker, 'You are either brilliant or rubbish. I cannot afford to gamble with you at the moment.' It was reported that Bert Head of Crystal Palace and Malcolm Allison of Manchester City were prepared to offer £180,000 for the unsettled Kindon although nothing transpired.

Kindon wasn't the only mercurial star in Adamson's side. England under 23 winger, Dave Thomas, also performed spasmodically, sometimes lighting up a game with his brilliant footwork, while at other times disappearing from view. After First Division strugglers Huddersfield dismissed Burnley from the FA Cup at a windy Turf Moor in January '72, one reporter carped: 'Thomas always seemed to be trying wastefully to win the match on his own.'

Young goalkeeper Peter Mellor was proving less reliable, too. It had been his mistake which gifted Huddersfield their winning goal. Despite the club reporting an annual loss of £27,000, Adamson was permitted to sign a replacement: Alan Stevenson, the Chesterfield and England under 23 keeper. His acquisition cost £55,000, although almost half of the fee was recouped as Mellor moved to Fulham.

The left-back problem had not been solved, either. Adamson tried four players in this position: youngsters Harry Wilson and Eddie Cliff, former Chelsea right-back Jim Thomson, and utility player Geoff Nulty, without success. Adamson's patience was sorely tried not only by his stars' inconsistency but also by the impatience of the home fans. He was so incensed at the fans' criticisms of Harry Wilson's performance against Fulham in March 1972 that he snapped: 'He is only a youngster and yet they expect him to play like Terry Cooper. Look at Peter Mellor, a confident, composed goalkeeper – because he was playing for Fulham. He got so much stick here we had to sell him. There is a message there, surely?' Former Blackburn, Everton and England full-back, Keith Newton, would remove this problem, but he did not arrive until the season was over.

February 12 was another grisly day. Grubby clouds squatted overhead, spattering the town with insistent icy rain. Traffic hissed past Turf Moor, leaving momentary trails on the road's sheen-like surface. Some people had better things to do. Cowering under their rain-darkened headwear and glistening brollies, a crowd of only 11,751 made haste for the shelter offered by the Longside and the Cricket Field stands. Surely, only the hated power cuts could have driven so many from their cold homes. The derelict Brunshaw Road Stand remained boarded up – an unsightly accusation – while the chairman, Bob Lord, glumly contemplated its indigestible replacement cost, then said to be around £500,000.

At the Bee Hole End, where the uncovered terraces were glassy with excess water, there was a scattering of ascetic misanthropes folded over their pet barriers, stoically defying the elements. A distorted version of T. Rex's 'Telegram Sam' emerged erratically from the club's PA system. Nobody seemed in the mood for electric boogie. Some stared into space as if afflicted by combat fatigue. With personal warmth a distant memory, others stamped and blew into their hands. Much of the pre-match talk focused on work shortages and home discomforts. Competitive deprivation was the rage, if lugubrious mutterings could be so described. Once the game was underway, these gripes receded, leaving embattled Jimmy Adamson to face the music.

Visitors Hull City were having a poor season. Despite thrashing bottom-placed Watford 4-0 at home on the previous Saturday, they remained in 20th position, where they had been for almost two months. They were only two points better off than Cardiff – a promotion rival just 12 months before – who had a game in hand. Hull had recorded just one league win away from home – a 2-1 victory at hapless Watford in mid-October. Despite their parlous league position, Hull had achieved an impressive FA Cup victory at Coventry in midweek.

Hull's form, this season, had been gravely disappointing to all at Boothferry Park. Twelve months before, they had been the Second Division leaders, on course to sample top-flight football for the first time in the club's 66-year history. Even as late as 9 March 1971, they were still in second spot, behind Cardiff, having just beaten promotion rivals Sheffield United 2-1 at Bramall Lane. Their late loss of form reduced them to fifth place, though, having been overtaken by both Leicester City and Sheffield United.

In 1963, Hull's chairman, Harold Needler, donated £200,000 worth of shares in his prosperous business, Hoveringham Gravels Ltd, to his club. This appreciating asset enabled Hull's manager, Cliff Britton, to assemble a brilliant, free-scoring side which took the Third Division title in 1966. Their promotion drive in 1970/71 owed much to big Chris Chilton's 21 league goals. Ken Wagstaffe was the only other Hull goalscorer to achieve double figures. However, Hull's lack of goals – only 54 were scored in 1970/71 – was compensated by their defensive tightness. The Hull defence kept clean sheets in almost half of their games.

Although Britton's Hull City side were renowned for their attacking flair, Britton was, by instinct, a defensively-minded manager. He was one of the first English managers to operate with a well-drilled flat back four, which frequently caught opposing forwards offside. After he 'moved upstairs' in 1970, his 28-year-old replacement applied an even sterner defensive discipline. Terry Neill had been a top defender with Arsenal and Northern Ireland. As a player-manager at Boothferry Park, Neill led by example, helping make the Tigers' defence one of the most niggardly around.

Chilton's goals had been indispensable to Britton and Neill. In his 11-year career at Hull, Chilton scored 222 goals in all competitions. So, when the strapping 28-year-old left for Coventry at the start of the 1971/72 season for a fee of £90,000, his presence was sorely missed. Stuart Pearson, a 22-year-old local lad, had been groomed to fill Chilton's boots but he made a slow start, not helped by the Hull fans' impatient criticisms.

Pearson was a different kind of centre-forward to Chilton. Whereas Chilton had muscular presence, Pearson had express pace and quicksilver mobility. Once he had found his feet, Pearson showed he had more in his locker than his predecessor. He could forage menacingly as a lone striker, creating space for himself and others. His first touch was immaculate. He was nimble but also strong, able to resist thuggish defenders at his back. He could bring others into the game with his accurate lay-offs. Although he did not share Chilton's aerial power, Pearson was competent with his head. He possessed a fierce shot to boot. Pearson was Hull's leading goalscorer in this difficult season, netting an impressive 15 league goals. Soon his detractors were singing his praises. So was eagle-eyed Tommy Docherty, snaffling Stuart for his resurgent Manchester United side in 1974, for a fee worth £200,000. Pearson would eventually play 15 times for England, scoring five goals.

Although Pearson represented a welcome introduction of youthful talent, Hull City's side was ageing. Two-thirds of Neill's first-team squad were around the 30 mark including Ian McKechnie, a former Arsenal reserve keeper; Bill Baxter, a championship-winning centre-back under Alf Ramsey; and John Kaye, a converted midfielder, formerly with Scunthorpe and West Bromwich. On the other hand, local full-backs Frank Banks and Roger Devries were in the early stages of their professional careers. Seasoned midfielder Ken Knighton was unavailable for the Burnley game, so his place was also taken by another experienced squad member, 29-year-old Billy Wilkinson. At Turf Moor, Wilkinson and the industrious Malcolm Lord played in central midfield – Lord having replaced long-serving Ken Houghton – while fiery Scot, Jimmy McGill, played on the right. McGill had made over 170 league appearances with Arsenal and Huddersfield before joining Hull in 1971. Playing on Hull's left flank was 28-year-old Ian Butler, who had racked up almost 400 league appearances at Hull and Rotherham. Up front with Pearson was Ken Wagstaffe. Wagstaffe had scored almost 250 league goals for Hull and Mansfield.

Burnley were in the midst of a goal drought, having managed just three goals in their previous five games. But lifted by their feisty victory over Norwich, Adamson selected an unchanged side, including the attacking talents of David Thomas, Frank Casper, Paul Fletcher, Steve Kindon and Leighton James. However, his young side got little change out of Hull's stubborn defenders. In the first 45 minutes, they created just one chance.

It came soon after kick-off. Fletcher – normally so ruthless in the air – unaccountably headed wide from Alan West's perfect cross. While James continued to impress on the left wing, Dave Thomas had a wretched game. Just two minutes after the restart, the Tigers showed they could bite as well as tame. Neill played a free kick to Wagstaffe, who quickly relayed the ball to the advancing full-back, Banks. Banks instantly sent over a low skidding cross which eluded everyone except Hull City's left-winger, Butler, who slid the ball in at the far post.

Burnley tried to raise the tempo. Despite their spluttering form, chances came but went with Casper, Kindon and James the worst culprits. However, Fletcher was unlucky with a goalbound header which beat Hull's keeper, McKechnie, only for the full-back, Devries, to head the ball over the bar. Not that Hull were restricted to all-out defence. They were able to exert a bit of pressure themselves, using long passes to good effect. Stevenson had to make athletic saves from Pearson and Lord and was at full stretch to prevent Colin Waldron scoring an own goal. But he was helpless when Wagstaffe scored Hull's second goal two minutes from time. With Burnley committed to a final all-out assault, Wagstaffe seized upon Casper's misplaced pass, just inside the Burnley half, and raced through for a fine individual goal.

The Longside supporters immediately began to chant 'Adamson out! Potts in!' Their demonstration lasted for several minutes after the game. Adamson offered no excuses. He told *Burnley Express* sports editor, Keith McNee: 'It was a poor game and one we shouldn't have lost. Generally, we had too many important players below par. When Hull scored the players got anxious, the crowd got anxious and we couldn't recover. Our supporters were fully justified in their criticisms. We can't put on an exhibition like that and hope to get away with it. We are entertainers and we must do a heck of a lot better than this ... But this is part of the hazards of being a manager and I have got to take it on the chin.'

Adamson had been in charge for 88 games. He had won just 27 per cent of them. The *Daily Mirror* football correspondent reckoned that 'Burnley needed someone like Jimmy Adamson out on the park ... Someone who can take stock, point the way and calm their hell-for-leather approach.' The *Daily Express* football reporter thought that Burnley's problems were due to a lack of mental toughness. He wrote: 'In short, Burnley's prodigies always look hurt and surprised if their dazzling footwork fails to bring goals. Lesser players than Terry Neill and Ken Wagstaffe smack their lips when they see that.'

Burnley supporters' letters to the local newspaper were unequivocally critical. One wrote that 'The booing of Jimmy Adamson has been on the cards for some time. In my opinion, Mr Adamson could bring internationals to play at Burnley and within a month they would be unrecognisable. The youth policy is a dead loss. I am honestly worried we will finish in the Third Division. What a disappointment this team is.' And yet another commented that 'Players valued at half a million pounds are giving Central League performances. What a disaster for the *Team of the Seventies*.' Just before their relegation from Division One, Adamson had boasted that his young side would become the 'Team of the Seventies'.

But chairman Bob Lord was not having it. 'It's not Jimmy's fault,' he retorted. 'It's the players who are not getting the results ... The fans will not get their own way.' Keith McNee reflected in his *Burnley Express* column: 'The manager and the team must expect to share a bitter reaction. Where the Clarets go from here, especially in their strained relationships with their own followers, remains to be seen, but the mood at the moment is black indeed and only a massive improvement on the field of play can move that monster cloud on to someone else's patch of sky.' After a subsequent defeat at promotion-bound Birmingham City, Burnley dropped to tenth place.

Belatedly, Adamson discovered his best team. Neither Kindon nor Thomas featured but Billy Ingham was included as a scrapping, fetching and carrying midfielder. Crucially, Martin Dobson was released to play a creative midfield role with Jim Thomson moved to centre-back to accompany Colin Waldron. A promotion-winning side was taking shape. Regrettably, Adamson's apparent inability to communicate with Thomas and Kindon about their value to the club left both players with bitter memories of him, souring their departures later that year.

Dave Thomas told his namesake, author of *No Nay Never: a Burnley Anthology*:

> *Jimmy Adamson was years ahead of his time, his free kick routines and tactics. Maybe it was me; I've got a determined streak in me and stood up to him when he wanted his own way. He always thought he was number one, always thought he was right. He was a sort of 'get your hair cut' sort of a bloke and he could be arrogant. Harry Potts, if he passed you by, always had something to say or a greeting. Adamson sometimes walked straight by. You never knew what mood he would be in.*

Steve Kindon recalled:

> *Towards the end of the '71/72 season, Jimmy Adamson sought me out. He put his arm around my shoulders and he told me, 'Next season I'm going to build a team around you, Steve.' It surprised me a bit because I never thought I was really his sort of player. I was the knock-and-run type whereas Adamson wanted the tippy-tappy, team-playing sort. Dave Thomas didn't fit in either because he was too individualistic. My fiancé and I decided to marry on 3 June and we were thinking about buying a house locally. I asked Adamson whether I should buy or rent as I didn't want to commit myself to a mortgage if I was about to move on. He told me emphatically that I should buy. Assured by this, we went ahead and bought a place ... I spent the summer doing it up. Then, just eight days after our wedding, I was transferred to Wolves ... As far as I am concerned, Jimmy Adamson is a two-faced so and so.*

But Steve would make a stunning return to Burnley eight years later, having been brought back by another returning hero, Harry Potts, who also left Burnley in that summer of '72.

Hereford's gain: Barrow's loss

Hereford's remarkable FA Cup victory on 5 February 1972 was achieved with two former Hastings United players: Bill Meadows and Ricky George. After watching George's slithering winner on *Match of the Day*, the significance of Hereford's victory eluded me as I morosely reflected upon Hastings' loss. A taste for sour grapes is easily acquired. Ricky George later told Phil Snow, a Barnet supporter:

> *The first couple of months [after my transfer to Hereford in January 1971] I played terrible. John Charles, the manager, a super guy who had done so much in his life, stuck by me and I stayed at Hereford. But in October he was sacked and replaced by Colin Addison. In the second round of the FA Cup we played Northampton and it went to three games. We beat them after extra time and*

by then we knew the winners would play Newcastle away, so our victory was amazing. The fans were fantastic. The first game up there was postponed due to a waterlogged pitch and it was played on the Wednesday night. There were 39,000 fans crammed into three sides of the ground because of refurbishment and we went 1-0 up after 17 seconds [through Brian Owen]. After ten minutes Newcastle had scored two, through Malcolm Macdonald and John Tudor. Everyone thought the floodgates would open, but Colin Addison, the player-manager, equalised with a 25-yarder. I was a sub that day and with 20 minutes to go I came on and the one good thing I did was get past a player and cross to the near post. Billy Meadows came in with a diving header which looked like we'd scored but it was tipped around the post. Great save. I've often thought that if that had gone in I wouldn't have had the glory from the replay! It would have been Bill who got the glory! He probably deserved it more than me!

Hereford's player-manager Colin Addison had enjoyed a successful career as an inside-forward at York City, Nottingham Forest and Sheffield United. He also spent a less successful 15-month spell with Arsenal in the mid-sixties. Addison told an *Observer* reporter in 2007 that

Hereford had good facilities and a nice little ground. I could see the League potential. They paid three grand to Sheffield United for me. It was my first management job – a real crash course. Everyone else was part-time and the players were scattered everywhere. Ricky George and Billy Meadows lived in London; Ronnie Radford in Cheltenham; Alan Jones in Swansea; Brian Owen and Tony Gough, the skipper, in Bath. I was lucky if I saw them one night a week. It was the games that kept us fit [Hereford played 79 matches that season] … The FA Cup was really special then. And there was a

> *bigger gap between League and non-League clubs – now many Conference teams are full-time. Centre-half, Mick McLaughlin, for example, had a job in Newport, so after the draw at Newcastle he travelled back on the supporters' train. He arrived at Hereford at 3am, had a few hours' sleep in his car at Edgar Street, then drove to work for eight ... During one of the periods when we were trying to put the game on, I was at the ground with Newcastle manager, Joe Harvey and his assistant, Keith Burkinshaw. When the match was called off again – this was the second occasion – Joe was absolutely distraught. I took them to my house. Joe had a whisky. And I thought, 'They're having to go home again, this will help us.' They absolutely did not fancy it at Edgar Street.*

Iam McFaul, the Newcastle keeper, also told the *Observer* reporter: 'It was a cold, windy, foggy, horrible day. The pitch was awful, but there was no excuse because both teams played on it. When the top sides go to places like Edgar Street there's always apprehension, but really our team had enough quality; our 2-0 defeat of Manchester United the following Saturday proved that. But that day we never took our chances. Radford's famous goal? Well, every time I see it I swear I'm getting closer. I only wish I was on the payroll every time it's shown.'

Malcolm Macdonald was Newcastle's top striker. After playing as a full-back for Southern League Tonbridge, at Luton he proved he was better employed leading the line. As a powerful and devastatingly quick centre-forward he scored 49 goals in 88 league games for the Hatters, earning himself a £180,000 move to Newcastle at the beginning of the 1971/72 season. At St James' Park he excelled, scoring 23 league goals in his first season. He added:

> *The tie ... was a saga that took five postponements, two games and three weeks to complete ... An awful lot is made of the goals scored in the replay, but people forget that Hereford produced two phenomenal strikes at Newcastle, long shots by Colin Addison and Brian Owen. The replay at Edgar Street was then called off three times. We were trying to fit in league games while*

seeming to live most of January in limbo land down in Worcester. The replay was scheduled for 26 January. We went down three times for it and it became a ten-day wait before we finally played the match. We packed an overnight bag for one of the trips and because we had to hang around for days, our clothes began to stink. Cecil Gees in Worcester had never known a time like it. We were their best customers. It was a very bizarre situation. On 5 February – fourth-round day – the pitch still wasn't fit enough, but the match had to be played. Seven minutes from the end, Viv Busby knocked over a cross and I headed in. We thought it was finally over. But of course there was Ronnie Radford's phenomenal goal. I was four yards behind him. The ball sat up on a divot. He didn't know that was going to happen. Without that, it would've been a throw-in to us ... Then, Ricky George came on and scored the winner. We hit the bar, we hit the post, the keeper made tremendous saves. You would think Ricky would never have a bit of luck like that again, but of course he did. He bought a jumper that won the Grand National (Earth Summit in 1998). On the coach back to Tyneside we felt utter disbelief because we hadn't played badly.

In Derek Watts' book *Football's Giant Killers: 50 Great Cup Upsets*, Ronnie Radford recalled:

Newcastle boss, Joe Harvey, admitted we'd been the better side up there. The Newcastle crowd were fabulous. They applauded our approach work and cheered us off at the end ... We wanted to do something for the town as the club's main ambition was to gain League status and the Newcastle match was our chance to show we were a decent side ... I liked to have a go from a long way out. I never got many because I played fairly deep ... in most cases, shots like that ended up in the car park, but I caught it just right ... to see the joy on the faces of all the kids streaming on to the pitch meant most of all to me.

In the 80th minute, Ricky George replaced right-back Roger Griffiths, who had played for most of the game with a broken fibula. He didn't know he was so badly hurt. 'I'm in pain but I'll be alright', he told Peter Isaac, as the club physiotherapist treated him for an injury early in the game. Isaac concluded: 'Adrenaline and the atmosphere must have kept him going.'

Regarding his winning goal, Ricky George told Phil Snow: 'Twelve minutes into extra time, Dudley Tyler knocked a ball in and I got it on the edge of the penalty area. I knew Newcastle defender Bobby Moncur was behind me so I turned to my left into the box. I got the ball under control, expecting a challenge ... Moncur tried to block the shot but it went under his foot inside the far post. I think it might have unsighted goalkeeper McFaul.' Once again there was a mass invasion by the parka-clad hordes. It took several minutes for the pitch to be cleared. But it wasn't enough for Newcastle to regain their composure. Sensationally, First Division Newcastle had been ejected from the FA Cup by a side 83 places below them.

Bobby Moncur admitted being close to tears at the end. 'After months of worrying if my career was finished I had to come back in this match and be labelled as the skipper of the first First Division side to be humiliated for 23 years [following Yeovil's FA Cup victory over Sunderland in 1949]. The upsetting thing is, looking back, we had only ourselves to blame. We wasted so many good chances throughout. And after Hereford equalised we went to pieces.'

Hereford then proved this result was no fluke by holding First Division West Ham to a 0-0 draw at Edgar Street in the next round. Having the immaculate Bobby Moore as his marker, Hereford centre-forward, Billy Meadows, did his very best to redress the imbalance in class by trying to wind up the great man. It failed spectacularly. But Meadows had the consolation of scoring Hereford's goal in the replay. Unfortunately for him and his team, another World Cup hero, Geoff Hurst, scored a hat-trick (1-3).

The willowy, composed playmaker, Dudley Tyler, was Hereford's outstanding player. Throughout their cup run he had showcased his elegant footwork and penetrative passing skills to a wide audience. West Ham were so impressed that they splashed out £25,000 for him – then a record deal for a non-league player. Hereford had also showcased their candidacy effectively for a Football League place. Although they completed their Southern Premier League season behind champions Chelmsford City, it was they who were chosen to replace the unfortunate Barrow. The Fourth Division Cumbrian side were voted out of the Football League despite finishing in 90th spot. Stockport and Crewe finished well below them with five and eight fewer points, respectively. Chester, in 88th place, who had narrowly avoided re-election, were only one point better off than Barrow while 89th-placed Northampton were only above the Cumbrian side on goal average. It wasn't as if Barrow had been perennial failures. They had been in Division Three a year before. Although Barrow drew just 2,000 fans to their home games, Crewe and Stockport could attract only 1,000 more. Barrow's ejection from the Football League was very rough justice. On the other hand, Hereford proceeded to justify their election, immediately winning promotion to Division Three and drawing an average crowd of 8,900. But in the Football League's election process, once again a southern club had been given precedence over a northern one. Previously, Peterborough had replaced Gateshead, Oxford had replaced Accrington, Cambridge had replaced Bradford Park Avenue and, in five years' time, Wimbledon would replace Workington. No regional bias there, then.

Almost 40 years on, Hereford remain above Barrow in England's football hierarchy although only 20 places now separate the sides. Relatively prosperous Hereford has a population of 55,000. A high proportion of those in work are self-employed. But despite the city's economic advantages its lowly league team now attracts crowds of little more than 2,000. Meanwhile, similarly-sized Barrow has a less favourable economy. It has a higher proportion of low-skilled labour and vulnerable occupations. This is a legacy of its past reliance upon marine engineering – the construction and servicing of nuclear submarines, in particular. Barrow supplies its modest Conference side with around 1,000 fewer fans than Hereford, not a huge difference. But gazing across the languid Morecambe Bay with its wide sky, shimmering sands and treacherous tides, Barrow seems miles away from everything. Whereas Hereford is located just 57 miles from Birmingham, only an 80-minute drive, Barrow, marooned on a peninsula and hemmed in by a wash of Lakeland hills, is over two hours away from Manchester, its nearest major city. In Barrow, faith needs to be valid. Here, underdogs need to scrap in order to survive. To their huge credit, AFC Barrow have done exactly that, defying liquidation and winning two FA Trophy finals at Wembley. Once again, they have spent the 2010/11 season fighting for their place in the Blue Square Conference Premier Division. Good luck to them.

Preston North End v Burnley

'Tie a Yellow Ribbon'
28 April 1973

Before the season began, chairman Bob Lord made his ambition clear – immediate promotion to Division One. With only 8,695 fans turning up for the midweek game with Watford on 8 April and only 9,800 attending the new season's opening home fixture with Carlisle, Burnley could not afford another underperforming season.

Jimmy Adamson believed he now had the right ingredients for satisfying Lord's ambition. He explained: 'We were apprehensive last year but now we know what to expect and we feel better equipped. The signings of Alan Stevenson and Keith Newton will strengthen the defensive part of our game and I don't expect to give away the vital goals that we were conceding last season.' Martin Dobson, Burnley's first-team captain, had total confidence in his manager, emphasising how well Adamson prepared his squad. He recalled:

> *When I arrived at Burnley in 1967 [after spending a year as an apprentice at Bolton] I could see straight away that this was an entirely different set-up. For a start, everyone was training with a ball: the internationals and the young players. There was two-touch and 'shadow' football going on, players were going through pass and move drills ... What impressed me, immediately, was that so much of the training centred on developing ball skills. There was instruction in what to do – not only in technique but in making runs, positioning and so on. I had never seen anything like this at Bolton. And at the heart of all this activity was Jimmy Adamson. He*

seemed to know exactly what he wanted from his players, blowing his whistle to stop the play when the exercises weren't being executed as he wanted, praising the players when they got it right and demonstrating what was missing when they didn't. He was outstanding. He commanded so much respect. Everyone knew what he'd achieved as a player.

Utility player Geoff Nulty, who enjoyed an extended run in Burnley's '72-73 side, agreed, stating:

What really impressed me was the training sessions were always very well planned. Jimmy Adamson and his assistant, Joe Brown, always worked out the training schedules in advance. This was quite unlike what I had experienced at Stoke. There, only the first team received any real attention from the coaches and even their training sessions did not seem that well prepared. The reserves were largely left to their own devices. But at Burnley the senior players, the reserves and youth team players trained together – at least for most of the week. Jimmy Adamson and Joe Brown would divide us into mixed groups and, typically, these groups would be made up of four first-team players, four reserves and four apprentices. Jimmy wanted everyone to be inducted in the Burnley style of play, so that when anyone stepped up, say from the youth team to the reserves or from the reserves to the first team, they were ready to make that transition.

The mixed group training routines took place on Mondays, Tuesdays and Wednesdays. There was always a strong focus on ball work. That was a key part of the Burnley approach. But on Thursdays we started to train in our team units in preparation for the Saturday games. As first-teamers we practised 'Shadow Football'. This is where we played against imaginary opponents. This really helped to tighten up our positional sense and interplay. Jimmy also organised this routine whereby the first team would be reduced to four defenders and a midfielder. They would be tasked with taking on a full reserve side. The only concession was that everyone on the reserve side was expected to fulfil their normal roles. For example, their defenders couldn't become extra attackers. This exercise really helped improve our defending. You had to play as one. It helped sharpen up our defensive instincts and organisation, our ability to cover for one another. We learnt how to spring the offside trap more effectively. We became better attuned to one another. Having no attacking outlet, the defence was under constant pressure – the ball kept coming back at us, so this training routine really helped us get our act together, defensively. Once we got ourselves organised we found we could keep the reserve sides out for some time.

We also used this other routine designed to improve our wing play. Burnley had a string of great wingers – John Connelly, Ralph Coates, Willie Morgan, Dave 'Ticer' Thomas, Leighton James and so on. It was a key part of the club's success over many years. So, in order to make the most of these assets, Jimmy Adamson devised these practice matches comprising 15 players per side with no goalkeepers, in which we could only score with our heads. In order to get goals we first had to work the ball wide to the point that it became instinctive. We scored a lot of goals from headers in league and cup games. I'm sure these practice sessions helped considerably. They also helped us in co-ordinating our attacks. When, say, Leighton James was attacking down one flank, the opposing defenders would be drawn over to his side to deal with the threat, so we then pushed up our full-back on the other flank to help exploit the gaps that this left.

Martin Dobson added: 'There was much practising of building attacks from the wing. Once again, Jimmy was meticulous about the type of crosses that were supplied from the wings. We would go through a series of routines involving whipped or hanging crosses, say. He paid so much attention to detail, which, of course, paid off.'

When asked about Jimmy Adamson's tactical awareness, Martin Dobson replied, 'I cannot recall Jimmy having the opposition watched prior to a game, not as they do today. Now, they have these Opta statistics to study. But Jimmy knew enough about other teams' strengths and weaknesses to devise good team plans. For example, we might have been playing a team with a big, commanding centre-half, who was capable of gobbling up all crosses pumped high into the box. So, in order to neutralise his strength we would assign someone to pull him out of position.' Centre-forward Paul Fletcher would sometimes be asked to do this. His primary job would be to occupy the centre-half so as to create more space for his team-mates.

Burnley clinched promotion to the First Division on Monday 16 April, in front of the largest Turf Moor crowd of the season – 22,852. Paul Fletcher's two goals were sufficient to defeat the eventual FA Cup winners, Sunderland.

Bob Lord was quick to praise Adamson. A *Burnley Express* article of April 19 1973 quoted Lord as saying:

> *Jimmy Adamson has brought me my finest hour. When Burnley clinched promotion to the First Division at ten past nine on Monday evening, it gave me more satisfaction than anything else I have experienced in football. We have had some great moments during the time I have been chairman at Burnley, but this was the best of all. When we won the championship in 1960 the maximum wage was still in force; there were not the huge amounts of money about, nor was football the rat-race that it is today. This is why I think it is wonderful that despite the very heavy odds against us, we have brought success to a town of this size. We have not only put Burnley back on the football map, we've put them back on the world map and this is something that the town should be grateful for. What has given me most pleasure is that everyone who criticised the policy of the club, and the policy of the manager, has now been proved wrong. I do not wish to deny the bouquets to anyone else, but one man must take the lion's share of the credit – manager Jimmy Adamson. This is HIS victory.*

> *He proved himself 12 months ago when there was a section of people who literally wanted his scalp. But never in the three years that he has been manager have I, myself, and the board lost faith in Jimmy Adamson. He has always had our 100 per cent support, and this must have helped him in his difficult task. I had faith in Jimmy Adamson the first time I met him in 1947; that faith grew by the time he made his first-team debut in 1951 and, by the late 1950s, we had become very attached to one another because his views in life are very much on the same pattern as mine. I realised that here was a person of principle who was dedicated to carrying through those principles. He was not prepared to accept half measures. So many clubs make the mistake of being impatient because of the impatience of their supporters. We value the support of our fans, but we have our own methods and we stand by them … We have achieved part of our goal of winning promotion. Now I am sure that everyone at Burnley FC will make every effort in the next ten days to carry off the Second Division championship.*

Despite Burnley's brilliant run of results, QPR had tracked them all the way. Burnley needed a point from the Preston game to secure the championship. By sharp contrast, Preston needed a point to avoid the drop. On a day of scintillating spring warmth, over 20,000 fans attended, twice Preston's average gate.

As it turned out, no one was disappointed. Preston took a first-half lead when Alex Bruce shot past Stevenson after a 40-yard run by Alan Lamb, but nothing was going to spoil the Clarets' party. Ten minutes after the break, Waldron's header rebounded to him 25 yards from goal. Without hesitation he struck a left-foot volley cleanly and crisply, high into the Preston net. As soon as referee Hunting's whistle sounded, on poured an excited, heaving churn of Bay City Roller-like pubescence. *Shang-a-Lang*'s shenanigans would not trump this.

THE 1973/74 SEASON

Leeds United v Burnley

'Jet'
23 March 1974

This was the season of the oil crisis. With the Arabs sore about a further defeat by Israel in the Yom Kippur War, we were made to pay for America's Zionist sympathies. There may have been oil in 'thar' North Sea but we would have a hell of a job extracting it. We had to contend with a scramble for petrol and a 50mph speed limit. For several months, petrol rationing seemed inevitable. To add to our winter woes, the coalminers, the railwaymen and the power workers presented us with more power cuts and more three-day weeks. Without sufficient investment in our long-neglected manufacturing industries, Tony Barber's 'dash for growth' merely fuelled a demand for more foreign goods, pushing up inflation. Even before we felt the Arabs' wrath, Barber had to scale back public spending and raise interest rates. We approached winter with trepidation.

That winter did for Ted Heath. It almost did for many small football clubs as well. Floodlit games were only permissible with a generator. Burnley bought one for £30,000, although Bob Lord reacted grumpily when less than 19,000 turned up for its christening. A vast majority of lower-division teams were forced to play their midweek fixtures in daylight. Gates fell through the floor. Just 450 people went to Spotland in February to watch relegation-bound Rochdale take on Cambridge in a Third Division game. But the top flight wasn't immune either. In March 1974, Chelsea versus Burnley attracted only 8,131 midweek fans.

Up until Christmas, Burnley tracked Leeds' hot pace valiantly. By mid-November home gates were averaging 25,000, the best for ten years, despite Turf Moor being reduced to three sides due to the reconstruction of the Brunshaw Road Stand.

The national press took notice, too. James Mossop of the *Sunday Express* wrote this report:

Cunning, That's Us, Says Adamson

When the rain comes slanting in at the dark hills and mills of Burnley, in the heart of Lancashire, a special comfort can be found in the deeds of the local football club ... Burnley are the little team from the sticks who are showing scrambling, frenetic, millionaire clubs how a soccer side should be run. On gate money insufficient to pay the wages, they have risen to the First Division and have produced and sold talent worth £2 million. A new stand is going up along one side of the ground and youngsters as yet unknown are bursting to get into the team. Last week, Chelsea, all smooth and sophisticated with their Kings Road charisma, arrived in Burnley, and were beaten. It was a night to remember ... The brass band playing in the fading light before kick-off; hot pork pies with their distinct flavour; men straight from work in overalls and bob-caps knowing they were about to see something special. This was football before it became political. This was Burnley on their first night back in the First Division. Nobody was let down, for even the winning goal was taken from every fan's dream as Frank Casper brought the ball down from chest high, swivelled and dug his left foot into it before it hit the ground and in a blur, it was there in the onion bag.

Jimmy Adamson said, 'You are always a bit apprehensive when you step up a division ... In the Second Division, a slightly lower class of football, you could generally tell what an opponent would do when he had the ball. The First is different. The players are cunning. They will outwit you. So we had to instil into the lads: "Don't buy anything. If a player shapes up to pass the ball don't always believe him. Don't let him sell you anything." They have shown great signs of mastering this. Peter Osgood, for example, was trying to kid them. He is a good player who will always do the unorthodox. He didn't kid us, though. Jim Thomson, our man watching him, fell for nothing. The greatest thing about this is that our players have shown their own cunning, their own ability to kid people at the highest level. Casper produced something the Chelsea defence was never expecting with his goal.'

Mossop was particularly impressed with the performance of Burnley's 28-year-old right-back Peter Noble, who had never played there before. Not that Noble had admitted this to Jimmy Adamson. When Mick Docherty was injured in the opening-day victory at Bramall Lane, Noble immediately volunteered. A perplexed Martin Dobson asked Noble when he had played at right-back before. He freely admitted: 'I haven't. But the football is so good in this team that I reckoned I could play in any position and not feel out of place.' Having been impressed by Noble's performance, Adamson added, 'Whenever we played against Swindon Peter was a torment to us, whether he was up front or in midfield. As soon as I knew I could buy him I did. He is a great professional who says he will play anywhere for us.'

Unlike other promoted sides, frugal Burnley could only afford one signing – Peter Noble on a 'play anywhere' basis. And to finance that deal out went five players with first-team experience: defender Eddie Cliff and midfielder Eric Probert were sold to Notts County for a combined fee of £35,000; midfielder Alan West was sold to Luton Town for £100,000; and in December, full-back Harry Wilson and midfielder Ronnie Welch went to Brighton for £30,000 each.

Although the national press picked out sturdy striker Ray Hankin and pint-sized midfielder Brian Flynn as exciting prospects, the Burnley production line was not delivering the volume of young talent it had done in the sixties. The emerging Bob Lord Stand began to assume a spectral presence as Burnley's 'sell to survive' policy began to run out of juice. Burnley needed to sell over £200,000 worth of talent each season in order to keep the wolf from the door. It was an impossible task.

As talented as his side was, Jimmy Adamson knew that he needed sharper game plans in order to prosper in the top flight. One area which Adamson prioritised was set plays. Martin Dobson remarked:

When Jimmy was a player at the club, he and Jimmy McIlroy were the tactical brains. The club were so fortunate to have two such brilliant thinkers, let alone two such brilliant players. We used to have this near-

post routine at corners. My job was to reach the near post at the precise moment that the ball arrived at just above head height. I would be at the back of the 18-yard box on the opposite side from the corner taker. From there I would make a curved run taking me along the goal line to reach the near post before anyone else could. But having got there I had to judge my jump just right, letting the ball just kiss the top of my head – no more than a deft flick – so that it would fall into the goalmouth at an unexpected angle. If a team-mate didn't get on the end of it, the resulting scrum could result in an own goal. It was really hard to get the required delicacy of the flicked header. Hour after hour went into this drill until we were really proficient. In 1973 we played Manchester City twice. The first game was staged at Maine Road in the Charity Shield final. Here, we used a set-play routine that worked to perfection. A free kick was awarded just outside the City box to the right of centre. We had a couple of lads standing over the ball – Dougie Collins was one. There was a bit of shuffling around – a false start – as if there was confusion between them as to what the plan was. In fact, the two of them started a mock argument, blaming one another for fouling up the routine. That caused the City defenders to relax and lose concentration. They thought our guys didn't know what they were doing. And just as the City lads had dropped their guard, Dougie suddenly clipped a lofted ball to the back of the six-yard box. 'Waldo', our centre-half, had anticipated the move. Unseen, he ran around the back of the City defence and met Dougie's chip with a diving header. It was the Charity Shield-winning goal.

City's Mike Summerbee suggested: 'This could be one of the greatest teams. The big-name First Division sides are going to get some shocks this season. Once Burnley have settled in the top flight they could easily become the team of the seventies.' Having been dismissed as deranged and deluded for making this boast three years before, Jimmy Adamson had finally found a believer outside the Turf Moor sanctum.

Martin Dobson continued: 'A few months later, we were due to play City again. This time it was in the league at Turf Moor. Jimmy said to us before the game: "Remember that free-kick routine that worked so well at Maine Road?" And we said: "Yes boss, but we can't pull that stunt again. They won't fall for it twice." But Jimmy replied, "But they might, if we change the players involved. They might be fooled into thinking it is a different set play." Well, we did as he suggested. This time 'Fletch' [Paul Fletcher] was the target. He, too, scored with a diving far-post header and we won easily by 3-0. That was typical of Jimmy's brilliance as a tactician.'

December began with three home wins, although the 2-1 victory over Arsenal was a lucky break. Alan Ball was taunted mercilessly throughout. To the tune of the *Dambusters' Theme*, the Longside choir sang over and over again, 'We all hate Ball and Ball and Ball….', concluding with an inventive crescendo: 'We all f***ing hate Ball!' As puerile as the chant was, the little man seemed rattled, much to the amusement of the depleted crowd. For the economic blight was beginning to take its toll – gates were now down to 13,000. But the Christmas period provided a welcome boost. On Boxing Day, 24,000 fans braved the sheeting rain to see Liverpool beaten in the Turf Moor mud with Hankin scrambling a late winner.

Derek Wallis of the *Daily Mirror* reported:

> *Billy Ingham's name seldom appears in print in a club programme. Usually it has to be written in by those keen enough to record the substitute's name. He has been Burnley's substitute so often this season that at one stage this 21-year-old midfield player – another product of the club's North East network – must have felt condemned to the dugout for ever. Not any more, though, I believe, because he must have established himself in the side after a performance largely instrumental in one of Burnley's rare victories over Liverpool in recent years. Ingham, as small as he is, was the most influential figure when Burnley out-numbered and out-played the Champions in midfield in the first half. And near the end, after Liverpool had been rewarded for second half pressure with a late equaliser, he supplied the cross from which Ray Hankin scored Burnley's winner. Burnley had*

so much possession in the first half that it was almost unbelievable. And Liverpool's defence was sorely pressed by lively and alert forwards. Emlyn Hughes tried to retrieve the situation with another impressive, enthusiastic performance, which was hardly matched by the players around him.

Burnley were ahead after only three minutes with a headed goal from Paul Fletcher after Martin Dobson had cleverly flicked on Leighton James' corner. Fletcher rose close to the penalty spot, and thumped a header down and wide of Clemence. Spray fizzed from the straining net as if an invisible dog had shaken itself. There is always something viscerally exciting about a bullet header. Not even a searing long-distance drive can match it. The explosive roar that greeted Fletcher's goal said as much.

In reflecting upon that game, Paul Fletcher preferred to focus on the skill of his team-mate Leighton James. He enthused: 'Leighton was a fabulous player. He had everything, he could tackle, he had pace, he could shoot, he could cross a ball, he could beat a man – but he took it all for granted. Most of us treasured what talent we had. We thought it was precious. Leighton was different. He was so casual about it.'

The Liverpool victory appeared to represent the summit of Burnley's league achievements for, despite an encouraging FA Cup run, helped by some fortuitous pairings, league form dipped alarmingly in the New Year. Burnley failed to register a further league win until 16 March, when Everton were defeated by an improbably late three-goal riposte, orchestrated and delivered by Leighton James. But surely Leeds, away, would be a very different matter?

Incensed by their 1973 FA Cup Final defeat by massive underdogs Sunderland, and frustrated again in their bid for the league title, Leeds took the First Division by storm in 1973/74. *The Mighty Whites* website described the first half of Leeds' season thus:

Elder statesman Jack Charlton, now 38 … called it a day. He retired to take over as manager of Middlesbrough, whom he led to the Second Division championship at the first time of asking. At the beginning of October, another old stager, Welsh international, Gary Sprake, moved on to Birmingham City in a six-figure deal, a record for a keeper. He was

> *replaced by the little-known David Stewart of Ayr United. Don Revie had rejected Everton's overtures in the end and chose to remain at Elland Road, his pride salved by an offer of improved terms from the board. He had also turned down an offer from the Greek FA, determined that his club would finally secure the second title they had missed out on so often. He somehow managed to inspire his troops to a remarkable swansong. Eddie Gray and Johnny Giles missed most of the campaign through injury, though Gordon McQueen [Charlton's replacement], Terry Yorath, Joe Jordan and Trevor Cherry proved more than adequate reinforcements, providing great support for the usual suspects. Bremner, Jones, Clarke, Lorimer, Madeley and Hunter were in imperious form as United swept all before them, earning unanimous acclaim from the critics. Leeds went off in unstoppable fashion, winning seven games on the bounce. They extended their unbeaten league run to 29 games, playing superlative football.*

Leeds didn't lose a game until 23 February, when Stoke beat them 3-2 at the Victoria Ground. Andrew Mourant, author of *Don Revie: Portrait of a Footballing Enigma*, recalled: 'Already without Jones, McQueen and Reaney, a 19th-minute groin injury to Johnny Giles, when Leeds were already two goals up, proved one knock too many … By the 67th minute, Leeds were 3-2 down, Bremner and Clarke were booked and tempers frayed. Revie's men plunged into intense recriminations with referee, John Homewood.' In the Leeds dressing room hung a sign with the inscription: 'Keep Fighting'. Each Leeds player seemed to take that message to heart.

The psychological burden of months of front-running started to eat away at Leeds. Once again, they began to choke in sight of the main prize. Peter Lorimer reckoned that every league game was contested with the intensity of a cup tie. He told Andrew Mourant that 'Teams would improve their game 70 or 80 per cent against us.' Second Division side Bristol City delivered another FA Cup embarrassment by winning a fifth-round replay at Elland Road with a goal from Don Gillies. Then, most excruciating of all, title challengers Liverpool beat Leeds at Anfield on 16 March to exert real pressure upon Revie's championship ambitions. Leeds' runaway lead had been cut to six points with Liverpool having two games in hand. Nevertheless, Leeds were still unbeaten at home in the league when Burnley arrived in the city a week later.

Despite the mounting pressure, Don Revie was not worried about Burnley. In fact, he was uncharacteristically dismissive of their chances in an ITV interview given before the game. His programme notes made no reference to the Clarets, either. He was entirely preoccupied with the spectre of crowd trouble following the game-changing pitch invasion at Newcastle. This forced Newcastle's FA Cup tie with Nottingham Forest to be replayed at a neutral venue. This outcome would have a significant impact upon Burnley's season.

There had been a lot of ill-feeling between Burnley and Leeds prior to this fixture. The spat between Burnley chairman, Bob Lord and his Leeds' counterpart, Manny Cousins, had hardly helped. This followed Lord's crass remark made at a formal dinner a year earlier. Lord said, 'We have to stand up against a move to get soccer on the cheap by the Jews who run television.' It is unlikely that Lord intended this to be a racial slur. He had a number of Jewish friends. He probably used the term in its, then, colloquial sense to denote stinginess. However, Manny Cousins, who was a Jew, found Lord's comment deeply offensive. Although Lord subsequently apologised, Cousins would have none of it and banned Lord from the Elland Road directors' box. Lord took umbrage and forbade anyone from his club to go to the game except the team, manager and physio.

Adamson prepared his players carefully, running through the niggling ploys used by the Leeds players designed to disturb their opponents and to place pressure on the match officials. Martin Dobson recalled how Adamson had warned them about the gamesmanship and intimidatory tactics employed by the likes of Hunter and Bremner. 'He insisted that we should not become involved in any fracas, no matter what the provocation was. 'That was firmly drilled into us from the start. He would always fine us if we retaliated. He would even discipline us for the use of bad language. If anyone used expletives in training, Jimmy would stop the play and make the offender do five press-ups. He would certainly not tolerate any of us sounding off to a referee. But he was equally insistent that we competed against these physical sides. The strange thing is that Leeds were such a good team they did not need to trade in these antics. Brian Clough was quite right on that score.'

After the 0-0 draw at Turf Moor, the Leeds players had targeted one Burnley player in particular – inventive midfielder, Doug Collins. They told him they would 'break his legs' in the return game. Adamson heard the threat and filed it away. Colin Waldron told Burnley author, Dave Thomas: 'Collins was not the most physically robust of players, he was no hard man. The Leeds players knew this. At Elland Road, Adamson, in front of Don Revie, informed the referee of the threats that the Leeds players had made. Revie was furious.' This game promised to be a joy.

Just before the game began, the powerful brassy introduction to 'Jet' boomed out of the Elland Road PA system. I wasn't much of a 'Macca' fan once the Beatles had fragmented, particularly after his abysmal Mull of Kindire. But the stirring opening to 'Jet' fitted this pumped-up occasion perfectly. In that moment, 'Jet' became stapled to my abiding memory of that splendid, sparkling spring afternoon.

Burnley started the game brightly, attacking the Scratching Shed End in the warm sunlight. They looked sharp and nimble, finding one another with quick, precise passes, riding the punches and dodging the jabs, just like Muhammad Ali in his prime. Don Revie turned to Les Cocker with a troubled, puckered expression, conceding, 'By —, they're a good side going forward.' It might have been a different story had Lorimer's 13th-minute shot found goal rather than the full face of the crossbar or had Stevenson not denied both Clarke and Lorimer at close range soon after Burnley had taken the lead. But this was to be Burnley's day.

James had been giving Leeds' full-back, Reaney, a particularly hard time during the opening exchanges. After enduring 15 minutes of this, Reaney took exception and felled the Welshman as he threatened to break free again. Unperturbed by the snarling remarks of the Leeds players, Doug Collins trotted over to take the free kick. Doug wasn't quick, but he was adroit; the accuracy and incisiveness of his passing was sublime. He rarely wasted a set play and he didn't waste this one. Floating the ball into the crowded Leeds box, Casper climbed above the ruck to head the ball back across the goalmouth. As quick as a flash, Fletcher nipped in to prod the loose ball past Harvey.

Fletcher nearly didn't make the game. 'I had been in bed all week with flu,' he remembered, 'and only a Dr Iven special anti-flu jab (two gallons of penicillin injected with a red-hot poker in the bum) had got me to the game. After I scored, Billy Bremner, foaming at the mouth, said to me, "What are your chances of playing at Hillsborough next Saturday, Fletch [this was the FA Cup semi-final with Newcastle] ... with two broken legs?" "Well done, Billy," I replied. "Where did you learn to put a FULL sentence together?" (I'd studied sarcasm at 'O' Level). I don't think he heard; he was too busy going over the ball and performing a vasectomy on Martin Dobson.'

Fletcher's goal was merely a catalyst. Supine Leeds reverted to 'Super

Leeds', intent on bloody retribution. Roared on by an incensed, agitated crowd, they threatened to score with each attack. Thanks to some desperate, full-tilt defending and Stevenson's frantic agility, somehow Leeds were repelled; that is, until six minutes before half-time. Forcing their fifth corner in quick concession, Bremner clipped a sharp head-high cross towards the near post. Although Noble blocked it, he failed to clear his lines, allowing Clarke to clatter in, with his header sneaking over the heavily-defended goal line. The whole ground trembled with a concerted bellowing of '*Leeds! Leeds! Leeds! Leeds!*' and the shuddering of so many stamping feet. Serious suffering seemed imminent.

Almost directly from the restart, Noble made progress along the right flank. Nulty and McQueen contested his high centre, the ball flicking off both their heads towards Fletcher, who had his back to goal. Despite Hunter's indecent close attention, Fletcher performed a stunning bicycle kick. The ball flew past Harvey in a blur. The cacophonous clamour that had greeted Clarke's goal was instantly silenced. It was as if a Neutron bomb had taken out the entire home support. The eerie silence that followed was surreal. The ecstatic celebrations of the Burnley players made it even more so. We watched, but did not recognise. We saw, but did not comprehend. It was left to an unusually audible tannoy announcer to confirm the reality – 'The scorer of Burnley's second goal was number nine, Paul Fletcher.' The adjacent Leeds fans glared at me maliciously; not that my thoughtful response helped. For having regained my faculties, but taken leave of my senses, I chirped, 'I bet you don't see a better goal than that in the next ten years.'

I'm rarely as wound up as I was on that afternoon. I've no problem with those fans who have hacked it through the hard times, whoever they support. It's the success groupies that get to me, those who indulge their flaccid egos by tagging on to the main event. I sensed that those who hemmed me in were probably of that order – 'Johnny-come-lately' glory hunters. In those rare moments of underdog triumph, nothing quite beats the odour of crushed invincibility on those who deodorise with hubris.

Meanwhile, out on the pitch the hero of the moment, Paul Fletcher, was exultant but suffering. He explained later: 'I was feeling awful. The week in bed was telling on my stamina … I had launched myself into an overhead kick thinking either the ball or Hunter's head would go flying into the net. In mid-air I felt my left foot come into perfect contact with a round, empty object – and for a moment I thought I'd kicked Hunter in the head. But as I landed I saw the ball crash into the net.' So relaxed, so confident, so well trained and so talented, Jimmy Adamson's team started to rip Leeds apart.

The second half was a breeze. Just past the hour, Martin Dobson dispossessed Paul Madeley in midfield. Like a smoothly orchestrated relay, the ball was passed along a line of Burnley players hunting hungrily for space; it went from Dobson to Casper to Fletcher and finally to Collins. Burnley's slick passing movement had opened up Leeds' defence like the proverbial sardine can, leaving Dougie Collins in oceans of space to do his worst. Dougie sized up his opportunity. He was 20 yards or more from goal, to the right of the Leeds box. Harvey was off his line. Dougie wasn't the best finisher at the club, often giving gravity far too much to do. But this effort was well and truly nailed. His delicate chip sent the ball sailing over the remaining home defenders and the furiously back-pedalling Harvey, before dropping exquisitely just below the bar and gently rippling the back of the net. Collins – targeted as a bottler by the Leeds bullies – had made his riposte. His tightly screwed-up expression conveyed the intensity of his satisfaction. He thrust both arms above his head, his fists clenched tightly, like a triumphant boxer. It was his moment of supreme vindication. Having just scored the 'goal of the decade', Paul Fletcher generously conceded that Dougie's effort was 'the goal of the game'.

Burnley's fourth goal came with 20 minutes remaining. Once again Dougie Collins was instrumental in its execution; it was his hat-trick of 'stuff yous'. Midfielder, Geoff Nulty, tells the story:

> *We had some really sharp dead-ball routines in our repertoire. We reckoned that if we were awarded a free kick within 35 yards of our opponents' goal we had a decent chance of scoring. At Elland Road we were awarded a free kick about 30–35 yards from the Leeds goal on our right. Doug Collins took the kick but instead of knocking it towards the far post, as the Leeds defenders were expecting him to do, he chipped it towards the near post. Colin Waldron anticipated Doug's intentions perfectly and made a late run towards the near post. Here, he back-headed the ball across the face of the goal, where I nodded it in, on all fours, at David Harvey's feet. At 4–1 up we were out of sight.*

I can still see them now, Colin Waldron and Geoff Nulty standing in front of the Leeds Kop, their arms aloft, totally oblivious of the feral surge tumbling their way. Today, they would have been stopped, but back then they had the freedom to indulge their moment of supremacy. 'What a joke!' sneered a nearby homer. I had to agree. It was Leeds' heaviest home defeat since returning to the First Division ten years before.

'We paralysed Leeds, we could have scored seven', claimed Peter Noble. The performance was so good it worried Jimmy Adamson. He said, 'I've got to bring them down to the ground again. They think they are a good team. We still have to put in a performance at Hillsborough. The team know they cannot live next Saturday on this Saturday's result.' As for Don Revie, he admitted to feeling 'terrible' after the game, adding that he didn't think the ball was rolling for his side at that moment. 'It will be tight now but Liverpool have still to win their two away games in hand. It is up to us to make the most of our last seven games.'

The one sour note concerned the serious injury inflicted on Frank Casper. Colin Waldron commented: 'Casper in fact was hardest hit and the tackle by Hunter that took him out of the game has never been forgotten by the players or the supporters who were there. It was savage and deliberate; the ball had long gone, and Casper in fact was a couple of feet off the field when Hunter connected. It effectively ended his career although he made a valiant effort at a comeback.' Paul Fletcher had this to say to author, Dave Thomas:

> *I didn't actually see it. I was in the middle, watching the ball. Next thing I see is Frank on the ground. I honestly wish we hadn't won 4–1. Hunter was wound up and just lost it because we had embarrassed and humiliated them. In those days if a player could smack another player and get away with it, he would. And our Waldo could dish it out. We had this rule, if the ref didn't see it then OK. A foul is only a foul if the referee sees it. I certainly know one player on my side who was told to smack an opponent hard on the side of the head in the first few minutes just to rattle him. 'I'll take responsibility and pay the fine if you get seen and sent off', the player was told. Today, the game is like netball, nobody is allowed to even touch another player. The thing is, Leeds did that kind of thing in every position. Most teams had one or two assassins, but with Leeds, it was the whole team. But OK, Hunter, you'd have him in your team. He won the players' award. Yes he did the things he did, but you'd have him in your team.*

> *We were already a good team, a very good team and had the makings of being a great team. We had skills, we had commitment and perhaps above all we had team spirit. We would have walked through walls for each other. And Jimmy Adamson, who had done so much to create that spirit, wanted to build upon it. All the players of that side had an incredible admiration for him. I asked him, 'what will happen next season?' He replied: 'I want to build a team but the chairman wants to build a stadium and I think he will win.'*

The sad thing about this result was that it counted for so little. Leeds deservedly went on to win the championship at a canter. Burnley failed to qualify for Europe and a week later lost a game of immeasurably greater significance, an FA Cup semi-final against Newcastle. However, just play me the opening bars of 'Jet' and I am immediately suffused with a warm, lingering glow.

Burnley v Wimbledon (FA Cup third round)

'Wombling Merry Christmas'
4 January 1975

Burnley's boss, Jimmy Adamson, began the new season in a morose mood. It wasn't just Mick Docherty's and Frank Casper's long-term injuries that troubled him. He had been right in what he told Paul Fletcher. Club chairman Bob Lord was prepared to sacrifice the team to build the stadium. The price of the new stand rested upon Martin Dobson's head. With the season barely underway, 'Dobbo' went to Everton for a Burnley club record fee of £300,000. 'The only classical wing-half left in the country', stated the *Football Digest* in 1974. Martin Dobson didn't want to leave. He told me:

> *It was so easy fitting in at Burnley. I was made to feel welcome. They looked after me so well. There were no big egos. The big-name players, the internationals, rubbed along with everyone else. I felt at home. And because I did, my confidence started to return. I owe so much to Jimmy Adamson. He saved my career. I was going nowhere until I arrived at Burnley. But he saw something in me that others hadn't. He could see I had some skill but he thought that I might benefit from having a bit more time when in possession. It wasn't as if I was slow. I'd always been very quick at school but there were so many young players with pace. He thought I might progress better in a midfield role rather than up front where there was so little time. I suppose he saw something of himself in me. He'd started off as an inside-forward but had been converted into a magnificent*

wing-half. He really should have played for England. He was that good. And he was right. Midfield did suit me better. No one else had seen that. I didn't want to leave Burnley. I was happy there. Besides, Jimmy was my mentor ... I knew nothing about the move until I read a paragraph in the Sunday paper. One morning I was told to go to the ground instead of training and Billy Bingham, Everton's manager, offered me £20 a week more than I was being paid at Burnley, which was about £140 all in [around £100,000 per year today]. I felt a little hurt but I suppose I was being naïve to think that Burnley could hold on to me. 'Waldo' used to say that Burnley had a 'revolving door' policy. Young players coming into the dressing room made their way around it before being sold. It was my turn, I guess.

Burnley's bottom line made grim reading. The balance sheet showed a loss of £224,000 for the previous year. The wage bill was becoming an increasing problem. Eleven players earned more than £10,000 during the '73/74 season. An annual wage of £10,000 was then £8,000 (over 400 per cent) above the national average wage. With Premiership players now earning over 20,000 per cent above the national mean that seems a trivial difference. But a £10,000 wage was a lot for little Burnley to find in 1974. Although Willie Irvine earned more at Second Division Preston than he did at First Division Burnley, Bob Lord continued to believe, rightly or wrongly, that his players were among the best paid in the country. He was proud of that record. Of course, his pay policy meant that there was a price placed on each of his players' heads. Necessary ground renovation increased his problem. When Martin Dobson was sold, Bob Lord defended his decision by stating: 'It will cost us £450,000 to run this club this season and we could not turn down £300,000. Four years ago, people were fed up with a three-sided ground and wanted a new stand, so we built one.'

Martin Dobson's departure wasn't just felt keenly on the terraces; this was a close-knit team with idiosyncratic ideas of fun, like 'bedroom golf'. 'I must admit I was intrigued to find out about this bedroom golf, but absolutely flabbergasted when the door opened to Paul Fletcher's and Alan Stevenson's shared room,' recalled Keith Newton. 'There they stood, both completely naked except each was wearing a jock strap, golf shoes, rubber soled, flat cap and Alan Stevenson was pulling a Jack Nicholson golf bag ...

on a trolley, with one club, a putter, in it … Great tournaments were played; "the Swindon Post House Masters"; "the Norwich Moat House Classic". And nobody ever won. Mainly because Stevo and Fletch were the biggest cheats I have ever come across … we may have acted like children but one thing is for sure, it was great for team spirit. This fun and laughter off the park gelled us together as a team …'

Despite making a stirring comeback at Stamford Bridge from a three-goal deficit, the season started slowly. After four games, Burnley were fourth from bottom. After a 1-2 home defeat by Chelsea, newly-appointed captain, Colin Waldron, rose to the occasion with this strident rallying cry:

> *Okay, so Martin Dobson has gone, but Burnley Football Club will go on with the players fighting like hell to improve the dreadful position we find ourselves in. Get one thing straight, there is no crying in the Burnley dressing room about the departure of Dobson. He is a loveable guy, extremely likeable and a great captain. But we are professional footballers with a living to make and much as we admire Martin and we wish him all the best at Everton, we can't, and don't intend to live off his memory. Unlike myself, Jimmy Adamson is not normally an emotional man but he was very emotional when he told us that the skipper was leaving. In midfield we have an abundance of cover, Doug Collins, Geoff Nulty, Billy Ingham, Brian Flynn and Peter Noble of whom the Burnley fans have not seen the best. I am one of those people who believe in straight talking. Dobson was the favourite player but not the best player. He has not had a good 12 months. When people ask me if we can manage without him it makes me angry. It is a ludicrous question for even with Dobson in the team we only picked up one point from three games. Football is a hard, cruel, ruthless game and we professionals know how to survive in it. We did not cry when Ralph Coates left or when David Thomas left, and they were great guys like Martin Dobson. We've got to get Coventry beaten and kick the club's critics in the teeth by doing well where it matters – on the field.*

Inspired by Waldo's gritty leadership, Burnley scrapped successfully to improve their position. Three wins came on the bounce, including a turbulent 2-1 home victory over Leeds, who were still mired by the *Damned United* saga. Better still, a 30-yard rocket from young left-back Ian Brennan defeated Liverpool at Anfield. Colin Waldron and his young partner, Billy Rodaway, were outstanding in a resolute rearguard action.

By the close of 1974, Burnley were in seventh spot, challenging for the title. Geordie Peter Noble had slotted into Dobson's place superbly, replicating his 'roving turret' role with interest. On 23 November, Burnley avenged their FA Cup semi-final defeat by Newcastle by ravaging the Magpies 4-1 at Turf Moor. Noble scored a superb hat-trick, lighting up the grey, grubby afternoon. However, a few weeks later, Bob Lord sold Geoff Nulty for £120,000 to the side that Burnley had just thrashed. He would be badly missed.

In his 'Team of the Seventies' article for the Autumn 2009 edition of *Back Pass* magazine, Martin Dobson said of Nulty: 'We had a lot in common. We used to think it was great if you were offered a one-year contract and unbelievable if it was two because we had that air of uncertainty about us. He went on to captain Newcastle but always said that everything he learned about the game, he learned at Burnley. Geoff was part of a dressing-room double-act, singing "Leaning on a Lamp Post" while Paul Fletcher played the ukulele. They eventually got on local TV.'

Geoff Nulty told me:

> *I felt well looked-after at Burnley. They found me digs very near to the ground. It didn't matter that some of the senior players were big names. They treated the younger players like themselves. They were not aloof or condescending. This was a family club and a very professional one. I am very grateful for what they did for me there. Although I enjoyed my time at Newcastle, Burnley was streets ahead of them in terms of professionalism, and its ability to bring players on. In fairness, when Gordon Lee took over at St James' Park things improved. He brought in fresh ideas. At Everton it was very businesslike, too … While I was helped to develop my game at Burnley, they certainly weren't soft with me. One week I found my name missing from all the team sheets. I wasn't down to play for the reserves or*

*the 'A' team. So I asked a team-mate what I should do. He said I should speak to 'the boss', Jimmy Adamson. I went to his office underneath the Cricket Field Stand. After knocking first, I put my head round his door and asked, 'Why am I not playing in any of the teams this week, boss?' His answer was curt but to the point: 'Not f***ing good enough.' Well next week, I was really wired, fighting and scrapping for the ball in our practice matches. Jimmy Adamson confronted me with 'How much do you really want this? I mean, is it everything to you? If it isn't everything to you, you're not going to make it. You are not as naturally talented as some of the other lads. That means you're going to have to work that bit harder.' I took that advice to heart ... The club was very good in encouraging players to look beyond their playing days. We were prompted to get our coaching badges. I went to Lilleshall in 1969 when I was only 20 years old. It was a bit early for me, to tell the truth. But it helped open my eyes to new possibilities of how the game could be played and how players could be developed. I turned to coaching at Preston for a spell after my playing career ended.*

Any hope that Nulty would be replaced by a new signing was scotched quickly. 'We have no plans to buy anyone at the present time,' Adamson said. 'But if we do get any injuries we will reconsider the situation.' Although the average gate remained around the 20,000 mark, on a par with the '73/74 figure, it was clear that the club were looking for another good FA Cup run to swell its dwindling coffers. A third-round home draw with a Southern League side, Wimbledon, offered a perfect start.

Wimbledon had become a semi-professional club only ten years before. They had swept all before them in the amateur game, winning the Isthmian League title three years in succession and lifting the FA Amateur Cup in 1963. Not that Division One of the Southern League offered them any tougher opposition. After a cautious start, the Dons were quickly into their stride, helped by the phenomenal goalscoring record of Eddie Reynolds, who notched 57 goals in 49 appearances. In April 1965, Wimbledon were duly promoted to the Southern League Premier Division, passing Hastings

United, who were on their way down.

Blessed with chairman Sydney Black's generous investment and local influence, Wimbledon successfully developed their Plough Lane ground and challenged immediately for the Southern League Premiership title. Reynolds moved on, but still the goals came in copious quantities. Westminster Bank employee Ian Cooke was the next top gun, eventually scoring 191 goals for the club in 427 appearances. However, Black's untimely death in 1968 seemed to cast a pall over the club's fortunes. Several league title challenges were lost as Wimbledon stumbled at the final hurdle. Roy Law remarked to Niall Couper, author of the marvellous oral history, *The Spirit of Wimbledon*: 'We seemed destined to never win the league. The Southern League was a tough one, certainly the toughest I ever played in. It was full of ex-professionals and players who were good enough to be professionals … those were the days when there was no fortune to be made in football, so for some there was no reason to step up.'

Manager Les Henley had lifted Wimbledon out of obscurity, turning the club into one of the best amateur sides in the country. But after Black's death he seemed to lose his enthusiasm for the job. By 1973/74, it wasn't only the team that was faltering. The club was struggling to make ends meet, too. After an early flush of enthusiasm – 3,432 supporters attended Wimbledon's first Southern League home game – by the end of the sixties, the average home gate had slumped to under 2,000. The club was forced into axing its reserve side despite strong protests from its supporters.

Although his side won the Southern League Cup in 1970, Les Henley was sacked a year later, whereupon Mike Everitt took over as player-manager. Everitt had starred in Northampton's startling rise during the early sixties. But he stayed for two years, only, before moving on to manage Brentford. His successor was the former Orient and Palace boss, Dick Graham, who had also guided Colchester to their stirring giant-killing feats. But Graham didn't stay long, either. He wasn't best pleased when the Wimbledon board re-designated his post as part-time. These were times of great financial hardship. No longer having Sydney Black to prop them up, and reeling at the impact of the power cuts and the three-day week, Wimbledon came perilously close to extinction. In early 1974, the club's debt stood at around £35,000 (£440,000 in today's values). Only a whip-round involving the board and the fans managed to raise the £5,000 sum needed to avert liquidation.

With the disgruntled Graham gone, the Wimbledon board turned to Allen Batsford, the successful Walton & Hersham manager. They weren't fazed by reports that Batsford had fallen out with his management committee. After all, the man was a winner. His Walton side had won the FA Amateur Cup in 1973 without conceding a single goal, a unique feat. Three of his players – Dave Bassett, Willie Smith and Roger Connell – had represented the England non-league side. To cap it all, Batsford's Walton & Hersham shocked the football world by winning an FA Cup replay, at Brian Clough's Brighton, by 4-0. A highly embarrassed Brian Clough was forced to concede that 'Walton were better than us in every aspect of the game – better technique, certainly, and better organisation.'

In conversation with Niall Couper, Allen Batsford recalled his arrival at Wimbledon thus:

> *I had been at Walton & Hersham for nine years. We had won the FA Amateur Cup and I felt I had gone as far as I could with the club ... I was desperate to get the [Wimbledon] job. I was so naïve. They had almost no money to spend and there were only seven players on the books ... I ended up signing seven of my ex-players ... with no reserves ... The two [sets of players] gelled well. Dave Bassett was on the one side and Ian Cooke on the other – they were both leaders and encouraged everyone to mix in ... [Former Colchester winger] Mick Mahon was an excellent player. He could easily have played in the Football League but wanted to be a schoolteacher. Ian Cooke played for 13 years and averaged almost a goal every other game. And then there was the goalkeeper, Dickie Guy. He was another great character with a good sense of humour. If there were two people who were going to get laughs among the players, it was Bassett and Guy ... We worked very hard and often. Sometimes we would be training every night of the week. Other clubs commented that they had never seen a club work as hard. Our organisation was superb and we had great spirit. The more we won, the stronger we became.*

Right-back, Bob Stockley, was already a Wimbledon player when Batsford arrived. He said in a *Back Pass* football magazine article of autumn 2009: 'We were run like a Football League club. We stayed in a hotel the night before away games and were well-drilled and organised. We practised free kicks, corners and set pieces religiously before every game. We knew exactly where every player should be – both attacking and defending. And we knew how the opposition would play, especially Burnley.'

Wimbledon made it to the third round of the FA Cup the hard way, having to extricate themselves from the four qualifying stages before reaching the first round proper. With money too tight to mention, a successful FA Cup run was imperative. In the first round proper, Wimbledon were fortunate to be drawn at home against tough Southern League adversaries, Bath City. With the nearby cup tie involving Palace and Tooting & Mitcham being postponed shortly before kick-off, the Plough Lane gate was expanded to 5,500. A desperately tight contest was won by Mick Mahon's 'screamer' in injury time. David Pleat's Kettering Town were expected to be equally tough opponents but goals from Cooke and Mahon (penalty) put them through with ease, watched by a 6,000-plus crowd. David Pleat remarked how difficult it was to play against Wimbledon. It was a salutary comment.

Typically thorough in his preparations, Batsford had Burnley watched prior to the Turf Moor game, producing a 15-page dossier on their strengths and potential weaknesses. 'We reckoned that Burnley were rather predictable,' he remarked. What he meant was that Burnley were over-reliant upon Leighton James' strong running and piercing crosses. During that season, at least 60 per cent of Burnley's goals came directly from James' strikes or his 'assists'. It was well known that if Burnley were to be neutralised, James had to be stopped. In his pre-match briefing, Batsford detailed Bob Stockley and Dave Bassett to double up on James. 'Dave was not the most cultured footballer nor a great passer of the ball,' admitted Stockley. 'But he had a huge will to win and loved to break play up. He was a fantastic player to have in front of you. Several times I got a tackle in or Dave did and Leighton James wasn't too happy. He also got plenty of banter from Dave. But he was quick and got past us a couple of times, but overall we handled him quite well. I'd had more difficult games.'

Despite the Dons' effective shackling of James, Burnley monopolised possession, pushing forward relentlessly. But the Wimbledon outfield players – from front to back – grafted incessantly to close their hosts down. And behind the Dons defenders, there was Dickie Guy, the London Docks tally clerk, who was in inspired form. I failed to recognise him as the hapless loanee who had gifted Barnet victory at Hastings eight years before. His transformation was extraordinary. He had not missed a game for Wimbledon in four years. His positioning seemed spot on, his handling so assured and as for his reflexes, they were simply astonishing. In the third minute he comfortably grasped Fletcher's cross-shot. On the half-hour he easily collected Ray Hankin's header after James had made a rare escape from his jailers, Bassett and Stockley. But Guy surpassed himself just before the break when he pushed over a scorching volley from Keith Newton. It was a stunning, lightning reaction save, which drew applause from all quarters of the ground.

Four minutes after the break, the unthinkable happened. Wimbledon scored with only their second effort on goal. Burnley centre-back, Jim Thomson, was slow to close down Ian Cooke. The Dons striker managed to get a shot away that keeper, Stevenson, could only parry. Mick Mahon recalled: 'The ball came to me on the edge of the box. I just hit it. There wasn't a lot of goal to aim at … before I knew it I was flattened. Everybody was on top of me celebrating wildly. It wasn't the staged celebrations you get nowadays – it was pure joy.' Mahon told Niall Couper 'It wasn't the greatest time to score … but we had a plan and stuck to it … Normally, I would play on the right wing, but with Dave Bassett playing there I was pushed into the centre of midfield. I didn't like playing there. On the flanks you only really had to concentrate on what was ahead of you. In the middle, you had to look everywhere.'

Although Burnley upped the tempo, laying siege to the Wimbledon goal, they could find no way past the brilliant Guy. He made a breathtaking stop to deny Fletcher's point-blank effort but was indebted to Collins' lack of composure as the midfielder blasted the rebound over the bar with the goal gaping. This was not one-way traffic, though. Revelling in the extra space granted by Burnley's hurried advances, the Dons' bearded strike partners, Connell and Somers, had several excellent chances to finish the game off. Between them, they managed to send three shots skimming just wide of the Burnley goal.

After the game, Jimmy Adamson muttered tersely that his 'players gave everything but their skills were off', whereas an ecstatic Allen Batsford said: 'In many ways Burnley only had themselves to blame … they were too complacent in the first 20 minutes and once they fell behind they panicked.' Burnley captain Colin Waldron admitted: 'We played ignorant football. Right from the first minute we kept hitting these long, high balls into their goalmouth in the hope that someone would make a mistake. This made their centre-halves look like crosses between Jack Charlton and Jairzinho.'

The press were as generous about Wimbledon's magnificent victory as they were scathing about Burnley's abject defeat. Paul Wilcox of the *Guardian* reported: 'The expected Wombling taunts from the crowd faded with Burnley's reputation. And little wonder. The only rubbish that Wimbledon picked up on Saturday were the First Division team's errors.' Local reporter, Peter Higgs, wrote, 'Hang your heads in shame after this defeat, Burnley. The match they said was a free pass into the next round of the FA Cup provided arguably the most humiliating result in the history of Burnley.'

Wimbledon's victory was no fluke. It was the product of immense effort, excellent planning, supreme team spirit and no little skill – the very qualities that had enabled Burnley to punch above their weight. My Leeds-supporting brother-in-law gave me a hard time. But his team, now restored under Jimmy Armfield's thoughtful management, would fare little better when they took on Wimbledon in the next round, only scraping through, after a replay, with the luckiest of goals. It was only the second goal that Guy had conceded in nine FA Cup games that season. Over the next 13 years, the football map would change completely. Wimbledon would swap places with Burnley. They would prove to be Leeds' masters, too. That was the beauty and the heartache of our game until the over-indemnified Premiership turned our league and cup competitions into a cartel.

Carlisle United v Burnley

'Fox on the Run'
1 April 1975

Curiously, the Wimbledon debacle did not destroy Burnley's season. They regrouped quickly, winning their next game at Loftus Road 1-0. They then put together a run of good results that lifted them into second place by the beginning of March. Although they had lost some of their former fluency, Burnley were dogged enough to grind out important victories. Unfortunately, the home fixture with Liverpool on 8 March was not among these. A win here might have put the Clarets on top. It was not to be. An attritional game ended as a 1-1 draw, with Liverpool ending the game as the stronger side.

On the following weekend Burnley were narrowly beaten by West Ham, the season's eventual FA Cup winners. Not helped by Fletcher's serious knee injury, Burnley's results fell away. Easter was a disaster. Just as the electricity board was raising prices by a whopping 33 per cent, we were hit with springtime snowdrifts. Middlesbrough outmuscled Burnley at a spitefully cold Ayresome Park on Easter Saturday (0-2). And then on a raw, brooding Easter Monday, Burnley were 'ram-raided' in the Turf Moor mud by Derby's Panzer Division, as Dave Mackay's side powered towards the title (2-5). Unabashed, my wife and I set out for Carlisle on the following day. Although Burnley's title prospects were in tatters, the European places were up for grabs. As for Carlisle, they were scrapping for their First Division lives.

Although Carlisle's rise from bottom to top was not as fast as Northampton's dizzying ascent, it was still a remarkable feat for a small, remotely-placed club. Carlisle remains as the smallest place to have had a top-flight side since Glossop's 'one-season wonder' in 1899/1900. Long-standing Carlisle supporter and historian, David Steele, accounts for Carlisle's celebrated rise in his fascinating book *Carlisle United: A Season in the Sun 1974-75*.

When its team broke into the top flight in 1965, Northampton had a rising population of around 115,000 – not at all big by First Division standards. But when Carlisle followed suit in 1974, it had an almost static population of 71,800. But it wasn't just a question of size. Northampton were promoted to the First Division on the back of five seasons of accelerating success. Conversely, Carlisle, like Leyton Orient, 12 years before them, managed to transform themselves from relegation battlers into promotion winners within the space of 12 months. Moreover, the Cumbrians achieved this astonishing turnaround with one of the smallest fan bases of any club reaching the top tier.

Orient weren't regarded as a particularly well-supported club when they went up in 1962. Around 14,000 fans watched their unexpected promotion. But that figure was almost twice as big as Carlisle's average gate during their promotion season of 1973/74. The Cumbrians' average gate for that season was 8,271. Had their total attendances not been boosted by a record 19,692 crowd for their penultimate home game with Sunderland, their average gate would have been little better than the 7,606 figure achieved during their previous, relegation-haunted season. On 22 September 1973, with Carlisle in 19th position, only 5,093 supporters attended their midweek win against Oxford – a record club low for a Second Division game. Even as late as Saturday 30 March 1974, with Carlisle on the brink of promotion, merely 6,544 fans turned up to watch their 5-1 victory over Swindon. Not helped by the nation's economic hardships, gates were falling everywhere. But these hardships were felt more keenly in the North.

Despite the promotion euphoria, the Cumbrians' bottom line was troubling. For the club reported a £106,000 loss for the 1973/74 season. That equates to around £1.3 million in today's values. The £33,000 rise in the wage bill easily exceeded the £16,000 extra revenue made on the gates. Although generally frugal in the transfer market, Carlisle racked up a £92,000 deficit in transfer activity. It was small wonder that the Carlisle board set about cashing in on the club's unexpected promotion. Admission prices were ramped up. The cost of a centre stand season ticket was increased by over 70 per cent to £24. The price of admission to the Paddock Terrace was raised by 30 per cent to 60p per game. Most enterprising of all, the board introduced a commercial sponsorship scheme for all home games, then a novel idea.

The club knew how to economise. They had to. During Bob Stokoe's time in charge, at the end of the sixties, the board decided to scrap the reserve team. The first-team squad was decidedly lean in number. There were only 19 full-time professionals available to Alan Ashman in 1973/74. Incredibly, he managed to guide his side to Division One – behind Middlesbrough and Luton – with almost the same squad which had successfully defied relegation a year before. The only additions were the 31-year-old former Ipswich, QPR and Shrewsbury striker Frank Clarke, (elder brother of Allan), and 22-year-old Hartlepool centre-back Bill Green, picked up for a bargain fee of £15,000. However, a succession of Carlisle managers proved they had a sharp eye for 'a steal'. They did not make many mistakes in the transfer market. Unfortunately, the £36,000 that Alan Ashman splashed out on Kenny Wilson was one of his very few mistakes. Wilson had been a prolific goalscorer for Dumbarton but only netted one for Carlisle. However, Ashman's other lads moved mountains.

In goal was Glasgow-born Allan Ross. He came to Carlisle as a makeweight in a 1963 player exchange deal. Some makeweight he proved to be! Ross racked up a club record 466 league appearances, playing in all four divisions. Ross was also selected for the Scottish senior squad final 16 in 1969/70 but unfortunately did not win a cap. His career began and ended with a clean sheet. With Carlisle's first game in the top flight, in August 1974, covered on *Match of the Day*, the nation was able to see what a fine keeper he was. At a sunny Stamford Bridge, Ross made a series of stunning saves to deny Chelsea's Sissons, Garland and Garner, helping his side to an astonishing 2-0 victory. He briefly worked in the club's commercial department after hanging up his gloves. He then joined the City of Carlisle Council's housing department, where he worked until his untimely death in 1999 at the age of 57. He is still regarded by Carlisle's supporters as perhaps the club's best ever player and certainly one of the most popular.

Right-back Peter Carr joined Carlisle from Darlington in November 1972 aged 21, but by then he had already played 100 league games for Darlo. Peter was a quick, enterprising defender, who formed a solid partnership with left-back John Gorman. He played in 204 league matches for Carlisle over five seasons before moving on to Hartlepool and thereafter to New England Revolution. He later opened a hotel on Cape Cod.

Glaswegian left-back Gorman was signed by Carlisle in 1970 after being released by Celtic. Gorman was a quick, skilful full-back who played 229 league games for Carlisle in a six-year stay. He became the club's 'player of the season' in 1971/72 and 1972/73. In 1976, he moved to Tottenham for a £60,000 fee. Although injury confined him to just 30 appearances there, he forged a close friendship with Glenn Hoddle, which continued beyond their playing days. Having completed his playing career in the USA, Gorman became Hoddle's assistant at Swindon, helping guide the Robins to the Premiership in 1993. Gorman then took over the managerial duties at the County Ground from Hoddle, who moved on to Chelsea after the play-off victory at Wembley. Gorman was also Hoddle's number two during Hoddle's time as England boss. He helped Hoddle at Southampton and Spurs, too. Gorman had other coaching or managerial stints at Northampton, Gillingham, Ipswich, QPR, Wycombe Wanderers and MK Dons. He is an accomplished cartoonist.

Centre-back Bill Green was a bargain buy from Hartlepool at the start of the 1973/74 season. Although he was then only 22 years old, he was a natural leader. He had been skipper at the Victoria Ground and soon took on this role at Carlisle. Green was a towering, intelligent defender who adapted well to top-flight football. Bill recalled: 'Carlisle were a fantastic little football side. The coaching from Alan Ashman and Dick Young was excellent. They instilled a way of playing the "right way". It was more of a level playing field then. Carlisle had a history of scouring the lower divisions for players. They did their homework.' Bill Green went on to play in 119 league matches for Carlisle before being sold to West Ham in 1976 for £90,000. He later moved to Peterborough and Chesterfield, for whom he played 160 league games. After his playing days finished at Doncaster, he took charge of Scunthorpe for two years in the early nineties, taking them to a play-off final, before turning to scouting duties with a number of clubs. He later turned to selling car transmissions in Birmingham. He was the scorer of Carlisle's first goal in the top flight at Chelsea. Bill told a local reporter, 'I tried to put it in on my right foot but I missed it. So I put it in with my left. Soon after, a fan wrote to me. He said "that was a great goal. Jimmy Greaves would have been proud of the way you dummied it with your right foot". I can't remember if I was honest enough to tell him the truth.'

Graham 'Tot' Winstanley was a central defender who played 166 league games in the first of two spells with Carlisle, but only one game in the First Division. He moved to Brighton for £20,000 in November 1974, becoming Albion manager Peter Taylor's 17th signing in a year! He returned to Carlisle in 1979 for one season only. He is fondly remembered for a spectacular goal he scored against Roma in the Anglo-Italian Cup tournament in June 1972, which secured Carlisle an incredible 3-2 victory in the Stadio Olimpico. 'We didn't go there expecting to win but it was a great result,' he recalled, 'and I remember they weren't very happy when Stan Bowles started keeping the ball up on the halfway line!' Graham worked subsequently for a wholesale electrical company.

Stan Ternent was a tenacious, ultra-tough midfielder who played 168 league games for Carlisle between 1968 and 1974 following his £4,000 transfer from his parent club, Burnley. His crunching ball-winning ability enabled the creative players, like Chris Balderstone, to express themselves so fluently. Graeme Souness described Stan as one of the hardest tacklers in the game. Coming from Souness this was quite an accolade. Stan recalled in his biography *Stan the Man*, written with current BBC presenter Tony Livesey:

> *If Souey shuddered when I rolled him over, it was hardly surprising. I flew into tackles, even in training. Each practice match was like a Cup Final to me. I'd go crunching in. I knew it narked some of the lads but it added needle, a sensation I thrived on. If I lost a match, I despised myself and moped around the house all weekend. I could hardly wait until the next game so I could be a winner again … I fought a battle to control my temper and win over the crowd. Whether I played at sweeper covering for Tot Winstanley, as a specialist man-marker or a straightforward half-back, I continually compensated for my lack of pace. Usually I picked opponents' brains and used my positional sense to outdo them. If that failed, Plan B was to hammer them into the ground … it was a tough league. Too many other teams ranged against us spent big money.*

Regrettably, a knee injury brought Stan's playing career to an end just after promotion had been secured in 1974. Stan remembered:

> *At Sheffield Wednesday I tore my cruciate ligament in a mistimed tackle … I didn't give in [but] I returned too*

> *early and aggravated the problem. I never recovered full mobility but I battled to compensate and regained my place … Crucially, we did the double over [promotion rivals] Leyton Orient. We beat Aston Villa 2-0 in our final game but then we had to wait six days to learn our fate … Villa were to play at Orient who would overtake us if they won … it was 1-1 when the referee contrived to add seven minutes of injury time … Cumbria held its breath … Eventually it was over … penniless, humble, unfashionable Carlisle had completed a remarkable rise from the Fourth Division basement to the First Division penthouse … I had a beer. Then they sold me.*

But Stan went on to enjoy a successful coaching and managerial career, notably at Chelsea, Bury and Burnley. He also saved Hull from relegation in 1990 and almost performed a similar service for Gillingham, much against the odds, in 2005. As a manager and coach, Stan retained his combative spirit which made him such a tough competitor in his playing days.

A midfielder or sweeper, Chris Balderstone signed for Carlisle in May 1965 for a 'snip' fee of £7,000. Carlisle coach Dick Young had watched him play for Huddersfield reserves and enthused, 'He was spraying the ball about as though he invented the game'. Although not blessed with great pace, Balderstone had tremendous vision and composure plus exquisite ball control. Chris was a Rolls-Royce midfielder who played for ten years at Brunton Park, clocking up 376 league appearances and 68 goals. During the 1973/74 season, manager Alan Ashman also used him in the role of sweeper. Chris said: '[The fans] gave me a bit of stick at first because I wasn't the quickest player or the hardest tackler. I used to think I made up for it with speed of thought and control of the ball. I always had confidence in my ability and I knew there'd be somebody in the crowd who appreciated a bit of skill. I won them over and they were very good to me after that.' Balderstone completed his playing career with Doncaster and Queen of the South. He also played county cricket for Yorkshire and Leicestershire, representing England against the all-conquering West Indians in 1976 with their ferocious pace attack of Roberts, Holding and Daniel. On one occasion he batted in a county championship game until the close of play at 6.30pm, whereupon he was whisked away to play for Doncaster Rovers an hour later, returning the next day to complete his century. Nobody else has scored a first-class century interrupted by a Football League appearance. Stan Ternent recalled in *Stan the Man*: 'When I was busy falling through ceilings on building sites during the summer to boost my wages, I'd telephone Balderstone as he prepared to walk out at Lord's and call him a lazy bastard.' But Stan recognised Chris' worth, describing him as 'a sublimely skilful footballer'. Chris became a first-class umpire after completing his professional cricket playing career in 1986. He died prematurely in March 2000.

Midfielder Les O'Neill was signed from Bradford City in 1972 for £6,000. He was then 29 years old, having made almost 300 senior appearances and scored 52 league goals in a ten-year professional career with Newcastle, Darlington and the Bantams. He played for Darlington on the night that Brighton seized the Fourth Division title in 1965. Writer and former Millwall midfielder, Eamon Dunphy, described O'Neill, in his football diary *Only a Game*, as '… unbelievable. He is useless if you use any of the textbook criteria. All he has got is a heart as big as the Den. He kept Carlisle going. They were dead and he would not stop. He was kicking and fighting and chasing.' But O'Neill was much more than an inspirational, waspish workaholic. He was both a ball-winner and a ball-carrier, adept at making penetrating runs deep into the opposition's territory. He was one of Carlisle's best players in Division One, scoring a spectacular goal at Chelsea. However, in 2009, he came clean about that effort when interviewed by the local football correspondent with the *Times and Star*. 'It was a fluke – a total fluke,' admitted O'Neill. 'I made an overlap for Dennis Martin, looked up and saw Hughie McIlmoyle making the run to the near post. I thought if I could get a decent ball in there, we had a chance. But instead of hitting the outside of the ball I came across it, and it flew over Peter Bonetti's head and went in at the back post. If you look at the footage, when the lads were running towards me, you can see I was delighted but a bit sheepish. The commentator was saying what a great goal it was. Let me tell you, it was a f****** fluke.' Les O'Neill stayed at Carlisle until 1977, playing 155 league games and scoring 20 goals. He later became a milkman before returning to football as a coach with Swindon, under John Gorman, and then as chief scout at Blackpool and Northampton.

Midfielder Ray Train was nicknamed 'puffer' not only because of his surname; like Les O'Neill, Stan Ternent and Joe Laidlaw, Train had an indomitable competitive spirit. He had considerable skill, too. As a 5ft 4in-tall apprentice at Coventry, he was considered too small for professional football but his performances grew in stature after moving to Walsall. Carlisle recognised his potential and paid £5,000 for him in December 1971. Train immediately impressed with his hard running, terrific stamina and his 'never-say-die' competitive zeal. Train was not merely a ball winner;

he had the ability to use it also. Many fans considered him to be their player of the year during the difficult 1972/73 season. Unfortunately, he sustained a slight fracture of the leg in the 1-6 debacle at Luton at the start of the promotion-winning season, sidelining him for 18 games. But he was ever-present in Carlisle's Division One campaign, often picked out by the *Match of the Day* commentators for his wholehearted displays. Thereafter, he sold himself as a promotion guarantee. Bob Stokoe paid £90,000 for him in March 1976 to help his Sunderland side seize the Division Two title. Train then helped Bolton achieve promotion to the top flight in 1978, whereupon he moved on to Watford, helping them to the Third Division championship in 1979. Train stayed four years at Watford before moving on to Oxford in 1982. Here, he helped lay the foundations for the incredible U's revival, before concluding his impressive playing career with Northampton, Tranmere and, finally, back at Walsall. He was then 36 years old. Ray Train then turned to coaching at Middlesbrough. He continues to work as a scout for various clubs.

'Smokin' Joe Laidlaw was a combative and bustling attacking midfielder who played for six English league clubs over a 15-year career spanning three decades. A local reporter described him as 'about as subtle as a bulldozer in the Amazonian rainforest'. However, Carlisle author David Steele described Laidlaw more accurately as 'a damaging and strong-running forward'. Laidlaw had previously spent five seasons at Middlesbrough. According to David Steele, 'He would prove to be one of the manager's most successful signings in [Ashman's] second spell at Brunton Park.' However, coach Dick Young needed to call him back for afternoon training sessions to improve his fitness. Young thought Laidlaw was carrying excess weight but believed that the midfielder could become an 'outstanding footballer by using his strength, shooting power and aggression'. Laidlaw's two cracking goals at Goodison Park, just before Christmas 1974, not only vindicated Young's judgement but also helped Carlisle to recover from a two-goal deficit and beat the title contenders 3-2. Laidlaw would become the club's top scorer in the First Division with 12 goals. He scored 44 goals in 151 league games for Carlisle between 1972 and 1976 before playing 254 league games for Doncaster, Portsmouth, Hereford and Mansfield, scoring 54 times. He later managed a Sussex non-league side.

Dennis Martin, a winger, was born in Edinburgh. He joined Carlisle from West Bromwich Albion in 1970 for £22,222 with Carlisle winger George McVitie joining the Baggies for £33,333; a curiously-priced exchange. In seven years at Brunton Park he played in 275 games, scoring 48 goals, including an exquisite chipped goal at Burnley in December 1974.

He was the last Carlisle player to score in the top flight, netting the winning goal against Wolves on 19 April 1975. He also played for Newcastle and Mansfield before ending his playing career with Kettering Town. He then went into the insurance business before retiring to Spain in 2004.

Striker Bobby Owen was a bustling centre-forward with a powerful shot. He began his career as an apprentice with Bury in the mid-sixties, making his first-team debut during the 1964/65 season after the former Burnley star, Ray Pointer, moved on to Coventry. He began to attract the attention of bigger clubs after scoring 23 goals during Bury's promotion campaign in 1967/68, which restored the Shakers to Division Two. 'My daughter even came home with a bubble gum card picture of me then,' recalled Bobby proudly. There were different measures of fame in the sixties. Having scored 35 goals in 87 league games for the Gigg Lane club, his impressive performance against the league champions, Manchester City, in a pre-season friendly in the summer of '68, persuaded the Maine Road board to stump up £35,000 for his signature. Owen made a spectacular start to his career under Mercer and Allison, scoring in the opening seconds of the Charity Shield game with West Bromwich in August 1968. Thereafter, Owen found First Division defences less obliging. He only managed three goals in his next 22 first-team appearances. After a short loan with Swansea, Owen was allowed to join Carlisle in 1970. Here, he rediscovered his form and confidence, scoring 51 goals in 204 league games over a six-year stay, with 11 coming in the 1973/74 season. Unfortunately, he is also remembered by long-standing Carlisle supporters for missing a fair share of sitters, too. Towards the end of his time at Carlisle he was loaned to Workington and Northampton before finishing his career at Doncaster and Gainsborough Trinity. After leaving football, he worked in a pub and managed a bowling club, before becoming employed as a forklift truck driver in Bolton.

Striker Frank Clarke was the eldest of five brothers, all of whom played professional football. He was the only brother not to have played for Walsall. Although not as famous or as gifted as his younger brother, Allan, Frank still had an impressive striking record. He scored 77 goals in 188 league games at lower-division Shrewsbury before netting 17 goals for QPR and 15 goals for Ipswich, mostly in Division Two. Ashman shelled out £36,000 for Clarke in August 1973 and he repaid this investment by becoming Carlisle's leading striker during their promotion-winning season with 16 league goals. Clarke and Owen found it more difficult to penetrate First Division defences, scoring just seven league goals between them. However, the unselfish Clarke frequently played as a lone striker in the top flight. Here, he took considerable punishment in his team's cause. Frank was not short of courage.

Midfielders Brian Tiler and Mike Barry only played supporting roles during the 1973/74 season. Tiler had spent long spells in defence at Rotherham and Aston Villa, joining Carlisle near the end of his career. He later became manager of Wigan and then chief executive at Bournemouth. He was killed in a car crash in Italy during the 1990 World Cup. His companion on that fateful day was Harry Redknapp. Mike Barry was a Welsh under 23 winger who began his professional career with Huddersfield. Ashman paid the Terriers £35,000 for Barry, seeing him as a long-term replacement for Chris Balderstone. Barry did not make the impact that Ashman hoped for, though. He spent four years at Carlisle, scoring 10 goals in 81 games before moving to Bristol Rovers in 1977, and on to America in 1979. He later became the director of coaching at the Thunder Soccer Club in Ohio where he now lives.

Alan Ashman was the architect of Carlisle's success. Having guided Carlisle to successive promotions in the mid-sixties and to within one place of the top flight in 1967, Ashman was selected for the West Bromwich managerial position. Despite steering the Baggies to FA Cup glory in 1968, almost repeating the trick a year later and then taking them to the League Cup Final in 1970, he was dismissed while on holiday in Greece in 1971. Admittedly, West Bromwich's league form had been declining and Arsenal's double-winning coach, Don Howe, a West Bromwich old boy, had become available for hire. Nevertheless, Ashman's sacking seemed harsh, even by football's cut-throat standards. Ironically, Ashman went on to manage a team in the country in which he was holidaying, although his stay at Olympiacos lasted for one season only – by preference rather than necessity. Given a choice between basking in the Mediterranean sun and shrinking from a Solway Firth gale, few would opt for the latter. But as a naturalised Cumbrian, Ashman had no qualms. He plumped for the rain-drenched, green, green grass of home.

Ashman was some man. He melted the heart of even his toughest player – Stan Ternent. 'Mac [Ian MacFarlane] was sacked at the end of 1971/72 and Carlisle turned to their ultimate hero, softly spoken, suited Yorkshireman, Alan Ashman,' remarked Stan. 'He was the genial figure who inspired the team … Ashman was a gentleman. Whenever he dropped a player he would hand over a Polo mint first to sweeten the blow. In his first season after his return to Brunton Park, we struggled to stave off relegation, but in the summer of 1973 he rallied his troops for a final push for that elusive, historic promotion. He inherited a decent team and part of his strategy was to take the lads to the Harraby Inn every Wednesday for a pint … Ashman was a modest hero but another great manager, Bill Shankly, put his performance into perspective.' Shankly said: 'I would say it is the greatest feat in the history of the game, Carlisle United getting into the First Division of the English league. It is an unbelievable achievement.'

To boost the club's survival chances, Carlisle's directors bought defender Bobby Parker from Coventry for a club record £52,500 and brought back legendary striker Hugh McIlmoyle for his third spell at Brunton Park. The nation's media were understandably curious. The local *Times and Star* football correspondent remembered: 'TV cameras made the unfamiliar trek up the M6, invariably preceding coverage of matches with shots of sheep in the fields behind the Scratching Shed ... few gave the Cumbrians much hope when the season kicked off at Stamford Bridge on Saturday August 17, 1974. A couple of hours later Carlisle, darting about in their yellow away kit, had won 2-0.'

'I don't think I ever believed we'd get there,' recalled Carlisle author David Steele. 'It always seemed so unlikely. Carlisle's history was the Third Division North. I postponed my holiday by a day to go to Chelsea. I'd say there were 2–3,000 Carlisle fans there. We cleared shots off the line and I remember thinking, "we'll never be as lucky again". And yet three days later United won 2-0 at Middlesbrough. The following Saturday they played Tottenham at Brunton Park, and won 1-0 with a Chris Balderstone penalty.' Bill Green added: 'Nobody could believe it. The football world was amazed. Little Carlisle were top of the First Division. The best team in England.' But as the *Times and Star* football correspondent said, 'It couldn't last, and it didn't.' David Steele continued: 'From early on I thought we'll do well to survive. When you start off like that you think you might have a chance. But we lost six on the trot in October and November. We had a whole sequence of matches that we lost in the last minute. If matches lasted 85 minutes we'd have stayed up. We lost 2-1 at home to Newcastle on Boxing Day. Malcolm Macdonald drove through in the last minute. Even though it was only Boxing Day, when we lost that match I thought that could be it. We had another bad run in the New Year, and when we lost to Luton, who were down there with us, the writing was on the wall.' Two days after Boxing Day, Carlisle lost again to another last-minute goal – this time, Burnley's Doug Collins was the executioner.

'It was always going to be tough,' concluded Bill Green. 'We couldn't really attract the better sort of players. The club had a strict wage structure which it wouldn't break. Everybody was on the same money. In some ways that was good. There was a great togetherness with no cliques. The senior players were on £70 a week plus £30 appearance money per match. If a young lad came in, they might be on £60 but their appearance money would be £40 to make it the same as the rest of us. Everywhere we went, we were always complimented for the way we played. It was no real consolation. We won a lot of friends, if not matches.'

Reflecting upon the events of April Fools' Day, I recorded the following entry in my diary a day later.

> *The day had started brightly with soothing, swishy breezes as we drifted through the Dales. But by the time we had reached the Lakes there weren't any lonely clouds. And upon entering Carlisle it started to rain. The red stone city centre was dripping and drab. We had lurched from Derby to Carlisle without any Jacobite joy. I was told that the city centre pubs were state-owned. As if to prove that anything sponsored by central government is mired with mediocrity, they seemed as hospitable as urinals. Carlisle United weren't very hospitable, either, not that they could afford to be. They were bottom despite their rousing 3-0 victory over second-placed Everton on Saturday. They tore into Burnley from the start and were soon two up through terrier-like midfielder, Les O'Neill, and sideburned striker, Joe Laidlaw. Burnley's diminutive debutant keeper, Mickey Finn, had no chance with either shot. Most of the 12,793 crowd roared their approval, making enough din for twice as many. Two other young Burnley reserves made their debuts tonight: Geordie striker Derrick Parker and former Enderby Town centre-back Richard Dixey. Both were drafted in after yesterday's fiasco. There was no obvious benefit as at first Burnley hardly managed a kick. Then, out of the blue, Parker took a wild swing at a loose ball. He was at least 30 yards from goal. Somehow the ball arced over Carlisle's reserve keeper, Clarke, and into the net for a fortuitous goal. Shortly after the break, James equalised with an expertly-placed penalty. However, Carlisle were the hungrier side. After the hugely impressive Ray Train scored with a scorcher, Joe Laidlaw ensured a deserved home victory with a late spot kick. Shrouds of*

> *fine rain drifted across the pitch, refracting and sparkling in the glare of the floodlights. A long dreary drive home awaited us. There appeared to be nothing beyond the far end of Brunton Park – just impenetrable darkness. Perhaps we'd come as far as we could.*

Despite their tendency to leak late goals, Carlisle were a good side, much better than their position suggested. They reached the quarter-finals of the FA Cup for the only time in the club's history, and were unlucky to lose to eventual finalists, Fulham. Derby County were that season's league champions and yet Carlisle beat them 3-0 at home and drew 0-0 away. Everton finished fourth and yet Carlisle beat them twice. United also defeated third-placed Ipswich, as well as Arsenal and Manchester City. A late revival brought Carlisle four wins in their last nine matches, but it was too late. The pundits were right. Little Carlisle went straight back down, never to return. However, 12 wins from 42 games was a better return than most relegated Premier League teams manage.

'I've got some good memories,' said Bill Green. 'My three years at Carlisle was the best time of my career. It was a lovely club; a nice place to live. Carlisle getting to the First Division gave other teams hope – maybe they could come through the divisions.'

Carlisle author David Steele summed up the incredible journey thus: 'If you're a glory-hunter you don't follow a team like Carlisle. It was disappointing to be relegated but you have to ask yourself, is it better to have loved and lost than never to have loved at all?' As I would soon rediscover, supporting an underdog can sometimes grant unbelievable highs. You have to be emotionally strong, prepared to contend with a diet of dross and disenchantment without renouncing your faith. Beware of supporting underdogs if you need regular shots of success; it's strictly for frugalists.

THE 1975/76 SEASON

Blackpool v Burnley (FA Cup third round)

'Bohemian Rhapsody'
4 January 1975

After making an awful start, Burnley managed a brief revival during the early autumn. League champions-elect, Liverpool, were beaten in the League Cup. Frank Casper signed off with a late, scorching free kick which defeated Queens Park Rangers, who were then heading the table. Another stunning drive, this time from Leighton James, saw off Coventry at Highfield Road. Although Fletcher was crocked, the versatile Peter Noble filled in admirably as Hankin's strike partner until November, when he, too, succumbed to injury. In the summer, Jimmy Adamson had been allowed to spend £50,000 in bringing Mike Summerbee and old boy, Willie Morgan, to bolster his slim first-team resources. But they couldn't cover the widening gaps left by injuries to Burnley's leading players. After the QPR game, Casper made only three more starts. Fletcher, Collins, Brennan and Noble were also missing for significant periods. James' inexplicable loss of form added to Adamson's woes. Burnley's strength in reserve was not good enough. Hankin, Flynn, Rodaway and Brennan had graduated successfully from the youth system but few others seemed capable of stepping up. After relegation rivals Wolves had stuffed Burnley into the Turf Moor mud in November (1-5), James left to join ambitious Derby for £300,000. Burnley desperately needed the money. Besides, James was unsettled. Adamson noted how much better he had performed for Wales. However, up until New Year we clung to a wispy hope of salvation. On Saturday 3 January this hope was whisked away in a Blackpool storm.

The previous night was wild. A violent gale rampaged across the country, causing 26 deaths and £100 million worth of damage. In some parts of the country gusts reached 80mph. My wife Liz and I were staying with friends in Bristol. Throughout the night the wind buffeted their windows and growled in their grate. In the neighbouring gardens loose gates and shed doors groaned and slammed.

We rose early on that bright Saturday morning, unrested and irritable, with a long drive ahead of us. The debris of the night's torment lay everywhere: fallen trees, torn branches, collapsed fences, overturned dustbins and scattering litter. The deep-blue morning sky seemed free of impurity but soon the clouds gathered.

Holding the car on course was a struggle in the buffeting wind. We arrived in Blackpool just before midday. With my eyes gritty with lack of sleep and concentrated driving, I left Liz in the car and took to the prom. There I stood, braced against the rusted railings, taking in the sea's fury. The towering, wrinkled, grimy grey waves lurched in and out of the flitting sun, their frenzied race for the shore urged on by an icy nor'wester. Only the booming sea wall arrested their charge, each repelled wave clawing back its glinting hostages with seething resentment.

I normally loved days like this. The west wind would usually stir my torpid spirits. But on this day I felt out of sorts. I returned to the car and slumped in the driver's seat, staring dully through the saline-smeared windscreen. The wind had been briefly refreshing but now my eyes smarted with salt as well as fatigue. My skin was tacky and my hair tugged on the comb. I felt a mess. Liz prescribed a pint and hotpot. She sensed we would need fortification for what we were about to receive.

As we approached the ground, snippets of 'Bohemian Rhapsody' were wafting erratically towards us on the gusting, eddying wind. The chanting, too, was whisked above the rooftops in waves of variable volume. It seemed as if there was a mass celebration of 'seaside air'. It took me a little time to twig that the chant was 'Seasiders'.

I loved the pre-match routine, particularly on smarting cold winter days such as this: the chirpy chatter in cosy, smoky pubs, heaving with unsegregated supporters, the banter, the put-downs, the grotesque caricatures, the surreal tales and the outrageous gossip. Then, there was the walk to the ground to stir the senses. I recall an Evertonian describing the time that his grandfather took him to his first game. Excited by the noise of the crowd as they crossed Stanley Park, he wanted to press on. But his grandfather held him back, refusing to increase his slow, measured step. Reflecting on his formative experience, this Evertonian reckoned that his grandfather had the perfect grasp of foreplay. On this stormy Saturday only foreplay was on offer.

Burnley's former league title-winning boss, Harry Potts, was in charge of Blackpool. He had taken over in 1972 when Bob Stokoe moved to struggling

Sunderland. Whereas Stokoe brought about an immediate revival at Roker Park, taking Sunderland to FA Cup glory several months later, Potts was unable to deliver what the Blackpool board demanded – a prompt return to Division One. Twice, his team had come close. Ironically, a defeat at Sunderland in their final game of the 1973/74 season tipped them out of the promotion places. In the following season, Blackpool were still in with a shout of promotion after beating West Bromwich 2-0 on 31 March, but they failed to win any of their five final games. Worst of all, there was a fatal stabbing during the home game with Bolton.

Nevertheless, Harry was popular with his players. As at Burnley, he gave enthusiastic encouragement to all – whether young or experienced. He restored a sense of fun to training sessions. He made the club more sociable. However, he did not have the full support of the Blackpool board. Some directors had actually opposed his selection. With results, crowds and resources dwindling during the 1975/76 season, Potts and chairman Dickinson came under increasing pressure. A boardroom coup was being prepared. Dickinson's and Harry's days were numbered.

On the day of the Burnley FA Cup tie, Blackpool were in 14th place in Division Two. No one at the club was satisfied. Goals had dried up; Harry's team managed only 40 league goals all season with Micky Walsh netting 17 of these. Only Middlesbrough loanee, Malcolm Smith, gave him support, after scoring five in his eight games. It was Blackpool's failure to land Smith in a permanent deal that helped seal Harry Potts' fate. As Harry prepared to face his old club he was under intense pressure. Blackpool had drawn a blank against relegation-bound York City in the previous home game (0-0). Harry was desperate for a cup run to revive the club's spirits and fill its coffers. He knew that only a run of good results would save his job.

With so much at stake and with both teams in such poor form, this was never going to be a fluent game. In fact, it was truly grim. The players had huge difficulties contending with the wind, which twisted, swirled and gusted, carrying away fluttering programmes, crisp bags and sweet wrappers. That wind howled ghoulishly under our rusted corrugated stand roof, tugging also at the furiously flapping club flag. Long balls became a hostage to fortune. Ball control was an embarrassment. Chances were fewer than hardy beach boys. Before the floodlights eclipsed this fading day, the sky began to clear. Only torn fragments of cloud remained, fleeing from the north-west approaches, their crimson reflections of a raw sunset entirely unappreciated by the anxious 20,573 crowd.

Liz and I had settled for a 0-0 draw. Then, Burnley's game fell apart. Hankin, Burnley's only striker of substance, was dismissed. Immediately afterwards, Blackpool defender, Bill Bentley, crashed in a free header from a corner. We bowed our heads as the home fans leapt around us. With Waldron's late equaliser ruled out, there was no way back.

Harry Potts was understandably jubilant. He dismissed the reporters' comments that it had been a petulant game littered with niggling fouls and reckless challenges. With his club £4,500 better off from the victory, Harry had good reason to feel chuffed. Besides, he had just put one over his former Burnley rival. 'We always seem to be playing uphill,' said a disconsolate Jimmy Adamson. 'We've been waiting for the tide to turn in our favour for weeks. But everything still keeps going against us.' The *Burnley Express* reporter's verdict was less forgiving: 'Scraping the Barrel', he wrote.

It was a lugubrious journey home. Liz drove. We hardly spoke. The branches of the overhanging trees still thrashed wildly in the stiff wind. The dead leaves were whipped up into twirls by the passing traffic. Outside, there was irrepressible energy but inside we felt flat and empty.

Little did we know that a savage dressing room row had been taking place at Bloomfield Road. When a local radio report conveyed the news it only added to the wretchedness of the day. Having been to see the referee, Adamson returned to find the dressing room door locked. It seemed an undignified affair. Two days later, Bob Lord requested Adamson's resignation. *Burnley Express* sports editor, Keith McNee, wrote:

> *I did not believe it when I first heard Jimmy Adamson had resigned. It was thought he was a permanent fixture at Turf Moor ... Everyone thought he had a job for life. He was not just a Burnley player. He WAS BURNLEY right up until those poignant moments when he shook hands with the players and then walked dejectedly out of their lives ... Life is full of irony, of course, but how strange that, after his playing career had ended with a match at Blackpool, his management term should end after another game [there] – and a dressing room argument, in which the only part he played, was to end it.*

Picking up on the evidence of internecine strife, James Mossop wrote in the *Sunday Express*:

> *There is little doubt that problems have arisen between Adamson and the man who has succeeded him, his friend*

for 25 years, Joe Brown, and the coaches. Said Adamson: 'I will not make any comment that could be detrimental to Burnley. They have given me a wonderful career and a wonderful home and many happy times. I have no quarrel whatsoever with the chairman, Bob Lord, the directors, the players, or the office staff.' When I pointed out that he had omitted to mention the assistant manager and coaching staff, he smiled a wry smile. It seems that a gulf has developed between the men who did so much together. On the unhappy ride back from Blackpool, Adamson decided it was time to leave them to it.

Mossop was unsurprised by Adamson's departure. He recognised that 'The Burnley boss had a losing and dispirited team; a poor relationship with Bob Lord; some players who were not in tune with him; and a gulf between him and his coaching staff; plus the inevitable thoughts that all good players would eventually be sold to meet the bills.' Burnley captain, Colin Waldron, added: 'This is no secret to Jimmy. There are possibly three or four players at the club who don't like him quite as much as I do.' Mossop also wrote of abusive calls that Adamson and his wife had received, some in the early hours of the morning, forcing them to go ex-directory.

It was a sorry end for Jimmy Adamson and the club. Although Jimmy went on to manage Sunderland and Leeds United, he seemed embittered. His heart was buried at Turf Moor, where he had performed so splendidly as player and coach. As for Burnley, they had no chance. Joe Brown's appointment was wholly inadequate. He managed to win just 20 per cent of his 45 games in charge, threatening to take Burnley into the Third Division for the first time in the club's history. Bob Lord allowed him to sign Preston's talented winger, Tony Morley, for £100,000 but as promising as Morley was, he had little chance of filling James' boots so soon after his arrival. Despite an occasional sop to hope, like the 3-2 victory in the Everton snow, Burnley slumped towards relegation. A resurgent Manchester United delivered the mortal blow on 19 April 1976. Burnley's 'Indian summer' was over. A harsh winter awaited them.

Adamson finally broke his silence when he wrote in 1988: 'I think it is fair to say that Bob Lord helped to build up one of the finest club set-ups in British football; AND THEN DESTROYED IT.' As angry as Adamson was that his dream should have been stifled by Bob Lord's financial priorities, once Burnley were relegated it was apparent how bad the finances were. During the relegation season the club sustained an annual loss of £146,871 despite Leighton James being sold for £300,000. Debts stood at £400,000 (equivalent to £3.4 million today) and were rising at around £4,000 per week. It was inevitable that there would be further sales. Young Ray Hankin played his last game for Burnley in a 2-1 defeat at Carlisle in September 1976. Leeds snaffled the muscular striker for £180,000. More sales followed. Winger Paul Bradshaw went to Hillsborough for £20,000 while young keeper, Gerry Peyton, went to Fulham for twice that figure. No longer having strength in reserve, Burnley had to bring in young Coleraine winger Terry Cochrane for £15,000 and Middlesbrough striker Malcolm Smith for £25,000. Although Cochrane's stay was relatively short, with Middlesbrough paying £238,000 for him in 1978, Burnley had little option but to trade as buyers as well as sellers. Ultimately, a further fall from grace was only arrested by the reappointment of Harry Potts as manager in February 1977. While his expansive 4-2-4 playing style resulted in some spanking defeats it also produced some sparkling victories. However, safety was only secured at the beginning of May 1977, following a fluent home victory over Notts County in the spring showers. It was the game in which Tony Morley gave notice of a talent that would flourish at Aston Villa during the early eighties. As with Dunkirk, the euphoria of Burnley's escape in 1977 subsided quickly into lugubrious reflection as we took in the scale of the club's decline and its diminishing prospects.

THE 1976/77 SEASON

Carlisle United v Matlock Town (FA Cup third round)

'Don't Give Up On Us'
8 January 1977

It has taken me a long time to appreciate arid places. Being my parents' son, limited horizons were taken for granted. For years, my idea of a holiday jaunt was a grey, choppy trip along the 'Costa Geriatrica' fortified by a zipped-up windcheater. This seemed so much better than cowering in the quavering heat of those dusty, sun-bleached Mediterranean resorts. But my blinkered calculation was confounded by the British summers of the mid-seventies. If the summer of '75 was unseemly hot, that of '76 was hotter still. Rivers dried up, ponds disappeared, trees wilted and crops failed just like 'grovelling' Tony Greig and his humiliated England cricketers. Among the many receding reservoirs, Ladybower, in the Peak District, revealed the village it had once drowned. The summer seemed like an exhumation.

It wasn't just the land which was drying up; so was the nation's industry. Wilson's answer was a 'social contract'. It seemed like a holding measure to keep the industrial peace. While attempting to limit inflationary wage demands, it didn't address the core problems of productivity and growth. Cabinet minister, Shirley Williams, objected. She found 'the TUC conservative, self-interested, fairly sexist, not all that interested in poverty or those not in full-time work'. Many saw TGWU general secretary, Jack Jones, as more powerful than the prime minister. The underdogs were running the kennel business. A graffiti message suggested 'Vote Jack Jones, cut out the middle man.'

Wilson's successor, Jim Callaghan, confronted the 1976 Labour Party Conference with grim news, announcing reduced government spending and demanding better productivity and reduced labour costs. His chancellor, Denis Healey, looked to the International Monetary Fund (IMF) for financial help. The price was punitive – swingeing cuts in public spending of between six per cent and eight per cent over the next two years. As it turned out the crisis was not as bad as was first feared. While the Treasury's figures were not to be trusted, the crisis gave Callaghan the political leverage to turn off the subsidy tap on unproductive ventures such as at British Leyland. In February 1977, the BL bosses laid down the gauntlet to 'Red Robbo' and the striking car workers: 'End the strike or face plant closure.' It was about time.

'Bleak chic' helped define the times, spawning punk rock and fashion. There was a surge of grim films such as Chris Pettit's *Radio On,* Lindsay Anderson's *O Lucky Man!* and Derek Jarman's *Jubilee*. In step with this, there were tales about emotionally impoverished lives, including Margaret Drabble's *The Ice Age*, JG Ballard's *High Rise*, Martin Amis' *Dead Babies* and Ian McEwan's *The Cement Garden*. Our TV sitcoms lampooned the mood – more gently in *The Good Life* and perhaps less so in *The Fall and Rise of Reginald Perrin* and *Fawlty Towers*. Dull, inflexible provincialism and moribund commuter strife became laughing matters.

If Peter Swan, the disgraced ex-Sheffield Wednesday and England centre-half, was looking for a way out of his dissatisfying existence, this didn't include renouncing his chosen profession. On the contrary, he was desperate to recover his former career, having been deprived of his right to play football following a grave error of judgement.

Peter Swan and two of his Sheffield Wednesday team-mates, David Layne and Tony Kay, were jointly convicted of conspiracy to defraud by betting that their side would lose a match at Ipswich in 1962. The bet was made as part of a larger fraudulent betting scandal, orchestrated by ex-Everton and Charlton forward Jimmy Gauld, and involving several lower-division players. Once their actions were uncovered by an investigative journalist with the *People*, Swan, Layne and Kay received four-month jail sentences plus life bans from playing any form of organised football. As the ringleader, Gauld was jailed for four years with £5,000 costs.

In 2006, Swan told Nick Johnson, who helped him write his book *Setting The Record Straight*: 'It was later claimed in court that I had bet on numerous lower-league games I knew to be 'bent' but that was totally untrue … the Ipswich game was a one-off.' Swan, Kay and Layne made £100 each out of an action which netted various gamblers thousands of pounds. Each of the three players lost glittering careers at the very top of the English game – in the cases of Swan and Kay, they lost a chance of World Cup glory, too, as Alf Ramsey rated both of them highly. The overwhelming impression was that the 'Wednesday Three' had probably been guilty of gross unprofessionalism and bewildering naivety rather than calculated fraud. But it took the FA until 1972 to relent and lift Swan's lifetime ban. *Daily Mail* football journalist,

Brian James, wrote in his 1977 book *Journey to Wembley*: 'For years the game followed him vengefully: a pub team for whom he played a friendly match one Saturday was banned as a punishment. Not until 1972, after he kept out of football for eight years (selling cars, scrap metal, running a bread round), was the ban lifted on appeal. Swan trained like a demon to lose weight, regain sharpness ...'

By then, Swan was approaching his 36th year. He had little time left to enjoy what remained of his truncated playing career. He was determined to make up for lost time. After a season of making sporadic appearances for his forgiving former club, by then a pale imitation of the top-flight side he had left in 1964, he joined Bury for the start of the 1973/74 season. He made 35 league appearances for the Shakers, captaining them to promotion to Division Three in 1974. However, after falling out with Bury manager Bobby Smith [not the Spurs one], Swan left Gigg Lane at the end of the season. He was offered and accepted the job of player-manager at Northern Premier League club, Matlock Town, which was situated close to his home in Chesterfield. He insisted he would only continue playing until a suitable replacement emerged.

Having outgrown the Midland Counties League, which they had won in successive years, Matlock joined the newly-established Northern Premier League in 1969. The step up proved to be a daunting challenge, and for the first few seasons they struggled. Then, Peter Swan came along to transform their fortunes.

Swan was impressed with the standard of play in the league. He thought that the top six sides could have held their own in Division Four. But he was well aware that Matlock Town were not of that calibre yet. There was much room for improvement. As a new manager he sought advice about how he should go about his task. Former England colleague and Leeds manager, Jimmy Armfield, invited him to Elland Road to watch their training sessions. Swan noted the greater attention paid to speed work but felt that little else had changed in the intervening years. Swan still held his former boss, Harry Catterick, in high esteem. Catterick was a tough, demanding boss who had uncompromising standards. He was a shrewd tactician and very explicit about what he wanted from his players. Applying Catterick's approach to his own good-humoured style, Swan instilled greater professional discipline within his team. They learnt quickly. In December 1974, they created a new club record by winning 10-0 at Lancaster City.

Peter Swan said in *Putting The Record Straight* that 'Working with players on a part-time basis wasn't easy because they had to juggle playing with their day jobs. There were always some players who missed training because of work commitments so you never had a full squad. If players couldn't get time off to play we would still pay their wage. You'd sometimes get a player pulling a fast one, saying they were working when they weren't.' Non-league players could earn decent money playing professional part-time football on top of their day jobs, as Swan told journalist Brian James. 'Many of the team were recruited on the promise of wages as low as £2, £4 or £6 per game,' he explained. 'It's unlikely that they average more than £15 a week from football [The average national wage at that time was about £38 per week].' Matlock's total wage bill was around £200 per week and once rent, rates, travel and other expenses were taken into account, the club needed a fortnightly gate of about 1,000 to break even. Approximately £100 per week came in from the Auxiliary Association pool, which had 7,000 members, equivalent to one for each Matlock household.

In his book, Swan continued:

> *[Before the game] we would meet at a hotel in Matlock Bath. I'd get them in at twelve o'clock for a meal of poached eggs, beans on toast, or whatever they wanted. It made the players feel as though they were at a big club … Their attitude changed, acting more professionally … I used to like playing the old way with wingers. I got two good wingers: Colin Oxley on the right, Andy Wilson on the left. If the ball was lost on the left wing, the right winger would come into midfield, so that we'd have the midfield packed. As soon as we retrieved the ball the winger would go back out wide. It was like playing a 4-2-4 system all the time and, with two fast, tricky wingers, it worked out very well. We had a brilliant midfield player called Brian Stuart, who was watched by league clubs. And then there were the Fenoughty brothers, Mick, Tom and Nick. Mick went wide when he retrieved the ball and Nick was very clever with the ball. I got him a trial at Burnley but he wasn't bothered … If he had the right attitude, I think he would have been a First Division player. Tom, who played for Sheffield United and Chesterfield, sat in midfield and sprayed the ball about. Keith Scott, who'd also played for Chesterfield, was a great lad and a very good centre-*

> *half … putting his head in anywhere. Keith was an old pro who would often claim that he wasn't fit to play … I wouldn't say another word to him and then he'd go out and play, well, more often than not. You have to know how to handle different players … When Harry Catterick told me 'Swanny, you're the best centre-half in England', I felt ten feet tall going out.*

Swan told journalist Brian James: 'People have a big thing about there being three Fenoughty brothers in one team. In fact it is though they are *all* brothers … they have a hell of a family thing going. The whole team thinks as one, in a way I have never known anywhere else.'

Peter Swan led Matlock to the first round of the FA Cup in the 1974/75 season. Although they lost 1-4 to Third Division champions-elect Blackburn, over 5,000 fans packed their tiny Causeway Lane Ground, a remarkable attendance given the town had a population of only 20,000, and that was including all the surrounding villages. The fact that so many could be accommodated was a testimony to the terrific efforts of the club committee members. After ten days of relentless rain, they levelled a section of banking and laid 100 tons of stone chippings to accommodate an extra 2,500 people. They had previously helped to rescue the club's possessions after the River Derwent had broken its banks and flooded the ground. Five of them also turned up at little notice to spread 14 tons of steaming tarmac after an unexpected early delivery. The club chairman, Cliff Birtland, was very hands-on. He would invariably visit the dressing room before a game and remark, 'Whatever happens lads, just make sure you enjoy it'. These guys were no stick-in-the-mud, talk-shop, petty-minded officials. Cliff Birtland epitomised the committed, grounded and modest approach. He was a caretaker at the local magistrates' court. There were no airs and graces about him. It was small wonder that the club drew such strong loyalty. At Matlock everyone pulled together.

Swan's crowning glory came in the FA Trophy, in which his little side progressed successfully through six ties to reach Wembley. In the semi-finals they faced a strong Burton Albion side which featured the former Forest, Manchester United and England winger, Ian Storey-Moore. Burton won the first leg at Matlock 1-0 in front of a record 5,123 crowd. Burton's cause was helped by Swan's dismissal after the Burton centre-forward had supposedly 'made a meal' of Swan's 'little dig in the ribs'. However, much against expectation, Matlock won the return leg at Burton 2-0 with goals from the tough, wise-cracking coalminer Peter Scott and Nick Fenoughty.

Peter Swan said of Scott: 'He was being wasted before the team was reshaped. They were playing daft formations – one upfield in away matches. So Scottie was left battering about on his own. Soon as we started to play more free, getting a bit of width, he looked a new man; a real rough, tough centre-forward of the old school.'

Matlock were through to the final where they would meet Scarborough Town, managed by ex-Hull and Rotherham inside-forward, Ken Houghton. Scarborough were in fifth position in the Northern Premier League, six places above Matlock, and were much fancied to win, particularly by their complacent chairman, Don Robinson. Robinson had perhaps overlooked Matlock's 3-1 victory at Seamer Road.

Swan took his side down to Wembley the day before the final, helping them to relax and acclimatise to the stadium. It worked. The overnight stay in Ealing helped focus the players' minds and conserve their energies. Swan insisted that they should play their natural game and not try to alter their style to suit the bowling green surface. Although the 21,000 crowd left the huge stadium looking comparatively empty, this was a massive turnout for two small clubs. Although they rode their luck in the earlier stages, Matlock defied the odds by winning emphatically, 4-0. The opportunistic Colin Oxley scored in the first half with a shot that went through the Scarborough keeper's legs and then just after the hour Colin Dawson added the vital second from a corner. Finally, Tom and Nick Fenoughty put Matlock out of sight. First, Tom struck with a 35-yard fizzer of a free kick before his brother, Nick, scored the fourth with a header from Oxley's cross. As the fourth went in, the 10,000 Matlock fans broke into a chant of 'easy, easy!' It was a proud moment for Peter Swan, who had performed so immaculately on the same surface for Walter Winterbottom's England side in the early sixties. He had been given a final opportunity to redeem his past and, on the biggest stage in the land, he and his doughty team had seized it gloriously. Not content with that, Matlock also lifted the Derbyshire Senior Cup that season for the first time in their history.

Brian James likened the Matlock team to the *Seven Samurai,* a group of avenging Yorkshiremen (apart from the Crewe-based Keith Scott). They lived, worked and trained in their native county but routinely travelled to the attractive little Derbyshire town of Matlock, huddled in its steep, wooded, limestone vale, to sort out the invading bandits. Tom Fenoughty told Brian James:

> *It may seem daft us all trooping across for a town we never otherwise see but it never occurs to anyone to*

think of it that way. We go there because we enjoy our football there and that means more than anything else to us. It's a smashing place, where we're made to feel welcome when we arrive … and it's obviously very important to the town when we happen to win. It's a nice relationship between the club and team. They've got it right. For example, when we went to Wembley they started a fund in the area to make sure we did it in style. The lads went down and had two days in a posh hotel. Then they brought our wives and girlfriends down on the day of the match, treated them right, and gave us all a party when it was over. Remember, the club was just about getting by; yet they spent money on the team and probably only just broke even on the big day.

Buoyant at their success, Matlock enjoyed a successful 1975/76 season in the Northern Premier League, finishing in fourth position. Peter Swan thought that his success at Matlock might recommend him as a potential league club manager but he was to be disappointed. 'I left Matlock to try to show people that what I did there was no fluke,' he explained to Brian James. 'I thought if I went to another club [he went to Worksop in the summer of 1976] I would make some league chairman sit up and take notice. I keep reading in the papers that I'm on the shortlist for this job … but that's all it is – newspaper talk. I just never even get the chance to put my case. Maybe people who live in boardrooms have never made a mistake in their lives and can't make allowances, or forgive those who have. They don't seem to see that all I'm trying to do is give something back to the game. But I won't give up!' Sadly, Peter Swan made a mistake in moving to Worksop. Here, the club committee tried to run the team. His stay was short. He also missed out on Matlock's stirring 1976/77 FA Cup run, managed, upon his recommendation, by Tom Fenoughty.

Matlock's journey began at Telford in the fourth qualifying round. World Cup hat-trick hero, Geoff Hurst, was Telford's player-manager but he was finding life hard, as he explained to Brian James.

It's more physical, people scrambling away at you all the time. But harder still is the service you get, the positioning of players you are trying to reach [he'd been endeavouring to instill the art of the near-post cross – a

West Ham speciality]. It's hard work just getting the ball from place to place … that part of the game you used to take for granted. I don't want them afraid to stick in a 25-yard killer ball when they got the ability to do so … The one thing I hate hearing is the excuse, 'oh well, we're only Southern League, playing part-time'. In football you are what you aim to be … not what outsiders think of the league you play in … the only real frustration is with myself. I wind up for a shot I know I would have buried ten years ago, and mis-kick. Or I scoot past someone and he comes tanking back to catch me. That hurts.

Matlock, described by Geoff Hurst as 'the best non-league side in the North', were heading the Northern Premier League by six points. In order to titivate the occasion, Hurst told his players that because Telford were a leading Southern League team, the unofficial English non-league 'title' was up for grabs. Regrettably for Geoff, he was way off beam in his estimation of his team. Despite fighting back from a two-goal deficit, having a stonewall penalty claim denied and enduring a hotly-disputed Matlock goal, Telford were unable to live with Matlock's pace and power. They were trounced 5-2. 'They're the best side we've played this year,' conceded the sporting Hurst. 'They're good enough to frighten quite a few in the [Football] League. They did for us, no messing.' This wasn't the end of Telford's woes. Far from being a leading Southern League outfit, Telford were relegated to the lower division in 1977. Meanwhile, Wimbledon, the eventual Southern League champions that season, were on course to join the Football League.

Colin Oxley was Matlock's star at Telford, having scored one goal and assisted with three others. Brian James described him as 'a slim, sharp and deadly quick winger'. Oxley was one of Peter Swan's 'finds'. Swan told Brian James: 'There were times when he used to turn up for training absolutely green; tired out after working all day in the steelworks. He'd never complain so I just used to look at him and say, "thanks for coming, Col. Now sod off and get some rest. See you Saturday".'

Swan understood how to manage the part-timers he had at his disposal, as he went on to explain: 'You have to take into account what the blokes have been doing in the day. Some of 'em are down the pits at 5am, others have been sitting behind a desk for eight hours … In a Football League club it's easy: you have training schedules and everybody works as a group … Football at this level requires understanding and diplomacy. If you sicken 'em in training on Thursdays, you're going to suffer on Saturdays … they'll fade on you or clear off back to their pub teams where they can have a bit of fun with their football.' Tom Fenoughty added: 'Colin Oxley doesn't say a lot but he does it all. He has this odd habit of being at his most dangerous when he looks to have the least chance, down on his knees, or off-balance yards from the ball. It's about quick reactions, the ability to see how things are shaping before they happen. And it's about being a fantastic enthusiast in play and training.'

In the first round proper, Matlock were drawn at home against Wigan, one of the strongest sides in the Northern Premier League. Wigan had spent 40 years fruitlessly trying to find a way into the Football League. They had thrown money at their ambition – lots of it. In the mid-seventies they ran up a wage bill of £800 per week. This was on a par with a full-time lower-division league team. They over-reached themselves, though, and subsequently reduced their wage bill to £170 per week, a much more realistic figure.

It was a bright, sharp November afternoon. As dusk approached a wintry haze infiltrated the deep valley, smoothing away its cragginess and softening the stark hilltop silhouette of Riber Castle. The absorbed 3,336 crowd were oblivious to its chilly presence, though. Wigan started well but fluffed two presentable chances. Gore blasted a shot over the bar while Braithwaite fired wide. Matlock made their visitors pay for their profligacy. With Wigan's defensive wall failing to do its job, Tom Fenoughty's free kick was deflected into the net, eluding the visitors' 19-year-old keeper, who seemed culpably leaden-footed. The young custodian was quick to make amends, though, producing a blinding save to turn away Nick Fenoughty's scorching volley. Matlock's keeper, Brian Arblaster, followed suit, denying Wigan's Gillibrand. Brian was formerly with Sheffield United, Barnsley and Chesterfield. He then became a lorry driver with the Coal Board but his will to win remained undiminished. He wasn't averse to giving his defenders a right ear-bashing.

This was a tight game but Matlock played to their strengths, pushing forward at every opportunity. Despite Worswick's lightning pace on the flanks, Wigan could not make much impression on their hosts' defence, so they pushed up their centre-half, Ward, to lead the line. Having given Matlock centre-forward Peter Scott a bit of a battering, he turned his attention to Scott's namesake, Keith. It was to no avail. With little time remaining, Nick Fenoughty seized upon a loose ball and hit a bobbling winner. It was a historic moment. Matlock had never ventured so far in the FA Cup before, not that this meant too much to the players. They were a grounded lot.

Matlock's prize for beating Wigan was a tie with their near neighbours, Mansfield Town, who were enjoying a successful season at the top of the Third Division under former Ipswich and Norwich midfielder, Peter Morris. The Stags would ultimately take the title ahead of Brighton and Crystal Palace in April 1977 but at this stage they were outside the promotion frame in seventh position. They had been unbeaten at home since Boxing Day 1975. The tie had to be postponed twice on account of ice, snow and fog. But now a thaw had set in. Playing conditions were expected to be heavy.

Mansfield were well-supported by Third Division standards. They attracted an average gate of 8,500, but their outgoings were high. Their players were among the best paid in the division, receiving around £75 per week. But the scale of club debts had forced the sale of centre-forward, Ray Clarke, to Sparta Rotterdam for £60,000 at the start of the season. Morris was still looking for a replacement. He had his eye on Chesterfield's big, raw-boned striker, Ernie Moss, who had partnered his current centre-forward, Kevin Randall, at Saltergate.

Mansfield were sound defensively. Colin Foster and Ian McKenzie were two of the strongest centre-backs in the division and Rod Arnold was one of the best lower-league goalkeepers. In deference to his age (he was 33 years old) and his declining speed, player-manager Morris retreated into a full-back role. Mansfield's danger men were their wide men: Jim McCaffrey, a former Forest left-winger, and young Johnny Miller, a £10,000 buy from Norwich. Miller had been Morris' only purchase, thus far. Tom Fenoughty identified McCaffrey as the player his team needed to subdue after watching his starring performance in Mansfield's victory over Huddersfield in the first-round replay. 'Give McCaffrey too much room and he can tear you apart', he announced, shifting one of his quicker players, Colin Smith, over to his 'wrong' side to mark the Mansfield left-winger.

During the first 20 minutes, McCaffrey caused Matlock's defence no end of problems, almost putting the hosts ahead with a shot that squirted past the post. But then the Fenoughtys took control of the midfield. They appeared to be perfectly attuned. Mansfield seemed perturbed, particularly after Matlock snatched the lead. Nick Fenoughty produced a cross for Peter Scott to chest down, allowing steelworks shunter, David Goodwin, to nip in and beat Arnold. Goodwin was Matlock's 'hard as nails' full-back. This was foreign territory for him. Stung by Matlock's impudence, the Mansfield forwards buzzed around Arblaster's goal, forcing him into a superb point-blank save. Although Mansfield managed to find a way past the agile lorry driver, Nick Fenoughty promptly restored Matlock's lead after

Peter Scott had chested Goodwin's free kick into his path. Nevertheless, when Colin Foster headed Mansfield level after an hour, it looked as if Matlock's resistance would be broken. Not so. Parity lasted two minutes as Nick Fenoughty turned in Scott's pass for Matlock's third. Surprisingly, Mansfield caved in. With the Matlock fans impertinently demanding a fourth, Colin Oxley answered their call by stabbing home yet another Scott 'assist'. Finally, Oxley returned the favour for Scott to poke in an incredible fifth to the Matlock fans' exultant strains of 'Easy! Easy!'

While the Mansfield players slouched sullenly off the field, their chairman, Arthur Patrick, did better. Sportingly, he was the first to offer the Matlock players his congratulations. 'After what you have done tonight there's no need to go to Carlisle thinking it's the end of the road,' he told them. 'Play like this and you can win.' He was quickly followed by Matlock committeeman George Bensall, who, according to Brian James, cautioned his team: 'Now then, lads, don't get carried away. After all, you only got … BLOODY FIVE!!' As for the chairman, Cliff Birtland, he seemed so befuddled by the euphoria and his five tots of whisky – he'd promised himself a swig each time Matlock scored – that he mixed up most of his players' names. 'Bloody hell,' one of them retorted. 'We've become so famous even our sodding chairman can't recognise us.' The national media did, though. But player-manager Tom Fenoughty kept his head. He refused to play along with the hype. He gave the media no easy sound bites. About as much as he was prepared to say was, 'I think we can give a good account of ourselves at Carlisle.'

Despite Arthur Patrick's generous encouragement, Brunton Park proved to be a game too far. Carlisle were well prepared. They had taken careful note of Matlock's strengths. After all, they had been plastered all over the nationals. The *Cumberland News* also told them that 'Matlock are now supposed to be the best non-league side in the country … their goalscoring is phenomenal. In their last 23 league games they have hit the back of the net 64 times.'

Carlisle could not afford to take any chances. The club were in a perilous position. Their brief shaft of First Division sunlight had been eclipsed two years ago. Now, more relegation clouds had clustered over Brunton Park. Their First Division stalwarts – Chris Balderstone, John Gorman, Bill Green, Joe Laidlaw and Ray Train – had moved on. Bobby Owen was no longer a contender. Their inspirational manager, Alan Ashman, had gone, too, replaced by the burly former Newcastle defender, Bobby Moncur. Player-manager Moncur hadn't been able to work the Ashman oracle. On 8 January 1977, the day of the Matlock tie, Carlisle were perched precariously in 19th position in Division Two, just above the relegation zone, which was then inhabited by Burnley, Orient and Hereford, all of whom had games in hand. After a brief spike in popularity – gates had averaged 14,500 in Division One – Carlisle were now drawing league crowds of less than 6,000. Money was short. Moncur knew that a lucrative cup run was essential. Having been a culpable member of Newcastle's losing side at Hereford five years previously, he was determined there should be no repetition. He impressed this upon Brian James, saying: 'I've been drilling it into my players that this could be much harder than a league match.'

Heeding Moncur's caution, Carlisle pulled everyone back into the box to defend an early Matlock corner, prompting a bemused Matlock fan to holler, 'We're only Matlock, you know, not bloody Manchester United.' The Carlisle players got the message and proceeded to put the Matlock upstarts in their place. Carlisle swamped the midfield where Matlock had been so dominant in the earlier rounds. With the Fenoughtys fragmented by Carlisle's brusque, bustling brawn, Matlock could not mount their customary swift charges. Up front, Peter Scott was easily outrun and outmuscled by Moncur. Tom Fenoughty reckoned that Carlisle's boss was much slower than in his prime but Moncur had too much in his tank for the Yorkshire miner. Matlock were pushed back and, unaccustomedly, forced to defend in depth. Their increasing anxiety was reflected by Arblaster's impetuous clearance when the ball was rolling harmlessly out of play.

Carlisle had managed to score just one goal in their previous three games. Confidence was low and yet, encouraged by their ever-increasing dominance, they began to find their feet. With 25 minutes gone and most of the Matlock team entrenched in their goalmouth, Carlisle midfielder Phil Bonnyman clipped a knee-high cross into the box. The low trajectory caught the Matlock defenders by surprise. Before they could react, Carlisle's Scottish striker, Billy Rafferty, had swivelled and blasted a volley into the roof of their net. Rafferty's technique was astounding, his power astonishing. Now there was blood in the water. Carlisle's forwards snapped and thrashed like frenzied sharks. Within minutes, Rafferty had levered himself above the Matlock defence and thumped a header against the bar. There was no respite. Returning Carlisle old boy, George McVitie, bent an exquisite drive past Arblaster. This was finishing of the highest calibre. Matlock looked overwhelmed. As if their woes weren't great enough already, they then lost their midfielder, Mick Chambers, after a horrible tackle. The Carlisle boys seemed to be fed on raw meat. The half-time break came as a welcome respite for Tom Fenoughty's shaky team.

Any hope Tom had of salvaging anything was dashed quickly. Within five minutes of the restart, Frank Clarke ended his goal drought by heading in Carlisle's third. To their credit, Matlock scrapped to redress the imbalance. Once again, Colin Oxley came to their aid by scoring with a remarkable long-range effort that curled over the Carlisle defenders and past the desperately leaping Martin Burleigh to find the top left corner of the net. For a brief period, Carlisle seemed rocked. Their poor league form had left them vulnerable to sudden setbacks. Matlock upped their game. The contest became heated, littered with battering, belligerent challenges. Nick Fenoughty and Phil Bonnyman went beyond the rules of engagement and were both booked. But Bonnyman came off best after riding a series of vicious challenges to put Carlisle beyond reach. It was left to Rafferty to tap in a fifth after Arblaster could not cope with Clarke's jostling presence at a corner. Arblaster was furious, believing he had been obstructed. It was to no avail. Arblaster's incensed two-fingered gesture at the referee merely earned him a booking.

Tom Fenoughty had warned his central defenders about Rafferty's and Clarke's aerial strength. 'You can't hope to beat them, but challenge them, put them off,' he urged. Afterwards, a bruised and exhausted Colin Dawson confided to Brian James: 'We'd no idea they could be that good … strong, big, quick, great in the air. What the hell are two men like that doing playing in the *Second Division* anyway?' Turning to his uncharacteristically solemn striker, Peter Scott, Dawson added: 'He's just told me he's never taken such stick.'

The Matlock players might have taken malicious delight at the 6-0 spanking that the FA Cup holders, Southampton, handed out when they visited Carlisle for a Second Division match a week later. Nick Fenoughty's bitter adversary, Phil Bonnyman, was picked out as one of the guilty men in the Carlisle post-mortem. Brian James recorded: '[Coach Hughie Neil said to Bonnyman] "You're good at turning and beating a player, but you tend to overdo it. By all means take a man on in tight situations in the box. But there are times, especially in your own half, when you must give it first time. Otherwise we're all in the shit." Bonnyman looks down, examining his presumably guilty feet and mumbles something inaudible.' Brian James' *Road to Wembley* is football journalism at its very best; it is strongly recommended.

Matlock took consolation from the financial proceeds of their cup run. Before the Carlisle game they had banked over £2,800, thereby exceeding the return from their FA Trophy triumph. They were understandably disappointed that they didn't draw a bigger fish in the third round but they were still able to take a half share of Carlisle's 10,000-plus gate to add to their swelling purse. With their Northern Premier League gates boosted by their FA Cup success, Matlock averaged crowds of 1,250 during the 1976/77 season, 25 per cent above their break-even threshold. Disappointingly, though, they failed to take the Northern Premier League title after topping the table for most of the season. A defeat by Northwich in their final game reduced them to third spot, although, once again, they won the Derbyshire Senior Cup.

In the following season, Matlock defeated the league champions, Boston United, by 3-0 to win the Northern Premier League Challenge Cup at Maine Road, also adding the Derbyshire Senior Cup to their swelling trophy cabinet. Boston were beaten again as Matlock won the Northern Premier League Shield in the following August. This win granted them entry into the prestigious Anglo-Italian Non-League Tournament, in which they finished as English runners-up to Sutton United.

Tom Fenoughty resigned in November 1980 due to business commitments and Peter Swan returned. 'I was asked to get rid of all the old players in order to cut the wage bill,' Peter recalled. 'It was a hard job to get rid of the players I had success with previously but I carried out instructions. I had no money to replace them so I was getting young players from the local leagues and pubs … We were losing games but were playing some good football … you could see things were on the right track … [But they told me] "we want you to resign".' When Swan refused, the Matlock committee sacked him. Even in the most mutually supportive of non-league clubs football can be a harsh business.

Mick Fenoughty replaced him in 1981, and although Town had to apply for re-election they made a strong recovery in the mid-eighties. In 1982/83, striker Bobby Mountain smashed in a record 49 goals in a productive partnership with Wayne Biggins, who would enjoy a successful career at Burnley, Norwich, Celtic and others. In 1983/84, Town achieved their highest ever Northern Premier League position, when they finished as runners-up to Barrow. But the club had to wait 20 years to have as much success again.

As for Carlisle, they lost their fourth-round tie at Anfield. They were no match for Bob Paisley's side, who was en route to European Cup glory. The season ended badly for Carlisle as they slid back into Division Three. I watched their crucial relegation contest at Turf Moor on 26 February – Harry Potts' first game back in charge of Burnley. Despite playing with three strikers – Rafferty, Clarke and former Celtic star, Dixie Deans – Carlisle hardly managed a shot in anger, leaving a relieved Burnley to snaffle the precious points. Bob Stokoe's return in 1980 did spur a revival helped by gifted players such as Peter Beardsley. Having won promotion back to Division Two in 1982, they threatened to scale the summit once more in 1983/84 but then fell away badly in following seasons, finding themselves back in the basement by 1987. They did not return to the the third tier until the mid-nineties, when the club was owned by Michael Knighton. Despite having one of the best strikers in the lower divisions, in David Reeves, they were relegated immediately. Carlisle's subsequent progress has been erratic. The 2004/5 season was spent in the Conference. Nevertheless, Carlisle came close to returning to the second tier in 2008 and since the mid-eighties they have progressed to six Football League Trophy finals, winning the most recent one, in 2011, against Brentford.

Brighton & Hove Albion v Burnley

'Heart of Glass'
3 March 1979

1978 was a year of Fundamentalist Islamic revolution. So while the Sex Pistols imploded, Iran exploded. The *Amoco Cadiz* went down while Jeremy Thorpe got off. A test tube brought life but an umbrella tip brought death. Rhodesia killed its rebels while Jim Jones murdered his followers. We were given May Day. Tom Robinson was 'Glad to be Gay' although the stuffy BBC was not. The 'Mods' were back, helped by the 'bard' of Woking. Fifteen-year-olds once again swanned around in olive, fur-trimmed parkas with 'The Who' emblazoned on their backs. It was as if 1965 had never ended. The decade began with 'glam' rock but ended with the 'glum' kind. As compelling as their music was, the acerbic Fall, joyless Joy Division, bleak Bauhaus, jabbing Gang of Four and caustic Killing Joke weren't much fun. They produced jagged, jarring, desolate sounds; a fitting soundtrack as the rubbish piled up and the dead remained unburied. The wintry dereliction of the Northern mills and factories seemed to belong to a wasted Eastern European state, touched by *Blade Runner* morbidity. 'Labour isn't working', insisted the Saatchi brothers. It was hard to disagree.

Once again, England had failed to qualify for the World Cup finals. Our club teams were dominating the European Cup competition but our national side choked in big games. Don Revie's selection as England's boss was a scandalous mistake. But while England played the hapless losers, the Scots were Great Britain's sole standard-bearers. They were unluckily eliminated on goal difference in the 1974 tournament. Inspired by this near miss and pumped up by their brash, bragging manager, Alistair MacLeod, the Scots travelled to the 1978 finals in Argentina more in expectation than hope. A swathe of malicious England fans waited for them to stumble. Despite producing a terrific final performance against Holland, Scotland fell at the first hurdle, having lost badly to Peru and drawn lamentably with Iran. This was the backdrop to Burnley's Anglo-Scottish Cup tie with Celtic.

On 26 September 1978, Celtic supporters came to Burnley in force. The Anglo-Scottish Cup was less at stake than bruised Scottish pride. Chrysler had pulled the plug on 'Ally's Tartan Army', leaving the sour English fans to scoff at MacLeod's shattered hubris. There were scores, ancient and modern, to settle on this hostile night. Some 30,000 people, most of them Glaswegians, crammed into Turf Moor. A closed turnstile was no obstacle to the thousands of well-oiled Scots fans. The Longside terraces became like a boozy, sectarian Rorke's Drift. Roared on by their belligerent hordes, Celtic came to slash and burn. But Burnley's ageing team, now reinforced by the returning Leighton James, defied them determinedly.

If the first-half stalemate stoked Scottish frustration, Steve Kindon's breakaway goal after the interval caused it to combust. Not content with singeing the Celtic defenders, Leighton James and Kindon had the temerity to humiliate them also. With their team incapable of satisfying their fierce chauvinism, the Celtic fans began to rampage, pulling the segregating fence out of its concrete emplacement and hurling the posts, like spears, on to the pitch and into the Burnley supporters. Play had to be held up. Burnley's manager, Harry Potts, was clearly shaken by the violence. The referee suggested that Potts and Billy McNeill, the Celtic boss, should jointly appeal to the crowd for order. Instead of presenting himself, Potts tried to persuade the irrepressible Steve Kindon to do the deed. 'You are much more popular with the crowd. They'll listen to you,' he enthused. Steve was sceptical. 'Harry, I think you're overlooking a small detail here. It was my goal which started the bloody riot.' Order was eventually restored and Burnley clung on to win. Just to rub salt into already inflamed wounds, Burnley won the away leg, too, thanks to a ferocious free kick from Brennan and another fine solo goal from Kindon. Avenging Culloden, the Boyne or Argentina would have to wait for another day.

Burnley went on to win the Anglo-Scottish Cup that season but their overriding priority – promotion back to Division One – eluded them. As with so many other clubs, Burnley suffered from the ravages of one of the harshest winters for 16 years. They managed just one game in January – a 2-0 FA Cup victory at baleful Birmingham. Their backlog of league fixtures was horrendous. When Burnley arrived at the Goldstone Ground on an overcast Saturday 3 March, this was their fifth game in 11 days.

After leaving Hastings, I had lost touch with Brighton. After that jubilant night in '65 when Brighton went up as Fourth Division champions, I had expected them to prosper. But they didn't. They stalled for six years. Archie Macaulay couldn't take them any further. Neither could Freddie Goodwin, despite Alex Dawson's best burly efforts. Bubbly Pat Saward did, although it proved to be a one-season wonder. Saward paid for that failure with his job. His dismissal was the first major act carried out by the new chairman, Mike Bamber. Bamber, a one time jazz drummer and property millionaire, set about placing the club on a commercially sustainable footing. The club's overdraft of almost £200,000 was brought down. Bamber also established a property development company as a subsidiary arm of the club. He reconstituted the board, helped by Harry Bloom and Keith Wickenden, who later became an MP. Wickenden was responsible for financial affairs while Bloom took care of fund-raising. Bamber turned to Brian Clough and Peter Taylor to replace Saward. He would be tested to the hilt. However, Bamber knew that for all his irksome game-playing, Clough was good for Brighton. The crowd trebled in size, to 16,500, for his first match in charge. The national press descended upon the Goldstone Ground in droves. Clough even appeared on American television. Extra publicity meant extra revenue. Besides, Bamber had Clough's measure. The results weren't good, though. A shocking 4-0 home defeat by Walton & Hersham was followed by an 8-2 home drubbing by Bristol Rovers. If Bamber expected Clough to rollick the players he was mistaken. Clough reserved that for when they won.

Although Clough left for his *Damned United* experience, Taylor remained and managed to stop the rot. Under Taylor, Albion rose to fourth place in Division Three in 1975/76. At the close of that season, however, Taylor resigned to resume his partnership with Clough at Nottingham Forest. History was about to be made at the City Ground. Meanwhile, Bamber sought a replacement. It did not take him long to decide that Alan Mullery was the man for the job. History was about to be made at the Goldstone Ground, too.

Alan Mullery had been a superb midfielder – skilful, dynamic, quick and tough. He played over 360 league games for Fulham and 312 for Spurs, scoring 62 times. He also represented England 35 times, scoring England's opening goal in the World Cup quarter-final defeat by West Germany in 1970. He had no time for half-measures. He hated losing. He hated cheating, too. During the semi-final of the 1968 European Championship he was dismissed for reacting angrily to Yugoslavia's niggling foul play. Mullery was quick-witted, intelligent but down-to-earth. He was generally affable and enjoyed a joke but was also fiercely focused with an explosive temper when crossed. Mullery was a natural leader, shrewd and consumed with driving ambition, but despite his moments of volatility he was also adept at relaxing his players before big games. He took them to out-of-town hotels, away from the glare of publicity, where they could play golf and chill out. Mullery was very loyal to his staff but he wouldn't stand any nonsense. Bamber didn't need to study Mullery's CV too closely to see that he was the man to take Brighton forward.

As a new manager, Mullery acknowledged his debt to his mentors – to Sir Alf Ramsey, Bill Nicholson, Bedford Jezzard and Alec Stock. In *Alan Mullery: The Autobiography*, Alan told writer, Tony Norman:

> *Alf was very studious; when he spoke to you he gave you words of wisdom. He trusted his players to do the job he'd selected them to do for the team. Bill Nick was a fantastic coach with a photographic memory. He knew everything about the game and, tactically, he was superb. Bedford Jezzard knew how to boost the confidence of his players. He was very tactile; when you played well he'd give you a big hug and say 'well done'. Alec Stock had a different skill. In my opinion he was the biggest bullshitter I'd ever met. I've seen him give the Fulham players a real rollicking after a game, then go out and tell the press there were definitive positives to take from the team's performance. He taught me how to do deal with journalists. His PR skills were exceptional.*

Alan Mullery knew what he wanted: two good attacking wingers, two good strikers, hard-tackling ball-winners and a reliable keeper. He was lucky. The rudiments of such a side already existed at Brighton. He had a reliable keeper in Peter Grummitt. He had a skilful, attacking winger in Peter O'Sullivan. The surprise package was young Peter Ward, though. Peter Taylor had bought Ward from Burton Albion for £4,000. Ward was an unknown quantity to Mullery. That was until Ward started banging in goals in the pre-season practice games. It didn't matter which defenders Mullery set up against Ward, the Burton Albion boy would get past them. Ward had a sharp eye for a half-chance, quick reactions and quicker feet. Give him an inch and he was 'in like Flint'. He had the look of a natural predator, the strut, the bristling intensity, the zest, the pace and the composure when in on goal. Ward was a huge, unexpected bonus.

But Mullery knew that he needed to trim his squad. When he arrived at the Goldstone he had 36 professionals on the books. At least a third of them were surplus to requirements. That left him with his first difficult decisions. Among those lined up for the chop were two close mates – Joe Kinnear and

Phil Beal – former Spurs colleagues. They were past their best and sitting on lucrative contracts. He couldn't show favouritism. That would compromise his position with the entire squad. After talking the issue through with Bill Nick, Mullery told Beal and Kinnear the bad news. Phil was philosophical. Joe wasn't. Joe wouldn't talk to Mullery for years. But Mullery knew he'd done the right thing.

The next difficult decision was to drop crowd favourite, Fred Binney. Supporters are particularly hard on managers who drop top guns. During the 1975/76 season, Binney had scored 23 times. In his first six league games under Mullery he scored three more. When he was dropped, the crowd were perplexed and so was Fred. Cheekily, he offered Mullery his advice. 'You're very new,' Fred told him. 'The little, skinny fella, Wardy. He's not strong enough for the Third Division. You should play me. I got over 20 goals last season, you know.' Mullery was cool. He thanked Fred for his advice but continued to play Peter Ward, partnering him with Ian Mellor, who was pushed up from midfield. Ward and Mellor scored 44 league goals between them that season – 32 coming from the young, wild haired former Rolls-Royce apprentice. As for Fred, he was sent to Exeter. Alan Mullery clocked what he saw, spoke as he found and was as good as his word.

Mullery's other major find was Brian 'Nobby' Horton. 'You couldn't ask for a better leader than Brian Horton,' he enthused. 'He had real authority on the field and led by example. He won nearly every 50–50 ball and never stopped urging the team on. I've seen him flying into tackles in five-a-sides at the club because he hated to lose … [He] represented everything I believed in on the field.'

Mullery's first season went like a dream – promotion back to the Second Division in April 1977, behind champions, Mansfield. Wickenden and Bamber were ambitious. They had the top flight in their sights and were prepared to pay the price. Mullery told them he needed more quality at the back. Preston's 19-year-old central defender, Mark Lawrenson, fitted the bill. Mullery said: 'Mark had a calm, strong temperament, he never caused any problems and he always performed brilliantly on the field.' When Wickenden and Bamber saw Lawrenson in action they were impressed. Liverpool were in for Lawrenson, too, but were only prepared to bid £100,000. Brighton got him plus Preston full-back, Gary Williams, for £12,000 more. However, Lawrenson failed his medical. 'I was fit and raring to go,' Mark explained, 'so you can imagine my shock when the doctor told me I'd failed. He thought I was a diabetic – my sugar levels were so incredibly high. He thought I had a sweet tooth, but I'd been on the lash [on holiday in Spain] for a fortnight. I'd been drinking Guinness and blackcurrant out of my ears and my sugar levels had sky-rocketed.' Fortunately, the problem was solved quickly and Lawrenson joined Brighton's pre-season training.

Anxious to make the most of his generous war chest, Mullery added further players to his squad. In came Fulham's young, sturdy centre-forward, Teddy Maybank, for a record £238,000 fee. So did Cardiff's winger or midfielder, Peter Sayer, for £100,000. Malcolm Poskett, another striker, was also enticed down from Hartlepool. Mullery knew Peter Ward – as good as he was – needed more help. During his first season in Division Two, Ward once again headed the scoring charts, but with a much reduced return of 14 league goals. This was a much tougher division.

However, Brighton came so close to promotion to the First Division at the end of that season. Spurs beat them to the line only on goal difference. Spurs' 0-0 draw at the Dell in the final game of the season was just enough to deny Brighton. It was a bitter blow but one which strengthened the club's resolve. The support was certainly there – Brighton's average home gate in 1977/78 was over 25,000. On the back of this increasing success, Gerry Ryan, a wonderfully balanced, loping Irish winger, was signed from Derby in the early part of the new season. Local boy Tony Towner and Eric Potts were, therefore, no longer needed. Towner moved to Millwall for £65,000 while Eric Potts went to Preston for £40,000. Mullery was equally good at selling.

The 1978/79 season started erratically. Emphatic victories sat alongside unexpected defeats. Much to his dismay, Mullery heard that Maybank and Sayer had been in a nightclub on the evening before the 1-4 loss at Leicester. He dealt with the matter quickly and authoritatively. Under pressure from their team-mates, Maybank and Sayer owned up, paid a fine – each made a £250 donation to the Guide Dogs Association – and the matter was put to rest.

The results were not good enough, though. With the Albion bouncing around in mid-table, the supporters became restive. Mullery's promise of promotion was wearing thin. Some fans started carping about Maybank's performances. Supporters tend not to see the value of strikers who don't score. Maybank became hacked off. He stopped giving press interviews and refused to acknowledge the fans. The fans' moans and groans grew louder when Maybank kept his place while the out-of-sorts Ward did not. Malcolm Poskett came in for him. Mullery knew Maybank's worth better than his terrace critics. He knew that Maybank's high work rate gave more to the team than the misfiring Ward.

Mullery was right. Results began to improve. Albion went on an eight-match unbeaten league run between 2 December and 3 February, lifting

Brighton into top spot. Moreover, Mullery's new strike partnership hit gold over Christmas. On the Saturday before the festive period, Poskett scored a hat-trick in a 3-0 win at Charlton. Then, on Boxing Day, Maybank followed suit as Albion went nap against Cardiff (5-0). Ward remained confined to the sidelines although he was recalled to the first team one week before Burnley's arrival. He played brilliantly in Albion's 1-0 victory at Fulham.

On Saturday 3 March, Brighton were in second place, one point behind Stoke City but a point ahead of West Ham and Crystal Palace, who both had games in hand. Meanwhile, Burnley were in 13th position, nine points behind Albion but with four games in hand. They had already met twice that season – both times at Turf Moor. Brighton had won the League Cup game 3-1 when popular full-back Chris Cattlin had contained Burnley's 'Welsh Wizard', Leighton James, brilliantly. But Burnley had their revenge in the league game shortly afterwards (3-0).

Burnley were continuing to sell their young talent. Three members of their squad had been sold in the last nine months, netting the club around £240,000. Tony Morley would also leave shortly for Villa for £220,000, raising the club's post-war sales receipts to £3 million. While Burnley's younger talent was on the move, former stars were returning. Steve Kindon had come back for £80,000, as had Leighton James for £165,000. Martin Dobson would rejoin the club, too, in the summer for £100,000.

It was a sombre day. As Liz and I strolled along the empty promenade, fine rain wafted in on a stuttering Channel wind. It left a dull sheen on the tarmac and the green, thickly-painted benches. Despite the damp, ruffling wind there was an indolent feel to the day. Mucky waves emerged out of the creased, swishing swell and staggered listlessly to the shore, their soiled surf collapsing on to the shingle with resigned sighs. We had little enthusiasm for the game. With the club apparently selling its future in order to commemorate its past, we felt as if we'd been invited to the *Last Waltz* for the 'Team of the Seventies'.

Actually, the team paid due respect to its estimable past. Shaking off the fatigue of its punishing schedule, Burnley immediately turned on the heat. They mounted one attack after another on Eric Steele's goal. Had he not been in such superb form, denying headers from Fletcher with breathtaking agility, Burnley would have been deservedly two goals in front at the break. If Cattlin had been James' master in the League Cup tie, the tables were turned here. Linking well with Burnley's attacking left-back, Ian Brennan, James roasted the Brighton full-back, jinking one way, only to flash past him on the other. One cross after another arrived in the Brighton box. Even the combative Horton seemed powerless to prevent the incessant aerial bombardment. With the spring-heeled Fletcher frequently outjumping his markers and Kindon acting as a shuddering battering ram, Rollings and Lawrenson were unexpectedly at sixes and sevens.

As the teams left the field at the break – Burnley in sprightly fashion and Brighton pensively – we were relieved that our lads had done us proud. We were concerned, though, that they hadn't made their domination count. While Debbie Harry's tinkling voice took us through 'Heart of Glass', Alan Mullery was tearing strips off his team. He berated them for not heeding his warning. He had impressed upon them beforehand that Burnley were a tough nut to crack. Smarting from their first-half chasing and from Mullery's half-time lashing, Brighton began the second half fired up. Adopting a higher defensive line, Horton and Clark began to express themselves in the centre of the park. Ryan and O'Sullivan had more of the ball and as a result Maybank and Ward were able to push up more against Burnley's slow-turning central defenders. Now it was Burnley's turn to feel the heat. They were unable to commit so many men forward. Their suspect defence became sorely stretched.

Within five minutes of the restart, a penalty was conceded which Horton put away decisively. But Burnley didn't buckle. Within one minute they were back on terms as Ingham stole into the box, unseen, to poke home a loose ball at close range. The game then turned into a nip-and-tuck affair, but one which began to tip increasingly Brighton's way. The contest was settled in the 69th minute by a goal of sublime quality. Lawrenson began to make probing runs. It was no wonder that Mullery was so keen to snaffle him. His sublime technique and composure were underpinned by throbbing power. He proceeded to turn the game. Seizing the ball in midfield, he strode forward effortlessly, gliding through the Burnley defence as if he was an apparition. Upon reaching the edge of the box, he easily evaded Jim Thomson's desperate lunge and sent a skimming shot past Stevenson's helpless dive at the speed of light. A huge roar greeted his effort. After the commotion had dimmed, Liz and I agreed reluctantly that a goal as good as that deserved to win any game.

Since I saw Burnley play at Brighton, in January 1961, the clubs' prospects had completely reversed. Brighton were destined for a four-year stay in the First Division while Burnley were to embark upon a slide that would take them to the trapdoor of oblivion. The 'Team of the Seventies' was a shattered dream.

With a child shortly on the way we found quickly there was less time or money for football. Saturdays became consumed by morose meanderings around heaving supermarkets, packed shopping centres or, worst of all,

MFI, where we sought affordable flat packs to bless with our incompetence. For the first time in my life football became expendable, subjected to financially-constrained choice rather than obsessive necessity, often only heard or seen peripherally, until our daughter became old and wise enough to want to go. The addiction doesn't expire, though. It is merely suppressed by the weight of parental duty, waiting for the moment when the trailing guilt of parenthood thins sufficiently for it to pop up again. That prospect was hard to imagine, sat on those penal MFI benches, waiting to collect our chipboard ensembles. There, my unseeing eyes would be fixed on the cartoon channel but my attention would be elsewhere, possibly speculating on events at the Shay or Spotland or wherever lowly Burnley were then playing. I would have to wait. The radio was always a car park away. Setting aside the contradictions in warmth, I felt like a beached expat, comatosed by Spanish wine and the Tenerife sun, indulging maudling home thoughts from abroad.

Watford's 'miracle maker'

Graham Taylor understands real pressure. I don't mean the tabloid turnip kind; nor do I mean the 'do I not like that' sort. I mean the pressure that descends upon a rookie 28-year-old manager when his impoverished Fourth Division club has achieved no wins in his first 11 games in charge, while he has a family to look after and a mortgage to pay. That's the kind of pressure that makes or breaks people. Fortunately, Graham Taylor is made of the right stuff. He has mental strength, self-belief and resourcefulness in spades. Not only did he cope with these pressures, he obliterated them triumphantly. Having been the youngest person to obtain his FA coaching qualifications, at the age of 27, he was offered his first job as a football manager with Lincoln City. He was fortunate. The club's directors seemed a rare breed. They had fortitude, patience and prescience. In other words, they knew a thing or two. Within four seasons of his appointment the Imps had won the Fourth Division, scoring 111 goals and achieving a points total that has never been beaten in any division before or since, making allowance for the modern conversion rate. In an article written for the *Independent* in 2009, Steve Tongue said:

> *In 1977, [Graham Taylor] went back to that lowest division with Watford after Elton John offered him a five-year contract and said he wanted his local club to*

> *play in Europe [having spent only two seasons outside the lower divisions in their entire history]. Rather than enquire what substances the chairman was on, Graham Taylor accepted the outrageous challenge and met it in the space of six seasons, finishing second to Liverpool and defending his direct style against all-comers, as he continues to today. 'If people think all we did was whack the ball and chase it, it must have been a very poor First Division! I was brought up watching the kind of football where teams went forward trying to score. I enjoyed my team doing that.' In five seasons among the big boys, Watford never finished lower than 12th place, but attendances in a town of 80,000 dropped off, Elton John suffered personal and drug problems and the local council refused to back a new stadium, all of which persuaded Taylor to try a new experience with Aston Villa and the rather more hands-on approach of their infamous chairman Doug Ellis. Winning promotion, then repeating his runners-up achievement [to Liverpool, again] confirmed Taylor as the obvious candidate to replace [Bobby] Robson [as England manager after the Italy World Cup of 1990].*

Taylor's win proportion, in his 31 years as a manager at Lincoln, Watford (twice), Wolves and Aston Villa (twice), and spanning all four divisions of the Football League, stands at an impressive 43 per cent. Sir Alex Ferguson trumps that with almost 58 per cent, but for two-thirds of his managerial career the United boss has had to contend with an embarrassment of riches. Neil Warnock's record provides a more comparable benchmark. Taylor is ahead here as Warnock's win percentage is just under 40.

Like Dave Bowen of Northampton, Graham Taylor took Watford from the bottom division to the top in five years but unlike Bowen, he kept his club there. To achieve that degree of success, so quickly, and at such a small club, requires considerable skill in spotting, developing and selecting the right players. But that's not all. There needs to be an extraordinary team ethic. There needs be as much inspiration as perspiration. There needs to be good game plans. Graham Taylor had excellent game plans. Like Alf Ramsey at Ipswich and Dave Bassett and Joe Kinnear at Wimbledon, he found ways of dumbfounding his mightier opponents. Notwithstanding Elton John's fortune, Watford punched well above their weight.

Graham Taylor told Oliver Price of the *Guardian*: 'In 1977 I was manager of Lincoln City when Don Revie, the England coach, called, saying he'd recommended me to a new chairman. I was thinking, "Blimey, which top club is this?" When he told me it was Elton John at Watford my heart sank. They were in the bottom division. I thought: "Rock star in charge of a Fourth Division club. This is crazy!" But Elton invited me to his house in Windsor and said he wanted to take the club into Europe. I said I didn't think he'd see any change from a million pounds, which back then was a lot of money [about £4.5 million in today's values]. He just said, "Right, we'll give it a go." Six years later, when we got into Europe, he worked out that he'd spent £790,000 [around £3.5 million today]'. In football terms, this is hardly paying the earth, particularly when put alongside the scale of Graham Taylor's achievements.

The direct, pressing style of play adopted by Graham Taylor's Watford was given a bad press in some quarters – unfairly so. As Steve Coppell pointed out in Andrew Ward's and Rogan Taylor's oral history, *Kicking and Screaming*:

> *It always amazes me that the long-ball theory is looked upon as simple – 'you just welly it and win games' – whereas the passing style of football is harder because 'there's more coaching involved'. My experience is that long-ball teams are coached, they are told what to do, they are allowed to express themselves but only in certain areas of the field, whereas passing sides are just told to go out and play. The Liverpool sides are famous for their training in five-a-sides whereas the more direct teams spend a long time getting formulae right and getting positions right and the shape of their side correct and they spend a long time in dead-ball situations … A lot of people say that bad players can play that style of football. They can, but they can't play it successfully. You need good players to play that style successfully.*

Graham Taylor found that his direct, high tempo, high-line pressing game paid rich dividends as Watford progressed onwards and upwards through the divisions. Most teams, even leading ones, had difficulty in dealing with it. This was a tactic which maximised his side's attacking possibilities while minimising those of the opposition, for his overriding intention was to win each game. However, for his system to work his players had to be extremely fit, capable of continually harassing their opponents deep within their territory, cramping them for space, pinning them down and restricting them to hurried, inaccurate clearances. It required his team to produce a level of energy over 90 minutes which is usually summoned when a team finds itself behind with little time left. When operated successfully he found that this approach upset the cohesion of other sides, isolating their wide midfielders and leaving them with the dilemma of staying or retreating. Graham Taylor told Andrew Ward and Rogan Taylor:

> *... Charles Reep had a system that recorded the movement of the ball and exactly what happened ... He would say that 'you've got to put in more long passes and you've got to regain the ball back'. You can't do the two. If you're winning the ball back in the opposition's third or half of the field, it's staying in there so you can't put in the long passes. But it opened up my mind to looking at professional football ... from a science point of view ... In 1975/76, I hadn't met Charles Reep, but Lincoln scored 111 goals and won the Fourth Division championship. I was already keeping a record of how many goals we scored and conceded from restarts ... [When playing under Jimmy McGuigan at Grimsby Town] nobody ever talked about the 'long-ball' then. People talked about 'third man running', so the ball was played from the back up to your front man, he played it back to your midfield man and your midfield man played it into the space behind the defenders for a third man running through. Never mind about Watford, we were playing that at Lincoln. We were scoring goals. We played with wide men and we got the ball in early. It began to hit the media when suddenly Watford were coming out of the Second Division and into the First Division, and we upset people because suddenly we beat the big clubs ... We had a centre-forward called Ross Jenkins who was 6ft 4in and had lovely chest control*

> *and we had a fella called Luther Blissett who wanted the ball in front of him, so why give it to him with his back to goal?*

To maximise the assets of his front men, Graham Taylor's team attacked swiftly, employing the long pass and the early cross. This was not 'hoofball'. The long pass had to be executed with great accuracy in order to catch opposing defences at their thinnest. And in players such as Ian Bolton, Graham Taylor had skilled exponents of the art. It mattered not that they were not household names. They were simply very good at what they did.

As Derek Mountfield pointed out to a BBC sports reporter, Graham Taylor's tactics did not focus exclusively on the long-ball game. The ex-Villa defender who played under Taylor in the late eighties said at that time: 'Graham's attention to detail is fantastic, not just on the playing side, but also ensuring the players' families are happy and everything around the game is looked after. He is often saddled with a long-ball label, but this is completely unfair. He often used to have lengthy team meetings on tactics and planning, and he never just advocated use of the long ball. He would not have had the success he has had ... if he had been as limited as that.'

Graham Taylor's alchemy was underpinned by a strict attention to basics. Firstly, he worked on technique, achieved by relentless, unstinting practice. Secondly, he insisted on phenomenal standards of fitness. Thirdly, he declared war on complacency. He had a perfectionist's commitment to constant improvement. Fourthly, he remained on the lookout for better players, those who could apply his methods with greater proficiency. But Taylor's success had almost as much to do with his singing as his song – and I don't mean his embarrassing rendition on *Match of the Day*. His inspirational, positive leadership was a key part of the equation.

Graham Taylor has a reputation for being some talker – a constant threat to donkeys' hind legs. But he has shown himself to be a careful listener, too. He was eclectic in his choice of advisers. He didn't just listen to those inside the game or freelance 'gurus', like Charles Reep. He listened to fans, too, even relatively young ones. Watford fan Stuart Clarke remembered Taylor, as the newly-appointed Watford manager, visiting his school in Berkhamstead. Taylor spoke with a group of teenage Watford supporters, saying, 'Tell me which players excite you and why. But don't tell me which ones you don't like. What about their style of play, what pleases, what frustrates?' Stuart and his brother told Taylor that they thought Watford passed too much without shooting enough, suggesting they needed to be more direct. Apparently, Taylor probed and probed – taking in what the two teenage boys told him with apparent seriousness. Stuart's anecdote emphasises how open-minded and accessible Graham Taylor was. Many successful entrepreneurs have this quality, too: personally seeking out their customers' opinions, affirming their stake in the enterprise. It's not a bad habit. You can learn a thing or two.

Former Watford commercial manager, Ed Coan, commented: 'It also quickly dawned on me that Watford FC was one of the focal points of the town – one of the things which gave the town its identity and its sense of pride. The football club had really taken this on board, and Graham Taylor embodied that. I suppose having played for and managed a 'town' club beforehand, Graham realised how vital it was to get a level of mutual understanding going between the football club and the locality.' Fellow supporter, Graham Walker, added: 'We belonged … the great achievement of the season was encapsulated in seeing a young Asian girl looking after her little brother in the Rookery, in her traditional dress plus Watford shirt, no parents to be seen anywhere. They were safe, they felt safe. A community club indeed!'

Taylor wanted to build more than a successful team at Watford. As has been shown at so many small clubs that have punched above their weight – Wimbledon, Matlock and Burnley, to name only a few – community engagement is of critical importance. Successful underdogs are usually more than just football clubs.

Former player Ian Bolton told Joe Whitbread of the *Watford Observer*, 'I would have run through a brick wall for Graham when I was at the club and I think the supporters felt the same way. He developed the team but I also think he developed the fans to make it a family club. He insisted that the players lived in Hertfordshire so that when they received their wages they invested their money back into the local economy. I think the fans enjoyed that because it was a commitment to the club. He formulated the family club.'

Graham Walker was present when the Taylor revolution first took to the road, on 20 August 1977, at Edgeley Park, Stockport. He wrote the following for the Watford fanzine, *Blind, Stupid and Desperate*:

> *So we now have Mr E John as chairman, and a new manager in a Mr Taylor. Okay, so Taylor had managed that massive Lincoln side that two years previously had stomped all over the Fourth Division by a record margin but, hell, why should we expect the same? We only have a couple of close-season signings; Taylor's old captain Sam*

> *Ellis, now approaching veteran status, and some bloke called Bolton from Notts County. Ah well, old habits die hard and here we are at Stockport on a sunny afternoon, watching the usual scapegoats and the two new boys. There is Andy Rankin, who surely deserves to keep goal for a better team than this, there is the mercurial Mayes, there is Ross Jenkins, taken to our hearts because he epitomises the club – enthusiastic, clumsy, continually under-achieving and just a little embarrassing, bless 'im! He is taller than everybody but 'aerial dominance' are two words that no reporter has ever yet written regarding the Watford front line.*
>
> *We hope for the best but expect the worst. But wait ... We take an early lead as Ross Jenkins nods in a free kick. County then equalise and press hard. Half an hour gone and Mayes is put through in a one-on-one with the keeper ... The referee decides it's a penalty, despite the fact that the foul happened at least a yard outside the area. It isn't so much that Sam Ellis converts the penalty ... but that he then stands in front of the Watford supporters with arms aloft and fists shaking. It has been years, literally years, since a Watford player actually acknowledged the presence of away supporters. This is weird and encouraging. Half-time comes and we still lead. Second half and Watford, not to put too fine a point on it, do the business. Professional, they stop County from doing anything much, close them down, strong, hard and determined. When was the last time Watford were not a soft touch away from home? And then, to crown it all, a towering centre from the right and there is Ross again at the far post. 3-1! What the ...? Normally our first away win of the season comes around November time against no-hopers like Southport, Workington, Rochdale. What's going on?*

Successful teams need scrappers. Ramsey's World Cup-winners needed Nobby Stiles. Upwardly-mobile Carlisle needed Stan Ternent. Roger Joslyn performed this role and more besides. Watford supporter, Colin Wiggins recalled:

Roger Joslyn was an appalling sight. We hated him. Sweat-stained, teeth bared, saliva foaming from his mouth ... 'That man's an animal!' we used to shout, 'GET HIM OFF!' Then, he signed for Watford. He was still an appalling sight, but now he was our appalling sight. Suddenly, we loved him. He was signed from Aldershot by Mike Keen in November 1974, shortly after putting in a particularly savage midfield display against the Hornets. Joslyn's contribution to the early years of the 'Great Era' was crucial. He was tireless. Tackling back, ball-winning and saving desperate situations in his own penalty area were all part of his game. Seconds after clearing his own lines, he would be forcing his way through defenders in his opponents' box, to score with one of his trademark downward headers from the edge of the six-yard box. Whether he would have survived in today's climate is debateable, but times then were different. Dirty, no; reckless, yes ... But in his day, Roger Joslyn was a supremely effective lower-division player, who left the club shortly after helping them arrive in Division Two. He was a vital component in the side that won two successive promotions and one of several heroes bequeathed to Graham Taylor by Mike Keen.

On 3 October 1978, Watford went to Old Trafford to play Manchester United in the third round of the Football League Cup. United had nine international players in their team – Paddy Roche, Brian Greenhoff, Sammy McIlroy, Gordon McQueen, Martin Buchan, Stewart Houston, David McCreery, Steve Coppell and Joe Jordan. Watford had none. Manchester United had just beaten their city rivals 1-0 in front of a 55,000 crowd, placing themselves in seventh position in Division One. Watford had just beaten Tranmere 4-0 in Division Three in front of a 10,700 crowd, with two goals from Ross Jenkins, keeping themselves in second place. Watford were expected to turn up, politely defer and return home empty-handed. They would have none of it.

Dave Sexton had replaced Tommy Docherty as United's boss after Docherty was dismissed for having an affair with the wife of a club employee. Docherty had transformed Manchester United's fortunes after their relegation in '74, converting them rapidly from lost losers into winsome winners. He had led them to an FA Cup triumph over the prospective European Cup winners, Liverpool, in 1977, expunging United's astonishing defeat by Second Division Southampton in the previous year's final. Dave Sexton proceeded to build upon Docherty's success, just as he had done previously at Chelsea. Sexton would guide United to a further FA Cup Final in May 1979, albeit in a lost cause. Graham Taylor faced his sternest test. According to Watford supporter Ian Poole,

> *The first half quickly settled into an ominous pattern of regular United attacks. Sporadic raids from the Horns never really looked like piercing the Man U rearguard and Luther Blissett and big Ross Jenkins became increasingly isolated up front as the red tide flowed remorselessly towards Andy Rankin's goal. The inevitable finally occurred just before half-time when the defence failed to clear a corner and that toothless gargoyle, Joe Jordan, hooked the ball home. Half-time was a depressing experience. Was there any way back? Flicking forlornly through the glossy programme just reminded us how many good players they had. They did, however, have an Achilles heel in the form of Paddy Roche – possibly the worst goalkeeper ever to play in the top flight and clearly an early role model for Jim Leighton. So perhaps there was still hope as the boys trotted back on to the pitch.*
>
> *For many years after this game I suffered from the delusion that Graham Taylor's team talks must be masterpieces of inspiring eloquence and Churchillian rhetoric. Do I not believe that anymore. However, whatever the 'master tactician' said, the Horns were a team transformed. Gradually Dennis Booth and Roger Joslyn wrested control of the midfield and the red tide started to ebb. For the first time in the match the defence looked in control while Ross and Luther started to hold the ball up well up front. Then suddenly it happened – we were level. A left-wing cross was whipped in and*

there was Luther rising unopposed to head goalwards. Good old Paddy Roche didn't let us down as the ball rudely brushed his fingers aside and nestled improbably in the back of the net. For a second or two there was an eerie silence until us travelling Horns leapt to our feet more in disbelief than celebration.

You could feel the unease spreading among the assembled multitude as the Golden Boys proceeded to hand out a footballing lesson. When it came, the winning goal had a certain inevitability about it. Another sortie down the right was repulsed and the ball was played back to Dennis Booth coming up in support. An instant cross pinged into the box and once again Luther rose head and shoulders above the United defence. He seemed to hover in the air for an eternity before a flick of the head rocketed the ball past the hapless Roche, who never even moved. Seventh heaven descended on our ecstatic band of Horns high up in the North Stand. We were at least going to die happy.

The police kept us behind for ages – an exciting novelty at the time but one that's worn pretty thin since. The net result was that by the time they let us out only the real lunatics were still around and were those boys mad. Our convoy of coaches had a non-stop police escort out of town with sirens wailing, lights flashing and to hell with the traffic lights – which at least gave the Neanderthals a moving target. A couple of cracked windows later and we were safely back on the motorway, at last able to savour a famous victory on the long coach trip home. It was a happy band of travellers indeed who disembarked in Occupation Road in the early hours and took the plaudits of our colleagues at work the next day like conquering heroes.

Watford reached the Football League Cup semi-finals that season, ultimately losing to Clough and Taylor's Forest, who proceeded to lift the cup and take second place to Liverpool in Division One. The Old Trafford victory was clearly no fluke. This was underlined two years later as the Second Division Hornets staged an incredible turnaround to defeat title-chasing Southampton 7-1 in the second leg of a League Cup tie, having lost the first leg by 4-0. This remarkable recovery caught even the irrepressible Graham Taylor by surprise.

Before the game, Taylor wrote in his programme notes:

> *Tonight, we face what almost everybody considers is an impossible task – and that is, to pull back a four-goal deficit against a Southampton team which includes players of not only outstanding ability but of proven international stature. My biggest disappointment is that this situation should have arisen in the first place. It is by now common knowledge to all associated with the Club, not least the players, that our display in the first leg at Southampton last week I considered to be inept and woeful. Not only did we miss a wonderful opportunity to show people our true capabilities both as a team and as individuals, we did in fact let down ourselves and our supporters. We are fortunate that tonight we have another chance to redeem ourselves. While it may be asking the impossible for a five-goal win, it is not asking the improbable for a win in this leg and it is asking for nothing in demanding full and total conviction from all of the players in Watford shirts tonight. Anything less than that is a complete let-down of everything this Club is trying to stand for. There is a way to win and a way to lose in this game, and whilst no one likes losing, I am prepared to tolerate it providing I keep my pride. I was not able to do that at Southampton. Whatever tonight's result, I expect all Watford players to walk off the pitch and be able to look people in the eye … If I may have the temerity to offer any advice to Southampton in their efforts to achieve this, it would be the following – forget about the League Cup – it may affect your league title chances!*

'Second Division Watford humiliated Southampton, second in the First Division, in the Football League Cup last night,' announced the following day's *Daily Telegraph*. 'Facing the seemingly impossible target of hauling back a 4-0 deficit from last week's first leg, Watford sent the game into extra time and scored twice more. Their fans were ecstatic and rightly so. It was the first time Watford have scored seven goals since they trounced Grimsby by the same score 13 years ago [Graham Taylor, ironically, was the Grimsby left-back in that game]. Watford's manager, Graham Taylor, said: "This is without doubt the greatest result of my career. I thought we could beat them but I did not believe we could go through to the next round. This is the sort of result you dream about but don't really expect to happen."'

Watford then went on to avenge their 1978/79 Football League Cup semi-final defeat by thrashing Nottingham Forest 4-1 at home in the next round. As Watford marched towards the summit of English professional football, Taylor continued to shuffle his pack. He never stood still and never allowed sentiment to stand in his way. He looked to reinforce what he had. Taylor was brilliant at uncovering or rediscovering neglected talent – Les Taylor, Steve Sims, Steve Sherwood and Wilf Rostron were cases in point. Ian Grant of the Watford fanzine *Blind, Stupid and Desperate* wrote: 'There's a truism that claims that Graham Taylor took a side of affordable journeymen to the First Division and Europe. Nonsense! He signed players whose qualities had gone unharvested at other clubs – they were outstanding footballers but outstanding in ways that didn't demand eulogies in newspaper columns or drooling from sheepskin-coated managers.'

Taylor was also brilliant at developing talent in his own backyard – John Barnes, Nigel Callaghan, Kenny Jackett and Steve Terry are the most obvious examples. Graham Taylor had this to say about Barnes and Callaghan: 'We had John Barnes; an outside-left who loved the ball at his feet and loved to take people on and could bend crosses in. We'd got Nigel Callaghan, an outside-right, who off half a yard could hit in quality crosses.' Taylor demanded both width and quality.

Ultimately, money swears and like so many other small clubs who have upset the odds, a time of reckoning is never too far away. What makes Graham Taylor's feat so magnificent is that he not only took Watford to such dizzying heights so quickly but he managed to keep them there for as long as he did. It is sad that his legacy has been sullied by that puerile 'turnip' joke and that ill-advised fly-on-the-wall TV documentary. Taylor deserves much more credit than that. Remember, he took Watford into the top flight twice, having guided them to a play-off success in 1999. As a supporter of a small-town club in a declining area I can take heart from what he has achieved. Well done, Mr Taylor. Without doubt, you are one of the very best football club managers of my lifetime. Besides, you don't get an OBE for nothing.

'Video Killed the Radio Star': the end of the seventies

It's been said that the length of a skirt or the height of a new building are measures of national optimism. Certainly, the miniskirt was a product of the hopeful sixties. So were many of our high-rise tower blocks. Notwithstanding the incorrigible hot pants, as we entered the seventies hemlines fell. And by the end of that decade we had become rightly disenchanted with our high-rise schemes. The rapid technological advances continued, of course. We had everything from the first test tube baby to the cheap electronic calculator. And yet when we were still in the afterglow of the first moon landing we began to question some of the advances that took us there as the environmental problems mounted. Our rapidly modernising world was costing us a bomb. As British house prices increased by almost 1,000 per cent between 1970 and 1979, we became more and more reliant upon credit. We seemed to be spending more than we were earning. This was partly due to the actions of the oil sheikhs, who made sure we paid through the nose for our support of Israel. As a result inflation grew, helping to create a wider rift between the left and the right. Meanwhile, Pol Pot's Killing Fields proved that the pathology of the Stalinist and Nazi death camps was still alive and sick, defying our resolutions of 'never again'. And despite a tentative thaw in Cold War relations, terrorism abounded at home and abroad.

For a brief period in 1978, there was hope that Callaghan's minority administration might survive. But once the unions pushed for wage rises in excess of the agreed five per cent threshold, one dispute followed another. Adding to the misery was the weather – the coldest British winter since 1963. There were fuel shortages, surgical operations were cancelled, the rubbish piled up and the dead remained unburied. Callaghan's government seemed impotent. Ultimately it lost a vote of confidence on 3 May 1979 – the only time that a government had fallen in this way during the 20th century.

There was little surprise about Mrs Thatcher's rise to power. In times of despair, quick-fix bandwagons abound. Mrs Thatcher traded on despair. Her bandwagon was fuelled by mounting exasperation with union activitists, fear and loathing of festering towns and cities and rising alarm about disaffected youths, whether represented by punks, Rastas or football hooligans. In decaying Britain, punk articulated despair and boredom, but the youth of

Thatcher's Britain wanted escape, not confinement. This may help explain the allure of the 'New Romantics'. Surrounded by so much shabbiness, we were ready for a dash of colour. And with the growth of MTV, vision trumped sound as a pop vehicle. Video killed the radio star.

'BLUE MONDAY' 1980–1987

'Anything that consoles is fake'
Iris Murdoch

In R. Harries' *Prayer and the Pursuit of Happiness*, (1985), p.113

THE 1980/81 SEASON

Oxford United v Burnley

'To Cut A Long Story Short'
6 December 1980

In the spring of 1980 there were signs of serious unrest. A riot in the St Paul's area of Bristol started a trend of disturbances up and down the country, but notably in Toxteth and Brixton. This time football could not be blamed. Chronic unemployment, poor housing and racism probably supplied the tinder. A breakdown in family discipline and overzealous policing possibly provided the sparks.

When the new football season began, the unemployment figure passed the two million mark. This was the highest level since 1935. Mrs Thatcher remained resolute. 'The lady is not for turning,' she insisted. 'We have paid ourselves 22 per cent more for producing four per cent less.' She was adamant that commercial salvation lay in the growth of financial services and tourism. High interest rates and an overvalued pound were savaging British manufacturing industries; for the first time since the Industrial Revolution we were experiencing a deficit in manufactured goods. Mrs Thatcher reduced subsidies for council rents, rates, gas, electricity, school meals and public transport fares. After the 1979 budget, the burden of taxation shifted more to VAT, driving up the prices of staple goods as well as those of luxury items. The less well-off suffered most of all, particularly those living in the languishing manufacturing areas such as Burnley. But the pain was also felt in areas of post-war economic boom, such as in Oxford, Coventry and Bristol, where Liz and I now lived.

Reflecting their troubled local economies, both Burnley and Oxford were now in the Third Division. During the previous decade, Oxford had dropped a division while Burnley had dropped two. Average gates had plummeted at both clubs. Ten years before, Oxford had attracted an average crowd of 11,000 to their home games. And yet only 2,526 supporters watched their 1-0 league victory over Chester in November 1980, their first home win that season. Their other home gates were scarcely better. Only a New Year revival lifted their average crowd figure to 3,905. As for Burnley, their average crowd had fallen from 16,000 in 1970 to 6,500 during the '80/81 season.

Burnley had continued to sell but, by the early eighties, their returns were much less lucrative. There were rumours that Brian Laws, their highly-talented right-back, would be sold for £300,000 but nothing transpired. With three notable exceptions – Brian Laws, Trevor Steven and Michael Phelan – Burnley's conveyor belt was not delivering the youthful talent of yesteryear. The Clarets were forced to buy more players than they sold, albeit on more modest terms.

The 1979/80 season was a disastrous one for Burnley. Their total of 27 points spelt relegation. They failed to record a single victory in their final 16 league games. Their season began with an identical poor run, bringing about Harry Potts' departure. Burnley's humiliating 7-0 defeat at QPR, watched by the *Match of the Day* cameras, underlined how far their standards had fallen. The careful preparations and strict professional discipline that had been a hallmark of Jimmy Adamson's days had disappeared. After Potts' exit, Brian Miller was asked to step up, helped by Frank Casper. Despite recent failures, Burnley ran their club as a family concern.

Saturday 6 December was a tingling winter day of radiant sunshine. The honeyed light slanted low across the Manor Ground, refreshing what rustling foliage remained in the adjacent trees. Apart from the piercing aerial vapour trails, only patches of smudged high cloud disturbed the sky's milky blue hue. Burnley did their very best to match the occasion. Playing composed, elegant football, they capped this impressive display with two goals of ferocious power. The first came in the 13th minute when midfielder Derek Scott was allowed unaccountable freedom to run at the Oxford goal. With the home defenders still backing off, he let fly from around 25 yards. The ball screamed into the top right-hand corner of the net. Two minutes after the break, Burnley confirmed their superiority when fellow midfielder, Kevin Young, blasted home another long-range effort, leaving the Oxford keeper, Roy Burton, without a prayer. Oxford's fragile morale fragmented. Thereafter, they produced hardly one shot in anger. It was clear why they were in trouble. The U's were above the relegation zone on goal average only. Meanwhile, Burnley had managed to insert themselves among the promotion contenders, having recovered from their slow start. Little did we know that the fortunes of Oxford and Burnley were about to take unexpectedly divergent paths.

'Maxwell's Silver Hammer': Bust to boom and back again

With Bill Asprey struggling in the 'hot seat', Ian Greaves, a former 'Busby Babe', was asked to take over. Greaves had already guided Huddersfield and Bolton to Division One. Here, his job was to protect Oxford from the drop. He did just that, helping Oxford achieve mid-table safety by the season's end. Their rugged central defensive partnership of Gary Briggs and Malcolm Shotton stopped the rot and provided the platform for better things to come. Helped by Kevin Brock's guile and the goals of Mark Thomas and Keith Cassells, Oxford began to rise. But after their emphatic FA Cup victory at Brighton in January 1982, Greaves decided to head off for Wolves – an ill-fated move as it turned out.

Greaves had inspired a significant improvement on the pitch but it was action taken off it that shaped Oxford's immediate future. When Greaves took over in December 1980, Oxford's financial situation was dire. The club had a bank overdraft of £162,000. It owed creditors in excess of £30,000. Around £1,500 was being lost each week. The club reported an operating loss of £77,104 for the 1980/81 season alone (worth around £300,000 today). Chairman Bill Reeves, a local dentist, explained to John Ley, author of *Rags to Riches: the Rise and Rise of Oxford United*: 'There was a crisis in football generally. Clubs like Portsmouth and Luton were close to going to the wall. Basically, the problem was a drop in attendances and the gate figures were getting lower. There just wasn't any commercial input in the game … We introduced a lottery which went on to produce a net profit of around four to five thousand pounds a week. That was enough for the club to survive on. But everybody jumped on [the lottery] bandwagon … Suddenly the lottery interest evaporated … the board members had to put money into the club and give guarantees of around £20,000 each to the bank … all we had to sell were Keith Cassells, Mark Wright [a future England centre-back] and Kevin Brock.'

According to John Ley, Oxford were given ten days to live. And then someone suggested approaching the tycoon Robert Maxwell, a Czech émigré with a distinguished war record. Maxwell was then managing director of an Oxford-based company owned by the multi-million pound Pergamon Press, which Maxwell also controlled and ran. Apart from once professing an interest in Arsenal's progress, he had no prior involvement in football. Maxwell ignored the advice of his accountants and agreed to help the languishing club, putting £128,000 immediately into its bare coffers. Maxwell told John Ley that 'As a business it may not have seemed commercially viable by normal standards, but my accountants failed to appreciate the full value of the players and their potential. Effectively led, United looked an attractive turnaround venture, and, with my many Oxford connections, I felt a strong obligation to try and save the club.' Although Maxwell insisted that he had no wish to take the chair at the Manor Ground, he changed his mind quickly. He stipulated that the manager, Ian Greaves, should support him and that the local council should support the club's search for a site for a new stadium. Maxwell was frustrated on both counts. Greaves left within two months of Maxwell's arrival and, despite the businessman's acrimonious demands, the local council did not satisfy his ambitions, either.

As for the running of the club, Maxwell made important changes instantly. The composition of the board was altered. Two directors resigned, although one later returned, and three officials of the supporters' club were invited to join. Maxwell wanted the supporters' club to have more of a stake in developing the football club, so he made it a subsidiary company. Maxwell changed the club's banks, relieving the directors of their former bank guarantees. Within two years of taking charge at the Manor Ground, he appointed his grown-up children – Ian, Kevin and Ghislaine – as board members to ensure his interests were upheld while he was engaged with his other business concerns. He also brought in others from his business empire in order to ensure he retained a tight control of the club's finances.

In March 1982, Maxwell chose Jim Smith to replace the departed Greaves. Smith had recently been sacked by Birmingham City. With uncompromising directness, Maxwell told Smith that he expected him to deliver promotion to the Second Division within two years. Maxwell backed his ambition with cash. During Smith's three years in charge of Oxford United, around £600,000 was made available for team strengthening. In football currency that is probably worth about £15 million today. Smith used this windfall wisely, bringing in a stream of talented players, many of whom he helped to improve. His acquisitions included goalkeeper Steve Hardwick from Newcastle (£20,000); defenders Bobby McDonald from Manchester City and David Langan from Birmingham (both free); midfielders Trevor Hebberd from Southampton (worth £80,000 in a player exchange), George Lawrence from Southampton also (£45,000), Ray Train from Watford (£10,000) and Peter Rhoades-Brown from Chelsea (£85,000); and strikers Steve Biggins from Shrewsbury (free), Mick Vinter from Wrexham (£25,000), Neil Whatmore from Birmingham (£25,000), John Aldridge from Newport (£78,000), Billy Hamilton from Burnley (for a net fee of £80,000), Brian McDermott from Arsenal (£45,000) and

Jeremy Charles from QPR (£100,000).

However, once Maxwell's investment began to pay off on the park, he applied his hard-nosed commercial acumen. Local traders weren't too impressed as Maxwell bumped up the price of ground advertising space well above the going rate for the big cup ties. He was oblivious to the retailers' protests, believing that TV coverage granted them a much wider market. Maxwell indicated that he wasn't prepared to be a 'sugar daddy' *sine die*. He wanted the club to stand on its own feet. But for that to be possible, Maxwell knew the club had to be successful, not only on the field of play but at the turnstiles, also. To achieve both objectives he needed a bigger stadium. The Manor Ground wouldn't do.

New manager Jim Smith was initially impressed with his chairman. Soon after his appointment, Smith remarked: '[Maxwell] made his money because while others have sat and pondered, he has made decisions ... They ought to let him run football.' Club secretary, Jim Hunt, added: '[Maxwell] expects things to be done at the utmost speed. He can be considered a hard man but I've always found him to be fair and ready to change his opinion if you can prove your case.' In the early eighties, Maxwell was considered to be the club's saviour. Having put his money where his mouth was, few saw any reason to quibble with the tycoon's ambition. If Maxwell was a Trojan horse few saw beyond its craftsmanship. The threat inside would soon emerge, though.

Oxford completed the 1981/82 season in fifth position, eight points short of the third promotion slot and nine points behind the champions, Burnley. The club were progressing in the right direction. Despite the harsh winter and harsher economy, which brought about a nine per cent fall in attendances at Football League games, Oxford's average home gate had grown by two per cent to 5,851.

Oxford seemed set to meet Maxwell's objective in the 1982/83 season. All four of Oxford's opening fixtures were won. And after relegation-bound Reading were beaten 3-0 at Elm Park on 3 January – Oxford's sixth league victory on the bounce – promotion seemed probable. But the injuries sustained by key players – Briggs, Hebberd, Brock, Lawrence, Thomas, Vinter and Fogg – slowed them down. A surprising FA Cup defeat by Fourth Division Torquay hardly helped. Then, on 16 April 1983, came Maxwell's bombshell.

Up until then, Maxwell had been largely unchallenged. He bestrode Oxford United like a colossus. When an outbreak of violence occurred during a home game with Portsmouth in September 1982, he pitched in alone to quell the trouble. Maxwell certainly did not lack courage. Although the incident enhanced his reputation as 'a man of the people', his love affair with the Oxford fans fell apart after he announced his plan to merge Oxford United and Reading football clubs. He claimed that this venture was supported by Reading chairman, Frank Waller, and the Football League.

The 1994 merger between two Inverness clubs – Caledonian and Thistle – was a bitter affair, but at least the clubs were situated within the same small city. Reading and Oxford were separated by 30 miles! There was nothing to bind these clubs together. Maxwell and Waller seemed quite prepared to ignore their lack of proximity and, much more importantly, the historical and cultural implications for both communities, out of commercial expediency. It was suggested that the merged club would play its home games at Elm Park and the Manor Ground alternately until a new stadium could be built, probably in the Didcot area. The only beneficiaries of such a deal would have been the footloose, football-starved residents of Didcot, or Newbury, perhaps, much like the later Milton Keynes Dons fiasco. In 2003, Milton Keynes was disgracefully donated the remnants of Wimbledon FC, abetted by the Football Association. British football is sustained by tribal identities, which do not transfer easily to alien communities, as various ground-sharing arrangements have shown. Irrespective of any financial advantage to the clubs concerned, 'cuckoo' set-ups please neither the host fans nor the 'cuckoos'.

Maxwell's and Waller's joint proposal caused outrage. Mass protests were organised at both clubs. Maxwell was given airtime on BBC Radio Oxford. With his iron fist protruding through a thin velvet glove, he insisted he would close the club if the merger failed. Maxwell accused the city council of reneging on its promise to provide the club with a new ground on the Marston site. Whether this accusation was justified or not, Maxwell knew the club needed to draw in bigger crowds if it was to thrive.

Ed Horton was one of many Oxford fans angered by the proposed merger. In a piece written for the book *My Favourite Year*, Nick Hornby's anthology, Ed wrote:

> *When Maxwell bought Oxford United he was getting the same sort of deal he got with the New York Daily News. For a relatively small amount he got, through gratitude and fear, a free hand to do as he pleased; and crucially, a new arena into which his empire could spread. Whether this was his original intention, we can't know … [When] he announced the merger of the club with Reading under a flag of convenience the plan*

> *was, he told us, utterly irreversible ... Managers and journalists like to say football fans are fickle. The truth is, we're not remotely fickle enough ... [But] some fans at least learned to see Maxwell as the enemy within, even at the time of his greatest triumphs [promotion to Division One in 1985].*

Maxwell's vice-chairman, Bill Reeves, was put in a difficult position. He supported Maxwell in his stand against the city council. He even led a fans' protest march about the council's failure to find the club a new ground. However, he wasn't sold on Maxwell's merger plan. 'I appreciate why supporters both here and in Reading felt the way they did,' Reeves later commented. 'The football club is part of the social structure of the city. To convince people that their city has to become a part of a bigger unit was very difficult.' But if Reeves was protesting, Maxwell wasn't listening.

To compound the crassness of Maxwell's announcement, it was made just as misfiring Oxford were attempting to grasp an outside chance of promotion. Jim Smith told John Ley: 'The first I heard about it was an hour before kick-off [at Doncaster on 16 April 1983]. [Maxwell] rang with the news that I would be the manager of the newly-formed Thames Valley Royals, and Reading's manager, Maurice Evans, would become my assistant. I didn't know what to think. The Doncaster game was a very important match for us and the news of the merger made it very difficult from my point of view to motivate the players. All I said to them before kick-off was that something big could happen and if you want to be a part of it you must play your hearts out for the club.'

Eventually, the merger collapsed. Under pressure from a Reading protest group led by former player Roger Smee, Reading's chairman, Waller, failed to gain boardroom approval for the plan. He and two other directors resigned immediately, leaving Maxwell to announce that the deal was dead. Maxwell was unrepentant, though, stating: '[Club merger] is an essential way for football to survive. It won't happen now with Oxford because there are no teams close enough in our division. But for other league clubs it will prove to be the only alternative to closure. I believe that no local area, apart from the big conurbations, like London, Liverpool and Manchester, for example, can support two viable, successful clubs.'

The merger failure left Maxwell feeling frustrated. Having found the football business to his liking, he looked covetously at bigger and better prospects elsewhere. In February 1984, he made a £10 million bid to buy Manchester United. But when the price rose to £15 million, Maxwell pulled out. It was rumoured that he then turned his attention to Spurs but nothing came of this, either. According to football journalist Ian Ridley, 'His attempts to get his hands on a really big club failed despite his use of the *Daily Mirror* newspaper he owned, to promote his own case and denigrate those of others.' Ridley also maintained that, at various times, '[Maxwell] had interests in Reading and sought to acquire Watford, until the League acted with legislation to contain his spreading, fragmented footballing interests.' In the early spring of 1984, with Oxford closing in on the Third Division title, Maxwell stated that he would 'remain with Oxford United for as long as I can do anything useful.'

Despite the ructions off the pitch during the '83/84 season, Jim Smith calmly steered his team to glory in both league and cup competitions. After stunning victories over Newcastle and Leeds, Oxford produced another outstanding Milk Cup performance to defeat Manchester United 2-1 in round four. The underrated former PE teacher, Steve Biggins, headed the winning goal in the second replay at the Manor Ground in front of a 13,912 crowd. Thanks to a Bobby McDonald goal, Oxford also led a woeful-looking Everton for most of their home Milk Cup fifth-round tie until a tragic error by Kevin Brock let in Adrian Heath for a late equaliser. Oxford lost the replay 4-1. Brock's gift proved to be a turning point for Howard Kendall's Everton side as they cast aside their spluttering form and lifted FA Cup that season, followed by two Football League championships and a European Cup Winners' Cup triumph.

Maxwell's ambition was realised during the 1983/84 season as Oxford took the Third Division by storm, winning 28 games, scoring 91 goals and racking up 95 points, eight ahead of second-placed Wimbledon. The season's surprise package was Steve Biggins, who led the league goalscoring charts with 19 successful strikes. Signed on a free transfer from Shrewsbury in June 1982, Biggins hardly had a look-in during his first season. In the summer of 1983 he was made available for transfer. However, with Mick Vinter showing poor pre-season form, Biggins was selected for the opening league game against Lincoln, partnering Neil Whatmore. He proceeded to score the opening goal in a 3-0 win and thereafter never looked back. But Smith remained unconvinced. In reflecting upon his headed winner against Manchester United, Biggins told John Ley: 'When I saw the ball drop into the net two reactions flashed through my mind. I was delighted for Oxford and the team and I was thrilled that once again I had shown Jim Smith that I can score goals … [Jim] didn't say anything to me after the game and that has been our relationship for some time.'

Biggins proceeded to break Colin Booth's club record for the number of league and cup goals scored in one season, but Jim Smith still thought the club could do better. In October 1984, Biggins was transferred to Derby County for £20,000. Out went Neil Whatmore (to Burnley) and Mick Vinter (to Mansfield) as well. Smith had set his sights on a new striking partnership for Division Two – Newport's John Aldridge and Burnley's Billy Hamilton. It would cost the club over £150,000 to bring the two to the Manor Ground but the outlay was justified. The sharp, predatory Aldridge proceeded to feed hungrily off Hamilton's muscular aerial strength. Until Hamilton sustained a knee injury in January 1985, breaking up their productive partnership, the pair had scored 42 goals between them in 29 league and cup games. Smith spent a further £100,000 in bringing in Jeremy Charles from Queens Park Rangers and Brian McDermott joined from Arsenal for £45,000 to provide cover for the injured Hamilton. Regrettably, Hamilton's injury brought his career to a premature end. After a short hiatus when Hamilton was first sidelined, Aldridge went on to smash Steve Biggins' recently-established club scoring record by hitting 34 league and cup goals. Oxford were promoted to the top flight in 1985 as Second Division champions.

In winning Division Two, Oxford won 25 league games, scoring 84 goals and accumulating 84 points. They seized the championship emphatically by thumping Barnsley 4-0 at home in the final game of the season in front of 13,196 ecstatic fans. An average home gate of 10,579 represented a rise of almost 3,000 on the previous season. Although this figure seemed insufficient to sustain top-flight football, this Oxford side looked capable of holding their own against the biggest and best clubs in the country. During the 1984/85 Milk Cup competition, the U's beat another big top-flight club, Arsenal, by 3-2, watched by a crowd of just over 14,300.

The Oxford team which was to compete in the top division would not be Smith's, though. He resigned in the summer after failing to agree new contractual terms with Maxwell. Maxwell stated: 'Ours was a good partnership, but in the end his departure was because of money. He wanted more than we were prepared to pay. Just like a housewife, I am governed by the law that states you can spend only what you have.' Possibly, there was more at stake than just money. Smith was understandably alarmed at Maxwell's threat to withdraw the club from Division One if the city council did not contribute £250,000 towards necessary ground improvements. As it turned out, an amicable agreement was struck, but Smith was placed in an embarrassing position when news of Maxwell's threat was put to him, without prior warning, on ITV's *On the Ball* programme.

'Now after Maxwell had abused the celebration party to attack the council and threaten closure once more, [Smith] decided he'd had enough,' recalled Ed Horton. 'Maxwell refused to pay him the wages appropriate to a First Division manager.' In his three years at the Manor Ground, Smith won 53 per cent of his league games, an impressive record which is only five per cent inferior to that of Sir Alex Ferguson's. It was small wonder that the players and fans were so desperately sorry to see him go. Smith left to become QPR's new manager, while Maurice Evans, his chief scout at Oxford and the former Reading manager, replaced him, helped by Ray Graydon. Ironically, Oxford would meet QPR in the final of the Milk Cup at Wembley almost a year later. Oxford won at a canter with outstanding performances from Kevin Brock and Ray Houghton. With memorable generosity, Maurice Evans asked long-serving physiotherapist, 72-year-old Ken Fish, to collect a winners' medal in his place. Unfortunately, Oxford were denied the opportunity to play in Europe on account of the ban imposed upon English clubs after the Heysel stadium disaster.

But as well as Oxford played at Wembley, they were not certain of First Division survival until the final game. A 3-0 home victory over Arsenal, with goals from Aldridge, the injury-plagued Hamilton and the sparky Houghton, ushered them into 18th position, with one point to spare over relegated Ipswich. Once again, Oxford were indebted to Aldridge's goals – he scored 23 league goals and 5 more in the Milk Cup. Once Aldridge moved to Liverpool in 1987, to replace the departing Ian Rush, Oxford's top-flight prospects crumbled. With average gates of around 11,000, they could not attract the calibre of players needed to keep them at the top. By then, Maxwell had become Derby's chairman, leaving his son, Kevin, in charge. Ed Horton's view was that 'United had risen as far as possible: so Maxwell threw them overboard ...' Yet some fans felt Maxwell continued to pull the strings at the Manor.

Although Oxford's revival owed much to inspirational team management, without Maxwell's patronage Greaves', Smith's and Evans' efforts might well have been in vain. Maxwell's initial outlay was relatively small but, as Ed Horton conceded, 'Jim Smith had two advantages not permitted to other managers. First, he did not have to sell: he could keep the players he desired. Second, he could offer the wages required to get these players in the first place.' Given that Oxford's average gate did not breach the 8,000 mark until the club's promotion season of '84/85 and, even then, only crept into five figures, it is highly probable that the club were reliant upon Maxwell's continued benefaction, irrespective of their money-spinning Milk Cup heroics. But after Aldridge departed, Oxford's dream became an ever-worsening nightmare.

When the new manager, Mark Lawrenson, took over from Maurice Evans in March 1988, it was already too late to prevent Oxford's relegation.

But Lawrenson promised to make dramatic changes to combat the defeatist attitudes he found at the club. He proposed to instill a Liverpool-style approach to help restore the players' sense of pride, professionalism and positivity. His methods seemed to be paying off as Oxford made an encouraging start to the new season – drawing at Leeds and Chelsea and beating Brighton and Hull at home. By 10 September, Oxford were in fifth position. But then, leading goalscorer, Dean Saunders, was sold suddenly to Derby by Kevin Maxwell. Ed Horton recalled: 'Mark Lawrenson, who'd just persuaded Saunders to sign a three-year contract, knew nothing of the sale, and was sacked for objecting [Lawrenson maintained he resigned]. "What are we now but Derby's reserves?" asked one of the players. Four thousand fans signed a petition demanding that the Maxwells get out of football ... [Meanwhile] attendances plummeted.' Oxford would complete this troubled season in 17th place. The following season was no better. And although Oxford managed an improvement in 1990/91, reaching tenth spot, this was merely the prelude to the trauma of '91/92.

Journalist Ian Ridley wrote of Oxford's anguished 1991/92 season in his book, *A Season in the Cold*. In a chapter titled 'Oxford Blues', he wrote:

> *[By Christmas 1991] Oxford were bottom of the second division ... The man who had saved them, then handed them over to a branch of his family to run, had died six weeks earlier after falling from his luxury yacht ... Now Oxford were all at sea, too, in danger of sinking. The £3 million they owed was perhaps as nothing compared to some of the sums being bandied about in connection with other institutions in which Maxwell was involved – indeed to other football clubs – but, to them, it was frightening. Maxwell's sons, Ian and Kevin, were under pressure to repair, or at least explain, their father's tangled business dealings and had said that their support for the club must end. In addition, they would require back the £2 million invested by the Maxwell family: the other £1 million was owed to the club's bank.*

According to Ed Horton, not only were club debts climbing alarmingly but a group of supporters found allegedly suspicious discrepancies in the club's accounts. Four directors resigned just before Christmas 1991, stating they were unable to inject more capital. All 26 professionals were put up for sale. Striker Lee Nogan went to Watford for £275,000. Winger Paul Simpson was on his way to Derby for £500,000. Ironically, the council had just approved a new ground and leisure complex on the city's outskirts. But would there be a club to play there?

These were grim times for the city. The Cowley car manufacturing plant was facing closure. Oxford's Blackbird Leys estate had become notorious after the national media portrayed it as a 'no-go' area, inhabited by hooded night-time joyriders. Shots of wrecked, burning cars flashed across our TV screens – not so much dreaming spires as screaming tyres.

And yet out of this mire emerged a heart-warming tale of defiance. Oxford's manager, Brian Horton, previously a battling midfielder with Port Vale, Brighton, Luton and Hull, led an improbable and heroic rearguard action, despite two-thirds of fans calling for his head. He told journalist Ian Ridley, 'We're not resigned to having financial troubles and getting relegated. That's rubbish. We're going to make the best of it. Sometimes, things like this can pull people together. I've told the players that they might even benefit. Some might get a move elsewhere and do better. Then it's there for the younger ones to make names for themselves.' Local lads Joey Beauchamp and Chris Allen did just that. Both had starring roles as hated local rivals, Swindon, were stuffed 5-3 on 7 March 1992. Despite missing a series of gilt-edged chances, Beauchamp scored the vital winning goal at Tranmere in the final game of the season. Oxford were indebted to Premiership-bound Blackburn, though. Rovers' victory at Plymouth sent the Pilgrims down in Oxford's place, along with Brighton and Port Vale, two of Horton's former clubs.

However, Oxford dropped back into the third tier in 1994, ten years after their initial promotion under Jim Smith. Although they had a brief revival in the late nineties under manager Denis Smith, life became progressively harder thereafter. By the late nineties Oxford's debts had reached £15 million. FOUL, a supporters' pressure group, emerged to draw attention to the club's plight. Fans rallied to provide unpaid backroom staff with food parcels – talk about 'Manor from heaven'. The debts were eased when the club's new ground and leisure complex was sold by their new owner, Firoz Kassam. A Company Voluntary Agreement was negotiated. But even the returning Jim Smith could not halt Oxford's slide into the Conference in 2006. Ironically, Accrington Stanley replaced them, reversing the events of 1962.

When our small clubs are sagging under heavy defeats and heavier debts, how often we yearn for a platinum-plated plutocrat, who will erase our strife at a stroke and propel our team towards stratospheric heights.

The message here is beware of all who bear gifts, whether they are Greeks, Arabs, Americans, Russians, Asians, Brits or 'bouncing Czechs'. It may cost you more than you think.

THE 1981/82 SEASON

Swansea City v Leeds United

'Tainted Love'
29 August 1981

On a warm, sunny afternoon on 23 August 1975, I made the mistake of watching a wretched Fourth Division game between Rochdale and Swansea City. Fittingly, it ended in a scoreless draw. Rarely have I seen a match so bereft of punch, pace, passion, poise or point although, disgracefully, both teams received one apiece for their dismal efforts. I've had more fun cleaning the cat's litter tray.

Rochdale had completed the previous season in 19th position. Swansea had fared worse, having had to apply for re-election after finishing next to bottom. Coincidentally, this was because they lost 1-0 at Spotland in their final game. The local residents of Rochdale and Swansea shunned their teams with emphatic disdain. Rochdale attracted an average crowd of 1,506; Swansea did only slightly better with 2,070. Unsurprisingly, both clubs were in deep financial difficulties. The Rochdale programme had a dedicated 'Money Page' which screamed 'REMEMBER THIS IS YOUR TEAM – YOUR CLUB – YOUR TOWN – SUPPORT THEM ... THIS CLUB MUST HAVE MONEY TO EXIST ...'

I read these hollered messages with my hands over my ears. Swansea's financial plight seemed worse, though. Having lost £223,657 during the 1973/74 season and £40,000 in the season that followed, potentially their last in the Football League, the club went cap in hand to the city council. In January 1975, the council agreed to buy the Vetch Field ground for £50,000 and to give the club a grant of £150,000 to help clear their massive overdraft. This was no act of charity, though. As noted by Terry Grandin in his absorbing book *Swansea City: Seasons in the Sun 1981-82 & 1982-83*, club chairman Malcolm Struel had stressed: 'If further financial pressures forces us out of the League, the terms of the sale would mean that we would have to surrender the lease to the council with vacant possession. If League football was ever lost, tenure at the Vetch Field would cease. It is a bad deal for the club but if they had not come in with their offer we would have been out of the League by now.' In other words, the city council had agreed to fix the high wire only to snatch away the safety net.

With only 503 season tickets sold for the 1975/76 season, new manager, Harry Griffiths, was told by Malcolm Struel that he had to make do with just 15 full-time professionals. And yet six years later, Swansea would kick off against Leeds in Division One. Two members of Swansea's 1975/76 squad – Robbie James, a crunching, combative, barrel-chested youngster with a fearsome shot, and Alan Curtis, a highly promising young winger – would be in their Division One line-up. In the realms of incredible journeys, this one takes some beating.

John Toshack would ultimately deliver the prize of top-flight football, but in climbing the first rung of the ladder, in April 1978, Toshack was quick to recognise the part played by his late predecessor – long-serving clubman Harry Griffiths, who died of a heart attack during the 1977/78 promotion run-in. As Swansea fan and writer Huw Richards put it: 'Harry's appointment, just before re-election, obeyed an ancient football rule: when *in extremis* appoint the honest and valued retainer.'

'Harry Griffiths was everything to the football club – player, physio, coach, trainer, assistant manager and manager – and if he had been asked to wash the kit and paint the Centre Stand on a Sunday he would probably have done it,' wrote Liam Sullivan of the *South Wales Evening Post* in August 2008. 'He loved Swansea Town when he was a player and he loved Swansea City just as much when he worked his way through the backroom staff at the Vetch to eventually take the top job. Whatever role he had he went about it with a twinkle in his eye and often a cheeky grin, but he knew his football. It was Griffiths, during his stint as manager, who turned Alan Curtis from a midfield player of promise into a striker of great talent – a move which paid rich dividends for both club and country.' At Griffiths' funeral, John Toshack, who had been with the club only a matter of weeks, paid him this tribute: 'This is Harry's team, not mine. It's his triumph. He was Swansea City.'

Apart from a brief spell at Merthyr at the end of his playing days, Griffiths had been at the club since 1949. He had made 422 first-team appearances for Swansea. He was the obvious choice as manager after the volatile Harry Gregg had moved on to Crewe in 1975. Gregg, a former Northern Ireland international keeper and Munich survivor, had struggled to contend with the club's mounting financial difficulties. Upon hearing of the club's £223,657 annual loss in October 1974, Gregg snapped: 'I'm sick and tired of hearing about the club's financial state. I would much rather talk about the practical side of football.' But when reminded that his team's abysmal disciplinary record wasn't helping their situation, Gregg retorted: 'Manliness has been taken out of the game and we are now pandering to the demands of Europe and changing our game to that played on the Continent which, after all, is only played by a bunch of fairies.' Swansea then had the worst disciplinary record in the Football League. The team's reputation was so bad that it was given the sobriquet 'Vetch Wretches' in the satirical football magazine, *Foul*. With only 15 players to call upon, Griffiths could ill afford to have suspensions cutting into his ultra-thin squad.

However, Griffiths had some talented youngsters in his squad: Robbie James, Alan Curtis, Jeremy Charles and Nigel Stevenson. Also, new chairman Malcolm Struel was determined to hang on to them. Griffiths had to fill in the gaps with free transfers such as George Smith, an experienced and fiercely-competitive half-back from Cardiff; Micky Conway, a fleet-footed wide man from Brighton; and Paul Harris, a defender from Orient. Griffiths paid one fee only, £1,000 to Manchester City for their young keeper, Stephen Potter. To his enormous credit Griffiths delivered entertaining *and* successful football – at least at home. Swansea won 14 and lost only one of their home league games in 1975/76, scoring 51 goals. Reading (5-1), Stockport (5-0), Crewe (4-0) and Watford (4-2) were hammered by the Swans at the Vetch Field. Attendances improved. Over 4,000 watched the Newport and Reading games, helping lift the season's average gate by 50 per cent. Although away form was dismal, Swansea finished in 11th position. The corner had been turned.

Building upon this platform, Griffiths' team pushed on during the 1976/77 season, failing to secure a promotion slot by just one point. A 1-4 defeat by Watford in the final home game, in front of 11,000 fans, ultimately denied Swansea that prize. Griffiths' find of the season was 16-year-old apprentice Jeremy Charles, son of Mel Charles and nephew of the great John Charles. Jeremy played in all but ten league games and led the scoring charts with 23 strikes. Curtis and James followed him with 14 goals apiece as Swansea netted 92 times. Unfortunately, the team had one of the worst defensive records in the division – conceding 68 goals.

Despite Swansea's narrow miss, the mood was lifting at the Vetch Field. The average gate had risen to around 5,000 while the League Cup home leg with Bolton drew in 13,600. The rise in gate revenue enabled the club to make an annual profit of £30,000 – worth around £250,000 in today's values. Notwithstanding the humiliating FA Cup home defeat by Minehead, chairman Malcolm Struel was sufficiently optimistic about

Swansea's progress to invest in a floodlight improvement scheme, the first phase of which would cost £7,500. By now, the Swans' young guns were attracting the interest of bigger clubs. Curtis had recently been selected to play for Wales – Swansea's first international honour in five years. But Struel remained resolute in repelling all boarders. 'None of our young stars are leaving Swansea City,' he declared. 'They are not for sale and that is that.'

For the 1977/78 season Griffiths brought in three new players, including Keith Barber, a keeper from Luton, to replace the error-prone Potter. However, after a bright start, Swansea's form fell away in the autumn months. With attendances falling, Malcolm Struel decided it was time for a change of management and relieved Harry Griffiths and his coach, Roy Saunders, of their jobs. In an act of remarkable loyalty, Griffiths agreed to carry on as temporary boss until his successor was appointed. Meanwhile, results began to improve. By mid-January, Swansea had returned to the promotion places.

Struel had initial difficulty in finding a successor to Griffiths. Although former Hereford boss, Colin Addison, was set to come, he ultimately turned down the offer. Struel had no more success with Eddie McCreadie and Bill McGarry. Finally, he struck gold when he persuaded the Liverpool and Welsh international striker, John Toshack, to take the job. Not that Toshack's first sight of his charges did much for the sales pitch. It came on a cold Monday evening at Rochdale. Rochdale were then bottom of Division Four. Their 2-1 victory was only their fifth in 32 games.

Toshack wasn't fazed, though. Fifteen thousand turned up to watch his debut against table-topping Watford on 3 March. Although resilient Watford pulled back a two-goal deficit to earn a 3-3 draw, six victories on the bounce put the Swans back in promotion contention. Tragically, Harry Griffiths collapsed and died on the day in which Swansea beat Scunthorpe 3-1 to put promotion firmly within their grasp. Toshack duly sealed that promotion with a thumping free kick against Halifax in front of 16,130 euphoric supporters. The 1977/78 average crowd of 8,100 was up by almost 40 per cent on the previous year's figure. This helped net an annual profit of £15,000. The ambitious Swansea board decided that it was time to speculate.

During the close season, in came former Halifax, Liverpool and Leicester striker, Alan Waddle, for £24,000. He was followed by legendary Anfield hard man, Tommy Smith, on a 'free'. Goalkeeper Geoff Crudgington was brought in from Crewe. Then Toshack invited two more of his former Liverpool team-mates to join him. Phil Boersma was signed from Luton for £35,000 and 36-year-old former England winger Ian Callaghan came from Anfield, also on 'a free'. Looking for more quality at centre-back, Toshack signed Leighton Phillips from Aston Villa for £70,000. And just after Christmas, Cardiff City defender Brian Attley joined the club for £20,000. Arguably Toshack's greatest coup, however, was in persuading Alan Curtis to remain at the Vetch Field after scoring 32 league goals during the previous season.

Swansea invested £150,000 in new players to boost the '78/79 promotion push. This was an astounding turnaround given the club's impoverished state just four years before. But the board's ambition paid off as Swansea had a storming season, securing a successive promotion behind Shrewsbury and Watford.

Belying his reputation as a striker who rarely struck, the tall, imposing Waddle led the Swans' charge with 19 league goals. Huw Richards wrote of Waddle in *My Favourite Year*:

> *The unmatched idol of the crowd was Alan Waddle – a selfless Stakhanovite targetman whose battles with opposing centre-backs and his own limitations struck an immediate chord of identification in the man on the North Bank. Opposing defenders were inclined to dispute the crowd's favourite chanted preposition, 'There's only one Alan Waddle' – his chasing and harassing left the distinct impression that there were two or three. His contribution was recognised graphically if unsubtly by a vast banner at the Swindon game proclaiming 'Alan Waddle lays on more balls than Fiona Richmond'. Deft flicks to supporting attackers assisted a high proportion of 83 league goals – 19 of which he claimed himself, none in a losing cause. His finest goal was yet to come on Boxing Day 1979; a stunning diving header whose minor defect was that it counted for Bristol Rovers.*

With the average attendance pushed up to 13,633 and the club's Cashcade lottery realising a £100,000 gain, Swansea enjoyed a £320,000 profit during that season, the biggest in its history. The club's coffers were also swollen by the sale of Curtis to Leeds for £400,000. With the Swansea board providing a further £350,000 for team strengthening, Toshack went on a spending spree. He brought in defender Dave Rushberry from Sheffield Wednesday for £60,000; midfielder Tommy Craig from Aston Villa for a club record fee of £150,000; midfielder John Mahoney from Middlesbrough for £100,000;

full-back Neil Robinson from Everton and midfielder David Giles from Wrexham, both for £70,000 fees; goalkeeper David Stewart from West Bromwich for £55,000; and, just before the close of the season, winger Leighton James from Burnley for £130,000. Meanwhile, Crudgington left for Plymouth and Bartley joined Hereford.

As Toshack expected, life in Division Two proved to be a lot tougher. Nevertheless, a final position of 12th was a satisfactory result bearing in mind that Swansea completed the season only ten points behind promoted Birmingham. They also finished ahead of the two other sides promoted with them, Shrewsbury and Watford. But goalscoring had been a problem – only 48 were put away in the 42 league games. David Giles was their leading marksman with eight goals.

The biggest problem the club now faced was the cost of upgrading the Vetch Field. In the summer of 1980, it was estimated that around £700,000 worth of improvements would be required to meet the standards set out in the Safety of Sports Ground Act (which equates to around £3.5 million today). Actually, the total bill was much higher. Two years later, and with £2 million already spent on various repairs, renovations and upgrades, it was readily apparent that there was still much to do. The Vetch Field had been neglected for years. Time had finally caught up with the club and its dilapidated arena. By the summer of '82, club chairman, Malcolm Struel, was forced to concede: 'We have no capital available to spend on the ground and we will just have to sit tight, hope we get a good season, and see where this takes us.'

Swansea's rise had been ballistic, severely challenging its capacity to manage its escalating liabilities: improved facilities, higher wages and larger transfer fees. Nevertheless, the Swansea board were determined to back their dream, believing that success at the highest level would guarantee the necessary resources with which to balance the books. They reasoned that with a catchment area comprising a population of around 600,000, the club had a potentially huge fan base, easily enough to support its ascending ambitions. They saw the club as a sleeping giant ready to be awakened. As if inspired by the film *Field of Dreams*, the Swansea board reckoned that if they built the stadium and laid on top-notch football, the people would come, not just in their thousands but in their tens of thousands. That misplaced expectation would prove ultimately ruinous.

The red alert signs were flashing at the very start of the 1980/81 season, one that would conclude with Swansea's historic promotion to Division One. The cost of reinforcing the team to meet Second Division standards had been high – arguably prohibitively so. The club reported an annual loss of £400,000. Struel attempted to reassure himself and others, stating that there was 'no cause for alarm. As we had a good profit the previous year, our working loss over two years was only £71,000 and in that time we have built a team worth £3 million.' Toshack had spent almost £600,000 more than he had received in sales receipts but he, too, was confident that his playing assets were depreciation-proof. They weren't; not by a long chalk.

Swansea started their second season in Division Two strongly. Despite initial goal-shyness, they had climbed to fourth place by the end of October. Two Yugoslavian internationals – Dzemal Hadziabdic and Ante Rajkovic – were added to the defence for £160,000 and £100,000 respectively. Nevertheless, there were still places for four local lads – full-back Chris Marustik, tall central defender Nigel Stevenson, and attackers Jeremy Charles and Robbie James – alongside the expensive imports. Alan Waddle was on his way out, though. He was sold to Newport for £80,000. His departure made way for the return of Alan Curtis for £175,000. After the festive period, Swansea were in second spot but a catastrophic 0-5 FA Cup home defeat by Middlesbrough knocked them out of their stride. The next five games were lost. Leighton James' hat-trick turned the corner at the end of February when visiting Bolton were beaten 3-0. Swansea lost only one the following ten games but once again they needed a victory in their last match of the season to secure promotion.

Being up in the north-west for a few days, I decided to go to their game at Preston. Arriving early, there was time to saunter through budding Fulwood Park in the salubrious spring sunshine. Nearly 19,000 fans pushed their way into the groaning, creaking anachronism that Deepdale had become. This gate more than doubled Preston's average crowd of 7,631. Apparently, 10,000 fans were from Swansea. As in the final game here, in April 1973, the result was crucial to both sides for opposite reasons. A victory for Swansea would grant them promotion to Division One, while a win for 'Proud' Preston – then managed by Nobby Stiles – might help them avert relegation to Division Three, where they would join local rivals, Burnley.

These were the days of caged terraces. The Swansea hordes were squeezed into the then covered Town End. Their many home-made placards and banners were pressed against the grilled fencing. Their belligerent chanting was incessant. In front of the Swans' fans, the Preston keeper, Roy Tunks, prowled warily. The opening exchanges were frenetic. The hard, scarred surface produced awkward deviations and steepling bounce prompting straining, leaping challenges all over the pitch. Avoiding any risk, both sides preferred to thump the ball forward, long and hard, for their pent-up forwards to scamper after. High on adrenaline, both teams began with more pace than guile, more power than skill. One clattering challenge followed another. Play was peppered with full-tilt muscular lunges. At the first sign of danger, both sides drew almost everyone back behind the ball. Swansea were quicker to settle, though. After the frenzied opening 15 minutes they were more adept in controlling the bouncing ball, killing it adroitly and providing probing passes.

After 25 minutes, Curtis knocked a high pass out to the left wing. James trapped it instantly without breaking stride, and confidently approached Preston right-back Taylor. Suddenly, James jinked right, leaving the dumbfounded Taylor sprawling on the turf. North End's centre-back, Blackley, attempted to block James' path but hesitated fatally, allowing the Swansea winger the time and space to curl a shot around him, past the diving Roy Tunks, and into the top right-hand corner of the net. It was James' 15th league goal of the season, his best return thus far. Ignoring the ecstatic Swans fans, James headed straight for the home supporters, situated in the Pavilion Stand, bearing an expression of malicious delight, his fists clenched above his head. Former rivalry still rankled, it seemed. However, Toshack remained unmoved. He simply instructed his players to hold a higher defensive line.

Two minutes later, a skilful exchange between Curtis and Robinson allowed the full-back to advance far down the right flank. Showing immaculate skill, Robinson cut in, beating two Preston defenders with nifty footwork, before clipping a lofted centre across the face of their box. Home centre-back Mick Baxter tried to intercept, but the ball skewed off his forehead into the path of the unmarked Tommy Craig in the inside-left channel. The little red-headed Swansea midfielder shot immediately with his left foot. Tunks got his left hand to the ball, but was helpless to prevent it bobbling over the line. The delirious Swans' fans scrambled to the top of the perimeter fencing with the agility of baboons.

After the break Preston rallied. Stiles had done his half-time work well. Finding that they could not outplay Swansea, North End tried to overpower them. They proceeded to hit the corners, attempting to find opportunities to bombard the Swans' box with high balls. It was a crude tactic but with keeper Stewart uncertain on crosses, Preston began to rattle their more skilful opponents. With 12 minutes left to play, a Preston player, near to Swansea's right corner flag, attempted a speculative overhead kick. The ball looped high into the crowded Swansea box. Stewart came out to claim the ball but spilled it under a challenge from a Preston forward. The ball ran loose, allowing the predatory Alex Bruce to rifle in his 13th goal of the season.

Now Preston had more than huff and puff; they had belief. Exploiting Swansea's vulnerability on high balls, one after another arrived in the Swans' penalty area. Stewart was at sixes and sevens. Shortly after Bruce's goal, the visiting keeper raced from his line to punch clear another aerial cross. But he found only thin air as Preston's burly centre-back, Mick Baxter, powered into the mix to send a thumping header just wide of the left upright. Home centre-forward Stephen Elliott then got away from his markers to smash a rising drive just over the bar. Toshack's coolness evaporated. Frantic instructions were relayed to his besieged team.

But, with Preston compelled to throw caution to the wind, Curtis seized his chance to seal the game. Picking up a short clearance in his own half, and finding only substitute defender John Anderson facing him, Curtis took the Preston man on. Having greater pace and power, Curtis wriggled past his opponent close to the right touchline. With Robbie James and Jeremy Charles advancing quickly, Curtis saw that they had the numerical advantage. Curtis cut in and laid a ball across to James. Although the ball bobbled badly, bouncing off James' shins, the youngster recovered quickly enough to push it wide of the challenging defender and into the path of the unmarked Charles. Charles took one touch before blasting the ball left-footed past Tunks. It was game over; Swansea were up and, after Cardiff's 0-0 draw with West Bromwich, Preston were down. Their subsequent victory at Derby County would prove fruitless. Across the sun-bathed Preston pitch Swansea players embraced one another, while scores of their fans scaled the Town End fencing, twirling their black and white scarves above their heads. A heady night would follow.

According to author Terry Grandin, club chairman Malcolm Struel declared: 'Providing we sell the expected number of season tickets and providing gates are good we will find the money to strengthen the squad. We have never said "no" to the manager and hopefully we won't have to in the future.' Struel was as good as his word. In came 29-year-old striker Bob Latchford from Everton for £125,000, as did Welsh international keeper Dai Davies, from Wrexham, for £75,000. A record £350,000 was then splashed out on Liverpool centre-back, Colin Irwin. He was accompanied by 24-year-old defender Max Thompson, signed from Blackpool for £20,000. Meanwhile, Dave Rushberry left for Carlisle for £40,000 – £20,000 less than Swansea had paid for him. Also leaving was Leighton Phillips, who joined Charlton for £25,000 – £45,000 less than Swansea paid for him. Toshack's spending over this three-year period in charge amounted to £1.8 million. This amounts to around £8 million in today's values and, if converted into present transfer currency, possibly £50 million. This was a phenomenal outlay for a club whose average gate was only 13,140 and whose ground improvement costs equated to around £8 million in today's prices.

Swansea's first game in Division One was at home against Leeds – the team of the early seventies but, by the eighties, a pale shadow of Revie's former side. Nevertheless, Leeds had finished the previous season in ninth place, despite scoring only 39 goals. It was small wonder that Alan Curtis felt disillusioned with the limited opportunities he had at Elland Road. Leeds' leading scorer was fellow Welshman Carl Harris, with a modest tally of ten league goals.

The Leeds United directors had been spoilt by success. After Clough was sacked in 1974, they became increasingly impatient when his replacement, Jimmy Armfield, failed to deliver the silverware they were used to. Just before the start of the 1978/79 campaign they dismissed him. It seemed a strange decision and even stranger timing. Armfield had led a strong recovery after the Clough debacle. Helped by his coach, Don Howe, Armfield had kept Leeds among the top ten First Division clubs and had taken them to a European Cup Final in 1975, just months after Clough's departure. Unfortunately, his side lost to Bayern Munich after dominating the game, not that this ill fortune excused the appalling behaviour of their rioting fans. It was rumoured that for all his tactical ability, Armfield relied upon Howe to keep the players in check. Once Howe left to take on the Arsenal post, Armfield was thought to be less effective, at least by a strong contingent of Leeds fans.

After a brief period with Armfield's assistant, Maurice Lindley, in charge, the famous Jock Stein was drafted in. Having just been ousted at Parkhead by his former skipper, Billy McNeill, Stein was deeply resentful. It seemed that his move south was motivated more by spite than by any ambition to revive Leeds' fortunes. He was not keen to uproot his Glasgow-based family, either. After six weeks at Elland Road, he resigned, preferring to take over the Scottish national side after the departure of Ally MacLeod. In October 1978, the Leeds' board invited ex-Burnley and Sunderland boss, Jimmy Adamson, to take the post.

Adamson faced a troubled situation. Leeds had won just three of their first ten league fixtures. Although Paul Reaney and Allan Clarke had moved on, Adamson still had a number of Revie veterans on board: keeper Harvey, defenders Frankie Gray, Paul Madeley and Trevor Cherry, and forwards Peter Lorimer and Eddie Gray. Realising Leeds would struggle to compete with the top teams, he decided: 'I want to see Leeds win first and entertain second.' There was early promise. A 16-match unbeaten run in the league lifted Leeds up to fourth spot by mid-March 1979. After the earlier traumas,

Leeds had achieved a highly creditable final position of fifth, which granted them another opportunity to conquer Europe, albeit in the UEFA Cup. Adamson also guided Leeds to a League Cup semi-final which they lost to Southampton.

Adamson had two big, burly, battling strikers: Ray Hankin, a former Burnley protégé, and John Hawley, formerly of Hull. They led the league scoring charts with 25 goals between them. Meanwhile, Tony Currie, Arthur Graham, Eddie Gray, Carl Harris and another former Burnley protégé, Brian Flynn, pulled the strings in midfield. At the back Adamson was able to call upon the imposing former Blackpool centre-half, Paul Hart, plus the Revie boys – Madeley, Cherry and Frankie Gray. Blackburn's attacking full-back or midfielder, Kevin Hird, was added to the squad in March 1979 for a massive fee of £357,000, a move which coincided with the cancellation of Lorimer's contract. It seemed to be so far, so good.

But the next season was one of mediocrity, resulting in a fall of six places to 11th spot. Leeds were soon out of Europe. Leeds supporters were upset to see talented players such as Tony Currie, John Hawley and Frankie Gray sold and replaced by largely unsuccessful big-money signings: Swansea's Alan Curtis, Manchester United defender Brian Greenhoff, Rangers centre-forward Derek Parlane and Sheffield United's Argentinean playmaker, Alex Sabella. Their purchases cost Leeds almost £1.5million. When Kevin Hird's fee was taken into account, Adamson had shelled out nearly £2 million in less than a year. With the big buys failing to deliver, Leeds' fans turned on Adamson. Mounted police had to break up an angry demonstration after a dire 0-0 home draw with Coventry in March 1980. Only 15,541 then turned up for a subsequent game with Stoke, the lowest home attendance in 17 years.

Leeds United supporter Gary Edwards, author of *Paint it White and Second Coat*, recalled: 'By now the "Adamson Out" brigade was out in full force at every game … At that time the Yorkshire Ripper was still on the loose. Everyone thought the Ripper was a Geordie because of the famous hoax tape and the police would come into the pubs in the city, playing the tape of the man reputed to be the Ripper to see if anyone recognised the voice. At every pub the police would be met with shouts of, "that's not the Ripper, it's Jimmy Adamson – lock him up". Eventually, in October 1980, Adamson bowed to public pressure and resigned, leaving football behind him for good.' As Burnley author Dave Thomas wrote: 'When you add the tragic deaths of both his daughters, his story really is one of broken dreams and personal tragedy.'

After Adamson's resignation, the Leeds board eventually turned to Allan

Clarke, their goalscoring hero of the Revie era, who was then managing Barnsley. Clarke had just helped the Tykes to promotion from Division Three. Like Adamson, Clarke inherited a Leeds side that had started the season badly. Although Clarke's Leeds finished in ninth spot, two places up from their 1980 position, the attritional football played by his team was not to the fans' liking. The average home gate for the 1980/81 season was only 21,378, representing a fall of 13,443, almost 40 per cent, since the championship-winning season of 1973/74. At the start of the following season, Clarke gambled hugely, paying a club record fee of £930,000 for former Manchester City and West Bromwich winger, Peter Barnes. Barnes lined up in the Leeds side for the opening game at the Vetch Field, which featured John Lukic in goal; defenders Hird, Frankie Gray (who had returned from Forest), Hart and Cherry; midfielders Flynn, Barnes, Graham and Eddie Gray, with Parlane and Harris up front. Swansea fielded Davies in goal; defenders Robinson, Hadziabdic, Irwin and Rajkovic; midfielders Mahoney, Robbie James, Leighton James and Charles, with Latchford and Curtis leading the line.

August 29 was a day of sparkling heat. A crowd of 23,489 wedged itself into the sweltering Vetch Field to watch 'Tosh's' lads take on what was once one of the strongest sides in Britain. Terry Grandin provided this account of the game in his book *Swansea City: Seasons in the Sun*:

> *The teams emerged on to the lush Vetch Field turf to a tumultuous welcome. [The expectant crowd] didn't have long to wait, as Jeremy Charles netted Swansea's first goal in the First Division after just five minutes. Latchford dummied the cross and the ball ran to Charles, who wrong-footed Leeds keeper John Lukic. Leeds were level midway through the first period when Scottish international Derek Parlane headed home a Harris centre. Immediately after the break, Swansea took over, with Latchford striking a hat-trick inside ten minutes. Charles nodded down a Robbie James centre for the former Everton man to lash in the first. He then tapped in at the near post, and claimed the match ball with an unstoppable header from a free kick by Leighton James. But the best was yet to come. Curtis ghosted past Trevor Cherry before uncorking a fierce shot that swerved high into the net at the near post. Flynn had worked hard for*

the losers, as had Harris, but little was seen of £930,000 signing Peter Barnes.

Alan Curtis told Terry Grandin: 'That 5-1 scoreline was beyond our wildest dreams. We were unstoppable in the second half. Two saves from Dai Davies probably won us the game but after that hat-trick it was goodnight and the game was over.' A discontented Allan Clarke grunted, 'I've nothing to say – the result speaks for itself.' The Leeds fans expressed their fury by hurling missiles on to the pitch, forcing the local police to mount a cordon of 30 officers in front of them while dog handlers moved into the menacing crowd. It was an ugly way to complete a perfect afternoon.

Chairman Malcolm Struel was not only delighted with the result, but with the 24,000 crowd, which had yielded record club receipts of £32,181, excluding season ticket sales, which stood at £650,000. An average gate of 24,000 would realise annual gate revenue of around £1.3 million, excluding cup games, although the first-team players' wages alone probably accounted for at least half that amount. However, Struel's hopes of achieving a regular 24,000 gate figure proved wildly optimistic. Twenty-two thousand fans turned up to see Spurs beaten by Alan Curtis' blistering 35-yarder in September, and similarly-sized crowds were drawn to the Vetch for the visit of other top clubs: Liverpool (2-0), Manchester United (2-0), Ipswich (1-2), Arsenal (2-0) and Southampton (1-0). On the other hand, lesser lights, such as struggling Middlesbrough and Stoke, drew crowds of less than 13,000. The European Cup Winners' Cup hardly set the pulses racing, either, with just over 10,000 paying to watch Lokomotiv Leipzig eliminate Swansea at the first hurdle.

Nevertheless, the spending spree continued. With Swansea seizing top spot in October following a victory at Stoke, Struel was persuaded to shell out a further £150,000 for Everton midfielder, Gary Stanley. And shortly after being awarded an MBE in the New Year Honours, Toshack was allowed to sign Liverpool midfielder, Ray Kennedy, for £160,000. Kennedy joined after Swansea's dismal 2-0 defeat at an icy Elland Road. The winter of '82 was particularly harsh. Rumours circulated that Toshack was about to pay £200,000 for Leeds' pint-sized midfielder Brian Flynn, but his assistant, Phil Boersma, dismissed this, stating the club couldn't afford such a fee. Kennedy was quick to impress, though, performing brilliantly in Swansea's 2-0 win over Manchester United on 30 January. He also scored against his former club, Arsenal, in a 2-0 victory at Highbury at the end of February.

On 20 March, Swansea returned to the top of the table with a 1-0 win at relegation-bound Wolves. Former Palace striker, Ian Walsh, opened his account in this game, having been exchanged with David Giles. But thereafter, Swansea's title challenge fell away. Only three victories were recorded in their final 12 games, reducing them to sixth place. This would be as good as it got for Toshack's team. A year later they would be back in Division Two, following in the footsteps of downward-bound Leeds. For having spent so much on the disappointing Peter Barnes, Clarke had little left as his Leeds team became mired in a relegation struggle, which they finally lost. Frank Worthington and Kenny Burns were brought in to try to stop the rot, but to no avail. In June 1982, Clarke paid with his job.

Chairman Malcolm Struel stated: 'I was very disappointed that the '81/82 average crowd was only just over 18,000 when we had such a successful season. It is also a surprise that we remain one of the few First Division clubs yet to attract a major shirt sponsor, particularly as the commercial potential for a sponsor allied to this club is tremendous.' Not for much longer, though. The 1982/83 season was an unmitigated disaster. Injuries to key players, dressing-room tensions and mounting financial pressures tore the guts out of the team that Toshack had skilfully assembled and led. Back-to-back home victories over Coventry (2-1) and Norwich (4-0) at the start of the season took Swansea up to second position, but by the end of October they had dropped 15 places. And they kept falling.

During the second half of the season, Swansea recorded just three wins and six draws in 21 league games. Latchford did his best by scoring 20 goals in 38 league appearances but only Robbie James, with nine successful strikes, gave him any significant support. Swansea's defeat at Old Trafford on 7 May sent them down alongside Manchester City and FA Cup finalists, Brighton. Just 9,226 turned up for Swansea's final home game – a gloomy 0-3 defeat by Nottingham Forest.

Swansea's average home gate had dropped by 36 per cent to 11,681. Malcolm Struel warned the supporters that 'It is not feasible to keep all the players on top of gates of 12,000.' This was something of an understatement. By October, the extent of Swansea's financial malaise was made clear. The club was £2 million in debt and losing £10,000 per week. The bank refused to make any further payments. If Struel thought he could make up this loss in player sales, he was badly mistaken. The club were forced into a fire sale. £100,000-plus signings such as Latchford, Kennedy and Leighton James left for no fee at all, as did £75,000 purchase, Dai Davies. As for the rest, it was one bargain-bin sale after another. Gary Stanley went to Portsmouth for an 80 per cent loss on his purchase value. Prize assets Robbie James, Jeremy Charles and Alan Curtis went for a fraction of their considered price. James, valued at £350,000, went to Stoke for just £130,000. Charles went to QPR for around £100,000 and Curtis went to Southampton for

£85,000. Although Toshack spent over £2 million on players, less than a third of that figure was recouped from their sales.

Having resigned in October 1983, Toshack returned briefly, only to be sacked five months later. At his resignation, Toshack had refused compensation despite having 18 months left on his £48,000 per year contract. He also donated £1,000 to the Swansea City youth development scheme. But even draconian economies weren't enough. By September 1985, Swansea owed £700,000 to Barclays Bank and over £100,000 to the Inland Revenue. Substantial sums were owed to other creditors. Some showed generosity, like Liverpool, who waived the £300,000 Swansea owed them in unpaid transfer fees. But it was no surprise that the club was wound up in December 1985. New manager John Bond and his entire playing staff were dismissed. Thanks to some canny negotiations, the club managed to arrive at receivership rather than liquidation. A 28-day reprieve was crucial. It was shown that the depleted club could be run at a small profit. Swansea narrowly survived.

Meanwhile, on the pitch, the team bombed, careering back to Division Four by April 1986. Like Northampton, the speed of the club's descent was as fast as its rise. The Swans' support reverted to a hard core of 4,000 loyal fans.

After years of hardship, the unexpected prospect of success must have seemed so intoxicating to those well-intentioned Swansea directors. As novice gamblers find, an early hot streak can turn the head. Perhaps that's why the directors bet the ranch in pursuing unsustainable success. These were, after all, very difficult times for British working people, particularly those dependent upon receding industries, as was the case in and around Swansea. For Swansea fans to turn up in the numbers that the board expected to see, they would need to have more disposable income than seemed likely in this time and place. As a measure of the economic hardship commonly felt, the average Division One gate fell by 18 per cent between '81 and '83. What chance was there, then, of Swansea doubling its average '80/81 gate of 13,000? In any event, hard-core support takes many years to build. Floating supporters will always be drawn to glorious events but rarely stay in times of strife. In trying to live the dream, the Swansea board consigned everyone to the nightmare. In those rare moments when the Icarus spirit moves within us, we might do well to consider Clint Eastwood snarled words in *Magnum Force*: 'a man's gotta know his limitations'.

Almost 30 years later, Swansea completed a magnificent recovery, returning to the top tier of British football after winning their 2011 play-off final against Reading. It is very unlikely that Brendan Rodgers will have the financial freedom that John Toshack had. As almost every Swansea fan knows, the price is far too high.

Bristol City: the price of loyalty

On 28 November 1981, I watched Burnley play Bristol City at Ashton Gate. With money very tight, Liz and I took in lodgers. Going to a game became a rare treat. But at least we weren't as badly off as Bristol City, for our local club was in a real mess. Having defied the odds in reaching the top flight in 1976, they strived too hard to stay there. Manager Alan Dicks had cannily, but expensively, recruited a clutch of experienced top professionals to boost the club's lofty ambitions. Joe Royle and Norman Hunter, in particular, played their parts well. But it wasn't just these ageing stars that enjoyed well-paid contracts. Manager Dicks awarded long, lucrative contracts to his home-grown players in order to keep them at the club. While City attracted an average gate of around 22,000, ends might have been met. But a day of reckoning had to come if the club fell from its perch. And that's what happened in April 1980. A year later, City were in Division Three along with local rivals, Rovers.

Dicks had departed and was replaced by one of our brightest young coaches – Bobby Houghton – who had been given a three-year contract with an annual salary of £25,000. Houghton was one of Hastings United's diaspora of coaching talents, which included the wonderfully eccentric Colin Murphy, Des Anderson, who was Dave Mackay's sidekick at title-winning Derby in '75, and the unsung Ted Ballard. Like George Raynor, Houghton was almost unknown in this country until he took his Malmo side to the 1979 European Cup Final. Like George Raynor, he taught Swedish sides how to beat acclaimed opponents, albeit by adopting a direct, pressing, style of play. And, like Raynor, he never received the recognition that his skills merited in his country of birth. It is ironic that imported Swedish coach, Sven-Goran Eriksson, should credit Houghton's influence on his early career.

Sadly for Houghton and Bristol City, he never had much of a chance at Ashton Gate. The club was in free fall. When I arrived at Ashton Gate in November 1981, the club's debt stood at £700,000 (around £3 million in today's values) with £120,000 unpaid tax payments. The Robins were reported to be losing £3,000 a week.

On that sunny but chilly afternoon, there was a threadbare crowd of 4,862. A mood of chuffing dissent had settled on the home fans, even before the game began. It was hardly helped when Burnley's young midfielder,

Kevin Young, prodded his side into a third-minute lead. But Burnley had yet to hit their stride. They were still in a dicey position – just four places off the bottom. Confidence was shaky. Realising this, City managed to turn the tables. First, Jimmy Mann put away an 11th-minute penalty and then, seven minutes after the break, Chris Garland put City in front. Whereas Burnley's early advantage had caused them to freeze, adversity spurred them into positive action. They retaliated furiously to Garland's goal, rediscovering their penchant for sharp one-touch football.

The instigator of this change was Burnley's 18-year-old midfielder, Trevor Steven. Oblivious to the frenetic tackling, he played with his socks bunched around his ankles. He was in the centre of everything. He played quick one-twos with his fellow midfielders, Kevin Young and Tommy Cassidy, as he probed for openings. Whether passing short or long, he executed his service with composed precision. He looked for runners on one side of him, only to suddenly reverse direction and pick out an unmarked colleague on the other. Nothing seemed to trouble him. He was unruffled by the rough and tumble stuff, creating space around himself with nonchalant calm. He seemed to have so much time on the ball. With a feint here, a drop of the shoulder there, he continually eased away from trouble. On a heavy, churned surface he played as if on a bowling green. I knew then that he was destined for the very top.

With Steven continually wrong-footing the home defence, Bristol were forced to pull more men back. Burnley grasped the initiative. With Burnley's back four posted on the halfway line and sweeper Martin Dobson reinforcing their advanced midfield, the game became a turkey shoot. However, it took two late goals from Paul McGee for Burnley to snatch their just deserts. At the end the Bristol players slouched off the field in despair as a chilly mist drifted in from the Avon, enveloping the ground in a damp shroud. The illuminated suspension bridge and the twinkling lights of Clifton lent a festive air to the winter evening but there were no celebrations at Ashton Gate.

Early in the New Year Bobby Houghton resigned, admitting: 'There is nothing more I can do.' The debts had then risen to £850,000. His assistant, Roy Hodgson, took over. With losses reaching more than £4,000 a week, accountants were called in to try to save the club. Their solution was drastic. Among their recommendations was the immediate termination of eight first-team players' contracts. The players were Peter Aitken, Julian Marshall, David Rodgers, Geoff Merrick, Gerry Sweeney, Trevor Tainton, Chris Garland and Jimmy Mann. Those on longer and / or more lucrative contracts had already left the club, including Joe Royle, Norman Hunter,

Terry Cooper, Clive Whitehead, Tom Ritchie and Gerry Gow.

Deryn Collier, who became a director of the reborn Bristol City (1982), recalled the grim events of 1981/82 in an article he wrote for the Bristol City fanzine *Three Lions and a Robin*. Deryn wrote:

> *I owned £500 worth of shares, about half a per cent. I went along to the club's AGM around about October 1981, and you did not need to be 'Brain of Britain' to see the club was in the proverbial. I asked a few pertinent questions … We agreed to pay for an independent financial report … They came up with an enormous debt, which we all knew was there, but had been hidden. They formulated a rescue plan which was quite simple: form a new company; place a moratorium on the creditors; unload your biggest liabilities. The accountant said you might be able to struggle on if you get rid of your liabilities.*
>
> *Terry Boyle, [a Welsh international defender], Jan Moller, [a Swedish keeper] and [centre-forward] Mick Harford were players who had value. So the rescue plan was: do a deal with the creditors; do a deal with the Football League (for whom this was a new situation); do a deal with the old company on the sale of the ground; and do a deal with the eight players who comprised a large slice of the liabilities. All of them were equally important. The company could not afford the eight players. If they had not torn up their contracts the club would have folded … All [the new club] had was what the seven directors had put in, which was about £10,000 each. And around £50,000 of that had to go to the Football League as a guarantee, so the working capital was about £20,000.*
>
> *We were living from hand to mouth, week in week out. Often we had board meetings where we all had to stick £300 in the pot, put it in the club, and the club would buy this or that or pay wages. The Ashton eight all walked out with around £10,000 each and if they*

had not taken it the club would have gone down and the other staff would have lost their jobs … Gordon Taylor of the Professional Footballers' Association realised it was not brinkmanship or gamesmanship … A lot of the creditors had to accept 10p, 15p, 20p in the pound, and they did it without whinging. A lot of them were pragmatic … [They] got more than they would have got if the club went belly-up. We were surprised at the level of debt … I do not believe Alan Dicks was responsible … The board, individually and collectively, had to be responsible for the decline of Bristol City.

The report came out just before Christmas 1981. [We] suggested certain routes … one being the BCFC (1982) Plc route. The directors [of the former club] realised they were in 'no win' land. It was almost a relief for them that other people were prepared to take over. They cogitated for four or five days and agreed. Then we all had to find £12,500 each, as a minimum of £50,000 is needed to launch a new plc … And of course we had the 'Ashton Eight' business to deal with, which went to the wire because Gordon Taylor and his advisers [initially] believed it was a double bluff. But one thing I know to be true … that the club was going into liquidation if the players had not signed that document. The Football League wanted guarantees which we couldn't give paying those wages.

I was under a lot of stress. I nearly lost my house and my job. My marriage came close to finishing. I was doing eighteen hour days at City, as was Ken Sage. We finished one particular board meeting at half past four in the morning … The amount of times that we had a board meeting where we needed to pay a bill of just £600; so the directors would put £75 or so each in the pot to pay that bill, and that happened more times than I cared to remember. It doesn't seem like much now – but it was a lot of money in those days. My total commitment in to

Bristol City for the first six months was over £70,000 which was all I ever had in the world and I kept it from my wife, because she would have gone absolutely ape if she had known. She did find out subsequently and went absolutely ape … The 'first type' friends of Bristol City groups collected around £4,000 after writing to all the secretaries of local football clubs, and that made an enormous difference. A lot of people rallied round in very, very small ways. But those small ways made a big impact.

In an article which appeared in the April 1982 edition of *Marxism Today*, Peter Ball wrote: 'The PFA estimate that only around 25–30 per cent of contracts will come up for renewal in the summer… With a short career expectancy and a rough average wage of £175 a week (obviously top First Division stars get much more, but a young player on the fringe of a Fourth Division team may only get £50 a week), footballers are hardly to blame for the economic mess the game finds itself in.'

As for the eight players, each of them gave their account in interviews conducted with a BBC Radio Bristol presenter in 2006. All, bar one of them, indicated that they had been entirely unaware of the severity of the club's financial situation prior to its shocking announcement.

Jimmy Mann was annoyed that the club directors described the eight players as being on long, lucrative contracts, an assertion he described as 'nonsense'. He continued:

Clive Whitehead had been on an 11 or 13-year contract and Tom Ritchie had one of about seven or eight years, because Alan Dicks wanted to hold on to his big players, but we weren't. I had a contract of three years, which was the longest among the eight of us. The press said we were on £30,000 or £40,000 a year. That was nonsense. What we had was a decent living wage but it wasn't a fortune. We were put under a lot of pressure. It was said that the club could fold and everyone would lose their jobs. It was on the TV and on the front pages of the Evening Post. The PFA were in a difficult position being confronted with this by the directors and their accountants. The PFA put our names around other clubs but nothing came of this. Other clubs must have thought there was something wrong with us, being picked out for the chop. I rang Norman Hunter at Barnsley and he gave me a trial, then a short contract. But I kept getting injuries and ended up working for Securicor before becoming a jetty master at Goole docks.

Captain Geoff Merrick added:

I had been with the club for 17 years. We had grown up together. We socialised together. The seventies had been the best period of my football life. We didn't really know what was happening. There was no real feeling that Bristol City was in such a state and about to fold. After returning to Ashton Gate following a reserves' match at the Arsenal, I met Jimmy Mann. He had some names written in biro on a tatty piece of paper. He told me that we needed to meet the directors on the Monday morning. Jimmy didn't know the reason. He was asked to pass this on to me and the others in the reserves. This summed up their lack of feeling for us. It was very sloppy. If I was to sack someone I would deal with it on a first-hand basis … We were innocent really, unprepared for the macabre situation we were about to face … I was supposed to be the players' representative with the directors and the PFA. I had to deal with the media and the supporters, too. We ended up with two weeks' pay in cash. Fortunately, my wife was really strong: she only admitted how upset she was afterwards. I found I lost two stones during the crisis … I ended up playing in Hong Kong for a while. I had to do something. We had a mortgage to pay and a family to look after – one boy of ten years old and two aged four and five. I could have gone to Portsmouth but by then I'd promised them in Hong Kong I'd go there. I didn't want to break my word but I didn't stay long, though. I came back and decided to go into farming and, because that didn't pay enough,

I went into the construction business, setting up my own firm. It took around ten years to put our life together again.

Chris Garland said:

I was disappointed with the club directors. Seven out of eight of them were successful businessmen, yet they made a real mess of things at the club. They went on to be successful businessmen afterwards. They wouldn't let their own businesses get in that way … We were offered 10p in the pound only on our contracts, although this was eventually lifted a bit. Mine didn't have long to run anyway. I felt sorry for the lads with longer contracts. We did get a testimonial game: Southampton played Ipswich at Ashton Gate. I got one, myself, too, after I had Parkinson's disease. Alex Ferguson kindly agreed to bring his Manchester United side down for this if I could wait 18 months, as he said 'they were a bit busy at the time'. That really helped me out with the mortgage and so on … After leaving Bristol and playing in Hong Kong and Sweden, I came back and played as and when needed for City under Terry Cooper for £20 per week. I was so pleased the club survived. I was just proud to wear the red shirt again. Four of us were local boys – Geoff, Trevor and David. We all grew up with the club. It's still my club.

Gerry Sweeney recalled:

I wasn't at the meeting with the directors to start with. I hadn't been asked. Then they phoned me and asked me to go to the club straightaway. I had been cleaning the car so I was in an old tracksuit. But I had to go as I was because they told me I had to be there in ten minutes. When I arrived at the meeting, I couldn't work out what was going on. They just carried on with what they'd been saying. It took me five minutes or so to cotton on. I thought, 'this can't be right'. I thought it must be a prank, like one of those Jeremy Beadle things. I was 37 years old and had only 14–16 months left on my contract. This last contract was a little bit longer than those before. It was given as a reward for what I'd done for the club. I knew I didn't have much time left but I wasn't ready for it to end just like that … The directors kept blaming the players but no one is going to take less money if you can get more. We couldn't say anything to anyone although people kept asking – team-mates and supporters … The Football League and the PFA got together and, although the original club was wound up, they were allowed to finish the season before becoming Bristol City (1982). That wouldn't happen now. The team would go out of the league like Newport County did and have to work their way up through the non-leagues. We got the Ipswich versus Southampton game. That helped a bit. We got 10–12p in the pound from the proceeds of that game … Afterwards, I went to York with Peter Aitken for a few months to help them avoid re-election. Then I worked for Securicor; became a postman; began coaching; did some scouting and was an assistant manager at Walsall for two years. I also coached the schoolkids and the youth side here.

Peter Aitken said that, among the 'Ashton Gate Eight', he was the least surprised about the news of their fate. He explained how

… attendances were falling. Violence on the terraces was causing fewer families to go to games. There were lot of financial problems in football then. Many clubs were letting experienced players go and carrying on with the younger ones. I came across from Bristol Rovers. I could see things were pretty tight. It didn't look as if the club was going forward. Most of the players had seen better days. But I still assumed that a contract was binding. I assumed the directors would deal with the finances … I remember we had just been beaten 1-0 by Aston

> *Villa in the FA Cup. We'd played really well against the next European champions. We'd only lost because of an unlucky deflection. Roy Hodgson told us, 'the chairman would like to meet the players on Monday morning'. I said straightaway to the others: 'we'll be getting the sack'. Trevor Tainton said, 'no, we are on contracts'. I said to him, 'look around you' … There were loads of photographers and newspaper people outside the offices in Bristol where we held one of the meetings. Gordon Taylor didn't realise how big this was going to be. He didn't want to see Bristol City go under because the players were his responsibility. Some people tried to split us but we stayed close … After helping save York, I went to Hong Kong for a year. I needed the money. The interest rates had just gone up. My mortgage repayments were £50 per month higher. After I came back I worked at Rolls-Royce and played for Bath. I then worked alongside Tony Pulis at Gillingham before becoming a postman. Then I went to work with Bristol Rovers, my first club.*

Trevor Tainton said:

> *I had been at the club 20 years, playing around 400 games. I had signed a contract and had been expecting that it would be honoured. Family members and friends kept telling me to stick it out. 'Someone will come in and save the club', they said. I had been Bristol born and bred. Playing for my home club was special. So, leaving was a wrench. I've still a lot of feelings for the club … I went to Torquay for a couple of months but they didn't have any money either, so they had to let me go. I'd always enjoyed playing so I continued to do so at Trowbridge. I wasn't interested in managing or coaching so I became a security officer, first at Patchway then at Oldbury Power Station. The money we got from the club wasn't outstanding but I recognise that people are in and out of jobs all the time. Life goes on.*

David Rodgers was equally philosophical. He said:

> *There was a lot of flak from the supporters. It wasn't personal, though. People would stop you when you were out shopping and ask what was happening. However, the attention we received from the press and public wasn't as intrusive as it is today. It happened so quickly. It is debatable whether the PFA did their job or whether we should have called the club's bluff. I had been at City for 14 years. I played briefly at Torquay. They couldn't afford another player. So I took a huge cut in pay to play at Lincoln for a couple of months. Then I returned home. My wife was working. I had to find something, too. I eventually got work at Bristol Grammar School, then Clifton College where I became a housemaster. Looking back, although we were sad and bitter at the time, why should we have had more consideration than anyone else, like those laid off at Aerospace, for example?*

Julian Marshall remembered:

> *I had just signed a two-and-a-half-year contract. I didn't expect it to be torn up. Although I kept away from the city, my girlfriend worked there and picked up a lot of the gossip. World in Action did a TV documentary about the club's plight. It was then that I realised how big this story was. It would have been a good time to have had an agent to help us but we had to help ourselves and one another. Apart from organising the Southampton–Ipswich game, which was a wonderful gesture by those clubs, Bristol City did not offer any support. I wasn't even allowed to train with the club after our contracts were ended. So in order to keep fit, I had to train on my own because I was still hopeful of getting another club. I was then only in my mid-twenties. I had a short-term contract with Blackburn as Bobby Saxton was looking for cover at centre-back. I was very grateful for the offer but it was a big wrench*

leaving Bristol. Although I went to Walsall for a while it wasn't a happy time so I decided to start a different career in financial advice. I'd always been interested in money matters – stocks and shares and so on. Now I have my own business.

As at Swansea, Bristol City suffered on account of the club's unsustainable ambition and imprudent stewardship. During the fifties and early sixties, aspiring underdogs, such as Ipswich, Dundee or Burnley, could scale football's summit without paying the earth. But even by the mid-sixties this had become much more difficult, as Northampton found. By the early seventies, Carlisle and Burnley found their modest means were insufficient to secure their survival in the top flight, let alone achieve success. Indeed, by the eighties, it had become almost impossible for a small club to emulate Ipswich's achievement of 1962, notwithstanding Wimbledon's, Luton's and Watford's outstanding efforts. For those without significant resources, a dream triumph, at least on Ipswich's scale, was usually just that. To try to live that dream carried a huge risk of ruinous collapse, as Swansea found. In more recent times, Ipswich Town, Bradford City and Portsmouth have all failed to heed that lesson. Although Brighton exercised greater prudence in attempting to stay at the top table, they, too, suffered financially on account of their 'seasons in the sun'. Even when a small club attracted the patronage of a major 'benefactor', as Oxford United did briefly, the 'Icarus' risk was certainly no less. At Swansea, Bristol, Oxford and, more recently, at Brighton, catastrophic collapse has only been averted by the brave, unstinting efforts of their supporters, whether they happened to be owners, staff or simply fans. BBC commentator and City fan, Jonathan Pearce, was right to acknowledge the legacy of the Ashton Gate Eight in Bristol City's survival. He said: 'People should never forget in this city that without those eight players there would not be a Bristol City Football Club here today. I don't think they've ever been given due recognition.' At a time when players are castigated for their wanton selfishness, it is worth remembering the loyalty shown by these eight men and the price they paid for it.

Put out more flags: the Falklands factor

Once again the shadow of the bomb spread its chilly presence over the land. US–Soviet relations became increasingly hawkish and edgy. When the USSR moved its SS-20 rockets into Eastern Europe, Reagan reacted by shipping his Cruise missiles across the Atlantic. Mrs Thatcher liked Ronnie

Reagan. He shared her trust in a free market ideology and her abhorrence of communism. Our 'Iron Lady' traded in smug folksy virtues, too, while taking a hard line with her political opponents at home and abroad. She had an equally pitiless view of how her policies affected the disadvantaged and the dispossessed.

At her behest, Britain became the first NATO country to accept Cruise missiles. She seemed unconcerned about the public protests which came thick and fast. These culminated in a 400,000-strong protest rally in Hyde Park. Meanwhile, the Greenham Common women maintained a state of constant vigil. Fears of mutually assured destruction began to infiltrate popular culture. In 1981 the BBC revived a dramatic version of John Wyndham's apocalyptic novel, *Day of the Triffids*. In 1982 Raymond Briggs published his mocking tale, *When the Wind Blows*. Messages about 'what to do in the event of nuclear conflagration' featured in TV shows as widely ranging as *Only Fools and Horses*, *Juliet Bravo* and *The Young Ones*. Meanwhile the adult comic *Viz* ran a feature on how to 'Improve Your Golf after the Bomb'.

But when it came to the crunch, the nation was deeply ambivalent about war, at least the conventional kind. It wasn't just the Argentineans who were susceptible to a shot of jingoism to distract them from their troubles at home. Despite Botham's heroics and our European Cup successes, many of us believed our country was 'going to the dogs'. Even one of Mrs Thatcher's Cabinet ministers said as much. In 1981, 'Wet' Ian Gilmour announced: 'Company profits fell by 20 per cent during 1980, output fell by nearly six per cent, manufacturing output fell by 15 per cent and unemployment rose from 1.3 million to over two million.' Actually, the jobless total wouldn't stop there, reaching three million by 1983.

Mrs Thatcher's popularity fell to 25 per cent, the lowest satisfaction rating with any British prime minister. And yet she seemed unchallengeable. The opposition was useless. Labour was riven by internecine squabbling as doctrinaire left-wingers insisted upon political agendas few would buy. As for the new party at the centre, the Social Democratic Party (SDP), it appealed only to footloose privileged types with prickling consciences. Despite the efforts of the estimable Shirley Williams, the party seemed unable to rid itself of an image of suave wealth.

It was no surprise that the eighties should have spawned a growth in self-help and direct action groups. Frustrated by the perceived restrictions in the democratic process, many campaigning and protest groups emerged or strengthened. Some were anti-discriminatory. Others were concerned with special needs, such as the Alzheimer's Society. Certain environmental, animal rights and nuclear disarmament groups were prepared to make their presence felt forcibly, and in some cases violently. With the opposition parties so weak, the allure of direct action grew.

Popular culture charted the malaise felt among the hard-up and the oppressed. We had the chirpy duckers and divers in *Only Fools and Horses.* We had the cheery strength of kith and kin in *Bread.* We had the solidarity of mates working abroad in *Auf Wiedersehen, Pet.* But we also had the abject despair of *Boys from the Blackstuff.*

Then came the news of the Argentinean invasion of the Falkland Islands. 'We're a Third World country, no good for anything', wrote the despairing MP, Alan Clark. There was no place for hand-wringing, though, as Mrs Thatcher ordered a direct military response. Some sneered but more cheered. It wasn't just the 'Ere we go' pub jingoists who became excited. Reminded painfully of the sins of past dictators, a bellicose Michael Foot lent his support to the government. Yet, was our support of armed action principally motivated by protective instincts or by a desire for a supposedly restorative military victory? Was this the growl of a cornered underdog, albeit one clad in threadbare imperial finery? Was the British Empire trying to strike back? Like a latter day Palmerston, Mrs Thatcher sent her task force cruising. The *Sun* played cleverly upon the basest of terrace tribal instincts, printing T-shirts bearing the slogans 'Stick it up your Junta' and 'Buenos Aires is full of fairies'. After the *Sun*'s controversial 'Gotcha' headline, *Private Eye* was moved to lampoon its crassness with a spoof invitation: 'Kill an Argie and win a Metro'. Of course, Mrs Thatcher took an almighty risk. Had the task force failed, her political prospects would have sunk quicker than the *General Belgrano.* But thanks to acts of outstanding bravery and flawed enemy fuse timings, the task force prevailed – just. No wonder Mrs Thatcher was exultant. 'Rejoice' she exclaimed once victory was assured. Many of us considered she had put the 'Great' back into Great Britain.

The Falklands victory came just before the start of the 1982 World Cup finals in Spain. Ron Greenwood's boys had squeezed in. Large contingents of England fans yomped aggressively around northern Spain like a ragged, xenophobic army of occupation. It did not take them long to face heavy reprisals from the outraged locals. Andrew Ward and John Williams quoted some of the England fans' angry protests in their book, *Football Nation.* 'There's all this Las Malvinas stuff going about,' said one. Another exploded: 'These f***in' barbarians don't have the British sense of fairness.' To which, his mate added: 'For f***'s sake, we *invented* fairness.' The Falklands victory did a lot for Margaret Thatcher, catapulting her to further electoral success. But the doughty Churchillian spirit, which she sought to evoke with 'Yet we fought alone', had resonance among those she angrily disowned. Much to her dismay, the unruly England fans fought battles of their own abroad that summer. They, too, flew the flag. But their patriotism was of a snarling, stunted kind. A West Ham hard man explained to Ward and Williams: 'When you boil down to it, the British are a violent people … we've always been outnumbered by whoever we fought, whether we've fought in India, the Germans, whatever.' He spoke for the rabidly savage strain of British underdog, one which sees threats all around, bragging rights to be scrapped for, real or imagined scores to be settled, beatings to be avenged. *Grrrrr!*

THE 1986/87 SEASON

'They came to bury Burnley ...': a near-death experience

It shouldn't have happened. On 18 May 1982, in front of almost 19,000 fans, Burnley were on the brink of seizing the Third Division title. The club's years of decline had been arrested. With a team boasting the last bumper crop of home-grown talent, including Brian Laws, Trevor Steven, Mike Phelan and Vince Overson, there were hopes of further glory. The average gate was up to almost 7,000 and despite the intense disappointment of an immediate relegation, successful FA Cup and Milk Cup runs netted substantial revenue. With the average gate also lifted by a further 2,000, the club was solvent once more. Trevor Steven's transfer to Everton in the summer of '83 brought in a further £300,000. And then it all went horribly wrong.

Breaking with a club tradition of keeping it within the family, John Bond was chosen as the new Burnley boss before the start of the 1983/84 season. In an effort to restore Burnley's fortunes quickly, he made sudden and expensive changes. As a former member of West Ham's academy, the 'Cassettari café society', he came with innovative ideas about how the game should be played – at least, that was the view of the home-grown Burnley midfielder, Derek Scott. The trouble was, Bond proved too impulsive, too eager to sweep the decks clean after the relegation woes of the previous season. Out went young talent including Brian Laws, Kevin Young and Lee Dixon, all on relatively low salaries, and in came a wave of ageing 'stars' on contracts which cost the club two or three times as much. Around £100,000 was added to the wage bill at a stroke. Had Bond achieved an instant return to the Second Division, all might have been well, but a tragic injury to striker Kevin Reeves knocked those hopes on the head. As for midfielder Gerry Gow and centre-half Joe Gallagher, their knees had gone even before their arrival. Having brought in former First Division players such as Reeves, Gow, Gallagher, Tommy Hutchison, Dennis Tueart and Steve Daley, Bond required the club to draw average gates of 13,600 in order to break even.

The reality was that, during the 1983/84 season, the average home gate was less than half that number.

On the rueful admission of one of its former directors, the Burnley board did not exercise sufficient control over Bond's spending. In a situation requiring more checks and balances, there were too many cheques and too little balance. Burnley were in serious trouble. Under pressure from their bank, the remaining family silver was shed in a fire sale. Out went Northern Irish centre-forward Billy Hamilton (for £80,000), centre back Vince Overson (for £25,000), centre back or midfielder Mike Phelan (for £70,000) and striker Wayne Biggins (for £40,000). The transfer receipts did not reflect their worth. For example, Norwich received ten times as much for Phelan when he was sold on to Manchester United in 1989. As a result of the austerity measures, the club dropped like a stone. Not even the Fourth Division seemed to arrest its fall.

At the beginning of the 1986/87 season, Burnley's situation was so dire that the board decided that it was time to call upon their 'honest and valued retainer' once again. Brian Miller had been sacked as manager on his birthday in 1983, just before a stirring League Cup triumph at Spurs. He might have been forgiven for refusing the club's call. But when chairman Frank Teasdale came to his newsagent shop in 1986 desperate for his assistance, it wasn't in Brian's nature to refuse. When all's said and done, this was the club he had loved from childhood. He was steeped in its illustrious history, having helped make it, playing alongside the likes of Jimmy McIlroy and Jimmy Adamson.

Miller's normally calm but quietly determined personality would be tested to the limit by the task he was given. He was left with a squad of just 13 players. The reserve side had already been axed. His club was allegedly £800,000 in debt and losing £10,000 per week. The future existence of the once proud Burnley FC rested upon the efforts of a team comprising the halted, the lame, the grey and the green – the green being Phil Devaney, the 18-year-old YTS lad who played up front for £25 per week. Just 25 years earlier, Burnley had competed admirably in the European Cup. Now, their non-league neighbours, Colne Dynamos, seemed a better prospect.

On 24 January, languishing Hereford United came to Turf Moor and, in front of 1,955 diehard or already dead fans, won heavily. The Red Rose Radio reporter at the game told local listeners: '… and the crowd is gathered outside the offices right now and they're chanting "rubbish" and "we want football". Well I can't say anything which would add to Burnley's misery. The players know it. The management know it. And all I can do is repeat that sad, final score of Burnley 0 Hereford 6.'

On 9 May 1987, Burnley played Orient. In order to protect their Football League status and, perhaps, also the club's future existence, Brian Miller's team needed to win and hope that other results went their way. Orient also needed to win to grasp a play-off place. The day began grey and misty but warm sunlight soon pierced the murk, leaving an unblemished blue sky. It seemed like a day to tantalise the condemned. And yet in front of a 15,696 crowd – 13,000 more than the club's average gate – Burnley scrapped for their lives, scraping a 2-1 victory. The tension was so unbearable that some supporters were forced to leave the ground prematurely and pace anxiously up and down outside, like expectant fathers. Here, they had to surf the waves of sound from within, attempting to interpret the unseen course of events. But with Swansea defeating Lincoln, it was the Imps, not the Clarets, who became the first Football League club to be automatically demoted to the Conference. The Turf Moor pitch became engulfed by excited young people. A shambolic conga began. Meanwhile, up in the stands, strangers clasped one another in tearful relief. A television camera seized upon a middle-aged woman helplessly consumed by gulping sobs. A near-death experience usually brings a family closer together. This is what happened here. As Joni Mitchell sang in *Big Yellow Taxi*, 'you don't know what you've got til it's gone'. Realising that something precious had nearly been snatched away, the prodigal supporters began to return. Burnley's gates doubled in the following season and, after a euphoric trip to Wembley 12 months later for the Sherpa Van Final (81,000 fans attended), the interest continued to grow. The TSB recovered its ability to say 'yes'. By the narrowest of margins, Burnley were saved from oblivion.

'RISE' 1987–2010

'I'm movin' on up now, gettin' out of the darkness . . . '
Robert Young, Andrew Innes, Bobby Gillespie
(Primal Scream, Sony Music)

'Movin' On Up' on the album *Screamadelica*,
(1991 Sony Music)

THE 1987/88 SEASON

Wimbledon v Liverpool (FA Cup Final)

'Perfect'
14 May 1988

Wimbledon were elected to the Football League at the third time of asking in June 1977. Successive Southern League championships helped their cause. So did a courageous losing battle with First Division Middlesbrough in a third-round FA Cup tie played in January of that year. But, arguably, the tipping point came with new chairman Ron Noades' well-presented and persuasive PR campaign. Three thousand pounds was invested in getting his 'Dons 4 Div 4' message across. The ambitious and energetic Noades orchestrated a relentless push for votes. While Lord Faulkner ably managed the media side of the campaign, Noades pulled off a major publicity coup by enlisting the help of England cricket captain, Tony Greig. However, team manager, Allen Batsford, had his doubts. He knew the club was hard-up. Wimbledon's little Plough Lane ground would need around £19,000 worth of improvements if it was to meet Football League standards. The first-team squad, still mostly part-timers, needed strengthening. Participation in a nationwide league meant higher overheads. Batsford later told Niall Couper, author of the splendid *The Spirit of Wimbledon*: 'I was full of mixed emotions … I remained apprehensive: we weren't in the right shape to make the transition but we had to take our chance … but my abiding memory of that [election] afternoon was the Workington people. They were devastated. Their whole world had been taken away from them and it was our fault.'

After the euphoria of Wimbledon's promotion, their opening Football League game, at home against perennial strugglers Halifax, brought them down to earth. Although goals from Bryant, Leslie and Connell were sufficient to secure a 3-3 draw, no one was impressed, least of all Allen Batsford. He called it 'a disgraceful performance'. Alan Ball senior, then manager of Halifax, agreed, suggesting: '[Wimbledon] won't set Division Four alight'. Both managers were right. Wimbledon struggled. It took them another six games to notch their first win.

Batsford complained that Noades made his job impossible, citing Noades' alleged unwillingness to pay players' expenses for attending training sessions. Batsford maintained that Noades interfered with his scouting arrangements, too. Then there were the difficulties between Batsford and his assistant manager, Dario Gradi, whom Noades had appointed. Batsford complained that Gradi wouldn't help him with first-team coaching, whereas Gradi felt that he was being sidelined by Batsford. The ill feeling reached a peak on Boxing Day 1977. Wimbledon were playing at Rochdale, and according to Batsford, Noades refused to pay for a coach, insisting that the players use their own transport. Wimbledon lost. After another shambolic defeat, this time at Swansea, Batsford left his post. He complained that Noades' constant interference created chaos. Given what Batsford had achieved in three years, it was a sad departure. However, with the club struggling to make or pay its way, Noades seemed to be in a difficult position.

Ron Noades first asked Dave Bassett if he would replace Batsford but Bassett refused, so the job was offered to Dario Gradi. Noades was deeply worried. His club was perched just above the re-election places. He reckoned he had made enemies when campaigning for the Dons' inclusion in the Football League. He thought Wimbledon might not survive a re-election vote. Noades told Gradi, 'Whatever you do, just make sure we don't finish in the bottom four.' In turn, Gradi told Noades he needed £20,000 for reinforcements – younger ones at that, because his was an ageing side. Gradi also insisted that the club be put on a full-time professional footing. Only the veteran stopper, Dave Donaldson, was exempted.

Dario Gradi had previously been a youth, reserve and first-team coach at Chelsea. He had also spent a short time managing nearby Sutton United before becoming Colin Murphy's assistant manager at Derby. He used his past connections to good effect. He persuaded the new Derby manager, Tommy Docherty, to release Alan Cork and Steve Ketteridge. Gradi employed the bustling Cork as a foraging forward. He also persuaded Chelsea to part with youngsters Steve Perkins, Glyn Hodges and Paul Fishenden, on free transfers. Millwall's reserve goalie, Ray Goddard, was bought for £4,500 to replace Dickie Guy, who had become less reliable. And another former Chelsea youngster, Les Briley, was snaffled from Hereford for a record £16,000 fee. His dynamic presence did much to bolster the midfield in the latter half of the season. However, Gradi was astute enough to retain a core of five or six experienced players who had taken the club this far. He was keen to preserve the 'old Wimbledon spirit', which he hoped his youngsters would feed off.

Gradi's recipe worked like a dream. Helped by his various changes, Wimbledon's form improved dramatically as they won ten and drew six of their final 21 league games, rising to a respectable 13th position. The returning Roger Connell rediscovered his striking powers, too, netting 11 times in the final 18 fixtures.

For the following season, Gradi chose the ultra-competitive Bassett as his assistant. Bassett's playing days were almost over, but Gradi realised he was too much of an asset for the club to lose. It was a winning combination. Their youngsters seized the third promotion slot in May 1979, behind Reading and Grimsby, with Alan Cork and John Leslie scoring 41 league goals between them – with 22 coming from Cork. Not even a traumatic 8-0 defeat at Everton in the League Cup could hold them back. Gradi continued to develop his squad, shelling out a record £45,000 fee for QPR and former Chelsea defender, Tommy Cunningham, to replace Donaldson. Yet another youth team product, 17-year-old Wally Downes, a nephew of the former world middleweight champion boxer, Terry, made his mark in only his second game. His goal in a 1-1 draw at Barnsley confirmed Wimbledon's promotion to Division Three. Alas, the promotion proved to be too much, too soon as the Dons were relegated immediately. Remarkably, the club bounced back straightaway, winning promotion once again in May 1981. Cork and Leslie continued to provide the firepower but now Dave 'Lurch' Beasant was the main man between the sticks. More remarkably, the club had sustained the promotion drive while rumours were circulating about an impending merger with neighbouring Crystal Palace.

The rumours intensified after Wimbledon's chairman, Ron Noades, bought Palace midway through the 1980/81 season. While Noades was insistent that Dario Gradi should join him as his new team's manager, the merger proposal was dropped in the face of strong supporters' protests. Following Gradi's move to Palace in February 1981, Dave Bassett took over as Wimbledon's new manager. He wasted little time in putting his team on the right track. When he took over Wimbledon were in 12th place, but by the end of the season they had seized the final promotion slot. Bassett attributed the team's success to the adoption of a more direct style of play.

Kevin Gage, at only 17 years old, became the youngest player to represent Wimbledon when he was selected to face Bury in the final game of the 1980/81 promotion season. He believed that while Gradi made the club a professional unit, 'Harry' [Dave Bassett] reinstalled the spirit of the club. 'People like Glyn Hodges, Mark Morris and me just lapped it up,' he told Niall Couper. 'All your mates were there and you could have a laugh. It was like playing for a really good pub team. Most of us had grown up together and created a bond that was to see us through the next five years.' Kevin recognised, though, that there needed to be professional discipline as well as fun.

But once again, Wimbledon stumbled in the higher league. It took them 12 league and cup games to record their first victory. By the year's end, with the country caked in ice and snow, they were rock bottom and nine points adrift of safety. A New Year revival was halted abruptly by successive heavy defeats at Fulham and Gillingham. Their plight was hardly helped by the loss of Cork as the result of a broken leg. He would be sidelined for a season and a half; medical treatment in the eighties was still fairly rudimentary. Bassett never lost faith in his youngsters, though. With eight games left they finally found their feet. Six victories in late April and May almost saved their bacon. Frustratingly, only goal difference denied them. But this late, hot streak would provide the momentum for an astonishing assault on the summit. Within four years Wimbledon would be playing in Division One.

Wimbledon's relegation woes paled into insignificance, though, after it became known that their former England full-back, Dave Clement, had ended his life. Clement had become deeply depressed following a serious leg fracture. Tragically, he saw no future for himself either inside or outside football.

Continuing their wild yo-yoing form, Wimbledon lifted the Fourth Division championship trophy one year later, having recorded 29 victories, scored 96 goals and accumulated 98 points. In the continued absence of Cork, John Leslie stepped up to the plate, netting a quarter of the Dons' 96 goals with the giant, former Sheffield United centre-forward, Stewart Evans, adding 14. But an average gate of 2,500 was worrying. The recession was partly to blame, so was fierce local competition – nearby Crystal Palace, Chelsea and Queens Park Rangers offered First or Second Division football. But some felt that Wimbledon's style of play didn't help, either. There was a view that Bassett's team had learnt to 'win ugly'. Bassett refuted the charge, maintaining that his team provided more goalmouth action than most other teams.

Ten years later, Bassett qualified his bleak pragmatism in discussion with Rogan Taylor and Andrew Ward, authors of *Kicking and Screaming*. He said:

> *There's a lot of claptrap talked about the direct style. Some people say that you just welly the ball down the field and get goals. Well, it's not quite like that. A lot of thought went into what we did, believe it or not. At Wimbledon we felt that we wanted to get the ball into their half of*

the field where we could get good crossing positions or good shooting positions or situations where we could pass a ball which resulted in a shot at goal. It amazed me how people reacted, but I think a lot of it was jealousy because Wimbledon came through the divisions … I think a lot of teams tried to pick up things that Wimbledon have done. We see that most goalkeepers dribble out of the box now … that was something that Wimbledon did before anybody else.

Wimbledon were developing a reputation for being a physically intimidating side, determined to win at all costs. Rough tackling and time-wasting were said to feature strongly in their play. Not that these carping criticisms dented the team's jubilant mood as they sprinted to the Fourth Division title. Dons' captain, Gary Peters, a future manager at Preston, Exeter and Shrewsbury, remembered the raucous train journey home after winning their final game at Bury in May '83. He told Niall Couper, 'Harry was supposed to get off at Watford [to meet his wife] but we wouldn't let him. We kept him on the train to Euston and left him stark-bollock naked at the station … We must have been the only Football League club to have ten players in the bar at midnight after a home game.'

The 1983/84 season followed on seamlessly from the one before. At the beginning of October Wimbledon were in fifth place, having won four and drawn two of their opening eight fixtures. Cork celebrated his return to first-team action with a hat-trick in the club's record 6-0 win over Newport on 3 September. The Dons then went on to dump Clough's Forest out of the League Cup, 3-1 on aggregate. Unfortunately, Third Division Rotherham halted their impressive cup run. But a 100 per cent return from their four festive games took Wimbledon up to fourth position, level on points with third-placed Sheffield United, whom they defeated 3-1, at home, in the New Year game. Crucially, Wimbledon also won a feisty game at Bramall Lane in May, with ex-Blade Stewart Evans ramming home a recriminatory goal. Once again, Wimbledon produced an impressive acceleration to the line – eight victories were recorded in their final 11 games. This run saw them promoted in spring 1984 behind Maxwell's Oxford United. Cork's return to fitness made a huge difference as he put away 29 goals, supported by Glyn Hodges, who added 15 from midfield. Hodges had cause to remember this season with pride as he became the first Wimbledon player to represent his country, having made his senior Welsh debut in a friendly game with Norway in Trondheim.

It came as a huge shock when Dave Bassett took off for Selhurst Park after winning promotion to the Second Division. Within three days he was back, though, saying, 'I loved Wimbledon too much and I knew I still had a job to do.' A further plus was the average gate figure – up by almost 1,000. But the club's detractors were not silenced. After Wimbledon had beaten Chris Cattlin's Brighton, the *Evening Argus* reporter, John Vinicombe, was moved to write: '[Wimbledon] are a poor man's Watford when four front men adopt a cavalry charge formation in pursuit of high passes slung from behind.'

Wimbledon's first season in Division Two was a bit of a roller coaster. There were successive 5-0 thumpings of Crystal Palace and Sheffield United. But these emphatic victories were counterbalanced by diabolical defeats at Carlisle (1-6), Leeds (2-5) and at Second Division champions-elect, Oxford (0-4). However, their final position of 12th was satisfying. Lawrie Sanchez had strengthened the Dons' midfield following his £20,000 transfer from Reading in November 1984. Andy Sayer was another successful addition to the side during their typically strong finish to the season. After the slaughter at Carlisle, Wimbledon only lost one of their remaining 12 fixtures. Although the goal and victory count were down, the local fan base obviously approved, as the average gate rose by almost another thousand to 4,424. But this figure still remained well short of Plough Lane's capacity, which was listed at 13,500.

After scoring a hat-trick in the 5-0 victory at Palace, Fishenden treated his marker, Jim Cannon, to a volley of post-match 'verbals'. But Fishenden later found himself on the receiving end when his team-mates strapped him to the top of a Transit van and drove him down the A3 as far as the M25 and back again – a 30-mile round trip. According to *Daily Mirror* journalist Tony Stenson, who first dubbed the Wimbledon team as the 'Crazy Gang', 'No one batted an eyelid' at this incredibly dangerous escapade. 'It was just one big laugh for them', Stenson said.

For the historic 1985/86 season, the fiery midfielder, Ian Holloway, was enticed to Plough Lane after Bassett had agreed a £35,000 fee with 'Ollie's' home-city club, Bristol Rovers. Former Southampton apprentice Dennis Wise also emerged from the reserves, as did a tall local defender named Andy Thorn, who made his league debut in the opening day's 3-0 victory over cash-strapped Middlesbrough. In front of a pitifully small crowd of 2,844, Evans, Gage and Sanchez were on target. Despite losing 0-4 at Bramall Lane on 24 August, Wimbledon started the season strongly. A 0-0 home draw with Oldham on 7 September was sufficient to nudge them into second place. But still only 2,749 turned up. Although Blackburn were hammered 5-0 at home in the second round of the Milk Cup, with Cork scoring a hat-trick, goals were hard to come by. In Wimbledon's first 16 league games they managed to score just 13 times. But by virtue of maintaining an 'iron curtain' defence – only seven goals were conceded in that run – they managed to rack up seven victories and four draws, putting themselves into fourth place by the end of October 1985.

Although visiting Carlisle were beaten 4-1 at the beginning of November, successive defeats by Leeds (0-3) and Middlesbrough (0-1) reduced them to seventh spot. A topsy-turvy period ensued but the Dons' 1-0 defeat at Oldham on 11 January was their last of the season. Wimbledon won nine and drew seven of their remaining 16 fixtures, with clean sheets kept in eight of these.

Bassett brought in former Tooting & Mitcham striker Carlton Fairweather in place of Stewart Evans during the run-in. Five of Fairweather's six goals netted his club eight points, helping see off Portsmouth's challenge in the promotion race. Bassett also persuaded the chairman, Sam Hammam, to part with £125,000 for Millwall's gangling and aggressive 6ft 3in centre-forward, John Fashanu. It was a club record fee but Fashanu proved to be excellent value. Bassett believed that Fashanu had the greater strength to upset opposing defenders. The black striker had shown how he could pull his markers around, creating opportunities for himself and others. Finally, Bassett restored Mark Morris to the defence. Morris made an already mean Wimbledon defence even tighter – only nine goals were conceded in those final 16 games.

John Fashanu was known as 'Fash the Bash' at Millwall. The nickname was apt. By his own admission he took few prisoners. He made his debut in the vital promotion clash with Portsmouth at Fratton Park on 29 March 1986 which ended 1-1. Pompey were then in second position with Wimbledon one place behind. In front of an almost capacity 18,859 crowd, Fashanu steamed into the torrid action. He told Niall Couper:

> *After every tackle there was a punch-up. I was having a non-stop battle with [Portsmouth centre-half] Noel Blake and their goalkeeper [Alan Knight]. It was never-ending. Everything was going on off the ball. The referee just took the attitude to ignore it all. The players couldn't believe it; my style was new to them. But at the end, Sanch, Corky and everyone were right there steaming in. I had cut eyes and bruises everywhere. I can't remember the score – I am not even sure if I touched the ball, but it was a great battle. The lads immediately accepted me.*

I first saw John Fashanu play 'in the flesh' in September 1992 – in the very early days of the Premiership. Wimbledon were playing an expensively-recruited Blackburn Rovers side, which included the best centre-forward of his generation, Alan Shearer. Blackburn were bankrolled by Jack Walker's millions, managed by Kenny Dalglish and destined shortly for a Premiership title. By this time, Wimbledon had ceased to play at Plough Lane and were sharing Selhurst Park. Previous home games had been watched by bulging crowds of 3,800 or less. Although a bumper 6,117 crowd attended the Blackburn game, there were vast sections of Selhurst Park cordoned off as redundant space.

The belligerence of the game seemed out of place, as if the Ali–Foreman 'Rumble in the Jungle' had been staged for a local gardening club. Not that these guys needed a baying crowd to fire them up. Vinnie Jones played the pantomime villain, a scowling, muscular big hitter, hissing with aggression, intent on battering Blackburn's ball players. Fashanu's hostility seemed less combustible. I do not recall him acting like the brute he had made himself out to be, despite the bad press he received for his later infamous clashes with Gary Mabbutt and Viv Anderson. What I saw over several performances was a tough competitor, prepared to give as good as he got, but not a roving assassin who had to knock seven bells out of his opponents to prove his physical supremacy. Perhaps I had been watching 'Fashanu – the sanitised version', but to me he played with a cool, breezy confidence as if he had nothing to prove.

It was John Fashanu's strength which first impressed me, even more than his towering height. He would persistently show for the ball at the edge of the box, and although hemmed in by big, bruising defenders, he had a knack of making space for himself. Playing with his socks bunched around his ankles, but his shin guards still in place, he seemed totally unconcerned by the knocks he took. Once he had decided the patch he would hold, he would plant his studs unshakeably into position, as if thrusting giant stabilising stakes into the Selhurst soil. Centre-backs would try to jostle him this way and that by wrapping their arms around his elongated frame or tugging at his drooping arms. He was not bothered. He seemed able to shrug them off at will, as if they were tiresome pets. It wasn't just his thighs and calves which were so powerful – he had immense upper-body strength as well. With his back to goal and the ball at his feet, he would embark upon a one-man rolling maul, using his backside as a battering ram. His rhythmic jigging of the shoulders, while calmly shielding the ball from the snapping snafflers, suggested that he was in some hip world of his own; perhaps wired for sound from an unseen personal stereo. I had never seen such cool aggression.

I cannot remember watching many better target men, or anyone who was as fearsomely effective in the air. With his aerial dominance there weren't too many high balls, struck or flung into his zone, which he couldn't reach. Besides, if a ball, pumped high into the box, did manage to elude him, his heaving, buffeting aerial challenges were often sufficient to wrong-foot his opponents, prompting unforced errors which he or others could capitalise upon. 'Harry' certainly knew what he was getting with 'Fash the Bash'. Apart from the masses of chances he created for others, he went on to score 107 league goals in his 287 games for the Dons over an eight-year stay. Alan Cork surpassed that record with 145 league goals in 430 appearances, but almost all of Fash's goals were in the top flight. He was also capped for England. That £125,000 fee was some snip!

John Fashanu had graduated from the school of hard knocks. He and his older brother, Justin, were brought up 'in care' from an early age. Although they were fortunate to have had a stable foster home, John's entry into professional football was particularly tough, but he proved quickly he was made of the right stuff. In a reply to a *Four Four Two* reader's question he recalled:

> *I came down to Millwall with Lincoln City once and bashed the hell out of their defence, so after the match I had to get a police escort to take me from the changing rooms to the coach. The Millwall fans were shouting, 'Nigger, black bastard, we'll kill you', and throwing cups of urine at me. I remember seeing the hate and the venom in their faces as we drove off. Then I signed for them shortly afterwards and the fans loved me. I think they respected me because I played football the way some of them lived their lives. It was the Millwall fans who christened me 'Fash the Bash'.*

When he arrived at Wimbledon he knew all about their initiation ceremonies but thought he could ward off the pranksters with his self-styled 'Fash stare'. John had been a boxer. But that didn't deter Wally Downes. Downes had a former world middleweight champion in his family. John told Niall Couper: '[Wally] filled my tea with salt and tried to burn my socks, my favourite silk socks. We had a bit of a confrontation after that, nothing too serious: that was left for Lawrie Sanchez …'

Daily Mirror journalist Tony Stenson recalled: 'The battle between John Fashanu and Lawrie Sanchez was probably the most famous fight ever to happen at the club. Fights were common at Wimbledon. They always had been. Harry encouraged them.' John Fashanu added: 'We had an agreement at Wimbledon that we would never stop a fight if it started. You can join in, but you can't stop it … But that was Wimbledon and I loved it.' Tony Stenson remembered one occasion when even Sam Hammam reprimanded one of his players, Terry Gibson, for breaking up a team scrap, giving Gibson a slap for good measure. This was a different land.

As for the clash with Lawrie Sanchez, Tony Stenson's version of events was that Sanchez resented the 'new boy,' Fashanu, calling the shots. Being 'one of the strongest players, mentally, you will ever meet', Lawrie Sanchez refused to comply with Fashanu's instructions. John's version of events as told to *Four Four Two* magazine was:

> *I don't like Sanch and he doesn't like me. Hate is a strong word, but we tend to disagree. Anyway, Sanch and I had a disagreement in training. I told the boys, 'I'm taking training this morning – everybody start jogging'. Sanch saw it in his wisdom not to comply and when I pointed my finger at him he went to slap me … So I said, 'Listen, this has been going on too long. We're two men, let's sort it out, let's take a walk. Lads, you carry on jogging …' It was like something out of a film: two people who don't like each other, and now they're going to fight. Anyway, Sanch gave me a shot and, give him credit, it wasn't a bad shot. But I thought, don't hit Sanch, don't mark his face, and my mind went back to when Muhammad Ali fought against the martial artist in New York, and the martial artist just kicked the back of his legs until it broke the tissues in his calves and he submitted. So I thought I'd teach Sanch a lesson and gave a sweep of the legs, but Sanch has calves like most people have thighs and he didn't move. So I gave him another couple, but Sanch came back at me. So I thought, 'I'm gonna take this guy out', and I hit him with one of the best shots I'd been training with – BAM! Take that, Sanch! – right in the solar plexus, a shot that would supposedly knock a horse down. And still he stood there. Then Terry Burton came over to break us up.*

Lawrie Sanchez was a man for the big occasion. On 3 May 1986, it was his scorching free kick, in the Huddersfield rain, which gave Wimbledon the three points needed to reach Division One. What an incredible feat this was for the little club from south-west London. They were supported by less than 5,000 fans, had spent less than ten years in the Football League and had paid less than £250,000 for their players. It was small wonder that 'Harry' Bassett was touted as the 'manager of the season'. He had an intuitive grasp of how to prompt this tiny club to punch way, way above their weight. 'Punch' is perhaps an apposite description, for team spirit at Wimbledon was certainly not of the 'hearts and flowers' type.

Not that all of Harry's squad were sold on the Crazy Gang's antics. Ian Holloway's Wimbledon career lasted for just one year. Laid low by undetected glandular fever and preoccupied with the health of his Bristol-based girlfriend – she was being treated for cancer – 'Ollie' was not at his best at Plough Lane. His form, fitness and spirit suffered. He recalled in his autobiography, *Ollie*:

> *Harry was an open and honest bloke whom I really liked … [Geoff Taylor had] been with Harry for years and also worked with the kids a lot and he was probably the only person who showed me a little bit of sympathy regarding what was happening in my life at that time. Mick Smith and Lawrie Sanchez were different class, too, because they would do anything to help me and stayed out of the piss-taking and the wind-ups. I made other good friends in Kevin Gage, Glyn Hodges, Nigel Winterburn and Stevie Galliers, but the fact that I couldn't really socialise with the squad and get to know them better meant I was viewed as some kind of outsider. I wasn't a country bumpkin, but I thought some of their antics and humour went over the top … 'what's it like dating a baldy bird', was one of their comments …*
>
> *The one occasion I did go out with the lads, I realised not being out with them regularly was a bonus after one of them spiked my drinks. The next day I had to be brought off at half-time, but none of them told Harry why I was struggling and that it hadn't been my doing. There was definitely a bullying culture at the club and if you were*

> *on the receiving end, as I was quite often, you'd better have a thick skin otherwise they'd destroy you … Harry had a couple of chats with me about it, saying I was too honest and had to lighten up … Some of the things the lads did to each other, like cutting the bottom of your jeans pockets so your money falls through or cutting the crotch of your pants so when you pull them up they go right up to your chest, just didn't make me laugh … I would still think it childish at best … Lawrie Sanchez was on the end of a lot of Wally's wind-ups but he wasn't having any of it and just let it wash over him. He'd read a book, listen to music or concentrate on the successful wine bar he owned – he didn't give a toss what they thought.*

Lawrie Sanchez was very much his own man. He obtained a degree in management science at Loughborough University while playing at Reading and remained aloof from the anarchic antics of the Crazy Gang. He was no less committed to the cause, though.

Having reached the top flight, it was widely believed that Bassett's team would slink back into the shadows. Not so. An opening day defeat at Manchester City was overturned quickly with home wins over Aston Villa (3-2) and Leicester City (1-0). More remarkably, still, subsequent 1-0 away victories at Charlton and Watford put Wimbledon at the top of Division One in September 1986.

Midfielder Steve Galliers told Niall Couper: 'I had played in the club's first-ever League game and now we were on top of the whole thing. Roy of the Rovers would have struggled to write that script … We were under no illusions that we were going to win the League but we were keen to prove our critics wrong … Our strength was that we had all been together for so long. We had spent the early years slogging around Rochdale and Hartlepool, so we were going to make damn sure we enjoyed playing the likes of Manchester City and Tottenham.'

He added in an interview given for the Wimbledon v Manchester United programme in April 1999: 'Every time we went up a rung it was always, "that's as far as you will go", but what people didn't realise was that Harry had instilled a certain self-belief in us that made us realise that we had to take our opportunities. We never got into a situation where we were close to promotion and failed, we always made it at the first attempt as there was a feeling in the camp that it may never come around again.'

The 'long-ball' criticism from sections of the media also irked some of the players. 'We had a lot of talent in the side,' continued Galliers, 'and we were better players than people gave us credit for. When I scored in the win against Forest in the Milk Cup in 1983 we were still in the Third Division. It gave me a great deal of confidence and belief that we could compete against the top sides. From then on, the apprehension left us.'

After the win at Watford, things got harder – only two wins but eight defeats came in their next ten games, although the Dons did manage to overturn Spurs 2-1 on their own turf on 1 November. Their League Cup elimination by Fourth Division Cambridge United was an unpleasant surprise, too. 'Harry' realised he needed more bite in midfield, shelling out £15,000 for a non-league part-timer with a rough, tough reputation. Wealdstone's 'hard man', Vinnie Jones, made his home debut on 29 November against Manchester United, who had just appointed Alex Ferguson as their manager. Wimbledon were then in 13th position, four places above United. The game at Plough Lane did not improve Ferguson's sombre mood as his side slumped to a 1-0 defeat. Vinnie Jones was outstanding, ruggedly commanding the midfield, persistently breaking up United's forays and driving his new side forward. This prestigious victory restored the Dons' brio and they immediately followed it up with a 4-0 thrashing of Chelsea at Stamford Bridge. Glyn Hodges told Niall Couper:

> *You could sense when another club didn't fancy playing us. I've never felt that anywhere else. It happened a lot in the lower divisions. We used to dominate teams, intimidate them, bully them, but it hadn't happened against a top team. But that day [at Chelsea] you could feel it. They didn't want it … no one was going to get away with degrading us and we weren't going to give in. If someone dropped off there would be someone to pick him up and drive him on. Dave Bassett would wind us up. But we had a couple of leaders on the pitch. That's the way Harry wanted it. It all began with Gary Peters years before. He wouldn't take any crap and I had a few run-ins with him. If he thought I wasn't playing well he would tell me. He was a great captain. And then there was Wally [Downes]. He was another motivator and he took on Gary's role when he left … He had the drive and desire to win and that was instilled in all of us.*

Vinnie Jones added: 'What the fans like is firstly goals; secondly skills – good passing or a good header – and thirdly they want you to play the way they feel, with passion and a desire to win. I have been a supporter on the terraces looking down and saying, "how can they just stroll about?", "how can they not fancy it when they are on a stage like that?" A lot of players are like that, but a lot of players have had it too easy [Jones had previously been a hod-carrier]. They haven't seen the other side of it. They don't get the fans' view. I've always got that.'

By the end of February, Wimbledon were up to ninth place and into the sixth round of the FA Cup, having beaten league champions-elect, Everton, at Plough Lane (3-1). This fifth-round tie was covered live on TV and featured a starring display from a young Don, Andy Sayer. But the home supporters weren't just baying for Everton's blood, they were also incensed with their club chairman, Sam Hammam, who had recently reignited the Palace merger controversy.

From an entirely business perspective, Sam Hammam reasoned that the Plough Lane gates of around 7,800 were insufficient to support First Division football. Defender Mark Morris said, 'The lads were earning peanuts at the time. We were on about £180 a week.' Not only was this wage much lower than those paid in the top flight – Peter Ward was earning £600 per week at Brighton six years before – it was significantly below the rate paid at many lower-division clubs also. For example, three years before, Third Division Burnley were paying most of their first-team players around £300 per week, with a £200 win bonus on top. Even the Clarets' young reserve full-back, Lee Dixon, received a basic wage of £140 per week. Like Burnley had done years before, Wimbledon had to buy cheaply and sell big in order to survive.

Once again the merger ambitions were thwarted. Wimbledon's supporters might have been small in number, but just like their team, they were well organised and strongly determined. An apparently contrite Hammam undertook to work with the Wimbledon Independent Supporters' Association in an attempt to secure an alternative ground in the Wandle Valley. That objective was not achieved. Hammam blamed Merton Council. Others, such as journalist, Tony Stenson, blamed Hammam. Ultimately, Hammam signed a deal with Ron Noades for Wimbledon to ground-share at Selhurst Park in 1991. The club went into exile.

Once the merger had been brushed aside, Wimbledon completed their first season in Division One in style – racking up four consecutive victories. Wimbledon completed their debut season in Division One in sixth place – a hugely impressive feat. Manchester United, Chelsea and Sheffield Wednesday had been beaten twice. Although Spurs deprived them of an

FA Cup semi-final appearance by beating them 2-0 at Plough Lane in the sixth round, Wimbledon earned a further feather in their cap by defeating Liverpool 2-1 at Anfield two weeks later. Bassett had good reason to feel proud, having taken his club from the bottom division to within striking distance of the very summit. But this would be as far as Bassett would go with Wimbledon. Much to everyone's surprise, he left to take over at Watford, following Graham Taylor's departure for Aston Villa.

> 'Harry' spoke to Niall Couper about his decision.
> *It was very difficult. Part of me didn't want to go, but Sam and I had fallen out. My contract was up and I felt Sam wanted me to go. I think Sam felt I was too big for the club and he felt he wasn't getting enough credit … I think Sam had never really forgiven me for walking out and joining Crystal Palace for three days after we had won promotion to the Second Division … I had tears in my eyes. And I didn't really know what to tell the players. There was Nigel Winterburn … I knew he would go on to become a great player. Then there was Lawrie Sanchez, he was a great player … And then there was Vinnie Jones and John Fashanu. Those two were unique. But most of all there were the players who I had known for years and had been with me at the start – Dave Beasant, Kevin Gage, Glyn Hodges and Mark Morris. I didn't know what to say to them. They knew it was the end of an era … It was a homely club. There was the Nelson's nightclub where the fans and the players would mix. I remember the characters among the fans as much as the players. The players, the management and the fans, it was unique. There was a feeling at Wimbledon that everyone was in it together …*

During the close season, Bobby Gould replaced Dave Bassett. Gould had formerly been a centre-forward with Coventry and Arsenal and had previously managed Bristol Rovers. His first job was to bring together a new coaching team, as Dave Bassett had taken all of his assistants with him to Watford. Gould drafted in top-rated coaches Don Howe and Ron Suart, both of whom had managerial experience, at West Bromwich and Blackpool, respectively. Gould was sufficiently shrewd and self-confident to allow his senior players their heads. He and Don Howe welcomed Lawrie

Sanchez, Vinnie Jones, Alan Cork and Dave Beasant setting out their their stall, stating what they expected of their coaches, their training routines and their style of play. These expectations were shared with the whole team.

'They told everyone what they expected ... getting the ball into the box 104 times each game, with 44 crosses. It was that precise,' recalled Bobby Gould in an interview with Niall Couper. 'They totally bossed it. In management, that's exactly what you want. You want your players to take over, to make yourself almost redundant. All it needed was a little bit of tinkering here and there. Terry Phelan [from Swansea], John Scales [from Bristol Rovers], Eric Young [from Brighton] and Clive Goodyear [from Plymouth] were my own additions, and very early on they were all told what was expected of them – not by me, but by the likes of Lawrie and Vinnie.' Gould had no intention of disturbing the Wimbledon way of doing things. Gould's motto was, 'If it ain't broke, don't fix it'.

Don Howe told *The Times* journalist, Simon Ritter, of his introduction to Wimbledon in 1987: 'Bobby rang and said, "could you help me through pre-season training, just for four weeks?" I stayed for two years. As much as Wimbledon were criticised for some of the silly things they did off the field, they had been brought up well and understood tactics. A lot of that must have been down to Dave Bassett, the previous manager. Alan Cork, Lawrie Sanchez, John Fashanu – they all wanted to get it right. That was refreshing.' In those days, Wimbledon did not have a training ground and were reliant upon a local public park. Don remembered it being 'a big park, and people were always there, walking their dogs. They used to wander over and watch us. The players just got on with it.' There were no airs and graces with this lot. Although the Dons' ability to keep clean sheets was an important ingredient of their success, Howe dismissed the suggestion that he was a defensive coach. 'I'm a defending coach, not a defensive coach,' he countered. 'It's knowing how to instruct individually and as a unit, how to defend.' Howe pointed out: 'You can't win a match if you're a defensive coach, only draw it.'

Bobby Gould also signed former Spurs, Coventry and Manchester United striker, Terry Gibson, for a club record fee of £200,000. Through the out door went Nigel Winterburn to Arsenal for a £350,000 fee. Accompanying him was Glyn Hodges, who joined Newcastle briefly before moving on quickly to Watford. Hodges would be missed. He had scored nine league goals for the Dons from midfield during the preceding season. Kevin Gage left for Aston Villa while Mark Morris decided to join 'Harry' Bassett at Watford.

Wimbledon began the 1987/88 season in stop-start fashion. However, an emphatic victory at Spurs prompted a rich vein of form up to New Year, in which Wimbledon recorded seven wins and only two defeats in 13 league fixtures. Once again, Manchester United were beaten 2-1 at Plough Lane. After thrashing Oxford 5-2 at the Manor Ground on 2 January, Wimbledon rose to fifth position. Thereafter, the Dons' attention shifted to the FA Cup.

The Dons' road to Wembley started at Plough Lane on 9 January. Second-tier visitors, West Bromwich, were thumped 4-1 on a cold afternoon helped by a vicious 25-yarder from Dennis Wise. Third Division Mansfield provided much sterner opposition at Field Mill in the next round, but thanks to Beasant's smart save from a spot kick, they came away with a narrow victory. A week later, Wimbledon played hosts to Newcastle, their fifth-round opponents, in a league game. It was a chance to soften up the Magpies, for the Dons liked to get in the faces of their opponents. On this occasion, Vinnie Jones lowered his sights, taking young Gazza in hand while they lined up for a free kick, with excruciating effect, apparently. While the league game at Plough Lane ended in a 0-0 draw, the FA Cup tie at Newcastle was a breeze. On a freezing late February afternoon, Wimbledon crushed the Magpies 3-1. With Andy Thorn in commanding form, Vinnie's unique ball-winning skills were not needed. After his outstanding display, Thorn was quick to credit Don Howe's expert coaching. This was the season in which the ex-Raynes Park High School centre-back came of age. Fittingly, he won the first of his England under 21 caps.

The quarter-final saw Wimbledon paired with Watford. 'Harry' Bassett was no longer in charge. He had left the Hornets in January 'by mutual consent' following a disastrous run of league results. Watford were staring down the barrel, although their performance at Plough Lane suggested otherwise. They began by taking an early lead. Dons' centre-back, Brian Gayle, hardly helped matters by lashing out at Watford striker Malcolm Allen, earning an immediate dismissal. But Wimbledon had lost none of their fighting spirit – the legitimate kind, that is. Much to the home crowd's perplexion, Gould took off a striker, Alan Cork, replacing him with a giant centre-back, Eric Young. But Gould's gamble paid off, as Young headed Wimbledon's equaliser from Wise's free kick four minutes into the second half. Gould commented: 'We were always good from dead balls. Something like 84 per cent of our goals came from set pieces and most of them came from Wise.' Fashanu, who had been receiving rave ratings in the national press, sealed a tight victory by scoring with 15 minutes remaining.

Luton Town were Wimbledon's semi-final opponents. Guided in turn by David Pleat and Ray Harford, little Luton had performed magnificently in the top flight, reaching seventh spot in 1987, the club's highest ever position. They also won the Littlewoods League Cup Final of 1988 against Arsenal, thanks to Brian Stein's last-gasp goal.

Howe detailed Cork to play in an unaccustomed right-wing slot against Luton. Although Cork wasn't convinced this was his best position, he trusted Howe's judgement. As a result of openings he created, Wimbledon should have been out of sight by half-time. Capitalising upon the Dons' wastefulness, Luton's Mick Harford stole in to put the Hatters ahead. Luton's lead was short-lived, though. Eight minutes later, Terry Gibson was pulled down in the box and John Fashanu despatched the resultant penalty with characteristic nonchalance. As further proof of Howe's tactical wisdom, Cork laid on the winning goal. It was his cross which Dennis Wise converted with an exuberant two-footed thrust. Incredibly, Wimbledon had reached Wembley, where they would meet Football League champions, Liverpool, the wonderfully fluent, but physically imposing team of the decade, which had cost a colossal £6 million to assemble. The Reds had lost only twice in the league that season. They were hotly tipped to win the league and FA Cup 'double'.

Liverpool were then managed by Kenny Dalglish, who had succeeded Joe Fagan in 1985. This had been a controversial decision. The Liverpool 'boot room' line of succession had been broken. But the board of directors knew what they were doing. Dalglish, one of the finest players ever to grace Anfield, was single-minded, vastly knowledgeable and steely. Above all, he was a born winner. Each of his expensive acquisitions had improved his side. He was unfazed about leaving crowd favourites on the bench. Rush and Beardsley were cases in point. Criticism left him unmoved. If he ever felt any explanation was needed, this was usually conveyed tersely, perhaps garnished with acid wit. Unlike Shankly, he never played to the gallery. He prickled rather than purred.

Dalglish assembled a formidable team, arguably as good as any of those prepared by Shankly or Paisley. In goal, he had the eccentric showman, Bruce Grobbelaar. Grobbelaar's early error-strewn performances were soon put behind him. His gymnastic agility and startling reflexes helped him to become a supreme shot stopper, while he learnt to use his powerful physique in dominating his box.

Dalglish's back four comprised Steve Nicol, Alan Hansen, Gary Gillespie and Gary Ablett. Like so many Liverpool footballers, Nicol could play in a variety of roles. As a full-back he was a sturdy stopper, a robust tackler, pacey, with terrific stamina. But he had subtlety; his first touch was delicate and sure. To top it all, he was a classy finisher. His opposite number, Gary Ablett, was also versatile. Compared to the muscular Nicol, Ablett seemed gaunt and spindly. He was not the fastest defender but he timed his tackles well and was unfussy in his distribution. Alan Hansen was approaching the end of his illustrious career but he was still an immaculate footballer. He had a perfect grasp of positioning, instinctively judging the point of his opponents' attack, often before anyone else realised. Although a strong tackler, his uncanny ability to read the game enabled him to make timely interceptions without muddying himself. His silky distributional skills helped him turn defence into attack at a stroke. In Lawrenson and Hansen, Liverpool had, arguably, their best ever central defensive partnership. Michael Robinson, the former striker turned Spanish TV football pundit, said, 'Mark used to fly into slide tackles, everyone would applaud and he'd be a hero. But Hansen would have seen it long before. Lawrenson was never on his feet; Hansen never needed to be on his bum. Lawrenson was brilliant but Hansen was a genius.' Following Lawrenson's Achilles tendon injury in 1988, which brought his playing career to a premature end, another versatile performer, Gary Gillespie, became Hansen's partner in central defence. Gillespie was a swift, mobile and composed defender, renowned for his long, loping forward runs, often sprinkled with slick one-twos. He had excellent distributional skills, too. But he was also a redoubtable defender, strong in the air; he was an imposing presence in both boxes.

The Liverpool midfield comprised Nigel Spackman, Steve McMahon, Ray Houghton and John Barnes. Spackman was the unsung linkman in central midfield. Most of his passes were short, but delivered quickly and with great accuracy. He left the showy skills to others. Partnering him was Steve McMahon, a powerhouse box-to-box midfielder, who was prepared to bomb forward knowing Spackman would stay at home. McMahon was an abrasive ball winner, but having stolen the ball he knew how to use it. He was also a dynamic attacker with a ferocious shot. With his pounding energy and his fiery demeanour, he seemed Jimmy Case's natural heir. Ray Houghton was a busy, bustling right-sided midfielder with a strong attacking instinct. He was a good crosser of the ball and shot well from distance. On the left side of midfield was John Barnes. He was no longer an orthodox winger. At Liverpool he sometimes undertook more of a central striking role. The fluidity of Dalglish's team meant that his players were not confined by prescribed patterns of play. Barnes thrived in the freedom he was given, combining surging power with delicate guile. He had a sumptuous first touch and once into his stride he proved incredibly difficult to stop, as Brazil once found to their cost. Not only did he have mesmerising ball control but he had the strength to ride the rough tackles. His deceptive turn of speed left many of his markers for dead. On top of that he was a composed and reliable finisher who, like Jimmy Greaves, often chose to pass the ball into the net rather than blast it home.

Up front were John Aldridge, a recent replacement for the departed Ian Rush, and Peter Beardsley. Despite his prolific scoring record for Liverpool, Aldridge was perhaps undervalued as the 'poor man's Rush'. However, he was better in the air than Rush and equally clinical in front of goal. Certainly, Aldridge's goalscoring record at Liverpool – 61 goals in 88 games plus 15 substitutions – spoke for itself. Aldridge scored 26 goals in 36 league games during the 1987/88 season, placing himself well ahead of Beardsley and Barnes, who netted 15 apiece. Peter Beardsley positioned himself slightly behind spearhead Aldridge, playing in the 'hole' as Teddy Sheringham would do. He was a classical inside-forward who had wonderful balance and ball control. He also possessed a teasing change of pace. His scurrying runs from deep positions spelt danger for retreating defences. These regularly resulted in deadly, penetrative passes that pierced the most stoutly-defended back lines. His shooting ability was erratic, but when he got it right he scored some spectacular goals.

Liverpool had carried all before them during the 1987/88 season. They won the league title with ease – it was their tenth championship in 18 seasons. Under Alex Ferguson's exacting management, Manchester United improved sufficiently to take second spot, but they still finished nine points adrift of their great rivals. As if any further proof was necessary, Liverpool turned on a devastating display of attacking football to crush third-placed Nottingham Forest 5-0 on 13 April in front of the BBC cameras. Three of their goals were nominated for the BBC *Match of the Day* 'Goal of the Season' award.

If Wimbledon were to beat Liverpool, they needed to do more than get in the mugs of their opponents – they needed to get inside their heads, too. Bobby Gould recalled the mind games with Niall Couper: 'Liverpool feared us – I don't care what anyone says. We spent the entire day trying to get under their skins and it worked. It started from the moment we went to meet the ref. We put all the clocks and our watches back five minutes and convinced Liverpool that their watches were wrong. That meant they were waiting in the tunnel for five minutes. Then there was our yell of euphoria: "Yidaho!" They were petrified. Despite what they've said since, it did upset them. I saw it in their eyes.'

'Yidaho!' added John Fashanu. 'It was a wild war cry. We were all shouting and hollering but everyone remembers Vinnie more than most. He spits when he shouts … Vinnie pulled me to one side and said, "none of this old shaking hands stuff, let's just stick it straight up 'em." Vinnie wanted to get me going, get the aggression pumping – and it worked … I said to everyone that nobody should shave or wash for 24 hours before the game. In the end it was only me, Jonesey and Wise that didn't. My thinking was that if we go out there looking like fancy dans, we will play like fancy dans. I wanted us to play like Raggedy-Arse Rovers.'

Andy Thorn remembered watching Liverpool on the television in their coach on the way to Wembley. 'Alan Hansen was being real cocky. He said: "Can you see any Wimbledon fans? This is all Liverpool." That's what kicked off the stuff in the tunnel. He was so arrogant. We couldn't wait to ram it down his throat. Bobby Gould didn't have to say a thing. Just listening to Hansen on the coach lit the touchpaper.'

Actually, Bobby Gould did have something more to say, as he told Niall Couper. 'The papers were saying that if Wimbledon won it would set the game back centuries. They criticised us for taking free kicks on the left with the right foot, and on the right with the left foot. And then there were the long throw-ins. In the years that followed, every club in the top flight followed suit … But those sorts of comments just helped us. It just added to the build-up of the whole day.'

While most teams retire early on the night before a big game, this wasn't the Wimbledon way. Off they went to the pub for some typically boisterous play. However, the mood darkened when it was rumoured that one of the tabloid papers was about to run a scandalous story concerning Fashanu. He was so incensed that he put his fist through a hotel door. Bobby Gould remembered: 'It took ages to calm [Fashanu] down… In every room there was something I had to deal with – that was the hard part of being manager of Wimbledon ... to be honest, being manager that week … was more about keeping an eye of them and making sure they didn't burn themselves out emotionally.'

But for all their antics and traumas, Wimbledon played to a carefully-prepared game plan. They had studied a video of Liverpool's 5-0 demolition of Nottingham Forest. 'We found that all of their attacks had stemmed from Alan Hansen,' revealed Terry Gibson. 'The key was to stop him playing the ball out of defence. My job was to mark Alan Hansen man-to-man. It was the most defensive role I'd ever been given, and yet I was still playing centre-forward. We planned to just let Gary Ablett get the ball. The rest of their team could pass but all he ever did was hit the ball long – and that would be meat and drink to our defence.'

Right-back Clive Goodyear added: 'Dennis Wise and I were told by Don Howe to stop the ball getting to John Barnes. That year he had torn so many defences apart. We didn't want Barnes to end up one-on-one against me. The idea was to make sure he had to face Dennis first and then I would clear up if he beat him. It was simple but it made a huge difference.' Don Howe suggested switching Wimbledon's wide men, Cork and Wise. This blocking tactic had been employed by Allen Batsford during Wimbledon's '74/75 FA Cup run.

Vinnie Jones also had his own game plan. 'The papers were all saying that Steve McMahon was going to do this and that to us, and I had had enough of it,' he told Niall Couper. 'I said to Fash that I was going to get him. And Fash said: "If you whack him early you'll be all right. It's the Cup Final, you're playing in front of 100,000 people, he can't send you off that quickly." That said, when the referee reached for a card I was bricking it. That tackle was the first key point of the game. It set the tone for what was to follow.' Left-back Terry Phelan agreed. 'That was our mark on the game,' he said. 'It said no one was going to come through the middle.'

The *Mail on Sunday* reported:

> *… the Final was not a pretty sight. But it was hardly Wimbledon's fault that not one of Liverpool's celebrities could fathom the basic strategic puzzle posed by Howe's redeployment of Dennis Wise, a winger hardly bigger than the average mascot, to cut off the supply to John Barnes. No wonder Kenny Dalglish was as disappointed with his own players as by the referee. Not that Wimbledon could be blamed either, because Brian Hill failed to give Peter Beardsley the advantage of a legitimate goal, then got in such a tangle over his penalty decisions that he is unlikely to be entrusted with a match of such importance ever again. But for the referee's premature whistling for an idiotic foul on Beardsley, Liverpool would have been one-up in the 34th minute instead of one down in the 35th, to the orthodox header which Sanchez applied to a straightforward free kick.*

That was churlish. Alan Cork told Niall Couper that Dennis Wise's delivery was so good 'that we almost expected to score every time. Nine times out of ten it would have been me who scored the goal … It missed me by maybe an inch. But it was destined to be Sanch's moment.' Terry Phelan had this to say: 'Don Howe told us to head out wide and look for the overlaps and get free kicks. Liverpool were terrified of us in the air. They had all the big six-footers but once the ball swung in the air, we were always favourites. We were never going to score from neat passing outside the box. We were going to score from a free kick or a corner. We had worked on that ploy all week and all the time I was at Wimbledon.'

The *Mail on Sunday* reporter continued: 'But for Beasant's defiant saves, Liverpool could have been heading for their expected landslide by half-time, instead of berating the referee for his Beardsley blunder. It became confirmed as Wimbledon's day in the 61st minute when Mr Hill's ruling that Clive Goodyear had fouled Aldridge looked to have made dubious amends to Liverpool, only for Beasant to inflict on Aldridge his first penalty miss under Dalglish's management, at the least welcome moment.'

'I clearly toed the ball back to Dave Beasant,' commented right-back Clive Goodyear, 'and the whistle went. Peter Beardsley had played a nice reverse pass but I read it and slid in and won the ball. John Aldridge had just fallen over my leg.'

Dave Beasant remembered the incident clearly. 'It was never a penalty. Andy Thorn and Eric Young were incensed, but I am more level-headed, so I pushed them aside … I headed back to my goal line and suddenly I couldn't breathe properly. I had to put my hands on my knees and try and get some air into my lungs.

'I've always studied penalties,' continued 'Lurch', '[but] when we were in the Fourth Division it wasn't easy. I used to look for pictures of penalties in the opponents' programmes, and I could normally tell by the angle of the penalty taker's foot where the ball had gone and how they had hit it. But against John Aldridge it was easier. Liverpool were on the TV every week and he had scored something like 13 penalties that season. I had seen his technique over and over again. A little shuffle and it would go to my right; no shuffle and it would go to my left. There was no shuffle, and I saved it.'

The *Mail on Sunday* reporter concluded:

> *… and the question left over Wimbledon is why they found it necessary to play so brutally for so many excruciating months when they would come to Wembley for their biggest day of all, control themselves, and still score a 1-0 win over the best team in the country. The answer may be found in Howe's coaching. Instead of blatant assault, Wimbledon employed the nudge and the partial obstruction to supplement firm tackling and solid organisation … it was a tale of the unexpected; a custard*

> *pie in the face of predictability. No-hopers of the world unite. You have nothing to lose but your inferiority complex.*

Or, as John Motson so memorably put it, 'The Crazy Gang have beaten the Culture Club!'

'In 1977, when we got into the league, only a nutter would have said that we'd get into the First Division and win the FA Cup,' reflected Alan Cork. 'Yet, 11 years later, here we were, winners. It will never happen again. It's impossible now; the gap financially is too huge. No club will ever emulate Wimbledon.'

Dave Beasant said: 'Stanley Reed had wanted to take us to the Hilton no matter what the result, but that wasn't our style. So we went for a marquee on the pitch at Plough Lane … I didn't figure that the Cup Final would be my last game for Wimbledon … Bobby called me and said that the club had accepted an £850,000 offer for me. And I suppose there was no better way to leave Wimbledon than having won the FA Cup.' Beasant would be accompanied by centre-back Andy Thorn, for whom Newcastle forked out over £1 million. With their profile now so high, the Dons could demand huge fees for the talent they had discovered and nurtured. Reserve centre-back Brian Gayle left after the final, too, when Manchester City paid £325,000 for him. Vinnie Jones remained for one more season before helping revive Leeds' fortunes under Howard Wilkinson. The Dons pocketed £650,000 from his sale, although he would return to the club in 1992, via Chelsea, to boost Joe Kinnear's new regime.

One by one, the remaining members of the class of '88 departed. Thorn's partner in central defence, Eric 'Ninja' Young, was sold to Crystal Palace in 1990 for £850,000 – a huge fee for a 30-year-old – while midfielder Dennis Wise joined Chelsea in the same year for a £1.6 million fee. Wise never lost his feisty combativeness. Sir Alex Ferguson once said that he 'could start a fight in an empty house'. Left-back Terry Phelan transferred to Manchester City in 1992 for £2.5 million. He, like John Scales, had endured a difficult initiation at Wimbledon, suffering damning criticisms from his team-mates. It was no good being a shrinking violet at Wimbledon. John Fashanu moved on to Aston Villa in 1994 for £1.35 million. However, he sustained a career-ending injury at Old Trafford in the following February. He was later accused, and subsequently cleared, of match-fixing. Centre-back John Scales, a substitute at Wembley, would also move. He went to Liverpool in 1994 for £3.5 million.

Right-back Clive Goodyear suffered a serious knee injury in the ensuing Charity Shield game and never fully recovered his form. Alan Cork stayed on for four more years before joining 'Harry' Bassett at Sheffield United on a free transfer. He had been a stalwart performer in Wimbledon's rise from the basement. Terry Gibson stayed on, too, until 1993.

As for Wimbledon's goalscorer, Lawrie Sanchez continued to play for the club until 1994, racking up 270 appearances. He joined Swindon, briefly, as the Robins attempted vainly to retain their Premiership place, before becoming Sligo Rovers' player-manager. But in 1995 he rejoined Wimbledon as a coach under Joe Kinnear.

The FA Cup-winning team of 1988 was eventually sold for over £12 million. That was twice the value of the team they faced on that sun-drenched spring day. It seems an extraordinary sum to pay for a rabid rabble. Perish the thought that there were actually players of skill in that Dons side. Bobby Gould and Don Howe had done well. They had helped Wimbledon to achieve their greatest triumph by harnessing rather than directing its driving force. But Gould stayed for only two more years. He left in 1990 following a dispute with Sam Hammam over terms. His replacement, Ray Harford, didn't stay long, either. He also fell out with Hammam, apparently.

Following Peter Withe's short-lived appointment, Joe Kinnear took over the managerial reins in 1992 and successfully re-established the spirit that had taken this club to such dizzying heights. It was then that my daughter, Lydia, and I began to watch Wimbledon. Her introduction to football had come at a similar age to mine. A distressing family event had been the catalyst, too. It is strange how a game that generally causes more heartache than joy should be selected as some kind of shelter from the storm.

Wimbledon continued to hold their own under Joe Kinnear. They played with passion and no little skill. It certainly wasn't just 'hoofball' as their detractors, such as Gary Lineker, claimed. Like 'Harry' Bassett, Kinnear knew how to turn out a disciplined, winning side, while allowing his players their heads and sense of fun. He brought on home-grown talent and discovered overlooked gems in the lower divisions, turning them into top Premiership performers. Although Wimbledon continued to buy small and sell big, the club was hugely reliant upon TV revenue. Despite achieving top-half finishes in seven out of their 14 seasons in the elite division, Wimbledon never enticed enough people to watch them – perhaps too many were watching on Ceefax?

In the three seasons that followed their move from Plough Lane, the Dons' average gate was pitiful. Selhurst Park attendances were no better than those at Plough Lane. Thereafter, their gates grew at funereal pace, peaking at 18,235 in 1999, the year of Kinnear's heart attack. This 'peak' figure was less than little Burnley drew in their solitary Premiership season in 2009/10.

Relocation raised its ugly head once again. In Ron Noades' time in charge there had been a rumour of a possible shift to Milton Keynes, but his purchase of Crystal Palace scotched this. During the late nineties the prospect of Dublin was raised, although there were murmurs about Basingstoke, too. The margins were getting tighter, on and off the field. Once Joe Kinnear stumbled, Wimbledon slipped. And that slip soon became a slide. Deprived of Sky TV money, Wimbledon probably had little chance, with or without the Norwegians' controversial ownership. However, the MK Dons fiasco remains as an indelible blemish on the face of English football. Milton Keynes' absorption of a club that had lost its capacity to sustain itself seemed like a marriage to an exhumed corpse. Surely necrophilia has no place in the modern game? Perhaps the last word on the subject should be granted to Wembley match-winner Lawrie Sanchez. He told Niall Couper:

> *What saddens me is my history has been extinguished with the demise of Wimbledon FC. With the move to Milton Keynes, how can they claim a credible line to Wimbledon? I have a great respect for what AFC Wimbledon have done – and the fans have the same great memories as I do – but AFC Wimbledon have never won the FA Cup. The 1988 FA Cup Final has been consigned to history – it belongs to neither club. It belongs solely to the players who played in it and the fans who watched it.*

'Two Tribes': Fear and loathing in Thatcher's Britain

On the upside, the eighties saw the ending of the 40-year-old Cold War. The Berlin Wall fell and the Soviet Empire fragmented, although new threats emerged from the bandit states of North Korea, Iraq and Libya, as the Lockerbie horror underlined.

The Thatcher years were generally good for the 87 per cent or so of Britons who remained in work. Even during the sharp recession of the early eighties, those with jobs experienced a rise in their standards of living. Big was beautiful. We had the 'big' fashions – 'Super Bowl'-sized shoulder pads and wildly sprouting hairstyles. And there were the massive mobile phones, too. This was the decade when the gulf between the well off and less well off grew exponentially. Towards the top end of the scale were the 'yuppies' while at the bottom end was the ever-expanding population of 'cardboard city' residents, surviving largely with charitable help.

While Margaret Thatcher's curbing of trade union powers was long overdue, she failed to deliver an economic revival that all might benefit from. During her premiership, annual national growth averaged 1.8 per cent. Even Labour had managed 2.4 per cent during the sluggish seventies. North Sea oil revenue was frittered away in supporting a rising jobless total, which reached over three million by 1983. When Mrs Thatcher resigned as prime minister in November 1990, there were 60 per cent more people dependent upon welfare benefits than at her accession in 1979. Around ten million people in the UK were then living at or below the poverty line, with black families disproportionately represented in that figure. While the 'right to buy' policy increased home ownership, helping revive previously drab and depressed council estates, this was at the expense of reducing the availability of social housing for those on low incomes. Homelessness doubled during the first half of the decade. By sharp contrast, before the crash of the late eighties, property values soared, particularly in and around London, where annual rises of 25 per cent were not uncommon.

The sharply divergent divisions in income had strong geographical features. Around 75 per cent of the new jobs emerging between 1983 and 1987 were created in the south-east. Meanwhile, youth unemployment reached horrifying proportions in the 'industrial' North. In areas of Liverpool, up to nine out of every ten young people were without work. In 1984, Tory MP Matthew Parris attempted to live for a week in Newcastle on a basic social security income. He failed. In a *World in Action* TV documentary, he stated: 'Perhaps the sharpest lesson I drew ... was that unemployment is not only a problem of the pocket but of the spirit; and once the spirit is broken neither money nor training can easily help.'

It was small wonder that coalmining folk chose to defend their livelihoods and communities so tenaciously when the NCB threatened pit closures. Mrs Thatcher strode into the conflict with the swagger of a newly-decorated prize fighter, framing it in familiar Falkland terms. To her, Arthur Scargill was a dictator to be crushed like the Argentinean, General Galtieri, although Ogreave was nearer to her 'Gettysburg' than her 'Goose Green'.

The eighties saw the birth of groundbreaking charitable initiatives, spearheaded by *Band Aid* and *Live Aid*, later to be carried forward by *Children in Need*, *Comic Relief* and *Sport Relief*. As if we needed any reminding, Mrs Thatcher pointed out that we wouldn't 'remember the Good Samaritan if he only had good intentions. He had money, too'.

But while some of us learnt to make serious money in the 'Thatcher Years', most of us lost our knack of making things, although that didn't apply to our knack of developing successful football club teams. Indeed, we produced some of our best ever club teams during this decade. Before the post-Heysel ban, Liverpool, Nottingham Forest, Aston Villa and Everton ruled the roost at home and abroad. It was ironic that Liverpool – beset by economic decline, a reducing population and fractious local politics – should boast two of our finest sides.

In 1982/83, the Football League became sponsored by *Canon*, a Japanese multinational corporation. Spurs also became the first British football club to be floated on the stock market. Their manager, Keith Burkinshaw, who learnt his trade in Workington and Scunthorpe, walked away, remarking bitterly: 'There used to be a football club over there.' And to compound the growing divisions in the game, the Football League changed its rules, allowing home clubs to keep all of their gate money, thereby benefiting the rich clubs at the expense of the poorer ones. Some fans played mischievously upon these divisions. London-based 'Casuals', clad in their expensive designer gear, wasted no opportunity in mocking their 'sartorially-disadvantaged' northern cousins. It was their obnoxious contempt which provided Harry Enfield with the inspiration for his 'Loadsamoney' character.

The game desperately needed investment – not in lucrative signings, but in improving our archaic grounds. Many of them had seen little upgrading since before the Second World War. That level of neglect would have catastrophic consequences at Bradford in 1985. The situation was no better at some places abroad. The Heysel Stadium disaster illustrated this so starkly, although here, the aggressive behaviour of certain Liverpool fans – such an offence to their proudly-held self-image – brought about the fatal crush. English clubs were then banned indefinitely from European competitions. The unruly behaviour of England fans at the 1988 European Championship finals hardly helped. However, in 1990, UEFA relented. While many Conservative MPs remained Europhobic, our club sides could compete once more with the best European teams.

At home, outbreaks of crowd disorder became tiresomely frequent; the most repellent of which was possibly the riot perpetrated by Millwall fans at Luton in March 1985. £20,000 worth of damage was caused inside the ground, £10,000 outside and £45,000 on the trains back to London. The rampaging violence of the Leeds fans at St Andrew's, two months later, had more tragic consequences – the death of an uninvolved teenager. It had been his first game. Supporters were penned behind high wire fences.

Luton banned away fans. Mrs Thatcher pushed for an identity card scheme. The upshot was that many genuine fans fell out of love with the game. Average gates were down by nine per cent at the start of the 1985/86 season. Whereas *Match of the Day* was watched by 13 million viewers during the late sixties, 20 years later, less than half that number tuned in. 'The beautiful game' had become defiled. And so were we, as supporters, at least in Mrs Thatcher's eyes. We became treated like pariahs.

To cap it all, there was the appalling tragedy of Hillsborough in 1989. Here, the police's fatal decision to open the gates at the Leppings Lane End was compounded by their subsequent inability to distinguish crowd disorder from mass distress. The adversarial circumstances hardly helped. The heaving caged pens were regarded by the police with a mixture of fear and loathing. The pre-match police briefing at Hillsborough focused exclusively on combating disorderly behaviour. Unsurprisingly, the police were predisposed to seeing their duty as one of control, not care.

In the early nineties, there was a re-emergence of rioting in British towns and cities, just as there had been ten years before. The nightly TV news bulletins carried new footage of hooded adolescents 'burning rubber', if not burning their joyridden vehicles, on the mean streets of Oxford, Tyneside, Cardiff and Birmingham, while the authorities looked on, apparently powerless to stop the mayhem. As abhorrent as the young people's behaviour was, this seemed like their seething riposte to a government which had fostered such divisive social and economic policies. Here were the snarling underdogs of an eighties underclass, stripped of purpose, ambition, hope, conscience or inhibition. Seen in this context, the construction of Canary Wharf seemed like a latter-day Babel; its occupants apparently oblivious to the disadvantaged communities scattered around them, as they paid blind homage to the voracious demands of high finance. How ironic it was that the new docklands development, a paean to eighties affluence, should be built where working men and women once toiled; where commerce was once measured in tangible commodities. Here, there and everywhere, eighties regeneration became gentrification.

THE 2007/08 SEASON

Exeter City v Aldershot Town

'I Will Possess Your Heart'
15 April 2008

My uncle introduced me to the former Aldershot club. Like so many others, our appetite for the game had been sharpened by England's World Cup triumph. Attendances rose by six per cent in the season which followed, halting the inexorable decline of the previous 17 years. On that balmy, late August evening, he had higher expectations than I. He remembered that the visitors, Luton Town, had recently been a top-flight team. He'd forgotten how far and quickly they had fallen. If he was preparing himself for haute cuisine, I was prepared for a Vesta Curry. Not that this was a problem. The Aldershot ground was enchanting. We queued outside the turnstiles housed in Edwardian huts of frosted, coloured glass. Behind them were meticulously maintained flower beds and shrubs, etched into a closely clipped lawn, which sloped upwards. A row of mature, elegant trees provided this verdant garden with swishy shade. I half expected to receive a putter in return for my admission fee. I was sure that over the brow was a putting green and may be a boating lake. Had anyone had their f***ing heads kicked in here? There seemed more chance of a ruck at Evensong.

Actually, I enjoyed the game. It was a League Cup first leg match between two Fourth Division sides. While Luton had seen better times – they had been FA Cup finalists seven years before – Aldershot had no head for heights. Since joining the Football League in 1932, the Shots had never ventured out of the basement. The bottom division had been renamed and restructured in 1958 but Aldershot's status remained unaffected. Thus far, their best finish was seventh place in 1962. They couldn't blame their pitch. It was an immaculate surface, like neatly-pressed Subbuteo baize.

For this game, Shots' manager, Dave Smith, picked the following team. In goal was Tony Godfrey, a small but agile former Saints keeper. Ron Davies, formerly of Cardiff, was right-back, and Dick Renwick, previously at Grimsby, was his partner. Player-coach and future club manager Tommy McAnearney played at right-half. He served under Harry Catterick at Sheffield Wednesday. At centre-half was another future club manager, Lennie Walker. He was a Geordie, and previously at Newcastle. At left-half was 22-year-old Malcolm Dawes, whose only red card offence was when he punched Stan Bowles. He later played for New York Cosmos until Franz Beckenbauer acquired his number six shirt. On the right wing was David Dodson, formerly with Portsmouth, and on the left was Ken Maloy, a hard-working wide man who later served Plymouth well. The inside trio comprised burly young striker Jack Howarth, previously with Chelsea and Swindon, veteran centre-forward Ron Rafferty, who had been a prolific goalscorer at Grimsby, and inside-left Bobby Howfield, a talented but fiery midfielder, once with Watford and Fulham.

Now that their record goalscorer, Gordon Turner, had moved on, Luton were left with none of their former Division One players. However, they did have a young Bruce Rioch at inside-left and David Pleat on their right wing. Their goalkeeper, Tony Read, had spent the previous season playing up front and scoring 12 goals. It wasn't clear whether he had been put between the sticks as a prize or a punishment.

This nip-and-tuck game finished as an entertaining 2-2 draw. It hadn't been pretty but it had been a highly competitive, evenly matched affair. I had been impressed with 21-year-old Jack Howarth, a buffeting, barging centre-forward of the old school. He wasn't so hot on the tippy-tappy stuff, but each time his wingers pumped the ball high into the Luton box he was a bundle of trouble. The former Durham miner would score almost 200 senior goals for Aldershot. Over 40 years later, the self-deprecating Howarth told *Backpass* magazine:

> *I was never greedy for goals. Maybe if I had been, I'd have got a lot more. I used to be the big striker who knocked the ball down for others … I never saw myself as a star … I was down the pits as a 15-year-old. I've always taken praise with a pinch of salt. Coming from a mining background kept me grounded. But I enjoyed a good rapport with the fans. They used to sing 'Grocer Jack, Grocer Jack, score a goal, don't let us down' to the tune of Keith West's 'Excerpt from a Teenage Opera'. Dennis Brown stood out for me as my best striking partner. He was at Chelsea when I was there and did his kneecap. He had a plastic replacement. I don't know*

> *how he carried on playing. He was like lightning, he played off me and I nodded it down for him. We had a great understanding. Neil [Warnock, who joined the club in the seventies] has done all right as a manager ... but he wasn't a good player ... He couldn't cross the road let alone the ball. I used to have a go at him at half-time. I said I'd been waiting for crosses I could reach ... He didn't like it. He's the same now in that he can talk a good game. But he couldn't do it out on the pitch. He was a nice enough bloke but he got on my nerves. He's never been quiet in his life.*

The 171 league goals that Jack scored for the Shots weren't just in defence of the club's league status. In November 1972, Tommy McAnearney rescued him from his brief exile at Third Division Rochdale to boost the Shots' first successful promotion campaign. Howarth had left Aldershot 12 months earlier after falling out with the previous manager, Jimmy Melia. Jack explained: 'Jimmy Melia was player-manager. He was a good touch player and never passed the ball more than three or four yards. It didn't suit our game, which was for the players to knock a long ball to me as the target man.' Once Jimmy had left, Jack did not need much persuasion to return.

Whereas Jimmy Melia was a footballing purist, Tommy McAnearney was a pragmatist, as one might expect from someone who had played under Harry Catterick. It was not that Jimmy Melia did not prepare a good game plan. In three years as the Shots' boss, between 1969 and 1972, his team dumped Frank Worthington's Huddersfield out of the FA Cup – Len Walker scored with a cracker in the first game at Leeds Road. Aldershot also gave both Manchester United and Liverpool real scraps in other cup games. Against United, Howarth made a whole heap of trouble for United's centre-backs, Ian Ure and David Sadler, winning most of the aerial duels. As Jack admits, he might well have played at a higher level had he been more determined. 'I could have done better if I had put my mind to it,' he reflected. 'But I had an absolutely brilliant time playing for Aldershot.' Despite their disagreements, Jack had reason to feel grateful to Jimmy Melia. Before he hung up his boots, Melia fixed him up with an opportunity to play with South California Lazers. It was a well deserved bonus for a thoroughly committed team man.

Although Jack Howarth's 25 league goals in the 1973/74 season took Aldershot to their highest ever final placing – eighth in Division Three – the club's stay in the higher division was short-lived. By 1976, Aldershot were back in the basement. Once Jack moved on to Bournemouth, at the start of the 1977/78 season, Tommy McAnearney had to seek a replacement. Providentially, he found one without shedding a penny. John Dungworth's record gave no evidence of his predatory skills. Before signing for Aldershot, the former Huddersfield striker had found the net only five times but Tommy McAnearney had a hunch that the tall striker had a lot more to give. Dungworth repaid McAnearney's faith by tucking away 23 league goals in his first season. He then went on to break Jack Howarth's club record, a year later, by scoring a further 26. Dungworth's eight FA Cup goals granted Aldershot their joint-best cup run. Disappointingly, it was ended by Third Division Shrewsbury in a fifth-round replay. But those 34 senior goals were enough to win Dungworth the Adidas Golden Boot award. John Dungworth established a productive central striking partnership with Andy Needham. They both benefited from the excellent service from the wingers, Murray Brodie and Alex McGregor.

The former Sunderland and Oxford boss, Malcolm Crosby, played 294 league games in midfield for Aldershot between 1972 and 1981, before Len Walker transferred him to York in return for Ian McDonald. Almost 30 years after his departure from 'the Rec' (the local nickname for Aldershot's Recreation Ground stadium), Malcolm told Aldershot Town's Craig Matthews: 'I suppose my fellow midfielder, Will Dixon, wasn't totally appreciated as much as he should have been because under Tommy McAnearney we used to play what was in effect a 4-2-4 with Murray Brodie and Alex McGregor out very wide. It was a very hard job in that formation when you had only two midfielders … Tommy Mac was a very good coach … there's a lot of things I do even now with teams that I picked up from Tommy. As a player Len Walker was good because he would really get into you if you weren't doing your job.' Although Walker transferred Crosby to York, the Geordie midfielder didn't have any recriminations. Malcolm considered his best game for Aldershot to be against Sheffield United during the Shots' 1978/79 FA Cup run. He recalled that he was up against the Argentinean midfield ace, Alex Sabella. Malcolm must have done his job well as Sheffield United were defeated 1-0 in a replay at the Rec in front of an 8,300 crowd.

Shots' centre-half Joe Jopling added: 'Everyone blames Malcolm for giving away the lead in the home fifth-round tie with Shrewsbury but they forget the previous game when he scored the winner. Nobody said anything to him – we were all sick as dogs after playing so well for so long. Still, we gave a good account of ourselves in the replay and were very unlucky again with Andy Needham and John Dungworth hitting the post. John Dungworth was the best finisher I've ever seen at the club, though Jack Howarth was the best centre-forward I ever played with.'

Unfortunately, Dungworth's stay at the Rec was a two-season wonder. In October 1979, he left for Shrewsbury after a Football League tribunal fixed his fee at £100,000 – half of what Aldershot wanted for him. But he left his magic dust behind him. He was never as prolific again. After Dungworth left, McAnearney paid a record £54,000 fee for Portsmouth striker Colin Garwood. After narrowly missing out on promotion in the previous two seasons, Tommy hoped that Garwood would help the club to be successful third time around. It was not to be. Garwood scored ten times in only 16 games but he was unable to prevent his team's late slump in form.

As was the case elsewhere, Aldershot's gates fell sharply during the eighties. During the sixties and seventies the club had regularly attracted crowds of between 4,000 and 5,000 for their league games and five-figure gates for the big cup games. But in a time of recession, the town of Aldershot was suffering. Because it had a higher than average level of unskilled labour, its economy proved less resilient than the surrounding areas. Their average gate halved. In 1986, it fell to under 1,500. The club began to face increasing financial difficulty. By this time Tommy McAnearney had called it a day. In January 1981, his place was taken by his former team-mate, Len Walker. In Tommy's 471 games in charge, he achieved a winning percentage of 39 – on a par with Neil Warnock's current record – which was particularly good given the limited resources available to him. His attacking instincts gave much cause for cheer until the recession left its mark. Tommy won 31 more games than he lost, making him Aldershot's most successful boss.

Tommy McAnearney might have been sold on bright forward play but he understood the need for tight defence as well. His solid central defensive partnership of Tommy Youlden and Joe Jopling was the bedrock of his side's successes in the late seventies. Youlden was an uncompromising, hard-tackling centre-back who served an apprenticeship at Highbury before moving on to Portsmouth, where he played in 90 league games. He then transferred to Reading, where he made 163 more league appearances. Nevertheless, he was in awe of his new central defensive partner, Joe Jopling, when they first teamed up together at the Rec. Tommy told interviewer Craig Matthews:

> *Joe was as brave as a lion, a terrific centre-half. I'm very surprised he never played at a higher level for longer than he did at Leicester. We were like chalk and cheese,*

> *though. He used to like a drink and I didn't drink at all but for some reason we hit it off from the word go. I remember when I came into the side … We were away at Exeter. Joe said to me, 'when I say mark tight, that means we come out for the free kick, so every free kick we get against us, we line up on the 18-yard box, and if I look at you and say "mark tight" that means we're coming up'. It's the first game I've played. I'm concentrating like mad. They get a free kick. Joe says 'mark tight' and I'm marking tight, the ball has come over and the whole back four, apart from me, have gone up. I'm now standing there with about five Exeter strikers bearing down on Glen Johnson in goal and Joe comes screaming back at me, 'I said mark tight' and I said I am ******* marking tight what do you think I'm doing, and then suddenly the penny's dropped. 'Sorry Joe'. Luckily, they missed, but he's never let me forget that!*

Len Walker took over the management of the club in increasingly cash-strapped times but he made a decent fist of things. As if the resource shortfalls weren't bad enough, he had to cope with a boardroom coup which temporarily deprived him of his job. That was in November 1984 when a rival consortium moved in, took over and installed Ron 'Chopper' Harris as manager in his place. In fairness, Harris did well during his eight months in charge, winning 42 per cent of his 31 league games. But come June 1985, the coup was overturned and Walker was restored.

Walker was responsible for bringing a number of talented players to the club including Dale Banton, Martin Foyle, Bobby Barnes, Glen Burvill, Ian McDonald, Steve Claridge, Andy King, Adrian Randall, David Puckett and Tony Lange. Many of Walker's signings were free transfers or low-cost acquisitions who were soon sold on for a profit. For example, striker Martin Foyle signed from Southampton for £10,000 in 1984 and was sold to Oxford in 1987 for £140,000. He was later bought by Port Vale for a club record fee of £375,000. The fast, tricky, goalscoring winger, Bobby Barnes, was obtained from West Ham in 1985 for £15,000 and then sold on to Swindon two years later for £50,000. Goalkeeper Tony Lange was a 'freebie' from Charlton but was sold to Wolves for a Shots record £150,000 fee in 1989. It was rumoured that in 1984, Millwall's boss, George Graham, offered Walker the chance to make loanee, Teddy Sheringham, a permanent signing if £5,000 could be found. Graham doubted whether his young striker would make it on account of his slightness of stature. Of course, four years later, Sheringham helped power Millwall into Division One, sharing 42 goals with twin striker Tony Cascarino. A stellar career with Spurs, Manchester United and England awaited him. Walker came close to delivering promotion in 1981 and in 1984. In '83/84, his new striking partnership of burly George Lawrence and nippy Dale Banton struck goals – 41 of them in the league. Glen Burvill and Ian McDonald also shared 23 more from midfield. Len's side had several points of attack.

However, Walker achieved his ambition three years later. In 1987, his side finished sixth in Division Four on 70 points, thereby qualifying for the inaugural Football League play-off competition. Walker's team rose to the occasion magnificently. First they defeated Bolton Wanderers, to consign the Trotters to Division Four for the first time in their history. Then, his plucky lads beat Wolverhampton Wanderers 3-0 on aggregate to take them up. Bobby Barnes scored the crucial goal at Molineux when he cut in from the right and fired the ball across the Wolves keeper. Wolves had been in the top flight only three years before. Walker had other causes for celebration, too, as his team thrashed First Division Oxford 3-0 in the third round of the FA Cup. Oxford's prolific striker, John Aldridge, was so well marked that he hardly managed a kick before being substituted. Two weeks later, Aldridge left Oxford for Liverpool in a £750,000 deal.

The Oxford game was played in January 1987 on a frosty pitch. Shots midfielder, Glen Burvill, had been doubtful whether the game would be played. He remembered that the conditions 'effectively ironed out any difference in class. In short, Oxford didn't fancy it.' It took Aldershot just six minutes to take the lead through centre-half Colin 'Smudger' Smith, who had recently recovered from Hodgkin's disease. The Shots defended tenaciously but broke with menace. Tommy Langley, Mike Ring and Bobby Barnes remained a constant threat up front, while McDonald played immaculately in midfield. Friar was outstanding at left-back, too. In fact, it was Friar who set up the decisive goal just before the hour. His through pass was capitalised upon by the advancing Burvill, who blasted the ball past Hardwick in the Oxford goal. Bobby Barnes completed an outstanding performance by lashing in a third after Hardwick had parried his first effort. His goal prompted a joyful conga on the East Bank.

As if this wasn't enough, Aldershot also managed to reach the Southern Area Final of the Associate Members' (Freight Rover) Trophy. Being gluttons for hard work, Len Walker's side played 64 games that season. Just

15 players covered the lion's share of this burden. The hot 'Shots' were Bobby Barnes, Martin Foyle and ex-Evertonian Andy King, who scored 11 league goals apiece. The former Chelsea, QPR, Palace and Wolves striker, Tommy Langley, contributed seven also.

The only sour note was struck when the Aldershot directors hiked up the admission prices for the Oxford FA Cup tie. Graham Brookland, then the chairman of the Shots Supporters' Club, and a future director of the Aldershot Town football club, recalled:

> *It should have been an exciting time but the mood changed when the club announced exorbitant admission prices … In those days £11 for seats and £9 for the terraces were crazy prices. [These prices amount to around £30 per ticket today.] From the club's point of view, they were trying to capitalise because the capacity of the Rec had been severely reduced to 3,400 on account of more stringent safety requirements, following the Bradford City fire, while the supporters were up in arms because they deemed that their loyalty was being taken advantage of. It was no surprise that a sub-2,000 crowd attended; the lowest in FA Cup third round history … Even if the club had arranged a scheme by which regulars were offered tickets at a more reasonable price it would have been acceptable but that wasn't the case … Unfortunately 'PR' wasn't the strongest facet of the club in those days. It seems a shame that perhaps the biggest upset in the history of Aldershot FC is not recalled with the euphoria it deserves.*

It wasn't just the home fans who complained. Many visiting supporters were denied access also, not knowing this was an 'all ticket' affair. Around 150 Oxford fans decided to take out their frustration in the town, making a lot of work for the local police.

Club chairman Colin Hancock refuted a charge of profiteering, stating: 'If we had played this game at a loss we would have been faced with winding-up orders.' Aldershot were then £300,000 in debt (equivalent to £800,000 today). Hancock also stated that the club faced extra costs because of necessary ground improvements, pointing out that they had applied unsuccessfully to Rushmoor District Council for a £30,000 grant. It seemed that while progress on the pitch had never been better, the club's financial situation was grimmer than ever. Nevertheless, Hancock assured the fans that the prices would be reduced for the next round and that the tie would not be switched if a good draw was obtained. It wasn't. Mid-table Second Division Barnsley were their next opponents. The horse had bolted. After a 1-1 draw at the Recreation Ground, the replay was lost 0-3.

After a slow start to the 1987/88 season, Len Walker's team took to life in the Third Division. Although non-league Sutton dumped them out of the FA Cup, the Gander Lane side were then tough opponents, good enough to beat Coventry, the 1987 FA Cup champions, a year later. Besides, a 3-0 home win against Bristol Rovers on New Year's Day, with goals from Langley (2) and Burvill, took Aldershot into 11th place in Division Three. This win came just four days after Gillingham had been put to the sword (6-0). The fans had returned. The average home gate during the festive period was 4,600. At that point, the club's sights were set expectantly upwards rather than nervously down, but their optimism didn't survive long. Aldershot's sharp dip in form was not helped by injuries to key players. With only 16 players on the books, Len Walker had difficulty in putting out a team. Only four of the Shots' last 23 fixtures were won. On the upside, his injury-depleted team managed to defeat champions-elect Sunderland, 3-2, in a switchback game at the Rec on 27 February, in front of over 5,000 fans. Midfielder Ian McDonald scored a stirring hat-trick, too, as Chester were beaten 4-1. But Aldershot still needed to draw their final game at Grimsby to ensure safety. Grimsby were in deep trouble, too. A crowd of fractionally under 6,000 watched this tense relegation battle.

Shots' keeper, Tony Lange, had been voted the 'player of the season' in 1987. Twenty years later, he told Craig Matthews: 'It was a strange old game because it is a horrible place to go and get a result at the best of times. They were more nervous than us. We scored early but they equalised quite quickly and as the game progressed they became more and more frustrated. Paul Roberts gave away a penalty. I think the lad who took it was Mark North but he wasn't confident at all, you could see that, and luckily I guessed the right way and saved it.'

Aldershot were safe. Despite losing two of their best forwards – Barnes to Swindon and Foyle to Oxford – the Shots had clung on to their Division Three place, just. Langley's 14 goals had helped considerably. He had scored the crucial opening goal at Grimsby. But Langley had terrific support from Burvill and McDonald who, between them, had netted 17 times from midfield. The Shots' average gate of 3,203 gave cause for satisfaction. It was easily their best for seven years and almost 1,000 higher than in the preceding season. However, the extra gate revenue and the net transfer receipts of £150,000 from Foyle's and Barnes' sales were insufficient to counter the mounting debts. In the accustomed fashion, Len Walker released the vastly experienced Tommy Langley and the injury-prone Andy King and brought in greener replacements. In came 22-year-old striker Steve Claridge from Crystal Palace for £14,000 and 19-year-old midfielder Adrian Randall from Bournemouth on a free transfer.

Steve Claridge was paid £350 per week and given a £12,000 signing-on fee. Although he thought his weekly wage to be 'a pittance', barely enough for married men to support their kids and pay a mortgage, it was almost twice the wage paid to First Division Wimbledon players, equating to around £50,000 per year now.

Steve joined Aldershot in order to secure regular first-team football but his debut at Craven Cottage, in 1988, was best forgotten as the Shots were hammered 5-1 by Fulham. By this time the club were struggling badly. Aldershot's goal was scored by midfielder Giorgio Mazzon. Surreally, Giorgio had a disabled sticker on his windscreen on account of a back injury he sustained in a car accident. Mazzon wasn't the only crocked Shot, either. Striker Dale Banton's knees were so battered that he had to spend all week icing them so that he might manage a game on a Saturday. Mazzon took a lot of ribbing on account of his sticker. Steve wasn't exempt from the mickey-taking, though. He became known as 'Worzel' after his team-mates heard his father's 'farmer's accent'. Steve's attire probably didn't help him, either.

I saw Steve play at Brentford several years later. I don't think I've seen any professional player look so dishevelled. His shirt and shorts seemed to belong to someone else – someone who hadn't reached puberty. His boots didn't match, either. This wasn't the modern affectation for footwear of contrasting colours. Steve had odd boots on. And then there were his shin ties, which trailed from his ankles. As he pirouetted, the ties were whipped up into a dervish-like frenzy. Eventually, the referee tired of this mess. Steve was ordered off and told to tidy himself up. I'm not sure which FA regulation covered this situation but the referee's decision did wonders for his popularity. But let it not be said that Steve could not play. He could – and how! For someone with an ungainly gait, he had good balance and a sharp turn of pace. His ball control was excellent, his footwork was dexterous and, once on the ball, he was very difficult to shake off. He was a good finisher, too. On top of this, he had a terrific engine. You felt he could run all day. Len Walker knew what he was doing when he signed Steve. Arguably, it took others, in higher places, too long to recognise what Len had seen long before.

As for 19-year-old Adie Randall, Len's other close-season signing, he quickly became a first-team regular, having failed to break into Bournemouth's side. Randall had been capped at England youth level but hadn't kicked on. Like Steve Claridge he had huge potential but seemed to lack Steve's drive. I saw him play a couple of times at Aldershot but wasn't aware of his ability until he moved to Burnley, for a £40,000 fee, shortly before the Shots folded in 1992. Having made irregular appearances in Burnley's first team, during his first 18 months at Turf Moor he finally demonstrated what he was capable of in a two-legged League Cup tie with Spurs in 1993. Here, he showed he had the ability to confound top quality defenders. He could run with the ball from deep positions, evading challenges with a feint, a step-over, a switch of direction or a dab on the accelerator. Driving forwards with the ball at his feet, Randall seemed focused, composed, well-balanced and entirely confident. He had that quality possessed by the very best players – an ability to create time and space around him, even in the most crowded, pressurised situations. While driving forward you had the sense that he was calmly assessing his options: a sweeping pass to the flanks, a penetrative through ball, or a shot on goal, perhaps prefaced by a quick one-two. At his best, Randall executed these skills with aplomb.

But while he had terrific technical ability and a zestful attacking drive, he was rarely much help to his defence. Only once did I see him get really stuck into the opposition; that was, when he was playing at Swindon, watched by his extended family. He had been brought up in nearby Amesbury. Adrian Randall had the talent to become a Premiership player. He'd even had a trial with top-flight West Ham while at Burnley. I suspect, but do not know, that Adie didn't want it enough. When asked at Burnley what his career ambitions were, he replied, 'to stay fit and free of injury'. And when asked how he saw his future beyond football he said, with a smile, 'just relaxing'. Len Walker recognised his considerable ability. Perhaps he hoped Adie had the application to match. Many Burnley fans found him to be a really nice, easy-going, unassuming bloke. Perhaps he was happy with what he had. Whatever the truth is, I'm still unclear why my daughter named her sexually voracious guinea pig after him.

Despite the addition of Claridge and Randall, Aldershot were relegated at the end of the 1988/89 season. Their season started badly and didn't improve. Goals were hard to find, although Northampton were thumped 5-1 at the Rec midway through the campaign, Len Walker brought in the former Saints bench man, David Puckett, from Bournemouth. He did his bit, scoring 11 times in 21 league appearances and helping player of the season Steve Claridge give the Shots greater firepower. But ultimately it was in vain. Aldershot finished 17 points short of safety. Their average gate fell by almost a fifth to 2,600, adding to the club's considerable financial woes.

The 1989/90 season proved to be particularly depressing. Training facilities and routines became shambolic, the showers didn't work properly and, worst of all, the money dried up. Halfway through the season, Len Walker told his players he could not pay them. They continued to play, but most of them stopped turning up for training. The supporters' 'Save Our Shots' campaign started. Games at the Rec were characterised by the sound of clinking collection buckets. Shorn of a living wage, the club secretary began to sleep in his office. The PFA helped out temporarily but now everyone and everything was up for sale. Although Claridge was sold to 'hoofball' expert John Beck at Cambridge United for £75,000, the wolf prowled and growled outside the door. Aldershot finished 22nd in the Fourth Division that season, narrowly avoiding relegation to the Conference.

However, there was no cause for relief. On 31 July 1990, Aldershot were wound up in the High Court with debts of £495,000. The winding-up order was lifted, though, on 7 August 1990, when a 19-year-old property developer, Spencer Trethewy, paid £200,000 to save the club and allow them to start the new Fourth Division campaign. But the ambitious youngster had overreached himself. Meanwhile, Aldershot's problems on the pitch continued as they finished the 1990/91 season as the second-worst team in the Football League. Len Walker became general manager in March 1991, allowing the former England international midfielder Brian Talbot to take over as player-manager. Briefly, there was hope of a revival under Talbot. But this was dashed quickly as he departed in November 1991 after finding there were again insufficient funds to pay the players. He was succeeded by the ever faithful Ian McDonald. However, now the die was almost cast. Despite appearing on the *Wogan* TV show as Aldershot's young saviour, Spencer Trethewy was not the 'white knight' he professed to be. Following an unforgiving trial by tabloids, his business credentials unravelled alarmingly. He was a bust flush and paid heavily for his business hubris.

On a wild Saturday just before Christmas 1991, Lydia and I watched our rapidly improving Burnley side take on Aldershot at the Recreation Ground. As much as it delighted us to see Burnley top the division it so nearly toppled out of, we were touched by the desperate sadness engulfing our opponents. The Burnley fans contributed generously to the blanket carried around the ground – the situation was too dire for buckets. Some might say our generosity was borne out of self-interest – a concern to keep our promotion booty. But we could see the writing on the wall. It read 'Please directors don't let the Shots die'. We wondered what the 2,000 or so loyal fans would do if their club folded. Many appeared of advanced age, huddled in their thick winter clothing as protection against the viciously spiralling wind. We wondered what might happen to the local pub, so often bulging with custom on a football Saturday, and the nearby newsagent, once their football business was yanked away. This was not a wealthy town. The losses would be hard to bear. The Pet Shop Boys' lush, pulsating cover of 'Always On My Mind' swept around the ground in the howling gale, pricking consciences into thinking that we may not have loved as we should. Like Elvis, Aldershot FC was a goner. On 25 March 1992, the club finally died. As with Accrington Stanley in 1962, the club was unable to fulfil its fixtures. The Burnley game, like all others Aldershot FC played that season, was expunged from the record. At the dawn of the Premiership, Aldershot FC had expired with debts of around £1.2 million.

Aldershot's financial troubles were not unique. Dr Simon Pitt, formerly of the London Business School, reckoned that the collective Football League club debt in 1992 stood at £130 million – equivalent to quarter of a billion in today's currency. Pitt reported that turnstile revenue during the eighties had dropped by 28 per cent while transfer fees had soared by 323 per cent and players' wages had more than doubled. Moreover, policing costs had also increased by 200 per cent, to £6.1 million in the previous year alone. It was small wonder that Aldershot FC found that there was a dearth of genuine 'white knights' in their hour of need. Former Shots right-back, Kevan Brown, told Craig Matthews:

> *We had our last pay cheque in December. Some of us were coming into training and some weren't … It was difficult because we all had mortgages to pay … We were told it was important that the players stuck with it because there was someone waiting in the wings to come in and keep the club alive … Although people were struggling to make ends meet, it pulled everyone together and those lads that did stay seemed to have a strong bond. It was really touching to go to away grounds and the reception we got before and after the games was great … There was talk that we would be a feeder club for Crystal Palace but I don't think it ever got that far because of all the hidden debts …. I don't know exactly what went on but there seemed to be a lack of accountability on the finances and due to the fact*

> *that the club didn't own the ground or have any assets, survival was always going to be a long shot really ... We were struggling to field a team. I think we had the groundsman's son playing centre-half. We had nothing to lose I suppose in the end. We just had to get out there and try to keep the club afloat by fulfilling fixtures and to make sure we weren't humiliated in any of the games and tried to give the best account of ourselves that we could. I think we managed to do that in the end.*

The brave dignity shown by Ian McDonald's threadbare squad was truly admirable.

A dedicated band of diehard supporters immediately set about recreating a football club to represent their town. The movers and shakers included local businessman and lifelong supporter, Terry Owens; a former chairman of the 'Save Our Shots' campaign, Graham Brookland; the chairman of the Shots Supporters' Club, Peter Bridgeman; David Brookland and Nick Fryer. As a result of their dynamism, Aldershot Town FC (1992) saw the light of day less than a month after the former club had expired. A new board of directors was subsequently formed, comprising Terry Owens as chairman, Graham Brookland, Peter Bloomfield, John McGinty, Malcolm Grant, Karl Prentice and Kevin Donegan.

As testament to the depth and breadth of local enthusiasm for restoring an Aldershot football team, 600 fans attended the inaugural public meeting on Wednesday 22 April 1992. Thanks to the relentless efforts of Owens and his colleagues, the Diadora Isthmian League was persuaded to accept Aldershot Town FC as a new entrant to their Division Three in time for the new season. This was the first time that the Isthmian League had accepted an application from a club that had not previously existed. Owens et al were equally persuasive with Rushmoor Borough Council, who agreed to lease the Recreation Ground to them, initially for three years. This was a heavy undertaking. Isthmian League gates were microscopically low. Their Third Division gates often failed to break into three figures. Aldershot Town FC would need many more than that to pay their way – an average home gate of around 700 was what the new board had in mind. Then, the fledgling directors had the problem of finding a team to play for them. As summer approached Aldershot Town had just one player on their books – Chris Tomlinson, the son of head groundsman Dave.

Helped by the acquisition of players from folding Farnham, by August 1992 Aldershot Town had assembled a full playing squad under the management of a former Shot, Steve Wignall. On Saturday 22 August, the new club played their first ever match at the Rec. It was quite an occasion. The local mayor attended; so did a host of local dignitaries alongside almost 1,500 fans, a higher turnout than for the former club's final home game in the Football League. Clapton FC were Town's first visitors. Their chairman, Mike Fogg, thoughtfully presented his Aldershot counterpart with a cask of rum to celebrate the rebirth of his club. But the Aldershot directors agreed that the rum would remain unopened until their new club had obtained re-entry to the Football League. Sixteen years later, the Clapton chairman was invited back to the Rec to share a toast with Shots' chairman, John McGinty, after Aldershot Town had lifted the Blue Square Conference Premier League title. I was there on that euphoric night of Tuesday 22 April 2008 to see this. Although the 5,800 crowd included some, like me, who were not diehard Shots fans, there probably wasn't a dry eye in the house. And rightly so, for this was a magnificent collective effort – not only by the players who had hacked their way up the football ladder; not only by the dedicated board of directors and management and coaching staff; but also by those scores of unseen people who gave freely of their time, week in and week out, to support the club's steady upward climb. You can keep your Premiership passion. This is the real McCoy.

In an outstanding first season in the Isthmian League, Aldershot won the Division Three championship by 18 points. Mark Butler and Steve Stairs formed a deadly partnership up front. It was their four goals – two apiece – which turned Aldershot's fortunes in that sunny, opening game against Clapton. For the visitors proved less generous than their chairman, quickly putting themselves into a two-goal lead and seeming intent upon upsetting the Shots' baptism party. After their rescuing act, Butler and Stairs never looked back. Helped by their consistent firepower, Aldershot Town won their first ten matches and remained unbeaten at home all season. An average crowd of 2,090 was drawn to the Rec – way above the new board's projections. A home Hampshire Senior Cup tie with neighbouring Farnborough Town trumped that figure by some distance – the 6,000 fans that came along created a febrile atmosphere for a fiercely-fought local derby. This was an astonishing turnout given that Aldershot were then five divisions below the Football League. A successive promotion was achieved at the end of the following season and, although manager Steve Wignall left to join Colchester, Steve Wigley took over and almost guided the Shots to a third rise. After Wigley had also moved on in July 1997 to become youth development officer at Nottingham Forest, the combustible George Borg was appointed as his replacement. Borg came with excellent credentials. He was a proven winner in non-league football, having secured an Isthmian League Premiership title at Enfield with his assistant, Stuart Cash. It was clear that Borg had the contacts and motivation to secure another promotion for the Shots.

In November 2005, *The Times* football correspondent, Russell Kempson, described Borg as someone who 'tells it as it is, warts, moles, bunions, blisters and all. Firing from the lip, hip and every other part of his anatomy, he is a controversy waiting to happen.' Whenever I mention George Borg's name to my non-league referee friend, he always raises his eyes in exasperation. I know what he means. I've witnessed the Borg hairdryer – make that, road drill – treatment, the frothing fury, the dugout bashing, the angry remonstrations. There's no room for prisoners when George Borg is about. Borg's rages make Neil Warnock's antics seem like a Sunday school sulk. When Kempson met him, just before Braintree's FA Cup tie with Shrewsbury, he was as wound-up as ever. On this day, he had Paul Gascoigne – recently appointed as Kettering's manager – and Sven-Goran Eriksson in his sights. Borg expostulated:

> *The likes of us get brushed aside just because we haven't played or coached at the highest level … And half of those who do get the decent jobs can't coach to save their lives, anyway. You just get fed up with being shafted. I mean, look at Gazza. He's done this and done that, he's taken this and taken that, he's been ill and yet suddenly he turns up at Kettering. In three months, it could be turmoil there [George was being generous on the timing] … I'm sorry, but watching England bores the pants off me. We're losing to Northern Ireland and Sven just stands there like a wet lettuce. He's a Swede, no disrespect, but can't we find a manager here, someone with a bit of fire in them? We need someone with balls to stand up and be counted.*

Borg's impact at the Recreation Ground was immediate and spectacular. Having been mired in mid-table before his arrival, way behind leaders, Grays Athletic, the Shots suddenly started to fire – with machine-gun intensity. They proceeded to take Division One by storm, winning all of their post-Christmas home games and eventually lifting the league title with an 11-point lead. The gate for Aldershot Town's final home fixture with Berkhamstead Town was a staggering 4,289. The occasion proved to be a valedictory appearance for record goalscorer, Mark Butler. He was given a standing ovation as he made his 303rd and final appearance for the club, having netted 155 goals in pushing the club three rungs up the ladder. Chairman Terry Owens then decided it was time to stand aside and allow his vice-chairman, Karl Prentice, to take the club onwards and upwards.

Borg splashed out £8,000 on prolific goalscorer Gary Abbott. He wasn't disappointed. Abbott won the non-league player of the year award in 2000 for scoring an astounding 48 goals. However, despite winning various cup competitions, George Borg failed to deliver the much-coveted prize of Conference football. The pressure on him began to mount. After his acrimonious departure in January 2002, the more relaxed but equally ambitious Terry Brown took charge. Straight-talking Brown also had an excellent record, having taken Hayes into the Conference, keeping them there for six years and almost achieving promotion to the Football League in 1999. This was in spite of the tiny gates at Hayes' Church Road ground.

Like Borg, Brown wasted little time in lifting the Shots' fortunes. During the summer of 2002 he was allowed the extra resources to sign 11 new players with Football League and Conference experience. He clearly knew what he was doing because by mid-November Aldershot Town were top of the Ryman's Isthmian League Premier Division. Brown's success was based upon having an agile, strong and dependable keeper in Nikki Bull; a back line of tough, no-nonsense defenders such as Ray Warburton, Dominic Sterling and long-serving Shot Jason Chewins; a clutch of crunching, combative midfielders such as Paul Buckle, Nick Roddis and Jason Cousins; and an array of ultra-swift, ball-playing forwards such as Roscoe D'Sane, Stafford Browne, Lee Charles and Aaron McLean. Under Brown's guidance, Aldershot had a fast, fluent attack and a steely, uncompromising defence. Despite their best efforts, closest rivals Canvey Island could not catch them. The title was effectively decided in deepest Essex on Tuesday 15 April 2003, when Roscoe D'Sane's penalty consigned Canvey to defeat in front of over 3,500 fans, two-thirds of them from Aldershot. The final home games against St Albans (5-1) and Hendon (6-2) were played in a sunny, carnival atmosphere in front of around 3,000 home fans. The lightning quick, spring-heeled 20-year-old, Aaron McLean, gave an early indication of the ability that would flower at Peterborough some years later, scoring a memorable hat-trick against Hendon. The Shots' brilliant keeper, Nikki Bull, joined the fun, too, scoring with a penalty kick in the same game. With the ball placed on the spot by a thoughtful colleague, Bull began his run in his own box, not breaking stride until he had blasted the ball past his opposite number. The Football League was just a division away.

Brown strengthened his Conference side by bringing in Kingstonian's muscular target man, Tim Sills, and St Albans' creative midfielder, John Challinor. The combination of Sills' strength, particularly in the air, and D'Sane's dazzling speed and footwork delivered almost half of Aldershot Town's 80 goals in their first Conference season. Promotion to the Football League almost followed immediately. Unfortunately, Terry Brown's side endured the heartache of a penalty shoot-out defeat by Shrewsbury in the play-off final at Stoke. However, he remained philosophical about the Shots' near miss, stating: 'To be brutally honest we were nowhere near ready to have turned full-time in the environment of the Football League. Being in the Conference has allowed us the luxury of learning from our mistakes while still being able to maintain a promotion challenge … the obvious difference between the Conference and Division Two is the forwards. Almost every Division Two side have forwards who could currently hurt us at the back.' This was Jason Chewins' tenth and final season with the club, having made a record 489 appearances. He left with a flood of good wishes. Chewy's gritty determination on the field of play epitomised the club's fervent ambition to regain what it had lost.

Brown had the added frustration of failing in the play-offs again, one year later, when Carlisle eliminated them in a semi-final penalty shoot-out at Brunton Park. The loss of D'Sane to knee injuries was a major blow, also, forcing Brown into bringing in loan signings Jonny Dixon from Wycombe and Jake Robinson from Brighton. With the Aldershot board having made the historic decision to become a full-time club, Terry Brown concluded, 'We were training the players too hard at the beginning and that resulted in some tired performances and a good few injuries, the most notable being the loss of Roscoe D'Sane. As a youngster at Palace he had the tendonitis problem, but he has never trained daily since then and so it went undiagnosed.' D'Sane never recovered fitness at Aldershot although he later played briefly for Accrington Stanley and Torquay in the Football League. However, Brown had no qualms about stepping up the fitness requirements. 'Other members of the squad are now beginning to look like athletes after a year's training,' he said. 'One area where the differences between the Conference and Division Two are not so stark is the physical side – the league players are physically strong and hugely fit … we would need to continue the progress we have made.'

Despite the dual disappointments, Terry Brown kept a cool head. He was not fazed by criticism, remarking: 'I think it's a mistake for managers and players to read message boards. We're gods one moment and devils the next. The truth, of course, is that we are neither.' He needed that coolness in the season to come as a succession of injuries halted the Shots' progress. Brown was forced to field no fewer than 47 players in this battle-scarred campaign, including 14 loan signings. It was small wonder that Aldershot mustered only a disappointing 13th place. The fans began to turn away, too. After averaging attendances in excess of 3,000 for their first two seasons in the Conference Premier League, the mean figure for the 2005/6 campaign fell by a quarter to 2,294. Despite the addition of Marcus Gayle and Ricky Newman, players with extensive Football League experience, the 2006/7 season was scarcely better. There were major distractions, though. In March 2007, Terry Brown resigned to spend more time with his seriously ill wife, leaving his coach, Martin Kuhl, to hold the reins temporarily.

After a short break, Brown returned to football management with AFC Wimbledon. Together with his assistant, Stuart Cash, he steered his new club into the Blue Square Conference Premiership in 2009 and, in 2011, took Wimbledon into the Football League. George Borg is right to be angry about the restricted opportunities for non-league bosses at a Football League level. Surely Martin O'Neill and Neil Warnock have shown how well a non-league manager can perform at a much higher level in the game? The reality is that taking a non-league club into the Football League and keeping it there is one of the hardest managerial jobs in football, particularly because many of these clubs draw only modest support and have few resources to call upon.

In May 2007, Gary Waddock, a former Republic of Ireland international midfielder with over 500 senior appearances for QPR, Luton, Millwall and Bristol Rovers, took over as the new Aldershot boss. Wisely maintaining the continuity of his coaching team, he invited the highly experienced Martin Kuhl to be his running mate. Waddock was given full control over all football matters – he took responsibility for the first team, reserve, youth and junior football and for all football-related budgets.

Waddock made a clutch of crucial pre-seasons signings. He assembled a powerful central midfield unit. The scrapping 21-year-old non-league international, Lewis Chalmers, joined from Altrincham. Strong-running, fierce-shooting Ben Harding, a former loan signing, came in having had previous experience with MK Dons and Grays Athletic. Waddock also persuaded Reading to allow their energetic, combative 19-year-old midfielder, Scott Davies, to join the club on a season-long loan. Anthony Charles, a strong, tall and composed defender, was brought back to the club from Barnet and a couple of progressive full-backs, Rob Gier and the pacey 19-year-old Anthony Straker, were snaffled from Woking and

Crystal Palace, respectively. Waddock did not neglect the forward line, either, signing target man Rob Elvins from West Bromwich.

The season began erratically. A 2-1 win at Kidderminster on the opening day was followed by an abject 0-3 home defeat by the bookies' title favourites, Torquay, under the management of an ex-Shot, Paul Buckle. Another former Shot, Tim Sills, put the boot into his old club by scoring a sixth-minute opener. Sills had left the Rec in the summer of 2006 in an unsuccessful attempt to revive his Football League career, initially with Oxford and subsequently with Hereford. While the strapping striker found goals hard to come by in the higher league, a return to the Conference restored his goal rush. He became the Gulls' top scorer during this season with 19 successful strikes, not that he wished to gloat. He told Graham Brookland, 'I didn't want to celebrate my opening goal for Torquay at Aldershot … I didn't want to be disrespectful. Aldershot is close to my heart. I grew up as a local lad and have an affinity with the area and the club. The fans were absolutely fantastic to me on my return for Torquay … I think I scored 46 goals for the club and I would have loved to have rounded it up to 50 … there will always be a piece of me that belongs at Aldershot.' It is gratifying to hear such sentiments from a professional footballer in a game decimated by ruthless avarice and self-interest.

With so many fans disappointed by the Torquay performance, the gate for the Droylsden home game, three days later, was down by almost a half to 1,773. This was scarcely better than some of the club's attendances in its lower Ryman League days. The Shots' first-half showing against a limited Droylsden side was scarcely better as they trailed to Nicky Fearns' lob. However, helped by the contributions of two second-half substitutes, the swift Kirk Hudson and the wily Jonny Dixon, Waddock's young side produced a vastly improved second-half performance, winning comfortably by 3-1 with goals from John Grant, Chalmers and Harding. Gary Waddock remarked: 'When you have a group of young players – the oldest is 26 – you will have a period when they get nervous, but the crowd got right behind them … This is a squad game. We put Jonny Dixon up front and he played his part in the goals … with Kirk Hudson who gave us a bit more pace in a wider area.'

Young Scott Davies' first-half brace at Histon secured a successive 2-1 away victory, but then visiting Crawley spoilt a sunny August Bank Holiday by sneaking an outrageously fortunate 1-0 victory at the Rec. Not that Crawley's explosive manager, Steve Evans, saw it that way, as he castigated the referee for awarding Aldershot '76 second-half free kicks'. Evans was no stranger to controversy after his chequered time in charge at Boston.

But Aldershot recovered quickly, winning 2-1 at Altrincham and 3-2 in Gloucestershire against Forest Green Rovers, where John Grant scored twice. With their club facing financial meltdown, visiting Northwich Victoria presented the Shots with an easy home victory on 8 September (5-0). Having copious shooting opportunities, Scott Davies grabbed another pair of goals from midfield. His ferocious long-range shooting was proving to be quite an asset, as were Lewis Chalmers' prodigious, skimming throw-ins. This cakewalk lifted Aldershot briefly into top position, ahead of Torquay, who lost 1-3 at Nigel Clough's Burton.

On a day of startling beauty, Aldershot travelled to Oxford. The U's manager, Jim 'Bald Eagle' Smith, included the burly ex-Burnley defender Arthur Gnohere in his team. At his best, Gnohere was a pacey, powerful and resolute defender. However, the centre-back fell out of favour at Turf Moor after Burnley's boss, Stan Ternent, found Arthur with 'his head up his arse'. On this showing, Arthur was still in the dark. Following a first-half display of gormless defending, in which his reckless tackle gifted John Grant a soft penalty, Arthur was summarily removed from Smith's team and, soon after, from the club.

Inspired by his good fortune, Grant scored a magnificent second two minutes before the break, weaving in and out of some desperate lunges before coolly picking his spot. But Oxford were not beaten yet. Shortly after the restart they were level. Another Burnley old boy, Paul Shaw, showed greater distinction by blasting a 55th-minute equaliser past Shots keeper Nikki Bull. At this point it looked more likely that Oxford would win the game. But it was here that Waddock's boys showed their resilience, as Lewis Chalmers tucked away a late winner from a corner. This was the Shots' fifth away victory on the bounce.

Aldershot then proceeded to win their ensuing home games against York (2-0) and Farsley Celtic, the league's only part-timers (4-3), extending their run of victories to six. However, the Farsley game provided a timely warning. After apparently coasting with a 2-0 second-half lead, the Shots allowed their visitors to peg them back, not once but twice, before John Grant seized their winner six minutes from time. Thereafter, Waddock's lads stuttered for a few games. Goals from Louie Soares (brother of Tom) and new signing Joel Grant enabled them to beat a well organised Exeter side. Also, late strikes from skipper Rhys Day, with a penalty, and Soares were enough to see off obdurate Ebbsfleet. But there were two losses on the road at promotion-chasing Stevenage (1-3) and Burton (0-2), although an 87th-minute equaliser from giant defender Dave Winfield grabbed a vital point at yet another title contender, Cambridge United. Despite struggling to beat financially-troubled Halifax on 20 October, Jonny Dixon's 90th-minute winner set Aldershot off on another run of victories – seven came on the bounce before Grays spoilt their festive party on 29 December.

The acquisition of Joel Grant from Watford proved instantly successful. The English-Jamaican winger had spent four months on loan with the Shots during the previous season, after progressing through Watford's highly impressive academy. Grant demonstrated quickly his ball artistry, speed, strength and eye for goal. With his sinuous dribbling, his step-overs and deft touch he seemed like the Cristiano Ronaldo of the Conference. The word got around rapidly. Soon, he became a doubly marked man. Not that Grant was troubled by such irritations. At his best he could take on several opponents without a qualm, confounding them with his wizardry and outpacing them with his speed. He seemed to need a lot of encouragement, though. Frustratingly, his head would drop far too easily. My football scout friend told me that Joel became unsettled after his folks left Hammersmith, his place of birth, for their native Jamaica. Whatever the truth of the matter, Grant was a brilliant but fitful talent. Judging by Dario Gradi's recent remarks, this reputation has not left him. Grant was transferred to Crewe in June 2008 for an Aldershot Town record fee of £130,000.

As far as wingers went, Waddock was spoilt for choice. Not only did he have the glittering, if erratic, skills of Joel Grant, he also had the pace, robustness and versatility of Louie Soares. For, at Reading, his parent club, Soares had been tutored as a full-back by the first-team captain, Graeme Murty. If Grant was more of a Ronaldo, Soares was more of a Steve Coppell, a predecessor of the pouting Madeiran on Manchester United's right flank. But Waddock's blessings did not end there. He also had 21-year-old Kirk Hudson, a wide man with blistering pace who had the balance, the swerves and the control to run with penetrative directness at the heart of opposing defences. What's more, Hudson could garnish his mesmerising approach play with spectacular goals. With so much menace on the flanks and so much driving energy in midfield, it was hardly surprising that Aldershot overwhelmed many of their opponents. Centre-forward John Grant had cause to count his blessings.

Admittedly, Aldershot's defence was sometimes vulnerable. A swift counter-attack sometimes caught the back men playing too square. Balls played over the top sometimes found them slow on the turn. Centre-backs Day, Charles or Winfield could be troubled by nippy opponents like Forest Green's Stuart Fleetwood. However, Waddock's tactics were largely based on taking the game to his opponents, pinning them deep inside their own half.

It was small wonder that many games were won because the Shots' pressing style resulted in so many shooting opportunities. Besides, their midfielders were adept at letting fly from distance. Ben Harding and Scott Davies could be lethal from long range. Despite the surfeit of rich entertainment – fast, fluent football, stacks of goalmouth action and sizzling goals – the local support remained frustratingly modest. Before the Christmas period, only two home games attracted crowds in excess of 3,000. These were the Torquay debacle and the stirring 2-1 home win over Rushden & Diamonds on 17 November. The festive derbies with Woking proved very popular, though. Over 4,300 watched the tight Boxing Day victory at Kingfield while over 4,700 came to the Rec on New Year's Day to see Kirk Hudson score his second decisive goal of the holiday period to seal a double victory over the Cards (2-1). Four days later, Hudson and Joel Grant put paid to impoverished Northwich at the Victoria Stadium (2-1).

With Cambridge United putting an end to Waddock's FA Cup ambitions, Aldershot were free to make progress with their league programme. Not that this was plain sailing. Forest Green arrived on a damp, glowering Saturday afternoon in mid-January and tore the home defence to shreds. Day and Charles were at sixes and sevens as Rovers' Stuart Fleetwood continually shot past them. Had Nikki Bull not been in the form of his life, this could have been a cricket score rather than just 0-1. The jitters continued at York on the following weekend as the Minstermen recorded an untroubled victory (0-2). Fortunately, Oxford were next on the agenda. Since that scintillating September contest at the Kassam Stadium, Oxford's fortunes had drooped. Jim Smith had left the club and was replaced by Darren Patterson. Despite making wholesale changes, goals had dried up. After being red-hot favourites for promotion in 2006/7, Oxford came to the Rec in a spot of bother. Although Patterson's men defended doggedly, they finally succumbed to John Grant's goal just after the hour. The Shots were back on track. On 17 February I saw their *piece de resistance*, a magnificent 3-1 victory over promotion rivals Stevenage in front of the Setanta TV cameras. I cannot remember spending a better Sunday evening. After the loss at Bootham Crescent, Aldershot would not lose another game in their remaining 16 fixtures. Their self-belief was such that defeat seemed inconceivable. Even with their backs to the wall they retained the conviction that they could win the game. The top-of-the-table clash on Monday 3 March, at a freezing Plainmoor, illustrated this perfectly.

With a part-time work assignment taking me to Devon, I gladly joined the 4,500 throng for what promised to be a title decider. Both sets of fans stoked up a ferocious atmosphere under the Plainmoor lights, helping keep the piercing cold at bay. Paul Buckle's Gulls flew at the Shots immediately. There were no frills, just bullish, full-on competitiveness. With the ball habitually pumped long and high, there was little opportunity for fancy footwork, although Joel Grant managed to buck the trend for a while. The frost-hardened pitch hardly helped, producing steepling bounce. It was like watching two packs of hounds in snarling competition over an elusive balloon. The ugly, physical challenges that ensued caused the ball to ricochet at unexpected angles and heights. The frenzied flock of Gulls seemed quicker to bear down upon the second ball. However, it was Aldershot who drew first blood – after only six minutes, too. The Torquay back line parted briefly allowing the nimble, home-grown striker, Danny Hylton, just enough space to nip through with the ball at his feet and only keeper Andersen to beat. Although Hylton managed to evade Andersen's mad dash from goal, his touch was a tad heavy, leaving him with barely enough space to squeeze the ball into the unguarded net. But, just in the nick of time, he managed to wrap his left foot around it and scored.

Whereas the pace of the opening period had been merely fast, after Hylton's goal it became totally frantic. Aldershot were forced to defend in numbers. With only Joel Grant offering much relief up front, the ball kept pinging back into their box. Another former apprentice, Dave Winfield, defended magnificently. With the slender Day buffeted in the air by both Sills and Phillips and troubled on the ground by the nifty Zebroski, Winfield came frequently to his aid. Aldershot were compelled to fight fire with fire. Shot after shot was charged down. Any unclaimed ball was hacked clear unceremoniously. The game fizzed with bustling energy, bruising challenges and scurrying pursuits. Beaded sweat glistened on the players' foreheads; their shirts became darkened with heavy sweat. There was hardly a moment in which to draw breath. Half-time came and went but still Aldershot managed to hang on. Disappointingly, just past the hour mark, Torquay breached the Shots' previously resolute defence, scoring from a right-wing corner. Culpably, the goal came from a free header. The magnificent Nikki Bull was finally beaten as Phillips' forehead made firm contact with the ball, sending it whistling into the roof of his net. A huge roar emitted from the home crowd. It didn't seem possible that a few thousand voices could create such a din.

Torquay threw ex-Shot Roscoe D'Sane into the fray. They needed all three points. One wouldn't do. Gary Waddock brought on Scott Davies for the punch-drunk Chalmers while the neutralised Joel Grant was replaced by Kirk Hudson. The Shots managed to repel Torquay's desperate charges but seemed unable to take the attack to their hosts, even when their speedy recent signing, Junior Mendes, came on for Hylton. But with only seconds remaining, Scott Davies seized upon a loose ball 25 yards to the left of the Torquay goal. He had a posse of home defenders bearing down upon him. But without hesitation Davies fired in a typical stinging drive. It had pace, power and above all, unerring accuracy. Andersen didn't have a prayer as the ball zipped past him and into the bottom right-hand corner of the net. The startled home fans around me couldn't believe what they had just seen. The dancing Shots fans at the other end could, though. The muggers had been mugged. The title was now Aldershot's to lose. Torquay would need a miracle to take it from them.

Aldershot didn't lose their nerve. They steadily racked up the points, progressively widening the gap between them and all of their rivals. So, it came to pass that they needed just one point from their 43rd league game at St James' Park, Exeter on Tuesday 15 April 2008, to achieve their dream and clinch a place back in the Football League. Once again, I was blessed by a convenient work arrangement.

I arrived well before kick-off. It was a magnificent evening with the sinking sun casting a pastel pink glow over the quaint ground and surrounding Victorian houses. Despite the bubbling euphoria among the Shots fans, I felt strangely detached. I was calmly confident that the script had been written. No other outcome was possible. Promotion would be won, here, tonight. My mind went back to that stormy, dark December afternoon in 1991 when Lydia and I had stood in the Rec's North Stand, like a pair of bashful ghouls, watching a Football League club fade sadly from view. For reasons I don't fully understand, it seemed appropriate that I should be here on this sumptuous evening to balance the score. Scott Donnelly's deflected drive did just that, giving the Shots the point they needed. I declined to stay for the celebrations. This wasn't my victory. Aldershot are not my team. I was simply a well-wisher who wanted those who had worked so hard to resurrect their club to have their just reward. Because of that, I went to their final home game with Weymouth to applaud those who had contributed so much to the Shots' renaissance. The club arranged a half-time parade of movers and shakers, some prominent, others previously unseen. Together, they enabled the small town of Aldershot to have a Football League team again. It was a thoughtful and entirely appropriate response. The game was almost irrelevant – a forgettable 0-0 draw. But I made sure I stood in the same place as I had done 16 years before.

Although I still look out for Aldershot's results, I have only visited the Recreation Ground occasionally since their promotion. I gather that times are hard once more. The League Two club now manage to attract only as many as they did when in the Isthmian League. Realisation of their fervent ambition has perhaps sapped their momentum. More to the point, running a Football League team is a very expensive business. Many of those extra costs have had to be passed on to the fans. Besides, recession bites hard in places like Aldershot – an island of financial modesty in a sea of plenty. I do hope the Shots come through, and that those tremendous restorative efforts will not be in vain. I have similar hopes for the likes of AFC Wimbledon and Accrington.

On the journey back to Totnes on that starry night in April 2008, I heard a track on the radio by an American band, Death Cab for Cutie. It is called 'I Will Possess Your Heart'. This is a stalker's song that seemed all the more creepy because of the circumstances in which I heard it. As I drove alone along the deserted Devon lanes, with the wan moonlight filtering through the bare beseeching branches, I began to wonder whether my preoccupation with football wasn't equally perverse and obsessive. There is a state of mind called 'Stockholm' or 'hostage' syndrome. This is the deal. You find yourself captive, trapped by abuse. You begin to lose sense of your own identity. The only thing you can turn to is that which is giving you a bad, bad time. This becomes your cause, your reason for living. Isn't this the fate of most underdog fans?

'Things Can Only Get Better': the nineties and noughties

Just as the sixties were framed by two obscenity trials – the *Lady Chatterley* and *Oz* court cases – so the nineties were framed by two demolitions – the Berlin Wall and the Twin Towers. Tim Footman wrote in his book *The Noughties*: 'It is quite possible to argue that the 1990s never happened at all; the decade was merely a history-free buffer zone between the ideological polarities of the 1980s and the socio-religious anxieties of the noughties.' That comment could apply only if we ignore what was happening in the world outside Britain. Certainly, in the Balkans, Rwanda, Burundi, Angola and Somalia there was bitter, bloody conflict. 'Ethnic cleansing' meant genocide. Elsewhere, there were dramatic revolutionary changes, as with the dissolution of the Soviet Empire and with the emergence of Nelson Mandela and the South African Rainbow Nation. Here in Britain, life may have seemed as grey as John Major's *Spitting Image* visage, but we had the Northern Ireland peace initiative to brighten our prospects.

Rampant commercialism tried to present itself in more benign, if spuriously caring, empathic ways – 'what can we do to make it happen?', 'every little helps', 'because life is complicated enough', 'because you're worth it' soothed the advertising slogans. Perhaps it was because we felt so cosseted by our paternalistic corporate giants that regressive behaviour became more appealing and permissible. Can the huge popularity of Harry Potter be attributed to such a partiality? Is it this which fed the new lad and ladette culture? If so, does this help to explain the popularity of *Viz* and *Men Behaving Badly*? The *Fantasy Football League* TV show of the mid-nineties seemed to trade on a predilection of this kind, creating a cosy, if ironic, image of regressive student life in faux bedsitter land. Not that we were alone on the regressive beat. The Americans exported to us their cartoon slackers *Beavis and Butthead* and the knowing, puerile humour of *Wayne's World* and *Austin Powers*.

Perhaps it was this regressive inclination that also helped spawn a taste for pop nostalgia. Surely, Britpop was one of its manifestations with Pulp perhaps becoming the new Kinks, Blur the new Small Faces or Who and Oasis, possibly, a gobbier, reworked Beatles? The mid-sixties taste for slumming it – remember *Up the Junction*? – was revived with the appalling 'mockney' affectations. Damon Albarn and Nigel Kennedy, you stand accused. Even a Spice Girl flew the flag on her mini skirt as if 'swinging London' had never gone away.

But in terms of popular culture, probably the biggest splash was made by the growth of the celebrity market. In days of yore, celebrities were remote, unobtainable, glitzy, Hollywood-style icons. But during the nineties and noughties a new accessible, fallible, endlessly-confessing model emerged, one which has greater resonance and identification with ordinary people, it seemed. Canonised Princess Diana seemed to embrace both the old and new style of celebrity – in one sense a pure Hollywood-like fabrication, with her iconic glamour and immaculate costumes, but in another sense, a reality TV queen with her array of personal confessions and intimate disclosures. Having fed and served such a wide, divergent celebrity market, perhaps it was no surprise that her death should release the mother of all necrothons.

With the escalation in surveillance gadgetry, hacking, spyware and any unintended consequences of Facebook and Twitter activity, there seems to be fewer places to hide. Advertisers now target us individually, based upon the profiles we build up in our internet activity. It is unsurprising that identity fraud has become a growing concern.

The 'Age of Anxiety' has been applied so variously and profusely so as to lose any meaning. But I cannot remember any other period during my lifetime that has featured so many dire warnings about the precariousness of our future existence. The threats seem to trip over one another. We are warned of imminent economic meltdown, of environmental catastrophe, of lethal pandemics, of escalating terrorist threats and of frightening food and fuel shortages. With so much to trouble us, it is small wonder that so many of us find refuge in football trivia and a celebrity culture.

As for the state of modern football, the Bosman judgement signalled the total reversal of the pre-1961 balance of power between player and club. With the international impact of satellite television, more and more foreign owners have been attracted to our game, some with their own fortunes, but most with borrowed capital. The growth in live TV coverage and the high cost of Premiership tickets has also meant that more people watch games in their pubs or front rooms than in our football grounds. As the game has become awash with TV money there has been a massive growth in the number of agents. Footballers' wives and girlfriends command almost as much media coverage as their partners. Who we are seems more important than what we do or produce.

Football clubs once represented the communities in which they were based. That seems much less true now, particularly with many of the larger clubs. We have had franchise commercial outlets, such as McDonald's; we even have franchise terrorism with Al-Qaeda, so what protection is there against further franchise football? If football clubs are run essentially as business ventures with little (if any) strong consideration for their community or cultural roots, then a recurrence of the MK Dons fiasco cannot be ruled out. And while the rich clubs get richer (or alternatively more mired in debt) and the poorer ones become simply poorer, the prospects for our underdogs recede. This is regrettable. The game thrives on surprise. Without this, it will die. Thank God we have heart-warming tales of triumph against adversity supplied by the likes of Aldershot Town, Accrington Stanley and AFC Wimbledon. Long may this continue. Massive financial meltdown in English football might rebalance the odds and allow smaller clubs a better chance of success, but until it does, hell might as well freeze over. Thankfully, we are not all prey to football osmosis whereby we become drawn inexorably to thicker and richer substances. Some of us are content to 'live frugally on surprise'. Amen to that.

Final Word

What my dad gave to me was not just a love of football but an overwhelming urge to see the little guys prevail. He never hitched his wagon to the big names, never attempted to ride on the coat-tails of glory. He supported Brentford, for Christ's sake. When I was in my teens we used to stay up late together, listening to the fights from America. No matter how much Dad grunted and growled at the radio, one after another of our brave, but basically horizontal, heavyweights became battered into oblivion by some smart, preening Yank. It wasn't so much that he turned me on to failure. His message to me was not to expect too much. Actually, that lesson has served me well. While my support for modest causes has left me frequently disappointed and defeated, the unexpected triumphs have been so much sweeter. How can I ever forget that sultry day in May 2009 when Burnley confounded all expectations and won a Premiership place at Wembley? How can I erase the memory of Robbie Blake lashing a blistering volley past Ben Foster to defeat Manchester United at a packed, rocking Turf Moor, a few months later? I suppose our choice of favourite team says a lot about how we view ourselves. There's no point supporting a big team if you can't even talk the talk. I'm more comfortable in being pleasantly surprised at my achievements and at those whom I support. Great expectations sit too heavily on my shoulders.

My dad's final years were blighted by dementia. It's an awful degenerative condition that strips its sufferers of their talents, independence, personality and dignity, and causes so much work and heartache for those who care for them. Perhaps because the world around him appeared so strange and unpredictable he became increasingly agitated. And yet whenever I took him back to Griffin Park he seemed to find an elusive sense of calm, notwithstanding the baying voices around us. As we sat in the Braemar Road Stand, a contented smile played frequently upon his lips as his pallid, watery eyes focused on a small corner of the ground opposite him, where he and his friends used to stand during the late thirties. I wondered whether he saw his old mates standing there, as the young men they once were, puffing on their Woodbines in the late summer warmth, in their open-necked shirts, baggy flannels with broad leather belts, ghosts of a generation decimated by war. I was also unsure whether it was Robert Taylor that he could see out there on the pitch or Dave McCulloch, Brentford's centre-forward of pre-war days. It didn't matter. In fact, it hardly mattered that he couldn't remember a thing about what he'd seen. He liked going back to Griffin Park. The football didn't need to be any good for him to enjoy a brief time of respite, sanctuary, even. I guess that was what football gave me all those years ago. If I should ever live beyond reason, as he sadly did, I hope someone might consider taking me to a game sometimes, too.

REFERENCES

Football books and journals consulted

A Case of Vintage Claret: Fifty of the best Burnley footballers of all-time: David Wiseman: Hudson & Pearson (2006)
A Century of Soccer: Terence Delaney: Heinemann (1963)
A Game of Two Halves: Stephen F. Kelly (Ed.) Mandarin (1992)*An Entirely Different Game: British Influence on Brazilian Football:* Aidan Hamilton: Mainstream (1998)
A Season to Remember: Bill Evans: Tempus Publishing Ltd. (2002)
Accrington Stanley: The Club That Wouldn't Die: Phil Whalley: Sports Books (2006)
Alan Mullery: the autobiography: Alan Mullery with Tony Norman Headline (2006)
Among the Thugs: Bill Buford: Arrow (1992)
Arsenal Football Club Handbook 1960-61: Arsenal Football Club (1961)
A Strange Kind of Glory: Sir Matt Busby and Manchester United: Eamon Dunphy: Aurum (2001)
At Home with 'The Hammers': Ted Fenton: Kaye (1960)

Backpass magazine: issues 1-15: Mike Berry (ed): PCP: (2007-11)
Banksy: Gordon Banks – the autobiography: Penguin (2002)
The Best of Charles Buchan's Football Monthly: Simon Inglis (Ed.): English Heritage & Football Monthly Ltd. (2006)
The Big Book of Football Champions: 1956–1962 annuals: Purnell
Sir Bobby Charlton: The Autobiography: The Manchester United Years: Headline (2007)
Billy: a Biography of Billy Bingham: Robert Allen: Viking (1986)
Biting Talk: Norman Hunter – My Biography: Hodder & Stoughton (2004)
Blackpool: The Glory Years Remembered: Mike Prestage: Breedon Books / DB Publishing (2000)
Bobby Collins: The Wee Barra: David Saffer: Tempus (2004)
Bogota Bandit: The outlaw life of Charlie Mitten: Richard Adamson: Mainstream (2005)
Bolton Wanderers: The Glory Years Remembered: Mike Prestage: Breedon Books/DB Publishing (2000)
Bolton Wanders: Percy M. Young: Sportsman's Book Club (1965)
The Bonnie Prince: Charlie Cooke – My Football Life: Charlie Cooke with Martin Knight: Mainstream (2007)
Book of Football: 60 Memorable Matches: Richard Widdows (Ed.): Golden Hands/Marshall Cavendish (1973) Rights acquired by Eaglemoss Publications Ltd.

The Book of Football: Norman Barrett: Purnell (1981)
The Boys Book of Soccer: 1958–1963 annuals: Evans Brothers Ltd.
Brighton & Hove Albion Miscellany: Paul Camillin: Pavilion (2006)
Brighton & Hove Albion on This Day: Dan Tester: Pitch Publishing (2007)
Burnley: A Complete Record: Edward Lee & Ray Simpson: Breedon Books Sport (1991)
Burnley Football Club: The Complete A to Z: Dean Hayes: Sigma Leisure (1999)
Burnley: The Glory Years Remembered: Mike Prestage: Breedon Books/DB Publishing (2000)
Burnley Football Club 1882-1968: Images in Sport: Ray Simpson: Tempus Publishing Ltd. (1999)
Burnley's Greatest Goal and the last of the golden boys: Peter Fyles

The Clarets Chronicle: The Definitive History of Burnley Football Club 1882-2007: Ray Simpson with Darren Bentley, Wallace Chadwick, Edward Lee & Phil Simpson: Burnley Football Club (2007)
Carlisle United: A Season in the Sun 1974-75: David Steele: Desert Island Books (2006)
Champions: Manchester City 1967/8: Phil Goldstone & David Saffer: Tempus (2005)
Charles Buchan's Football Monthly magazines: 1959–1969: Charles Buchan's Publications Ltd.
Charles Buchan's Soccer Gift Books: 1957-8–1968-9 annuals: Charles Buchan's Publications Ltd.
Claret and Blue: The Story of Hastings United: Philip Elms: 1066 Newspapers Publications (1988)
The Clarets Collection 1946 – 1996: A Post-War Who's Who of Burnley Football Club: Ray Simpson: Burnley Football Club (1996)
Clough: a Biography: Tony Francis: Stanley Paul (1987)
Cup Final Extra: How the Finals were Reported 1872 – 1980: Martin Tyler: Hamlyn (1981)

The Daily Mail History of the Wembley FA Cup Final: Andrew Thraves (Ed): Weidenfeld & Nicolson (1994)
The Deepdale Story: An A to Z of Preston North End FC: Dean Hayes: Sport in Word (1996)
Dell Diamond: David Bull: Hagiology Publishing (1998)
Determined to Win: George Eastham: Sportsman's Book Club (1966)
Don Revie: Portrait of a footballing enigma: Andrew Mourant: Mainstream (1990)

The Double: The inside story of Spurs' triumphant 1960-61 season: Ken Ferris: Mainstream (1999)
Double Bill: The Bill Nicholson Story: Alan Mullery & Paul Trevillion: Mainstream (2005)

Eagle Football Annual 1963: Hulton Press Ltd.
Eagle Sports Annual: 1959 & 1962 annuals: Hulton Press Ltd.
East Lancashire Derbies: Blackburn Rovers v Burnley: Dean Hayes: Sigma Leisure (2001)
Empire News and News Chronicle Football Annual: 1958–1963 annuals: Thomson & Co.
England: The Quest for the World Cup: A Complete Record: Clive Leatherdale: Two Heads Publishing (1994)
England Managers: The Toughest Job in Football: Brian Glanville: Headline (2007)

FA Cup Giant Killers: Paul Harrison: Stadia/Tempus (2007)
Flat Back Four: the tactical game: Andy Gray with Jim Drewett: Boxtree (1998)
Football Against the Enemy: Simon Kuper: Phoenix (1994)
Footballing Fifties: Norman Giller: JR Books (2007)
Football's Giant Killers: 50 Great Cup Upsets: Derek Watts: Book Guild (2010)
Football in London: David Prole: Sportsman's Book Club (1964)
Football in Sheffield: Percy M. Young: Sportsman's Book Club (1964)
The Football League: 1888 - 1988: Bryon Butler: Macdonald Queen Anne Press (1987)
The Football League: Match by Match 1959-60: Tony Brown (Ed.) SoccerData (2007)
The Football League Directory 1985-87, 1993-94: Tony Williams (Ed): Newnes/Hamlyn/Harmsworth/Burlington
The Football Man: Arthur Hopcraft: Aurum (2006)
Football Nation: Sixty Years of the Beautiful Game: Andrew Ward and John Williams: Bloomsbury (2009)
Forest: 1865 – 1978: John Lawson: Wensum Books (1978)
Forever & Ever: A Rock 'n' Roll Years Diary of Burnley Football Club: Tim Quelch in collaboration with Burnley FC and the London Clarets (2000)
From Rags to Riches: The Rise and Rise of Oxford United: John Ley: Queen Anne Press (1985)
Fulham: The Complete Record: Dennis Turner: Breedon Books / DB Publishing (2007)

Glory Glory: My Life with Spurs: Bill Nicholson: Macmillan (1984)
The Glory Game: Hunter Davies: Mainstream (1972)
The Golden Age of Football: 1946 – 1953: Peter Jeffs: Breedon Books (1991)
Golden Heroes: Fifty Seasons of Footballer of The Year: Dennis Signy & Norman Giller: Chameleon (1997)
The Great Ones: Joe Mercer: Sportsman's Book Club (1966)
Greavsie: The Autobiography: Jimmy Greaves: Little, Brown Books (2003)

Harry Potts – Margaret's Story: Margaret Potts & Dave Thomas: Sports Books (2006)
Hastings United Through Time: A Collection of Football Recollections: Roger Sinden: Flying Free Management Ltd.
Hastings Reunited: A Collection of Football Recollections: Roger Sinden: Flying Free (2005)
He Shot, He Scored: The Official Biography of Peter Ward: Matthew Horner: Sea View Media (2009)
The Heart of the Game: Jimmy Greaves: Little, Brown Books (2005)
The Insider's Guide to Manchester United: John Doherty with Ivan Ponting: Empire Publications (2005)

Inverting the Pyramid: The History of Football Tactics: Jonathan Wilson: Orion (2008)
Ipswich Town: Champions of England 1961-62: Rob Hadgraft: Desert Island Books (2002)

Jack and Bobby: A story of brothers in conflict: Leo McKinstry: Collins Willow (2002)
Jimmy Greaves: Four Four Two Great Footballers: Matt Allen: Virgin Books (2004)
Johnny Haynes: Football Today: Arthur Barker (1961)
Journey to Wembley: A Football Odyssey from Tividale to Wembley: Brian James: Marshall Cavendish Ltd. (1977) Rights acquired by Eaglemoss Publications Ltd.
Just Like My Dreams: My Life with West Ham: John Lyall: Penguin (1990)

Kicking and Screaming: an oral history of football in England: Rogan Taylor & Andrew Ward: Robson Books / Anova Books (1996)
The King: My Autobiography – Denis Law: Bantam /Transworld Books (2003) Reprinted by permission of the Random House Group Ltd.
Kings of King's Road: The Great Chelsea Team of the 60s & 70s: Clive Batty: Vision Sports Publishing (2007)

League Football and the men who made it: Simon Inglis: Willow Books (1988)
Leeds United: Second Coat: Gary Edwards: Mainstream (2005)
Leyton Orient: The Untold Story of the O's Best-Ever Team: Tony McDonald: Football World (2006)
The Life Story of Doncaster Rovers Legend Alick Jeffrey: Peter Whittell: Chronicle Publishing (2003)
Liverpool: Player by Player: Ivan Ponting: Crowood (1990)

Manchester City: The Mercer-Allison Years: Ian Penney: Breedon Books /DB Publishing (2008)
Manchester United: The Official History: Tom Tyrrell & David Meek: Hamlyn (1988)
Masters of Soccer: Terence Delaney & Maurice Edelston: Naldrett Press (1960)
Match of My Life: Brighton & HA: Paul Camillin: Know the Score Books (2008)
Match of the Day: 40th Anniversary: Martyn Smith: BBC Books (2004)
Matches of the Day 1958 – 1983: Derek Dougan & Patrick Murphy: Dent (1984)
My Father and Other Working Class Heroes: Gary Imlach: Yellow Jersey Press (2006)
My Favourite Year: A Collection of New Football Writing: Nick Hornby (Ed): Witherby (1993)
My Fight for Football: Bob Lord: Stanley Paul (1963)

News of the World Football Annual: 1965–1995 annuals: Thomson & Co. / Invincible Press
Never Had It So Good: Burnley's Incredible 1959/60 League Winning Triumph: Tim Quelch: Know the Score Books (2009)
No Nay Never: A Burnley FC Anthology: Dave Thomas (2004)
No Nay Never: A Burnley FC Anthology Volume 2: Dave Thomas: Burnley Football Club (2008)
Northampton Town: A Season in the Sun 1965-66: Mark Beesley: Desert Island Books (2005)

The Official Illustrated History of Arsenal: Phil Soar & Martin Tyler: Hamlyn (1997)
One Hundred Caps and All That: Billy Wright: Robert Hale (1962)
Only A Game?: Eamon Dunphy: Viking (1976)
Ollie: The Autobiography of Ian Holloway: Ian Holloway with David

Clayton: Green Umbrella Publishing (2007)
Ossie: King of Stamford Bridge: Peter Osgood with Martin King & Martin Knight: Mainstream Sport (2002)
Paint it White: Following Leeds Everywhere: Gary Edwards: Mainstream (2004)

Peter Broadbent: A Biography: Steve Gordos: Breedon Books (2007)
Peter Swan: Setting the Record Straight: Peter Swan with Nick Johnson: Stadia (2006)
Preston North End: The Glory Years Remembered: Mike Prestage: Breedon Books/DB Publishing (2000)
Provided You Don't Kiss Me: 20 Years with Brian Clough: Duncan Hamilton: Harper (2008)
The Pride of Manchester: A history of Manchester derby matches: Steve Cawley & Gary James: ACL & Polar Publishing (1992)
Prophet or Traitor: The Jimmy Hogan Story: Norman Fox: Parrs Wood Press (2003)

The Real Mackay: The Dave Mackay story: Dave Mackay with Martin Knight: Mainstream (2005)
The Rivals: Blackburn v Burnley: Mike Holgate: Tempus Publishing Ltd. (2005)
'Right Inside Soccer': Jimmy McIlroy: Nicholas Kaye (1960)
Ron Reynolds: the life of a 1950s' footballer: Dave Bowler & David Reynolds: Orion (2003)
The Roots of Football Hooliganism: An Historical and Sociological Study: Eric Dunning, Patrick Murphy and John Williams: Routledge (1992)
Rothman's & Sky Sports Football Yearbooks 1973-2011: Macdonald's & Jane's/Headline

Season in the Cold: A Journey through English Football: Ian Ridley: Kingswood (1992)
The Sixties Revisited: Jimmy Greaves with Norman Giller: Queen Anne Press (1992)
Soccer in the Fifties: Geoffrey Green: Ian Allan (1974)
Soccer Partnership: Walter Winterbottom and Billy Wright: Bob Ferrier: Heinemann (1960)
Soccer the British Way: Kenneth Wheeler (Ed.) Sportsman's Book Club (1965)
Soccer Top Ten: Ivan Sharpe: Stanley Paul (1962)
Soccer Who's Who: Maurice Galsworthy: Sportsman's Book Club (1965)

The Spirit of Wimbledon: Living Memories of the Dons from 1922 – 2003: Niall Couper: Cherry Red Books (2003)
The Sportsview Book of Soccer: 1958–1963 annuals: Vernon Holding & Partners Ltd.
Stan Cullis: The Iron Manager: Jim Holden: Breedon Books (2000)
Stanley Matthews: My Autobiography: The Way It Was: Headline (2000)
Stan the Man: A Hard Life in Football: Stan Ternent with Tony Livesey: John Blake (2003)
Striking for Soccer: Jimmy Hill: Peter Davies (1961)
The Sunday Times History of the World Cup: Brian Glanville: Times Newspapers Ltd. (1973)
The Sunday Times Illustrated History of Football: Chris Nawrat & Steve Hutchings: Hamlyn (1994)
Swansea City: Seasons in the Sun 1981-82 & 1982-83: Terry Grandin: Desert Island Books (2005)

Tales from the Boot Camps: Steve Claridge with Ian Ridley: Vista/Cassell (1997)
Together Again: Willie Irvine with Dave Thomas: Sports Books (2005)
Tom Finney: My Autobiography: Headline (2003)
Tommy Docherty: My Story: Hallowed be thy game: Headline (2006)
Topical Times Football Book: 1960–1963 annuals: Thomson & Co.
Training for Soccer: An official coaching manual of the Football Association: Walter Winterbottom: Heinemann (1960)
Trautmann: The Biography: Alan Rowlands: Breedon Books (2005)

The Ultimate Drop: George Rowland (Ed): Tempus (2001)
Up, Up, And Away: Brighton & Hove Albion's Rise to the 1st Division: John Vinicombe: George Nobbs (1979)

West Bromwich Albion: Peter Morris: Sportsman's Book Club (1966)
West Bromwich Albion: The Complete Record: Tony Matthews: Breedon Books (2007)
Winning isn't everything...: Biography of Sir Alf Ramsey: David Bowler: Orion (1998)
The Wolves: An Encyclopaedia of Wolverhampton Wanderers: Tony Matthews: Paper Plane Publishing Ltd. (1989)
World Sports magazine March 1959, May 1962: March 1963

Plus football match reports and additional material from: *Aldershot News & Mail*, *Backpass* magazine, BBC Radio Bristol, *Bletchley Gazette*,

Burnley Express, Cumberland News, Brighton Evening Argus, Daily Mail, Daily Mirror, Four Four Two, The Guardian, Hastings & St Leonards Observer, The Independent, Lancashire Evening Post, Mail on Sunday, News of the World, Oxford Mail, Sunday Pictorial, Daily Sketch, Carlisle Times & Star, The Times, The Sunday Times, Northampton Chronicle & Echo, the Observer & Observer magazines; *South Wales Evening Post, Sunday Express, Watford Observer, When Saturday Comes* and club programmes and websites. Particular thanks go to the help offered by freelance journalist with Cumbrian papers, John Walsh, and club and supporter websites, notably Ian Grant and Matt Rowson at Watford's 'Blind, Stupid and Desperate'; Paul at Bristol City's 'Three Lions and a Robin'; Tony Scholes at Burnley's 'Clarets Mad'; Phil Whalley of 'Clarets' Archive'; Graham Brookland at Aldershot FC and shotsweb; Workington's 'Workipedia' site; QPR's 'Independent Review' site; Fulham's 'Hammy End Chronicle'; Swansea's scfc.co.uk and Leeds 'Mighty Whites' site. Thanks also to Phil Snow, Barnet FC supporter for the extract of his interview with Ricky George.

Non-football reference works consulted

A Rumor of War: Philip Caputo: Pimilco (1999)
A Writer's Britain: Margaret Drabble: Thames & Hudson (1979)
Absolute Beginners: Colin MacInnes: MacGibbon & Kee (1959)
Anatomy of Britain: Anthony Sampson: Hodder & Stoughton (1962)
As It Seemed To Me: Political Memoirs: John Cole: Phoenix (1996)

Babylon's Burning: From Punk to Grunge: Clinton Heylin: Penguin/Viking (2007)
Billy Liar: Keith Waterhouse: Penguin (1959)
Bomb Culture: Jeff Nuttal: MacGibbon & Kee (1968)
Brighton Rock: Graham Greene: Vintage Classics (2007)
Bring the Noise: Simon Reynolds: Faber & Faber (2007)
The Captive Wife: Conflicts of Housebound Mothers: Hannah Gavron: Pelican (1966)

Challenge to Civilization: A History of the Twentieth Century 1952–99: Martin Gilbert: Harper Collins (1979)
Chronicle of the 20th Century: Derrik Mercer (Ed.): Longman (1998)
Crisis? What Crisis?: Britain in the 1970s: Alwyn W. Turner: Aurum (2008)

Dancing in the Street: Tony Palmer: BBC Books (1996)
The Diaries of a Cabinet Minister: Volume 1: Richard Crossman: Book Club Associates (1975)

The Faber Book of Pop: Hanif Kureishi & Jon Savage (Eds.): Faber (1995)
The Female Eunuch: Germaine Greer: McGraw-Hill (1970)
From the Velvets to the Voidoids: A Pre-Punk History for a Post-Punk World: Clinton Heylin: Helter Skelter Publishing (2005)

The Golden Years of Burnley: Peter Thomas: True North (1998)

A History of Modern Britain: Andrew Marr: Macmillan (2007)

The Neophiliacs: Christopher Booker: Collins (1969)
Never Had It So Good: A History of Britain from Suez to The Beatles: Dominic Sandbrook: Little, Brown (2005)
The Nineties: When Surface was Depth: Michael Bracewell: Flamingo (2003)
NME Rock 'n' Roll Years: John Tobler (Ed.): W.H. Smith (1990)
The Noughties: A Decade That Changed The World: Tim Footman Crimson (2009)

Rejoice! Rejoice! Britain in the Eighties: Alwyn W. Turner: Aurum (2010)
'Annus Mirabilis' in High Windows: Philip Larkin: Faber & Faber (1974)
Rough Guide to Cult Fiction: Rough Guides (2005)
Rough Guide to Cult Movies: Rough Guides (2004)
Rough Guide to Cult Pop: Rough Guides (2003)
Rough Guide to Cult TV: Rough Guides (2002)

The Seventies: Christopher Booker: Penguin (1980)
The Sixties: Arthur Marwick: Oxford (1998)

Thatcher's Britain: The Politics and Upheavals of the 1980s: Richard Vixen: Pocket Books (2009)

The Ultimate Hit Singles Book: Dave McAleer (Ed.): Carlton Books (1998)
When the Lights Went Out: What Really Happened to Britain in the Seventies: Andy Beckett: Faber & Faber (2009)

White Heat: A History of Britain in the Swinging Sixties: Dominic Sandbrook: Abacus / Little, Brown Books (2006)
Wigan Pier Revisited: Beatrix Campbell: Virago (1984)

The 1950s & 1960s Scrapbooks: Robert Opie: Global Publishing (1998)
The 50s: Peter Lewis: Cupid Press (1978)
The 50s & 60s: The Best of Times: Alison Pressley: Michael O'Mara Books (2003)